In Many a Strife

General Gerald C. Thomas, U.S. Marine Corps (Retired). *(Portrait by Peter Egeli for the Army and Navy Club, Washington, D.C., with permission of the Army and Navy Club)*

In Many a Strife

General Gerald C. Thomas and the U.S. Marine Corps 1917-1956

Allan R. Millett
Colonel, U.S. Marine Corps Reserve (Ret.)

Naval Institute Press
Annapolis, Maryland

© 1993
by the United States Naval Institute
Annapolis, Maryland

All rights reserved. No part of this book may be reproduced without written permission from the publisher.

Library of Congress Cataloging-in-Publication Data
Millett, Allan Reed.
    In many a strife : General Gerald C. Thomas and the U.S. Marine Corps, 1917–1956 / Allan R. Millett.
        p.   cm.
    Includes bibliographical references and index.
    ISBN 0-87021-034-3
    1. Thomas, Gerald C., 1929–   . 2. Generals—United States—Biography. 3. United States. Marine Corps—Biography. I. Title.
E840.5.T46M55   1993
359.9′6′092—dc20
[B]   92-31557
                                                                                                                                                       CIP

Maps 1, 5, 6, and 13 were reprinted from *Semper Fidelis: The History of the United States Marine Corps,* revised and enlarged edition, by Allan R. Millett (copyright 1990, 1991 by Allan R. Millett). They are reprinted here with the permission of The Free Press, a Division of Macmillan, Inc.

Printed in the United States of America on acid-free paper ∞

9 8 7 6 5 4 3 2
First printing

"Here's health to you and to our Corps
Which we are proud to serve;
In many a strife we've fought for life
And never lost our nerve."
— *The Marines' Hymn*

Contents

	List of Maps	ix
	Foreword	xi
	Preface	xv
	Acknowledgments	xxi
Chapter I	**Molding the Man, 1894–1917**	1
Chapter II	**Becoming a Marine, 1917**	13
Chapter III	**Marine Sergeant at War, 1918**	22
Chapter IV	**Belleau Wood, 1918**	34
Chapter V	**Soissons, 1918**	46
Chapter VI	**Surviving, 1918**	56
Chapter VII	**The Long March and an Occupation, 1918–1919**	66
Chapter VIII	**Haiti, 1919–1921**	74
Chapter IX	**Renaissance of a Career, 1921–1925**	85
Chapter X	**The Long Watch, 1925–1934**	98
Chapter XI	**Preparing for a War, 1934–1938**	113
Chapter XII	**Inside the Marine Corps Elite, 1938–1941**	127
Chapter XIII	**Observing World War II, 1941**	137
Chapter XIV	**Once More to War, 1941–1942**	150
Chapter XV	**The Road to CACTUS, June–August 1942**	160
Chapter XVI	**Division Operations Officer on Guadalcanal, 7 August–22 September 1942**	172
Chapter XVII	**Division Chief of Staff on Guadalcanal, 22 September–10 December 1942**	194
Chapter XVIII	**Marines in the South Pacific, 1943**	211

Chapter XIX	**The War at Headquarters Marine Corps, 1944–1946**	225
Chapter XX	**The Unification Crisis, 1945–1947**	245
Chapter XXI	**Watch on the Yellow Sea, 1947–1949**	260
Chapter XXII	**More Wars on the Potomac, 1949–1951**	276
Chapter XXIII	**Commanding General, 1st Marine Division, 1951–1952**	288
Chapter XXIV	**Reforming the Marine Corps, 1952–1954**	318
Chapter XXV	**The Last Tour, 1954–1955**	336
Chapter XXVI	**Sunset Parade, 1956–1984**	344
	Bibliographical Essay	353
	Notes	363
	Index	437

List of Maps

Map 1:   Marine Operations in France. p. 24
Map 2:   American 2d Division, 3 June 1918. p. 32
Map 3:   Belleau Wood. p. 41
Map 4:   Operations of 2d Division, July 1918. p. 49
Map 5:   China. p. 118
Map 6:   South Pacific Theater. p. 161
Map 7:   South and South Western Pacific Theaters, 1942. p. 170
Map 8:   The Solomon Islands. p. 173
Map 9:   Guadalcanal. p. 175
Map 10: Lunga Perimeter. p. 188
Map 11: Lunga Perimeter II. p. 195
Map 12: Tsingtao. p. 261
Map 13: Marines in Korea, 1950–1953. p. 289
Map 14: 1st Marine Division, Korea, 1951. p. 299
Map 15: Punch Bowl. p. 308

Foreword

"Certain battles have a special quality," I remember General Gerald Carthrae Thomas saying. "Belleau Wood and Guadalcanal were two such battles."

He had good reason to say this. He was a veteran of both, but was speaking not entirely of himself but of larger things. As he would say, Belleau Wood and Guadalcanal were alike in that both were opening offensives in the First and Second World Wars respectively. Both brought the fighting qualities of the United States Marines to the forefront of American consciousness and to international attention. Both provided a yardstick by which later Marine Corps battles of the two wars would be measured. Both would be of lasting influence on the Marine Corps itself, and veterans of these two campaigns would have a special status. For Gerald Thomas, the Marine and the man, they would prove overwhelmingly important.

He went into Belleau Wood as a sergeant and intelligence chief of the 1st Battalion, 6th Marine Regiment. His commission as a second lieutenant would come late in the war. This put him behind those commissioned in 1917, such as Clifton B. Cates and Lemuel C. Shepherd, future Commandants and already of considerable reputation.

Thomas landed at Guadalcanal as a lieutenant colonel, serving first as division operations officer and then as chief of staff of the 1st Marine Division, coming off the island a colonel. Many of the lieutenant colonels and colonels in the 1st Marine Division at Guadalcanal had been with the 4th Marine Brigade in France, and of this number a high proportion had been at Belleau Wood or in the battles that followed: Soissons ("Worse than Belleau," said Thomas), Saint-Mihiel, Blanc Mont, and the Meuse-Argonne.

In the small Marine Corps between the two World Wars, all the officers knew each other, if not personally at least by name and reputation. They came and went, rubbing elbows in ships detachments afloat and small garrisons ashore, with occasional action in such places as Nicaragua, Haiti, or Santo Domingo, exotic tours in China, and a country-club life at Quantico, Parris Island, and San Diego. Thomas himself served in occupied Germany, Haiti (twice), and in China, where he was adjutant to then-Colonel Alexander A. Vandegrift.

After China and just before the U.S. entry into World War II, Thomas was detailed to accompany Captain James Roosevelt, USMCR, on a round-the-world politico-military mission ordered by Roosevelt's father, the President. It gave Thomas a first-hand look at the war-torn world and some of its leaders.

At Guadalcanal, Vandegrift, as a major general, commanded the 1st Marine Division. Guadalcanal was a testing. Some of its officers, all old comrades, proved out well. Some did not. The ones who did not test out well would be sent quietly to the backwaters of the war. The ones who did well, and Thomas was one of them, were in line for command of divisions or other high posts, either in the Pacific or later in Korea. Three—Vandegrift, Cates, and Randolph McC. Pate—would become Commandants of the Marine Corps. Thomas never made the last rung of the ladder, but he stood close to several who did, notably Vandegrift and Shepherd. He has been called the Richelieu of the Marine Corps—the "gray eminence"—and that is not far off the mark.

I remember the first time I saw and heard Thomas. It was in the winter of 1942–43, and Headquarters was bringing back selected officers from Guadalcanal to talk to us at the Marine Corps Schools at Quantico. I was a second lieutenant, a platoon leader in the Officer Candidates Course, just past 21 years old, and very, very impressionable.

I can still see the square-built man on the platform of Breckinridge Auditorium, shining dark hair worn longer than Marines do now, slicked back on both sides of the part, and heavy, jutting eyebrows. His advice to us, and I have never forgotten it, was: "We're not in Haiti or Nicaragua now. We're fighting in the big leagues. The Marine Corps has to learn staff work, logistics and the like. A man with a rifle can go only so far; we have to learn to back him up."

When Vandegrift, after Guadalcanal, went on to be Commandant, he took Thomas with him to Washington. I did not see Thomas again until the war was over. In 1949 he came to Quantico for duty as a brigadier general, after commanding the last of the Marine occupation forces in North China. I was a captain and managing editor of the *Marine Corps Gazette*. I was much flattered when he visited the offices of the *Gazette*. Straining for small talk, I told him that a man from my small hometown in New Jersey had served with him in France.

"What was his name?" asked General Thomas.

"Rudy Mattson," I answered. "He was a policeman and he went back into the Corps during World War II as a Class IV Reserve."

"I remember him well," said the general.

"How could you?" I asked. "When there were so many."

"Not that many," he answered.

It was then that I learned of his remarkable memory, how he never seemed to forget anything but filed it away in his mind for future use. He had the facility, very gratifying to a young officer, of picking up on a conversation where he had left off three or six months earlier.

After Quantico I saw him next in Korea, when he came out in March 1951 to command the 1st Marine Division. He led us well in those harsh times, a sturdy figure climbing the hills with a walking stick in hand. A *cocomacaque,* we were told, from Haiti, the twin to that carried by Commandant General Shepherd.

Years passed before I saw the general again, by then a retired four-star. I saw him chiefly on social occasions. He was grayer now and a bit heavier, but still with the beguiling habit of picking up on a conversation where he left off: "Simmons, the last time we talked you said . . ."

He was the honorary president of the 1st Marine Division Association and ruled that sometimes unruly organization with a firm but benign hand. He walked almost daily from his home in Northwest Washington to the Army-Navy Club in Farragut Square. There hangs in the club the portrait of Major General James G. Harbord, USA, who as a brigadier commanded the 4th Brigade of Marines at Belleau Wood. In the background of the portrait, in the nineteenth century style of things, stands the hunting lodge at Belleau Wood, a landmark well remembered by all who fought there. Funds for the portrait were raised by subscription by Marine officers who had served under Harbord in France.

A group of latter-day Marine officers, mostly retired and habitués of the Army-Navy Club, decided that there should be a like portrait of General Thomas in the club. The general as painted by former Marine Peter Egeli is in dress blues. In the background of the portrait, almost inevitably, is a map of Guadalcanal. My contribution was the collection and mounting of the general's large medals that had accumulated in careless fashion in a bureau drawer over the years. Those medals include the Army's Distinguished Service Cross and Distinguished Service Medal, the Navy's Distinguished Service Medal, the Silver Star, two Legions of Merit, and the Purple Heart.

After the general's death in 1984, the Elizabeth S. Hooper Foundation of Philadelphia gave the Marine Corps Historical Foundation a generous grant to support the writing of a biography. Mrs. Hooper's son Ralph had been a four-year roommate at the Naval Academy, class of 1951, of Gerald C. Thomas, Jr., now a retired colonel. Ralph's brother Bruce had served as a Marine Corps aviator on active duty from 1953 to 1957, with seven more years in the Reserve, reaching the grade of major.

It took no great search to determine that Colonel Allan R. Millett, USMCR, would be the ideal author for the planned biography. In civilian life Dr. Millett was, and still is, a professor of history and an associate director of the Mershon Center at Ohio State University. He graduated from DePauw University, magna cum laude and Phi Beta Kappa, in 1959. His master's and doctoral degrees were taken at Ohio State in 1963 and 1966. He taught at the University of Missouri as an assistant professor and then moved to Ohio State in 1969. Since then he has built up what is probably the largest graduate program in military history in the United States. There have also been many academic honors, including a stint as a Fulbright lecturer in Korea.

Amazingly prolific as an author and editor, Millett has to his credit a considerable number of books and many published essays. Of these the most important stepping stones to his writing of the Thomas biography are probably his *The General: Robert L. Bullard and Officership in the United States Army, 1881–1925* (Greenwood Press, 1975); *Semper Fidelis: The History of the U.S. Marine Corps*

(Macmillan, 1980, 1991); and *For the Common Defense: A Military History of the United States of America, 1607–1983,* in collaboration with Dr. Peter Maslowski (The Free Press, 1984).

With more than a full plate of academic activity, Millett has also managed a parallel career in the Marine Corps Reserve. He served successively in all officer grades, with frequent periods of active duty (including command of the 3d Battalion, 25th Marines, USMCR), from his commissioning in 1959 as a second lieutenant until his retirement in 1990 as a colonel. The quality of his contributions to the Marine Corps has been recognized by a Legion of Merit.

His academic and military interests have frequently merged, as in his repeated assignments as an adjunct professor at what is now the Marine Corps Combat Development and Education Command, where he has left his imprint in the shaping of the new Marine Corps University.

In the classic German scheme of things he would be "Colonel Professor Doctor Millett." He brings all these skills and a near-lifetime of experience to bear in this biography, which he has developed in the time-honored style of "the life and times" of General Thomas.

> Edwin H. Simmons
> Brigadier General, U.S. Marine Corps (Ret.)
> Director of Marine Corps History and Museums

Preface

The clouds swept high across the clear spring sky, and the gas in my car ebbed as I pulled into a service station in downtown Marshall, Missouri, in late March 1988. On my way to a Marine Corps Reserve meeting in Kansas City and research at the Eisenhower Library in Abilene, Kansas, I had left Interstate 70 for a side trip to Slater and Marshall to see the birthplace and childhood homes of Gen. Gerald C. Thomas. I also planned to visit the cemetery where the general's mother and first wife had been interred. Beyond these modest missions, I had no other plans.

While a young attendant worked on the car, I walked into the service station. An older man sitting in the office—where he looked very much at home—asked me if I were a Marine. Since I was wearing a red baseball cap with the Marine Corps emblem and a flight jacket with my name and rank on it, I did not marvel at his acute powers of observation, but I answered that, yes, I was a colonel in the Marine Corps Reserve. The man sneered slightly, then added that he had been a *real* Marine during the Korean War. He then said that he had heard that some Marine named Thomas had come from Marshall. Had I heard of him? I laughed and said yes, that in fact I was writing a biography of Jerry Thomas and that I had come to town to see where Thomas had grown up.

"Was he a good Marine?" the man asked.

"Well, he made lieutenant general before he retired."

"Yea, but was he a *good* Marine?"

"Jerry Thomas was a very good Marine," I responded.

Any biographer of a military officer faces the same question I did in the service station in Marshall, Missouri: was General Rifle or Admiral Keel a *good* soldier or Marine or airman or sailor? The question implies that the biographer should provide some judgment about the subject's effectiveness in the role of a military officer, especially in wartime. It seldom has anything to do with the officer's personal life, whether he or she was an honest person, a constant friend, a loving spouse, or caring parent. The measure of a military officer is the ability to move a military organization toward some common goal. The mission is the message. However clear and obvious the mission may be—and it is seldom clear above the tactical level—only civilians think that all an officer has to do is to devise a plan and issue the appropriate orders, and all that the officer hopes to accomplish will be done. On the battlefield, of course, the enemy is also moving and shooting—and probably thinking—all of which multiplies the chance for human error, not to mention sudden death and incapacitating fear. Even in peacetime, Clausewitzian friction affects all organizational activity by grinding down the most ambitious and urgent efforts to improve institutional effectiveness.[1]

The challenge any officer faces, regardless of rank and station, is to contribute to the organization's core competence. If the officer is a commander, he or she bears the formal responsibility for maintaining or increasing the command's mission performance, even though there may be finite limits to the officer's skill as a leader, the resources available, and the time to make improvements. Although it may be assumed that an officer wants to contribute to his or her service's core competence, the task of reconciling the individual's sense of accomplishment and the service's requirements defines every military career. The process is continuous and relational. A military career proceeds through stages of professional maturity, intellectual and emotional growth, accumulated occupational expertise, and physical energy. Today's zealous lieutenant who flies an aircraft or commands a platoon with a self-confident competence that makes colonels cry may be a miserable failure as a field grade officer. Uncertain young officers who appear to be living examples of Mort Walker's "Lieutenant Fuzz" may blossom (provided, of course, that they have understanding seniors) later in their careers, especially if they work in fields where technical expertise counts more than charisma. On the other hand, senior officers face the peril of arrested development—of placing the expansion of their core competence at parade rest.

The seven ages of man that Shakespeare describes in Act II of *As You Like It* have their counterparts in a military career. The first of "the many parts" played by an individual—the infant and the schoolchild—occur before he or she becomes a commissioned officer. The challenge of the service, then, is to transform the lover, "sighing like a furnace, with a woeful ballad" of emotional self-indulgence, into a soldier, "full of strange oaths, and bearded like the pard; jealous in honor, sudden and quick in quarrel, seeking the bubble reputation even in the cannon's mouth." The next transition, however, is more difficult, for the soldier may not become the senior organizational leader ("the justice") who guides the service toward improved performance, using all "soldiers" for purposes that serve the state and enhance the reputation of the military profession. Some officers simply move directly to the sixth and seventh stages of humankind, in which progressive intellectual, emotional, and physical impairment bring their useful careers to an end. The challenge for the *good* officer is to play the part of "soldier" and then move on the stage of "justice" and to make that fifth "act" the longest of the play.

In writing a biography of Gen. Gerald C. Thomas, who fused "soldier" and "justice" into a thirty-nine-year career, I have been most influenced by four other works (three historical, one fictional) on officers of the American armed forces.

The first, in all immodesty, is my own biography of Lt. Gen. Robert L. Bullard, USA. In that work, I attempted to demonstrate how the career of a single officer reflected fundamental changes in the nature of the U.S. Army and its officer corps. Bullard proved an apt model for such study; he heard his first rifle shots fired in anger on the New Mexican frontier in the 1880s and heard his last shells exploding in complete fury on the Western Front in 1918. His life in microcosm took the Army from its role as a frontier constabulary to the land force of a modern industrial power that faced the prospect of battle outside the Western Hemisphere. I did not claim, however, that Bullard, however successful he became in his Army, played a leading role in guiding the Army toward its twentieth-century role. He had been acted upon more often than he acted when the issue became institutional change. His significance to a biographer arose from the fact that he understood what was happening to his Army, he approved of the change, and he wrote about it with perception and objectivity, at least most of the time.[2]

Although the historic importance of Robert L. Bullard—even in the history of the U.S. Army—is limited, two other Army officers provide ample examples of the relationship between an individual career and great events: Generals of the Army George C. Marshall and Douglas MacArthur. Although both of these giants in the history of the Army, the United States, and the modern world have found several biographers, their lives are best described and interpreted in the multivolume biographies written by Forrest C. Pogue and D. Clayton James.[3] Pogue and James define the biography of the modern American officer, although I have also read with admiration Stephen Ambrose's biography of Dwight D. Eisenhower, E. B. Potter's biography of Chester W. Nimitz, Thomas B. Buell's biography of Ernest J. King, Barbara Tuchman's biography of Joseph W. Stilwell, Martin Blumenson's biography of George S. Patton, and Donald Smythe's biographies of John J. Pershing.[4] For an institutional historian, however, these biographies present a common problem with the partial exception of Smythe's works about Pershing. All of the subjects played pivotal roles in the American participation in the two world wars, so their historical significance is inextricably linked with those global conflicts, not just the development of their services. In fact, other officers of their generation have a stronger claim to the role of organizational reformer, although all of these officers (with the exception of Eisenhower) had some significance as institutional leaders before they marched onto the center stage of a world war. Their biographers, therefore, tend to deal with their "prewar" careers (which may actually include service in an earlier war) as simply a prologue to greatness rather than an entire adult life lived within the unique environment of a military service. The phenomenon is well known to military historians; for example, Lloyd Lewis and Bruce Catton wrote one volume of their biography of Ulysses S. Grant on his life before 1861 and two on the Civil War. This proportion of the treatment between "unhistoric" and "historic" phases of an officer's career is common in military biographies, to some degree driven simply by the more extensive documentation of the "historic" phase of one's career.[5]

Any historian worth his or her ink knows the difference between historical truth and Truth. Both objectives worthy of a lifetime of pursuit (even if one objective remains untaken), historical truth and Truth should be at least compatible or complementary, a challenge accepted by some historical novelists. This book owes an intellectual debt to one such work, Anton Myrer's *Once an Eagle,* a novel that follows the lives of two Army officers, Sam Damon and Courtney Massengale, from World War I into the Cold War.[6] Like many other professional military historians, I find Sam Damon too good to be true and Courtney Massengale too bad to be true. As an officer and historian for more than thirty years, however, I have seen some Damon and some Massengale in most of the officers I have known. I cannot speak for the U.S. Army, but I believe that Marine officers, sometimes to their own and their service's peril, are more Damon than Massengale. Should I start again as a second lieutenant in some other life, I would choose again to be in a service that reflected the disabilities of "simple soldiers" like Sam Damon rather than one that functioned efficiently from the Machiavellian manipulations of a Courtney Massengale. Yet *Once an Eagle*—its anachronisms and historical errors forgiven—reminds students of officership that personality, peer relationships, and service reputation mean everything in an officer's life. To the degree that I could blend historical truth and Truth in the life of Gerald C. Thomas and the Marine Corps in which he served, I have tried to do so.

My nameless acquaintance in Marshall, Missouri, still does not have an answer to his implied question: Why was Gerald C. Thomas a *good* Marine? It was not just because he became a general. Hundreds of thousands of good Marines did not reach flag rank, some because they died in battle for Corps and country. Although he fought in three wars, Thomas cannot claim the same sort of historical significance as George C. Marshall or Douglas MacArthur. The highest wartime billet Thomas held was commanding general, 1st Marine Division. In fact, one is hard pressed to identify *any* Marine general who made any difference in American military history writ large, although a case might be made for two Commandants, John A. Lejeune and Thomas Holcomb. Many Marine generals, however, made a great deal of difference to Marines and the Marine Corps. Gerald C. Thomas deserves a place in the first rank of such officers along with (and this is not an exhaustive list) Charles Heywood, George Barnett, Alfred A. Cunningham, John H. Russell, A. A. Vandegrift, Roy S. Geiger, Clifton B. Cates, O. P. Smith, Lemuel C. Shepherd, Jr., David M. Shoup, Wallace M. Greene, Jr., Leonard F. Chapman, Jr., Lewis W. Walt, Keith B. McCutcheon, and Lewis B. Puller. Only three such officers have thus far been the subjects of definitive biographies, Smedley D. Butler, Lejeune, and Holland M. Smith, although Barnett and Vandegrift wrote memoirs and Puller and Geiger have received biographical treatment. There is also a biography of Shepherd under way, and all the Commandants will receive scholarly attention in a forthcoming anthology.[7] If the U.S. Marine Corps has made a difference in American military history (since World War II, can one realistically doubt this assertion?), then these officers, including Thomas, belong in the libraries as well as in the memories of their families, friends, and comrades.

Gerald C. Thomas lived through the creation of the twentieth-century Marine Corps. He was impressed by the reputation of Marines who had taken part in the colonial campaigns of 1898–1916, when Marines brought the eagle, globe, and anchor to Cuba, China, the Philippines, Nicaragua, Mexico, Haiti, and Santo Domingo. Thomas enlisted in the Corps when the United States entered World

War I. He fought in France as a sergeant and lieutenant, with distinction and courage appropriate to his rank, and discovered his calling as a Marine officer. He entered the postwar Corps just as the Navy and John A. Lejeune realized that any future war with Japan, whose imperial ambitions and geographic reach had expanded in World War I, would require the seizure of advanced naval bases in the Pacific by amphibious operations. After twenty-two years of preparation for this military specialization (regarded by most experts as only a faint possibility), Thomas played a critical role in the Marines' first offensive action in the Pacific war, the capture of Guadalcanal. This operation validated the operational concept of amphibious warfare and proved that the reputation for valor bought with blood in France still defined *good* Marines.

Had his career ended with World War II, Thomas would have earned his place, however small, in Marine Corps history. His niche would have widened some when he left the South Pacific in 1943 as a brigadier general to assist the new Commandant, A. A. Vandegrift, his division commander on Guadalcanal, in completing the formation and employment of the Fleet Marine Force for the defeat of Japan. His career, like Bullard's, would have mirrored the "coming of age" of his service in twentieth-century total war.[8] Thomas, however, served another ten years as a general officer. Before his retirement at the end of 1955, he worked with boundless determination and considerable success to give the Fleet Marine Force the organizational foundation in law and practice as the nation's "force in readiness" for any Cold War contingency mission "as the President may direct." He himself commanded the 1st Marine Division as part of the force in one of these missions, the American intervention in the Korean War.

His contributions to the development of the modern Fleet Marine Force, however, were not related to his distinguished service as a division commander. In fact, the 1st Marine Division had already won enough laurels to please a Roman legion before Thomas became its commander. When Thomas returned to Headquarters Marine Corps in 1952, he continued his struggle to create a truly integrated air-ground Marine Corps that not only could conduct amphibious operations in the nuclear age but also could use its sea-based capabilities for contingencies that fell short of general war with the Soviet Union. No one officer, certainly not Gerald C. Thomas, would have claimed the title of "father" of the modern Fleet Marine Force. The reform of any military organization above the tactical level requires multiple paternity, a coalition of senior and junior officers who share a common vision of where their service has been and the direction it must take to serve the nation. By the testimony of officers who brought the concept of helicopter vertical envelopment to life, Thomas provided timely, effective leadership on several occasions when the very future of the Fleet Marine Force was at stake.

The Marine veteran I met in Marshall, Missouri, may still doubt that I have made my case that Thomas was a *good* Marine. He may have to read this book and make up his own mind, a common trait among Marines and Missourians. However, one of General Thomas's closest associates in the adaptation of the Fleet Marine Force, the late Colonel DeWolf Schatzel, USMC, testified to what made Thomas so effective and influential:

General Thomas was deeply dedicated to the Marine Corps, and a devout believer in its importance to the security of the United States. He chose for his close friends and associates those about him who shared his feelings, although his judgment in this matter was not always accurate, and caused him a few disappointments. He also put a high premium on demonstrated military proficiency and leadership, even though it might be narrowly focused, and oblivious to the wider issues which concerned him. Beyond this rather small circle, his friends included many individuals who disagreed with him on matters which he considered of prime importance, and many whose abilities he held in low esteem, but for whom he had, through long or old association, developed a fondness. Beyond the outer limits of his friendship, though not his civility, were those whose integrity he doubted, and those who, in his opinion, used the Marine Corps to serve their private interests.

Not all Marine officers were as magnanimous as General Thomas in extending their friendship. If my recollection is correct, he was "spot promoted" to the rank of brigadier general, and this was resented by some of his seniors as well as some of his peers. A larger group, extending lower in rank, was antagonized by his persistent efforts to secure to the Commandant more effective control over the Corps's fiscal, supply, and aviation agencies. These had long enjoyed a high degree of autonomy which they were unwilling to relinquish, and many of [these] officers, field as well as general, translated their unwillingness into a personal animosity toward General Thomas, although some of the most senior officers remained his warm personal friends.

Regardless of their personal feelings toward him, I know of virtually no experienced Marine officers of his era who questioned General Thomas's outstanding competence as a commander or staff officer. Although I know only by hearsay of his performance as a "field soldier," and more particularly as a troop leader, I cannot imagine that so fine a student of human nature, and an officer so well versed in the military art, could have failed to perform with distinction in the three wars in which he faced the enemy.[9]

No *good* Marine could ask for a better appreciation. Gerald C. Thomas deserves the "Well Done" that this book strives to provide.

Acknowledgments

Battlefield heroism and book writing have much in common. The convention at a Marine Corps awards ceremony is for the battlefield hero to say a few words to the group gathered to honor him, whether it is a regiment on parade or a handful of friends in an office. The recipient of the decoration steps forward and says that he is only representing the many Marines of his command that won him the decoration and that he accepts it in their names. He may mention some of his Marines—all good and often too few—who survived the battle and those who did not. The words are sincere, the sentiment genuine. Nevertheless, the recipient will wear the decoration. The names of the other Marines will disappear from history, but his will not.

A biography, like a decoration, brings a touch of historical immortality to two people, the subject and the author. It is, nevertheless, a collective enterprise. If one characterized books like military operations, this book would be a campaign, an extended effort by many participants. Although the residual shortcomings of the book remain the responsibility of the author, its strengths—its ultimate success, in fact—represent the contributions of many people, whose desire is to honor the memory of the late Gen. Gerald C. Thomas, USMC, and to preserve the memory of the Marine Corps as he knew it and the Marines with whom he shared his thirty-nine-year career.

This book would have been impossible without the general's autobiography. He began writing it shortly after his retirement in 1955, an effort that deepened in the 1960s after a second retirement from government service allowed him more time. In 1966, Thomas provided a lengthy oral memoir of his career to Benis M. Frank, then the chief of oral history for the History and Museums Division, Headquarters Marine Corps. The central source of this book is Thomas's autobiography, which went through several revisions into the 1970s, as supplemented by the oral memoir, which does not depart in any important way from the autobiography. Wherever possible, of course, I corroborated events and Thomas's opinions with additional documentary evidence and the recollections of his family and friends—and even a couple of critics. General Thomas had a reputation for having an amazing memory for names and events. I found this reputation deserved but did not depend on it alone.

Two people assisted General Thomas with his autobiography, thus contributing in important ways to this book: the general's youngest son, William H. Johnson Thomas, a professional writer and editor; and the late Col. Angus M. "Tiny" Fraser, USMC (5 March 1913–6 July 1985). An admirer of General Thomas and a frequent companion during the general's retirement, Tiny Fraser planned to write a biography of Thomas, and he began the process of interviewing the general, collecting some documents and letters, and even writing a couple of draft chapters before his death (the result of an accident). Although I found some of the material Fraser collected to be useful, as I did his interviews with Thomas, his greatest contribution was to keep the idea of a Thomas biography alive after the general's death, an idea shared by the entire Thomas family.

My own principal collaborator on this book was Col. Gerald C. Thomas, Jr., USMC (Ret.), whose skills as a historian make him a research assistant and critic without peer. Mrs. Gerald C. Thomas, his mother, provided critical family information and her own and the general's views on people they knew and experiences they shared. William H. Johnson Thomas and his sisters, Mrs. Joseph A. (Tina) Bruder and Mrs. J. Richards (Virginia) Andrews, also provided family information and their own perceptive views of their father, their family life, and the general's Marine Corps associates. All male members of the immediate Thomas family, including sons-in-law Col. Joseph A. Bruder and J. Richards Andrews, are Marines. I had insisted in my contract that the Thomas family should have no editorial control over the book. All of the family members, however, made essential and willing contributions to the project, even though they and I sometimes differed in our assessments of people and the meaning of events. We also occasionally disagreed about why General Thomas had said or done something, and, whether correct or not, my interpretations are the ones in this book, not theirs, and they should not be held responsible for any of the controversial judgments the reader may find here.

I want to thank the Elizabeth S. Hooper Foundation, in collaboration with the Marine Corps Historical Foundation, for its financial support for a Thomas biography and the Mershon Center, The Ohio State University, for its continued and generous support for my research in the history of the U.S. armed forces.

Through his counsel as the representative of the Marine Corps Historical Foundation, Brig. Gen. Edwin H. Simmons, USMC (Ret.), director of the History and Museums Division, played a key role. He was the principal reader of the draft manuscript as I wrote it, and only he read the entire manuscript before I submitted it to a panel of reviewers chosen by the Marine Corps Historical Foundation, the Naval Institute Press, and myself to read the manuscript. These additional readers, all valued friends and established professional historians, are Marine officers with doctorates in history: Col. John W. Gordon, USMCR, Department of History, The Citadel, biographer of Commandant Thomas Holcomb; Lt. Col. Merrill L. "Skip" Bartlett, USMC (Ret.), biographer of Commandants George Barnett and John A. Lejeune; and Lt. Col. Donald F. Bittner, USMCR (Ret.), historian of the Marine Corps Command and Staff College and biographer of Commandant John H. Russell.

In addition, I profited from the criticism of Henry I. "Bud" Shaw, Jr., and Benis M. Frank, two senior historians of the History and Museums Division, both of whom knew General Thomas. As historians and Marines, Bud and Ben are the reigning experts on the history of Marine operations in World War II and the Korean War. Although we occasionally differed in our assessments of Marine officers and events, I found their suggestions, without fail, to be informed, thoughtful, and objective.

A major source of information about General Thomas and the Marine Corps of his era is the testimony of his contemporaries, those officers who, as senior commanders and staff officers of the Fleet Marine Force, fought in World War II and then, as general officers, brought the Marine Corps into and through the dark days of the Vietnam War. Two of Thomas's closest associates contributed written commentary on his career, their own experiences, and my draft chapters from World War II through 1956. From the South Pacific campaign into the postwar struggles to save the Fleet Marine Force, through the Korean War, and to the "New Look" Marine Corps of the force-in-readiness, Gen. Merrill B. Twining, USMC (Ret.), and Lt. Gen. Victor H. Krulak, USMC (Ret.), worked closely with General Thomas and matched his dedication to building a Corps that could fulfill its own high promises. I owe them a special debt of gratitude for their sage advice and untempered opinions.

Many other retired Marine officers who knew Thomas provided written commentary about the general's career. I want to thank Generals Wallace M. Greene, Jr., and Robert E. Hogaboom; Lieutenant Generals William K. Jones, Edward W. Snedeker, William J. Van Ryzin, and Henry W. Buse, Jr. (deceased); Major Generals John P. Condon and Jonas M. Platt; Brigadier Generals James D. Hittle and Frederick P. Henderson; Colonels DeWolf Schatzel (deceased), Warren P. Baker, Sanford B. Hunt, Clarence R. Schwenke, Drew J. Barrett, Jr., Jeremiah A. O'Leary, Jr., and Walter F. Murphy; and Lt. Col. Sherman W. Parry, for their assistance. In some cases this extended to reading the draft chapters that covered their respective common service with General Thomas in war and peace. For their contributions to my understanding of the Guadalcanal campaign, which included access to diary entries and personal notes, Maj. W. F. Martin Clemens, CBE, MC, formerly of the Australian armed forces, and Herbert L. Merillat, former Marine captain and 1st Marine Division historian, deserve special thanks. I also want to thank Wallace Edwin Dibble, Jr., for his photographs and recollections of service as a lieutenant in Thomas's headquarters during the Korean War, 1951.

In doing research for my history of the Marine Corps, *Semper Fidelis* (1980 and 1991), I learned to trust the cooperativeness and expertise of the staff of the History and Museums Division, Marine Corps Historical Center, Washington, D.C. Again, these dedicated professionals made my search for information more often rewarding than frustrating: Joyce E. Bonnett of the archives section, Danny J. Crawford and Robert V. Aquilina of the reference section, Evelyn A. Englander and Pat Morgan of the library, and J. Michael Miller of the personal papers collection.

I want to thank other historian-archivists and researchers for their assistance: David Haight of the Dwight D. Eisenhower Library; Marilyn B. Kann of the Hoover Institution for War, Revolution and Peace; Betty Collins-Van Sickle of the U.S. Army Infantry School library; Rose Snellings of the Marine Corps Research, Development and Acquisitions Command; Robert W. Frizzell of the Illinois Wesleyan University library and archives; Timothy K. Nenninger of the National Archives and Records Administration; Charles H. Cureton of the U.S. Army Combined Arms Center at Ft. Leavenworth; Ronald H. Spector and Dean C. Allard, both directors of the Naval Historical Center; Carl F. Cannon, Jr., of the U.S. Army Transportation Command; Richard J. Sommers of the U.S. Army Military History Institute; A. O. Fisher of the U.S. Information Service who tried to find medical records in Port-au-Prince, Haiti; Marilyn Haggard Gross of Sweet Springs, Missouri, and Mr. and Mrs. John J. Hughes of Marshall, Missouri, all of whom provided information on the Thomas and Durrett families; David Brown and his staff of the James C. Breckinridge Library; and the staff of the Franklin D. Roosevelt Library.

Special thanks go to Claudia Riser, Josephine Cohagen, and our student assistants at the Mershon Center, especially Todd Miller, Douglas Plummer, and Richard Meixsell, for their careful typing and editing of the original manuscript.

The Naval Institute Press deserves a "Bravo Zulu" for its careful attention to this project from its inception to completion, in particular Deborah Guberti Estes, Paul Wilderson, Mary Lou Kenney, Terry Belanger, and Anne Fenelon Collier-Rehill. The cartographer for the book was John Fehrman, Center for Teaching Excellence, The Ohio State University.

I dedicate this book to my wife, Martha E. Farley-Millett, in recognition of her immeasurable contribution to my dual career as historian and Marine Reserve officer, and to our daughter, Eve Noelle, who landed on 25 July 1990 just as this book neared completion.

Allan R. Millett

In Many a Strife

[CHAPTER I]

Molding the Man
1894–1917

THE WAR CAME TO Bloomington, Illinois, before the warm weather in April 1917, but the passionate patriotism of its citizens provided heat that the warmest spring could not match. The *Daily Pantagraph,* a Republican newspaper and no friend of President Woodrow Wilson's administration, preached national honor, loyalty, and military preparedness as it carried war news on the front page with headlines bolder than those of stories about Bloomington's most pressing domestic issues, the prohibition of alcoholic drinks and the price of grain. In early April, the city went on a flag-buying spree, and on 5 April, the day before Congress approved Wilson's call for war against the Central Powers, Illinois Wesleyan University started daily military training for its male students. The university also began first aid classes for women so they could serve as Red Cross nurses. According to a plan made by the Reverend Theodore Kemp, the energetic president of Illinois Wesleyan, the university decided to show its commitment to Americanism and democracy by dedicating a new flag and flagpole in front of Old Main, the university's venerable office and classroom building.[1]

The university's ceremony of 18 April proved to be only the prelude to an emotional binge that affected most of Bloomington. "Not since the Civil War times," the *Illinois Wesleyan Argus* reported, "has the population of the city been so united on one issue."[2] The Illinois Wesleyan convocation included songs, patriotic readings, and speeches in support of American entry into the war from President Kemp, Mayor E. E. Jones, and law professor Hal M. Stone, the university's most famous orator. The proceedings opened and closed with prayers by the Reverend J. N. Elliott, pastor of the prestigious Second Presbyterian Church and father of the famous athletic Elliott brothers. After the Reverend Mr. Elliott's last prayer, the group of hundreds formed a square around the flagpole. The male battalion, commanded by math instructor and all-sports coach Frederick L. Muhl, formed one side of the square, the women students another. The members of the

Grand Army of the Republic (GAR), aged veterans of the Union army, formed the third side, and the townspeople made up the fourth. A squad of coeds raised the flag, "a moment of full emotion," and the assembly sang "The Star-Spangled Banner." The students returned to class, but they could not have been too interested in their studies. The day's pageantry had just begun.[3]

That evening, the city of Bloomington mustered ten thousand marchers and twenty-five thousand onlookers, a host close to the city's official population, for a mass march and patriotic rally. McLean County, Illinois, was once more going to war as a community. Down Main Street came the marchers, formed in columns of fours, almost all carrying flags. Amid the ranks of the first division rolled a float with Miss Sylvia Herbig dressed as "Columbia." On the units marched: the state and city employees, the GAR, a mixed group of union members, the Grange, the clubs of Bloomington's churches. The Illinois Wesleyan contingent of one thousand (much larger than the student body) marched behind a trio of men dressed as "The Spirit of '76" and the Reverend President Kemp. The parade ended in the city square in front of the McLean County courthouse for another round of patriotic poems, prayers, speeches, and songs. Then the people dispersed, perhaps to wonder in more private ways what the war would mean to each of them.[4]

The war could not have been more important for one Illinois Wesleyan marcher. In less than a month, Gerald Carthrae "Fats" Thomas, the darkly handsome, muscular center of the Titans football team, would pull on the uniform of a private in the United States Marine Corps. Unlike 160 other McLean County men, Thomas escaped death; unlike most of the county's military survivors, he remained in the service. Thirty-nine years later, he would retire as a general and a veteran of three wars. In many a strife with the enemies of his country and the critics of his service, Gerald C. Thomas would prove as determined as he must have felt on 18 April 1917 when he stood in his first military formation and watched the flag of the United States fly above a country at war.

The journey of some thousand miles that separated the Blue Ridge Mountains and the great bend of the Missouri River between Boonville and Lexington, Missouri, did not change the sturdy Virginia farm families that trekked westward before and after the Civil War. Seeking fertile land to sustain the rural culture of their ancestors, the migrants from Virginia joined other Anglo-Irish-Welsh families from Tennessee and Kentucky to settle along the Missouri. One of the river areas, known collectively as "Little Dixie" to Missourians, became Saline County. Its county seat, Marshall, was a town by 1839, thirty years after the first settlers appeared amid the oak woods and grass prairie south of the Missouri. About fifty miles from both Lexington and Boonville, Marshall became the center of town life for the corn, wheat, and livestock farms that provided the economic base for Saline County. One small Civil War battle brushed the town in October 1863, but the war did not wreck the county or the town, which numbered 924 people in the 1870 census. The outlying towns of Malta Bend, Shackelford, and Arrow Rock were little more than crossroads graced by a nest of churches and country stores. Another crossroads town, Slater, some fifteen miles northeast of Marshall, served as the meeting place of the Thomas family—hard-working, hard-living

Virginians who had come to Missouri from their farm at the base of Southwest Mountain in western Albemarle County.[5]

At the time of the Civil War, the reigning patriarch of this Southwest Mountain family, David Wyatt Thomas (1816–84), and his wife, Frances Ellen Wood Thomas, farmed the lands settled by Thomas's grandfather after his service in the Revolutionary War. Known as "Young David" in contrast to his grandfather "Old David," David Wyatt liked farming, but he also liked corn whiskey, which he made and drank with distinction. He fancied fine horses and fox hunting. Fortunately, his wife brought money to their marriage in 1846, for her family, the Woods and Marshalls, had land and one of the biggest whiskey stills in Albemarle County. The Thomases needed every penny—between 1846 and 1872, they had nine children, six daughters and three sons. The youngest, Vander Wyatt (1872–1963), was born when his father was fifty-six and his mother forty-four. The Thomas family, burned out of their home by Union cavalry, was living in Louisa County with kin while Young David earned enough money to rebuild the farmhouse at Southwest Mountain. Whether or not they knew, the Union raiders had not punished an innocent, for Young David, although a civilian, had spied for the Confederacy while buying cattle and horses in the Shenandoah Valley and the western Virginia Piedmont. Vander Wyatt grew up on the restored Thomas farm, worked hard, and learned some basic mathematics and English at the rural academies his father could sometimes afford. Twelve at the time of his father's death, Vander Wyatt depended on his unquenchable optimism, physical strength, native intelligence, skilled hands, and great energy to succeed.

Two years after her husband's death, Frances Thomas sold her property and left Virginia with her three youngest children for Saline County, Missouri, where two of her older daughters, Laura Thomas Yowell and Madeline Thomas Norford, already lived with their own growing families. The Thomas family bought a farm in Saline County and settled into the reconstructed life of former Virginia farmers in 1887. Vander Wyatt did not stay at home very long because he did not get along well with his older brothers, Lemuel and Joseph, or his mother. Working as a farm laborer, he saved enough money to rent the George place, a farm of 120 acres near Slater. A massive young man at 6'2" and 240 pounds, he was not yet twenty, but he was ready for a life and family of his own. The only thing he lacked was a wife. Like his male forebears, he was drawn to a woman of more distinguished origins than his own.[6]

Virginia Harrell Young (1870–1938) was also the descendant of colonial settlers in Virginia and had many relatives in central Missouri. Her mother's family, the Carthraes, had also immigrated to Missouri in 1855 from Albemarle County. The moving spirit in the relocation was her grandmother, Sidna Brown Carthrae (1820–82), who brought her aging husband, children, slaves, a whole wagon train of household goods and equipment, horses, cattle, and hogs to a new 5,000-acre farm south of Waverly, a river town halfway between Marshall and Lexington. In the face of depression and war and widowed in 1864, Sidna preserved the family's relative affluence and genteel traditions. One of her several children, Adeline "Addie" Sidna Carthrae (1846–73), had sufficient musical talent that her mother sent her to the Boston Conservatory of Music after the Civil War.

In Boston, Addie met Jacob Harrison Young (1834–1906), a fellow Missourian who also had Virginia roots. Harrison must have been an unusual student. He was thirty-four years old and had already been married once and had two children when he met Addie Carthrae, who was twenty-two. Whatever his magic—and Thomas family lore suggests that he had ample charm—Harrison Young and Addie Carthrae married in 1868. They left Boston and music forever and returned west to find fortune and to start another family. Two children quickly followed; the second child, Virginia Harrell Young, arrived while the couple was examining mining property in the Dakota Territory. Then tragedy struck. During another childbirth in 1873, Addie and her third daughter died.

Harrison's mind was still alive with dreams of instant wealth in western mining. He returned to Missouri long enough to leave his two young daughters with his adoring younger sister, Margaret Young Dawes Marshall, who lived with her second husband, James Robert Marshall, near Orearville, Missouri. James and Margaret Marshall became Virginia Young's parents for all intents and purposes; Harrison Young had virtually no further contact with his two daughters by Addie Carthrae or their children. James Marshall provided wealth and an extended family large enough to give Virginia a real home.[7]

The Marshalls, who had no children of their own, lived comfortably on their farm along the Marshall-Slater road. Robert preferred hunting and fishing to farming, so he hired another family to work his land. He also enjoyed long discussions with fellow veterans about the War Between the States, in which he had served in the Confederate army. Their interest in the war did not flag with age. Margaret matched her husband in probity and religiosity but had more education; she had attended a female academy in Winchester, Virginia. Both Marshalls were strong people who transferred their values to the Young girls. Virginia proved to be an apt student, especially in math and Latin, and completed public school in Saline County. She then attended a small college near Marshall before returning home to become a teacher at a one-room school close to both the Marshall farm and the George place, the farm operated by Vander Wyatt Thomas. The young farmer and the schoolmarm met, and they were married on 2 September 1892. Because the Marshalls did not think much of Vander—too little Bible, too much bottle, too little education and future—the couple eloped to Marshall. Lawfully wed, they settled in to work the George place and started their family.

Vander and Virginia soon proved what the Marshalls feared, that the marriage would not duplicate the ordered calm of the Marshall household. Stubborn to the point of willfulness and separated by tastes and expectations, Vander and Virginia did not get along well. Incompatibility being no barrier to parenthood, however, they soon had a son, Robert Shelton Thomas (1893–1952). Shelton's birth probably forced them to reconsider their long-range economic prospects. They soon moved to a farmhouse near Slater, and Vander took employment with the Chicago and Alton Railroad, a major rail company that had built its western branch across Saline County in 1878 and brought a new measure of prosperity to the area. During Vander's first short spell as a railroad employee, he and Virginia had a second son, Gerald Carthrae Thomas, born 29 October 1894. The Thomases then returned to farm the George place, and Virginia was able to regain the emotional support she so badly needed from the Marshall family.[8]

Gerald C. Thomas remembered his childhood as both puzzling and fulfilling, for he sensed the tension between his parents and between his father and the Marshall family. His mother made sure that he and Shelton grew up under the influence of "Uncle Robert" and "Aunt Meg" Marshall. Except when they were in school, Shelton and Gerald spent most of their time on the Marshall farm and often did chores there when they were old enough. Virginia took her two sons—but not Vander Thomas—to her adoptive parents for Sunday dinner by walking the three miles between the two farmhouses. She often helped the Marshalls' housekeeper with canning and preserving and usually brought food home with her from the Marshalls' ample pantry and smokehouse. The Thomas boys also found a friend in "Uncle Robert's" tenant farmer, who allowed them to earn a little spending money and once gave Gerald the pelt of a mink he had killed near the Marshall corncrib. Gerald thought the $2.50 he earned from the pelt a small fortune. Even after they moved away from the Slater area, the Thomas boys returned to work on the Marshall place and other neighboring farms as hired hands.

In the meantime, Vander Thomas looked for more promising ways to make a living and, one suspects, a job that reduced his dependence on his wife and her adoptive family. He found work with a firm, Zimmerman Brothers, that was experimenting with fattening cattle for market. When Zimmerman Brothers went out of business, Vander looked again to the Chicago and Alton Railroad. For about two years, the Thomases lived near Marshall while Vander learned about constructing railway bridges and maintaining shop machinery. A gifted mechanic, he began to make his way in the Chicago and Alton's water and coal service department, and the family moved to Slater.

Meanwhile, the Thomas family expanded. In 1900, Virginia had a daughter who died the following year. In 1903, she gave birth to twins, a son, Louis O'Vander (1903–83), and a daughter, Inez, who survived only a year. Three years later Vander and Virginia had their last child, Mary Frances (1906–72). Throughout the family traumas of moving and childbearing, Virginia Thomas ensured that her two oldest sons attended the Marshall and Slater schools and did their homework, which she supervised. Shelton proved an indifferent student, but Gerald liked schoolwork and responded to his mother's tutoring. Virginia also exposed her sons to music. She played the organ at the Methodist church and sang to her children, but she probably could not afford to have them take lessons or to buy a piano for her home, however much she wished they might inherit this part of her life that was so different from the rough tastes of her husband.[9]

After a promotion in 1906, Vander Thomas transferred to Bloomington, Illinois, a major hub of the Chicago and Alton's operations. He went to Bloomington first and then moved his family during Christmas week, six weeks after Mary Frances's birth. The move represented a dramatic change for the Thomas family. From Slater, a rural town of 2,000, they entered the life of a prosperous, optimistic north-central Illinois city of 26,000. The city fathers of Bloomington estimated that they served a region of 700,000 people, many of whom farmed the rich

Illinois lands opened to settlement after the War of 1812. Although Chicagoans might have viewed Bloomington, the twelfth largest city in Illinois, as an overgrown farm town, the Thomases must have seen it as a metropolis. Rich in public buildings and parks—especially Miller Park on the south side of town—the "evergreen city" boasted forty miles of paved streets, an efficient public utilities system, twelve primary schools, four parochial schools, five music schools, a business school, and a host of thriving banks, restaurants, and businesses, including what became the Funk Brothers agribusiness conglomerate.

Bloomington had about one hundred businesses and intended to have more. Although a fire in 1900 had destroyed much of the downtown area, the city business elite had rallied to rebuild the lost blocks at a cost of $2 million. The citizens of Bloomington could be justly proud of their most prominent sights: the McLean County courthouse, the massive Soldiers and Sailors Monument in Miller Park, the homes of the Hill, Livingston, Holton, and Wochner families, the Masonic Temple, and many churches of all the major Protestant faiths, several Catholic churches, and a Jewish temple. The town had been settled by Anglo-American immigrants from the mid-Atlantic states and Kentucky and also had a large German-American community with its own churches, a German-American bank, and active *Turnverein* and *Maennerchor* societies. Bloomington was a town of associations: the Masons, the Hibernians, the St. Patrick Total Abstinence and Benevolent Society, Knights of Pythias, the Independent Order of Odd Fellows, and an active lodge of the Grand Army of the Republic. Although Bloomington had been an early bastion of the Republican party, its active Democratic party, built around the Catholics and "wets," made elections occasional contests. The citizens of Bloomington considered their home "a city of refinement."[10]

For Vander Thomas, the important thing was Bloomington's position as a railroad town. Track, flowing through and around the city in fourteen different directions, linked major lines between Chicago and St. Louis and between the graineries across the Mississippi and the cities of the Midwest. The Chicago and Alton Railroad had built large shops to service and repair locomotives and railway cars. Local businesses provided all sorts of goods and services to the railroads, principally the Chicago and Alton and the Illinois Central. To be near his office at the Chicago and Alton's eastern division headquarters, Vander purchased a small, one-story house at 904 West Locust Street at the foot of a viaduct that crossed the Chicago and Alton's right-of-way. The home was west of Main Street, which divided the affluent and less affluent neighborhoods of Bloomington. Relocating to a house on West Locust Street meant that the Thomases entered a neighborhood of railway workers, many of them Irish and German Catholics, rather than one in which Bloomington's polite society moved. Preferring to spend his time, even his nonworking hours, around the railroad yards in the company of railroad men, Vander probably did not care about the social implications of living in west Bloomington. Virginia, on the other hand, saw little merit in her new neighborhood or her house on West Locust Street, a busy thoroughfare. She did something about the house, for within a year or so the family moved to a two-story frame house with a yard on the next street to the south, 905 West Mulberry Street. Virginia still did not like the neighborhood school on West

Market Street. She wanted her children to attend a more demanding upper middle-class school across town. Shelton and Gerald probably did not share their mother's educational ambition because they were set back half a grade when they entered the Bloomington school system.[11]

The move to Bloomington offered Virginia Thomas several potential compensations for leaving her family in Missouri—if she could drive Vander to earn enough money to exploit Bloomington's opportunities. She could see her children educated through high school in the Bloomington public school system and reasonably hope that they might continue on to college at Illinois Wesleyan University, a sober Methodist institution just north of downtown Bloomington. An alternative was Illinois State Normal University, located in the adjoining town of Normal. A life-long Methodist, Virginia probably preferred Illinois Wesleyan, a liberal arts college that stoutly maintained "a Christian atmosphere," banned drinking, and offered tuition assistance to eager but impoverished students. Moreover, Bloomington was a city devoted to music. The Amateur Musical Club brought professional musicians to perform in the city's acoustically renowned coliseum and arranged local concerts and recitals. Bloomington had an ardent city band; musical instructors abounded. (Not surprisingly, Louis and Mary Frances Thomas started music lessons as young children and became proficient singers and pianists.) Bloomington was also a city of churches and churchgoers, whose values provided a stark contrast to the values of Vander's railroad friends. Virginia Thomas seems to have made a bargain with a husband she no longer respected and may not have loved: she would not interfere with his life as long as he provided enough money for her children to advance in the world. Gerald admired his mother's ability to spend his father's modest salary for the family's benefit, but he saw no family savings and decided early in life to become as financially self-sufficient as possible.

Gerald went to work for the Bloomington *Daily Pantagraph,* the city's morning newspaper. The *Pantagraph* provided a steady source of employment for a serious, energetic teenager. Gerald carried papers and then graduated to the address machine in the mailroom. He enlarged his savings account with much harder summer jobs. When Virginia went west in 1910 with Louis and Mary Frances to visit her sister in New Mexico, Vander hired his two oldest sons to work on the right-of-way crew of the Chicago and Alton at twenty-five cents an hour for a ten-hour day of back-breaking labor. The boys relished living in the gang's special boxcars and the chance to travel to jobs throughout the state. During the next three summers, Gerald worked in construction, both for the money and to harden himself for football, which he played with reckless abandon and considerable success for Bloomington High School. Gerald used much of his college savings in 1914, however, to help his father pay Shelton's medical bills when his older brother had an almost fatal case of typhoid fever.

The years 1910–14 were not easy ones for the Thomases. Plagued by sciatica and rheumatism, Vander left the railroad and went to work as a carpenter and then a foreman for H. M. Saleh Brothers Construction Company. In 1915, he left Bloomington to work on a new factory being built for Caterpillar Tractor in Peoria. His family moved to a home east of Main Street on Beecher Street, which bordered the Illinois Wesleyan campus.[12]

Gerald had decided that his entry to college would come through athletics and part-time jobs. He and his brother Shelton had haunted the YMCA since they had moved to Bloomington. Gerald became a passable basketball player, although he was not physically imposing at 5'9" and around 160 pounds. Football, in which he played offensive and defensive line, proved to be his best sport. Aware that he was not academically well prepared for college, he courted, and was courted by, several preparatory schools to play football for the 1914 season while he completed high school. He considered going to either Mercersberg Academy or Staunton Military Academy, both in Virginia, but chose instead to attend Evanston Academy in Evanston, Illinois. Gerald did not last long at the academy. After breaking his arm at football practice during the second week of school, he returned to Bloomington to finish high school. He then became ill with appendicitis and required surgery. Losing one semester of high school, he successfully appealed to Illinois Wesleyan to admit him as a special student. He completed his high school requirements by the spring of 1915 while working for the *Pantagraph* in the mailing room; he became the supervisor with the princely salary of $10 a week. His determination and persistence paid off. Illinois Wesleyan admitted him as a regular student for the 1915 fall semester, with advanced credit in sociology, economics, English, and history.

Gerald had entered college at the age of twenty. He burned the candle at both ends for the next two years. If the candle had had three or four ends, he would have burned them, too. He lived at home to save money, but he joined Sigma Chi fraternity and spent plenty of time with his brothers at the fraternity house on Main Street. He probably joined the fraternity through the sponsorship of Fred Young, another Bloomington High School athlete, who became a Titans star pitcher and (later) sports editor of the *Pantagraph*. The "Sigs"—cheerful, indolent, and independent—were the Illinois Wesleyan "jock" house and did not feel especially bound by campus rules against drinking. "They are in college, but not of it, seemingly misunderstanding certain rules," according to *The Wesleyan*. Thomas became an enthusiastic member of Sigma Chi; he wore a fraternity ring for the rest of his life and delighted at hearing and singing "The Sweetheart of Sigma Chi." His first love at Illinois Wesleyan was football. He played on a 6–2 Illinois Wesleyan team in the autumn of 1915. *The Wesleyan* reported, "'Fat' is a bear on defense . . . has played football all his life." In the 1916 season, the Titans, plagued by injuries, finished 1–6 but beat Normal, their traditional foe. The end of football season brought no end to Gerald's athletic interest. He went out for basketball and made the team for the 1915–16 and 1916–17 seasons, but he didn't play much. In the 1916–17 season, he appeared in five of nineteen games and didn't score for a .500 team. He joined the track team in the spring, although he hadn't run competitively since 1912. The picture in *The Wesleyan* shows Thomas in manager's garb with the 1916 track team.

Other demands competed with Gerald's love for athletics. He had to earn his tuition money, if not his room and board. He worked in the *Pantagraph* mailroom six days a week from 0230 until 0530, sometimes napping before going to class. He continued to attend class throughout the summer sessions and studied when he could. His grades were not distinguished: Cs in rhetoric, geometry, and algebra, and Bs in trigonometry and chemistry for seven courses in 1915–16. His academic performance did not improve in his second full academic year. He received two Cs in philosophy; failed German; and received a B in English history, a C in economics, and a B, two Cs, and a D in four different chemistry courses. These grades, however, did not reveal all that Gerald had learned.[13]

During his first chemistry course in the second semester (1915–16), he became the protege of Dr. Alfred W. Homberger, chairman of the chemistry department. The thirty-eight-year-old native of Wisconsin, who received his doctorate from the University of Illinois in 1910, matched Gerald's enthusiasm for campus life at Illinois Wesleyan. Not uncommon at a university of fewer than five hundred students and a small faculty, Professor Homberger did far more than teach classes. He and Thomas saw each other often. The professor served as a "friend" of Sigma Chi and faculty advisor to the chemistry club, and he sat on the athletic board. Professor Homberger had also seen a larger world than Slater, Missouri, and Bloomington, Illinois. He had done graduate-level research at Columbia University and the University of Göttingen. In order to supplement his faculty salary, the professor hired out his research skills to the Illinois Anti-Saloon League. He checked beer samples for excess alcohol content, and Gerald served as his laboratory assistant. (Under the city prohibition laws then in effect, beer could not have an alcohol content above 3.4 percent.)

The dapper, cerebral Homberger tested a lot of beer, which overwhelmed the laboratory's icebox. Homberger then sent the suspect beer over to the Sigma Chi house for group testing in which he, too, participated. In part for Gerald's able assistance as a beer-tester and in part because of the professor's trust in his drive and intelligence, Homberger recommended his student for a full scholarship at the Mellon Institute in Pittsburgh, Pennsylvania. Here, Thomas could finish his collegiate career without working full time and could receive a degree in chemical engineering. Gerald was supposed to transfer to the Mellon Institute for the 1917 autumn semester. Despite the fact that Professor Homberger assured him that he had a great future as a chemical engineer, Gerald may have wondered about a career as a chemist. Industrial chemistry was showing disconcerting signs of rapid change, and Illinois Wesleyan was not exactly on the cutting edge of the specialty. The entry of the United States into World War I spared Gerald from entering a profession in which he had little intrinsic interest and aptitude, but which his mother and favorite professor had chosen for him.

What kind of man had Gerald C. Thomas become when he sought military service in April 1917? He was, first of all, a young man of considerable practical intelligence and realism. He was accustomed to uncertainty and hard work. His parents, in their own and very different ways, loved and supported him, both for his own merit as their son and as an instrument in a classic clash of wills between an uncompromising husband and an ambitious wife. By some mysterious psychic chemistry, Thomas drew the best from both his parents: intelligence, physical hardiness, determination in the face of adversity, a strong sense of place and person and of belonging to the traditional America of the first Anglo-American Protestant settlers. Thomas never had to look for his roots because he knew where they were and what they meant. From his Thomas forebears and his exposure to the Marshall family, he knew he had an obligation to serve his country in time of war. He had already known considerable frustration and disappointment as a teenager—seeing his savings go to pay Shelton's medical bills and suffering disappointment at Evanston Academy. His two and a half years at Illinois Wesleyan had helped him to recover from these experiences. Thomas now saw before him a professional career that he knew offered social prestige and economic security, both of which would make his mother happy.

Yet when the United States entered the war, Thomas did not wait to see how his personal plans might fit into the national mobilization. He was among the first sixteen Illinois Wesleyan students to volunteer. If he had not sought military service, he could have certainly postponed, if not avoided, the draft. After the declaration of war on 6 April, a total of 27,304 Illinoisans joined the National Guard or enlisted in the U.S. Army. When the War Department established a 1917 draft quota of 51,653 men for the state of Illinois, the state received credit for voluntary enlistments that satisfied more than half of that quota. At the county level, McLean County had provided 287 volunteers against a draft quota of 681, which required the county draft board to provide 394 additional young men for military service. Judged against the county's performance in the Civil War, meeting a quota of 394 would not have been much of a problem. In fact, the student body of Illinois Wesleyan alone provided almost a like number of servicemen. That the initial draft would not bear heavily on America's young male population was well known, but this knowledge made no difference to Thomas. He was already planning to leave for Fort Sheridan, Chicago, to become an officer in the Army.[14]

Uncle Sam wanted men like Thomas to be officers. As the War Department assessed the officer requirements of a mobilized army of no fewer than one million men and probably no more than two million men (for such were the conservative estimates of April 1917), it calculated that it could not meet its needs without a massive program to commission "emergency" officers through a system of Army-controlled officer training camps. The War Department already had some experience in managing officer candidate schools. It had adopted a civilian-sponsored initiative, the Plattsburg Movement camps of 1914, and had operated camps in 1915 and 1916 for young men who wanted peacetime military training. The National Defense Act of 1916 allowed the Army to commission qualified graduates of the summer training camps in the Officer Reserve Corps, along with college students who completed military training courses on campus. Even before the passage of the Selective Service Act on 18 May 1917, The Adjutant General had announced on 17 April that the Army would open sixteen officer training classes on 15 May at thirteen Army bases throughout the country. Two classes would be held at Fort Philip H. Sheridan just outside Chicago. The officer candidate classes were designed to produce officers from the cream of America's young men: recent college graduates, college students (especially athletes), and high school graduates who had experience in white-collar occupations. In the month between the announcement and the course opening, the War Department screened 150,000 volunteers and accepted 43,000 for admission to the ninety-day precommissioning courses, from which 27,341 men eventually graduated. The administrative load, however, inevitably led to problems. The Army asked officer candidates to provide their own uniforms and two blankets.

The Marine Corps profited from another Army oversight: the Army did not initially enroll Gerald C. Thomas in the 15 May class despite his eagerness to attend. In mid-April 1917, an Army captain arrived in Bloomington to interview prospective officer candidates from among the male students of Illinois Wesleyan and Normal State University. Along with several of his football teammates, Thomas volunteered and began to collect the documents his application required. By 24 April, he had gathered letters of endorsement from the Illinois Wesleyan registrar and treasurer, the head cashier of the McLean County Bank, and the pastor of the Grace Methodist-Episcopal Church. On 13 May, Bloomington youths began to receive orders to Fort Sheridan, but no orders came to Thomas. He thought about other options, such as waiting for the draft or enlisting in the National Guard or the regular Army. He talked about his dilemma with Alfred Brown, president of the Public School Publishing Company. An enlisted Marine in his own youth, Brown encouraged Thomas to think about joining the Marine Corps, which was also seeking ardent volunteers for its expanding officer corps and enlisted ranks. Marine Corps advertising, saturating the country through 2,600 newspapers (but not in the *Pantagraph*), trumpeted an irresistible appeal: the Marines would be the "First to Fight" the despicable Huns, and the Corps would find many of its new officers from among the college men who enlisted now.[15]

Major General Commandant George Barnett saw the World War mobilization as a marvelous opportunity to enlarge the Marine Corps, to build its reputation as an elite fighting force, and to fill its ranks with the highest-quality new officers and recruits. Even discounting its possible wartime missions in 1917, the Marine Corps could not meet its peacetime requirement for an estimated 1,000 officers and 17,400 enlisted men. The Corps was supposed to maintain an Advanced Base Force to defend expeditionary naval bases, but its active forces had become absorbed in two brigades in the Dominican Republic and Haiti, both involved in the pacification and administration of these tumultuous Caribbean nations. In March 1917, the Navy Department, by an executive order approved by President Wilson, announced that the Corps would expand to its emergency enlisted strength of 17,400, as established in the Naval Act of 1916. (The Corps had only 341 officers and 10,056 men in June 1916.) As the likelihood of war increased, Barnett received authority to enlarge the enlisted strength by an additional 4,000 men. After the declaration of war, Headquarters Marine Corps established a new goal of 30,000 Marines, which was approved by Congress in mid-May. The new officer strength of the expanded Corps was 1,197. By the end of June, the Corps had 874 officers and, by September, 1,099, almost all lieutenants commissioned as "emergency" or Reserve officers.

General Barnett and Secretary of the Navy Josephus Daniels, whose ardor for social egalitarianism was matched only by his military ignorance, disagreed about the social base of the Marine officer corps. Barnett preferred Naval Academy graduates (of which he was one) and college graduates, preferably with campus military training like that provided by the Virginia Military Institute, a favored source of civilian candidates. Daniels, a North Carolina progressive who scorned a "Washington aristocracy" that included General and Mrs. Barnett, pressured the Commandant to reserve officer vacancies for meritorious enlisted men, a policy Barnett announced in June 1917. With all the promotions already granted or in process, there were fewer than one hundred vacancies by summer's end. During April through June 1917, the Marine Corps enlisted almost 14,000 new Marines, many of them potential officers. With no officer vacancies, however, and in accordance with Marine Corps policy, they would have to prove their merit by service as corporals and sergeants in the new Corps.[16]

Unaware of the higher politics of Marine Corps recruiting, an impatient Gerald C. Thomas and two of his friends, Leonard O. Prather and James T. Elliott, decided that they could no longer wait for orders to the Fort Sheridan officer training camp. Prather was the Titans' fullback and, as a Staunton Military Academy graduate, Illinois Wesleyan's best drillmaster; the blond, balding Elliott was an athlete from Normal State College. When no orders arrived on 14 May, the last day before the officer training class began, the three friends decided to go to Chicago and enlist in the Marine Corps, a decision they shared with the *Pantagraph* and, presumably, their families and Mr. Brown. At 0730 on the morning of 15 May, Gerald, Len, and Jim—"strong, robust chaps . . . well fitted for the life upon which they are to enter," in the words of the *Daily Pantagraph*—took the first train to Chicago, bound for the Marine Corps recruiting station. (Thomas took along his letters of recommendation for Army officer training but made no effort to contact Fort Sheridan.) The train had already left Bloomington when the telegraph office opened at 0800 and received the message accepting Thomas for Army officer training. Spiritually as well as geographically, as Thomas remembered, "happily we were long gone" when the telegram arrived.[17]

Gerald, Len, and Jim found the Marine recruiting station on South State Street, a storefront decorated with Marine Corps recruiting posters. The heroic posters of James Montgomery Flagg, Howard Chandler Christy, and J. C. Leyendecker fused the Corps' martial past of expeditionary duty in the Caribbean with the high excitement of intervention in the European war: "Want Action? . . . First to Fight . . . Join the Marines." A sergeant in dress blues, probably Barnett Neidle, made a quick judgment of the three men's physical condition and asked them a few questions about their background, health, and motives for enlistment. He then took them to a Marine first lieutenant, who administered the oath of enlistment. Under the existing regulations, Thomas, Prather, and Elliott agreed to serve four years, but the recruiters probably assured them (accurately in this case) that Congress would make such enlistments "for the duration of the war," not a full regular enlistment. In fact, even the oath of enlistment was tentative because the recruiting station staff could not provide careful physical examinations or complete all of the enlistment paperwork. Full processing would have to wait until the recruits reached a Marine base.

After enlisting, the three young men took a train to Evanston and had dinner with Jim's brother, a Northwestern University medical student, at his fraternity house. They then returned to the recruiting station where they found almost a hundred fellow recruits awaiting transportation. Ahead of them lay a two-day train ride south. Sometime during the night of 15 May, two carloads of recruits left Chicago for the Marine Barracks, Port Royal, South Carolina. The base, however, had become better known by its local name: Parris Island.[18]

[CHAPTER II]

Becoming a Marine
1917

MAJOR GENERAL COMMANDANT GEORGE BARNETT knew exactly why he wanted Gerald Thomas and the thousands of young men like him at the recruit depots at Parris Island, South Carolina, and Mare Island, California. The urbane Commandant, a veteran of Marine Corps politics and skilled with Congress, intended that the Marine Corps not only be "the first to fight," but that his Marines fight where the battle meant most to the country and the Corps. In the spring of 1917, that place was France, not the Caribbean. Barnett had sent a series of observation missions to Britain and France early in the World War. By the autumn of 1915, he had a sound grasp of the requirements for warfare on the Western Front. Barnett promised Secretary of the Navy Daniels and Chief of Naval Operations Adm. William S. Benson that the Marine Corps would not shirk its naval responsibilities. He also insisted that the Corps' participation in the war, should the United States intervene, would produce lasting benefits: it would eventually improve the Corps' ability to perform its principal mission, the seizure and defense of advanced naval bases. Serving abroad as part of an American expeditionary force would enhance the Corps' reputation for prowess in battle—the foundation of its public appeal—and undoubtedly increase its size. In addition, the wartime Marines would receive invaluable experience in all phases of modern warfare, including the employment of field artillery, aviation, trucks, all sorts of crew-served weapons, communications, and engineering equipment. Even when reduced in size after the war, the Corps was likely to be larger than its prewar strength, and its new cadre of officers and noncommissioned officers would be unparalleled in leadership qualities and combat experience. Such was Barnett's vision, shared by his assistant, Brig. Gen. John A. Lejeune. From Headquarters Marine Corps, housed in a rented office building in downtown Washington at the corner of New York Avenue and 14th Street, the orders flowed out to the recruit depots to make Marines that would turn the vision into reality.[1]

The demand to make Marines fell most heavily on the cadre of a new command, the Marine Corps Recruit Depot, Parris Island. Although the depot had been created by the Navy Department in October 1915, little had been done to build a training base from six thousand acres of tidal island and assorted buildings that had survived episodic Navy and Marine Corps use since the Civil War. Barnett wanted the depot to house seven thousand recruits at a time and to have the two critical requirements for recruit training, a massive drill field and a large rifle range. The location could not have been less appealing. Surrounded by dark tidal mud flats, the island's pathetic groves of pines and live oaks, stunted by Atlantic winds, huddled like outcasts among the marsh grasses and sand flats. There was water everywhere, but too salty to drink; all fresh water for human consumption had to be trucked or piped in from mainland wells. On this primitive seascape, the Marine Corps erected more than five hundred new buildings during the years 1917–18 and trained 46,202 of its 58,103 wartime enlisted men. It also created a mystical experience that embodied all the twentieth-century Marine Corps came to mean. As one World War I Marine later reflected, Parris Island was to the Marine Corps what the parochial schools were to the Catholic church.[2]

In May 1917, however, Parris Island had barely begun to function as either a school or holy place. Hurriedly assembled from various posts and stations, the officers and noncommissioned officers (NCOs) who would make young men into Marines had just started to organize and train the first recruit companies. Much of their effort went into the sheer burden of administrative processing, medical examinations, and physical survival in an extemporized cantonment that was short of everything but people. Working eighteen-hour days, the cadre had but eight weeks to turn the eager recruits into passable basic Marines. In this, they succeeded and left a lasting impression. As one recruit wrote his parents:

> The first day I was at camp I was afraid I was going to die. The next two weeks my sole fear was that I wasn't going to die. And after that I knew I would never die because I'd become so hard that nothing could kill me.[3]

Two days and a thousand miles from Chicago, Gerald Thomas, who had become "Jerry" to his fellow Marines, arrived in Port Royal by train on 17 May 1917. The two coaches with "400 of us all fine fellows" had come south through Cincinnati and Atlanta, where the recruits had spent one night in the Kimball Hotel, a notorious sporting house temporarily sanitized in the name of the war effort. For the next ten days, Jerry and his comrades plunged into the hectic life of the seven thousand recruits at Parris Island and finished the enlistment process. There were a series of shocks. Shorn of their hair like so many sheep, the recruits, with identification numbers painted on their skulls with iodine and clad only in white cotton pajamas, marched from one processing station to another. Jerry lost his civilian clothes somewhere during the processing, but he found the food "coarse but good" and in ample quantity. He passed his physical examination with ease: hearing and vision normal, tonsils slightly enlarged, complexion "ruddy," hair brown, eyes brown, height 68 inches, weight 167 pounds, and general physical condition excellent. Just as the novelty and anxiety began to ebb, the Illinois recruits finished processing and joined training companies. Jerry, Jim Elliott, and Len Prather found themselves in Company 32-M with forty-seven other recruits under the supervision of Gy. Sgt. James Borden, a veteran NCO. The company was "putty in his hands and in a manner common to DIs [drill instructors] he never let us forget it." With a rich vocabulary but no need for physical abuse, Sergeant Borden began to make Marines of Company 32-M, "a pliable group" that "readily adapted ourselves to the discipline and rough routine of our new life."[4]

During the next six weeks, Company 32-M followed an unfaltering schedule as Sergeant Borden taught discipline, teamwork, and the importance of being Marines. Billeted in tents, the recruits slept on cots with a single blanket (no sheet, no mattress). They tumbled out for breakfast, greeted the sun, and policed up their area. Then Sergeant Borden, inspired by the *Landing Party Manual* and his own experience, drilled the company on the packed sand flats near Spivey Beach. Like his comrades, Jerry Thomas became intimately familiar with the weight and balance of the "U.S. Rifle, .30-caliber, Springfield, Model 1903." As the company marched and countermarched or practiced the manual at arms, the recruits' sweat spread along the base of peaked campaign hats, streamed through rough khaki cotton shirts, dripped down trousers, and seeped into canvas leggings.

The drill went on and on, up to nine hours a day, broken only by sessions of bayonet practice, physical training both with and without rifles, bouts with the obstacle course, and other labors. The men spent an hour each day washing clothes, shined shoes at least twice a day, and carried buckets of crushed oyster shells to pave the company street. By the end of June, the company was hiking in full field gear, which weighed fifty pounds a man. The recruits found their living conditions improved, however, when they moved into wooden barracks that boasted the ultimate luxury, real "heads."[5]

Jerry Thomas thrived on the training. By the end of June, he had already thought of applying for a commission. He had served as an acting squad leader for a month and liked the responsibility. He thought he would become a corporal shortly after he left Parris Island, whether he went to France or Santo Domingo. "Marines can . . . take care of themselves wherever they are." His only serious complaint was that he couldn't get enough candy, and he asked his mother to send some. In fact, he worried about his family, for Virginia Thomas had decided to follow her husband to Peoria. Jerry promised to send some money when he could to help with the move. He doubted that he would miss Bloomington since it was no longer his home. In the meanwhile, he survived a round of inoculations and a sudden rainy spell that turned Parris Island into a steaming quagmire. He relished the fact that Company 32-M would leave the drill field and spend a full two weeks on the rifle range, the long-awaited opportunity to see if his Springfield, so lovingly cleaned and oiled, could really shoot.[6]

Jerry found marksmanship training just as exciting and rewarding as he hoped—until the official qualification day. Like thousands of Marines, Jerry learned that the Springfield, built around a Mauser action, put bullets where they were supposed to hit, provided one mastered the intricate sight adjustments for windage and elevation and maintained a tight sling and firm firing position. At 8.69 pounds, the rifle could become a test to hold on target. The 30-06 ball cartridge, propelled by 46 to 50 grains of powder, left the muzzle at 2,700 feet per second, generating a recoil of 14.98 foot-pounds. The 1917 marksmanship course demanded emotional calm and polished technique. Each Marine fired 60 rounds from six different combinations of ranges, positions, and time. For the slow-fire positions (one minute maximum for each shot), he fired 10 rounds each at 200 yards (standing), 500 yards (sitting or kneeling), and 600 yards (prone) at two different sized targets with concentric scoring rings. A "possible" at each position was 50 points; each bulls-eye rated a score of 5 points. The rapid-fire positions required the Marine to fire 10 rounds in one minute at a silhouette target from a sitting or kneeling position at 200 yards, 10 rounds in one minute and ten seconds from the prone position at 300 yards, and 10 rounds in one minute and twenty seconds from the prone position at 600 yards. The rapid-fire stations also produced a "possible" of 50 points each, for a course total of 300 points. Minimum qualification as a marksman required 202 points; as a sharpshooter, 242 points; and as an expert rifleman, 253 points.

The Springfield rifle, however, could be an inconstant friend. The recoil could bruise one's shoulder, and a loose union of trigger hand and right cheek over the stock and receiver could produce a swollen lip and purple cheek. There were other perils: the elevation leaf on the sight needed watching because it could slip, and a slight elevation of the bolt with one's right hand during sighting might cause a misfire because the bolt main spring would not then drive the firing pin with full force. Whatever the perils of marksmanship training, the Marine Corps wanted its men to shoot straight and true. It had fielded championship teams in national competition for more than twenty years. In 1917, the Corps boasted that 61.9 percent of its recruits qualified as marksman or better, a percentage higher than the Army's and a distinct improvement from the 1910 level of 20.9 percent. The Marine Corps and the Army both paid qualified shooters from $1 to $3 more a month, depending on one's score. If you could not shoot the Springfield, you were not a "real" Marine.[7]

Despite satisfactory scores in practice, Jerry Thomas did not qualify on record day, and "no one knew what went wrong." He thought that the heat, ninety-five degrees at 0600 that day, might have had something to do with his poor shooting. Irritated and anxious because of his "relapse," Jerry had a slight swoon in his self-confidence, but he found victory even in disappointment. If he had been a superior shooter like Len Prather, who qualified as a sharpshooter, he might have been held at the Parris Island rifle range as a coach. With Len Prather reassigned, the Illinois Wesleyan trio fell to two when Company 32-M returned to its barracks. Jerry was happy to leave the rifle range and to return to those parts of soldiering in which he excelled. As rumors about the fate of Company 32-M circulated, Jerry and his comrades stood guard duty, served on police details, drilled, attended some classes, and enjoyed a new freedom to visit the canteen and watch movies and boxing matches. For all intents and purposes, recruit training had ended. Jerry Thomas could now be called "Marine."[8]

Even before Company 32-M finished recruit training, the first Marines had sailed for France to become part of the American Expeditionary Forces (AEF) commanded by Gen. John J. Pershing, a hard-bitten cavalryman who combined a wealth of field service with political deftness. Although the War Department General Staff, overwhelmed with the mobilization of the wartime Army, showed no enthusiasm for a Marine contingent in the AEF, Secretary of War Newton D. Baker agreed to accept a regiment of Marines in the first contingent of troops (the 1st Division) dispatched to France, largely for psychological purposes. The Marines would have to equip and organize themselves to conform to Army infantry regiment standards, but Marine regiments already conformed in most of the important ways. The major change was the size (new to the Army as well) of the wartime infantry regiment, three battalions of four companies each. Although the Table of Organization (T/O) size of the standard AEF infantry regiment climbed from 2,709 to 3,699 officers and men in 1917 as it underwent two reorganizations, General Barnett was determined to meet whatever criteria the Army set—as long as he could get Marines into the fighting in France. His fondest dream, unrealized, was to field an entire Marine division; at a minimum, he planned to ship one full brigade (a headquarters, machine gun battalion, and two infantry regiments) to the AEF. He agreed that the Marines should be treated in the same manner in all matters of administration and supply as Army regiments. He also agreed to provide adequate replacements. When the War Department wavered, intentionally or not, in providing shipping, Barnett and Daniels found space on Navy vessels, a task simplified by the War Department's promise that it would provide all of the Marines' heavy equipment and weapons. By the end of June 1917, a hastily formed regiment, the 5th Marines, had gathered in Philadelphia and sailed for France. The 5th Marines, by 1917 standards, was a veteran outfit. One-third of its officers and men had at least one year of prewar service, and many of them came directly from field service in the Caribbean. Barnett's attention then turned to the second regiment of the proposed Marine brigade.[9]

Aware that the Marine Corps needed a reservation suitable for field training, General Barnett seized the opportunity of wartime mobilization to lease 5,300 acres of scrub pines, red oaks, brushy hills, and gullies west of the Potomac River in Prince William County, Virginia. Some thirty miles south of Washington, D.C., the new reservation became Marine Barracks, Quantico, in May 1917. Until the end of the World War, Quantico served as the principal site for officer and enlisted field training and for the organization of units and replacements for overseas duty. However large the reservation in total acreage, the 1917 base grew from the ground up (sand and clay) between Quantico and Chopawamsic creeks, bordered on one side by the primary highway between Fredericksburg and Washington and on the other by the Potomac River. The main line of the Richmond, Fredericksburg, and Potomac Railroad paralleled the river to the east and the main building site to the west. The sleepy village of Quantico, surrounded by the base, offered few attractions. Marines from all over the United States came to a base that was ill prepared to receive them. Contractors scraped roads from the woods, including Barnett Avenue, the base main road, and threw up wooden barracks, offices, and supply shacks from unseasoned wood. Tents served—more or less—to handle the excess demand for shelter. The summer of 1917 was unusually hot and humid. Welcome thundershowers only turned the ubiquitous dust into red mud tenacious enough to make glue. Quantico had not seen military activity in such primitive conditions since it had served as an encampment for both Confederate and Union troops during the Civil War.[10]

Pvt. Jerry Thomas arrived by rail at Quantico station on 14 August and was assigned with many of his Parris Island comrades to the brand-new 75th Company, 1st Battalion, 6th Marines. A new regiment housed in new barracks, the 6th Marines had even fewer experienced men than the 5th Marines. Only 7 percent of the regiment—the senior officers and NCOs—had more than a year's service. The veterans were a hardened lot. Col. Albertus W. Catlin, age forty-eight, had served as a Marine officer for twenty-five years, had survived the destruction of the *Maine* in 1898, and had commanded a regiment at Vera Cruz in 1914 and won the Medal of Honor. The 1st Battalion was commanded by Maj. John Arthur Hughes, known as "Johnny the Hard." The handsome thirty-seven-year-old Medal of Honor winner (again Vera Cruz) from Brooklyn had led Marines into action in the Philippines, Mexico, and the Dominican Republic, where he had been wounded in his leg. Major Hughes more than lived up to his nickname in matters of discipline and field performance. His meager sense of humor was exhausted by the daily pain of his unhealed wound. Among the regiment's senior enlisted men were Marine Corps legends: Sgt. Maj. John Quick, 1st Sgt. Dan Daly, and 1st Sgt. Daniel O'Brien. Colonel Catlin liked his cadre, but he liked his wartime officers and men as much. They impressed him as athletic, serious, intelligent young men capable of great battlefield feats. He estimated that half of them had even attended college. (Jerry Thomas's own estimate of the 75th Company was that perhaps one-third of his comrades were "college men.") From the standpoint of Thomas and other ambitious new Marines from Parris Island, the important thing about the 6th Marines was that it had many unfilled NCO vacancies and little time to fill them.[11]

Thomas and his comrades turned to their training with high purpose because they assumed that the regimental policy on furloughs (none) meant that they were bound for France. The training, however, had less to do with war than blending into the AEF. Although the men of 75th Company received some instruction on trench warfare, they spent most of the next four weeks learning the complicated Army eight-man squad drill, a martial ballet that had lost its tactical meaning in the Civil War. Under the watchful eyes of its platoon commander, 2d Lt. David A. Redford, a short, hard Rhode Islander, and nineteen-year-old platoon gunnery sergeant, Jeremiah Dalton, a bright, forceful New Yorker with some naval militia experience, the 75th Company marched through "right front into line" and all the other variations of the complicated drill. It welcomed occasional hikes under full pack and a dose of hand-grenade practice. It spent one weekend in Washington in a review. On that occasion and one other, Jerry Thomas got a chance to meet some of his Virginia kin. In all, Jerry flourished at Quantico. He scored 100 on his corporal's examination, which meant that promotion became only a matter of time. When the company drew forest green wool winter uniforms, he knew that it would soon leave for France. He was impatient to get under way, even though he knew that not all the Marines who left Quantico would return. He wrote his mother that he and the company were ready: "I am pretty strong and should be able to hold my own." Finally, on 14 September 1917, the 1st Battalion received firm orders to depart for a port of embarkation.[12]

On the cold, rainy morning of 15 September, the 1st Battalion, 6th Marines, marched from its barracks to Quantico station where it found the regimental band fighting the weather with Sousa marches. To the cheers of the rest of the 6th Marines, the battalion headquarters and 74th, 75th, 76th, and 95th Companies boarded the train and tried to find room for bodies, weapons, and field packs, all dripping water and reeking of the distinctive smell of wet wool. Passing through Washington's Union Station, the Marines received coffee and doughnuts from Red Cross volunteers led by Mrs. George Barnett, the Commandant's wife. The battalion reached the Philadelphia Navy Yard that evening and filed immediately aboard the Navy transport *Henderson* to find a welcome dinner of franks and beans. The next morning, as the troops and ship's company came to attention for "To the Colors," the *Henderson* slipped its lines and steamed down the Delaware River. It then turned north toward New York harbor where it was to meet two other transports and its escort of one American cruiser and four destroyers, which appeared in black-and-gray zig-zag nautical camouflage. The *Henderson* remained at anchor off Staten Island for six days. The convoy assembled and sailed for France on 23 September. Swinging north to avoid prowling U-boats meant a twelve-day passage for the convoy through the first of the season's North Atlantic storms. The regiment was off to an unsettling start in its movement to the Western Front.[13]

The voyage to Europe, despite the rough seas, brought Thomas a welcome relief from four months of intense work. Unaffected by the pitching and rolling, Jerry complained that Navy food was good, but not plentiful enough, a problem that did not worry his seasick comrades. There was no room for training aboard the crowded *Henderson* and little time for anything but police details, eating (or rather standing in lines waiting to eat), holding "General Quarters" and "Abandon Ship" drills, and maintaining rifles and field equipment. While at sea, Jerry became Corporal Thomas and sewed red-trimmed chevrons on his uniforms with hoarded enjoyment. He thought about becoming an officer but worried about the cost of uniforms. As an NCO, he supervised working parties and checked to see that Marines assigned to gun crews and sentry duty arrived on time and in proper uniform. He enjoyed the few classes for the battalion NCOs, and even receiving another battery of inoculations did not dampen his spirits. He wrote his mother that he had "never felt better in my life" and asked for more mail and packages of cigarettes and candy. With only two false submarine sightings to break the shipboard routine during the voyage, the *Henderson* passed the tip of Cornwall on the ninth day at sea. In the early morning of 4 October, Jerry watched four small French destroyers join the escort for the final run into Saint-Nazaire harbor. The *Henderson* rode a favoring tide into the port and anchored that afternoon under the watchful eye of Marine Maj. Holland M. Smith, the liaison officer from the 5th Marines. The next day, after unloading the *Henderson,* the 1st Battalion marched to the huge American tent camp five miles outside Saint-Nazaire. The war now seemed much closer.[14]

Whatever the Marines thought they would do in France—and they probably thought they would divide their time between real combat training and sampling the local *vins* and famous French *amour*—the 1st Battalion arrived to work, not to fight. While it awaited the rest of the regiment, the battalion worked on the Saint-Nazaire docks as stevedores. Shipments from the United States had swamped the local work force, much reduced by conscription for the French army, so first the 5th Marines and then the 6th Marines got an unwelcome taste of backbreaking manual labor. Almost every day, now Sgt. Jerry Thomas, who had been acting platoon gunnery sergeant since Dalton departed for a school, marched with the 75th Company to the docks. The Marines worked long days, unbroken by lunch, because the battalion and the French apparently could not arrange to feed the troops. In desperation, they slipped off in the afternoon to dockside cafes for rum drinks and snacks, but indiscipline did not become a problem. The company welcomed the sight of its tents and cookhouse at the end of each day. This routine was broken only by Sundays off and occasional periods of drill, normally followed by a tour of sentry duty at the camp and port facilities. The Marines did not ignore the fact that their status was little better than that of German POWs and black Army labor troops.

> So here we are at Saint-Nazaire
> Our guns have rusty bores
> We are working side by side with Huns
> And nigger stevedores
> But if the Army and the Navy
> Ever gaze on Heaven's scenes
> They will find the roads are graded
> By United States Marines![15]

Although it regarded the Marines as the best disciplined, drilled, and uniformed troops in France, General Pershing's General Headquarters, American Expeditionary Forces (GHQ AEF), viewed the Marines as a mixed blessing. Plagued by administrative and logistical problems, General Pershing did not take kindly to constant Navy Department inquiries about the Marines and by predictable difficulties in arranging with the War Department to pay for all of the Marines' expenses. Pershing refused to add the 5th Marines to the 1st Division, but he promised to make the Marines part of the planned 2d Division as soon as all of the 6th Marines arrived in France. In the meantime, he thought the Marines made excellent security troops and work details. Part of the administrative confusion came from the fact that the Marines had brought with them their usual quota of Navy doctors, dentists, chaplains, and hospital corpsmen, a group of indigestible experts who insisted that *they* still worked for the Navy Department, not the Army. Even the matter of uniforms poisoned relations with the AEF. As the forest green service uniforms wore out, Headquarters wanted to replace them from Marine Corps stocks, but GHQ AEF ordered the Marines to shift to Army khaki, which they did. The Marines insisted, however, on using red-trimmed chevrons and the famous "Eagle, Globe, and Anchor" hat and collar insignias, and they replaced Army buttons with their own, which also bore the Marine Corps emblem. In addition, they exchanged campaign hats for overseas caps and canvas leggings for wrap-around puttees. The War Department had ordered Pershing to accept a Marine brigade, but it could not order him to like Marines or them to like him.[16]

Sergeant Thomas of the 75th Company, 1st Battalion, 6th Marines, proud of his stripes and conscious of his duty, felt only the daily demands of small unit leadership. He enjoyed the friendship of seven other Marines from Bloomington, including Jim Elliott, now also a sergeant in another platoon, but he missed football. This was the first autumn he could remember when he had not played. He wrote his mother that he would send some money when his pay account finally reached the blessed state of order that would allow a payday. His health was excellent despite the arduous daily routine, and his morale was good. He found France interesting, but he admitted that he had seen little but the Saint-Nazaire docks. He appreciated letters from his family but wondered what had become of the Christmas package of food they had sent. His pay eventually arrived—and he found that he had saved one hundred dollars—but Christmas came and went without the food package from Peoria. (When Thomas received the package on 19 January, he found that he had been robbed of all but a box of crackers and a jar of pickles.) Whether his pay record proved irritating or his food package arrived only as the evidence of criminal activity, Thomas took such personal disappointments in stride and never let it affect his performance of duty. He enjoyed Lieutenant Redford's confidence. The platoon commander kept him in Gunnery Sergeant Dalton's slot, even though Thomas was not the platoon's senior sergeant. During eight months of service, Jerry Thomas had become more than a Marine—he had become a leader of Marines. He would soon test his leadership in the crucible of combat.[17]

[CHAPTER III]

Marine Sergeant at War 1918

THE SOUL OF THE 4th Brigade belonged to the Marine Corps, but the bodies of its Marines belonged to John J. Pershing. In January 1918, the commander in chief of the AEF faced a dilemma of classic proportions that would affect the 4th Brigade and Jerry Thomas of the 75th Company, 1st Battalion, 6th Marines. Under instructions to cooperate with the Allies on the crucial Western Front, Pershing had also accepted an order to create an independent American army, an order in which he heartily concurred. Pershing knew, however, that such a force would not spring immediately to arms, even if the Allies provided most of the weapons and supplies. Pershing and his staff studied the war in France, pondered the plodding pace of American mobilization, gauged the training requirements urged upon them by Allied officers, and examined the American troops who arrived in France in 1917. Pershing concluded that he could mount only limited offensive operations in 1918 and that the major American effort would have to wait until 1919. The first stage of Pershing's plan required hard field training for the 1st, 2d, 26th, and 42d Divisions. They were assembled and introduced to battle in the region south of Verdun, where they would take the offensive later in 1918. In the meantime, he and his staff concentrated on organizing the training and logistical system that would support a much larger AEF.[1]

Pershing's dilemma arose from the fact that his plans did not fit the changed realities of the European war. By January 1918, the Central Powers had reduced a three-front war to a one-front war by defeating the Russians and the Italians. The two stunning victories allowed the German army to withdraw most of its divisions from the Eastern and Italian fronts, leaving those theaters to its Austro-Hungarian allies. Throughout the winter of 1917–18, German army headquarters, directed by Field Marshal Paul von Hindenburg and General Erich Ludendorff, redeployed, reorganized, and retrained its still formidable field forces. German activity for 1918, fully appreciated by both the British and French general staffs, clearly indicated that the Germans planned to regain numerical superiority (217 divisions to 169 divisions) on the Western Front and to take the offensive for the third time, to win what they had not won in 1914 and 1916.

Desperation affected all the opposing commanders. The Germans found war weariness, fed by famine and economic blockade, spreading in the army and the civilian population. The U-boat campaign of 1917 had not brought a similar level of despair to Great Britain. Germany's allies, the Austro-Hungarian and Ottoman empires, showed growing signs of military collapse. As the German General Staff appreciated, its army had one more major offensive in it and that campaign would have to win the war.[2]

The Allied armies in France took no comfort from Germany's problems; their own were equally disheartening. The offensive campaigns of 1915, 1916, and 1917 had brought the British Expeditionary Force (BEF) to the point of exhaustion. The French army emerged from the hecatomb of Verdun with its honor intact and its lines slightly bent, but it could not bear the shock of further offensives. The Allied governments and military staffs welcomed American soldiers but not an independent American army. They feared that Pershing would take too long to field anything more complicated than divisions, which were quite complicated enough. (By early 1918 Tables of Organization, an American division, built upon two infantry brigades and one artillery brigade, numbered some twenty-eight thousand officers and men at full strength.) The Allied preference, even before the German offensive of 1918, was to put American divisions under Allied commanders. Pershing found this suggestion anathema, a slur upon the skill of the U.S. Army officer corps and an open-ended invitation to Allied generals to use American troops with the same lethal thoughtlessness they had shown since 1914.[3]

Nevertheless, Pershing wanted to have at least four divisions ready for combat early in 1918. He ordered his staff to concentrate them as rapidly as possible to commit them to limited operations in relatively quiet sectors. In early January 1918, the 1st Division entered a sector on the southern side of the Saint-Mihiel salient south of Verdun and east of the Meuse River. Pershing's staff also arranged for the various parts of the 2d Division to concentrate in the Bourmont training area, also in the Department of the Haute Meuse and east of the Meuse River and the city of Neufchâteau. After combat training, supervised by French training detachments, the 2d Division would take its turn at the front. The 6th Marines joined the general redeployment and moved one step closer to the war.

On 4 January, Sgt. Jerry Thomas and the rest of the 75th Company boarded a train of small French boxcars ("Hommes 40–Chevaux 8") and headed east. The trip was an introduction to the hardships to come. The troop train took four long, cold days to reach its destination, the railroad town of Damblain, a journey of about 400 miles. Crowded in the boxcars with their packs, the Marines slept in huddled masses, ate cold corned beef and hardtack, and relieved themselves in buckets in the corner of the cars. Occasionally the train stopped to let the Marines stretch. At one stop at a French train station, the Marines found a ration of coffee laced with brandy, the trip's only memorable concession to morale. Arriving at Damblain on 8 January, the 1st Battalion marched four miles to the farm villages of Germanvilliers and Champigneulles, its billeting area. Most of the 75th Company

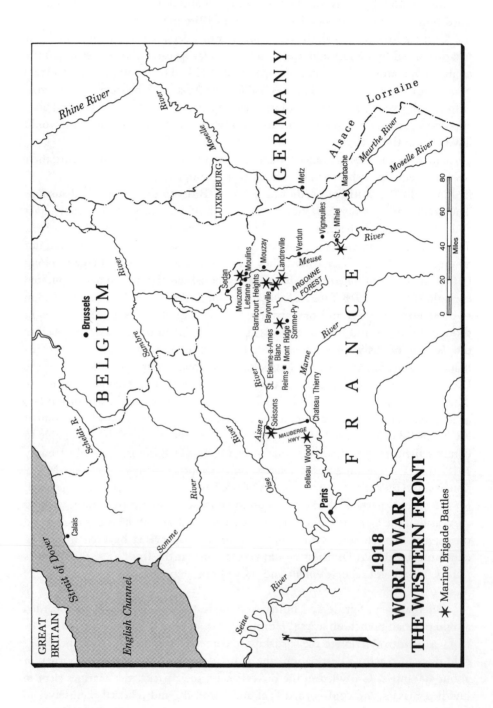

occupied two long, low wooden buildings known as Adrian barracks. The only heat came from two small stoves at either end of each building. The 95th Company moved into two other barracks on the other side of Champigneulles. Each barracks held one hundred men, so the officers and leftover enlisted men took billets in Champigneulles itself, principally in barns that provided the welcome insulation of stored hay.

The village itself had few attractions, and the Marines remembered little about it except its drab, worn, aged *paysans* and its large manure piles. They bought all the food in its one store within hours of arriving. Their enemy was the weather, for the winter of 1917–18 produced cold, ice storms, and biting winds that caused the Marines to compare their ordeal with that of the Continentals at Valley Forge. Their feet were always wet because the French allowed them to train only in marshy meadows unfit for cultivation. Each day began with moist socks, dried only by body heat as the Marines slept at night, and wet field shoes; each day ended with feet, socks, and shoes pasted together in one soggy mess. Baths were infrequent, and the laundry of wool uniforms and underclothes virtually unknown. The Marines bathed in the snow with a bucket of water; baths did not last long in the act or the effect. The Marines met their first lice and fought a losing battle to hold the biting mites at bay. Jerry Thomas could not imagine conditions "more calculated to toughen people. The outfit was so damn mean that they could have fought their own grandmothers."[4]

The 75th Company lived hard and trained hard within a schedule largely dictated by its French instructors. Trench warfare skills were the order of the day: bayonet practice on dummies, throwing and firing hand and rifle grenades, practicing the arcane skills of fortifying trenchlines and conducting trench raids. A typical training day began with a forced march out to a mock-up trench area and instruction and exercises that lasted well into the night, followed by a hike back to the barracks. A twenty-mile forced road march for conditioning purposes proved a welcome relief because the Marines warmed up and kept their feet out of the mud. Jerry Thomas and his comrades found their pleasures in the hallowed victories of infantrymen over unrelieved hardship: an occasional meal that combined some taste and warmth, a pair of dry socks, a good night's sleep, a nap in front of a villager's fireplace, a quiet moment hunched over a latrine hole, the passing humor of a joke shared with one's comrades, a sip of brandy, any slight diversion from the grinding routine of training.

As the training progressed, the 1st Battalion changed. Major Hughes departed for an Army school at Gondrecourt; Capt. Robert Emmet Adams, commander of the 75th Company, replaced him as acting battalion commander. The company command fell to the senior lieutenant until the arrival of Capt. Edward C. Fuller, the son of a Marine colonel, a 1916 graduate of the Naval Academy, and a conscientious officer eager to make good in the Marine Corps. In the rearrangements, 2d Lt. Carlton Burr, also of the 75th Company, became the battalion intelligence officer. Burr was a veteran, but not in the Marine Corps. A slight, cerebral graduate of Harvard University (1913), Burr had completed voluntary Army officer training in the summer camp at Plattsburgh, New York, in 1914 while he was employed as a junior executive in a utilities company. Drawn to the World War by his sympathy for France, he had served as the director of American

Ambulance Unit No. 9 on the Verdun front from February 1916 until February 1917. Exhausted from his exposure to shellfire and sickened by poison gas, Burr returned to the United States but became a Marine officer during the mobilization of 1917 and came back to France with the 6th Marines.

Burr was a perfect choice for his new assignment. He was familiar with the war and fluent in French, but he needed help. He turned to Jerry Thomas. In mid-February 1918, Burr asked Dave Redford if he could have his platoon gunnery sergeant as the senior NCO in the battalion's newly formed intelligence section. Redford agreed to the change and told Thomas: "I am sorry to lose you but you have been selected to head the suicide squad." Jerry welcomed the change when he learned that Burr intended to form an elite unit of scouts and observers. Burr and Thomas combed the 1st Battalion for Marines with exceptional field skills—or at least the intelligence to develop them. They chose fifteen scouts and ten observers who had shown some aptitude in scouting and patrolling exercises. Before Burr departed for an AEF school on terrain analysis and aerial photograph interpretation, he and Thomas began a rigorous training program in map reading, sketching, and night compass reading for the "suicide squad." Thomas taught himself as he taught his troops, and "a month of training gave us a reasonable degree of proficiency."[5]

Ready or not, the intelligence section of the 1st Battalion moved with the rest of the 6th Marines toward the front on 17 March and prepared to occupy the trenches held by the French 33d Division in the Toulon sector at the northwest corner of the Saint-Mihiel salient, ten miles southwest of Verdun. The 6th Marines were to hold the extreme left subsector of the line to be manned by the 2d Division, which was assigned to the French X Corps of the French First Army. The regiment detrained at Souilly on 18 March and then marched to the division headquarters at Sommedieue. While staff officers arranged the transfer of responsibility for Toulon, the regiment waited in reserve billets behind the lines. On 28 March, the 1st Battalion's intelligence section moved forward to man the observation posts on the Côtes des Heures, a five-hundred-foot high ridge behind the Bonchamp subsectors and the ruined village of Tresavaux. Jerry Thomas looked out on his first battlefield. He saw well-developed trench lines pocked with shellholes and separated by a thousand yards of barbed wire entanglements. For four years, the German and French soldiers on either side of this "No Man's Land" had dug fortifications and strung wire. Only about two hundred yards of open space separated the two wire systems; that two hundred yards of ruined earth constituted the battlefield in the Toulon sector, accessible to patrols from both sides by a series of intricate gates in the wire entanglements. Some of the wire ran in multiple strands from fixed posts. Closer to the enemy were hastily emplaced rolls of concertina wire. All of the wire was a deadly barrier to patrols.[6]

On the evening of 31 March–1 April, the 1st Battalion filed into its positions under the concealment of night, but it had to survive desultory German artillery along its line of march to Tresavaux and its outlying strongpoints. Only small parties of enlisted men manned the forward trenches, and all the Marines stayed under cover during the daytime unless duty absolutely required movement. There was little to see in any event, certainly no Germans. Col. Albertus Catlin found his battlefield as depressing as he expected:

> Through our loopholes we looked out upon a forlorn, desolate, uninhabited country. . . . The woods were splintered on every hand, the stone buildings in the villages were knocked to pieces, and some of the fields looked like freshly ploughed land. The whole countryside was pock-marked with craters. It was like a Doré vision of the end of the world—an abomination of desolation.[7]

The Marines did not like digging, but the harassing artillery of the Germans provided ample encouragement to maintain and improve the French trenches and protective dugouts. One Marine told his family that his rifle had become rusty, but his pick and shovel shined with use. The regiment lost its first casualties to a German shell, dropping on top of a working party, that killed two and wounded three Marines. The Germans, whose own scout aircraft and observation posts had identified the movement into the lines, immediately sent small patrols into the wire. French and American intelligence officers correctly identified the patrols as the preliminaries for a major trench raid. Having established observation posts, Jerry Thomas and his 1st Battalion scouts were about to get very close to the enemy.

Lieutenant Burr took his scouts into the wire for the first time on the evening of 4 April and verified what the lookouts had reported: the Germans had penetrated No Man's Land and seemed to be locating gaps and gates in the wire in front of the 6th Marines trench. Thomas learned that nighttime patrols—heart-pounding journeys into a strange land where nothing looks familiar and time and distances elude easy estimation—were far different from collating and analyzing observers' reports. Although his first patrol did not fight the Germans, it found them. On the basis of his observations, Burr planned a large patrol on 6 April, a joint French-American effort that involved about thirty Allied scouts. Its purpose was to kill or capture the Germans posted along the French wire and, if necessary, to fight any raiding party. Burr and Thomas led the patrol, moving through the friendly wire into the cleared area and then sweeping carefully across the 1st Battalion's front. Hardly had the Marines deployed than they ran into a strong German combat patrol, much better equipped and trained for trench warfare but too self-confident. The firefight swelled with the two patrols exchanging rifle and pistol fire, the crash of shots and blasts from muzzles dazzling the Marines. Everyone dropped into the nearest slimy shell holes. Someone fired flares to call in pre-planned artillery fire, which crashed into the battlefield. Machine guns from both sides of the wire raked the ground along a prearranged field of fire, the tracers whirring past the cowering men like vicious fireflies. Hell had come to Jerry Thomas and his comrades.

The very chaos of the engagement, however, meant that the Allied patrol had accomplished its mission, for no Germans would raid the 6th Marines that night. Noticing an opening in the barrage, Thomas found the French lieutenant and some of his own men, and they quickly rounded up the patrol and sprinted through the dead space to a gate in the Allied wire. Then Jerry realized that Carlton Burr was not among the party. He turned back into the mud. On his second sortie into the falling shells, he found the lieutenant, physically exhausted, in a shell hole. Gathering his energy as Burr recovered his own stamina, Jerry pulled the lieutenant to his feet and dragged him back into the friendly wire and past the Marine outposts.

As daylight broke, the patrol assembled in Tresavaux and found that it had lost one man killed (later found outside the wire along with four dead Germans) and several lightly wounded. Jerry marveled that he had escaped without a scratch and felt pleased that he had saved Burr, whom he regarded with great affection. He heard a rumor that he was going to be recommended for a French decoration, or the Medal of Honor, then learned that the battalion adjutant, Capt. Arthur H. Turner, would not approve an award for a Marine who was only doing his duty. Jerry went about his intelligence tasks with care and learned that his observers had provided verification of a major German movement from the Saint-Mihiel salient. He had no love for trench life—especially the rats and lice—but he told his mother that his work had been "highly interesting."[8]

Far from the Toulon sector, the war on the Western Front took a dramatic turn, setting off a ripple of decisions and orders that eventually reached the 2d Division. On 21 March, the German army assaulted the British Fifth and Third armies in the valley of the Somme and, in two weeks of heavy fighting, drove a forty-by-sixty-mile salient into the BEF's position in front of Amiens, a major rail center. According to existing plans, Field Marshal Sir Douglas Haig, commander of the BEF, called for French reinforcements from the quiet sectors of Lorraine. In the crisis, the British and French governments also asked for the commitment of American troops, especially fresh infantry brigades shipped directly from the United States. Pershing stood fast against amalgamation, but Secretary of War Newton D. Baker wavered. Aware that he might lose in Washington what he was winning in France on the amalgamation issue, Pershing on 28 March made an impassioned response to an equally warm plea for help from Gen. Ferdinand Foch, the new Allied supreme coordinator. Foch wanted hundreds of thousands of American troops brought to France in British ships without further training. What Pershing gave him when he promised "all that I have is yours" was the 1st Division for service with the French First Army in Picardy. The 2d Division extended its sector to the north to fill the gap left by a departing French division, and the U.S. 26th and 42d Divisions moved into quiet sectors to free additional French divisions for the battle to the north.[9]

Untouched by the great disaster in the British sector, the 1st Battalion, 6th Marines, suffered its own small tragedies without striking back at the Germans. For two hours in the early morning of 13 April, German artillery dropped an estimated three thousand shells on the Adrian barracks in Fontaine Saint-Robert and Bonchamp. At Fontaine Saint-Robert, the mustard gas shells felled 295 Marines, almost all of them from the 1st Battalion's 74th Company, which had just returned from working in the trenches. The sleeping Marines had donned their masks too late and removed them too soon. Forty Marines eventually died from the gas attack, the heaviest casualties suffered by the 4th Brigade in the Verdun area. Gas discipline in the 1st Battalion improved immediately. In the meantime, Jerry Thomas continued to work with his scouts and observers, even after the 1st Battalion left the Toulon section on 10 May. Then the battalion changed its mind about the value of the "suicide squad," probably a decision by the new battalion commander, Maj. Maurice E. Shearer, a thirty-eight-year-old Indianan who had come to France as the commander of the 6th Marines machine gun company. A handsome and methodical officer, Shearer showed no special flair for field operations; most of his sixteen years in the Marine Corps had been spent on sea duty or in staff and administrative assignments ashore. Perhaps the company commanders demanded that Burr return their skilled, experienced Marines to general troop duty. In any event, the "suicide squad" disbanded, and Jerry Thomas returned to the 75th Company's third platoon.[10]

The 2d Division also experienced some leadership changes above the 1st Battalion, 6th Marines. Dissatisfied with the division's senior officers, General Pershing sent four of his most trusted, hardest-driving subordinates to replace the division chief of staff and the three brigade commanders. Much to the dismay of the 4th Brigade and Headquarters Marine Corps, Pershing sent Marine Brig. Gen. Charles Doyen home as unfit for field service because of illness. Although the illness judgment had some validity, Doyen had fallen prey to "The Chief's" conviction that the 2d Division could not fight offensively. Of course, it had not been asked to do so. In any event, Brig. Gen. James G. Harbord, Pershing's own chief of staff, took command of the 4th Brigade, whose officers greeted him with cool correctness. The balding fifty-one-year-old Harbord, a college graduate who had won a cavalry commission after three years in the ranks, intended to make the 4th Brigade the pride of the AEF. Pershing told him he had no excuse for failure because the Marines were the most disciplined, most fit soldiers in France. A tireless worker, Harbord had seen ample field service in the Philippines, but he had no more preparation for the Western Front than any other officer. Harbord liked to talk with his Marines, but his style with his officers was abrupt, demanding, and sometimes impatient and ill-informed. The new brigade commander and the Marines had little time to learn about one another; on 15 May, the 2d Division entrained for a new concentration point near Beauvais, midway between Paris and the menaced Amiens.[11]

Pleased with his performance in the trench war, Sgt. Jerry Thomas shouldered his pack and marched north in the warming weather to another battlefield. The 75th Company felt hard and confident. The officers and men had learned to trust one another in the month's service in the Toulon sector; the company had suffered few casualties, yet had gained a feel for combat. Even the sun felt good—at first—until the packs, bulging with trench warfare equipment and extra clothes, became intolerable and heat casualties started to drop along the road. Completing the movement by 23 May, the 4th Brigade spent the next six days on brigade maneuvers that exercised the staffs as well as the troops. Rumors abounded that the 2d Division would join an Allied counterattack against the Amiens salient within the next week. The 1st Division was already fighting for Cantigny, a village near Montdidier, a major objective.

On Sunday, 30 May 1918, Thomas and a group of 75th Company Marines strolled from their campsite to regimental headquarters for a special Memorial Day religious service. The regimental chaplain preached in vague terms about the trials that faced the 6th Marines. His obsession with "the ultimate sacrifice" confirmed what the Marines had heard from 6th Marines clerks, that the 4th Brigade had just received orders to move to Beauvais to start the counteroffensive against the Amiens salient. But there were other rumors: the Germans had opened another offensive against Paris. Before he started back to the campsite, Thomas took his detail to the regimental galley. They ate as much as they could, a sensible precaution. As the detail strolled back to camp, a messenger found Thomas and told him that Lieutenant Redford wanted him as quickly as possible. When Thomas found Redford, the platoon commander told him that the regiment had orders to move that evening. Thomas already knew about the move, so he was not surprised. Redford told him to draw 100 rounds of rifle ammunition for each man and to distribute travel and reserve rations. Neither Thomas nor Redford knew the company's destination, but that was not a new experience. They would know where they were when they got there.[12]

On the morning of 27 May 1918, forty-three German divisions, supported by a short, intense barrage from 5,000 guns, attacked the Allied position on either side of Reims. The German attack east of Reims did not gain much ground in the face of a stubborn but flexible defense by the French Fourth Army. The major German effort west of Reims at Chemin des Dames ridge placed twenty-three first-class divisions against ten weak French and British divisions under the command of the French Sixth Army. Along the Chemin des Dames, the Germans caught the French Sixth Army deployed too close to the front where it took the full shock of the German bombardment and infantry assault. In four days (27 through 30 May), the German Seventh and First Armies had advanced more than thirty miles, inflicted 100,000 casualties, and taken more than 50,000 prisoners. French reserves, committed piecemeal by French generals who had lost their nerve, fought and disappeared "like drops of rain on white-hot iron."[13] The defeat had many of the same signs as Caporetto and the early stages of the First Battle of the Marne; for the French, it cast longer shadows that reached back to the dark days of 1870–71. The Germans were once again at the approaches of Paris as their patrols scouted the Marne River crossings between Reims and Château-Thierry. To the west of Château-Thierry, north of the Marne, the IV Reserve Corps of the German Seventh Army moved forward between the Ourcq and the Marne rivers toward the Paris-Metz highway. Dining with General Foch on the afternoon of 30 May, Pershing found the French in despair, full of doubt that their own reserves could block the way to Paris in time.[14]

At dusk, the 1st Battalion, 6th Marines, marched to an assembly area where it was supposed to meet the French truck convoy that would take it to Beauvais and the Amiens counteroffensive. Little did the battalion know that the movement had been canceled at 1700. Pershing had authorized the French to use the American 2d and 3d Divisions to blunt the spearhead of the German advance at Château-Thierry. American and French staff officers tried to organize the division's movement to the concentration point, the city of Meaux, some twenty-five miles southwest of Château-Thierry. The four infantry regiments would go by truck convoy; the rest of the 2d Division would move by train, then road march. The distance to Meaux was too far for the horse-drawn machine gun carts and field artillery, as well as all the field kitchens and supply and ammunition trains. Shortly after the first truck convoys departed around midnight, the 2d Division staff learned that the French could not provide the required railway trains, which meant that the infantry regiments would enter the battle without their own machine guns and artillery in support. Nor would they have adequate food and ammunition. The logistical foul-up provided added incentive for the 2d Division to delay its battle as long as possible. Col. Preston Brown, division chief of staff, arranged for AEF supplies to meet the division at Meaux, and he took the division's advance party to meet the French, who did not want the 2d Division to wait for anything. Fortunately, the staff of the French Sixth Army could not decide where the Germans would attack next, which gave Brown precious time to assess the situation for himself and prevent a premature commitment of the 3rd and 4th Brigades.[15]

Of the 2d Division's four infantry regiments, the 6th Marines departed last from the Bar-le-Duc area in the early morning of 31 May. Sgt. Jerry Thomas rode beside the Vietnamese driver of one of the two trucks that carried the third platoon of the 75th Company, but the language barrier and clouds of dust prevented Thomas from finding out anything about the convoy's destination. He doubted that the driver knew anyway. Around dawn, Jerry could see that the convoy was passing around a city, and he finally learned from the driver that the city was Saint-Denis, nine miles north of Paris. Now Jerry knew where the company was, if not exactly where it was going. He also could guess that it would soon be fighting the Germans somewhere along the Marne. The convoy slowed as it approached Meaux. It had to push forward against a swelling tide of refugees and defeated French soldiers. The traffic jam only dramatized the confusion that had already sent the leading two regiments—at least their advance parties—from one assembly area to another. The 2d Division managed to find its immediate tactical superior, Gen. Jean Degoutte, commander of the French XXI Corps, but Degoutte, exhausted and no keen student of operational planning, could think of nothing but counterattacking with the Americans north of the Marne as soon as possible. Finally, after much heated debate, Colonel Brown, General Degoutte and Maj. Gen. Omar Bundy, the 2d Division's elderly, limited commanding general, reached an agreement. The division would defend a line astride the Paris-Metz highway, facing roughly northeast, a position that could block a move either from Château-Thierry or from the other likely approach along the Soissons road, which ran from the north through Torcy and Lucy-le-Bocage.[16]

The 6th Marines truck convoy drove—or stalled—through the afternoon of 31 May into the morning of 1 June 1918 until it reached the site of division headquarters, the town of Montreuil-aux-Lions, forty-five miles from Paris along the highway to Château-Thierry. Most of the refugees had now passed on to the west, but the town burst with American infantry, staff cars, and supply trucks, as well as convoys of *camions* struggling to return to the rear. The 1st Battalion, 6th Marines, moved into a woods near the town to wait for orders. Small parties of Marines began to forage for food among the deserted houses, an activity French officers encouraged and American officers did not stop because the battalion had exhausted most of its travel rations. Roast rabbit and chicken, accompanied by the local *vin* and fried potatoes, raised the Marines' morale, and they basked in the sun until early afternoon.

Major Shearer then ordered the 1st Battalion onto the road, and it joined a great stream of infantry heading east. After about four miles, the 6th Marines swung north on the road to Lucy-le-Bocage and the U.S. 9th Infantry of the 3d Brigade proceeded to its positions on the Marines' right flank. Thomas watched

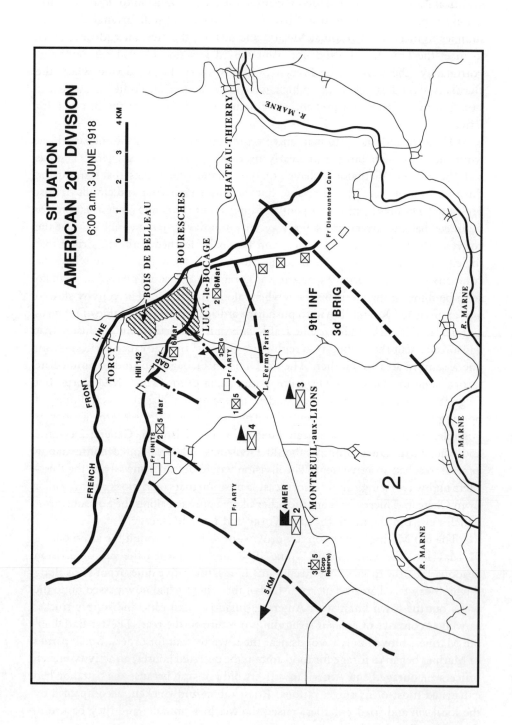

[32]

the 3d Battalion deploy in an extended formation of squad columns on the right of the Lucy road, while the 1st Battalion made a similar change in formation on the left of the road. As the two lead battalions marched toward Lucy, General Harbord and Colonel Catlin loaded the 2d Battalion on trucks and drove it directly to the village. When the 1st Battalion, moving slowly in the heat, finished its four-hour hike, Catlin deployed it to the left of the 2d Battalion. The 3d Battalion moved into a support position in a woods behind Lucy. With all four of its companies on line, the 1st Battalion still had over a mile of front to protect with little natural cover and concealment. The 75th Company was somewhat better positioned as it assumed responsibility for the defense of Lucy itself, but the village crossroads made the position an easy target for German artillery, aided by the smoke of the Marines' cooking fires. (Some rabbits, pigs, and chickens had also made the march from Montreuil.) To the front of the 6th Marines, the remnants of three French regiments still maintained contact with the Germans. The war had moved much closer to the 75th Company.[17]

Exhausted by forty-eight hours of travel, the 1st Battalion did little in the remaining daylight of 1 June to fashion an integrated defensive position. The Marines still did not have their regimental machine gun company, the brigade machine gun battalion, or support from the guns of the U.S. 12th Artillery Regiment. They had no influence over the three weak French artillery battalions in the 2d Division's sector, although the French guns still fired missions in the direction of Château-Thierry, which had fallen to the Germans the same day. Throughout the long dusk, small parties of French stragglers moved through Lucy and climbed the slight ridge to the village along the roads that led north to Torcy or from the east to the town of Bouresches. Some of the French bore wounded comrades on stretchers; others hauled small carts piled with *les blessés*. Many no longer carried their long Lebel rifles. The French had little to say except that they had seen many Germans. While the retreat continued, the Marines slept. Jerry Thomas watched the thin columns of *poilus* from his platoon's position along a hedge that bordered a vegetable garden, a position it had occupied at dawn on 2 June. As the daylight widened, with the weather warm and clear, Jerry could see to his left a field of early oats in which stray livestock browsed, oblivious to the occasional German shell that burst in the field. The Marines, however, noticed the shells and dug holes as deeply and rapidly as they could. From about a thousand yards to the 75th Company's front, scattered gunfire could be heard in the dark forest at the far edge of the field—Belleau Wood.[18]

[CHAPTER IV]

Belleau Wood
1918

A DARK FORTRESS OF TALL hardwoods, Belleau Wood stretched for about a mile along the edge of a low plateau between the roads to Torcy to the north and Bouresches to the southeast. It took its name from the farming village of Belleau, beyond the wood's northeast corner. Belleau's name comes from its only noteworthy feature—a clear, cold spring. Neither the wood nor the town would have had any importance except for the fact that they lay between two major roads. These roads gave the attacking German IV Reserve Corps a way to flank the Allied positions along the Paris-Metz highway, about four miles to the southeast, and the wood provided an excellent place to assemble safe from Allied observers. Moreover, German spotters on its western edge could see with ease the Marine brigade positions around Lucy-le-Bocage. The wood also made an excellent defensive position. Used by a rich Paris businessman as a hunting preserve, Belleau Wood deceived the Americans who watched it from a mile away. Inside the trees, it was a tangle of brush and second growth, cut by deep ravines and studded with rock outcroppings and large boulders. Only narrow paths and rocky streams provided access through the thick forest. Little light penetrated the trees in this haven for gamebirds and animals. Until 3 June 1918, Belleau Wood had been used for hunting animals, not killing men. The 4th Marine Brigade and the German 28th and 237th Divisions, however, soon converted it to an historic battlefield.

On the morning of 3 June, General de Infanterie Richard von Conta, commander of the German IV Reserve Corps, ordered a three-division attack on the French forces screening the 2d Division. As the fighting to the 4th Brigade's front swelled, German artillery, assisted by aircraft and balloon spotters, crashed down upon the Marines' defensive positions. The bombardment exceeded any of the shelling that the 1st Battalion, 6th Marines, had experienced in the Toulon sector. The battalion did not occupy well-built trenches, only quickly dug foxholes. As the shells dropped, shovels and picks rose and fell. Trips to and from the rear with water, food, and ammunition were an invitation to shell wounds. On the other hand, only a direct hit or a near miss would destroy a foxhole, so the 75th Company pulled the ground around itself and endured. Nevertheless, it suffered casualties: a curious Marine decapitated when he looked outside his hole, two men knocked senseless by a near-miss, the company commander wounded in the leg while checking his men, and a carrying party destroyed on its way forward with water. More French soldiers drifted back through Lucy. To the north, small-arms fire swelled as the first German patrols made contact with a battalion of the 5th Marines defending the woods and high ground west of the Torcy-Lucy road. The 75th Company could hear the noise of moving troops in Belleau Wood.[1]

The French delaying action had collapsed. The only sign of French combativeness was the occasional group of *poilus* who stayed with the Marines. In Jerry Thomas's position, the third platoon gained a Hotchkiss machine gun crew, a welcome addition, because Marine machine gun teams did not arrive until late in the day. The 6th Marines was spread thin, for Colonel Catlin had committed three of his four reserve companies to his endangered left flank where the 5th Marines had first met the Germans. The Marine brigade, however, finally received its own artillery support as the 12th U.S. and 17th U.S. Artillery Regiments moved into position and opened fire on suspected German positions, including Belleau Wood. In the late afternoon, the 75th Company shifted positions to meet an expected attack to its left, which meant that Thomas's platoon moved from the edge of the village into an open field. Hardly had the platoon scooped out shallow holes than a German battalion—probably between four and five hundred men—emerged from Belleau Wood in lines of skirmishers and squad columns and started across the fields toward Lucy. At a range of four hundred yards, the 1st Battalion savaged the German infantry with rapid, accurate rifle fire. The French Hotchkiss crew raked the Germans, and Jerry watched soldiers in baggy *feldgrau* uniforms spin and slump into the wheat and poppies. The German attack collapsed, and the survivors scuttled back into Belleau Wood where the rest of the 461st Infantry Regiment, 237th Division (about 1,200 officers and men), had concentrated for another attack.[2]

Uncertain about the nature of the new resistance his corps had encountered, General von Conta halted the advance on the afternoon of 3 June and instead continued his assault on the 4th Marine Brigade's lines with artillery fire. As the heavier German guns and trench mortars moved into range, the Marines felt the increased weight of the bombardment. They especially disliked the heavy mortar shells, which they could see curling in on top of them, detonating with fearsome noise and destructiveness. Before day's end, the 75th Company had suffered more casualties, but, despite hunger, thirst, and filth, the company held fast. That night, Thomas's platoon again shifted to the left and gained the welcome concealment of a small woodlot. Much of the artillery fire was now falling on positions to the rear where the Germans guessed the enemy (not yet identified as Marines) might have its reserve infantry and artillery positions. The next day (4 June), the infantrymen on either side remained in their holes as German and Allied artillery swept the front with a desultory bombardment. On the left flank of the 6th Marines' position, a German patrol found its first Marine corpse. General von Conta shifted to the defense while he awaited the German Seventh Army's decision on whether the IV Reserve Corps should make another maximum effort to reach the Paris-Metz highway from the north. In the meantime, the 6th Marines continued to improve its defensive position by building up its artillery and logistical support. Colonel Catlin, however, still sensed that he did not have a complete understanding of the regimental position, and he ordered the first systematic mapping of his sector.[3]

In the early morning hours of 5 June, Dave Redford found Jerry Thomas and told him that he had a new assignment. "Johnny the Hard" Hughes had returned to the 6th Marines during the night. Colonel Catlin returned the 1st Battalion to Hughes and relieved Maurice Shearer, a more junior major. One suspects that Catlin wanted Hughes, a proven combat leader, in command, although Shearer had performed competently. When Hughes resumed command of the 1st Battalion, 6th Marines, he learned that his intelligence officer, Carlton Burr, had just been evacuated with another dose of gas. He ordered the 75th Company to send Sergeant Thomas for temporary duty at battalion headquarters. After collecting his gear, Thomas reported to Hughes at the battalion PC (Post of Command) in a wooded ravine behind Lucy. Hughes told Thomas that he wanted an exact map of the battalion's positions. Hughes would scout from the left flank where the 6th Marines were supposed to tie in with the 5th Marines; Jerry should find the right flank with the 3d Battalion, 6th Marines, and move to his left until the two of them met, probably in Lucy-le-Bocage. Quickly recruiting two veterans of the "suicide squad" who were skilled map sketchers, Thomas began his trek along the lines. The men were harassed by shellfire, but they met Major Hughes about mid-day within the 75th Company's position. They had found the left flank of the 3d Battalion as instructed and had then plotted the positions of two 1st Battalion companies. Johnny the Hard liked their work but not their findings or his own. The entire 1st Battalion position had neither adequate cover nor concealment. In fact, Hughes told Catlin that the entire regiment was exposed and persuaded the colonel to order a withdrawal that night to a reverse slope defense two miles to the rear.[4]

General Degoutte, however, had other plans for the 2d Division, and a withdrawal was not part of his concept of operations. Degoutte's XXI Corps, for all practical purposes, consisted of the French 167th Division, the U.S. 2d Division, and some French artillery regiments; his other two French divisions no longer existed as effective fighting organizations. At midafternoon on 5 June, Degoutte ordered the 167th Division and the 2d Division to attack the Germans the next day in order to disrupt the massing of German artillery and infantry reserves in the Clignon River valley north of Torcy. The 2d Division received a second objective—Belleau Wood—which was to be attacked as soon as possible after the completion of the attack to the north. With little time to prepare for an early morning attack the next day, Colonel Brown and General Harbord concentrated on the first-phase attack on Hill 142 by the 1st Battalion, 5th Marines, supported by the 3d Battalion, 5th Marines, commanded by Maj. Benjamin S. Berry. Although Harbord did not issue an order for the Belleau Wood attack until 1400, 6 June, he alerted Catlin that his regiment would control the attack and that it would have the 3d Battalion, 5th Marines, and 3d Battalion, 6th Marines, for the operation. Because the 3d Battalion, 5th Marines, had a role in both attacks, it would replace 1st Battalion, 6th Marines, in the middle of the brigade sector. Hughes did not learn of the changes until Berry and his advance party reached the 1st Battalion's PC shortly after dark. Hughes did not like the attack plan, but he did not complain when Berry's battalion arrived around midnight and filed into the 1st Battalion's positions. The 1st Battalion then marched five miles to the rear into a protected, defiladed wood near Nanteuil, a village on the Marne, where it became XXI Corps reserve. Arriving by daybreak the Marines stripped off their sodden equipment, ate their first hot meal in a week, and collapsed in sleep in the welcome haylofts. In the meantime, the roar of artillery at the front introduced a new phase in the battle for Belleau Wood.[5]

The 4th Brigade attacks of 6 June 1918 produced a fury of heroism and sacrifice that remained fixed as a high point of valor in the history of the American Expeditionary Forces and the Marine Corps. Although Degoutte's and Harbord's conduct of operations on that day showed little skill, no one then or now has faulted the Marines for their efforts to transform bad plans into good victories. The first mistake was Degoutte's in insisting that the attacks begin 6 June rather than a day later, after the attacking battalions would have had time to enter the front lines, conduct some reconnaissance, and make their own analyses of the situation. Artillery fire support could certainly have profited by the delay. As it was, the battalions had to conduct a relief of positions and mount an attack within hours after a night movement—not ingredients for success. Moreover, a 6th Marines nighttime patrol reported that Belleau Wood was strongly defended, and this report reached the brigade. It made no difference. The attacks proceeded on the assumption that the German front was lightly held, which was reinforced by reports that French aerial observers saw little movement in the area.

The early morning attack on Hill 142, mounted by only two 5th Marine companies, produced a costly victory that widened with the arrival of four more Marine companies and supporting machine gunners, who beat back a series of German counterattacks. At midday, General Harbord ordered the Belleau Wood attack to begin at 1700. His order reflected an optimism unjustified by the stiffness of the German resistance in front of Torcy, for he expected Catlin to take Belleau Wood and the town of Bouresches with only three battalions. (Two of these battalions had additional assignments that prevented them from using all four of their rifle companies.) Presumably the fire of thirteen Allied artillery battalions would clear the way of Germans. Catlin mounted the attack as ordered—although Harbord's concept of "infiltration" changed to a standard battalion advance of two companies up, two back—and saw the better part of three battalions shot to pieces by German machine gun positions along the western and southern edges of Belleau Wood. From the west, Berry's 3d Battalion, 5th Marines, barely entered the wood; so shocked and exhausted were the few survivors that they could advance no farther. The southern attack by 3d Battalion, 6th Marines, commanded by Maj. Burton Sibley, penetrated the woods at sufficient depth to hold a position but only at great cost. Casualties in these two battalions approached 60 percent, with losses among officers and NCOs even higher. The two-company attack on Bouresches, on the other hand, produced success, even though the two companies also took prohibitive losses. The Germans quickly recognized that the loss of

Bouresches menaced their lines of communications. They counterattacked heavily and drew the rest of the 2d Battalion, 6th Marines, commanded by Maj. Thomas Holcomb, into the battle. Whatever its original tactical value, Belleau Wood had to be taken in order to protect the left flank of the Bouresches salient.[6]

As he analyzed the scattered reports arriving at his PC during the evening of 6 June, General Harbord began to understand that the Marine brigade had not taken Belleau Wood and that it had lost more than a thousand officers and men. The Marine Corps suffered greater losses in this battle than it had in its entire history. Although the attacks on Hill 142 and Bouresches had succeeded, the attack on the wood itself had not. Perhaps stung by his own shortcomings as a commander, Harbord lashed out at the new commander of the 6th Marines, Lt. Col. Harry Lee, and demanded that the attack be resumed. (Colonel Catlin had been wounded by a sniper's bullet while observing the afternoon attack of 6 June.) Basically, Belleau Wood remained German except for a corner of its southern edge held by 3d Battalion, 6th Marines, which had slid east toward Bouresches. The remnants of 3d Battalion, 5th Marines, were scattered from the western edge of the woods around Hill 181 to the left flank of Sibley's battalion. Germans remained both in front and behind them. As the situation cleared during 7 June, Harbord assumed that the 6th Marines, with help from the U.S. 23d Infantry Regiment to its right, could hold Bouresches, so he ordered Lee to continue Sibley's attack within the wood itself. The shattered 3d Battalion, 5th Marines, had withdrawn from the woods to a reserve position, and the 3d Battalion, 6th Marines, fought alone in Belleau Wood without making much progress. Neither side could mount overwhelming artillery support because their positions were imprecise and too close; the battle pitted German machine gun and mortar crews, supported by infantry, against Marine infantrymen, who depended primarily on rifles and grenades. By midmorning of 8 June, the battalion had little fight left in it, and Sibley withdrew from the wood.[7]

Harbord let the 2d Division artillery attack Belleau Wood for the rest of 8 June while he organized his next attack. Degoutte had decided that he would not press the attack against Torcy, so Harbord could use his two battalions that remained relatively unscathed, 2d Battalion, 5th Marines, commanded by Maj. Frederic Wise, and 1st Battalion, 6th Marines, for another attack on Belleau Wood. On the evening of 8 June, Harbord ordered Major Hughes to move his battalion into a woods southeast of Lucy-le-Bocage. Although Harbord had not yet committed himself to a particular plan, Hughes believed that Harbord wanted him in position to move into Belleau Wood on the afternoon of 9 June, a move Harbord was considering. Returning from the brigade PC in the late afternoon of 8 June, Hughes sent Sergeant Thomas up to Le Ferme Paris to locate the mouth of a sunken road that could lead the battalion back to the front along a gulley, which would provide some cover and concealment from the Metz-Paris highway to Lucy-le-Bocage, and south to a woods across from the southeast edge of Belleau Wood. Finding the mouth of the sunken road, Thomas jogged back to the battalion and reported to twenty-eight-year-old Capt. George A. Stowell, the senior company commander and a veteran of three Caribbean operations. Stowell would move the battalion while Hughes conferred with Harbord at the PC.

The battalion stepped out around 2100 and entered a nightmare. It did not reach the sunken road until midnight; at one road junction, a connecting file took a left turn and marched off in the wrong direction. At the sunken road, the column met 1st Lt. Charles A. Etheridge, a 75th Company officer who had taken Carlton Burr's place as the battalion intelligence officer. Thomas thought Etheridge knew the rest of the route, but Etheridge had not reconnoitered the trail because Hughes had not told him to do so. Harbord, in fact, had told Hughes that 6th Marines guides would meet his battalion at the Gobert Creek bridge, but the guides never arrived. As dawn broke, the 1st Battalion had strayed into the open fields west of Lucy-le-Bocage and into the view of German observation balloon spotters. Stowell ordered the battalion quickly into a nearby wood, where it would have to remain until night came. A furious Hughes rejoined his battalion and relieved Stowell of command, a decision Thomas thought unjust. Stowell's 76th Company went to 1st Lt. Macon C. Overton, a thin, handsome, twenty-six-year-old Georgian who had joined the Corps as an enlisted man in 1914. Later in the day (9 June), Harbord ordered Hughes to resume his approach march and to be in position on 10 June to enter Belleau Wood behind a crushing barrage. After dark, the wandering 1st Battalion set off again for the front, marching down the road through Lucy, then southeast into the woods on the far side of the Lucy-Bouresches road and Belleau Wood. This time, the battalion did not become lost. On the other hand, it also had nothing between it and the Germans but the outposts of one 2d Battalion company. The attack on Belleau Wood would have to start again from scratch.[8]

Despite the setback of 6 June, Harbord did not change his concept of attack for the 10 June operation. The 1st Battalion would attack the southern part of the wood from the south while the 2d Battalion, 5th Marines, would later attack the northern part from the west. The two battalions would swing north in order to join one another at Belleau Wood's narrow, middle neck. It was a maneuver that looked good on a map, but worked poorly on the battlefield. Fortunately, the extra day of shelling had persuaded the German defenders—still battalions from the 27th and 28th Divisions—to concede the wood's southern edge. But the combat teams still manned a thick belt of defenses that covered the wheat fields to the west and faced the trails inside the southern end of the wood. The Allied artillery bombardment had taken its toll but had not crushed the defenders. The Germans endured the intense barrage at daybreak on 10 June and then manned their positions to wait for the next two Marine battalions, one of which included Sgt. Jerry Thomas.[9]

Disobeying Major Hughes's orders to remain near the phones at the battalion PC, Jerry joined the waves of Marines as they started across the wheat field for Belleau Wood. The moment had seized him. The battalion, with two companies forward and two back in the standard French attack formation, marched steadily across the Lucy-Bouresches road. Rifles at the high port, bayonets fixed, and Chauchat automatic rifles pointed to the front, the Marines crossed the swale between the highway and the trees and entered the wood. Avoiding the bodies of Sibley's dead Marines among the wheat, Jerry ran until he caught up with the third platoon of the 75th Company. Much to the battalion's surprise, not a shot was fired at it. Instead of entering the wood, Jerry started back to the PC, for he recalled "that I had another job to do." He met Hughes, who was elated by the attack and wanted to report his success by phone. The battalion commander did not censure him for joining the attack, but told him to move the PC across the road to the raised bank at the edge of Belleau Wood. As Jerry helped establish the battalion PC, he heard the roar of gunfire within the wood. The 1st Battalion had discovered the Germans.[10]

The 1st Battalion's battle, which began around 1800 on 10 June, did not end until the battalion left the wood seven days later, an exhausted, smaller but still combative group of veteran Marines. Jerry fought with his battalion from start to finish and marched out of Belleau Wood a proven combat leader. He learned to cope with stress, fear, hunger, thirst, exhaustion, and the death of comrades over a protracted period of combat. Belleau Wood was not a place for anything but the sturdiest of warriors. The fighting on 10 June struck hard at the 75th Company, which moved through the wood with Overton's 76th Company on the left, in the center of the battalion front. When the company struck a strongpoint of three German machine guns, Jerry lost a dozen or so comrades from the third platoon. The Marines now crawled forward until they could throw grenades at the machine gun nests. In the battalion PC, Jerry managed scouts and collected reports throughout the rest of the day. He worked with the regimental intelligence officer, 1st Lt. William A. Eddy, in plotting the known German positions and planning artillery fire. Jerry undoubtedly agreed with Johnny the Hard that the 1st Battalion needed help.[11]

On the afternoon of 10 June, General Harbord committed the 2d Battalion, 5th Marines, to the battle and established its attack for 0430 the next morning. The 1st Battalion's left flank company, the 76th, was supposed to protect the right flank of Wise's battalion as it pivoted to the left and attacked along the long axis of the wood's northern section. Hughes assigned Thomas the job of ensuring that Overton's company contacted Wise's battalion as Harbord's order directed. As the rolling barrage lifted, Jerry and one of his scouts left the wood and found Wise's battalion moving across the deadly wheat field that had become the graveyard of Berry's battalion on 6 June. The passage was only slightly less disastrous for the 2d Battalion, 5th Marines, which was at three-quarters strength as a result of its brave defense of the brigade's extended left flank from 1 through 5 June. As the battalion neared Belleau Wood, German artillery fire crashed down on it and machine gun fire raked its front and left flanks. Instead of pivoting to the north, the Marines plunged straight ahead into the wood's narrow neck and across the front of the 1st Battalion, 6th Marines, which had joined the attack. Pressured by his own company commanders for help, Wise asked Thomas where the 76th Company was and why it hadn't appeared on his right flank. Again, Thomas went back into the woods. He found Macon Overton, whose company was indeed in action and successfully so. Under Overton's inspired and intelligent direction, the 76th Company had destroyed the last German positions around Hill 181 and opened Belleau Wood for Wise's battalion. Overton found Wise's concern mildly amusing and wondered why the 5th Marines could not use the available cover. Certain that Overton had the situation under control, Jerry returned to Hughes's PC and told Johnny the Hard that the 76th Company had fulfilled its mission.[12]

Belleau Wood
10-11 June, 1918

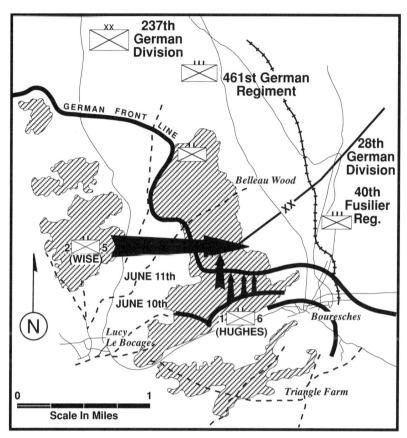

➤ USMC Attacks
— Paved Roads
- - - - Dirt Roads
▨▨▨ Woods

The two-battalion battle for Belleau Wood became a muddled slugfest, with Wise moving east when he should have been moving north. His battalion engaged the strongest German positions and suffered accordingly. At one point, Wise, Lee, and Harbord all thought that the Marines had seized Belleau Wood. Hughes knew better, but his battalion had its own problems as the Germans responded to the attack with intense artillery fire and reinforcing infantry. Thomas continued his duties in Hughes's PC. Each morning and evening for the next five days, he checked company positions and discussed the enemy situation with the four company commanders. "On occasion enemy artillery made my journey a warm one," he wrote. He helped to maintain situation reports, drafted messages for the regiment (which most often had to travel by messenger), interrogated messengers from the companies and occasional POWs, and carried messages to the company commanders. Thomas and Lieutenant Etheridge were the only operational staff Hughes had; the adjutant and supply officer had their hands full with administrative problems. As they watched the battalion's effectiveness wane from lack of sleep, water, and food, Thomas and Etheridge recognized their own limited capacity. Fatigue had dulled everyone's senses and ruined otherwise sound judgment.

Mounting heavy counterattacks in the early morning of 13 June, the Germans punished the Marine positions on the 1st Battalion's left flank still held by the 76th Company. Macon Overton asked battalion headquarters to investigate the fire coming from his rear because he thought it might be from the disoriented 2d Battalion, 5th Marines. Etheridge and Thomas, who were reconnoitering the lines, decided to check Overton's report. Working their way through the woods, now splintered and reeking of cordite smoke and souring corpses, the two Marines found an isolated 5th Marines company. The company commander, a young lieutenant named L. Q. C. L. Lyle, told them that he was sure the firing came from bypassed Germans to his rear. He had no contact with the company to his left. Etheridge volunteered to scout the gap in the 5th Marines lines. He and Thomas had not moved very far when they saw some Germans who had just killed a group of Wise's Marines and occupied their foxholes. Before the Germans could react with accurate rifle fire, the two Marines sprinted back to Lyle's position and told him about the Germans. Lyle gave Etheridge a scratch squad armed with grenades, and Thomas and Etheridge led the group back through the wood until they again found the German position. In the short but intense battle that followed, the Marines killed four Germans and captured a sergeant, who identified himself as a member of the 5th Guards Division. He also showed them another German stay-behind position, which the 6th Marines attacked and wiped out later the same day. Impressed with Thomas's performance in this affair, Etheridge and Hughes had him cited in brigade orders for bravery in combat.[13]

The German prisoner also provided Thomas with a temporary reprieve from battle. Brigade headquarters wanted to interrogate the POW immediately, and Hughes ordered Jerry to escort the sergeant to the rear, about a mile away at Maison Blanche farm. When he arrived at the brigade PC, Thomas reported to Harbord's aide, who asked him when he had last eaten a real meal. Jerry knew exactly: five days. The lieutenant sent him to the brigade mess. A sergeant, who had obviously not missed any meals at all, fixed him a large plate of bacon, bread, and molasses accompanied by hot coffee. To Jerry, food had seldom tasted so good.[14]

Thomas returned to a 1st Battalion that had reached the limit of its endurance. German shell fire, increasing with intensity and accuracy on 12 June, continued through the night and the next day. About 5,000 rounds had fallen on the two Marine battalions in the wood. Among the dead were Capt. Ted Fuller of the 75th Company and one of Thomas's best friends, Sgt. Douglas Laws, a Kentuckian. One barrage that fell on the battalion PC and the reserve 74th Company ruined the hard-luck company and killed old-timer Capt. John Francis Burns, the company commander. Much loved for his rough humor and affection for his pet toy bulldog, the former first sergeant bled to death from his severed legs. Before the end of 13 June, the 1st Battalion lost not only two company commanders but also its battalion commander. Major Hughes, his eyes swollen shut from gas and staggering from fatigue, allowed himself to be evacuated. His own condition, however, did not prevent his telling Harbord that his battalion could defend itself but could no longer advance: "Have had terrific bombardment and attack. I have every man, except a few odd ones, in line now. . . . Everything is OK now. Men digging in again. Trenches most obliterated by shellfire. . . . The conduct of everyone is magnificent. Can't you get hot coffee and water to me using prisoners?"[15] Before Hughes could receive an answer, he had been replaced by Maj. Franklin B. Garrett, a forty-one-year-old Louisianian who had spent most of his fourteen years as a Marine officer aboard ship, in administration of barracks detachments, and in other assignments that did not include combat operations in the Caribbean. At the moment, however, the 1st Battalion did not need a heroic leader. It needed rest.[16]

As the 1st Battalion continued to endure and suffer, division and brigade headquarters argued with XXI Corps and Pershing's headquarters about relieving the 4th Brigade. Generals Bundy and Harbord reported that the Marines' spirit was high (an exaggeration) but that their physical strength had been exhausted in more than two weeks of frontline service. They pointed out that by French standards the brigade had been in battle twice as long as it should have been. Even though Harbord had sent some Marine replacements forward to his battalions, they were not well-trained and did not last long in combat. The lack of sleep, food, and water had been severe, exacerbated now by German gas attacks. The Marines had to work in their gas masks, which had to be cleared often of condensed water and mucus, and to endure mustard gas burns over the rest of their bodies. All that Bundy and Harbord reported was true enough of the 1st Battalion headquarters group, huddled among the rocks on a small hill in Belleau Wood. The Germans tried no more infantry counterattacks, but they pummeled the battalion with heavy mortars and Austrian 77-mm cannon, which fired a flat-trajectory, high-velocity shell dubbed a "whiz bang." In the meantime, Wise's battalion (or rather, its remnants) and Holcomb's 2d Battalion, 6th Marines, had finally reached the northern section of Belleau Wood but could not advance farther without help. The 1st Battalion, 6th Marines, completed the occupation and defense of the southern woods. On 15 June, the battalion learned it would finally be replaced by a battalion of the U.S. 7th Infantry. Two days later, the 1st Battalion, 6th Marines, now less than half strength, shuffled out of Belleau Wood.[17]

Despite their exhaustion, the men of the 1st Battalion, 6th Marines, including Jerry Thomas, had proved themselves tough and skillful in Belleau Wood. After the "lost march" of 8–9 June, the battalion's performance had been exemplary. Largely because of Johnny the Hard's tactical skill and an extra day of artillery preparation and planning, the 1st Battalion, 6th Marines, was the only one of five Marine battalions to enter Belleau Wood without suffering serious casualties. If the 74th Company had not been destroyed by gas and high explosive shell fire on 13 June, the battalion would have fought within the wood with fewer losses than the other Marine battalions. It also captured its objectives and did not lose its cohesion because Major Hughes and his small staff (Etheridge, Thomas, and the scout section) kept themselves and the companies linked on the ground and on their poor maps. Unlike Lieutenant Colonel Wise, who declared the north woods seized on 11 June when his troops had not even entered it, Hughes submitted accurate reports, even when he knew the news would not be welcomed by Lee and Harbord. He misreported his frontline positions only once. Although no one could determine which infantry battalion killed the most Germans in Belleau Wood—from German accounts, Allied artillery probably inflicted the greatest casualties—the 1st Battalion at least shared with Wise's battalion the claim of destroying the German 461st Infantry Regiment, which fell from around 1,000 effectives on 5 June to 9 officers and 149 men a week later. In addition, the battle of 10–12 June cost the German 40th Infantry Regiment of the 28th Division almost 800 men killed, wounded, and missing. A battalion from the 5th Guards Division also fell to the Marines. The 1st Battalion and Wise's battalion captured ten heavy mortars, more than fifty heavy machine guns, and at least four hundred POWs. Within the woods, the 1st Battalion, 6th Marines, and 2d Battalion, 5th Marines, broke the back of the German defense, even though the battle did not end for another two weeks.[18]

The tactical effectiveness of the 1st Battalion, 6th Marines, to which Jerry Thomas had made an important contribution, became obscured by the valor of the entire 4th Brigade in the battles for Hill 142, Belleau Wood, and Bouresches. Paired with the performance of the U.S. 1st Division at Cantigny (28–31 May 1918), the 4th Brigade's fight proved to the Germans and Allies alike that the AEF would be a significant force in offensive combat on the Western Front. (The 2d Division's 3d Brigade reinforced this conclusion by seizing Vaux on 1 July.) The intelligence section of the German IV Reserve Corps filed a major report praising the valor of the Marines and predicted glumly that their tactical skill might soon match their heroism. French and American headquarters up to and including Pershing's staff and the French Grand Quartier General (or Army General Staff) praised the 4th Brigade's performance. At the emotional level, however, their reactions varied. Pershing and his staff believed that the Marines had received altogether too much newspaper coverage, especially for the attacks of 6 and 11 June. (The AEF censor was at fault, not the Marines.) The French, on the other hand, proved as always capable of the classic *beau geste*: they awarded the 4th Brigade a unit Croix de Guerre with Palm and renamed Belleau Wood the "Bois de la Brigade de Marine." For Marines of the twentieth century, Belleau Wood became the battle that established the Corps' reputation for valor. Sergeant Jerry Thomas had been part of it all.[19]

The battle for Belleau Wood really ended for the 1st Battalion, 6th Marines, when it returned to the rest area at Nanteuil-sur-Marne on 17 June, but the battalion did not leave the sector until the entire division departed between 4 and 9 July 1918. On the road to Nanteuil, the Marines found the battalion's kitchens and enjoyed hot stew ("slum") and café au lait that tasted like a five-star meal. For three days, the men did little but sleep and eat. The company first sergeants called formations only to assign replacements, mostly fresh privates in new forest green Marine uniforms, to the rifle companies. The Marne River became a welcome bathtub for the Marines. Ten-day beards and dirt came off; thin faces and sunken eyes took longer to change. The Marines had little patience in their search for creature comforts. When a woman proprietor of a store refused to open, the Marines nearly rioted and forced her to choose between selling her goods or facing destruction. Happily, a convoy of Red Cross trucks arrived with cigarettes, tobacco, and toilet items for the Marines to purchase. By 20 June, the 1st Battalion had regained most of its resilience and high spirits.[20]

The battalion returned to the Belleau Wood sector during 20–21 June in order to give Harbord two fresh battalions in brigade reserve. The battle in the northern wood had swelled as the Germans committed a fresh regiment, and Harbord had countered with an attack by the 7th Infantry and the 5th Marines. After attacks by the 5th Marines had finally cleared the northern wood on 26 June—Harbord could now report accurately: "Belleau Wood now U.S. Marine Corps entirely"—the battalion marched back into Belleau Wood, a doleful walk through clumps of unburied German and American dead, and occupied a sector at the edge of the wood facing east. Except for occasional harassing shell fire, the battalion did not have to deal with live Germans, although the dead ones smelled bad enough. Jerry Thomas spent most of his time in the PC or checking the battalion observation posts. His last special duty in Belleau Wood was to help guide the U.S. 104th Infantry, 26th Division, into the sector. On 4 July, he returned to Lucy-le-Bocage to meet the advance party from the 104th Infantry. Learning that the relieving "Yankee Division" had already lost men to German artillery fire, Thomas again proved his intelligence and force by persuading an Army lieutenant colonel to move the 104th Infantry into the woods by a longer, but more protected, route than the one the colonel intended to use. Thomas had no desire to add more Americans to the some eight hundred dead scattered throughout the 6th Marines' sector.

The relief that night went as planned. Just as dawn was breaking, the 1st Battalion left Belleau Wood for the last time. "Led by our chunky commander, Major Garrett, we traversed the three-quarters of a mile to Lucy at a ragged double time." Pushing along on weary legs, Thomas turned his back on Belleau Wood, at last certain that he would never see the forest again, at least in war. The battle, however, had made him a charter member of a Marine Corps elite, the veterans of the Battle of Belleau Wood. From this group, the Marine Corps would eventually draw many of its leaders for the next forty years, including four Commandants (Wendell C. Neville, Thomas Holcomb, Clifton B. Cates, and Lemuel C. Shepherd, Jr.). Thomas had entered Belleau Wood on 10 June 1918 as a conscientious noncommissioned officer, whose early performance in France had indicated his courage. He left Belleau Wood a proven leader of Marines in combat, a young man clearly capable of exercising greater responsibilities in the most desperate of battles.[21]

[CHAPTER V]

Soissons 1918

I**N ITS BILLETS, MOSTLY TWO-MAN** tents pitched among the woods between Montreuil-aux-Lyons and the Marne River, the 4th Brigade enjoyed eleven days of luxurious rest after it left Belleau Wood. Regular meals came again from the company field kitchens; formations and training occurred only when replacements arrived to fill the ranks of the ravaged infantry battalions. The Marines found plenty of time to visit friends, explore the small towns near their tent camps, and sleep without interruption. Even though the battle along the edges of the German salient between Soissons and Reims still flared, the Marines convinced themselves that they would leave the front for a more adventurous recuperation in Paris. The price they would have to pay for the Paris excursion was to march in the Bastille Day parade on 14 July. On 2 July, the regiment sent twenty officers and 300 men, chosen for the condition of their uniforms, to Paris for an Independence Day parade. A soiled Jerry Thomas did not make the trip. The rumor of another Paris parade that swept from campfire to campfire flushed away some of the Belleau Wood memories. The thought of a trip to Paris provided an inner excitement among the Marines that matched the naps in the sun, the shared bottles of wine, and the quiet meals among the trees. The Marines found it hard to believe that they would return to battle soon; they had already suffered much and won fame in the newspapers.[1]

The French high command had something rather different than a Bastille Day parade in mind for the U.S. 1st and 2d Divisions. Even before the fighting west of Château-Thierry slackened, Gen. Ferdinand Foch, Allied supreme commander, and Gen. Henri Philippe Pétain ordered Gen. Marie Emile Fayolle, whose Group of Armies of the Reserve controlled the Allied forces in the Second Battle of the Marne, to prepare a plan for a counteroffensive. His superiors wanted to cut the Soissons–Château-Thierry highway near the salient's western face; therefore, Fayolle turned the planning over to Gen. Charles Mangin, a sour Breton known as "The Butcher," because Mangin's Tenth Army was likely to mount the attack. Mangin had already conducted one corps-sized local counterattack on 11 June that had taken the Germans by surprise, primarily because Mangin reduced his artillery preparation to a short, intense bombardment at the point of the attack. As the planning developed between mid-June and mid-July, the concept of the counteroffensive broadened until it included one major attack north of the Ourcq River by Mangin's Tenth Army and another south of the river by the French Sixth Army. The plan would pit twenty-one French and three American divisions against about twenty German divisions. The German divisions were so depleted that the Allies enjoyed local superiority in infantry, reinforced with massed artillery (2,100 guns) and five hundred French tanks. Surprise, presumably, would give the Allies an additional advantage.[2]

As the French army's planning continued, the American role in the Aisne-Marne counteroffensive expanded with General Pershing's blessing. Of the two French armies to assault the western face of the salient, Mangin's Tenth Army received the primary mission: to drive the German Ninth Army away from the Soissons–Château-Thierry highway. Mangin, in turn, assigned the army mission to the French XX Corps, which was not French at all if one looked at its infantry regiments. Two of its divisions were American, the veteran 1st and 2d, fresh from the triumphs of Cantigny, Belleau Wood, and Vaux. The corps' center division was the 1st Moroccan Division, twelve battalions of Senegalese, Moroccans, and Foreign Legionnaires. Pershing would have preferred an American corps commander, but his recently created III Corps was not ready to function. In any event, Mangin, not the corps commanders, established the terms of the attack. The XX Corps commander, Gen. Pierre E. Berdoulat, had no more influence on the scheme of maneuver than did Sgt. Gerald C. Thomas. Mangin lobbied hard for reinforcements and received a total force of thirteen infantry divisions. He also succeeded in gaining control of the French II Cavalry Corps, which he planned to throw into the ruptured German lines in the best tradition of Marshal Michel Ney.[3]

The Germans upset the French plans when they attacked across the Marne River between Reims and Château-Thierry on 15 July. In a moment of concern, as the French Sixth Army gave way, Pétain suspended the concentration for the western counteroffensive; Foch then overruled Pétain. By the afternoon of 15 July, the French high command had reestablished daylight of 18 July as the beginning of the great counteroffensive. Mangin insisted that his Tenth Army artillery would open fire only as the infantry crossed the line of departure at 0435. On the XX Corps front alone, over one hundred batteries would pulverize the German positions with interdiction fire, counterbattery fire, and a rolling barrage so devastating that the infantry would sweep forward to count German bodies and to collect stunned prisoners, followed by the II Cavalry Corps. Napoleon himself could not have designed an operation of greater grandeur.

The U.S. 2d Division, now commanded by Maj. Gen. James G. Harbord, did not receive a clear picture of its role until it received the XX Corps operation order on 16 July. Even before Harbord issued his own operation order at 0430 on 17 July, a scant twenty-four hours before the division was to attack, the French army had sent trucks to the division rest area to begin the movement to the Forêt de Retz, the vast woods that would conceal the XX Corps as it concentrated for the attack. The division was not totally surprised by the movement because its artillery brigade had received orders to move north on the evening of 14–15 July. General Harbord, however, did not receive even a vague idea of his mission until the following evening. The infantry brigade commanders (Col. Wendell C. Neville in the case of the Marine brigade) had even fewer details about their missions. In vast ignorance of their critical roles, the infantrymen of the 3d and 4th Brigades shouldered their packs and weapons and boarded the French trucks that began to appear mysteriously at their billets during the night of 15–16 July.[4]

Because the 6th Marines had been assigned the role of XX Corps reserve for the attack of 18 July, the regiment, commanded temporarily by Lt. Col. Thomas Holcomb, did not leave its billets until the afternoon of 16 July. Nevertheless, the move came as a surprise, and some Marines still thought they were bound for Paris. The regiment's realists noted, however, that the French seldom wasted trucks on infantry headed for the rear. The move came so suddenly that the 1st Battalion had no time to draw ammunition and emergency rations. Once again, Jerry Thomas found himself seated beside a Vietnamese truck driver who could not tell him where the convoy was bound. As the trucks moved north through the gathering darkness, the Marines listened to the roll of artillery fire and watched the reddened sky to the east where the French Sixth Army struggled to hold the ground south of the Marne. Even though some of the Marines tried to keep their spirits up with bawdy songs, such as "Lulu and Her Baby," the prospect of a Paris leave disappeared that night, especially after German air attacks on the convoy. While they were passing through a French village, a bomb exploded in front of Thomas's truck, and the driver took a sudden detour to the west. When the errant section of the 1st Battalion's convoy found itself entangled in a French artillery position, the driver turned back to the east and found his ultimate destination just as dawn was breaking. Thomas disembarked with relief, but with little optimism about the operation.[5]

Relatively well concentrated on the morning of 17 July, the 6th Marines, already exhausted and hungry, started the twenty-mile hike to the front. As the Marines trudged along the Maubeuge highway toward the Forêt de Retz, their thirst climbed with the sun. The column started to lose stragglers to heat exhaustion. Around noon, the Marines entered the forest, some twelve square miles of tall oaks and beeches, and found a gloomy world crowded by thickening streams of infantry, horse-drawn artillery, supply wagons, field kitchens, and tanks. The inside of the Forêt de Retz was a military madhouse. Looking for food and water, the Marines found instead vast piles of artillery shells and small-arms ammunition. They found American cartridges at one dump, and the 1st Battalion took two bandoleers for each man. More men fell by the wayside as the column moved in fits and starts along the edge of a road jammed with wagons and trucks. The chaos enabled the Marines to pillage French ration wagons for bread and water; they marched on with loaves stuck in their jackets and wine and water bottles jammed in their packs. They finally found some of their own ration wagons toward evening, but by that time they were too tired to worry about food. They would have killed for water. As dusk fell, "Johnny the Hard" Hughes, who had regained command of the 1st Battalion on the eve of battle, led about fifty of his

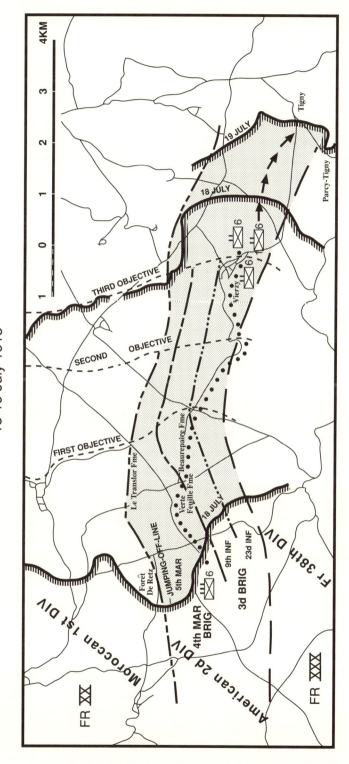

men off the road into a bivouac area. Still plagued by his own wounds, Hughes knew that the men needed rest, and he wanted the stragglers to rejoin the battalion (most did during the night). The Marines collapsed in exhaustion, huddled in their ponchos as a thunderstorm pelted the troops and tormented the trees above them. The rest of the 2d Division infantry struggled toward the line of departure.[6]

Jerry Thomas began the hike of 17 July as platoon sergeant of the third platoon, 75th Company. He was still with the vanguard when the battalion reached its assembly area. Johnny the Hard then plucked him from his company. As the battalion started to stir before daylight on 18 July, Hughes ordered Thomas to take a working party to the rear for water and food. He showed him the location of an American supply point on the map, and Thomas set off with his detail just as the Allied artillery opened fire. Deafened by the roar, Thomas and his men located some boxes of corned beef and hardtack, not exactly fit rations for thirsty men. Thomas found no easy solution to the water shortage. The thousands of men and animals in the Forêt de Retz had even drained the mud puddles left by the midnight thunderstorm. A battalion working party left behind that morning with canteens did not rejoin the battalion with water until that evening. During Thomas's absence, the last of the 1st Battalion's stragglers had arrived; by 0800, the battalion was ready to move forward. On orders from 6th Marines headquarters, the 1st Battalion assembled on the Maubeuge highway and again started east in search of the battle.[7]

Ahead of the 6th Marines, the other three infantry regiments of the 2d Division fought their way through the German outpost line along the eastern edge of the Forêt de Retz and started the drive for the Soissons–Château-Thierry highway, ten miles away. The enemy dispositions, the terrain, and the French concept of attack forced the division into a narrow frontage of two miles. Fortunately, the Germans had been truly surprised. Their initial machine gun and defensive artillery fires could not match the deluge of Allied shells that fell on every enemy position in the sector. For the 1st Battalion, moving by bounds behind the attacking regiments, the day brought constant wonder. The Marines gaped at the destruction caused by the Allied artillery and stared at the large groups of German prisoners herded to the rear by Marine walking wounded. The battalion followed the Maubeuge road to La Verte Feuille Farm, then turned directly east along a country road that led to another crossroads, Beaurepaire Farm. It seemed as if the whole French army was on the move. Trucks and ambulances moved slowly to the front, then sped back with their loads of wounded. Large Schneider and small Renault tanks, mixed incongruously with squadrons of French cavalry, clattered toward the battle. The Marines gawked as a column of cuirassiers and lancers swept past with the sunlight glinting from their helmets and lance tips. Batteries of horse-drawn artillery, well-formed men and horses of impressive size, galloped up to advanced positions, wheeled into battery front, and opened fire with the speed and noise distinctive to the famous French 75-mm field gun. Occasionally, the Marines saw groups of khaki-clad African infantry jogging across the fields like packs of hunting dogs. When the 1st Battalion discovered the initial collection of captured German artillery, its euphoria rose to wild heights, and rumors of a vast Allied victory ran through the ranks.[8]

Around midday, the 6th Marines reached Beaurepaire Farm, about six miles from the battalion's night assembly area. Burdened by their packs and equipment and baked by the ripening sun and battlefield dust, the Marines rediscovered their fatigue, thirst, and hunger. The orders to halt, which came from the brigade headquarters at Beaurepaire Farm, were welcome. The Marines fell out along the road and stripped off their loads. Jerry Thomas marveled at the lines of French artillery deployed to the east a mile or so ahead along the edge of Vierzy ravine, which cut the plateau on an angle from southwest to northeast. The battle around Vierzy ravine had brought the advance to a halt. The confusion among the attacking American infantry regiments, the 5th Marines and 9th Infantry, convinced General Harbord that he would have to reorganize his advance. Since the XX Corps had not released the 6th Marines for his use, he brought forward the reorganized 23d Infantry to spearhead the 3d Brigade's attack on Vierzy ravine and the town of Vierzy. The soldiers of the 23d Infantry, whose own early morning attack had been successful, had lost their regimental sector when the 5th Marines and 9th Infantry had executed a partial right wheel in the advance to Beaurepaire Farm. The veteran 23d Infantry passed through the 6th Marines on its return to battle. The soldiers and Marines exchanged insults about each other's parentage, courage, and sexual preferences as the Doughboys marched by.

Excitement grew with the arrival of a convoy of ration trucks loaded with crates of canned beef, canned prunes, bread, and canned tomatoes. The salty beef and suspect prunes did not please the Marines, but the bread and tomatoes provided the battalion a badly needed lift in morale. The tomatoes—especially the watery tomato juice—were the pièce de résistance of the battalion's primitive picnic. Except for weak, errant shelling, the only battle the Marines of the 1st Battalion saw took place above their assembly area. When a harried French Spad swooped toward the ground to escape two pursuing German aircraft, the battalion sent up a hail of rifle fire and drove off the Germans to the sound of cheering and catcalls. More French artillery and cavalry filled the fields above Vierzy as the infantry battle below the plateau swelled. The Germans continued to build up their defenses. As the remnants of two divisions held the ravine and its small town, the Marines' old foe, the German 28th Division, moved forward from its reserve position to add its weight to the main line of resistance. The result of the pitched battle for Vierzy ravine, which began around 1900 and ended before midnight, was an American victory, but the 5th Marines, 9th Infantry, and 23d Infantry were no longer combat effective.

The 6th Marines remained a witness to the battle for Vierzy because XX Corps still had not released it for Harbord's use. During the afternoon of 18 July, the battalion deployed once but did not advance. The French II Cavalry Corps massed west of Vierzy ravine but prudently drifted to the rear as German shells began to fall among the horsemen. The Marines speculated about the war's inverted values: horses seemed more precious than men. One Marine officer commented to another that he doubted they would see the II Cavalry Corps again until the victory parade in Paris. Jerry Thomas noticed the sparkle of the setting sun upon the retreating cuirassiers. His attention, however, shifted with the arrival of 1st Lt. Carlton Burr. Like others wounded at Belleau Wood, Burr had found his way back to the battalion in order to join the battle. Burr and Thomas greeted one another warmly. Burr did not look well, but he wanted to know about the battalion and their mutual friends. The two men talked for half an hour before the lieutenant returned to Major Hughes's command group. Burr told Thomas that he couldn't understand why Thomas had not yet received a commission but promised that they would both investigate the matter with the battalion adjutant as soon as they finished the battle of Soissons.[9]

While the 6th Marines slept fitfully under arms that night, harassed by German star shells and the rumble of more French tanks, General Berdoulat ordered General Harbord to use his two fit regiments, the 6th Marines and 2d Engineers, to attack at first light on 19 July. The objective would be the Soissons–Château-Thierry highway, some three miles from the eastern edge of Vierzy ravine. Because Harbord had already committed two battalions of engineers to the battle for Vierzy, the 19 July attack depended only on the 6th Marines, twenty-eight French tanks, and massed Allied artillery fire. The Germans would not be surprised by the attack; during that same evening, they had massed batteries among the woods above the Soissons–Château-Thierry highway. American observers could even see batteries of 77-mm field guns in the open. German infantry and machine gun teams established battalion-strength strongpoints from (north to south) Hill 160, the village of Tigny, and the village of Parcy-Tigny. Machine guns in Parcy-Tigny could be fired directly across the front of any advance from Vierzy—the enfilade fire that brightens machine gunners' dreams. The most vulnerable American unit would be the right flank battalion of the 6th Marines. In the regimental formation dictated by Lt. Col. Harry Lee, that would be Johnny the Hard's 1st Battalion, which would deploy with the 75th Company at the front right-hand corner of the battalion's standard two-company up, two-company back assault formation.

Although the 1st Battalion, which learned of its mission after midnight, arose early, the 6th Marines did not leave the Beaurepaire Farm assembly area until 0730. As they marched by the French artillery positions above Vierzy ravine, the Marines found the guns firing shells at the furious rate that usually characterized the rolling barrage preceding an infantry attack. (Not until after the battle did the Marines learn that the French were indeed firing *their* rolling barrage—about three hours before the Marines actually began the attack.) The regiment filed into Vierzy ravine, still ripe with poison gas and littered with dead. The 2d Battalion moved off to the left while the 1st Battalion marched all the way through Vierzy itself, climbed up the ravine's eastern slope, and deployed in an open wheat field. There the 1st Battalion waited, naked to German observation and direct artillery and machine gun fire, until the French tanks struggled up the steep road from Vierzy and also deployed. Although German machine gunners fired at them as they lay prone in the wheat, the Marines awaited the real attack. Allied artillery fire continued but with much reduced intensity. Finally, at around 0930, the 6th Marines—with shouts and the shrill sounds of officers' whistles—went "over the top" toward the division's final objective. With pounding heart and unsettled mind, Sergeant Thomas rose from the ground and shepherded his platoon toward the two villages and the woods visible about two miles to his front.

During the next hour, the 1st Battalion, 6th Marines, suffered and endured but did no particular damage to the German defenders. In the mind of Jerry Thomas, *his* 1st Battalion died on the second day of the battle at Soissons.

The massacre of the 1st Battalion, 6th Marines, severed Thomas from his most important human relationships within the battalion. Soissons was his last battle as a noncommissioned officer, but his transformation did not occur only because he became an officer. It happened because he lost his closest friends, Carlton Burr and David Redford, the two lieutenants who had helped him establish his own standards of military professionalism and personal courage and integrity. The horror began the moment the Marines of the 1st Battalion struggled to their feet—rifles and Chauchat automatic rifles at high port, bayonets bright in the morning sun—and pushed through the wheat. The German artillery and machine gun fire immediately swelled in volume, and Marines toppled, staggered, and twisted into the crushed stalks of wheat. The French tanks, dispersed at fifty-yard intervals among the infantry, drew the bulk of artillery fire coming from guns only four thousand yards away as the waves of Marines passed through the forward foxholes of the 23d Infantry. The Doughboys urged the Marines to take cover, but the lines of men pressed forward. Tank after tank burst into flames, showering the wheat with burning gasoline and bursting ammunition. The Marines skirted the pyres and marched forward, unconsciously leaning against the storm of fire that burst around them. When men were hit, they simply folded on their faces because they were already bent double. The worst threat to the 75th Company was the machine gun fire from Parcy-Tigny. Thomas quickly calculated that the battalion could not live unless it took the village, eliminated the guns, and masked the German artillery. A second quick calculation indicated that the battalion would not live long enough to reach Parcy-Tigny. Thomas's cool professional assessment did not mean he would stop his march into oblivion. For one thing, he owed David Redford his best, for Redford had become the acting company commander. As the 75th Company went into the attack, the new company commander, 1st Lt. Frederick C. Wheeler, had toppled with a leg wound. Redford had taken command without a pause, and Thomas became the 3d Platoon commander. Watching his ranks thin, Thomas urged his men forward until he and his platoon collapsed with exhaustion and futility.[10]

The 75th Company collectively decided it could go no farther when the last tank in its area exploded from a direct hit. Almost immediately, the remnants of the company fell into the thin concealment of the wheat field. Thomas dove into the wheat with his comrades. He and a veteran private, J. P. White, found themselves near a twelve-inch field roller left by a French farmer. The two used their shovel and pick-mattock to dig a shallow hole behind the roller, which deflected the machine gun bullets raking the field. Thomas was not in very good shape. Just before the attack stopped, another of his comrades, a member of the original 75th Company, had taken a machine gun bullet in the stomach and, screaming, had collapsed into the wheat, "which just shot my nerves."[11]

Although stricken and exhausted, Thomas went about his duty. He and White fashioned a respectable hole for themselves behind the French roller, and the hard work of digging a hole while flat on his stomach brought Thomas back to some semblance of control. He looked about. He could see few Marines, but he saw 1st Lt. Macon Overton, commanding officer of 76th Company, fifty yards away to his right rear, protected by a road embankment. Overton beckoned to him, so Thomas heaved himself to his feet and joined Overton, who seemed only slightly distressed by the halt. Overton had already assessed the situation but wanted Thomas's help before he went back to Major Hughes's PC, perhaps four hundred yards to the rear, to give Hughes his evaluation of the battalion's plight. Overton wanted a count of Thomas's effectives because Redford had apparently already gone to Hughes's PC for additional orders. Under fire, Jerry moved from foxhole to foxhole and counted about one hundred men, one-third of them from the 75th Company. Overton took this information to Hughes, and Thomas returned to his hole behind the roller.[12]

When Overton returned to the 75th and 76th companies, he brought good news and bad news. The good news was that the battalion would be relieved that evening by French colonial troops, who would continue the attack. The bad news was much worse. Before Overton had reached the battalion PC, a German shell had landed on top of Hughes's command group. Carlton Burr had died immediately, decapitated by a shell fragment. Among the other casualties was David Redford, who had suffered serious wounds and had been evacuated. (Although Jerry Thomas did not know it that day, Redford died from more wounds he received while being carried to an ambulance.) Because all of the other officers of the 75th Company had fallen or could not be found, Sgt. Gerald C. Thomas became the acting commander of the 75th Company, at least in the eyes of Macon C. Overton, whose opinion was the only one that counted at the front line of the 1st Battalion, 6th Marines, on 19 July 1918.

Overton told Thomas that the battalion would withdraw from the front, still about a mile short of the German defenses. Upon receiving this welcome news, Thomas immediately fell asleep. Around 2300, White awakened him as French colonial troops moved into the battalion area. Thomas led the remnants of the 75th Company back to the battalion PC, where he found a number of wounded too incapacitated to walk to the rear. Jerry organized the survivors of the 75th Company to construct litters from blankets and rifles and carry the battalion's worst wounded to the rear under the concealment of night. Although additional attacks by the French Tenth Army interdicted the Soissons–Château-Thierry highway in the days that followed, the 6th Marines in one day of battle had left the war for another period of reconstruction. An exhausted Jerry Thomas, one of the pillars of the 75th Company, went to the rear with a heavy heart.

Soissons left unpleasant memories for the 4th Brigade. Having taken almost 4,500 casualties in Belleau Wood, the brigade had now suffered another 2,000 in the two days of attack at Soissons. In these two battles, the brigade had taken more casualties than its authorized strength. The original 4th Brigade was gone. The fate of the 1st Battalion, 6th Marines, told the story. The battalion had been in battle about one hour on 19 July 1918. It had started the attack with 37 officers and 654 enlisted Marines. (Clearly, the losses of Belleau Wood had not been replaced.) The attack of 19 July ravaged the battalion. When the battalion finally got an accurate count of its "present and effective" Marines on 21 July, the 1st Battalion, 6th Marines, mustered 16 officers (some slightly wounded) and 247 enlisted men, which included a small party left in the rear. The 75th Company started the day with 6 officers and 173 men on its rolls and finished with 4 officers and 92 enlisted men. The battalion at full strength should have had three times as many officers and five times as many enlisted men. Jerry Thomas was surrounded by ghosts.[13]

At one-third strength, the 6th Marines marched back toward the Forêt de Retz after its one day of desperate battle. The 1st Battalion met its rear echelon and field kitchens at the edge of the forest at about noon on 20 July. The relief did not continue well. The regiment assembled at Le Translor Farm at the eastern edge of the Forêt de Retz. The Germans shelled the farm, an obvious concentration point, on the evening of 20–21 July. Tree boughs and shell fragments dropped on the exhausted Marines. The 6th Marines recognized the danger but made no changes in position. After its ordeal of 19 July, there was little the German army could do to make the Marines feel any worse than they had felt during the long evening of 19–20 July 1918.

[CHAPTER VI]

Surviving 1918

Having served with distinction in the two hardest and bloodiest battles in Marine Corps history up to that time, Sgt. Gerald C. Thomas marched to the 6th Marines assembly area at Nanteuil-le-Haudouin, some thirty miles northeast of Paris. The brigade received several days of rest behind the lines, where it found hot meals, some new clothing, and safety from German shelling. Scattered members of the 6th Marines, some from rear-area assignments and others the slightly wounded veterans of Belleau Wood, found their old companies—or what remained of them. More replacements brought the infantry battalions back to three-quarters strength. The changes in the Marine brigade reached from top to bottom. One of the most experienced and forceful senior officers of the Marine Corps, Brig. Gen. John A. Lejeune, arrived to take command of the brigade. After only four days, however, he became the 2d Division's commanding general when General Pershing reassigned General Harbord to reform the troubled AEF Services of Supply. Lejeune remained the division commander for the rest of the war, and "Buck" Neville, aided by Lejeune's brilliant, erratic protégé, Lt. Col. Earl H. Ellis, retained the 4th Brigade. Col. Harry Lee kept the 6th Marines, but "Johnny the Hard" Hughes left the 1st Battalion upon his promotion to lieutenant colonel. (As commander of the 23d U.S. Infantry Regiment, Hughes became gas poisoned again and left the war as a permanent casualty.)

The 1st Battalion's new commanding officer, Maj. Frederick A. Barker, impressed Jerry Thomas as "of equal caliber" to Colonel Hughes. The thirty-eight-year-old native of Charlestown, Massachusetts, lacked Johnny the Hard's charismatic leadership style, but he brought equal valor, considerable field experience, and solid professional skills to the 1st Battalion. Commissioned in 1904 after three years of service as a sergeant, 1st U.S. Cavalry Regiment (1899–1902), Barker had served on ships detachments and at Marine barracks until he saw two years of campaigning in Haiti and Santo Domingo. During operations in the

[56]

Caribbean, he had participated in seven engagements. His reputation stood high enough in the Marine Corps that he was assigned to command the 47th Company, 5th Marines, before it sailed for France. Barker's ability then took him away from troops. He was first assigned to command the regiment's headquarters company and then went to AEF Headquarters to command the American provost guard in Paris, a combat assignment of another sort. Promoted to major in October 1917, Barker finally returned to the Marine brigade—much to his own relief—after Soissons and took command of the 1st Battalion on 30 July. He undertook the job of rebuilding the battalion with patience and skill. His task was eased, no doubt, by the fact that the battalion adjutant, Capt. Arthur H. Turner, a martinet who prided himself on his immaculate appearance and administrative infallibility, had been wounded and evacuated at Soissons. The new battalion commander and battalion adjutant were officers closer to Jerry Thomas's own personality and leadership style than Hughes and Turner, whose rigidity and emotionalism contributed to the battalion's ups and downs in spirit.[1]

Along with the rest of the 2d Division, the Marine brigade moved by train to a divisional sector near Nancy, south of the Saint-Mihiel salient, for training and further reorganization. The brigade assumed a routine not unlike peacetime training. The veteran Marines of the 1st Battalion became increasingly aware of their historic importance as a new flood of replacements reached the brigade. After a pause in recruiting and commissioning new officers dictated by the Wilson administration, Headquarters Marine Corps had received welcome authorization to expand the Marine Corps to an ultimate strength of 2,500 officers and 70,500 enlisted men. If the 4th Brigade was to continue fighting at full strength—and General Barnett planned to send an additional brigade to France—the Marine Corps needed many more good men. The casualties in June and July alone had consumed almost one-fifth of the Marine Corps' total authorized strength. Pershing's headquarters did not want another Marine brigade, let alone a Marine division as Barnett planned, but it demanded that Barnett provide 22,500 Marines just to support the 4th Brigade and to perform security duties assigned by AEF Headquarters.

The expansion of the Corps sent ripples that eventually reached the 1st Battalion, 6th Marines, and shaped Jerry Thomas's career. As the recruit depots received new men (draftees who had volunteered to be Marines and who met Marine physical standards) and then sent them to duty, Headquarters pulled the 1917 volunteers from the Caribbean and stateside security duties and sent them to France. Although the replacements had not seen much action, they had trained hard for a year and arrived eager to continue the 4th Brigade's illustrious record, of which they were keenly aware. The veterans, glad to share the burdens of future battles, accepted their enthusiasm and innocence with bemused toleration. Jerry noticed that he and his old comrades no longer worried about the future and focused only on each day's trials and pleasures. Jerry had not, however, lost interest in one part of the present: becoming an officer in the new 6th Marines. On 25 August, he learned that the 6th Marines could recommend as many as forty enlisted men, ages twenty to thirty-five and of proven ability, for provisional commissions in the Marine Corps Reserve. The 1st Battalion received a quota of twelve nominations. Within the five days allowed to complete the application,

Jerry and his Bloomington friend, Jim Elliott, had applied again to become second lieutenants.[2]

The reorganization of the 4th Brigade, built on a stream of new NCOs and Marine privates, as well as the arrival of some new officers, started an unpredictable chain of events that probably saved Jerry Thomas's life in 1918. On 18 August, Jerry learned that he had been assigned as a student to an AEF infantry weapons course that would last four weeks. Four other NCOs from the 1st Battalion received similar orders. Jerry was not unhappy to leave the battalion because it was standing security duties along a quiet stretch of trench line, training in open warfare, and doing a lot of trench digging, the most unpleasant of tasks as defined by American soldiers. The infantry weapons school, held at Fort de Plenois in the fortified belt around the historic city of Landres, provided some new knowledge, but, more importantly, Jerry found time to distance himself from combat and to think about his future. He wrote to his mother that he would soon be promoted to gunnery sergeant (he had seen his name on the eligibles list) and had been approached about becoming a regular warrant officer. Instead, he wanted to be a second lieutenant. Jerry thought he and Jim Elliott would soon be lieutenants because Headquarters Marine Corps had announced that it would favor combat-proven NCOs when it made new officers. Rather than worrying about his own future, Jerry felt concern that his family was "breaking up" during the war, and he wondered whether his mother had enough money. He assured his mother that all was well. He did not tell her that he and his fellow students sensed that the new American First Army was about to start an offensive.[3]

The experienced NCOs in the infantry weapons course had ears to hear and eyes to see, and they were not surprised when the First Army attacked the Saint-Mihiel salient on 12 September. The next day—with every Paris newspaper carrying news of the offensive—the students became very restless. Concerned about mass desertion (if that is the proper term for returning to battalions in battle), the school's commanding officer called a formation and told the assembled students that the offensive had been so successful that it would soon end. He reminded them that they were close to graduation and that there would be other battles before the war ended. To Jerry Thomas and the four other Marine NCOs in his group, the plea for patience made no difference. That night the Marines packed their musette bags and simply walked through a sallyport for the local railroad station. They found an eastbound train for Nancy and talked their way aboard. In the Nancy station, they could get no clear information on the location of the 6th Marines until they found some wounded Marines among the casualties awaiting a hospital train. Learning that the regiment was somewhere around Thiacourt, the five Marine NCOs rode and walked for three more days until they found the 6th Marines still engaged in the Bois de la Montagne and Mon Plaisir Ferme, a strongpoint in the German rear guard positions. Not heavily engaged in the first two euphoric days of the Saint-Mihiel offensive, the 6th Marines had instead met a hardening German delaying action and lost about two-thirds of the brigade's 729 dead and wounded. The 75th Company had had another ten Marines killed in action, and it was still shooting when Thomas found it. Nevertheless, the Fort de Plenois "deserters" found the 1st Battalion just as it was being relieved. They had missed the battle.[4]

Billeted in tents in a wood near Toul and pelted by a cold rain that continued for four days, the 75th Company had little to celebrate after the Saint-Mihiel attack, but four sergeants received welcome news. On 20 September 1918, Gy. Sgt. Jeremiah Dalton and Sergeants William H. Busby, James Elliott, and Gerald C. Thomas reported to the PC of the 6th Marines to accept their commissions as second lieutenants, provisional, Class 4C, U.S. Marine Corps Reserve. First, they had to submit to the probings and proddings of two Navy assistant surgeons, who found nothing wrong with them that precluded their becoming officers. All of the new lieutenants had been with the 75th Company since its formation, although Dalton had spent the past year as an instructor at the AEF weapons school at Gondrecourt. Col. Harry Lee administered the oath of office to the new officers.

Jerry Thomas attained what he had sought for more than a year: to become an officer of Marines. "I am rather proud to have risen from the ranks of the finest fighting force on the Western Front," he wrote his mother. He also reassured her that he would now have better food and a place to sleep indoors. He had not changed his uniform much, simply substituting gold bars for red-trimmed stripes. An officer's tan raincoat and a Sam Browne belt (the marks of rank in the AEF) would have to wait. Also, he would not be commander of the 75th Company's third platoon, a position claimed with Jerry's happy consent by Jerry Dalton. The company now had too many lieutenants, so Jerry accepted a transfer to the hard-luck 74th Company, which always seemed to need officers. Jerry joined his new company just as the 6th Marines, revived by a move from the woods into houses on the outskirts of Toul and one day's liberty, marched to the trains that would take them to a new battlefield. On the day the regiment left Toul (27 September), the First Army was already again in combat, but the 1st Battalion Marines had little idea about their next operation.[5]

On 26 September, General Pershing launched an attack of three corps of nine divisions, supported by about four thousand guns, between the Meuse River and the Argonne Forest. The offensive did not point westward toward Metz and the German border as Pershing had planned, but north toward Sedan, a crucial railroad center along the north bank of the Meuse, and the edge of the Ardennes, the hilly anvil upon which the Americans were supposed to crush the German Fifth Army. The American offensive complemented a similar grand attack by the British Expeditionary Force through Belgium eastward into Germany, thus constituting in the words of its conceptual father, Field Marshal Sir Douglas Haig, a "compressing envelopment." The arc between the American and British armies would be filled by the French Army, which would advance with enough ardor to prevent the Germans from shifting divisions to their menaced flanks. In examining the challenges facing his own army, General Pétain thought the French Fourth Army, whose sector bordered the American First Army's west of the Argonne Forest, did not have enough strength to penetrate the German positions anchored on Blanc Mont ridge. Pershing examined his own reserves and assigned two divisions, the 2d (Regular) and 36th (Texas National Guard), for operations with the Fourth Army. The 2d Division would be concentrated by the evening of 30 September.

Moving ahead of his division, General Lejeune reached Fourth Army headquarters on 25 September and watched the start of the French attack. He learned two disturbing things. The first did not surprise him: the French attack on Blanc Mont had stalled. The second development alarmed him more: the staff of the Fourth Army, Lejeune heard, wanted to break up the 2d Division and use its brigades to reinforce French divisions. Fortunately, the French did not yet have operational control of the 2d Division, and Lejeune knew that such a piecemeal commitment would be anathema to Pershing. Before the French could act—and confident that AEF Headquarters would support him—Lejeune proposed that his division assault Blanc Mont. The Fourth Army commander, Gen. Henri Gourard, accepted the proposal on 29 September. When the 2d Division arrived by train at Châlons-sur-Marne, it immediately found trucks waiting to take it to the wrecked villages of Somme-py and Suippes where it would prepare for its fourth major operation.[6]

Still unaware of their impending attack, the men of the 6th Marines enjoyed two days' rest in a French cantonment near Châlons-sur-Marne because they had been among the first Americans to arrive on the new battlefield. The rains gave way to a welcome spell of Indian summer, and the Marines enjoyed being dry and eating prepared meals. On the night of 29 September, the regiment joined the division movement into the trenches as the chill weather and rain returned. Although the Marines did not know it, General Lejeune watched them dismount from their trucks, draw ammunition and flares, and head to the front. Taking up a position in a French antitank ditch about eight hundred yards behind the lead 2d Battalion, the 1st Battalion Marines huddled in their ponchos for a few hours of sleep and waited for sunrise. When he awoke, Jerry Thomas found himself in a wasteland far worse than anything he had yet seen in France. As Lejeune saw it:

> The area surrounding us had been fought over for four long years. We were in Champagne. The ground of that country consists of a thick layer of black soil beneath which is a deep layer of pure white chalk. Tens of thousands of mines, shells and bombs had churned and pulverized the ground into a fine white powder so that the men emerging from trenches or dugouts were grey ghosts. The debris of war was everywhere—broken cannon and arms of all sorts, partially destroyed trucks and other vehicles, here and there the body of a soldier, now French, now German, which burial parties had failed to care for. Across the road and several hundred yards away was the completely leveled village of Souain where not one brick or stone rested upon another. It was indeed a tortured land.[7]

While Lejeune's staff planned, the 1st Battalion waited for more details about the operation. The first hint of the difficulties ahead for the Marine brigade arrived in a "Division Order-of-the-Day" on 1 October. The 2d Division, General Lejeune told his men, had won a reputation, acknowledged by all the Allies, as a crack assault division. It had now been moved from reserve to mount the critical attack that would pierce the German lines on the French Fourth Army's front. Once again, it would defeat the enemy and add to its glory. No veteran in the 1st Battalion needed to have the division order translated. The operation had Soissons written all over it. Later in the day, the battalion received orders to march forward five miles to the trenches, held by the French, where the attack would begin at 0530 on 3 October. As the 74th Company made its final preparations, the company commander chose Jerry Thomas to remain behind with a detail of twenty men, a French practice of removing about ten percent of each infantry company from each attack. The role of this nucleus was to rebuild a shattered company after the engagement; its immediate duty was to help the division provost marshal to round up stragglers and to control traffic. The practice allowed a company commander to perform a rough act of mercy, for the practice was to put the unit that stayed behind under the most veteran officers and NCOs he could spare. The only officer in the 74th Company who had survived both Belleau Wood and Soissons, Thomas was a natural choice for the detail, but he felt guilty about missing his first action as an officer.[8]

For the next week, often under German shellfire, Lieutenant Thomas and his de facto military policemen performed their many duties with efficiency and, at least on the part of Thomas, a heavy heart. As he moved through the brigade's rear area, he sought information about the 1st Battalion, 6th Marines, especially the 75th Company. The news carried by the wounded from the front was that the battalion was taking its objectives but with heavy losses. Thomas learned that Jerry Dalton had fallen, badly wounded, at the head of his platoon in his first day in battle. Led by Major Barker and the new commander of the 95th Company, Capt. George Stowell, who had returned from his purgatory in a replacement battalion, the 1st Battalion drove forward across the trenches on Blanc Mont's western slope, reinforced by a battalion of the 5th Marines. On the second day of the attack, the 4th Marine Brigade lost more than 1,100 men, its worst day of the entire war. On 8 October, the battalion passed the crest of the ridge, and the 76th Company, still led by the indestructible Macon C. Overton and assisted by the 75th Company, captured the key German position at Saint-Étienne-à-Arnes. In the furious German counterattacks against Saint-Étienne, the 75th Company disintegrated under a deluge of shells and raking machine gun fire. The company commander, Capt. Henry E. Chandler, reported to Major Barker that he commanded no officers and 13 enlisted men. The next day he, too, died. The defense of Saint-Étienne fell to a patchwork force of Marines and Texas infantrymen, whose inexperience cost them dearly. The Texans brought only one advantage to the battlefield—so the Marines thought. They were armed with the new Browning automatic rifle (BAR), which the Marines "borrowed" whenever possible to strengthen their own positions. Accurate, heavy American artillery fire probably saved the Saint-Étienne salient, but the cost was dear. When the 75th Company finally left the battle in the early morning of 10 October, it mustered 11 Marines, commanded by the one surviving sergeant. Major Barker thought his entire battalion probably had fewer than 300 effectives, about one-third of the Marines that he had taken across the line of departure only five days before. The regiment had lost 940 officers and men. The 2d Division's attack on Blanc Mont, however, cleared the way for additional advances by the Fourth Army.[9]

While the 2d Division was providing the punch that moved the French Fourth Army's offensive forward, the American First Army had stalled in the Meuse-Argonne. Although the two flank corps of Pershing's army had made acceptable progress, the center V Corps, with the critical task of penetrating the *Kriemhilde Stellung* (the Germans' strongest defense position), had not carried its objectives. In truth, Pershing's concept of operation was too ambitious. Nevertheless, he continued the general attack after local attacks had brought some improvement to the First Army's position and allowed artillery to be displaced forward. On 14 October, the First Army made another general attack with the V Corps, composed now of the veteran 42d and 33d Divisions, attacking the crucial Romagne Heights in the center of the Army's sector. The Americans advanced again, but not much, and the two divisions of the V Corps lost heavily. They did, however, capture Romagne Heights. Their success left one major objective, Barricourt Heights, to be taken before the First Army could turn a slugfest into a war of maneuver. Pershing's thin patience with his army had disappeared in mid-October, in part because the Allies had lost patience with him. He sacked one corps and three division commanders. He gave the V Corps to Maj. Gen. Charles P. Summerall, who had commanded the 1st Division at Soissons and Saint-Mihiel. Summerall's leadership style was uncomplicated. He made his officers and men fear him more than they did the enemy. His technical skill and personal courage gained respect, but his constant threats to relieve and disgrace subordinate commanders did not make him the AEF's most beloved general. His reputation also meant that his corps would get the First Army's hard jobs, starting with Barricourt Heights.[10]

As the First Army began to reorganize for another general offensive, the 2d Division was still under the control of the French Fourth Army, which seemed uncertain just how much longer it would keep its two American divisions. In the meantime, the 4th Brigade came again to full strength with more replacements. The Marines received clean uniforms, bathed, resumed their war on lice, ate hot food, and did some training. Small parties of officers and men went to Châlons-sur-Marne on liberty. The 6th Marines staged a parade for General Lejeune and a distinguished visitor, Adm. Henry T. Mayo, commander of the U.S. Fleet. On 19 October, however, the brigade received strange orders to assume part of a French sector—orders never fully explained by either Lejeune or Gourard. The confusion required the Marines to make a sixty-mile forced march in new field shoes in a cold, steady rain. About 20 percent of the marchers went lame, and respiratory problems spread throughout the 6th Marines. Jerry Thomas, who had returned to the 75th Company, made the mystery hike and felt every kilometer. He and Jim Elliott were the company's only veteran officers, and Elliott's morale fell when he learned of his mother's sudden death back in Bloomington. Jerry's own spirits remained good, but for the first time in his life he felt permanently exhausted. In addition to a persistent cough and cold, he developed stomach problems. He investigated honorable ways to leave the battalion and considered applying for an assignment as an aerial observer. The new company commander, however, appealed to him to stay with the company for one more operation because he was the company's only dependable, experienced combat officer. Jerry agreed to remain with the 75th Company.[11]

By 23 October, General Lejeune had a clear picture of his division's next assignment and had arranged its immediate change of operational control from the French Fourth Army to the V Corps, American First Army. The mystery march ended, and the Marine brigade, after a day's rest, boarded a truck convoy that took it eastward to Les Islettes. After a march through the Argonne Forest to an assembly area near Exermont, the Marines received four days' rest. Even the weather cooperated as the days turned clear and reasonably warm. The Marines had their complete packs and overcoats, so the crisp nights did not bother them. On 29 October, the 6th Marines received twenty-five new Browning automatic rifles. Reconnaissance parties departed for the positions still held by the 42d Division, and high-ranking visitors came to see the 6th Marines. One visitor, General Summerall, insisted on making an "inspirational speech" to the regiment that left a sour impression on the Marines. Summerall's talks to the enlisted Marines stressed the importance of their attack with such fervor and blood lust that one veteran spontaneously responded with "hogwash" or words to that effect. Summerall promised the 6th Marines officers that he would relieve every field grade officer in the brigade if the Marines did not succeed. General Lejeune's request for three cheers for Summerall drew stony silence from the Marine officers. The brigade's scant regard for Army senior commanders did not increase in the Meuse-Argonne.[12]

Jerry Thomas marched to the front on the evening of 30 October at the head of the 3d Platoon of the 75th Company. The 1st Battalion reached its next assembly area before dawn on 31 October just north of the ruined town of Sommerance. Hardly had the company settled into holes on the slope of a deep ravine when German artillery fire began to fall on the Marines. Suspecting a major attack, the German Fifth Army artillery raked the entire V Corps front with a mix of high-explosive and gas shells. Mustard gas shells smashed into the 75th Company's position in the ravine. One shell exploded opposite Jerry's foxhole and splashed liquid gas all over the young lieutenant. Some of the gas reached Jerry's eyes and soaked into his uniform, which meant that he would soon have blistered armpits and crotch. After the shelling subsided, the battalion surgeon inspected the 75th Company and ordered about a quarter of the company to the rear. Jerry refused evacuation for several hours, but his condition worsened. The surgeon insisted that he go to the rear for gas prophylaxis. The doctor, apparently deciding that he would spare as many veterans as possible from the next day's attack, tagged the Marines with enthusiasm. By noon, Jerry was in an ambulance headed for Field Hospital 16 for treatment. The 75th Company would go on without its third platoon commander.[13]

Leading the 6th Marines attack on 1 November, the 1st Battalion lost one hundred men to German artillery fire before it even reached the line of departure. Nevertheless, the battalion plunged forward against a German strongpoint that had not been touched by the Allied barrage. In three hours of heavy fighting, the battalion penetrated the German main line of resistance but at high cost. By 0800, the 1st Battalion could no longer continue the attack. At the point of battle as always, Capt. Macon C. Overton of 76th Company died as his Marines and Army tanks crushed the German machine gun nests. Major Barker became ill from gas, and Maj. Benjamin S. Berry assumed command of the battalion until George Stowell, who was commanding a special flanking unit built around his 95th Company, could return to the battalion. Jerry Thomas learned of the battalion's plight as the first wounded arrived at the field hospital. After having his eyes washed out and submitting to a soda bath, Thomas did not feel too ill twenty-four hours after his gassing. When he found an ambulance headed back to the 6th Marines sector, he deserted his hospital bed and reached the newly taken town of Landres-et-Saint-Georges late in the day. There he found Jim Elliott, commanding the 75th Company's "stay-behind" detachment, in charge of a traffic control point. The ambulance was not going forward that evening, so Jerry accepted Elliott's invitation to spend the night in his temporary quarters. A real bunk looked attractive because Jerry was once again feeling sick. Before he could resume his journey to the front the next day (2 November), Jerry was captured—by Maj. Franklin B. Garrett, the division provost marshal. Garrett immediately recognized Thomas; the major had served briefly as his battalion commander at Belleau Wood. Garrett ordered Thomas to provost marshal duty and gave him a detachment to command.[14]

For the next week, the 2d Division drove the Germans northward toward the Meuse River and Sedan. Thomas's detachment, following behind the two infantry brigades, stayed busy as wagons and truck convoys jammed the available roads. While the division pursued the German defenders, whose resistance now amounted to little more than rear guard actions, Thomas twice saw Marines of the 1st Battalion on the road, but he resisted the temptation to flee Major Garrett. In addition, his stomach problems, gas-damaged eyes and body, and suffering lungs reduced his enthusiasm for more combat. As German resistance waned, Marine losses from exposure and exhaustion soon exceeded those from bullets, for the November weather had turned raw and rainy. Jerry did not have to rejoin the 75th Company to get sick. He already was. He still wanted to rejoin the company, and he and Jim finally wrestled a promise from Major Garrett that they could rejoin the 1st Battalion "in a day or so." On 9 November, after their detachments had been replaced, Jim and Jerry started back to the 6th Marines. The next day, they found the brigade headquarters in the city of Beaumont, not far from the Meuse. They learned that the 6th Marines would mount an assault across the river on the morning of 11 November, but that the brigade staff did not know the exact whereabouts of the 1st Battalion because the whole regiment was on the move toward the river. Jerry and Jim also found the headquarters ablaze with "very flighty rumors of a cease fire." Sleeping that night in a wine cellar, they escaped a sudden sleet storm.[15]

For Jerry Thomas, the last day of the war began at brigade headquarters and ended, five miles from Beaumont, with the 75th Company in a wood overlooking the Meuse. With more precise directions from the brigade PC, Thomas and Elliott marched out of Beaumont, first stopping at a field hospital in the shattered shell of Beaumont cathedral to look for members of the 6th Marines. They found American wounded but not members of their regiment. Although they did not know it, the regiment's early-morning attack had been canceled because only one of two bridges over the Meuse had been completed, and the Army engineers working on the bridge reported that the crossing site was clearly covered by German artillery and machine guns. The battalion commanders of the 6th Marines conferred and withdrew their troops to the Bois du Fond de Limon at dawn. Before the attack could be continued, the 1st Battalion learned that a cease-fire would go into effect at 1100. An hour after the war ended, Lieutenants Thomas and Elliott rejoined their company. They found no sign of celebration, only a company of very tired, hungry, and wet Marines trying to warm themselves around several bonfires. They did a final tally of their friends. Of the original 75th Company, only six men, including Thomas and Elliott, saw peace come above the banks of the Meuse. Since June 1918, more than seven hundred men had served in the 75th Company. Amid the deafening silence of a battlefield where the guns no longer roared, the Marines watched as flames leaped from their camp fires toward the dripping treetops above. When Jerry Thomas wrote to his mother three days later, he had little to say except that he had been slightly wounded but was back on duty with his company, part of the finest regiment in the AEF. As for news of the Armistice, he could only add: "well, this old war is over."[16]

[CHAPTER VII]

The Long March and an Occupation 1918–1919

As the guns cooled along the Meuse River and the 6th Marines enjoyed standing around the warming fires without the worry of danger, the Allied high commanders prepared to enforce the Armistice and to establish a military posture that would ensure that the peacemaking continued and the war did not. Responding to plans already drafted and approved by the Allied governments, General Pershing reorganized the American Expeditionary Forces for movement in two different directions, one toward the French ports and home, the other into Germany. If given a choice, the 6th Marines would have willingly marched all the way back to Saint-Nazaire. Instead, the regiment turned north and east and marched about 150 miles to an enclave near Koblenz at the juncture of the Mosel and the Rhine. The Marines did not see the United States again until August 1919. The 2d Division had become part of the U.S. Third Army, a special force of six divisions that occupied part of the Rhineland until the Allies and Germany concluded a binding peace treaty. The III Corps, composed of the 1st, 2d, and 32d Divisions, would defend bridgeheads east of the river while the IV Corps would remain west of the Rhine. For divisions that had just completed the Meuse-Argonne campaign, the new assignment posed new labors.[1]

The long march and the occupation provided an opportunity for 2d Lt. (Provisional) Gerald C. Thomas, USMCR, to think about his eighteen months of military experience and to assess his future. As the new year dawned, Jerry requested that his temporary reserve commission be changed to a permanent commission in the regular Marine Corps. He decided to stay in the Marine Corps during a phase of his service that provided every reason to go home a civilian, for the occupation of Germany (November 1918–August 1919) tested all of his leadership skills. His duties started the day after the Armistice. Maj. George Stowell, the acting battalion commander, sent Thomas and an enlisted detail back to the battalion's staging area near Sommerance to recover the battalion's personal baggage and blanket rolls, both sorely needed by the Marines. During the successful journey to and from Sommerance, Jerry's detail found the rest of the First Army seething with rumors about an immediate return to the United States. When the baggage detail returned to the 1st Battalion's bivouac, Jerry found that the rumors had flown ahead of his trucks. So, too, had real orders, which blew the rumors away. On 14 November, the 6th Marines learned that the regiment would begin its long march into Germany on 17 November.[2]

In seven days of hard marching through the southern rim of the Ardennes, the 6th Marines left France north of the Meuse, hiked across the southeast tip of Belgium, and struggled up one ridge after another until it reached the German border at Beforterheider on the Saar River. The march was no victory stroll. At the extreme left flank of the Third Army's movement, the 2d Division had farther to go—with no additional time—than the other divisions. Its march would have been longer if General Lejeune had not insisted that his men were on the verge of physical collapse and his transport, especially his horse-drawn wagons, could not handle the logistical burden. Even with a more direct route, the division quickly reached the edge of its endurance. Burdened with full field packs, ammunition, and weapons, the men bore seventy-pound loads. Many of them were still ill with intestinal disorders, respiratory congestion, influenza, and gas poisoning; some collapsed along the route, and a few even died. Their route could have been easily followed. Dead American horses littered the route, in addition to the dead German horses (some partially butchered) and piles of discarded German equipment and weapons. Lejeune remembered the march to the German border as a true ordeal: "I shall never forget those days of gloom. Even when the sky was cloudless the sun was hidden by the haze and mist until the afternoon, but most often it rained—a slow, misty, but chilling rain it was. Sometimes it snowed gently; sometimes the ground was frozen; but always the mud covered the roadbeds."[3]

Obeying the III Corps march orders, the division made the march in tactical fashion. It provided appropriate advance, flank, and rear security detachments, and also established outposts miles from the main bivouac. Warm meals were a sometime thing, even for the main body, and the outposts never saw a field kitchen. Although Jerry Thomas's lungs hurt during the march, he suffered most from a lack of warm, palatable food. During the first week of the march, he found good food and a warm billet only in Arlon, Belgium, where the jubilant citizens welcomed the 2d Division as liberators. Despite the discomforts, Jerry enjoyed his duties with the 75th Company that ranged from posting the outguards to billeting the battalion at the German border.[4]

The 1st Battalion rested for seven days along the German border (24–30 November 1918) because the Armistice terms provided that the Allied occupation forces could not cross into Germany until 1 December. The halt was welcome, but the battalion did not abandon its military labors. The process of replacing worn-out uniforms and equipment continued as the division trains caught up with the brigade. General Lejeune ordered the entire division to conduct close-order drill and smarten its appearance for the march to the Rhine. Like other infantry regiments, the 6th Marines held formations to announce promotions, and a detail of men went to division headquarters to receive Distinguished Service Crosses for valor in the Meuse-Argonne campaign. Thomas found every day a busy one for the 75th Company, but he appreciated the pleasant countryside and the Luxembourgers' reserved cooperativeness.[5]

On 1 December, the 6th Marines followed the 5th Marines across the Our River and began a nine-day march to the Rhine. The weather and terrain did not improve, for the route to the Rhine lay through the steep, heavily forested hills of the Schnee Eifel. The Marine brigade entered Germany with its colors and guidons flying, but the German civilians showed no special response to the American column. Thomas thought they seemed relieved that the war had ended and that their own army, whose vaunted discipline had collapsed in its stricken retreat, had now passed beyond looting range. Other Marines noticed additional things about Germany. The roads were much better than those in France, and the towns that the Marines passed through appeared neat but badly in need of paint and repair. The Marines thought that the Germans had more children than the French and kept them more warmly clothed and better fed. The most common German complaint about the war was that the German army had taken most of the grain supply and had thus reduced the quality of the local beer. Pondering their observations about German children and beer, the Marines crossed the divide between the Saar and the Rhine and marched down the Ahr Valley, a narrow river corridor that led to the Rhine. General Lejeune welcomed the level roadway and the new scenery: "A picturesque and beautiful valley it is—dwarf mountains, with corkscrew roads leading to ruined castles perched on their peaks; miniature river gorges and palisades; health resorts exploiting springs of every description; hot springs, cold springs, warm springs, Apollinaris springs everywhere—bath houses, too, were plentiful, and full advantage of this luxury was taken by officers and men."[6]

The Marines marveled at the terraced hillsides covered with massive vineyards. The advance elements of the 2d Division reached the Rhine on 7 December. Two days later, the 1st Battalion, 6th Marines, saw the great river for the first time. Like other officers of the Marine brigade, Jerry Thomas and his comrades strolled to the riverbank and urinated "to show I didn't give a damn about the Kaiser and his hosts."[7]

After a four-day halt for more drill and logistical organization, the 4th Brigade crossed the Rhine on the Andernach-Leutesdorf ferry. Thomas served as the embarkation officer for the 6th Marines and saw the entire 2d Division make the crossing by ferry or over the Remagen bridge. By 16 December, three days after its short Rhine boat ride, the 75th Company occupied its permanent position on the 4th Brigade's outpost line that guarded the northern approaches to the American enclave at Koblenz. Sharing its billets with most of the 74th Company, the 75th Company settled into the homes and public buildings of Bad Hönningen, a river town that straddled the north-south road on the east bank. The "watch on the Rhine" had begun as the last year of war ended.[8]

As the Third Army started one occupation, Second Lieutenant Thomas considered another occupation—his own. Although he had wanted to become an officer since he joined the 75th Company at Quantico, Jerry had not given his future much thought until he was sure he would have one. At Belleau Wood and Soissons, his odds for a career of any kind seemed dim. Even after he became a wartime officer in September 1918, his major concern was his family's disintegration and financial condition. While Jerry had been in France, his father had left Peoria (and Mrs. Thomas and her two youngest children) for an Army construction job at Aberdeen, Maryland. Vander Thomas's ill health and weakening commitment to his marriage and family, however, worried his son, who wrote his mother that he had saved $400 that she could use to pay bills in Peoria. Jerry's older brother, Shelton, had joined the Marine Corps, too, which meant that he could not contribute much to the family's support until the war ended. When Mrs. Thomas asked Jerry about his postwar plans, he responded in January 1919 that he intended to return to college if he could afford it. In the meantime, however, he had given serious thought to staying in the Marine Corps if he could be a regular officer. In February 1919, he learned from the 1st Battalion adjutant that Headquarters Marine Corps had published a bulletin asking Marine Reserve officers whether they wanted to remain on active duty (Haiti and the Dominican Republic beckoned) and encouraging them to apply for regular commissions. Jerry decided to do both, even though the postwar officer strength of the Marine Corps was uncertain. He assumed that Reserve officers who volunteered to remain on active duty, especially those commissioned on the battlefield in France, would be the strongest candidates for regular commissions.[9]

On 23 February 1919, Thomas applied for continued active duty and for a commission as a regular Marine officer. His request received the warm endorsement of Capt. Glen C. Cole, his company commander; Maj. Frederick A. Barker, his battalion commander; and Col. Harry Lee, his regimental commander. A regimental screening board, headed by Lt. Col. Thomas Holcomb, the executive officer, found him fit in every respect for a regular commission. The officers of the 6th Marines who reviewed his application found Lieutenant Thomas an ideal candidate for a Marine Corps career. He was intelligent, energetic, versatile, courageous, physically sturdy, and morally upright. He had almost completed his college education. Thomas had proved his ability as a combat leader, and he showed an aptitude for military life. He had demonstrated his commitment to the highest Marine Corps standards, and his strength of character assured his superiors that he would educate himself for higher rank and more responsible assignments.[10]

Only Mrs. Thomas objected to Jerry's plans. She wrote him that their friends in Bloomington reported that Jim Elliott planned to return home, finish college, and find a good job. She chided Jerry for not being as sensible as Jim. Although he did not go into the details of Jim's modest performance as an officer, Jerry responded that he and Jim had different ambitions and prospects. He told his mother that a career in chemical engineering did not now appeal to him and that the field had developed too rapidly for him to return to it. Although he knew that she could not understand his reasoning, he had decided that military life— especially as an officer of Marines—appealed to him and that he was a very good officer. Being an officer meant that he would have an adequate income and a secure job, and he wanted to provide money for his younger brother Louis's education so that Louis would not have to work his way through college. In addition, he could not envision himself settled into some boring job back in Illinois after his adventures in France. He did not relent under his mother's pressure.[11]

Proud of his recent promotion to first lieutenant, U.S. Marine Corps Reserve, and pleased that Captain Cole made him the acting company commander when the captain went on detached duty (which was often), Jerry Thomas waited for the American occupation to end and for his own career as a regular officer to begin.

The 2d Division, firmly commanded by General Lejeune, carried on its occupation duties with discipline and skill. Aware that the American military presence would prevent the disorders that plagued the rest of Germany, the Rhinelanders cooperated with the Americans. Both groups obeyed the Third Army's orders against fraternization, which limited contacts to those necessary to conduct official duties. No doubt there were exceptions to the nonfraternization policy, especially for young Marines and German *fräuleins*. One machine gunner noted: "The fact is chocolate and soap will get the fellows most anything they want." What they wanted most, however, were roofs over their heads, home-cooked meals, beds in which to sleep, and a place to drink beer off duty. The Army made all of these amenities possible. The Marines lived with German families; no single, male German was to have a bed until all the Americans had comfortable billets. The Marines could draw rations and have their German hosts cook their meals for them. The Americans controlled the best available food, a powerful instrument of population control in an area where the citizens were living on horsemeat and scant supplies of vegetables. Off-duty Marines went to bars that sold only beer and wine and operated under military supervision.[12]

The 2d Division made sure that its soldiers and Marines had little time for mischief. The 4th Brigade established a rigorous training schedule, barely allowing the Marines to rid themselves of lice and read their accumulated back mail before they returned to the field. In cold and snow, with the low clouds turning the Rhine valley into a gray-domed trench, the Marines took conditioning hikes, participated in tactical exercises, and fired their weapons. Company and battalion maneuvers increased as spring approached because the German government had not yet accepted peace terms. In the meantime, the division maintained its frenetic pace. It sponsored football and baseball leagues, held horse shows and elaborate military competitions, staged innumerable parades and inspections, and sponsored shooting matches. YMCA and Knights of Columbus canteens served the Marines. The brigade trucked liberty parties to Koblenz for free sightseeing holidays; off-duty enlisted men could attend high school and college credit courses established by the AEF or watch movies, plays, and vaudeville shows. Aware that misbehavior might slow their return to the United States and civilian life, the men followed the routine without official complaint. Some managed early discharges to support families at home or to attend college. The other Marines remained acutely aware that they could be released as soon as Congress declared the war over, and they largely avoided the ultimate perils of garrison life, drunkenness and reckless driving. Keeping the troops busy, of course, kept the officers even busier.[13]

Except for a week's leave to Brussels and Paris and a long weekend in Wiesbaden (where he noticed the large number of pretty girls), Lt. Gerald C. Thomas ensured that the 75th Company maintained high standards of readiness and discipline as the Marines waited to go home. Few of them believed the war would continue, although Jerry thought they all disliked the Germans enough to fight them again. The Rhineland remained peaceful enough within the occupied zones, but the Marines knew that an urban civil war had reduced the Germans to military impotence. Jerry was more interested in hunting the abundant local rabbits and game birds than hunting Germans, but his schedule allowed only marksmanship training, not sport. The routine paperwork for the 75th Company was mountainous enough, and the company, like all other units in the 4th Brigade, prepared summaries of service and letters of condolence for the families of the company's dead. Because the company would probably demobilize, Thomas had individual personnel records and property accounts to prepare. He left his office, established in the dank rooms of a castle ruin, to inspect the company's sentry posts, billets, and supply storerooms. His superiors recognized his steady, conscientious performance. Although they rated him higher in intelligence and personal qualities than they did in physical appearance and forceful leadership, Major Barker and Captain Cole judged Lieutenant Thomas of great value to the Marine Corps and a fully qualified infantry officer. He had quickly demonstrated that he could lead in garrison, as well as in the field.[14]

As spring widened along the Rhine, the chemical plant in Bad Hönningen offered some work, but most of the Germans turned to preparing their grapevines for the next harvest, which meant pruning and fertilizing them with natural manure. At Versailles, other types of fertilizing and pruning shaped the draft of the peace treaty and brought many American visitors as far east as the Koblenz bridgehead. The 4th Brigade entertained Secretary of the Navy Daniels, Assistant Secretary Franklin D. Roosevelt, and a delegation of Congressmen. British and French officers came and went, usually laden with decorations for the American senior officers. In June, the brigade had two exciting experiences. The first was a divisionwide celebration of the first anniversary of the Battle of Belleau Wood. Although few veterans of the battle remained in the brigade, the troops had a rare bacchanalia and drove most of the Germans into the safety of their homes. Two weeks later, the brigade prepared for field service. The III Corps had received orders to march inland to encourage the German government to sign the punitive peace treaty. The 6th Marines made two forced marches of fifteen miles in full field equipment, then returned to its billets at a less urgent pace when Germany signed the treaty. The citizens of Bad Hönningen welcomed the Marines back because they provided life to the local economy and tranquility to the Koblenz area. By July, the Marines knew they would be headed home; they had received orders to pack their equipment for a long journey and to submit to careful physical examinations. (Men infected with flu or venereal disease would not make the trip home with their comrades.) Jerry Thomas had little trouble urging the 75th Company to prepare for the journey.[15]

For the 1st Battalion, 6th Marines, the return to the United States brought no special trials. First, the battalion traveled by train across France to Brest where it entered the embarkation site, Camp Pontanézen. More administrative chores followed: additional physicals, a check of pay records, the screening of service records. A Dutch ocean liner carried the battalion across the Atlantic to New York City, where the Marine brigade reassembled at Camps Merritt and Mills on Long Island. On 8 August 1919, the entire, full-strength 2d Division—twenty-five thousand officers and men—marched up Fifth Avenue from Washington

Square to 120th Street. With a sixteen-man front, the division filled 5th Avenue and stretched in length for three miles. Despite the intense heat and the press of the hysterical thousands that crowded the parade route, the division held its formation. At 110th Street, General Lejeune left the head of the formation and joined other general officers who had served with the 2d Division for the last pass-in-review:

> For an hour we watched the serried ranks marching by. Each battalion as it passed gave us three mighty cheers—cheers which sprang spontaneously from their hearts to ours. It was the most exalted moment of my life. When all had passed, I turned to say goodbye to the officers who were assembled. On every weather-beaten face I saw tears streaming down. It was a sacred hour—an hour spent in communion with the living and the dead.[16]

The 2d Division had, in fact, made a record for combat valor contested only by the 1st Division, its staunchest rival in the AEF. Only the 1st Division had spent more days in active combat (93) than the 2d Division (66). Only the 77th Division had covered more ground in battle (71 kilometers) than the 2d Division (60 kilometers). The 2d Division had taken more prisoners (12,026), captured more cannon (344), and suffered more casualties (22,230) than any other AEF division. All of the infantry regiments of the division had won enough multiple Croix de Guerre to entitle their members to wear the green and red *fourragere*. (Members of the 5th and 6th Marines still wear the *fourragere* while serving in these two regiments.) Among individual soldiers and Marines in the division, 646 had been awarded the Distinguished Service Cross (DSC) for gallantry. The next largest number of DSCs (300) had gone to the 1st Division. Hundreds more of the 2d Division's members were entitled to wear small silver stars on their campaign ribbons for being mentioned by name in brigade or division special orders for gallantry and distinguished service. One of the Marines so entitled was Gerald C. Thomas for his service in the Battle of Belleau Wood.[17]

From the Army's perspective, the 4th Brigade (Marines) had been just a little too conspicuous, even within a very conspicuous 2d Division. Marines alone had won 363 DSCs (which had to be approved at the division level), more than the entire 1st Division. The brigade had taken almost 12,000 casualties, more than half of the entire 2d Division's killed and wounded. Just as the 4th Brigade returned to the United States, the War Department and Navy Department became embroiled over whether the Marines deserved to be listed for honors for "the battle of Château-Thierry." Vast confusion, stirred by inaccurate press coverage in both 1918 and 1919, surrounded the issue over who had fought whom, where, and when. High-ranking Army officers assumed that the Marines were once again building their reputation at the Army's expense. In fact, the public relations bureau at Headquarters Marine Corps had pursued the "Château-Thierry issue" with inordinate enthusiasm, even though the 4th Brigade was largely innocent of any special claims to honors outside of its fight for Belleau Wood, which was technically, by the Army's honors rules, a different engagement. As the Marine brigade left New York for demobilization at Quantico, Secretary of War Newton Baker and Major General Commandant George Barnett tried to quash the press controversy with soothing words, but the poison in Army-Marine relations, already spreading in the veterans of the AEF, could not be treated with interservice diplomacy. As Jerry Thomas was to see many times, the official and informal contacts between Army and Marine Corps officers could never quite rise above the jealousy stirred by the 4th Brigade's performance.[18]

After the New York City parade, the 4th Brigade entrained for Quantico where it prepared for one last parade in Washington, D.C., and its demobilization. First, it exchanged its hated Army olive drab uniforms and puttees for forest green Marine uniforms and distinctive tan canvas leggings. Although they wore helmets for the last parade, most Marines also bought new campaign hats, rather than wear the shapeless Army overseas caps on the trip home. On a hot 13 August, the Marine brigade, led by Brig. Gen. Wendell C. Neville, marched down Pennsylvania Avenue past a reviewing stand that held President Wilson, Secretary Daniels, and the senior officers of Headquarters Marine Corps. The parade brought another moment of high drama to the 4th Brigade, but the moment evaporated with the last details of demobilization at Quantico. Jerry Thomas saw the 75th Company one last time when he gave his men their final pay, savings, and travel funds. Then they were gone, marching to the Quantico railroad station and the trains that would take them home. Jerry watched them go with sadness: "I have seen many military formations since but I have never seen a finer one." He himself had little time to think long about how much had happened in the two years since he had joined the Marine Corps and had come to Quantico as a private in the company that he now commanded. Ahead was more uncertainty: would he remain in the Corps and, if so, where would his next assignment be? He, too, soon left Quantico to seek his future.[19]

[CHAPTER VIII]

Haiti
1919–1921

THE MOIST WEIGHT OF AUGUST along the Potomac River did not dampen Gerald Thomas's enthusiasm for a career as a lieutenant of Marines. After mustering out the 75th Company but before taking leave to visit his family and friends in Illinois and Missouri, Thomas took the train to Washington to determine his chances for a permanent appointment. Headquarters Marine Corps could now provide some information; the Personnel Section had the results of an officer retention board established by Major General Commandant George Barnett and chaired by Col. John H. Russell. When Thomas arrived at Headquarters, settled in its new quarters in the Main Navy Building on Constitution Avenue between 17th and 19th streets, he learned that he had been placed on a list of officers "tentatively to be retained," which meant he was some sort of an alternate. Uncertainty reigned about which wartime officers would eventually receive permanent commissions. First, Congress had not yet set a permanent peacetime strength for the Marine Corps. Instead, it had established a temporary strength of 1,093 officers and 27,400 enlisted men when it passed the Naval Appropriations Act for 1920 on 11 July 1919. These figures represented General Barnett's recommendation for the Corps' permanent strength, but Congress postponed acting on his plan.[1]

The recommendations of the Russell Board did not simplify the officer retention problem but added another controversy to the crisis building between Barnett and Secretary of the Navy Josephus Daniels and the House Naval Affairs Committee. In appointing Russell and the other board members, Barnett did not include officers who had served in France with the 4th Marine Brigade. Russell instructed the board members that they should apply prewar standards, not just reward combat leadership, and insisted they remember that they were selecting the next generation of Marine officers. The board should assess formal education, social acceptability, potential fitness for further military education and higher rank, and versatile service in the peacetime Marine Corps. This precept did a disservice to the prewar noncommissioned officers and some of the NCOs who had won battlefield commissions, and it encouraged the Russell Board not to give special consideration to the veterans of the 4th Brigade. Already outraged by Barnett's quest for promotions and decorations for his Headquarters staff, Daniels and the House Naval Affairs Committee, led by Representative Thomas Butler (father of Marine Brig. Gen. Smedley D. Butler), viewed the Russell Board findings as another reason to deny the Commandant any part of his legislative program. The continued uncertainty about Marine Corps strength meant that the officer retention issue would drag on for another year.[2]

The confusion over officer retention probably helped Thomas to remain in the Marine Corps. The uncertainty over numbers was compounded by such questions as whether the permanent officers would hold their wartime ranks or lower ranks, where they would stand in lineal precedence in their permanent ranks, and how soon they would be shifted from temporary, probationary rank to permanent commissioned status. In 1919, Headquarters proceeded on the assumption that it would have around three hundred permanent commissions to award. When Thomas visited Headquarters, the officers of the Personnel Section assured him that the number of vacancies already exceeded the number of officers who had applied for regular commissions. Some quality officers who might have become regulars would not wait another year to make career plans, and Headquarters later estimated that more than four hundred Marine officers with exemplary records (proficiency marks above 3.5 on a scale of 4) had left the service in the first year after the war. Thomas also benefited from the fact that General Barnett himself felt that the Russell Board had discriminated against former enlisted men with fine combat records, and Barnett agreed to accept Daniels's demand that social status not determine appointment. On 16 September 1919, Thomas learned that he would be offered a temporary appointment as a regular second lieutenant (date of rank, 19 August 1919) with a lineal precedence of 107, which meant he was at least in the upper half of the second lieutenants' list. Already on leave, he wired back his acceptance on 22 September. Although he was disappointed that he had not remained a first lieutenant, he had made a start on a postwar Marine Corps career.[3]

Before leaving Quantico for a month's leave, Thomas had taken additional steps to improve his chances for a permanent commission. He had volunteered for service with the 1st Provisional Brigade in Haiti. The officer assignment section accepted his offer with alacrity, as Thomas knew it would. General Barnett wanted to send as many experienced officers as he could to Haiti, for the Marine brigade and the Gendarmerie d'Haiti, the Marine-officered constabulary, were deep in a brutal guerrilla war with the Haitian *cacos*. Moreover, Barnett had learned enough about conditions in Haiti to suspect that his military forces had, in fact, sparked the *caco* revolt by mistreating the Haitians and that they were compounding the problem by conducting field executions and torture. Thomas was just the mature, stable, energetic, responsible lieutenant the Marine Corps wanted in Haiti, and Thomas, in his turn, must have concluded that successful work there would improve his chances for retention. When he headed west by train for a nostalgic visit to Bloomington and Marshall, Missouri, Second Lieutenant

Thomas knew that his leave would end on the next available Navy transport to Port-au-Prince. He was a satisfied man—"I had a job for which I appeared to have some aptitude and in which I was happy."[4] If not rich, he could count on a steady income of $1,200 a year, and the government had to provide him with two rooms of quarters or pay him an additional $12 a month. (The pay, fixed before the World War, had only one-half the purchasing power it had in 1908.) When he made first lieutenant again, he would receive an additional $300 a year and three rooms. After a brief stop in Bloomington, Gerald went on to Marshall, where his mother now lived as the housekeeper for her aging uncle and aunt, Robert and Margaret Marshall.

In a mad moment that may have matched the Soissons attack, Gerald Thomas, in less than a week, fell in love and married Mary Ruth Durrett, "one of the counties [sic] most admirable girls."[5] The daughter of Mr. and Mrs. Frank Durrett, a prominent Marshall family whose ancestors had also come from Albemarle County, Virginia, Mary Ruth had just graduated from Missouri Valley College and had become one of Marshall's most eligible belles. A tall, physically attractive brunette almost eighteen years old, Mary Ruth was an extrovert. Her major interests were glee club singing, debate, and horseback riding. Proximity probably had something to do with the sudden romance. The Durrett home was just across South Brunswick Street from the Marshall house; perhaps Thomas had already met her during one of his trips with his mother to Marshall after the move to Bloomington. Whatever the circumstances, the Thomas-Durrett romance developed quickly. On Saturday, 27 September, Gerald and Mary Ruth eloped on the morning train to Independence and returned, married, on the midday train—"a surprise to the relatives and closest friends." Less than a week later, the newlyweds caught "The Hummer" for Washington, D.C. Thomas does not appear to have confided in anyone why he married. Four years later, he discussed the matter with Miss Lottie Johnson of Charleston, South Carolina, who was to become the second Mrs. Thomas. At that time, he only mentioned that he had been married once before and that "it was the unhappiest time of his life." He never discussed the matter again, even with his family.[6]

After traveling east and then south by train, Lieutenant and Mrs. Thomas reached the naval base at Charleston, South Carolina, on schedule and sailed for the Caribbean aboard the naval transport *Kittery* on 20 October 1919. Despite the ship's notorious reputation for rolling, the newlyweds enjoyed the honeymoon cruise atop mild seas and in balmy weather. The ship's first call was Cuba, where it put Marines ashore at Guantanamo Bay and at Nuevitas, the headquarters of the regiment then guarding the Cuban sugar industry. Continuing its leisurely pace, the *Kittery* arrived off Port-au-Prince, Haiti, at dusk on 1 November. Fascinated by his first trip to the tropics, Gerald manned the rail as the ship dropped anchor in the harbor. "The night was warm and the gentle offshore breeze brought the acrid odor of many charcoal fires tainted at the last by passage over the 'Gut' a mess of several acres of filthy straw shacks that sprawled at the water's edge where the long pier landed." As he and seven other Marine officers awaited the expected call by the officer of the day, Thomas watched the city bloom with lights against the quick dark of the mountains and ocean.[7]

★★★★

Cupped between the clear green waters of the Gulf of Gonâve to the west and lush mountains to the east, Port-au-Prince, a tropical mix of limited opulence and general squalor, was the home of ninety thousand Haitians, a few hundred Europeans, and about a thousand Americans associated with the occupation. Although parts of the city, especially the business section of the *basse ville* and the suburb of La Coupe, boasted solid masonry buildings, only the partially rebuilt Palais National (victim of a rebel bomb) and the new *cathédrale* had glass windows. In 1919, the city showed some signs of prosperity, insured by four years of American occupation. It had an electrical system, a trolley line, paved main boulevards, and a reasonable sewage system, at least in the affluent suburbs and government buildings. Gardens and parks of palms, breadfruit trees, mangoes, Haitian roses, coleus, and poinsettias added green grace to the foreign section, which began at the sunbaked Champ de Mars, home of the buildings that housed the Marine brigade headquarters and the barracks of the Gendarmerie d'Haiti. In their homes clustered above the heat and dust of the lower city, the foreign community enjoyed fresh sea breezes, shade from high trees and canopies of vines, and freedom from the ripe smells of the city's native population and open marketplaces. Isolated from both the mainstream of Haitian life and the pseudo-Parisian life-style of the Haitian elite, the Americans went about their official duties and enjoyed the insular social life of their alien culture. Haiti might offer opportunities for an ambitious Marine lieutenant, but it offered little to a young Missouri bride once the novelty faded in the Caribbean sun.[8]

Thomas and his seven comrades, all former enlisted men and veterans of the 4th Brigade, had come to fight, not to sightsee, and Col. John H. Russell, commander of the 1st Brigade, wanted the new officers to join the battle against the *cacos* immediately. Russell was an aristocratic graduate of the Naval Academy (1892) and the State Department's favorite Marine officer. On his second tour in Haiti, he had inherited a revolt that the *cacos* had opened in the summer of 1918. In part an armed protest against the Gendarmerie's administration of the *corvée* (or compulsory road labor) and in part simply the return of bandit gangs into the vacuum of arms created by the withdrawal of Marines for France, the Second Caco War had just swung in favor of the 1st Brigade and Gendarmerie at the time Thomas reached Haiti. After seventeen months of inconclusive operations marked by vicious ambushes and atrocities on both sides and the death of almost 1,800 Haitians, the principal *caco* field commander, Charlemagne Peralte, ordered a mass attack on Port-au-Prince in mid-October. The attack was a tactical disaster and a major psychological defeat for the *cacos* because it proved that voodoo could not best Springfields. On 30 October 1919, far from Port-au-Prince, a Gendarmerie patrol led by Marines Herman H. Hanneken and William R. Button infiltrated Peralte's headquarters and killed the *caco* leader in a sudden firefight. With Marine reinforcements sent from Cuba and the United States, Russell ordered more intensive patrolling to exploit the disarray of the *cacos*. The principal focus of the campaign now became the band of Benoit Batraville that numbered perhaps half the *cacos* in the field (an estimated 5,000 armed men) and dominated the Mirebalais district of central Haiti. Lt. Col. Louis McCarty Little took command of the new 8th Marine Regiment and ran the combined Marine-Gendarmerie patrols that began to reduce Batraville's band through amnesty and action.[9]

Russell and Little, both of whom touched Thomas's life while he served in Haiti, were far different officers than "Johnny the Hard" Hughes or most of the other officers of the 4th Marine Brigade with whom Thomas had served in France. Russell had served in the field in Mexico, Santo Domingo, and Haiti, but he had made his reputation in command and staff positions that required a delicate mix of personal force and diplomacy. He had commanded ships detachments and Marine barracks, had served on the Navy Department's intelligence staff and at the Naval War College, and had done a tour with the legation guard in Peiping, China. He was an intimate friend of Assistant Secretary of the Navy Franklin Roosevelt and had easy access to the New York–Washington political and social elite. Little had even more impressive credentials. The son of a Navy captain, the forty-one-year-old Little had been educated in schools in France and Newport, Rhode Island, before graduating with an engineering degree from Rensselaer Polytechnic Institute in 1899. Commissioned the same year, he fought the Boxers in China and saw additional field service in the Caribbean. Handsome, urbane, polished in speech and manners, Little had a deserved reputation for intellectual accomplishment and interests. Already fluent in French, he learned Mandarin Chinese during a long tour in China. Then, in London during the World War, he was Adm. William S. Sims's principal planner for advanced base force operations. General Barnett sent Little to Haiti as soon as he returned from Europe in early 1919. Little's hard work that summer and autumn set the groundwork for Russell's successful command.[10]

Concerned about the brigade's lack of experienced leadership, Russell ordered six of the eight new lieutenants into the field. Three continued to northern Haiti to the 2d Marines, while five stayed in the south with the 8th Marines. Two 8th Marines officers who had landed at Port-au-Prince did not travel to the regiment's camp at Mirebalais. One of those held at the Marine barracks was Thomas, who believed that his rear-area assignment was directly linked to his marriage. Short on action and glory, the Port-au-Prince assignment offered much work and little time in quarters with Mary Ruth. Brigade headquarters seldom had more than two or three lieutenants to manage the daily business of a detachment that numbered between four and five hundred enlisted men, most of whom were close to discharge and disinclined to take soldiering seriously. Headquarters also provided a roof for a stream of Marine officers who had resigned their commissions during the postwar demobilization. Thomas found his work difficult and the environment depressing. Every other day he served as officer of the day, which meant a twenty-four-hour tour as the commander's direct representative. Often, when not on duty, he had to sleep in the office as commander of the Marine reserve force, alerted for provost marshal duty within the city. During the mornings, he and his fellow lieutenants supervised drill and then spent the afternoons serving as recorders and assistant judge advocates for the interminable numbers of courts-martial and boards that the 1st Brigade required. Although he received a valuable education on the garrison aspects of officership during the six months in Port-au-Prince, Thomas longed to escape the capital for the field.[11]

Lieutenant Thomas, however, had one opportunity to show that he had not lost his skill and enthusiasm for close combat. During the duty day of 14 January 1920, the Marines learned that the *cacos* planned a second attack on Port-au-Prince, with the objectives of killing American civilians and robbing the town. In the general defense plan, Thomas assumed command of a ten-man detachment assigned to reinforce the civilian volunteers defending the compound of the Haitian-American Sugar Company on the city's northern outskirts. Around 0200 on the morning of 15 January, the sugar company manager called and reported *cacos* moving through his area. Thomas ordered the Marine detachment to a truck and charged off to the rescue. When the truck was moving past the arcades and iron-grilled buildings of the city's central marketplace, Thomas saw the flashes of rifles up the street. He ordered his men off the truck and into the arcade on the right side of the street. As the patrol jogged by bounds from pillar to pillar, Thomas saw the head of a column of *cacos* emerge from a side street and ordered the Marines, who were hidden by the darkness of the arcade, into a hasty ambush. When the chanting Haitians closed to fifty yards or less, Thomas and his men opened fire with eight Springfields and two Browning automatic rifles. The surprise was complete, the slaughter considerable. The some two hundred *cacos* broke off the action within ten minutes and fled the city. The marketplace was blanketed with the dead and dying. Recovering his hearing and eyesight after the din and dazzling gunfire, Thomas discovered that his patrol had not survived unscathed; seven men had been hit. He sent the two seriously wounded back to headquarters in the truck and led the remaining seven Marines to the sugar company compound.

Thomas's patrol made a significant contribution to a *caco* disaster, identified by the Haitians as *le débâcle*. Brigade headquarters estimated that as many as six hundred *cacos* had entered the city. The column Thomas met had been the largest and was supposed to rob the central bank. The other columns had set fires near the foreign quarter and city radio station. Thomas's ambush had been the heaviest engagement in the nighttime battles, which continued into the next day. At the cost of one Marine, Private Lencil Combs, who died of his wound from the ambush, Thomas's detachment had dropped many of the sixty-six Haitians who were dead in the city's streets. The attacking *cacos* came from Benoit Batraville's band, and the disaster convinced many of Batraville's followers to accept the standing amnesty to become "bon habitants." The Port-au-Prince battle broke the back of Batraville's campaign in central Haiti.[12]

Shortly after the battle with the *cacos*, Thomas had another formative experience, his first meeting with the officer who became his most important acquaintance in the Marine Corps, Maj. Alexander Archer Vandegrift, then serving in the rank of colonel, Gendarmerie d'Haiti. The occasion was the convening of a military commission in Port-au-Prince to try the former city chief of police, Cadeus Bellegrade, with murder and cannibalism. On the evidence, the commission found him guilty as charged and sentenced him to death. Because of twists in Haitian law and Washington politics, Secretary Daniels refused to confirm the sentence and punishment, and Bellegrade fled the city to practice voodoo in healthier climes.

Thomas and Vandegrift, who met at the trial, had much in common. The spare, balding, athletic Vandegrift, then thirty-two years old, came from Albemarle County, Virginia, the Thomas family's eastern home. Like Thomas, Vandegrift loved football and attended but did not finish college (the University of

Virginia) before he received a commission in the Marine Corps in 1909. Scion of Confederate veterans, Vandegrift loved to read Civil War history; Thomas was developing similar tastes. Both Vandegrift and Thomas had served with "Johnny the Hard" Hughes, Vandegrift as a platoon commander in Hughes's company in Smedley Butler's Panama battalion. Although Vandegrift had not served in France, he had heard bullets whistle in Nicaragua, Mexico, and Haiti. Smedley Butler had virtually adopted Vandegrift, whom he called "Sunny Jim" for his optimistic disposition under fire. Otherwise impatient and easily angered, Vandegrift loathed staff work, so he could especially sympathize with Thomas's plight at headquarters. The relationship between Vandegrift and Thomas that began in Haiti in 1920 profited both of them for almost thirty years.[13]

In April 1920, Thomas left for the 8th Marines forward patrol bases and joined the exploitation campaign against Batraville's withering army. Little's plan of operations for the 8th Marines was simple in concept but demanding in execution. He saturated central Haiti with patrols of Marines and *gendarmes,* who were ordered to deny the *cacos* food, shelter, and rest from pursuit. During the day, the Marine patrols and *cacos* hid from one another; at night, they played hare and fox across the mountains of interior Haiti. "McCarty Little drove officers and men at a furious pace. We got little rest but more importantly neither did the cacos." Although the patrols seldom made contact, their pressure resulted in more and more voluntary surrenders. Sometimes atrocities marred the campaign. At one point, Thomas saw Lt. Louis Cukela, a Serbian immigrant of violent temper, execute a prisoner. (Cukela, a legend for his exploits in France for which he won two Medals of Honor, apparently did not understand the niceties of warfare.) The campaign received a major boost in May when a Marine patrol surprised Batraville's personal band and killed the *caco* leader. By the end of summer, the Second Caco War seemed near its end.

For both Thomas, who had been back to Port-au-Prince to see Mary Ruth only once since April, and the Marine Corps, the end of the campaign came none too soon. Alarmed by reports of Marine misbehavior in Haiti, Josephus Daniels had sent an investigating committee, led by Adm. Henry T. Mayo, to Haiti. Congress had anticipated an inquiry on the occupation and ordered its own investigators to Port-au-Prince. Having won the war, the 1st Brigade and Gendarmerie d'Haiti would now have to explain why the victory had required them to kill Haitians. John H. Russell cautioned his officers that they must quickly make peace with the Haitian people and show great restraint in "the maintenance of law and order and establishment and cementing of friendly relations with the inhabitants." Meanwhile, Little's patrols were pursuing the remaining bands of *cacos.* In November 1920, Thomas and his detachment fought one of the last battles of the campaign near Chapel Saint-Martin.[14]

As the *caco* war sputtered out, Thomas had reason to believe that his decision to come to Haiti would have some immediate career benefits. In June 1920, after a nasty personal feud that brought little credit to any of the principals, Josephus Daniels removed George Barnett as Commandant and replaced him with his obvious (and popular) successor, Maj. Gen. John A. Lejeune. Although Barnett's cavalier treatment of both Daniels and the Congress contributed to his downfall, the Commandant fell victim to Daniels's conviction that Lejeune deserved the job, that the Navy's senior officers wanted him to have it, and that a bipartisan coalition in Congress would approve the change, however controversial. Educated by his son Smedley about Barnett's shortcomings, Congressman Thomas Butler, the leading Republican on the House Naval Affairs Committee, helped to push Barnett into oblivion.

One price Lejeune had to pay to become Commandant was to order a reconsideration of the status of the company grade officers retained by the Russell Board, an act he was predisposed to do anyway. The sense of the Congress was clear in a provision of the Naval Appropriations Act for 1921 (passed 4 June 1920) that all company grade officers who had held temporary or Reserve commissions during the World War were eligible for some five hundred vacancies in the permanent rank structure, finally established in the same legislation. The Judge Advocate General of the Navy further interpreted the law to mean that any officer, regardless of when he received a regular commission during the war, did not have to be maintained at his temporary rank in 1920. In effect, Marine captains could become lieutenants and vice versa. Lineal precedence within grades also could be changed. General Lejeune ensured that the Russell Board's results would be moot when he convened a new board, headed by Brig. Gen. Wendell C. Neville, former commander of the 5th Marines and the 4th Marine Brigade. The heroes of the AEF would now get their just due—or so they anticipated. Required to screen some 1,200 potential permanent appointees and to assess the relationships between rank, lineal precedence, and service record in France, the Neville Board worked slowly through the winter of 1920–21.[15]

In the meantime, Gerald Thomas's personal fortunes fell. The months of two-week patrols with little rest had brought him to the verge of exhaustion and reduced his resistance to disease. Like virtually every other Marine in the 1st Brigade, he contracted malaria. Thomas collapsed during his November patrol, and two days of rest did not revive him. He then ordered his Marines to get him back to the Mirebalais base camp, a slow twelve-hour trip. Supported by two men, Thomas staggered back to Mirebalais. He was delirious and semiconscious for most of the agonizing march. After arriving by ambulance at the brigade hospital in Port-au-Prince, Thomas stayed flat on his back for three weeks and received daily intravenous injections of quinine. Although he had not been much of a letter writer since he and Mary Ruth arrived in Haiti, he must have let his mother know that he was sick, or Mary Ruth had written to her family. Somehow, Thomas's mother and brother Shelton thought Gerald wanted to leave Haiti because they asked Congressman Samuel C. Major (Democrat of Missouri) to intercede with General Lejeune. The Commandant checked on Thomas's condition and reported that he was in "no imminent danger" and would soon be fully recovered. Lejeune saw no reason to allow Lieutenant Thomas to take recuperative leave in Marshall, Missouri.[16]

On the very day the Commandant wrote Mrs. Thomas that her son could not come home, Mary Ruth Durrett Thomas died in Port-au-Prince. Critically ill with abdominal pains diagnosed as appendicitis, Mary Ruth went immediately into surgery with a team of Navy doctors and medical corpsmen and Haitian medical personnel. Gerald telegraphed her family: "Mary dangerously ill, following an operation for appendicitis." At dusk that same day, 15 December 1920, Mary Ruth died, and Jerry sent another, sadder telegram to her stricken parents. In the midst of his ordeal, Thomas learned that he owed $30.61 as his share of a mismanaged post exchange audit. On the day after his wife's death, he acknowledged his debt to the Adjutant and Inspector of the Marine Corps. He received leave to return to Missouri but only as the escort of his dead wife.[17]

The last two weeks of December 1920 must have been among the worst in Gerald Thomas's life. His father and Shelton met him in Illinois after his long train ride from New York City, and they all made the final leg of the journey to Marshall. Thomas spent Christmas Day on the train. Arriving in Marshall on Sunday, December 26, the funeral party took Mary Ruth to P. M. Walker's funeral home, where Gerald, Vander, and Shelton remained until the service at 1400 the next day at the Durrett home. Two ministers conducted the service. A quartet sang "Rock of Ages" and "It Is Well with My Soul." How Thomas felt as he buried a young woman he hardly knew, but whom he had taken to a sudden death far from home, remains lost. After the service, the family and friends accompanied Mary Ruth to the Durrett plot in Ridge Park Cemetery. Six school friends were pallbearers. According to *The Weekly Democrat News* of Marshall, "The beautiful flowers laid on the new grave were in great profusion and were typical in their loveliness and purity of the young life just ended." Thomas did not remain long in the United States. By mid-January, he had returned to Port-au-Prince.[18]

The collapse of the Second Caco War did not protect the 1st Brigade from a spring of discontent. As the war ended, the recriminations mounted. When Thomas returned to brigade headquarters for duty on 20 January 1921, he found the Haitian Marines angered by the news that their conduct of the counter-guerrilla campaign would now be investigated by the Mayo Board. Every charge of misconduct, including atrocities in the field, would receive official scrutiny. Louis Cukela was one of the officers named as a party to the investigation (from which he eventually escaped censure), but Gerald Thomas remained only an interested observer of the investigation, not one of its reluctant participants. Instead, he reassumed his earlier duties of a company officer at the brigade's headquarters and barracks detachment. Although the troop indiscipline and administrative turmoil of 1919 had largely passed, the continued officer shortage meant that Thomas worked every day and stood duty as officer of the day almost every other day. Staying busy did not remove his anxiety about his future as a Marine officer, a future now simplified in one sense because he was a widower and unfettered by the concerns of a wife and family.[19]

The 1st Brigade saw its strength decline as part of the personnel shortages throughout the Marine Corps. Although Commandant John A. Lejeune had insisted to Congress that the peacetime strength of the enlisted Marine Corps (27,400 men) should be fully funded, he had money to pay only about 20,000 men. Lobbying for more enlisted personnel became his highest priority, along with cost cutting at Marine Corps installations in the United States. He hoped to create an advanced base force at Quantico of 6,000 officers and men, a force trained and equipped to seize and defend expeditionary naval bases for the Fleet.

The last thing Lejeune needed in the spring of 1921 was another battle about the rank and lineal precedence of the Marine officer corps. On 21 March 1921, the Neville Board reported the results of its reexamination of the 1919 appointments of permanent captains and first and second lieutenants. Reflecting the sense of Congress, the Neville Board favored former enlisted men who had won battlefield commissions, and it rearranged rank and lineal precedence to favor officers with exemplary combat records in France. Of the 748 officers confirmed as permanent appointees, 489 had former enlisted service. The officers who most dramatically improved their rank or seniority within rank—including Clifton B. Cates, Murl Corbett, Louis Cukela, Charley Dunbeck, Walter Galliford, LeRoy P. Hunt, Henry L. Larsen, Alfred H. Noble, Keller E. Rockey, Lemuel C. Shepherd, Jr., and Merwin H. Silverthorn—had brought home Medals of Honor, Distinguished Service Crosses, and Navy Crosses from France. Others, such as Graves B. Erskine, were undecorated but had proved themselves as captains and returned to their wartime ranks. Wartime leadership had now been served and the Congress presumably satisfied. Lejeune adopted the board's findings immediately.[20]

Thomas drew no comfort or advantage from the Neville Board's reorganization of the rank and seniority of the Marine Corps' company grade officers. He had been commissioned late in the war and had earned no medals. He actually lost seniority on the second lieutenants list. He was ranked 107 on the list when he accepted a temporary regular commission in 1919, and vacancies during the following eighteen months should have advanced him by seniority alone. The Neville Board now placed him 104 among the 253 permanent second lieutenants. In effect, Thomas had been penalized by the Neville Board, largely in order to reward long-service sergeants who were too old for more field service and disinclined to view officership as an educated profession. Congress eventually allowed the Marine Corps to back-date the commissions from 4 June 1920 to the dates on which the officers had received their first commissions in World War I. There was no relative advantage in the change, however; the entire generation of World War I officers benefited by the change, largely for pay purposes. Basically, Thomas was 600 numbers down a "World War I hump" of 748 officers. Unless the Corps expanded or switched to some promotion system other than seniority, Jerry Thomas had little chance to advance beyond the rank of major before he neared the age of mandatory retirement. It was a grim prospect for an ambitious officer.[21]

Two days after he approved the findings of the Neville Board, the Major General Commandant invited Gerald C. Thomas to become a permanent second lieutenant in the U.S. Marine Corps. Instead, on 6 April, Lieutenant Thomas resigned his temporary commission, which was now due to expire on 30 June. He requested that he be ordered on terminal leave to Marshall, Missouri, where he would await the Commandant's action. His decision to leave the Marine Corps, as Thomas recalled, was the direct result of the Neville Board's action but probably also reflected his personal depression. Certainly, it did not reflect the attitude of his senior officers. Louis McCarty Little, endorsing his request with dismay, reported that the Marine Corps was losing "a young officer of sterling quality." John H. Russell added that he regretted Thomas's decision because Thomas had proved that he could serve with equal excellence in the garrison and the field.

Headquarters Marine Corps implied that it would accept Thomas's resignation by ordering him to report for temporary duty to the Marine Barracks, Norfolk, Virginia. On 12 May, Thomas once again boarded the *Kittery* and returned to the United States.[22]

Whatever Thomas's intent—and it was clear enough in his own mind in April—his resignation did not stir Headquarters to take action. He had not formally refused his permanent regular commission. Headquarters did not send it to him until 22 May, seven days before he reached Norfolk. The commission, in fact, did not even leave Headquarters but went instead into the desk drawer of Capt. Franklin Steele of the Adjutant and Inspector's personnel office. Steele added it to a file that contained Jerry's resignation. As long as General Lejeune did not accept his resignation and as long as Jerry did not refuse his new commission, he remained a Marine officer. When Jerry arrived in Norfolk, he found no orders that allowed him to continue his journey to Missouri, so he took a ship to Washington and eventually found Captain Steele's office. He asked Steele about his resignation and his orders home. Steele would not act until he saw Thomas in person. "Well," Steele said, "I've got your resignation in my basket along with a lot of others, and there have been a lot of others there. They come in to see me, and I talk them out of it. How about letting me just tear this thing up?" Steele went on to promise Thomas that he could even arrange a tour of duty with a ships detachment, an appealing assignment. On 4 June 1921, the day he met Captain Steele, 2d Lt. Gerald C. Thomas withdrew his resignation letter (it was not torn up) and wrote a letter accepting his permanent commission in the U.S. Marine Corps.[23]

[CHAPTER IX]

Renaissance of a Career
1921–1925

His return from Haiti marked the true start of Gerald C. Thomas's twenty-year march to leadership in the combat forces of the Marine Corps. By the time the United States entered World War II, Thomas had positioned himself by formal military education, self-study, and experience to assume responsibilities he could not have imagined as a lieutenant. Thomas did not have a career master plan. Indeed, the Marine Corps could not have provided him with definitive career guidance had Headquarters chosen to do so, which it did not. Promotions came to those who survived and moved up the lineal list by seniority, not by the meritorious performance of duty. Officer assignments stemmed from rank and the Corps' needs of the moment, rather than from a general system of officer development. Yet the postwar Marine Corps was not an unmapped land for an aspiring officer, and Thomas correctly read the existing guideposts of organizational development, however indistinct. Some of his success was accidental, most was not, and all of it rested on the superior performance of every duty assignment he received. The foundations of his interwar career grew from his service between 1921 and 1925, the period in which he made an irrevocable commitment to advance as high as he could in the Marine Corps.

Thomas was a twenty-six-year-old second lieutenant, who looked much younger and unmarked by life than he actually was, as he returned to Norfolk from Washington in July 1921. He could hardly have foreseen how different his life would be just four years later. He knew that, at some point in his career, he would be ordered to join a ships detachment, a high-status assignment, but that was the only certainty. For the next two years, in fact, he would serve at Quantico and Washington and see at close range the development of the Marine Corps' principal wartime mission—the amphibious assault of a defended naval base site—and the creation of the Marine Corps Schools and the East Coast operating base at Quantico, Virginia. Both the mission and the place (Quantico) would be at the center of Jerry Thomas's career. During this period, Thomas would attend the first of five different service schools he completed before 1941; the formal schooling would be supplemented by two tours as a schools instructor, usually more educational than a student assignment. He would also spend two years at sea on board a gunboat of the Special Service Squadron that patrolled the troubled ports of Mexico and Central America. Although he would find the exposure to Latin culture and American interventionist diplomacy fascinating, Thomas would learn even more about the conditions of service in the U.S. Navy, especially the skills and values of its officers. And, in 1924, Gerald C. Thomas would marry again, establishing the basis of a happy marriage that lasted until his death sixty years later. His family, a devoted wife and four admiring children, would give his career an emotional foundation, even within the unavoidable strains of a service marriage, that never deteriorated.

A changing Thomas had left Haiti for a changing Marine Corps. The results of World War I had set off a fundamental shift of sea state in international politics that profoundly affected the Corps. One of the major changes was the emergence of Imperial Japan as the dominant power in Asia and the Pacific. By siding with the Allies, Japan had received tacit approval for a whirlwind campaign against the German possessions in the central Pacific and the Shantung Peninsula of China. Seizing these holdings and defending them with obdurate diplomacy at the Versailles peace talks, Japan had only reluctantly agreed to part with Shantung and to withdraw its army from Russian Siberia. Japan retained its hold on the Carolines, the Marshalls, and the Marianas (with the exception of Guam, an American colony) through a trusteeship agreement that prohibited Japan from fortifying these islands. The fact remained that Japan, avowed champion of eliminating European and American influence from Asia and the western Pacific, now held potential advanced bases that interdicted the U.S. Navy's direct route to the Philippines and China. Moreover, the European coalition that had held Japan at bay seemed destined to weaken. Wracked by revolution, Russia could not be regarded as a deterrent on mainland Asia. Debilitated by war, Great Britain and France might hold their colonies of Malaya, Hong Kong, and Indochina but not contest Japanese expansionism to the north. The realities of postwar military power suggested only one major deterrent to Japanese imperialism—the United States Navy. The Navy now faced the prospect of a campaign across thousands of miles of ocean north of the equator and west of the international date line.[1]

The Navy's senior planners, principally officers assigned to the Office of the Chief of Naval Operations, the General Board, and the Naval War College, could read a map and the reports of the Versailles conference, and they doubted that the prewar assumptions of War Plan ORANGE, the contingency plan for a war with Japan, still held. A 1919 review of ORANGE produced the ominous conclusion that the fleet could no longer count on an unopposed transit to the Philippines. The Chief of Naval Operations, Adm. Robert E. Coontz, informed the Major General Commandant on 28 January 1920 that the Marine Corps should study the requirements for seizing advanced bases from the Japanese as an essential part of a naval campaign in the Pacific. This mission, which would be the Marine Corps' principal wartime function, ". . . will furnish a definite point of aim, which will permit of the logical development of the Marine Corps for the duties it will be called upon to perform under the War Plans."[2]

The turmoil of General Barnett's relief prevented any meaningful action at Headquarters until General Lejeune became Commandant, but Lejeune, who grasped completely the importance of the mission, assigned a protégé, Lt. Col. Earl H. Ellis, to the task of defining the Marines' new role in ORANGE. Ellis, whose planning genius was matched only by his alcohol-fueled neuroticism, produced Operations Plan 712, "Advanced Base Force Operations in Micronesia," in May 1921. Ellis concluded that defended bases *could* be captured by amphibious assault. This conclusion ran against the conventional wisdom, which rested on the British experience at Gallipoli in 1915. Ellis proposed that the Marine Corps form three assault brigades and one base defense brigade of twenty-four thousand Marines from its peacetime strength of twenty-seven thousand. Balanced against the Corps' traditional peacetime responsibilities, Lejeune could not make such a dramatic shift in priorities. He embraced Ellis's study, however, and ordered that the Marine Corps make its wartime mission of amphibious assault the focal point of officer education, troop training, and equipment development.[3]

However committed he might have been to the Marine Corps' future as an amphibious assault force, John A. Lejeune could not decree that the Corps jettison all its current missions and devote itself exclusively to preparing for a war politicians thought inconceivable in 1921. The political reality of postwar defense retrenchment pushed the Marine Corps toward tasks that had present, not future, value. Defending the Corps' budget, Lejeune stressed that the Marine Corps existed to provide ships detachments, occupation forces in the Caribbean, and security forces at naval bases. In June 1921, the Commandant reported to the Navy Department that his existing tasks would make it very difficult to form expeditionary forces for any duty, let alone an especially trained amphibious assault force. Marines in the continental United States (676 officers, 13,278 men) manned thirty-two posts, ranging from the bases at Quantico and San Diego to details at naval hospitals, cable offices, and radio stations. An additional force of 350 officers and 6,508 enlisted men provided security forces in twelve foreign countries and American territories. The major commitments in the "foreign service" category were the regular Marine units in the Dominican Republic and Haiti and the officers for the Gendarmerie d'Haiti and the Policia Nacional Dominicana. Another 56 officers and 1,975 enlisted men made up the thirty-six ships detachments required by the U.S. Navy.[4]

As a second lieutenant, Gerald Thomas did not have quite the same problems as Major General Commandant John A. Lejeune, but the problems were not dissimilar. He had been part of the wartime Marine Corps. He had been a minor figure in the 4th Marine Brigade, whose exploits in France provided General Lejeune with the political ammunition he needed to advance the interests of the future Marine Corps. But, in 1921, Thomas faced important decisions that would shape the rest of his career. Once a part of the Marine Corps that *had been*—the Marine Corps of World War I and the Caribbean interventions—Thomas was now an officer in the Marine Corps that *was*, not the Marine Corps envisioned in War Plan ORANGE. Lieutenants have little choice but to accept the demands of the service as they face them in the present. Yet, the intellectual and emotional choices they make may take them into the mainstream of some future Corps or isolate them in their specialization in peripheral missions. Thomas did not make a comprehensive assessment of his future career in 1921 (at least not one that he left for posterity), but by 1925 he had found his niche in the Marine Corps of the future, a niche that prepared him for World War II.

After a month of routine garrison duty at Marine Barracks, Norfolk, Thomas received orders to Marine Barracks, Quantico, where he arrived in August 1921 to find much of the garrison preparing for a field exercise. The maneuvers, designed by Brig. Gen. Smedley D. Butler and approved by General Lejeune, were the first for the small expeditionary force at Quantico and mixed real training with show business. Butler proposed to use a force of 3,000 Marines drawn from all East Coast posts and stations to reenact the Battle of the Wilderness (1864) at the original location, some thirty-five miles from Quantico and fifteen miles directly west of Fredericksburg, Virginia. Although Butler planned to organize the road march by World War I standards and to conduct tactical exercises along the way, the ultimate mission of the exercise was to demonstrate for Washington visitors (including President Warren G. Harding) and the press how efficiently the Marine Corps could fight a Civil War battle with modern weapons. When Thomas arrived at the headquarters, 5th Marine Regiment, he found the exercise in its late preparatory stages. The regimental commander, the stubborn and impatient Col. Frederic M. "Fritz" Wise of Belleau Wood and the Gendarmerie d'Haiti, asked Thomas what his major had been in college. When Thomas responded that it had been chemical engineering, Wise sent him to a patchwork engineering battalion under his control. Thomas found himself further assigned to the Corps' only battery of tractor-pulled heavy 155-mm guns, leftovers from the World War. Tractor and gun together weighed nineteen tons, far too heavy for the bridges along the roads to the battlefield. As engineer officer for the battery, Thomas had the chore of getting the guns to and from the maneuver area over Virginia's back roads.[5]

Lieutenant Thomas completed the Wilderness exercise wiser about the needs of artillery and the problems of overland movement, happily through success, not failure, of the mission. The artillerymen already knew they would have to stay off the paved roads and cross the Rappahannock and Rapidan rivers by fords, not bridges. In fact, the six-gun artillery battery used the same fords crossed by the Army of the Potomac in 1863 and 1864 and returned the same way. Although Thomas had to retrace the march with a detachment of engineers in order to repair some culverts and small bridges the tractors had ravaged, he enjoyed the experience. The maneuver rekindled Thomas's interest in Civil War history, especially the Eastern theater battles in which his Confederate ancestors had fought and, in the case of Col. Thompson Brown, CSA, had died. He also saw that the stage-managed exercise did indeed provide the Corps with an avid public audience and Congressional attention.[6]

Seeking additional interesting assignments, Thomas volunteered to take the place of a married lieutenant on a temporary detail to Washington in November. The occasion was the Conference on the Limitation of Armament, a diplomatic initiative by the Department of State and its Secretary, Charles Evans Hughes.

The "Washington Conference," as it became known, represented the Harding administration's alternative to the Fleet expansion program adopted by Congress in 1916 and reaffirmed in 1919. The negotiations, completed in February 1922 with the signing of three treaties, represented an American diplomatic triumph by linking naval strength to a reduction of tensions in the Far East and Pacific—at least in the administration's eyes. To the degree that capital ship tonnage represented power, the United States and Great Britain agreed to rough parity (eighteen battleships and twenty-two battleships in the half-million-ton range), and Japan accepted a third position with ten battleships of almost three hundred thousand tons. The Five Power Treaty on naval limitations also replaced a British-Japanese alliance (1902) that the United States and the Commonwealth countries wanted to terminate. The Japanese position of negotiated inferiority, however, was less onerous than it appeared because the Japanese refused any alteration of their trusteeship holdings in the Pacific and demanded that the treaty signatories maintain the status quo at naval bases outside their "home waters." For the United States, this provision meant that it could not develop the facilities or improve the defenses of the Philippines, Guam, the Aleutians, and the Hawaiian islands. Although the Navy's senior officers supported the concept of naval limitations, they opposed the basing limitation because it made War Plan ORANGE even less tenable. Pro-treaty advocates argued that the complementary treaties that pledged the political status quo for China and the signatories' colonies reduced the danger of war. Opponents were not so sure about Japan's benign intentions. Naval and journalistic circles seethed with debate during and after the conference.[7]

As one of three junior officers of the special Marine guard detachment assigned to provide special security for the Washington Conference, Jerry Thomas took a crash course on international diplomacy and strategy he could not have then received in the Marine Corps school system. The Marine detachment (120 enlisted) protected the sanctity of the foreign delegations' special offices located on the ground floor of the Main Navy Building. The Marine officer of the day's desk controlled access to the delegates' offices; on his tours, Thomas watched the diplomats come and go. During his off-duty hours, he attended plenary sessions to hear the diplomats trumpet their nations' claims, even though he knew that the significant negotiations were going on behind closed doors. He profited from listening to the discussions of the army of international journalists who clustered around his desk for interviews and to share their own views. According to Thomas: "To be truthful the news gatherers at the conference were of a caliber equal to the delegates." He wrote his mother that no newspaper, especially the Hearst chain in the Midwest, had the complete story of the negotiations. He also left the assignment convinced that Japan had surrendered none of its long-range goals of Asian hegemony. The Washington treaties had given Japan only a financial respite, and they would lull the other powers into even greater military impotence in the region.[8]

After hours, Lieutenant Thomas enjoyed other educational pursuits along the glittering margin of Washington military society. A regular attendee at the debutante balls and tea dances that involved the daughters of senior military officers, Jerry savored a sophisticated social life he had never experienced before. He marveled at the number of attractive, socially acceptable young women he met, but he reported to his brother Shelton that half of them were Catholic and hence unsuitable.[9] Among his new male acquaintances was another Marine officer who, like Vandegrift, would touch Thomas's future career. Handsome and polished, Capt. Lemuel C. Shepherd, Jr., was aide-de-camp to General Lejeune and special social aide to the White House. He occupied a natural leadership role for the Washington Marine lieutenants, both by his formal duties and his reputation for battlefield leadership (two medals, three wounds) in France. Moreover, he was a Virginian and a Virginia Military Institute classmate (1917) of one of Thomas's officer friends in the old 6th Marines. By the workings of fate and the Neville Board, Shepherd, who was eighteen months younger than Thomas, made major the same year (1933) that Thomas became a captain.[10]

Thomas's social life also put him in the middle of the winter's greatest disaster, the collapse of the roof of the Crandall's Knickerbocker Theater on 28 January 1922. When he took his date home from a tea dance at 2400 16th Street and dinner at the Army-Navy Club, Thomas learned from her father, a Navy captain, that a two-day snowfall had caused the roof of the Knickerbocker to cave in on the Saturday evening movie crowd. He was only a block from the theater, so he plowed through the snow to the disaster site (18th Street and Columbia Road) and found Washington Marines already involved in the rescue operation. The site was grotesque. The building's walls stood, and its marquee lights blazed. Inside, snow and wreckage had crushed and trapped hundreds of men, women, and children. For the next twenty-four hours, Jerry and his comrades labored to save the living and retrieve the bodies of the 107 dead. Jerry left the shell of the theater only once, to change from dress blues to his service uniform. He renewed his acquaintanceship with violent death and leadership in crisis.[11]

Although he extended his stay in Washington by volunteering for mail guard duty, Thomas returned to Quantico in the summer of 1922 in time to participate in the second of Smedley Butler's military extravaganzas, the reenactment of the Battle of Gettysburg. Again serving as an engineer officer, Thomas marched from Quantico to Gettysburg and back in an exercise that took more than two months to complete. Despite the publicity of the "long march" and the re-creation of Pickett's charge (led by a Marine officer from Virginia), the maneuver had considerable training value. The troops also probably enjoyed the hike and tactical exercises more than serving as labor troops at Quantico, where Butler had them busily engaged in developing the base and building a mammoth football stadium. Thomas did not expect to be at Quantico much longer, however; he had orders to the ships detachment of the battleship *Delaware*. His orders were then changed, and he found himself in the second Company Officers Course, a ten-month curriculum for captains and first lieutenants.

Surveying his forty classmates when the Class of 1923 formed in September, Thomas discovered that eighty percent of them were veteran former noncommissioned officers, many with World War I experience. Most of the students did not care to be students, and some of their lethargy spread to Thomas. He moved from the bachelor officers' quarters (BOQ) on base to a house in Quantico that he shared with old Haitian comrades Charles Connett and Edgar Kirkpatrick, and he did not devote his after-hours time to study. Because he had already studied for and passed the promotion examination for first lieutenant, he had had a large dose of naval law, ordnance, military administration, topography, and tactics. He used his evenings instead to read military history, for which he had developed an avid taste. He started with G. F. R. Henderson's life of "Stonewall" Jackson, then read all of Matthew F. Steele's *American Campaigns*, the Army's bible of American military history. His favorite subject was Civil War history. (Thomas later claimed that for the next fifteen years he seldom missed a military history reading period of two hours a day.) He did not respond to the formal curriculum of the officers' course, which he thought "not particularly good . . ." and especially ill-suited for officers who already knew all they cared to know. Thomas finished the course in the middle of his class (23 of 40); his tepid performance made not a whit of difference to his advancement to first lieutenant on the promotion list published in April 1923. On the other hand, he had developed an intellectual interest in his profession through reading military history, "no better preparation for a military career."[12] By graduation, he was ready for another leave period in the Midwest and the sea duty assignment for which he had been chosen the preceding year.

The romance of sea duty filled Marine recruiting posters. Young men, vague look-alikes to Douglas Fairbanks, strode across spotless decks or, more often, strolled along a tropical waterfront. In fact, enlisted Marines sought sea duty, for it gave them a full set of dress uniforms, a chance for foreign travel, and rapid promotion. In the 1920s, Marine officers understood that the romance of sea duty paled beside the reality of service as "sea soldiers." The ships detachments had brought the U.S. Marine Corps into formal existence in 1798. Despite the diminished importance of the Marines to discipline on board American warships and their irrelevance in sea battles, the Corps had fought to maintain the ships detachments even in the face of hostility from the Navy's officer corps. Article 711, Title 34 U.S. Code, continued to state: "Marines may be detached for service on board armed vessels of the United States, and the President may detach and appoint, for service on said vessels, such officers of said corps as he may deem necessary."[13] The law did not say what the Marines would do. Some of them manned part of warships' secondary batteries. All stood guard and performed the full range of nonspecialized ships work, which often meant that the Marines did the same menial tasks as the common "deck apes." Marine officers, chosen because they were "suitable" and "more efficient," went to sea to learn about the Navy, a requirement for useful service in Marine expeditionary forces. Their basic function was to organize and train the ship's landing force, which included the Marine detachment and part of the ship's crew. The success of this mission, however, depended on the interest of the ship's captain and the warship's station. Obviously, the captain of a battleship of the Main Battle Force was unlikely to view landing parties with the same concern as the captain of a light cruiser on the China station.[14]

For Thomas, sea duty represented his first close contact with the United States Navy, and, like his contemporaries, he found the duty instructive, if not always pleasant. Ordered to the aged light cruiser *Galveston*, whose home port was the Brooklyn Navy Yard, he learned that his new home for the next two years would actually be the *Tulsa* (PG 22), a 1,270-ton patrol gunboat nearing completion in the ways of the Charleston (South Carolina) Navy Yard. About a week after he reported to the *Galveston*, the cruiser slipped anchor and made what her crew thought would be its last voyage. Throughout the fall of 1923, the *Galveston* crew prepared the cruiser for decommissioning and worked up the *Tulsa* for its shakedown cruise.

Commissioned on 3 December 1923, the *Tulsa* had been built for one purpose, extended cruising in Latin America or Asia as part of the State Department's Navy. Officially home ported in Boston, the *Tulsa* was really bound for the naval station at Balboa, the Canal Zone, for cruising with the Special Service Squadron, the newly formed (1920) force of light warships that patrolled the coasts of Mexico and Central America. Authorized in 1919, the *Tulsa* was 241 feet in length, 41 feet abeam, and drew but 10 feet as mean draft. She maintained good habitability and shallow water-handling characteristics by sacrificing armament, armor, and power. She carried only three 4-inch, 50-caliber guns as a main battery (without turrets), supplemented by two 3-pounder and two 2-pounder rapid-fire guns. The oil-burning boilers could generate enough steam for only 12 knots' maximum speed from a single screw. On the other hand, the crew and work spaces, in addition to being new, provided more room than a larger warship. The *Tulsa* rated a complement of 9 officers and 184 enlisted men, but she put to sea with only 154 sailors. The Marine detachment had one officer, a first sergeant, one sergeant, three corporals, one trumpeter, and twenty-five privates. The ship's armory boasted four Lewis light machine guns, eight Browning automatic rifles, and ninety Springfield rifles, as well as two Model XII 3-inch landing guns. In sum, the *Tulsa* was a Caribbean cruise ship with considerable firepower against unfortified shore targets and men and arms enough to protect American lives and property—or sway the local military balance if the State Department so decreed.[15]

The routine at the Charleston Navy Yard allowed Thomas ample time to sample Southern social life, which he found in full swing with pre-Christmas parties and debutante balls. His tour in Washington had added to his social self-confidence, and his friends now called him "Jerry," not Gerald or "Tommy." His social swath narrowed rapidly after the evening of 11 November 1923. He and a messmate from the *Tulsa* had dates arranged by a female friend of the Navy officer. The fourth party, who was supposed to pair off with the Navy officer, was Miss Lottie Capers Johnson. Petite, blonde, lively, and twenty years old, she was the daughter of Dr. and Mrs. William H. Johnson, both members of old Charleston families, and the sister of Ensign J. Reid Johnson (U.S. Naval Academy class of 1922).

Dr. Johnson, an orthopedic surgeon educated at the University of Virginia medical school and teaching hospitals in Germany, France, and Russia, had a local reputation as a miracle worker. He not only set bones but designed and built his own braces and tension devices in a shop behind his Greek revival home at 107 Wentworth Street. Dr. Johnson also had some novel habits and hobbies. He never billed patients; he exercised by throwing an anvil around his backyard; he invented a portable pressure cooker that could be fixed to a car's radiator; and he practiced pistol marksmanship by potting away at bees in his backyard. His wife, the former Lottie Palmer Capers, was the daughter of the Reverend Ellison Capers, the seventh Episcopal bishop of South Carolina and a former brigadier general (at the age of twenty-six) in the Confederate army. The Johnsons' home, built in the late eighteenth century and rebuilt twice after that, belonged to Mrs. Johnson. The

Johnson and Capers families claimed ancestors from England, Scotland, the Netherlands, and France who had been among Charleston's earliest settlers. The family also had a respectable military tradition that dated to the Revolution. Dr. Johnson himself had served in France as a captain, Medical Corps, USA, and one of Lottie Johnson's favorite first cousins was newly married to another more distant cousin, 1st Lt. William Capers James, USMC.

It was well that the Johnson family liked military officers, for Lottie Johnson fell in love with Lieutenant Thomas at first sight. She saw him first in civilian clothes and had no idea that he was the Marine officer her friend coveted. "All I saw was Jerry! I never saw another man! I went through the motions of being a debutante with a filled dance card!" Between Christmas and 19 January 1924, Jerry and Lottie had nine dates. He told her he was a widower, but nothing else except that his first marriage had been a mistake. He would like to try again, and she agreed to be his wife.[16]

With its smitten lieutenant of Marines, but minus two of his detachment who had jumped ship, the *Tulsa* (captained by Comdr. MacGillivray Milne, USN) cast free of Pier 314 on 19 January 1924 and moved cautiously out of Charleston harbor bound for Galveston, Texas, on what was supposed to be a routine shakedown cruise. A storm off the coast of Veracruz decided otherwise. When the *Tulsa* reached Galveston on 27 January, Captain Milne learned that the light cruiser *Tacoma* had gone aground on the treacherous Blanquillia Reef. Because another civil war had brought a flood of American refugees to Mexico's eastern ports, Commander Special Service Squadron ordered the *Tulsa* south to replace the *Tacoma*. On 12 February, the *Tulsa* started across the Gulf of Mexico at nine knots, her three boilers putting out as much steam pressure (190 pounds per square inch) as they could. Except for one short trip back to Galveston, the *Tulsa* spent the next four months shuttling between Veracruz and the smaller ports of Tuxpan, Puerto México, Frontera, and Progreso and evacuating German, American, British, and French refugees, most of them oil workers. The port calls included much "showing the flag" and military courtesies but little liberty for the crew and ship's guard; the State Department wanted no incidents ashore. Jerry found his duties aboard the *Tulsa* easy enough for a seasoned troop leader, although Pvt. W. Barnes plagued him with disciplinary problems. He was not satisfied that his detachment could serve as an effective landing party and welcomed the order, received on 8 May, to return to Charleston.[17]

Thomas also anticipated his marriage to Lottie, scheduled for 2 June. Amid a sanctuary awash with flowers, white dresses, and white dress uniforms of the Navy and Marine Corps, Lottie Johnson and Gerald C. Thomas exchanged vows in Grace Episcopal Church. The best man was the groom's best friend from the *Tulsa*, Ens. Sherwood Smith (U.S. Naval Academy class of 1920).[18] The couple honeymooned in Richmond, where Jerry did some genealogical research on his own colonial roots. This impressed the Johnson family.

For the next sixteen months 1st Lt. and Mrs. Gerald C. Thomas led a nomadic life that followed the *Tulsa* from as far north as Boston to as far south as Panama. Much of the time they lived apart, Lottie with her parents in Charleston and Jerry in his stateroom and the wardroom of the *Tulsa*, where he whiled away the time by playing bridge and reading. Sherwood Smith remembered Jerry as a congenial, considerate officer respected by the ship's officers for his diligence and thoroughness. Although he had considerable reason to minimize his work during the three weeks the *Tulsa* spent in Charleston, he took his detachment to the Marine Barracks for large doses of drill and tactical instruction. Jerry's next major responsibility, part of the routine for any warship in the Special Service Squadron, came when the *Tulsa* arrived at the naval station, Guantanamo Bay, Cuba, on 20 June 1924. He took the Marines ashore, and the detachment set up tents near the Deer Point rifle range. Jerry put his men through the rifle qualification course and more tactical exercises; he and his men then served as coaches while the *Tulsa*'s crew fired the Springfield for record. Now an expert rifleman, Jerry impressed Smith with his patience and determination to teach the sailors as much marksmanship as they could master. At the conclusion of the training period, Jerry organized and trained the entire landing force, some ninety sailors and Marines. Again, he handled the landing force, especially Smith's crew of one landing gun, with understanding because he quickly recognized that manhandling a 3-inch gun from a whaleboat in the surf was not an easy task. It was Jerry's first practical experience with amphibious landings.[19]

From arid Guantanamo Bay, which resembled southern California more than the Caribbean, the *Tulsa* sailed for the Panama Canal, made the transit from Colón to Panama City, and took up station at the squadron anchorage off Balboa on 9 July. The *Tulsa,* like other squadron vessels, actually dropped her hook off the port only on weekends. During the week, she exercised at the squadron gunnery range at Taboga Island and conducted ships drills. Jerry found the drills boring after their novelty ended, but he used the gunnery practice as an opportunity to learn about naval gunfire. "This was my first experience with naval gunnery and I worked at it. There was always one ship or another firing and I was a more or less permanent member of umpiring teams."[20]

Following the *Tulsa,* Lottie Thomas arrived in Colón on 10 July, along with other *Tulsa* families, and Jerry met her the next day. The Navy Department did not pay for families to travel to Panama because Balboa was not a home port. Nor did duty make concessions to love. On their first full day together, Jerry stood shore patrol duty in Balboa and left the next day for gunnery at Taboga Island. Jerry and the *Tulsa*'s supply officer, Lt. H. D. Nuber, found an apartment for their wives and Nuber's young child in a former French hospital. The officers returned to their shared apartment on weekends. Lottie remained in Balboa, often alone, until she returned to Charleston in January 1925. Only four weeks after she had settled into her apartment, the *Tulsa* received orders to cruise the east coast of Honduras and protect American lives and property (principally the facilities of the United Fruit Company) from Honduran rebels. Twice during Jerry's absence, Lottie fell ill, first with a kidney infection and then with pneumonia, but she was successfully treated both times at an Army hospital in the Canal Zone. Despite the loneliness of her separation from Jerry, Lottie enjoyed the beauty of Panama, especially the mountains, ocean, and tropical flowers. In the meantime, Jerry sampled the exotica of Honduras.[21]

The Honduran cruise of the *Tulsa* provided no action for its Marine lieutenant, but he had several interesting experiences. The ship's first call at Puerto Cortéz found the sugar company town quiet, but the local American consul requested that Captain Milne provide him with a military escort for a trip inland to negotiate with the rebels. Thomas and Sherwood Smith volunteered for the two-day trip, made in an automobile body fitted to a handcar, on the company's narrow-gauge railroad. The consul's hidden agenda was to attend a party at the company's inland sugar plantation, which Thomas and Smith also may have found interesting. In any event, the trip had its moments. On the way upcountry, the party found a company train stalled in front of a body on the tracks; aware of the quaint Honduran custom of charging anyone around a body with murder, the workers had no intention of investigating the "corpse." Thomas checked out the body, which proved to be a breathing, but quite drunk, sugar worker. At the plantation, the Americans found a very hospitable manager who had organized a private cocktail party, complete with women, for his important visitors. The women, however, were the wives of some of his staff whom he did not invite. As the first drinks made the rounds, the manager learned that the husbands had decided to attend the party as well—complete with *pistolas*. The party hurriedly disbanded without incident, much to the Americans' relief. The highlight of the trip back to the ship was less menacing. A flood had driven the jungle wildlife onto the railway embankment, and Jerry observed "deer, myriad species of tropical animals and more snakes than I had ever seen . . . it was a veritable zoo."[22]

The *Tulsa* called next at the United Fruit Company headquarters at Tela, which was loosely besieged by a rebel force and defended by an equally inept group of Honduran soldiers. Jerry prepared the landing force, but the American did not go ashore for action. On his reconnaissance, Jerry admired the company's hospital and other facilities for its workers and decided that "dollar diplomacy was not all bad." During most of the *Tulsa*'s anchorage off Tela, Jerry performed his routine tasks with his detachment (drill and inspections) and took his turn as officer of the deck, which he shared with four junior Navy officers. During each twenty-four hour tour (the standard when not under way), he checked the condition of the ship, inspected the magazine and took air samples, noted events for the ship's log, inspected arriving stores, and ensured that all the watchstanders were at their posts.[23]

Relieved on station by another ship, the *Tulsa* turned north to make a prior date at Galveston, Texas, whose city fathers wanted a warship to help the city celebrate Navy Day, 26 October. The *Tulsa* was underway at noon on 15 October, but that night she was caught in a hurricane and could not escape, even by running south for four days. On the fourth day, her lifeboats ruined and the crew bruised and seasick, the *Tulsa* almost ran aground on a bar off Yucatán. The storm brought winds of up to 125 miles an hour and gave the *Tulsa* a pitch from trough to trough that Thomas thought stood the ship on end. During the height of the storm, the ship's doctor, an inexperienced Medical Corps lieutenant, diagnosed one sailor's agony as acute appendicitis. Even in the raging storm, he planned to operate, but Thomas talked him out of such heroic measures. The sailor survived with a simple kidney infection. Finally regaining some seaway as the storm shifted course, the *Tulsa* ran out of the storm to the east and then turned north to Key West to check for structural damage. Finding only minor damage that could be easily repaired, Captain Milne brought the *Tulsa* to Galveston for the parade. The parade did not impress Thomas, who led the *Tulsa*'s landing party along the line of march, but he liked the fireworks and the chance to give his stir-crazy Marines some liberty.[24]

Despite Milne's report that the ship's engines needed major overhaul, Commander Special Service Squadron sent the *Tulsa* back to the Honduran coast to show the flag at the port of Trujillo, but after another four weeks the ship returned to Balboa in time for the Christmas holidays and Jerry's welcome reunion with Lottie. The new year began with a cruise up Central America's western coast to take Dr. Leo S. Rowe, director-general of the Pan American Union, to the capitals of Costa Rica, Nicaragua, and Honduras. The stop in Nicaragua was marred by a tragedy. During a liberty outing on Lake Nicaragua, a sudden storm capsized a small craft serving the lake steamer. Three sailors and one Marine drowned. Jerry led the hunt for the bodies, found his Marine, and then buried him at the Isla de Guerrero cemetery. The sailors' bodies were also later recovered. After the stop at Honduras, the *Tulsa* received orders to sail for "home," meaning the Boston Navy Yard, for overhaul, so the ship reversed course, transited the Canal, and steamed north for the United States and the end of its cruise. When she arrived, the *Tulsa* resembled Noah's Ark—the Navy allowed sailors to bring home pets on the last leg of a foreign cruise. The *Tulsa*'s main deck "resembled a zoo, macaws, other varied colored birds, honey bears and what not." Unenthusiastic about being a keeper and anxious to see his wife, Jerry left the ship in New York, traveled to Charleston for two weeks' leave, and then brought Lottie with him when he rejoined the *Tulsa* at Boston. Finding an apartment on Bay State Road overlooking the Charles River, the Thomases set up housekeeping for two idyllic months while workmen replaced the *Tulsa*'s propeller and adjusted her engines.[25]

As the mild winds of May bathed Boston harbor, the *Tulsa* set sail once again with a new captain, nine new Navy junior officers, twenty-three new .45-caliber Colt automatic pistols, and one veteran Marine first lieutenant who was already thinking about his next assignment. Jerry had seen Lottie off for Charleston because he knew he would leave the *Tulsa* sometime in the fall. Whether they knew it or not, the decision was especially wise, as well as frugal. Lottie had just become pregnant. Jerry had had enough troop duty and foreign service for awhile; he had requested recruiting duty well away from the sea in Des Moines, Iowa; Indianapolis, Indiana; or St. Louis, Missouri. The first stop on the voyage to Panama was again Guantanamo Bay for field and range firing. Jerry tackled his now familiar range chores with vigor and skill. Except for burning his hand on a warm BAR barrel and being annoyed by the local mosquitoes, he enjoyed the activity, but he was not satisfied with his Marines' marksmanship. He felt especially well but worried that he was eating too much. At night, the tent camp was alive with games and songfests. Jerry liked to sing "Sweetheart of Sigma Chi," because he pretended he was singing it to Lottie, whom he missed worse than he had during the first cruise. He paid special attention to the incoming message traffic aboard the *Tulsa* as he awaited orders.[26]

Because relations with Mexico remained strained, the *Tulsa* steamed to Tampico and Veracruz on her way to the Canal Zone. The worst violence encountered by the ships detachment consisted of liberty fights with American oil workers in

Tampico. The officers dined and drank with the foreign community, which left Jerry exhausted and glad to be off for Veracuz after a week of showing the flag. From Veracruz, the *Tulsa* stopped again at Puerto México, Frontera, and Progreso before reversing course and making her way south through the Canal. Again stationed in the Balboa-Taboga Island waters for two months, the *Tulsa* conducted the required drills and gunnery. The ship took a break by visiting a prime fishing ground near the Peralos Islands. Jerry continued his routine duties at sea and served as permanent shore patrol officer on weekends in port. Although individual violence was not a problem, political unrest brought rioters into the streets of Panama City in the summer of 1925, followed thereafter by fully armed infantry battalions of the U.S. Army from the Canal Zone's garrison. The local Navy commander, however, did not suspend liberty, so Jerry took his customary detail into the city and reported for duty to the Army brigadier general in command. The senior officer took one look at Jerry and began laughing: "My gosh, here we are armed to the teeth with mortars and machine guns in position and the Navy sends one Marine lieutenant armed with a riding crop!"[27]

In the meantime, another civil war had begun in Nicaragua, a fratricidal struggle over the presidential succession and the future of the Liberal and Conservative parties, two armed gangs led by uncompromising traditional rivals, such as the Chamorro, Sacasa, Diaz, and Moncada families. As the Special Service Squadron deployed to meet the latest challenge to American diplomacy, the *Tulsa* transited the Canal back to the Atlantic side of the isthmus and took station without incident at Bluefields and Puerto Cabezas, although neither was then in any immediate danger. Neither port impressed Thomas, but he preferred Puerto Cabezas. He kept the landing party prepared to go ashore, but the orders never came.

After six weeks, the *Tulsa* returned to Balboa. Jerry was anxious to be off for the States. He had a pregnant wife he desperately wanted to be with, and he knew where he was going: Marine Barracks, Charleston, South Carolina. The assignment could not have pleased him more. His last days with the *Tulsa* brought few regrets about his detachment. He took the shore patrol into Balboa, supposedly for the last time, on the weekend of 13–15 October but had to return once more on 18 October because of a small riot. In the meantime, the Army troops had withdrawn, leaving the bars closed and the streets open. The last gasp of hooliganism did not last long, and Jerry's Marines went unmolested. Their only action was to capture S2C. C. G. Cochran, a constant problem, who dove over the side and tried to swim to shore. The Marines gleefully fished Cochran in. Jerry had had enough of such valiant engagements. Sometime during the forenoon watch on 20 October 1925, he requested permission to leave the *Tulsa*, saluted the flag at the fantail and the officer of the deck, and descended into a cutter that would take him ashore for transportation to the United States. Although he could not know on that sunny day off Panama, fifteen years would pass before Jerry would again see duty aboard a vessel of the United States Navy.[28]

[CHAPTER X]

The Long Watch
1925–1934

Gerald C. Thomas stood the long watch between demobilization from one war and rearmament for another during the decade after his return to shore duty. In a personal sense, those ten years brought Thomas satisfaction in his career and contentment with his family, which would include a son and two daughters by 1935. In 1932, fourteen years after he received his first commission, Thomas would become a captain of Marines. His next six assignments would provide variety and professional development: three tours at Marine barracks in the United States, two assignments to U.S. Army schools, and another tour in Haiti. He also began to feel that his fellow Marine officers regarded his abilities highly and viewed him as a candidate for important assignments when he became a field grade officer. Thomas was not yet within the Marine Corps' operational mainstream, however, for he did not participate in any of the three major landing exercises held during the period of 1922–26.

In 1927, the Army and Navy Joint Board, the high temple of service roles and missions and interservice relations, published a revision of its bible, *Joint Action of the Army and Navy*. This edition of *Joint Action* approved the wartime role John A. Lejeune sought, "the initial seizure and defense" of bases during a naval campaign.[1] The only such campaign that any planner in the Navy and Marine Corps could really envision was a war with Japan, but, during the ten years that followed the Washington Conference, Japanese-American diplomacy preserved a strategic environment that promised peace. The years between 1925 and 1935 did not allow the Marine Corps to develop its amphibious assault forces. In 1927, civil wars in Nicaragua and China convinced the State Department and Navy senior officials that American interests required military intervention. By the summer of 1927, virtually all the field forces of the Marine Corps had deployed to China (the 3d Marine Brigade) or Nicaragua (the 2d Marine Brigade); in Nicaragua, Marines were fighting the guerrilla forces of Augusto César Sandino.

Jerry Thomas did not serve with the crack 4th Marines in Shanghai, and he did not join Smedley B. Butler's brigade in North China as it deterred any breakdown of communications between Tientsin and Peiping. In Nicaragua, some of Jerry's contemporaries enhanced their troop-leading reputations as combat commanders by leading Marines and soldiers of the Guardia Nacional de Nicaragua against the Sandinistas. "Bush warfare" proved to be the forge of greatness for Merritt A. "Red Mike" Edson, Lewis B. "Chesty" Puller, and Wilburt S. "Big Foot" Brown. Jerry Thomas had no nickname, no tropic war stories, no new patrons, and no official praise. If opportunities for distinguished field service lay ahead, he would have to wait.[2]

For the World War I generation of Marine officers, the wait for advancement in the peacetime Corps would be a long one. An aging officer corps threatened the Marine Corps unless Congress gave the Commandant the power to prune his senior ranks. In 1927, John A. Lejeune decided to change the Corps' system of promotion and advocated some procedure like that of the Navy, which linked promotion to board selection by merit, age-in-grade requirements, and compulsory retirement for those officers who failed to advance in rank. A board headed by Brig. Gen. Ben H. Fuller gave the Commandant the bad news. In 1928, the Corps would have a World War I "hump" of 650 officers, more than half of the Corps' total officer strength. Some officers in this group might serve fifteen years as lieutenants (Thomas served fourteen) and then another fifteen years as captains before they made major. Given the current personnel laws, 150 members of the "hump" could still be on active duty in 1956 as majors before they had to retire for age. Unless the Marine Corps received some relief, its lieutenant colonels in 1942 would have thirty-three years' commissioned service and probably be too old for field service; all field grade officers in 1942 would be, on average, five years older than their 1928 counterparts. Moreover, the aging officer corps might bankrupt the Marine Corps. The Joint Pay Act of 1922 had established that officers within each grade would receive raises based on their length of service, not just promotion. Officer pay, therefore, would increase each year by an estimated $45,000; in twenty years, it would be almost $1 million more than in 1928, just to reward longevity. Officer pay problems might dominate the Corps' fiscal planning, rather than the equipment modernization and increases in enlisted strength that the Commandant wanted.[3]

After publishing the conclusions of the Fuller Board and listening to the opinions its report stimulated, Lejeune asked the board to reconvene in 1928 and write an officer personnel act that he could submit to Congress. The Fuller Board's second report actually provided more emphasis on board selection and promotion by merit. Its first plan, which recommended using age in grade as the way to identify officers for compulsory retirement, was a not too subtle assault on the former enlisted men commissioned during the World War. The new scheme was designed to create sixty more officer vacancies a year across the entire rank structure and allow an additional twelve lieutenant colonels and twenty-three new majors to be promoted each year. Officers would be selected on an annual basis by a board of general officers, who would match the estimated vacancies in each rank with the qualifications of the senior four-sevenths of officers in each grade. Each year, the board would also select one-seventh of the eligible officers not selected for promotion to be retired, but no officer would be required to retire unless he had completed thirty years' service. The board would certify that officers were fit for "field service," as well as "sea service," which implied that lack of such fitness might be grounds for nonselection. Just what criteria the selection board might apply would be determined by the Commandant.[4]

With the approval of the Navy Department and the Bureau of the Budget, Lejeune sent his officer personnel reform act to Congress in May 1928. By December, the House of Representatives had passed the act largely unscathed. In the Senate, however, the reform languished because key members of the Senate Naval Affairs Committee (a bastion of seniority) thought that such a change penalized the decorated veterans of the World War, especially the former sergeants of Neville Board fame. Also, as Lejeune admitted, some additions to the field grade rank structure, however justified by the Corps' increased responsibilities for war planning and expeditionary duty, would require immediate additional funding. The Hoover administration, already devoted to reducing military spending, would not support any measures that required more money, especially after the autumn of 1929. The officer personnel act went into legislative limbo.[5]

Stymied in reforming the Corps' promotion system, General Lejeune could, on the other hand, establish an inner elite of operational and technical experts among Marine officers by sending a chosen few to advanced schooling. The Marine Corps Schools, Quantico, served this purpose, but Lejeune (himself a graduate of the Army War College) admired the Army's school system and recognized that Marines had much to learn about land warfare from the Army. Lejeune was not the first Commandant to send Marine officers to Army schools, but he was the most ambitious in doing so. By the time of his retirement in 1928, Lejeune had established regular Marine officer quotas at the Army's Infantry School, Air Corps Tactical School, Command and General Staff College, War College, Industrial War College, Field Artillery School, Subsistence School, Signal School, Chemical Warfare School, and Motor Transport School. The Commandant intended that Marine officers study their profession, and he also intended that school completion be regarded as part of an officer's fitness for special assignments. It also might serve as a moral equivalent of promotion and the key to rapid advancement if the Corps went to war again.[6]

The newest officer at Marine Barracks, U.S. Navy Yard, Charleston, South Carolina, showed few signs from a medical standpoint that might have differentiated him from any thirty-year-old businessman. He weighed two pounds less (165) than when he enlisted, and his chest and waist measurements showed no change. His vision was perfect, and he no longer felt any residual effects of being gassed or having malaria. His hearing, however, showed some loss and continued to worsen until the loss stabilized in 1932. Lieutenant Thomas's hearing problems might have been related to the six to eight cups of coffee he drank daily and the pack of cigarettes he smoked, for his pulse and blood pressure were slightly higher than normal. His diet was conservative: one heavy meal (dinner) with an emphasis on chicken, vegetables, and fruit, but not meat and fish. He liked bread and potatoes. Thomas also liked to sleep—eight to nine hours every night, if possible. His functions were normal. He preferred walks, but he also did physical exercises in the morning and evening. The Navy doctors (no Prohibitionists they) who examined Lieutenant Thomas noted that he admitted to being a light drinker. Except that they recommended removal of his tonsils, and out they came in 1927, the doctors found Thomas fit for duty at sea or in the field.[7]

Duty at the Navy Yard presented no threat to the regularity of Jerry Thomas's life as a Marine officer, husband, and father-to-be. Arriving on station on 2 November 1925, Jerry took up his principal duties as an officer of the guard and instructor with ease: "The transition from a ships detachment to the equal 'spit and polish' of a navy yard guard was an easy one." He also became the barracks athletic, school, and morale officer. He coached the Marine basketball team. The barracks commanding officer thought that Jerry would make a better post quartermaster and post exchange officer than the captain who had those duties; in March 1926, Thomas found himself immersed in the details of accounting and inventories. He found the quartermaster experience educational, if not his life's work. The barracks had only four officers, so there was work enough for all, even though the Navy Yard itself was in a period of inactivity. The naval base offered little social life, but the Thomases would have spent most of their time with the Johnson family and Lottie's many kin and friends in any event. At the center of the family's life was its newest member: Lottie Capers Thomas, born 17 January 1926 and called Tina. From the beginning, the love of father and daughter could not have been stronger.[8]

Although Jerry fully enjoyed the pace and nature of his duties and social life, as well as the time to continue his reading of military history, he did not expect to remain in Charleston very long because he knew the Corps needed officers for foreign service in Nicaragua and China. The barracks processed officers and enlisted men assigned to the 2d Brigade in Nicaragua. As they came through Charleston bound for the field, Jerry noted, "I experienced great regret at seeing others go off for field duty and leaving me behind." In 1927, the barracks guard lost half its enlisted strength of 130 to the newly reconstituted 6th Marines bound for China. Marine Barracks, Charleston, was supposed to provide one officer with this levy, but another lieutenant received the assignment. Jerry expected the assignment—and sought it—but instead he received orders in July 1927 to report as a student-officer to the Army Quartermaster Corps' Motor Transport School at Camp Holabird, Maryland. His performance as a post quartermaster had impressed the Quartermaster General of the Marine Corps, who recommended to the Commandant that Lieutenant Thomas prepare for additional logistical assignments through formal training.[9]

The Marine Corps and the Army had both committed themselves to an extensive program of motorization by 1927, and the Quartermaster General of the Marine Corps wanted more school-trained motor transport officers, at least one for every major command. Because the Corps' annual bill for automotive spare parts now exceeded $200,000, increased officer supervision of drivers and mechanics seemed essential. The Marine Corps should provide four or five officers a year for the Camp Holabird training; the Commandant decided three would be enough for the 1927–28 class. Thomas arrived at the Motor Transport School at a propitious time. Critical of the "trade school" character of the school, which specialized in training enlisted men as mechanics, the War Department General

Staff had just directed that the course for motor transport officers contain classroom instruction in logistics and management. The class of twenty-seven officers (three Marines) had seven months of formal instruction in the intricacies of internal combustion systems, electrical systems, and metallurgy; Thomas thought he learned the equivalent of a year's worth of college physics. He also received instruction in how to plan entraining and detraining; to organize and manage motor marches; and to plan the consumption of petroleum, oil, lubricants, and spare parts. In the afternoons, the class went to the Camp Holabird motor transport shop and learned to be mechanics: "We became adept at motor repair and rebuild as well as in welding, tinsmithery and battery building." Jerry took the mechanic's training with some anxiety because he had no mechanical aptitude. Nevertheless, he plunged into both phases of the instruction and finished the course fourth in the class with an 89.5 average; the three officers who finished above him (one a Marine) had some prior experience in motor transport work.[10]

By the time the class reached its final practical exercise, a four-week field trip to the Midwest, Jerry knew he would be the next motor transport officer at the Marine Corps Recruit Depot, Parris Island. He had no illusions about the task ahead of him. His predecessor had left for Nicaragua early in 1927, and the number of deadlined vehicles awaiting repair had climbed with each month. He knew he had been especially selected to clean up the mess.[11]

Jerry prepared for the challenge. Sending Lottie and Tina home to Charleston on 21 April, he turned to preparations for moving and making the motor road march to Ohio and Michigan. In early May, the convoy set out across the Appalachians and reached Greensburg, Pennsylvania, after turning north toward Pittsburgh. Jerry commanded the convoy during a night march through a cold rain on the final leg into Greensburg. The convoy arrived in time for lunch, but Jerry fell asleep while he was eating. The rest of the trip west proved less arduous, at least in terms of terrain and weather. The class visited plants that made tires and component parts and assembled automobiles and trucks in Cleveland, Detroit, and South Bend. Although Jerry enjoyed the tours of the Chrysler, General Motors, Packard, White, and Ford plants, he ducked out of the continuous round of parties the automotive companies arranged for the officers. The grand tour ended at the Quartermaster Corps depot in Columbus, Ohio, where each officer drew a three-ton "Standard B" truck, serviced it, and then drove it all the way back to Baltimore. The road march back to Camp Holabird took six days, and the officer-drivers slept in the trucks to save time and money. The trip ended on 1 June, but the class had no rest. It had its final classes and exams to complete by graduation day, 15 June. Jerry finished the Motor Transport School satisfied that he had performed well and learned much.[12]

After a brief leave with Lottie and Tina in Charleston, Jerry Thomas arrived at Parris Island on 30 June 1928 and found the motor transport situation as bad as reported. Moreover, he learned that his household goods had not yet arrived from Camp Holabird and Charleston. He found his new quarters comfortable, clean, and freshly painted, however, and he quickly hired a servant to help Lottie. The motor pool disaster took somewhat longer to fix, but Jerry brought his vehicles up to inspection standards by November. He found an easy way to get better work and longer hours out of his sixty drivers and twenty mechanics: he kept them out of jail. Most of Jerry's enlisted men were not Marines at all, but sailor-convicts imprisoned at the Parris Island Naval Disciplinary Barracks for minor felonies and crimes against good order and military discipline. (One suspects that deserters were the majority.) Prisoners whose good behavior had earned them "trusty" status worked at various places on the base. The motor pool was a favorite employer—no sailor could resist a truck or car and the additional freedom it provided. Jerry learned that he could demand extra hours from his personnel because the alternative to the motor pool was the disciplinary barracks with its unsympathetic Marine guards. "Overtime" posed no problems at Parris Island. When a quartermaster inspector visited Parris Island, he found the improvements dramatic. He also told Jerry that he would go to Nicaragua in less than a year to tackle some more logistical problems.[13]

The prophecy of neither place nor time proved accurate. Thomas received orders to report to headquarters, 1st Marine Brigade, Port-au-Prince, Haiti, the same month he passed the motor transport inspection. His specific assignment was aide to the commanding officer, Col. Mason Gulick. How Thomas received this assignment (which he welcomed) was and is a bit of a mystery because Gulick was not his patron. The most likely explanation is that Thomas was the senior available first lieutenant who had prior experience in Haiti, probably a prerequisite. Also, he had already served more than two years in the United States and was therefore eligible for foreign service. Assignments to China and Nicaragua with either of the Marine brigades would have meant a family separation; he could bring his family for the longer tour (two years or more) to peaceful Haiti, but he decided against it. Lottie was four months' pregnant, and Jerry probably did not want to risk his second wife in Port-au-Prince. Also, the *Kittery* would be carrying gasoline and oil to the Caribbean on its December run, and dependents could not travel on transports so loaded. Jerry returned to Haiti and remained there alone until July 1929, when Lottie and Tina arrived with his first son, Gerald C. Thomas, Jr., born in Charleston on 6 May 1929. The Thomas family set up housekeeping in the comfortable foreign quarter of Port-au-Prince, where living conditions, especially with the absence of malaria, had improved since 1920.[14]

Jerry found the 1st Brigade headquarters, a fashionable former French consular building above the city near the Champs de Mars, an interesting place to work but not seething with action. The Thomas family had ample time to visit other American families, especially other Marines, on evenings and weekends. As they mounted the family car, Jerry inspected Tina's dress and cautioned her that the Thomases had an obligation to represent the highest standards of the Marine Corps and the United States. In addition to his duties as Colonel Gulick's aide, Jerry became the brigade press and mail officer as well as decoding officer, which gave him responsibility for the headquarters' classified files. Gulick ran the command like a sinecure. In Jerry's words: "He was a typical old-time officer. He had no particular ability. He just lived." The two had worked well together, but Jerry welcomed the chance to serve his next commander, Col. Richard M. Cutts. "Cutts was a very brilliant fellow, a brilliant man." A handsome, dynamic officer, Cutts had a high reputation in the Corps as a Caribbean military reformer (he had formed the Policia Nacional Dominicana) and inventor of firearms modifications. (His Cutts Compensator reduced the tendency of the Thompson .45-caliber submachine gun to climb while being fired.) In April 1929, probably attracted by the increased pay and troop duty, Thomas had applied for a transfer to the Garde d'Haiti; the Marine commander of the Garde reported that he was fully qualified, but there were no openings. Once Cutts took command, Jerry had to match his commander's high pace of work, and, in part, he unofficially performed some of the tasks of the small brigade staff (four officers) that Jerry thought "of indifferent quality." At Cutts's side, he worked and learned.[15]

Service in the 1st Brigade no longer required field operations, but Jerry saw that its standards of dress, discipline, drill, and training had improved dramatically since his first tour. The demands for troops in China and Nicaragua had reduced the brigade to about 800 officers and men, most of them stationed in Port-au-Prince. The only other detachment (150 Marines) manned a barracks at Cap-Haïtien in the north. Most of the routine work rested with the operational units, the 8th Marines and Marine Observation Squadron 9 (VO-9M). Brigade headquarters had a considerable administrative load, however, and had to investigate all complaints of American troop misconduct, most of it minor in nature and related to the off-duty misuse of alcohol and automobiles, traditional traps for young Marines. The brigade work day began at 0730 and ended for lunch at 1330. In the afternoons, Jerry read military history, exercised, and visited with his fellow officers. He probably saw the American High Commissioner, Brig. Gen. John H. Russell, only in the line of duty. One old friend, Capt. Lemuel C. Shepherd, Jr., arrived in July 1930 fresh from duty with the 3d Brigade in China. Shepherd became commander of the Garde barracks at Caserne Dartiguenave. Thomas also associated with Capt. Gilder D. Jackson, twice wounded and six times cited for courage in France, and Capt. O. P. Smith, a taciturn, cerebral Texan with no combat experience but some reputation as a tactician. His contact with them probably encouraged Thomas to think about his next assignment because both Jackson and Smith had requested assignment to the U.S. Army Infantry School, a mecca for fighting infantrymen.[16]

As for the purpose that brought the 1st Brigade to Haiti, Thomas saw little prospect that the American-driven reforms would survive in Haiti's political culture. Another bout of unrest in late 1929 ratified his pessimism. In October 1929, the president of Haiti, Louis Borno, announced that, instead of holding a popular election for a legislature in 1930, he would continue to rule through his American advisors and his captive Council of State, a haven of Borno cronies. The client-president publicly said that Haiti was not ready for democracy, which he intended to make a self-fulfilling prophesy. Members of the anti-Borno elite organized a series of protests that culminated in November with several student strikes and protest rallies. The rallies turned ugly. Rioters and looters flooded the streets of Port-au-Prince, Cap-Haïtien, Jacmel, Petit-Goâve, and Cayes. Russell and Cutts shared some concern that the Garde d'Haiti would not be adequate to restore order, and Russell declared martial law, suspended newspaper publication, placed the Garde under Cutts's command, and called for reinforcements, which he received in the form of a scratch Marine infantry battalion. On 6 December, the crisis reached dramatic proportions when a twenty-man Marine patrol in downtown Cayes, menaced by a mob of 1,500 rock-throwing peasants, opened fire on the howling crowd. The riot collapsed, with 12 to 24 Haitian dead and 23 to 51 wounded. The killings, later judged by the Navy Department as justified, broke the fever, aided no doubt by President Hoover's announcement that he would immediately review the status of the occupation. The Haitian elite quickly called off the anti-American mobs and pledged its undying cooperation with Hoover's investigative commission.[17]

The Hoover administration's policy of Caribbean disengagement kept Colonel Cutts and Jerry Thomas busy through most of 1930. In February 1930, the President's special investigating commission headed by the former governor-general of the Philippines, W. Cameron Forbes, held six weeks of hearings in Haiti, with its administrative requirements met by the Marine brigade. As the result of its findings, the commission urged the abolition of the post of high commissioner, the "Haitianization" of all executive departments, and a transition of power that would bring all of the Americans home by 1934. In the short term, however, Jerry noticed little change in Haitian-American relations, which remained strained by mutual agreement and were limited to official occasions. He thought another political operation, equally doomed, appeared more interesting.

In 1930, the commandante of the Policia Nacional Dominicana, Rafael Trujillo Molina, decided to run for president, an act that served only to ratify his domination of the Dominican Republic's political life since 1924. State Department officials did not like the implications of Trujillo's announcement because they knew his presidency was likely to become a dictatorship. Colonel Cutts, who knew Trujillo well and who had advanced his career in the Policia, received orders to meet his ambitious protégé and talk him out of his political plans. Twice Jerry accompanied Cutts to a secret meeting place in a customs house just over the Haitian border, and twice he heard Trujillo tell Cutts to mind his own business. Trujillo persuaded Cutts that only he could save the Dominican Republic from chaos, and Cutts reported to the State Department that he could see little reason to block Trujillo, even if the means were available. After Trujillo's inevitable election, Cutts assisted the Dominican government to organize relief after a hurricane and to negotiate another loan from an American bank.[18]

Whatever Jerry may have done to make Colonel Cutts's difficult problems in Haiti and the Dominican Republic more manageable, his grateful commander offered to help him with his next assignment. Jerry should have returned to the United States in December 1930, but Cutts persuaded him to extend his tour by six months, which would take Cutts through the end of his own tour in May 1931. Cutts's successor would be the popular Louis McCarty Little, and Jerry found the idea appealing. He found it even more appealing when Cutts offered to use his influence at Headquarters Marine Corps to get Jerry orders to the Army Infantry School. Cutts's influence was considerable; his brother-in-law, Brig. Gen. John Twiggs "Handsome Jack" Myers, was then serving as assistant to the Commandant and as chief arbiter of assigning Marine officers to schools. What General Myers wanted, he got—he was a Corps legend for his command of the Peking legation guard during the Boxer Rebellion. Cutts wrote Myers that Thomas wanted to go to Fort Benning. After Myers replied that Thomas had no letter requesting such duty on file, Thomas promptly produced a copy of his request. Cutts sent it to Myers with a stronger plea that Thomas receive the coveted assignment. (Thomas suspected that an enemy of his in the personnel section had destroyed the original letter.) In any event, Myers arranged that Thomas fill one of the three slots for Marine officers at the Infantry School's basic course. On 7 June 1931, the Thomas family left Haiti on the SS *Nickerie*, bound for New York City and temporary duty at Marine Barracks, Charleston, until the new class assembled at the Infantry School.[19]

The heat beneath the forest of pines and oaks did not match the pressure in the classrooms of the U.S. Army Infantry School. Under the leadership of Lt. Col. George Catlett Marshall, the school had emerged by 1931 as one of the world's premier schools for combat leaders. Even the German Reichswehr sent officers to endure ten months at Columbus, Georgia. The school offered two basic courses, one to train officers in battalion operations and the other in company operations. Colonel Marshall, assigned to Fort Benning as the school's assistant commandant in 1920, which meant control of the instructional program, had made the Infantry School an alternative mecca to the Fort Leavenworth schools. His own reputation was beyond reproach in the interwar Army. A splendid staff officer at Leavenworth and in the field before the World War and one of the most brilliant planners in the AEF, Marshall had guided the 1st Division and U.S. First Army to success. He had concluded, however, that the Army's tactical training had atrophied from a heavy dose of German and French formalism that was inappropriate for an army of wartime officers and citizen-soldiers. He wanted to train officers who could think independently and quickly under stress.[20]

By 1931, Marshall had a directing staff that represented his judgment about the Army's most promising future commanders. Among his subordinates were Lt. Col. Joseph W. Stilwell, the acerbic but brilliant head of the tactics department; Maj. Omar N. Bradley, an outwardly modest and unimpressive officer from Missouri who combined burning ambition and quiet intelligence; Capt. J. Lawton Collins, whose charisma and skill matched his self-esteem; Maj. Harold R. Bull, who knew that the best operations rested on logistical feasibility; and Maj. Forrest Harding, a military historian who could tie the students to the nation's military past and open the universe of experience through his didactic comments on generalship. The directing staff and student body from Marshall's five years at the Infantry School provided two hundred generals in World War II. Age and opportunity (particularly the confidence of wartime Army Chief of Staff George C. Marshall) had something to do with the Infantry School's success, but the school's reputation had something to do with whom the services assigned for instruction. The curriculum was tough, the peer pressure even tougher. The only officers who were probably immune to the competition were 10 foreign officers from China, Cuba, and the Philippines. The 134 American officers tackled the 1,341-hour course with varying zest, but the staff and curriculum ensured that no one could hide. Colonel Marshall wanted and got realistic training: exercises; performance testing; demonstrations; tactical problem solving; field leadership that could not assume the availability of time, information, and accurate maps for decision making; and constant observation and evaluation by the staff.

The Marine Corps had five slots for the 1931–32 classes. Headquarters selected

Captains Gilder D. Jackson and O. P. Smith for the "senior course," and Capt. Dudley S. Brown and First Lieutenants Lewis B. Puller and Gerald C. Thomas for the "junior course." Jerry Thomas, one of the oldest students in the class, attacked the course with a vengeance. He enjoyed the classroom instruction, especially the classes on military history, but he also profited from the weapons instruction (476 hours) that gave the officers a chance to learn and fire every infantry weapon in the Army's inventory. The students exchanged roles on crew-served weapons and assembled and disassembled every weapon they fired. The Infantry School did not spare the ammunition for its students; their only complaint was a bad lot of rifle ammunition that reduced most of the Springfield experts to curses on the rifle range. In preparation for the tactical exercises that dominated the second part of the school year, the students received 43 hours of equitation instruction. Jerry preferred the instruction in motor transport, a bias he shared with Stilwell but not Marshall, who was a compulsive horseman. The best thing about the Infantry School curriculum was that it required no after-hours study, the bane of Leavenworth students. Jerry discovered the excellent Infantry School library and devoted his evening hours (after time with his children) to reading about the lives of British generals and Victorian military operations. Other students spent their spare time playing golf and hunting. The evening social life also could be demanding, but, with young children, the Thomases avoided excessive socializing. The field exercises and tactics instruction (388 hours) dominated the second half of the course. The students spent much of their time in the field with troops, principally the 24th and 29th Infantry and 6th Cavalry. Jerry's field command was the machine gun troop of the 6th Cavalry commanded by Capt. Henry Hodes, whom Jerry would see again in Korea almost thirty years later.[21]

The field training at Fort Benning provided experiences that Jerry had reason, years later, to appreciate. The reservation—some 97,000 acres of sandy forest and slow streams with little change in elevation—made it difficult to call in observed artillery fire. Engagements in the thick woods began and ended swiftly with the umpires distinguishing between the quick and the dead. The 1931–32 course devoted more time to nighttime combat, also an investment from which Jerry profited. He advanced through the tactics exercises with an unbroken run of passing grades. For "Chesty" Puller, no whiz at classroom instruction and graded assignments but cursed with a mouth that worked faster than his brain, the tactical instruction proved an arena for his innovative approach to fighting and his stubborn, forceful leadership. Already a veteran of guerrilla warfare in Haiti and Nicaragua, for which he was about to receive the first of his five Navy Crosses, Puller could not avoid challenging the directing staff or arousing his fellow students, who persisted in tiresome remarks about the intelligence level of Marine officers. Jerry Thomas went about his business without arousing the interest of his classmates. He made friends with two garrison officers, both accomplished World War veterans, Majors Barnwell R. Legge and Jens Bugge. (As a young captain, Legge had been the 26th Infantry's senior surviving officer at Soissons.) Jerry completed the course with a B+ average and felt that he had done very well; Marshall, Legge, and Bugge had told him and his classmates that they thought the Class of 1932 was the best yet to complete the Infantry School's "junior course." Jerry finished the school year—his fifteenth year as a Marine—with expanded confidence about his ability to command a company and even a battalion.[22]

The five Marine officers who attended the Infantry School in 1931–32 returned to a Corps reeling from the effects of budget cuts and a thorough organizational review. The Navy Department, alerted by rumors that the War Department wanted to absorb or abolish the Marine Corps as a way to cushion its own budget cuts, completed a careful examination of the Corps' roles and missions. The Navy's General Board reported that the advanced base seizure role was indeed essential to a naval campaign. Chief of Naval Operations Admiral William V. Pratt went even further, recommending that the Corps be increased, not reduced, in personnel and modern weapons. The political reality of 1932, especially the obsession of the Hoover administration in reducing military spending as a crisis fiscal measure, produced the opposite results. At the President's urging, Congress pared the Corps' budget from $16.4 million to $15.3 million, which translated into a cut in enlisted personnel from 17,500 to 15,343. The austerity move bore more heavily on the Corps than on the Army and Navy, and Marine officers took an annual salary reduction equivalent to one month's pay so that the Commandant would not have to sever ninety-seven officers. As for organizing and training amphibious forces, the Corps could not provide the troops. Only about one-third of all its officers and men were serving somewhere within the United States. The rest were on board ships, serving as security forces at naval bases abroad, or providing expeditionary forces in Haiti, Nicaragua, and China. Even with skeleton units at Quantico and San Diego, Major General Commandant Ben H. Fuller reported that "it is impossible for the Corps to carry out its primary mission of supporting the United States Fleet by maintaining a force in readiness to operate with the fleet. . . . The Marine Corps is not prepared to perform its allotted task in the event of a national emergency."[23]

Although Jerry Thomas shared the Corps' summer of anxiety, his own sense of professional fulfillment continued to grow. In 1932, he received more tangible recognition for his individual heroism during the World War, the award of the Silver Star and Purple Heart medals. The War Department was his benefactor because the Army, faced with its own morale problems and the veterans' protests of that year, first decreed that the Order of the Purple Heart, introduced in the American Revolution for distinguished service, be reintroduced to commemorate the bicentennial of George Washington's birth. Although the decoration could be awarded for service, its principal purpose was to recognize wounds received in action. Any World War veteran who rated a wound stripe now rated a Purple Heart. The Army also provided for the conversion of silver stars for commendations-in-orders (worn on the World War Victory Medal) to a distinct medal, awarded for gallantry in action at the high risk of life. When the Navy Department ruled that both medals might be awarded to Marines of the 4th Brigade, Jerry applied for and received both, which he now added above his ribbons for his Victory Medal and Haitian Campaign Medal, all set off by the green and red *fourragère* of the unit Croix de Guerre awarded to the 6th Marines. The new bearers of the Silver Star were a select group; only thirty-seven active Marine officers not previously decorated received the medal.[24]

★★★★

After fifteen years of service in the Marine Corps, Gerald C. Thomas became a captain in 1932, thus reaching the rank that marked full professional competence in the interwar Corps. Alerted to his eligibility in May, Jerry reviewed the standard references, many of which were the same ones he had studied for the first lieutenant's examination. He had learned much of the data for the examination on naval ordnance while serving on the *Tulsa*; the tactics examination mirrored the training at Fort Benning and the official Army training regulations. A disciplined reader of key service publications, such as the *Marine Corps Manual*, the *Landing Force Manual*, and *Naval Courts and Boards*, Jerry did not anticipate trouble with his examination, and indeed he had none. His promotion physical examination on 5 July also went well, although the Bureau of Medicine and Surgery had to review whether his hearing loss disqualified him; it did not. In November 1932, when Jerry became a captain, he felt he had attained a rank for which he had been qualified since 1919.[25]

His next assignment also suggested that Thomas, regardless of rank and medals, had entered the Corps' inner elite. He was selected to be an instructor at The Basic School, where the Marine Corps taught its new second lieutenants the rudimentary skills of officership. Since John A. Lejeune's time, an assignment as an instructor in the Marine Corps Schools, of which The Basic School was a part, indicated that Headquarters viewed an officer with esteem. Instructors normally had to complete formal schooling themselves, which required special selection; the assignment of the five Marines to the Army Infantry School in 1931–32 meant that they had been already selected for duty with the Marine Corps Schools (MCS), especially The Basic School. Upon certification of graduation, all of the officers except "Chesty" Puller received orders to report to the commandant of The Basic School for duty as instructors. (Puller returned to duty with the Guardia Nacional de Nicaragua and soon won another Navy Cross as the commander of Company M, the Guardia's mobile reserve.) The Basic School was no longer at Quantico; it had moved in 1923 to the Marine Barracks, Philadelphia Navy Yard, where it had more classroom space and quarters for officers. The school, however, still received its orders from Quantico and had its curriculum shaped by the faculty of the company officers and staff officers courses. The students of The Basic School were themselves an elite, for the restricted number of vacancies in the officer corps meant that forty-two of the fifty-one Marine officers commissioned in 1932 and 1933 were new graduates of the U.S. Naval Academy. As Academy graduates who had chosen to be Marine officers, they already viewed themselves as an elite within an elite—against the chidings of their classmates—and with few exceptions they took their additional classroom and practical experience seriously. The Basic School instructors had little concern about their students' enthusiasm and concentrated on giving them the best possible instruction they could provide.[26]

Jerry Thomas learned that he had considerable talent as a teacher, and he found his assignment one of the most fulfilling he had yet had in the Marine Corps. First, however, he had to get his family settled. Filled with their own anxieties, Jerry's young students could not have known that he found his quarters in a multiple-family barracks unsatisfactory; at that time, he did not rate captain's quarters. Jerry wrote Lottie, still in Charleston with the children, that the Marine Barracks had some very attractive quarters. "We did not get that kind, however."

The household goods and his uniforms were slow arriving from Fort Benning, and he had to live with the barracks' commanding officer until his apartment had been cleaned and repaired. About the only thing Jerry liked about his family's living arrangements was that it was cheaper than living in Philadelphia.[27] When the school year began in September, however, Jerry was ready to dazzle his students as the principal instructor of the functioning and use of the .45-caliber Colt semiautomatic pistol, the Browning automatic rifle, and the Browning family of .30-caliber and .50-caliber machine guns. He used Infantry School techniques, in which Colonel Marshall demanded that the teachers not use extensive notes. Jerry's students remembered him as patient, serious, entertaining, thoroughly prepared for his courses, and equally adept at group and individual instruction. They noted his flashing smile and World War sweater. He especially enjoyed the class range training each spring at the Pennsylvania National Guard's range at Mount Gretna. In the meantime, he continued his own reading program and vowed that he would improve his writing ability.[28]

As much as he enjoyed teaching lieutenants, Captain Thomas also recognized that he was working in the least exciting part of the Marine Corps Schools. At Quantico, the faculty of the company officers and field officers courses had emerged as the doctrinal elite for amphibious warfare. During the academic year 1931–32, Brig. Gen. Randolph C. Berkeley, schools commandant, had established a four-officer board (three Marines, one Navy) to write a text for instruction in landing operations that Commandant Ben Fuller hoped would become the basic doctrinal statement of the Corps' wartime mission. The Landing Operations Text Board soon expanded its membership by including other members of the MCS faculty and student body. Under the lash of Lt. Col. E. B. Miller, as dogged and unpleasant as "Vinegar Joe" Stilwell of the Infantry School, the research on the text came to dominate the curriculum of the Quantico field and company officers schools. The work reached an even higher intensity under the direction of Brig. Gen. James C. Breckinridge and Maj. Gen. John H. Russell, the new assistant to the Commandant. Encouraged by the Navy's commitment to the advanced base force concept and the planned withdrawal of the Marine brigades from Nicaragua and China, Russell and Commandant Fuller announced in the summer of 1933 that henceforth Marine operational units assigned to the Fleet would be designated the "Fleet Marine Force" and train for base seizure. The term "expeditionary force" was no longer approved for describing Marine tactical units. Even though the landing operations text had not been completed, the officers of the Marine Corps Schools (including Jerry Thomas) recognized that it would soon be the "bible" for the core curriculum of officer instruction.[29]

Another issue dominating the interests of Marine officers from 1932 through 1934 was the renaissance of legislation that would make future promotions a matter of board selection, not seniority. Under the continued prodding of Headquarters Marine Corps, the House Naval Affairs Committee, led by Congressman Carl Vinson, reopened the clogged legislative path to officer reform. Building on its successful lobbying effort to halt any further reductions in its strength and in its missions in 1932, the Marine Corps mounted a comprehensive effort to interest Congress in its reform, and it succeeded. Jerry Thomas played a small part in the lobbying, his first real foray into service politics. His mentor was another of

Lottie's cousins by marriage and a Virginian, Col. Ralph Stover Keyser, director of the division of plans and operations at Headquarters—"one of the bravest and ablest officers the Marine Corps ever had." Commissioned in 1905, Stover Keyser was a veteran Caribbean campaigner and Headquarters staffer. As one of the 4th Brigade's most distinguished battalion commanders, he had received the Navy Cross, Army Distinguished Service Medal, two Silver Stars, and the Purple Heart. He had learned to speak Japanese and shoot weapons at national match standards. To aid Keyser, Jerry introduced him to the wife of a fellow Marine officer, the kin of an influential congressman, and personal access to the politician helped the issues of both Corps strength and officer reform. Jerry himself discussed the issues with his own congressman and met Representative Melvin Maas, a Marine reserve captain and the founder of the Marine Corps Reserve Officers Association. Thereafter, Keyser viewed Thomas as a protégé to be encouraged.[30]

As part of its general effort to improve the Navy's readiness after 1933, Congress not only approved an increase in shipbuilding that would bring the Fleet to Washington Treaty strength, but it also enlarged the officer strength of the Navy and Marine Corps. It was easier to add officers than sailors and Marines; in the 1934 personnel legislation, the Navy gained about one hundred new officer billets, the Marine Corps seventy-three. Significantly, all the new billets in the Marine Corps were in the field grades, although the Corps had to surrender some numbers of company grade billets to compensate for the change. The most important aspect of the Marine Corps Personnel Act of 1934 (P.L. 263), however, was the provision for promotion-by-selection to colonel, lieutenant colonel, and major. Nonselected field grade officers would have to retire at the completion of 21, 28, and 35 years of service. The new system, so Headquarters estimated, would provide about 10 percent more new officers in each field grade and arrest the age creep among the Corps' senior officers. In practical terms, the Marine Corps could now prune the World War I "hump" of its oldest and least accomplished officers. Some officers suggested that John H. Russell would now have his revenge on John A. Lejeune, Congress, and the Neville Board, but Jerry Thomas, a junior captain of thirty-nine when the new law passed (29 May), welcomed the change. He also noted that the law did not require officers to pass promotion examinations if they graduated from an appropriate school while serving in their current rank. His interest in amphibious warfare and an accelerated promotion to major made him think seriously about exchanging his podium for a classroom seat at the field officers course at Quantico.[31]

Convinced that two years at Philadelphia had been enough, Jerry conducted a reconnaissance at Quantico and Headquarters in the spring of 1934 to see what kind of reassignment he might arrange. His official reason for visiting Quantico was to get a copy of the newly approved *Tentative Manual for Landing Operations* for The Basic School. He met the famous E. B. Miller, whom he didn't know, and learned (as others had) that Miller, a tall, thin, nervous, and ill-tempered officer, was never easy to deal with when one wanted something from him. After his ration of abuse, Thomas left with a copy of the *Tentative Manual,* the beginning of his flowering study of amphibious operations.

Thomas had found the personnel situation in chaos at Headquarters. Because of another civil war in Cuba, the Marine Corps had dispatched an expeditionary force to float off Havana; it had stripped Quantico of faculty and student officers in order to fill the force's staff and some of its troop billets. Other officers assigned to the next Quantico classes were also at sea. The new personnel act added further uncertainty. The first selection boards would convene in June, and no one could be sure which of the eligible officers would be promoted. The promotions would then force dramatic changes in the lists of officers due for foreign and sea service or available for faculty and student billets. Where the personnel assignment officers saw confusion, Jerry saw opportunity. He visited Stover Keyser and asked his help. Keyser agreed to arrange Jerry's assignment to the field officers course provided he would complete his assignment as a weapons instructor for the incoming 1934–35 Basic School class. Jerry readily agreed, and Keyser was as good as his word.[32]

Bound for another tour at Quantico and his fourth assignment as a student officer, Jerry felt buoyant about his own prospects and the signs of revival among his fellow officers. Meritorious performance of duty, not just seniority, would now shape promotions. No longer would the old criteria apply: "All you had to do was live and not get a general court." No temperance man himself, Jerry recognized that many Marine officers would rather drink than study, and he hoped that the new system would prune the ranks of the problem drinkers. He also looked forward to matching his intellectual skills against the best officers in the Corps; he knew that he would be the junior captain in the field officers course and that his fellow students would include some of the best officers of his generation, such as Clifton B. Cates and Franklin A. Hart. By later standards, Jerry would have been an overage captain at forty, but the youngest captain in the Marine Corps in 1934 was thirty-six and the oldest sixty-three. Jerry was, in fact, younger than the average age for captains, which was forty-two. The new promotion system promised to make him a major in far shorter time than he had served in the rank of first lieutenant, and he recognized that majors provided the key personnel for the staffs that amphibious warfare required. Although the Fleet Marine Force showed all the pain of infancy—and banishing the word "expeditionary" from the Corps' official language did not prevent the Navy Department from sending an expeditionary force to Cuba—Jerry and his contemporaries had become self-consciously committed to preparing themselves for a future naval campaign, probably against Imperial Japan.

[CHAPTER XI]

Preparing for a War
1934–1938

To A CIVILIAN VISITOR to the Marine Barracks, Quantico, the post appeared as placid as the silt-clogged Potomac River that flowed past its eastern rim. Continual construction—and its resultant red dust—was a fact of life at Quantico, but the most important building project for the Marine Corps proceeded in its classrooms and exercise areas. In 1934, the seed of the Fleet Marine Force had taken root within the Marine Corps Schools and the newly reconstituted 1st Marine Brigade, whose flag had come from Haiti and its troops from Nicaragua the previous year. The Marine Corps had conducted training since 1921 for its wartime mission—the seizure and defense of advanced naval bases in a naval campaign—in two phases, neither satisfactory. First, it had conducted landing operations for its troops, but it did not have a doctrinal statement that made the planning and training coherent. It then lost its troops to Nicaragua and China, but in the interim the faculty and students at the Marine Corps Schools had written the *Tentative Manual for Landing Operations* in a rush during the winter of 1933–34. The urgency felt by the sixty-seven officers who reviewed the draft document, largely written by a small committee chaired by Maj. Charles D. Barrett, reflected the priorities of Commandant John H. Russell, who had just persuaded Secretary of the Navy Claude A. Swanson to approve Navy Department General Order 241, the charter for the Fleet Marine Force. Neither knew how ominous the signing day really was—7 December 1933. The Marine Corps had less than a decade to turn its hopes into reality.[1]

The authors of the *Tentative Manual* had no illusions that they had resolved all conceptual problems of landing operations, even those that lay within Corps control. For example, the handsome, urbane Barrett, representing Headquarters, insisted that a Marine division should be the basic organization for amphibious operations, and E. B. Miller argued that British-style brigade groups represented the optimal force. The Marine Corps Schools staff, well drilled in the Dardanelles operation of 1915–16, emphasized the importance of the ship-to-shore movement and the critical nature of naval gunfire support. No less a student of the landings at Gallipoli, Barrett thought the problems of the ship-to-shore movement were not conceptual but rested on the development of appropriate landing craft and landing force weapons and equipment. The critical issue was to ensure that the concept of operations ashore and its logistical support shaped the landing, not vice versa. The planners disagreed about developmental priorities, which were indeed numerous: specialized naval transports, landing craft, vehicles and artillery for landing operations, radio communications equipment, and engineering equipment designed to support sustained logistical operations. Headquarters had already committed the 1st Brigade to landing exercises with the Fleet when it moved to the Caribbean for its annual maneuvers in late 1934. With troops available and doctrine to guide it, the 1st Brigade staff had to turn the concepts into capability. Quantico regained a level of organized, purposeful excitement it had not experienced since the mobilization of 1917.[2]

The Marine officers at Headquarters and Quantico felt an additional urgency to put the Fleet Marine Force in the field, for they wondered whether the senior officers of the Navy understood and really supported the assumptions of the *Tentative Manual* and the Marine Corps role in War Plan ORANGE. Some signs were positive. At the Naval War College, largely at the insistence of Col. Richard M. Cutts, freshly returned from Haiti, the curriculum now included the "Advanced Base Problem," which usually focused on the seizure of a fortified island complex in the Japanese-held Mandated island groups of the central Pacific. (With prescience, the problems included the *recapture* of the Philippines and Guam.) Marines also took heart that the Navy had at least embraced the concept of the Fleet Marine Force, even to the point where some admirals now thought that the Marine Corps could be dealt with as a Navy type command, not a separate service. The problem of service roles and missions, however, loomed ahead. The Army-Navy Joint Board had undertaken a comprehensive review of *Joint Action of the Army and Navy 1927*, and, as some Marines predicted, the emerging version of the new *Joint Action of the Army and Navy* (1935) gave the Army, for the first time, the secondary mission of amphibious assaults for the seizure of naval bases. The Marine Corps wanted to ensure that the Navy did not encourage the Army to take this mission seriously. Because War Plan ORANGE was the only contingency plan the War Department regarded as a real probability, the Army's sudden interest in amphibious warfare (at least at the doctrinal level) could not have been more worrisome.[3]

The urgency that Marine officers felt about testing the *Tentative Manual* had its roots in a growing international crisis in Asia, not just interservice paranoia about roles and missions or the annual campaign to wrest more money from Congress. By 1934, the government of Japan had slipped under military domination, and the Japanese armed forces had demonstrated their ability to shape national policy by defying the European powers and the United States over the future of Manchuria, a resource-rich region claimed by both China and the Soviet Union. In 1931–32, the Japanese army had occupied all of Manchuria, which Japan then governed through a puppet Chinese regime. The status quo established by the Washington Conference treaties had broken down. Investigations, reports, and negotiations by the League of Nations and by the United States did not succeed in forcing the Japanese to disgorge Manchuria as they had the Shantung Peninsula in 1919. The "Open Door," the American concept for relations with China, had started to swing shut. If the American public and its political leadership did not see the change—or saw it and chose to do nothing—the State Department and the military departments recognized that the nation faced an international crisis in Asia that might require military action.[4]

After settling his pregnant wife and two young children in a rented home in nearby Fredericksburg, Capt. Gerald C. Thomas reported to the Marine Corps Schools at Quantico for instruction in the Field Officers Course on 27 August 1934. Thomas marveled at the activity. The base still had some of the raw, treeless look of 1917 and 1921, but its very size and the ambitious construction under way demonstrated that the Marine Corps had begun another renaissance. In addition to the 1st Brigade, which meant two battalions of the 5th Marines; a mixed battalion of artillery (the 10th Marines); and smaller units of engineers and other support troops, Quantico was the home of Aircraft One, a composite group of fighters, scout bombers, and observation aircraft, located at a modern air station on a landfill north of the mouth of Chopawomsic Creek. For Jerry Thomas, however, the focus of interest was the Marine Corps Schools, housed in cavernous Barracks H. He entered a curriculum (about one thousand hours) dominated by the *Tentative Manual* and the problems of the Fleet Marine Force.[5]

A member of a small (twenty officers) but elite class, Captain Thomas—forty, neat but not imposing, most noticeable for his brushed-back long black hair and heavy eyebrows—grew with the demands of the classwork. In the first four months, he reviewed current Marine Corps organization, the principles of land operations up to the brigade level (largely taught from Army manuals), and military history. His attention must have been slightly diverted by the approaching birth of his third child, a daughter, Virginia, born at Mary Washington Hospital, Fredericksburg, on 25 January 1935. That same month, the course took on a more challenging character. The instructors and students divided themselves into three working groups to plan actual amphibious operations against real places. Furnished with tasks and general situations provided by the Naval War College, the class first planned to seize and defend an advanced base at Dumanquillas Bay, Mindanao, the Philippine Islands, a potential objective in War Plan ORANGE. Grounded in the principles of the *Tentative Manual*, the class tackled a more demanding task, the capture of the Japanese naval and air base of Truk, an island in the eastern Carolines. Navy and Marine Corps planners had long before identified Truk as an essential objective in any campaign by the Navy across the central Pacific. For the Truk problem, Jerry's group included Maj. Clifton B. Cates, a hero of the 6th Marines in France, and Capt. Louis E. Woods, a talented aviator; Cates served as the group's division commander and Woods as the division chief of staff. As the division operations officer, Jerry had the principal responsibility for planning the landing.[6]

The Truk problem gave Jerry a thorough understanding of the problems of an amphibious assault because the island, surrounded by a coral barrier reef and cursed with restricted lagoon entrances, presented formidable planning problems.

"For hours and hours I stared at the chart with never a single gleam that illuminated the task." Then Jerry began to see how the requirements for air and naval gunfire superiority and the necessity for a rapid buildup of the landing force ashore should shape the landing. His solution was to concentrate the force against one critical island within the atoll, not conduct multiple landings. There seemed to be no good way to avoid the estimated 50 percent casualties among the assault infantry battalions. Although the faculty liked its own solution better, "I could not possibly have had a more useful experience," and Jerry thought the report the faculty sent to the Naval War College resembled his own plan more than the "school solution." Cliff Cates thought the Truk problem (as well as other exercises that involved landings on Saipan and Guam) amply demonstrated not only the soundness of the *Tentative Manual*'s concepts but the still unresolved equipment and communications problems a Marine landing force would face in the Pacific.[7]

Another important part of Jerry's study at the Field Officers Course during 1934 and 1935 was instruction in air employment, his first involvement with aviation planning. His tutors were Louis Woods and 1st Lt. Vernon E. Megee. These two future Marine air generals were drafting a text on Marine air operations to supplement the *Tentative Manual* and were leading members of the Roy S. Geiger clique among Marine aviators, who had just emerged as the dominant force in aviation policy. The leadership of Marine air had fallen open in 1931 with the accidental death of the senior Marine air officer, Col. Thomas C. Turner. Although the next most senior aviator was Maj. Ross Rowell, Geiger could claim five more years' flying experience than Rowell, and he became the head of the aviation section at Headquarters Marine Corps. Geiger and his disciples, including Woods and Megee, used their influence to develop the air doctrine portions of the *Tentative Manual*. Not a brilliant pilot like Turner, Geiger relied on his strong personality and his conviction that Marine air existed only to support the landing force, rather than to carry on air superiority and interdiction operations as a small but interchangeable part of the Navy's carrier-based aviation force. The curriculum of the Field Officers Course not only familiarized ground officers with air operations but indoctrinated them in the emerging concepts of close air support. Impressed with Megee's spirited presentations on the potential of close air support and coached by Woods, who was a member of his car pool, Thomas finished the course as a convert to the concept of integrated air-ground operations, both for amphibious assaults and extended campaigns ashore.[8]

The Quantico tour also allowed Thomas to renew his acquaintanceship with Lt. Col. A. A. Vandegrift, the personnel officer of the 1st Brigade. Although their relationship in Haiti had been distant and casual—after all, Vandegrift had been a major and Thomas a lieutenant—Vandegrift remembered Thomas from Port-au-Prince and, in the close society of Quantico, must have heard from other officers that Thomas was one of the best pupils at the Field Officers Course. The more senior officer must have also learned that Thomas admired him, for Vandegrift placed a premium on personal loyalty as well as high competence. In any event, Vandegrift, who appreciated skilled staff officers but loathed the work himself, had just received orders to become the executive officer of the Marine detachment in Peiping, China. He was virtually certain of a promotion to colonel because he knew he would replace the current commander, Col. Presley M.

Rixey. Thomas was due for foreign or sea service, and he preferred an assignment where his family would be with him. Who approached whom about going to China is uncertain, but Vandegrift later claimed to have Thomas posted to Peiping: "I gathered that he was just the type of man that I would like to have with me out there, and it turned out exactly that way." Mediocre officers seldom went to Peiping—critics said that the "China Club" ran the Corps—and Thomas was probably flattered to be selected for such career-enhancing duty. Almost certainly, his studies of military history and operations made it attractive to visit north Asia firsthand and to spend two years within the vortex of Chinese-Japanese conflict.[9]

Stepping from the train coach into surging mobs at the Chien Men (East) station in downtown Peiping, the Thomas family began two years of life in a city within a city, each with a flow of life as foreign to the other as the world outside China. First, the Thomases joined the close community of the Marine Detachment, American Embassy, consisting of twenty-five officers and about five hundred enlisted men, a military island of exemplary Marines noted especially for the splendor of their uniforms and their public discipline. The Marine Detachment lived within the American part of the foreign section of Peiping. The foreign quarter, which hugged the southeast region outside the Forbidden City, provided not just a place but a style of life the Marines found nowhere else in the world, with the possible exception of Shanghai. In 1935, only five major powers, the United States, France, Japan, Great Britain, and Italy, maintained embassies in Peiping, but the foreign quarter of the 4,500-year-old imperial capital of China still drew a human stew of official visitors, students of China, entrepreneurs, tourists, political refugees, missionaries, and European waifs of all ages and both sexes who sought some personal haven among the teeming masses of the city. One officer of the Marine Detachment captured part of the ambiance of Peiping:

> The tourists are always with us in Peking. Some of us make a living from them, setting forth, at a price, such loot of the gorgeous East as they desire to take away. Some of us are exiled here on duties looking toward the protection of them and of their representatives. And all of us regard them with interest, because we are a small colony in an alien place, and new faces mean variety in our lives. Also we get a selected lot, grading, I think rather high. A hotel here has housed, at one time, three such celebrities as Zimbalist, Will Rogers, and the greatest living paleontologist, whose name I forgot. Our Legation guard has been reviewed on successive Saturdays by the British General Officer Commanding on the Asiatic Station, by a reigning prince of the Mongols with a pedigree back to Genghis himself, and by Mr. Douglas Fairbanks. Great whales of the arts and sciences are always thick among us, running about just like ordinary people. We seldom hear why they are traveling, and we never try to learn.[10]

The compound of the Marine Detachment, wedged between the Tartar Wall and Tung-Chiao Min (Legation) Street at the western end of the American quarter, provided all of the basic services the Marines needed. The major buildings held the detachment offices and barracks, post exchange, commissary, library, post office, and hospital. The compound included the horse stables, motor pool,

electrical plant, telephone exchange, bakery, waterworks, ice plant, swimming pool, and five sets of officers quarters. Imposing Johnson Hall housed a gym, theater, ballroom, and bowling alley. Most Marine officers rented quarters in the foreign quarter, hired several servants (all with rigidly defined duties), and lived comfortably off the economy because they received an extra financial subsidy ("exchange relief") to compensate for the diminished power of the Great Depression dollar. They also could draw upon the excellent services of the Union Medical College Hospital and the American School.[11]

Governed by the Protocol of 1904, the Marine Detachment existed to provide protection for the American compound in particular and the legation quarter in general. The presumed attackers, as they had been in 1900, would be xenophobic Chinese, either mobs or organized soldiery. The central fact of the American presence in Peiping, however, was the growing Japanese civilian and military presence in China's five northern provinces and Japan's efforts to subvert the tenuous political control of General Sung Che-yuan, the Nationalist governor. Arguing that Chiang Kai-shek's government could not protect its citizens from the warlords, bandits, and Communists, the Japanese had negotiated an agreement that allowed them to deploy an army in northern China. The American embassy provided a window on the confusing world of Chinese-Japanese rivalry. Its security, like that of the other diplomatic missions, however, depended essentially on the behavior of the Japanese military, specifically Col. Mataguchi Renya, the Japanese Protocol detachment commander, and Lt. Gen. Kawabe Shozo, the North China Garrison Army commander. But who would watch the watchman, particularly when the watchman wanted to be the burglar? The answer was the United States—the Marine Detachment also provided security for a radio intercept facility within the legation grounds. The radio security station collected Japanese diplomatic and military messages for decoding and use in charting the locations and patterns of Japanese radio traffic. The "on the roof gang" of nine Marines and one Navy radioman chief maintained their intelligence operation until July 1935. Beneath the ordered routine of American life rested a collective anxiety that Peiping sat in the middle of a brewing battlefield.[12]

Less bothered by contemporary Chinese politics than by the rigors of its journey, the Thomas family enjoyed the standard Marine Detachment welcome on 17 July 1935. They met Colonel and Mrs. Rixey and Lieutenant Colonel and Mrs. Vandegrift at the head of a delegation of other officers and their wives, accompanied by the detachment band. Jerry immediately recognized Rixey's new operations officer, Maj. Graves B. "Bobby" Erskine, a fellow veteran of the 6th Marines in France and Haitian service after the war. With the exception of Vandegrift, Erskine would be the most important officer with whom Thomas would work in China, thus starting a relationship that lasted until the end of their careers. Valedictorian of his Columbia, Louisiana, high school class, Bobby Erskine completed a degree at age twenty at Louisiana State University before he enlisted in the Marine Corps in 1917. Commissioned the same year, he served in the 4th Brigade until the second of two severe wounds forced him from the battlefield. He was a relentless, brooding, brilliant officer and had completed four school tours before coming to China. Although he was three years younger than Thomas, Erskine already looked older. A tall, muscular man with a seamed face, a short temper, and high military standards, he had an abrupt manner that cowed the timid and irritated the strong.[13]

The Thomases' trip to Peiping ended on a high note, as it had begun, but some low notes occurred in mid-passage. The first leg of the journey via Hawaii by the Army transport *President Polk* could not have been more relaxing—by military standards—and included a day of touring exotic Oahu. The thirteen-day trip to Kobe, Japan, went smoothly, in terms of both the state of the sea and shipboard conditions. Although the Thomases discovered the European hotels in Kobe were fully booked, they found lodging with an English woman, the widow of a Russian admiral who had fled the Bolshevik Revolution. Even as he and his family stared in awe at the unique beauty and inscrutable social life of Japan, Jerry realized that his trip had just become very complicated. There were no unbooked accommodations on any steamers going from Kobe to Tientsin for three weeks; under orders to report before then, Jerry accepted another option, a trip to Dairen, Manchuria, and then another booking from Dairen to Tientsin. The trip to Dairen was idyllic, a smooth voyage on a new Japanese vessel through the pine-forested islands of the Great Inland Sea. Three days later, the Thomases landed in Dairen to find that their last leg to China, only one day, would be aboard a *maru* carrying fertilizer. "Food and rooms aboard were impossible and we partook sparingly of both." Fleeing the ship when it tied up at Tientsin's port city of Tang-ku, the Thomases found the boat train for Peiping the same day and arrived at the capital that evening. For the novelty of the sights, sounds, tastes, and smells, it had been a long trip (twenty-six days) for a family with two active young children and an infant.[14]

With the excitement of arrival behind him, Capt. Gerald C. Thomas, commanding officer of Company B, Marine Detachment (July 1935–February 1936) and adjutant, Marine Detachment (February 1936–May 1937) began two years of "really marvelous duty, professionally and every other way." As the commander of Company B, Thomas faced much the same duties as he had while commander of the Marine guard on the *Tulsa*. Each company lived to some degree as an island within the Marine Detachment, and the company commander, assisted by two lieutenants, had the power to shape his company as he saw fit. An officer of "wide experience," Jerry commanded with his usual strong touch; his seven sergeants and ninety-one Marines knew who ruled Company B. Jerry was dissatisfied with his first sergeant and replaced him with a promising private first class. The company, however, qualified only 73 percent of its Marines with the rifle and pistol, below the detachment average of 80 percent, which irritated its captain.[15]

Thomas ensured that Company B prepared for its special duties within the defense plan for the two-square-mile legation area. Like the other two Marine companies, the "cannoneers" of Company B could serve as infantry or man crew-served weapons. Thomas's company trained on four Navy 3-inch landing guns, dubbed "Miss Lizzie Slats," "Kitty," "Hangfire Hannah," and "Thousand Yard Shorty." All four guns belonged in a museum, but their crews defended their virtues to the Marines of Company A, the Browning heavy .30-caliber machine gun detachment, and Company C, which manned six 81-mm mortars and six 37-mm antitank guns. The dual combat functions made training an intricate process because the detachment had to maintain sufficient force for its guard and ceremonial duties. The training season of 1935 began for Company B on the international rifle range outside Peiping and ended with artillery practice in November at the French Arsenal range near Tientsin. During the same period, Company B guarded the legation area and mounted parades in dress blues three times a week when the other companies trained at the U.S. Army range near Chinwangtao on the coast. With the end of summer and the rice harvest, the Marines could conduct field problems in the countryside. When a flu epidemic struck Peiping in the autumn of 1934, Colonel Rixey had canceled training. Under pressure from Vandegrift and Erskine, Rixey did not cancel field training in 1935–36. This pleased Thomas, although he himself had a bad bout with the flu that winter, probably exacerbated by the intestinal ravages of poison gas and malaria.[16]

When the Marines were in Peiping, the garrison routine provided ample time for athletics after the completion of military training in the early afternoon. Only the guard company was excused from individual or group athletics, which included baseball, basketball, bowling, ice hockey (on a frozen rink on the parade ground), track and field, shooting, swimming, tennis, polo, and boxing. Company competitions and military field days abounded and culminated each year with matches against the other international military detachments as well as the teams of the U.S. 15th Infantry, the Tientsin garrison. Rixey loved athletics and provided training tables and extra time for his teams. All Marines, however, did their scheduled training, and the athletes received no special liberty privileges. Under the whip of 1st Lt. David M. Shoup, a dour Indianan, Company B won the 1935–36 boxing tourney, small-bore rifle match, pistol match, baseball tourney, and swimming and diving meet. Shoup applied the same determination to his duties that he showed by working his way off a farm, through DePauw University, and into the Marine Corps in search of financial security and personal challenges. He impressed his company commander, who may not have known that Shoup's real passions were high-stakes poker and emulating Bobby Erskine. Jerry participated in the company's athletics. After becoming adjutant, however, he invested in a Mongolian polo pony named Black Peter and rode for exercise almost every afternoon in order to arrest the fleshiness that accompanied Peiping's social life. He had ridden as a boy, but his real introduction to the neuroticism of horses came in the equitation classes and staff rides of the Infantry School. Not skilled enough to make the Marine polo team, he nevertheless improved his riding skills and enjoyed watching competitive polo, which was Vandegrift's passion.[17]

Lottie and Jerry Thomas thoroughly enjoyed the foreign community's social life, and they attended the luncheons, parties, teas, dinners, and dances that seemed to occur every day. They danced late at night at the Grand Hotel, visited the Peking Club, and attended the spring and autumn horse races. They became protégés of Mrs. Lucy Calhoun, a social lioness of the European community. The Thomases lived comfortably with their three children and eleven servants in a home next to the pool and outdoor restaurant of the Peking Club and later moved to an even larger German-owned house at 5 Rue Gaubil in the French quarter. They had enough money to spend that they often visited the Fetté Rug Company on Tung Tan Street to buy Chinese rugs and the Old Friend Shop on Brass Street to purchase antiques, objets d'art, and brassware. The Thomas family visited the Forbidden City and other local sights and found plenty of time to see the Great Wall, the Ming Tombs, and the European vacation community in the Western Hills. Only in the autumn of 1936 did the social whirl slow, for Lottie was pregnant with her fourth child, William H. Johnson Thomas, born 17 March 1937. Lottie endured a high fever and difficult birth, but the Thomases remembered the Peiping tour as one of their family's high points.

The real benefit of the American diplomatic community's social life was Jerry's chance to listen to the political gossip and speculation of the "Old China hands." The American ambassador, Nelson T. Johnson, a Buddha-like career diplomat who followed the Taoist injunction *wu wei* (do nothing), did not capture his interest, but Jerry associated with a group of younger officials who saw the new China as well as the old: John Stewart Service, John Paton Davies, and O. E. Clubb. He also saw his old tactics instructor from Benning, Col. Joseph W. Stilwell, the military attaché, and a brilliant (and younger) Marine captain named Samuel Blair Griffith II (U.S. Naval Academy, 1925), who was attached to the embassy as a Chinese language student. Thomas and his friends speculated endlessly about the course of Japanese military politics, including the confrontation between the Japanese Army's two dominant factions, *kodoha* (Imperial Way) and *toseiha* (Control), which flared into a mutiny and purge of the Japanese officer corps in 1936. They also followed the mysterious comings and goings of Col. Doihara Kenji, "the Lawrence of Manchuria" and intelligence officer of the Kwantung Army, who was supposed to be the guiding force behind the Japanese Army's plans for the subversion of north China. If Thomas did not quite qualify as an "expert" on Japan and China, his two years in Peiping made him sensitive to the ways of the Japanese and Chinese military, knowledge he would later apply in two wars.[18]

As Colonel Vandegrift's adjutant in 1936–37, Captain Thomas demonstrated his skill in handling complex and diverse tasks. His additional duties depended on the availability of other company grade officers, but at one time or another he held the duties of post fire control officer, mail officer, morale/athletic and amusement officer, mess officer, officer-in-charge of the mounted detachment ("Horse Marines"), editor of the post newspaper, provost marshal, officer-in-charge of the post Chinese school, court-martial member, assistant intelligence officer, and assistant operations and training officer. He also performed yeoman service as Vandegrift's alter ego and agent in the commanding officer's relationship with Lieutenant Colonel Erskine, whose unrelenting devotion to military matters made him almost a martinet. With Vandegrift's consent and Jerry's assistance, Erskine drove the Chinese servants from the enlisted barracks, an unpopular act. In another episode, Erskine almost brought charges against an officer he found reading the *Saturday Evening Post* instead of a field manual during a tour as officer of the day. Jerry played a crucial role in muting any confrontation, which Vandegrift abhorred, between Erskine and the strong-willed company commanders, Captains Joseph C. Burger, John A. Bemis (Jerry's friend since their tour at the Motor Transport School), and Robert B. Luckey. For all-round education, Jerry believed he had drawn more benefit from his China experience than he had from any of his earlier tours.[19]

Happily, Colonel Vandegrift and Lieutenant Colonel Erskine shared Jerry's own assessment of his performance of duty, and both volunteered to boost his career. The officer selection board at Headquarters also agreed and placed Jerry on the list of qualified majors-select in 1937. As Jerry anticipated, the new system had indeed worked to his benefit, for he would spend only five years as a captain, even though the Marine officer corps had not appreciably expanded. Erskine urged him to apply for more formal schooling at the U.S. Army Command and General Staff School, Fort Leavenworth, Kansas. Erskine, himself a graduate of the school, told Jerry that after a year at Leavenworth he would never face an operational problem he could not solve. Convinced of Erskine's assessment, Jerry asked Vandegrift if he could arrange such an assignment. Delighted to reward one of his most trusted subordinates, Vandegrift reported to Col. John Marston, the responsible personnel officer at Headquarters (and Vandegrift's own successor at Peiping), that Major-select Thomas should go to Leavenworth. Before the Thomases left China in May 1937, Jerry had orders to report for the next class at the Command and General Staff School.[20]

For the Marine Corps, 1937 was the best of times and the worst of times. At Headquarters Marine Corps, where accomplishments in the field are translated into political influence and appropriations, a new Commandant, Thomas Holcomb, had succeeded John H. Russell on 1 December 1936. Holcomb brought with him to Washington a deserved reputation as a combat leader in France, staff officer, marksman extraordinary, field commander, and champion of progressive officer selection and education. Holcomb, like Russell, enjoyed a warm, personal relationship with President Franklin D. Roosevelt that dated to the Wilson administration. He gave his old friend's son, James F. Roosevelt, a commission in the Marine Corps Reserve and arranged for Jimmy, a large, handsome, and exuberant young man of twenty-nine, to "drill" as his father's aide. The political situation on "The Hill" looked no less promising. General Holcomb, however, found that Congress had reservations about funding the Fleet Marine Force, whose mission of base seizure frightened the isolationists. At the same time, Congress had given the Navy sufficient funds to enlarge and modernize the Fleet and shore establishment. The Navy, in turn, demanded that its eight new cruisers and new radio installations, air stations, ammunition depots, and naval stations all receive a Marine security detachment. Holcomb estimated that the two small brigades of the Fleet Marine Force could certainly not be manned much above four thousand officers and men, even though both Navy and Marine Corps planners thought the peacetime strength of the force should be nine thousand. Holcomb's request to enlarge the Marine Corps from about eighteen to twenty-one thousand had special urgency—in July 1937, Japan and China went to war.[21]

If Congress proved reluctant to expand the Fleet Marine Force, it did enlarge the Marine officer corps by fifty-one positions and supported promotion by selection. Congress cushioned the blow for those officers who would soon retire by choice or by law; it provided a one-grade advancement for any officer who had been cited for heroism or wounded in the World War. After two years of promotion-by-selection, Headquarters determined that seventy-five of the officers nonselected twice could still serve in their current grades because they had not yet violated the age-in-grade and years-of-service limits now attached to each rank. Nineteen officers, however, would have to retire. The plan to force a minimum annual vacancy rate of 10 percent was working. The most pressing problem involved the Naval Examining Board and the Marine Corps Schools, who were at war with one another over the content of Marine officer examinations, still required for promotion through the rank of lieutenant colonel for all but formal school graduates.[22]

Pleased by the leisurely return voyage from China, again through Japan and Hawaii with time out for sight-seeing, Thomas arrived on 8 June 1937 at the Marine headquarters in San Francisco and found his orders to the Command and

General Staff School. The next day, he, Lottie, and the four children crossed the continent by train to Charleston. Jerry left his family there while he went to Fort Leavenworth to arrange their quarters. Although quarters at Leavenworth were in short supply, his new rank and early arrival helped. He also discovered that an old friend from Camp Holabird, Maj. Lawrence Slade, Quartermaster Corps, USA, was the transportation officer for the post. Slade promised him that he would clear the Thomas household goods through customs at Kansas City and have the quarters ready for occupancy when the entire family returned with Jerry in September. During his trip west, Jerry picked up a new car from his brother Shelton in Illinois and visited his mother in Marshall. An invalid for several years and dependent on Jerry's sister Mary for care, Virginia Thomas had failed since 1935. Jerry returned east to Charleston. He and his family enjoyed a North Carolina mountain vacation and then drove to Kansas to find their spacious apartment ready.[23]

First established in 1827 as a frontier post on a bluff above the Missouri upriver from Kansas City, Fort Leavenworth had assumed its principal identity as the home of the U.S. Army Command and General Staff School late in the nineteenth century. The school occupied a converted brick arsenal marked by a large bell tower, Grant Hall, to which the Army had added additional classroom wings named Sherman and Sheridan halls. After the exemplary performance of its graduates in the American Expeditionary Forces, the school became a requirement for any Army officer who wanted to become a general. The Army picked the officer-students by board review, so sheer selection had a halo effect; to finish the course in the top 20 percent of the class virtually insured a series of important, challenging assignments with the Army's senior commands and the War Department General Staff. Developed upon German Kriegsakademie practices, including weekly graded requirements, the Command and General Staff School had a deserved reputation for rigor. Nervous breakdowns and suicides were not unknown among its students; others wondered if they had something in common with the prisoners at the federal penitentiary north of the post. Although the Marine Corps did not regard stellar performance at a formal school as the sine qua non for advancement, the Commandant had no intention to use his annual quota of three officers unwisely. Marine Corps graduates of Leavenworth had already proved their value at the Naval War College, at Headquarters, with the Fleet Marine Force staffs, and at the Marine Corps Schools. Marine officers were expected to do well at the school and show their Army peers that Marines knew about land warfare.[24]

With proven instructional techniques and doctrinal publications (which they themselves often developed), faculty members of the Command and General Staff School wasted little of their 1,125 instructional hours on anything but the study of division- and corps-level operations (786 hours), and they put their students under acute pressure that did not end until graduation. The faculty of seventy had been handpicked by the General Staff; sixteen of the 1937-38 faculty became general officers. The class of 1937-38 numbered 226 Army officers, 3 foreign officers (Chinese and Filipino), and 2 Marines. The other Marine was Capt. Homer L. Litzenberg, a blond, dogged, and humorless officer who eventually retired as a highly decorated lieutenant general. The students were divided into two groups and twelve conference sections by alphabetical order (Thomas was part of Section XI) in order to increase faculty supervision and evaluation. Most of the instruction involved planning exercises, war games, map problems, command post exercises, and terrain rides. The problems stressed the analysis of operational situations, combined arms planning, logistical planning, the decision-making process, and staff procedures, including formalized order writing. Although the school offered lectures on a wide range of military subjects and case studies from world military history, the class concentrated on shaping operations to the forces of the 1930s, including tactical aviation and mechanized units. Colored crayons and pencils were essential equipment—as well as scissors and paste. The students' "bible" was the 1923 edition of *Field Service Regulations*, supplemented by the forthcoming 1939 revision whose principles dictated the "school solution." The schedule demanded eight hours of class work a day, five days a week, and each week ended with an examination that determined each student's class standing. Even the evenings at Leavenworth had a monastic tinge. Each student apartment building had a study hall. Children were supposed to be quiet and safely housed, and no radios could be played after 1900. As Thomas recalled, "Leavenworth was a grind, a very, very useful one but a grind nevertheless."[25]

Working his way through all the problems and exchanging roles with the other nineteen officers of his conference group, Jerry Thomas studied hard but, as he himself admitted, without quite the same desperation as his Army classmates. Nevertheless, he finished the course "with genuine confidence in my ability," as Erskine had predicted. His major release from study was horseback riding, both for exercise and for the staff rides. Early in the course, he drew a fractious bay mare named Louise, a large, nervous animal dropped from the post's string of jumpers and hunters. Jerry suspected that someone gave him Louise as a challenge—or embarrassment—fit for a Marine major. He tackled Louise with the same determination he attacked his operational problems. Although he had no desire to make equitation his life's work, he appreciated that the mare gave him some rides so wild "that I was all cleared up" after also coping with "some of those wooly sessions in school."[26]

On weekends that he might have spent with his children or his studies, Jerry, as always devoted to his parents and kin, drove more than one hundred miles to Marshall, Missouri, to visit his ailing mother. After another stroke, Virginia Young Thomas, "a woman of high ideals sacrificing much for the best interests of her children," died in her home on South Brunswick Street on 19 January 1938. Jerry and his family joined his sister Mary and his brothers Shelton and Louis, an Episcopalian minister, for the funeral at the Methodist Episcopal Church, South, on 22 January. From a church filled with friends, relatives, and flowers, Virginia Thomas made her last trip to Park Ridge Cemetery where she was buried beneath the bare oaks next to James Robert and Margaret Marshall, her de facto parents, and thirty yards from Mary Ruth Durrett Thomas.[27]

On the surface, Major Thomas did not emerge as one of the distinguished graduates of his class. At graduation on 19 June 1938, he ranked 81st among the 228 American officers. (Litzenberg finished 37th.) Thomas received the evaluation of "very satisfactory," and the academic board certified him for additional schooling, proficiency in "theoretical training" for high command staff duties, and suitable for assignment as an instructor at service schools. The rating "very satisfactory" meant that Thomas's accumulated score had placed him in the 80- to 90-point range along with 70 percent of his classmates. He also had learned a great deal that could not be quantified. As during his tour at the Infantry School, he learned more about how the Army operated. Also, as during his tour at the Field Officers Course at Quantico, he became increasingly familiar with air operations, taught at Leavenworth by an air subsection led by Col. Lewis H. Brereton, an expert on tactical aviation. The logistical instruction at Leavenworth was also more demanding than at Quantico. In addition, Thomas learned that the Army really did intend to participate in amphibious operations; in fact, the school included eight days of instruction (including a problem) on amphibious operations and additional days on the defense of the Philippines, Hawaii, and the Canal Zone against attacks from the sea. Thomas also made lasting acquaintanceships with a number of Army officers, many of whom he would meet again in the Pacific and Korea during campaigns no longer theoretical. When he later assessed his success in analyzing operational problems and appreciating the complexity of joint operations, Thomas credited his year at Leavenworth as his most important single experience before 1941.[28]

[CHAPTER XII]

Inside the Marine Corps Elite
1938–1941

GERALD C. THOMAS, APPROACHING forty-two, returned again to Quantico in the summer of 1938 to join the faculty of the Marine Corps Schools. He and his family lived first in a Quarters 2 apartment, then in spacious Quarters 12. To his family and friends in the Marine Corps—and there were many—Jerry held no surprises and confounded no one with moods and methods that defied understanding. He had not changed dramatically in appearance since he joined the Marine Corps more than twenty years before. His dark hair and heavy eyebrows framed clear eyes and a strong face, as yet only slightly lined. Long-waisted and heavy through the waist and upper legs, Major Thomas counterattacked his tendency to put on weight with careful eating; his carriage was erect and he wore well-tailored uniforms. Except for walking, he had no exercise program, and he did not play games with his children. Outside of his military career, his passion was his family, generously defined to include a host of distant relatives scattered about Virginia. Although Jerry maintained his personal contacts with old friends in Bloomington, Illinois, and Marshall, Missouri, he thought of himself as a Virginian, in part because of his ancestry and in part because of his multiple tours at Quantico. His father had gone through the same metamorphosis. Vander Thomas had left his wife Virginia as the undisputed ruler of the Robert Marshall home in 1927 and moved from Missouri to Louisa County, Virginia. His contracting business destroyed by the Great Depression, Vander Thomas, the perpetual optimist, slumped into despondency and gave up regular work in 1931. Concerned by his father's depression, Jerry helped him settle in a small home in Gordonsville and stayed in close touch with him. About once a month while stationed at Quantico, he drove with all or part of the Thomas family to visit his father and then make the rounds of the homes of his father's many cousins. At the same time, Thomas helped support his mother until her death. He had also sent money to educate his brother Louis and sister Mary until both finished college in the late 1920s.[1]

Articulate and a born raconteur who could also listen to others' good stories, Jerry enjoyed the company of his fellow officers and their wives but only as an occasional release from work. Lottie ran the Thomas household, but Jerry watched the children's spending habits and academic performance with a knowing eye. As he had in China, he took young Jerry with him on trips when fathership did not interfere with officership. During 1938 and 1939, these trips were principally Civil War battlefield tours around northern Virginia, for Major Thomas had become the resident military historian for the Marine Corps Schools.

Although the dramatic creation of the *Tentative Manual for Landing Operations* had given way to a normal instructional program at the Marine Corps Schools, Thomas entered an emerging elite of amphibious planners and dominant Marine Corps officers when he became an instructor. Many were also old friends, or at least acquaintances. The directors of the Schools for the next two years were Brigadier Generals James T. Buttrick and Philip H. Torrey, neither of whom gave special attention to the Junior and Senior courses. The assistant directors, Lt. Col. Alfred H. Noble and Col. A. F. Howard, and the department heads ran the program of instruction. The department heads (lieutenant colonels or senior majors) in 1938 and 1939 were Graves B. Erskine; Lemuel C. Shepherd, Jr.; Louis R. Jones; W. Arthur Worton; James E. Betts; and O. P. Smith. Among the instructors were William P. T. Hill, Dudley S. Brown, Robert C. Kilmartin, Lester Dessez, John A. Bemis, Vernon E. Megee, Thomas A. Wornham, Merrill B. Twining, John C. McQueen, Robert O. Bare, Robert E. Hogaboom, and David M. Shoup. If stars were about to fall on the West Point Class of 1915, the same heavens would be equally kind to the Marine Corps Schools faculty. The faculty presented a curriculum that provided common instruction (usually lectures, demonstrations, and staff rides) for both the Senior and Junior courses but divided the two groups for the operational exercises and staff planning conferences. Thus, Thomas had contact with both groups. The Senior Course of 1938 (fifteen Marine and seven Navy officers) included William N. McKelvey, William E. Maxwell, and Harold E. Rosecrans; the Junior Course included Victor H. Krulak; Wallace M. Greene, Jr.; Frederick L. Wieseman; Samuel R. Shaw; Robert H. Williams; and Joseph C. Burger. The Senior Course (twenty-one Marine and seven Navy officers) and Junior Course (thirty-five Marine officers) of 1939 brought more old friends to Quantico, among them Bill Whaling, Ray A. "Torchy" Robinson, and Sam Griffith. The next gathering of many of these Marine officers would be under fire in the Solomon Islands.[2]

Thomas had no choice in his particular assignment. Bobby Erskine, chief of the F-1 section, recruited him for the newly vacated billet as Schools military historian. Thomas found the fifty-five hour bloc of instruction, bequeathed to him by Maj. David Nimmer who had departed for the Naval War College, in good shape. Thomas accepted from Nimmer (who had written it) one presentation on Germany's 1918 amphibious operations in the Baltic without change. The centerpiece of the historical instruction remained the analysis of the Gallipoli campaign, which first entered the instructional program in 1923. Inheriting a five-hour presentation designed by Capt. Arthur T. Mason and printed in abbreviated form in the *Marine Corps Gazette* in 1936, Thomas decided to expand it to seven hours. This allowed him to pay more attention to the battles ashore, especially the operations of the Australian-New Zealand corps. He returned to the basic sources: John Masefield, *Gallipoli* (1916); Gen. Sir Ian Hamilton's diary; and the British official history, Maj. Gen. Sir C. E. Callwell, *The Dardanelles* (1919). For the "Anzac Beach" story he read C. E. W. Bean, *The Story of Anzac* (two volumes, 1921, 1924), the Australian official history just released in an American edition. The presentation on Gallipoli by Jerry Thomas, rich with operational insights, anecdotes, and splendid visual aids, became a high point of the 1938 and 1939 courses. Working at his side, Dave Shoup spotted unit pins and handled slides and transparencies.[3]

With Erskine's approval, Thomas deemphasized a series of canned presentations on limited American amphibious operations of the nineteenth century and used the rest of his military history hours to study generalship in the Civil War. Influenced by his experiences at the Infantry School and the Command and General Staff School, he assembled a series of lectures on the first and second battles of Manassas, the battle of Fredericksburg, and the battle of Chancellorsville. Although Thomas already knew the battlefields well, he returned to all of the locations to test his knowledge against Douglas Southall Freeman, *R. E. Lee* (four volumes, 1934), which he had just read. He then organized two full days of touring the battlefields and conducted the classes in the best Leavenworth staff ride tradition. As Thomas had learned from his first postwar tour at Quantico, these battles had an endless fascination, from both professional and personal viewpoints, because he enjoyed identifying the places where his own ancestors had fought and fallen. The students remembered and appreciated his enthusiasm for his subject even if they wondered about the relevance of the case studies.

For all their lessons about the friction of command, Civil War battles did not replace amphibious operations as the focus of instruction at the Marine Corps Schools, and Major Thomas wasted no time in joining the analysis of the Corps' current war plans. Always quick as well as thorough, he found that his own teaching left time for other projects. Erskine asked his help in updating a study of the island of Trinidad, a key position for the control of the entrance to the Caribbean. Thomas seized the opportunity and produced a study that the demanding Erskine found acceptable. He rewarded Thomas with another major project, a current, detailed military analysis of the problems of attacking and defending the island of Guam. Thomas entered the vortex of naval planning, the continued analysis of War Plan ORANGE or, more properly, Marine Corps Contributory Plan C-2, ORANGE, MCWP-2, October 1932 (Top Secret). What he really inherited was an encyclopedic, four-volume study of Guam—complete with photographs, topographical maps, and beach studies—produced by Maj. William P. T. Hill. On a secret mission ordered by the intelligence staffs of the Navy and Marine Corps, Pete Hill had collected data on Saipan, Tinian, and Guam in 1935. The Japanese authorities on Saipan and Tinian did not welcome such a reconnaissance, and Hill had examined these islands through the periscope of a submarine. Guam was under American control and presented no problem of access, so Hill had turned his engineering skills and thirst for data into a bravura performance of terrain and hydrographic description. The Hill study, however, had not yet been reduced to an operational estimate of the situation.[4]

The study of Guam, as Jerry Thomas realized, was not just an academic exercise. Alarmed by Japanese expansionism in China, Congress finally broke from the constraints of the Washington treaties by passing the Naval Expansion Act of 1938 on 17 May, an act that provided a $1.1 billion, ten-year fleet expansion plan that would take the U.S. Navy 20 percent over the tonnage limitations of 1922. Congress balked, however, at appropriating money for base development outside the continental United States, a position encouraged by the State Department and the aviation enthusiasts of the War Department. Chief of Naval Operations Adm. William D. Leahy wrested a concession from Congress—its willingness to study the basing problem before the end of the year. Leahy turned the project over to Rear Adm. Arthur J. Hepburn, who already had a study of air base development on Wake Island, Midway, and Guam to begin his board's investigation. At the same time, the War Department General Staff also began its own analysis of Guam's defensibility.

The Marine Corps Schools suddenly became a popular place for Army and Navy planners to visit. A General Staff delegation, which included one of Jerry's Fort Benning instructors, asked Erskine for a copy of the Guam study. Thomas briefed the Army officers, who admitted massive ignorance of the island and the basics of base seizure and defense, and then gave them a copy of his analysis. On 1 December 1938, the Hepburn Board submitted its report to Secretary of the Navy Charles Edison, who transmitted it to the House Naval Affairs Committee and its pro-Navy chairman, Congressman Carl Vinson. The Navy recommended a $287 million program, 80 percent of it for air base construction. Guam, identified as the centerpiece of America's Pacific defenses, could be defended with a reinforced garrison, extemporized shore defenses, and an adequate airfield and submarine base. One Navy witness predicted that Guam, if adequately defended, could not be taken by 60,000 Japanese. Also called to testify, Jerry Thomas agreed with this assessment, largely because he—like Hill—thought the coral barrier reef around the island made it impervious to an amphibious assault.

Basing its judgment on reasons that had little to do with operational questions, Congress in April 1939 rejected any plan to strengthen Guam. Thomas's analysis, however, had not been in vain. Although he had faithfully supported the Navy Department's position that a modest investment would make Guam impregnable, he actually concluded that Guam *could* be seized or recaptured—but only if the Navy and Marine Corps developed an amphibian vehicle that could scale the coral reef with embarked assault troops. Thomas's Guam study became further justification for one of the Corps' high-priority development projects, the conversion of Donald Roebling's tracked swamp vehicle, the "Alligator," into a combat troop and supply carrier. Thomas could not claim a share of the paternity for the "landing vehicle tracked" (LVT), but he learned another important lesson about the requirements of the amphibious assault and understood the justification for developing the LVT.[5]

As a Marine Corps Schools faculty member, Thomas shared the further refinement of amphibious doctrine. The *Tentative Manual for Landing Operations* had become Fleet Training Publication, *Landing Operations Doctrine United States Navy 1938* (FTP 167), which made it the official guidance for landing exercises. It also had a companion piece, Marine Corps Schools, *Tentative Manual for Defense of Advanced Bases*, MCS-3 (June 1936). Much of the doctrine now contained principles well understood by Marine planners: the need for air and naval gunfire superiority, the requirement for the quick seizure of key objectives and the buildup ashore of a landing force capable of defending the beachhead, and the likelihood that the landing force would either succeed or perish ashore. Among the operational principles of the doctrine, there remained one ominous assumption: the concept of operations *must* allow the fleet to leave the amphibious objective area as quickly as possible in order to prepare for a sea battle. If the enemy contested the landing with its own naval forces, the major threat would be a counterlanding directly upon the beachhead. In fact, ". . . no base should be established that is going to necessitate the detachment of portions of the fleet for its defense." The landing force, including its aviation elements, must be adequate to hold the base in the fleet's absence. The doctrine conceded that this task might be extremely difficult if the landing force held a position that required the movement of reinforcing units and supplies along a long line of communications. The only consolation for the landing force was that the enemy could be equally or more greatly discomfited by a vulnerable supply line. As Jerry Thomas was to learn—and may have already learned from his own studies—the landing itself might be difficult, but the long campaign that could follow would be the ultimate test of the Fleet Marine Force.[6]

If omens appeared in the doctrinal publications on amphibious warfare, they did not trouble the measured life of the Marines at Quantico. The highlight of the spring seasons of 1938 and 1939, the 1st Brigade's annual field day for a delegation of congressmen and their attendants, came and went as scheduled. The brigade staged a mock war in the morning, provided a sumptuous picnic luncheon, and concluded the day with a softball tournament and a parade, complete with the base band. Work continued at the Marine Corps Schools, but so did play, most notably organized athletics and social events at the officers club. The faculty of the Marine Corps Schools stayed busy under the direction of Shepherd and Erskine. Its performance was still not much affected by promotion prospects, for the World War "hump," if somewhat reduced, had now bumped into the limited number of authorized colonels and lieutenant colonels. The Marine Corps rated 181 majors, but only 50 colonels and 100 lieutenant colonels. Jerry Thomas stood 135 in seniority on the majors list after eighteen months in grade. Headquarters Marine Corps estimated that majors would spend at least five or six years in grade before becoming eligible for promotion to lieutenant colonel, which meant that Thomas would not be promoted again (if selected) until 1943. Even a slight expansion of the officer ranks in 1940 did not help those near the bottom of the hump. The officers placed in greatest seniority by the Neville Board (commissioned in early 1917), including LeRoy Hunt and Clifton B. Cates, now began to reach the rank of colonel. Behind them came the next group of 4th Brigade veterans: Lemuel C. Shepherd, Robert Blake, Alfred H. Noble, and Bobby Erskine. Thomas moved only to the upper quarter of the major's list, still probably at least a year away from selection. If he felt any resentment at watching officers his age or younger pin on eagles or silver oak leaves, he did not let it dampen his enthusiasm for his work.[7]

★ ★ ★ ★

The outbreak of war in Europe in September 1939 increased the level of anxiety and interest at the Marine Corps Schools, but it did not have as much impact as preparation for Fleet Landing Exercise 6, a 1st Brigade exercise planned for Culebra, Puerto Rico. Such exercises were now routine for the Fleet Marine Force, and the 1st Brigade had made the same deployment from January through March of that same year. Headquarters Marine Corps, however, wanted as many officers as possible to experience an amphibious operation and to see all of the obvious defects in amphibious force and landing force size and equipment. Fleet Landing Exercise (FLEX) 6 produced no lessons Marine planners had not seen in FLEX 5—or FLEX 4, for that matter. Headquarters planned, however, to have solid tactical training during the landing and operations ashore, so it continued the two-year-old practice of assigning an extensive umpiring team to the 1st Brigade. As soon as the Chief of Naval Operations proclaimed FLEX 6 a "go" on 28 November 1939, Headquarters formed an umpiring team headed by Col. William H. Rupertus. Eleven officers under Col. Pedro del Valle went to the 5th Marines and four more to the 10th Marines. Jerry Thomas became a part of del Valle's team, an assignment he relished since it would take him on his first amphibious operation.[8]

Assembled off Hampton Roads in early January 1940, the amphibious force bore slight resemblance to future armadas of World War II. For transports and naval gunfire support ships, the Navy assigned four old battleships:

Battleship	Embarked Marines
Wyoming (BB 32)	38 officers, 649 men
New York (BB 34)	35 officers, 375 men
Arkansas (BB 33)	31 officers, 375 men
Texas (BB 35)	21 officers, 294 men

The *Manley*, a converted four-stack destroyer of World War I vintage, served as the transport for three officers and forty Marines. It was supposed to test the utility of the fast destroyer-transport, a new class for special operations, which meant raids and reconnaissance missions. The *Capella* (AK 13), one of the Navy's five general cargo ships, carried seventy-five of the brigade's seventy-eight vehicles and all of its thirty-five trailers. Thomas embarked on the *Arkansas*, the oldest battleship still in service, used principally as a fleet training ship and manned with a reduced crew. In keeping with its modest power, the amphibious force cruised south on smooth seas at slow speeds while Thomas studied his umpiring manual, operations plans, and maps and attended conferences on the problem.[9]

When the amphibious force arrived off Culebra, the 1st Brigade went ashore and set up a tent camp while the four battleships moved to the gunnery range at another part of the island. The Marines found most of the island's three hundred inhabitants awaiting them on the beach with beer, rum, and Coca Cola for sale. Penetrating this resistance, the Marines settled into garrison routine while their officers and the umpires organized a series of battalion and company tactical exercises. Jerry, Bob Bare, and another officer worked with Alfred H. Noble's battalion. Jerry enjoyed the outdoor work, the camaraderie of camp life, and the chance to serve with enlisted Marines again. He admitted to Lottie that he badly needed the exercise of hiking, but he did not relish washing his own socks, a field expedient that was the only sure way to prevent them from disappearing. In camp, he read his mail and the *Washington Post* for war news. He and the other umpires also sampled the good life of Charlotte Amalie, St. Thomas, on a liberty call. In the meantime, the battleships banged away in a series of exercises to test their ability to hit point targets. The results confirmed earlier experiments. At nine thousand yards, a safe distance from shore guns, the battleships had only 16 hits in 69 shells fired. The *Manley* made only 19 hits of 120 shells fired. When the battleships closed to two thousand yards, their accuracy soared to 78 hits of 120 rounds put downrange. With nothing left to prove in either tactics ashore or naval gunfire at sea, the force reassembled for the first of two landing exercises.[10]

After practicing the ship-to-shore movement, especially loading artillery on two experimental lighters, the task force conducted its first landing and field problem during 14–15 February on the island of Culebra. Two reinforced battalions assaulted the beach positions, but found that the defenders (the third battalion) had moved inland and established a strong, positional defense. In all, the ship-to-shore movement went well, even according to the demanding standards of the 1st Brigade commander, Brig. Gen. Holland M. Smith, and his staff, which celebrated the brigade's performance with a cocktail party. Jerry Thomas thought the landing had produced no surprises, an opinion shared by Smith. Within its limitations, the 1st Brigade had learned its trade; its infantrymen could scramble down landing nets, survive the ride in cutters to the beach, vault over the high gunwales into the surf, and then stumble ashore, even when they carried machine guns and mortars. The requirement for special transports, landing craft with bow ramps, amphibian tanks and tractors, and rapidly deployable artillery was obvious. The second major landing of 20–23 February on Vieques went smoothly, even the predawn assault of one company landing from the *Manley*. The defenders met the invaders close to the beaches this time, but the umpires ruled the landing successful because of the effect of the simulated air attacks and naval gunfire bombardment. The task force returned to Norfolk on schedule and in good spirits—even Holland M. Smith. Despite the war in Europe and rumors of new Japanese expansion plans in Southeast Asia, the ides of March 1940 came and went without disaster.[11]

Spring marches into Quantico uncamouflaged as the daffodils, wild onions, dogwood, and redbud spring to arms under the warm winds off the Potomac River. The Marines aboard the base celebrate the change of seasons by switching from the green service uniform of winter to the lighter shirts and trousers of summer. In the spring of 1940, the winter uniform for officers was a heavy, green serge uniform with blouse, leather Sam Browne belt, and barracks cap; the summer uniform was gabardine or cotton khaki, long-sleeved shirt, and matching tie, worn most often without blouse, topped by the barracks cap with khaki cover. As Jerry Thomas went through the spring rituals at Marine Corps Schools after his return from the Caribbean, he could not change his mood as easily as his cap cover. The spring of 1940 was not like other springs. With the migratory warblers came the bad news from Europe: in a lightning offensive against Norway, the Low Countries, and France, the German Army destroyed the Western alliance and drove the shattered British armed forces home to England where they sued for time, if not peace. Because Nazi Germany maintained its 1939 neutrality pact with the Soviet Union, it appeared that Adolf Hitler might really enjoy his fantasy of a thousand-year Third Reich. If Japan repeated its opportunistic imperialism, the irresistible product of a European war, the United States might find itself isolated in a hostile world or at war.

Thomas's grasp of the European disaster showed itself in little ways. When his daughter Virginia spent her savings on a red velvet dress, Thomas uncharacteristically exploded. The United States would be at war before the end of the year, he shouted, and who would then need red velvet dresses? "I was not able to throw off a deep feeling of depression and foreboding. . . . I particularly recall going for a walk on a lovely day in May in an unsuccessful effort to shake off a feeling of despondency. I returned with the conviction that the world as we had known it was passing and I was helpless to do other than ride with the tide." His teaching at the Marine Corps Schools now held little zest or gave him the sense that he was preparing the Marine Corps for war.[12]

The fall of France, however, at last mobilized sufficient public alarm to support accelerated improvement in the state of the American armed forces. President Roosevelt, already a secret convert to intervention on behalf of the Allies, and Congress found some common ground for increasing military readiness, if only for hemispheric defense. In July 1940, Congress passed the dramatic "Two Ocean Navy" Act, which authorized the construction of 326 warships and, for the first time, the construction or conversion of specialized transports for amphibious operations. The major challenge for the Marine Corps became the expansion of the two skeleton brigades of the Fleet Marine Force into two divisions; Commandant Thomas Holcomb submitted plans to mobilize the Marine Corps Reserve, both units and individuals, and increase the size of the regular Marine Corps. Commanding a Corps of 1,556 officers and 26,369 enlisted men on 30 June 1940, Holcomb wanted to double this force within the next year, a plan approved by the Navy Department. Roosevelt recognized the need but ordered the Marine Corps to postpone its plans for expansion until he was safely reelected for a third term.[13]

Relatively certain that he would soon command an enlarged Corps, General Holcomb could enlarge the officer corps without changing its authorized (active duty, paid) strength by increasing the number of college students in the Platoon Leaders Class (PLC) program. Initiated in 1935 to provide younger company officers for the organized Marine Corps Reserve, the PLC program provided two summer training periods of six weeks each for aspiring Marine officers. If the candidate successfully completed both training periods, he would become a Reserve second lieutenant when he graduated from college. The Marine Corps held two PLC camps, one at Quantico for Eastern students and the other at San Diego. The program started small (250 candidates the first summer) but grew steadily. The Marine Corps liked the quality of the candidates, whose social and educational profiles looked much like those of the college students commissioned in 1917. The 1939 PLC class at Quantico (305 candidates) included a heavy dose of campus leaders and varsity athletes; representatives of twenty-nine different fraternities made up more than half the class. Two candidates even had Phi Beta Kappa keys.

The PLC program not only produced Reserve lieutenants but enlarged the ties between the Marine Corps and the nation's political elite, a fact not lost on Lt. Col. Joseph W. "Buddy" Knighton, an assistant adjutant and inspector and a career congressional lobbyist for Headquarters. Buddy Knighton knew what sold on the Hill, and the PLC program sold. He proposed that the concept be expanded in 1940 to open officer training to college graduates who would accept Reserve commissions after completing three months of training. Holcomb ordered the First Officer Candidate Course to open at Quantico in November 1940.[14]

Jerry Thomas joined the first ripples of mobilization in July 1940 when he became executive officer of the Eastern Platoon Leaders Class and moved with Bob Bare (the operations officer) from Barracks H to Barracks A. The job change involved a greater adjustment than shifting offices a couple of blocks along Barnett Avenue; the PLC program required active supervision and daily crisis management, the latter just the thing to sweep away depression. The candidates themselves (114 senior course members, 220 junior course members) brought youthful eagerness and amazing ignorance of military life to Quantico, and the PLC training cadre had little time to waste. The executive officer was anything but a timewaster. From 7 July until 17 August, Thomas supervised the senior instruction in tactics and leadership and the junior class instruction in basic military skills and drill, a shortened version of the boot camp experience. When Headquarters activated the First Officer Candidate Course (OCC) in October, Holcomb appointed Lemuel C. Shepherd, a new colonel and head of the MCS F-3 section, to be the course commandant. Shepherd took Thomas and Bare, a proven team, back to Barracks A. Although Headquarters planned a class of 400, the First OCC began training with 269 candidates, unmarried college men under twenty-five years of age. A month later, Headquarters produced about 100 more candidates, which meant that the OCC had to run two different training programs, one four weeks shorter than the planned thirteen weeks. Thomas became acting commanding officer after one month's training. Shepherd rolled a horse he was jumping and broke his shoulder, which put him in Bethesda Naval Hospital until March 1941. This was a busy time for Thomas. He assigned Bare all of the administrative and logistical burdens so that he could supervise training.[15]

Under Thomas's guidance, the First Officer Candidate Course cadre ran "an amplified recruit depot." Unlike the PLC program, which treated its charges gently, the OCC had the task of assessing the candidates for leadership potential and discharging those men who did not measure up to the physical demands and emotional stress of combat officership. Thomas knew that the evaluation process at that stage was inexact, but he believed that the thirty-six candidates he disqualified were clearly not officer material. (Later attrition rates were much higher.) He believed that the candidates he passed, who were commissioned in February 1941, had at least rudimentary knowledge of leadership principles, Marine Corps drill and ceremonies, infantry weapons, and small unit tactics. Fortunately, the new lieutenants would begin their extended active duty as officers by attending the Reserve Officers Course, a shorter version of the traditional instruction of The Basic School. Thomas looked forward to retaining command of the Officer Candidate Course when Headquarters announced it would assemble a second OCC class in February as soon as the first class graduated. Instead, Col. A. F.

Howard, assistant commandant of the MCS, assigned one of his own protégés, a lieutenant colonel, to command the OCC, and Thomas reverted to executive officer on 24 February 1941. Although he did not know it, he had less than a month to serve in this billet.[16]

In March 1941, Thomas received orders to report on temporary duty to the Division of Plans and Policies, Headquarters Marine Corps. He had no clear idea of why he had received the orders until he reported to Lt. Col. W. Walter Rogers, an old friend he had first met in France in the 6th Marines when they were both sergeants struggling to earn commissions on the battlefield. A Headquarters insider, Rogers headed the M-3 (training) section of the Plans and Policies ("Pots and Pans") Division, created in 1939 to replace the Division of Operations and Training. Thomas soon guessed that Rogers was plotting to have the division director, Brig. Gen. Charles D. Barrett, accept Thomas as Rogers's replacement so that the latter could escape to a field command. Rogers probably guessed that Jerry Thomas would soon be a lieutenant colonel in the expanded Marine Corps. To direct the M-3 section would have been a choice assignment for one who sought a high-risk, high-visibility job; there was already talk that M-3 would absorb the functions of the M-5 section, which did war planning. With the Fleet Marine Force already in the process of expanding to two divisions and six base defense battalions, M-3 would be hard pressed to coordinate training on two coasts and revise contingency plans that now included possible employments in the Pacific and Atlantic missions that stretched from Iceland to Trinidad. As England fought on, Roosevelt had already redeployed part of the Fleet, renamed it the Atlantic Fleet, and slipped it behind the Royal Navy to protect the flow of American war materiel by sea to the British Isles. To Walter Rogers, Jerry Thomas seemed to grasp the complexity of the challenge and the sensitivity of the politics. He also probably assumed that Thomas would work well not only with General Barrett, commander of the 5th Marines during FLEX 6, but also with the assistant to the Commandant, Brig. Gen. Alexander Archer Vandegrift.[17]

[CHAPTER XIII]

Observing World War II
1941

IN MIDPASSAGE BETWEEN war and peace, President Franklin D. Roosevelt moved the United States into a closer relationship with Great Britain, the only unoccupied nation fighting Nazi Germany. From January through March 1941, the senior military staffs of the United States and Great Britain concluded a study of the world military crisis and recommended extensive American military assistance to the Allies. Even before the conclusion of the staff talks, which produced the strategy of "Germany First," Roosevelt asked Congress for legislation that would allow the United States to provide military equipment without immediate payment. The Lend-Lease Act (11 March 1941) authorized a new legal foundation for aid to Great Britain, provided that American industry could produce war materiel and that the Allied navies could escort the merchant ships through the waiting German submarines. Because the only active theater was the Middle East, Roosevelt and Winston S. Churchill recognized that Lend-Lease materiel had a long and dangerous trip before it reached the Commonwealth armed forces.[1]

The Mediterranean theater assumed central importance to the Allied war effort in the spring of 1941, largely because the British position in Egypt ensured the security of the Suez Canal and the vital links to Middle Eastern oil and the resources of India. Churchill and Roosevelt agreed that Lend-Lease materiel should go to the British forces in the Middle East. The Allied position, however, deteriorated rapidly in April 1941 when Germany's Afrika Korps began offensive operations in the Western Desert and its 12th Army invaded Greece and Yugoslavia. Although FDR had ample diplomatic sources in the area, he decided to send his oldest son and trusted political companion, Capt. James F. Roosevelt, USMCR, to the Middle East. Jimmy Roosevelt had been training with his Reserve artillery battalion at Camp Elliott in southern California and had just married for the second time. He already had word from his father (in a letter delivered by his mother) that he would soon depart on a trip for the purposes of fact-finding in the Middle East and stressing his father's support to the embattled governments of Yugoslavia and Greece. Other than receiving broad guidance that related to his observation of British military operations, he had no other instructions. He did learn, however, that Headquarters Marine Corps, which managed the trip, had assigned him a traveling companion, Maj. Gerald C. Thomas.[2]

Major General Commandant Thomas Holcomb, one of FDR's intimates, selected Thomas for the trip, but Thomas received no more precise instructions than those the President sent his son. Neither Assistant Commandant A. A. Vandegrift nor Brig. Gen. Charles D. Barrett, Thomas's immediate superiors, knew anything more. The trip began with no sense of urgency. Thomas left Washington by train on 14 April and enjoyed the transcontinental ride to San Francisco for its very dullness, which he exploited by reading. Arriving in San Francisco, he learned that he and Jimmy would depart on 19 April by the China Clipper, Pan American's flying boat, to Hong Kong via Pearl Harbor, Midway, Wake Island, Guam, and Manila. From Hong Kong, the route and means of transportation became uncertain because commercial air service in the Far East had become erratic and American or British military transportation was unscheduled.

The mission started on time, and nineteen hours later (0800 20 April 1941) Roosevelt and Thomas landed at Pearl Harbor. On the way into the landing area, Jerry saw the concentration of air and naval bases on Oahu, the most tempting target he had ever witnessed. His anxiety disappeared, however, after a round of calls on the senior Navy and Marine officers at Headquarters 14th Naval District. One was his old friend, Col. Gilder D. Jackson. Thomas also found time to talk privately with Jimmy and learned that the President had given Jimmy the letters of reassurance. Jimmy thought the mission was largely symbolic, that FDR wanted world leaders to see his son in uniform as a living example of America's military determination. Thomas had no doubt that Jimmy would be taken seriously because he was FDR's favorite son, and FDR had (in foreign eyes) "limitless power and bottomless money bags."[3]

The Roosevelt-Thomas mission had been observed even before it started its own observations. The British, of course, welcomed them and approved their assignment to the Naval Mission, United States Embassy, London, with actual posting to Cairo. The day the mission left Honolulu (21 April), the intelligence section of the Japanese consulate reported to Tokyo that Capt. James Roosevelt and "Rear Admiral Thomas" had left on their goodwill trip to China, but the Japanese concluded that the wandering Marines had no military significance.[4]

In the meantime, the China Clipper droned westward. The stops at Midway, Wake Island, and Guam allowed Thomas to visit with old Navy and Marine friends on each island and to marvel at the lack of military defenses at all three places. The fortifications for Midway and Wake were progressing slowly, but the authorities on Guam had done nothing at all, even with their local resources. Thomas still thought Guam more defensible than the atolls. That the Japanese would attack Guam he had no doubt, a conviction reinforced by an unscheduled diversion of the China Clipper over the island of Rota, a Japanese-held island some forty miles north of Guam. During the flight west, Thomas mentioned to the pilot that he had studied the defense of Guam and wondered if the Japanese would build a fighter strip on Rota. The captain had appeared unmoved at the time, but during the approach to Guam he called Thomas to the cockpit and told him to take the copilot's seat. The pilot then dropped the plane through the cloud cover and let Jerry see a Japanese aircraft taking off from Rota's completed east-west runway.[5]

When the China Clipper arrived in Manila in the afternoon of 24 April, Roosevelt and Thomas received red carpet treatment from the Philippine government, the office of the American High Commissioner (Francis B. Sayre), and the senior Navy and Marine Corps officers of the 16th Naval District. Again, Jerry found many old friends with whom to visit at the Cavite naval station, but he and Jimmy had to go by launch across Manila Bay to their air-conditioned suite at the Manila Hotel. That evening, High Commissioner Sayre held a lawn party in their honor, complete with a battalion of Filipino and American officers resplendent in tropical white dress uniforms. They met the High Presence, Field Marshal of the Philippine Army Douglas MacArthur, but the most assiduous of the people Thomas met were representatives of the Chinese Nationalist government, who urged that he and Jimmy visit their wartime capital of Chungking in western China.

Two days later, Sayre reported to FDR that the Roosevelt-Thomas mission would proceed to Hong Kong, then continue to the Middle East through Chungking. The change in the tentative itinerary had a practical excuse: commercial air service from Hong Kong to Singapore had been suspended. Nevertheless, the new routing had clear political implications. An awesome "Gang of Three"—Madame Chiang Kai-shek, Ambassador to the United States T. V. Soong (the Madame's brother), and retired Army colonel Claire Chennault (her advisor)—had mounted a determined effort to use $150 million of Lend-Lease money to turn western China into a bastion of air bases. Jimmy Roosevelt probably knew that his father, who supervised Lend-Lease programs to China through a special assistant, Lauchlin Currie, favored the air program. The War and Navy departments, however, did not view the plans with enthusiasm. Neither did part of the Nationalist cabinet, which welcomed American attention but preferred dollars to bombers. With a vacuum in the official American mission to China (FDR had just transferred Ambassador Nelson T. Johnson), the views of Sayre and the Chinese Nationalists in Manila probably reinforced Jimmy's inclination to see Chungking. Thomas was not a party to the decision, but he needed no urging to return to China, which he loved. On 25 April, the mission was on its way to Chungking via Macao and Hong Kong.[6]

If Roosevelt and Thomas worried about their lack of preparation for the Chungking visit—they had no official greeting for Chiang Kai-shek—their welcome in Hong Kong probably removed their doubts. The American consul-general greeted them warmly and announced that they would have a suite in the luxurious Peninsula Hotel in Kowloon with the compliments of the Chinese government. Personal representatives of both the Generalissimo and Madame Chiang Kai-shek announced their devotion to the mission's comfort and entertainment, a pledge sealed by a sumptuous Chinese dinner at the Hong Kong Hotel. Organized by O. K. Yui, head of the Central Bank of China, the dinner provided the opportunity for twenty-five or thirty Chinese educated in the United States to lobby Roosevelt and Thomas for aid to China. The militancy of the "returned students" compared favorably with the lethargy and defeatism Thomas found among the British civil and military officials he met in Hong Kong. Although Thomas thought that Hong Kong island's rugged terrain made it defensible, he doubted that the resident British brigade would offer more than token resistance. As he had in Manila, Thomas sensed the end of the European imperium in Asia, a shift of fortune that could not be concealed by brave talk, romantic news stories, and the attentiveness of Chinese servants.[7]

The eight-hour flight to Chungking, 1,500 miles up the Yangtze River valley, began on 29 April in early-morning darkness—the better to evade patrolling Japanese Zeros—and ended at an airport nestled below the cliffs on which Chungking perilously clung. Marine Maj. James M. McHugh, the naval attaché and intimate of the Chiang and Soong families, greeted Roosevelt and Thomas and led them on foot up Chungking's famous thousand stairs to the walls of the fortress city. They found Chungking a bomb-ravaged city of gray buildings and bamboo huts. One million Chinese, three-quarters of whom were refugees, crammed the streets and cowered in huts along the river. The travelers went to their quarters (a bungalow that belonged to T. V. Soong), cleaned up, and began a round of calls on their hosts: Maj. Gen. J. L. Huang, head of the New Life Movement to train Chinese youth, and Dr. H. H. Kung (also married to a Soong sister), the head of the Executive Yuan and minister of finance. Dr. Kung invited the Americans into the chambers of the Executive Yuan and introduced them to the rest of the Chinese cabinet, an unparalleled sign of political goodwill.

As Roosevelt, Thomas, and McHugh left the Executive Yuan building, McHugh said the surge of people in the streets meant that a Japanese bombing raid was on its way. Climbing down the stairs to the river, the Americans were borne by the mob seeking bomb shelters or the ferries to the south side of the river where the bombs seldom hit. (A month after Thomas left Chungking, four thousand people perished in a stampede for the city's largest shelter.) The party reached the docks for its trip to the American Embassy for lunch, but the launch was missing. McHugh hired a sampan, which carried them through the barrier of crowded ferries and fleeing small craft to the south bank. When the air alert ended in about an hour, the Americans entered the embassy to meet Ambassador Johnson, who had not yet left for his post in Australia. Johnson greeted Thomas warmly and reminisced about their days in Peiping, a cultural paradise compared with Chungking.[8]

The four-day visit to Chungking passed in a whirl of official calls, formal dinners, and visits to Nationalist military installations. No one in the "China Lobby" could have improved McHugh's itinerary. The remainder of the first afternoon started with meetings with the minister of war, continued with a call on the chief of operations of the Nationalist Army (unimpressive, thought Thomas), reached a high crescendo in a meeting with Foreign Minister Dr. C. T. Wang, and ended with a diplomatic epiphany, an audience with Generalissimo and Madame Chiang Kai-shek. The last call, which was supposed to be tea, turned into an intense discussion of China's plight dominated in flawless English by Madame Chiang. The Generalissimo struck Thomas as just another Chinese warlord, but Madame Chiang impressed him as a person of great strength, intelligence, and modern vision. She assured him that McHugh would show them anything they wanted to see and invited them to dinner their last night in Chungking. The day ended with a formal dinner for Ambassador Johnson, hosted by Dr. Kung. Thomas noted that all the Chinese he met were enduring their wartime hardships with dignity and patriotism and all regarded the United States with undisguised affection. (Of the eight Chinese at the dinner for Johnson, four were Yale graduates.) The trips afield further reinforced the impression that the Chinese had dedicated themselves to a long war of attrition against Japan, their despised traditional enemy. Roosevelt and Thomas visited a base for Chinese pilot training. They saw thousands of coolies building airstrips for the existing Russian fighters and the anticipated American fighters and bombers and watched Chinese officer candidates run tactical exercises with the traditional ardor of the German army, from which they drew their inspiration. They visited a university, walked through a museum of traditional Chinese art, and dined with the foreign minister—all during their second day in Chungking.[9]

On a somewhat reduced schedule for their last two days in China, Roosevelt and Thomas met the high officials of the Kuoumintang and Gen. Pai Chung Hsi, deputy chief of staff and a Moslem warlord of considerable power, who doubted America's support. Thomas suggested that General Pai should visit the United States to see its industrial power. In the meantime, he and Roosevelt sampled Chinese industrial might—actually craftsman might—in the underground munitions factories around Chungking designed and organized by the Master of Ordnance, Dr. Yu Ta Wei, who was a graduate of the Massachusetts Institute of Technology with further engineering education in Germany. By the time Roosevelt and Thomas dined with the Generalissimo and Madame on 2 May, they were full of schemes to deepen the joint war effort against Japan, a commitment encouraged by an "American dinner" organized by the Madame. Thomas sat next to Madame and recommended she draft a plan to train "overseas" Chinese as pilots in America and to send General Pai to the United States. Thomas thought both ideas appealed to the Madame, and she said she would raise them with the Generalissimo.[10]

His visit to Chungking convinced Thomas that the Chinese would not surrender and that the Nationalists' use of time, space, and population would prevent the Japanese from conquering the hinterland. He also concluded, erroneously he later admitted, that Japan could not disengage enough of its army for a war of conquest into Southeast Asia. Perhaps war with Japan was not as inevitable as the Navy had assumed since 1921. The key was materiel assistance to the Nationalist armed forces via the Burma Road, managed by the British to the Chinese border and then by the Nationalists to the terminus at Kunming. Chinese and foreign authorities agreed that the Nationalist armed forces required sixteen thousand tons of supplies a month and that the British delivered about that amount to the Chinese. Only about a quarter of the supplies reached Kunming, however, because the Chinese could not keep the trucks running and they found the lure of pilferage irresistible. Thomas and Roosevelt agreed to report the problem to Lend-Lease administrator Harry Hopkins, who took the lead in tightening control of the transportation system through a U.S. Army military mission. Thomas also decided that Madame Chiang and Chennault were correct in arguing that the available foreign assistance be focused on the Nationalist air force; such aid might produce immediate dividends and cause fewer political problems than reforming the Nationalist Army.[11]

Roosevelt and Thomas left Chungking as planned on 3 May on a Chinese National Airlines flight to Rangoon via Kunming. Due to leave around noon, the two Marine officers learned that their flight had been rescheduled to leave earlier—before a flight of Japanese bombers reached Chungking. McHugh got them to the plane on time, and they departed an hour before the Japanese arrived. When their flight arrived in Rangoon around 1900, Roosevelt and Thomas disembarked into a furnace of Burmese heat and humidity. Thanks to the ministrations of the American consul and the military secretary to the Governor-General of Burma, they arrived only fifteen minutes late to a black-tie dinner held for them by the Governor-General, Sir Archibald Cochrane. Cochrane used the occasion not only to brief the Americans but to educate his successor, Sir Reginald Dorman-Smith. The gist of the discussion over brandy and cigars was that the Burmese would not fight for Burma, which they thought had fallen into the hands of Indian entrepreneurs. During the following day of rest, shopping, and sight-seeing, Thomas could not shake a sense that disaster awaited the British in Burma as it did in Hong Kong. The trip did not allow time for additional reflection; on 5 May, Roosevelt and Thomas caught a British Overseas Airways Corporation (BOAC) seaplane flight for Cairo.[12]

The two-day trip from Rangoon to Cairo impressed Thomas with the fragility of the British position in the Middle East, for an Axis-supported coup in Iraq made the trip to Egypt more complicated than planned. One day's flying brought the Americans, along with a group of British officers of the Indian Army, to Karāchi, Pakistan. When they landed, Roosevelt and Thomas found the British officials reluctant to let them continue to Basra in Iraq on the BOAC amphibian. The flight could no longer proceed safely beyond Basra to the Royal Air Force (RAF) base on Lake Habbaniya (fifty miles west of Baghdād), which was under attack by Iraqi rebels. The plane could not carry enough fuel to fly directly to the next nearest landing site, Tiberias on the Sea of Galilee. The British offered the Americans a side trip into India until other passage could be arranged, but Roosevelt insisted that he continue to Cairo. Even reports of fighting near Basra did not deter him, and Thomas actually relished the chance to see British Commonwealth troops in action in an area he had studied. Misled by his reading about World War I, Thomas found Basra a garden spot with an excellent hotel and handsome buildings. He and Roosevelt enjoyed tea meant originally for their traveling companions, Lt. Gen. E. P. Quinan and Brig. William Slim—a tea held with traditional British imperturbability among the wounded brought to the hotel from a nearby skirmish with the Iraqis. The Americans later attended a cocktail party given by Sir John and Lady Ward, the leaders of the local British business community, and they learned from Slim that passage was available on a big RAF Sunderland flying boat taking a British military party, including a group of wounded RAF pilots, directly to Egypt. After a short, hot night in a blacked-out hotel room, the Americans left early the next morning for the final leg to Cairo.[13]

Flying over Saudi Arabia—"the most unpromising layout of sand . . . and jagged mountains I ever saw"—the flying boat brought Roosevelt and Thomas to the RAF base at Ismailia on the Suez Canal. After lunch at the mess, the Americans and Col. Roger Peake, a Middle East Command staff officer who had joined them in Basra, continued the trip to Cairo by car. At the American legation in Cairo, a crowded city made more hot and dusty by the British military presence, they found the minister, Alexander Kirk, expecting them. Kirk said that the RAF would handle all their local arrangements, including housing in a luxury suite in the ancient and honorable bastion of British influence, the Shepherd Hotel. After reporting to London by cable, Roosevelt and Thomas went to the hotel with Kirk, who also lived there, and unexpectedly met two Marine officer friends, Lt. Col. Walter G. Farrell and Capt. Perry O. Parmalee, naval aviators sent out from London to observe RAF operations. They also found the bar at Shepherd's the Egyptian rendezvous for American war correspondents, who became a great source of information.[14]

For the next three days (9–11 May 1941), the four Marine officers, using Jimmy Roosevelt's political influence and assisted by the able military attaché, Maj. Bonner Fellers, USA, educated themselves on the British position in the Middle East and planned their further itinerary. They judged the British situation desperate, largely because of a lack of fighter aircraft and armored fighting vehicles. The front at the Western Desert was for the moment quiet, with the exception of besieged Tobruk, but both sides had offensive preparations under way. To the north, British forces on Crete awaited a predicted German airborne and amphibious assault, and the Royal Navy fought to keep the lines of communications open to Malta and through the Mediterranean to Gibraltar. Although Palestine could be defended (in part because Jewish militia cowed the restive Arab population), Syria, under French Vichy control, posed a new problem. The French would not block German use of Syrian airfields, which allowed the Luftwaffe to support the Iraqi rebels. The British and a small Free French force could not cope with Syria until the situation in Iraq improved, that is, until a Commonwealth and Jordanian ground expedition relieved Habbaniya and another column from Basra reversed the Iraqi military coup against the pro-Allies government of Regent Amir Abdul Illah. The British campaign in Ethiopia had defeated the Italians, but the reduced threat to the Red Sea had been in part checkmated by German aerial mining of the Canal and its approaches.

Of all the British the Americans met, their official host, Air Marshal Arthur W. Tedder, proved the most helpful and candid. New to the command of RAF Middle East—he had been serving as deputy to Air Chief Marshal Sir Arthur Longmore—Tedder masked a keen operational mind and deft political touch with a dry sense of humor and a fascination for technology and administrative detail. He was an energetic introvert who could even charm Churchill (something Gen. Sir Archibald Wavell and Longmore could not and would not do). Overmatching his American guests, Tedder quietly deflected their persistent requests that they visit Crete and the King of the Hellenes, George II. Instead, Tedder and his staff guided the Americans toward a problem they wanted solved, the more efficient arrival of Lend-Lease aircraft. Using Roosevelt's influence, Thomas arranged for Farrell and Parmalee to study the reports on the RAF's assembly base at Takoradi, a Gold Coast port that received crated aircraft by ship from the United States and Great Britain. The two Marine aviators discovered that 320 American fighters awaited assembly and ferrying from Takoradi, which had the capacity to process only 120 aircraft a month. Of the completed aircraft, 10 to 20 percent failed to survive the 3,800-mile flight to Egypt. The greatest losses occurred among the fighters, which required frequent landings at dusty strips to refuel. Roosevelt and Thomas asked their RAF hosts about the problem but received no clarifications. Frustrated, they continued to press for a flight to Crete to deliver FDR's messages to King George. Again, the RAF stalled. Jimmy then cabled his father and received assurances that FDR wanted the messages delivered, regardless of the risk. Half an hour after Jimmy received his father's answer from Kirk, RAF Headquarters called him and said that he and Thomas should take a train to Alexandria the next morning (12 May), where they would find seats on a flying boat bound for Crete.[15]

The trip to Crete, a harrowing twelve-hour odyssey that ended in the early morning of 13 May, allowed Roosevelt to have his private meeting with King George II and gave Thomas a chance to see the vulnerable defenses of the island only a week before the Germans attacked. The flight on the Sunderland to Suda Bay took about four hours, most of it at less than one thousand feet, which gave the unarmored flying boat maximum protection (it had four topside turrets) from prowling German fighters. Approaching Suda Bay, the pilot took the plane to five thousand feet to clear the mountains and then plunged dramatically onto Suda Bay when he learned that he had German fighters below his altitude. Thomas found the flight path thrilling, but not repeatable. The British headquarters staff took the Americans in tow, wined and dined them to the best of their limited ability, and took them to King George, who impressed them with his appearance, self-control, and mastery of English. During his travels about the island, Thomas learned as much as he could about its defenses and concluded, along with his candid escorts, that Maj. Gen. Bernard C. Freyberg had an impossible mission because he lacked air superiority and heavy weapons. Given their limited air support, Thomas wondered why the British did not destroy the three major airports, the only place the Germans could land gliderborne heavy weapons of their own. He did not share the forlorn hope that RAF transports would fly in reinforcements over these same airstrips. When he returned to the Sunderland for the return flight to Alexandria—timed to give the flying boat the advantage of darkness before moonrise—Thomas concluded that Crete would fall. His foreboding did not lift when the flight had to divert to Aboukir Bay to avoid a German air attack on Alexandria, and the Americans had been on the road to Alexandria only an hour when another raid hit their landing place.[16]

With virtually no sleep, Thomas and Roosevelt visited the Royal Navy's Mediterranean Fleet, specifically HMS *Warspite*, the flagship of Adm. Sir Andrew B. Cunningham, and the carrier HMS *Formidable*. They found Cunningham and his staff, with whom they dined, jubilant that they had convoyed six freighters and tankers to Malta and returned with four heavy freighters, loaded with 238 tanks and 43 fighter planes, to Alexandria. The Americans received a more dour assessment from a firsthand observer, Marine Col. Roy S. Geiger, who had seen the whole convoy operation from the *Formidable*. Although the Royal Navy had lost only one freighter to a mine, Cunningham had deployed four times as many warships as he had freighters to get Convoy "Tiger" to Alexandria, and the *Formidable* had lost its entire air group fighting the Luftwaffe.[17]

Returning to Cairo, Roosevelt and Thomas found the British much more cooperative about the Americans' proposed travels throughout the Middle East. They also found senior British officers more interested in their possible influence on President Roosevelt. On the evening of 14 May, they dined with Air Vice Marshal A. C. Maund, chief administrative officer of RAF Middle East Command and the officer responsible for assembling aircraft in Takoradi and ferrying them to Cairo. Maund and another officer, the RAF chief of supply, admitted they had a problem, but their proposed solutions, all of which assumed continued RAF control of the operation, struck Thomas as only palliatives. During a two-hour discussion over brandy and cigars, Thomas proposed instead that the British arrange for an American company to assemble the aircraft at Takoradi and have it ferry the fighters to Egypt. The British officers thanked him for his suggestion but made no commitments. Still assertive, Thomas spent the next day discussing artillery procedures with Brigadier R. H. Maxwell, chief gunner of the British Army in Egypt, and the air support situation with Geiger, Farrell, and Parmalee. He finished a professionally stimulating day with equal social stimulation, a late-night dinner with Minister and Mrs. Kirk at their new residence near the Pyramids. Thomas and Roosevelt planned to leave Cairo the next day for a trip to Palestine to see King Peter II of Yugoslavia and to visit the British relief column already on its way to Iraq.[18]

The four-day visit to Palestine (16–20 May 1941) proved another highlight of the trip, although the audience with King Peter II produced no thrills. The immature monarch wanted only to request that the United States train Yugoslav pilots. The Roosevelt-Thomas mission made its key contact with Air Vice Marshal John J. D'Albiac, the commander of British forces in Palestine, who arranged for them to meet leaders of both the Jewish and Arab communities of Palestine, the Free French representatives, and the key British officers who were mounting simultaneous operations against both Syria and Iraq. As the British pondered just how much danger they wished Roosevelt and Thomas to encounter, they arranged for the Americans to see the holy places around Jerusalem and ferried them about Palestine to see *kibbutzim* and older historic sites. Reflecting his Bible training as a child, Thomas found the trips fascinating; reflecting his training as a Marine officer, he found the sight-seeing trips an unwanted postponement. Even though his vaunted energy fell to a sudden attack of diarrhea, Thomas wanted to be off for Iraq, and he welcomed the news from D'Albiac, a former Royal Marine who embraced Roosevelt and Thomas with unexpected hospitality, that they could fly with his chief of staff directly to Habbaniya. They thus could be on station to welcome the relief column then crossing the desert under the command of Lt. Gen. H. M. "Jumbo" Wilson.[19]

The trip to Iraq exposed Thomas to the first enemy fire he had faced since Haiti. He found he still had sound survival instincts and sufficient physical courage to fight another major war. Above all, he saw the trip as a professional challenge, a chance to involve himself in real operational problems. He learned that the major difficulties were logistical, not tactical, for the Iraqis had flooded the area over which the British planned to advance. Thomas and Roosevelt went on a tour with D'Albiac to the scene of the fighting and found themselves under air attack. A flight of German bombers pounded the British positions, followed by low-flying

Messerschmitt Bf-110's churning the sands about Thomas's party with cannon fire. Neither the staff car nor the men, who sought the scant cover of the sand dunes, took any hits, but the bombers destroyed several other targets. The D'Albiac party surrendered its car for ambulance duty, and Jimmy and Jerry hiked back to the RAF command post. The next day, they inspected British engineering efforts to control the flooded Euphrates and returned to their billets, only to be strafed again in the late afternoon at Air House. The attack did not spoil cocktails and dinner.[20]

That evening, Roosevelt and Thomas decided to return to Cairo on an RAF transport because they concluded that the British offensive toward Baghdād would develop only in the fullness of time. The major interest at the moment was the German attack on Crete, which had begun on 20 May. The Germans gave Thomas a going-away experience by bombing Air House again early in the morning. Half way between his pajamas and his uniform, Thomas ran nude to the first-floor shelter, but did not let his disarray prevent him from learning about a sudden Iraqi attack to the north, which the British successfully countered. The German bombs rearranged the lawn in front of Air House but did little damage. After breakfast, the Americans boarded a Lodestar for the flight back to Egypt.[21]

Even before the trip to Iraq, Jimmy Roosevelt had decided that he had spent enough time fact finding and too little time with his new wife. When he and Thomas returned to Cairo, they learned that the American naval attaché's office in London had issued them requested orders to return to the United States via Great Britain by the first available commercial aircraft. Although the debriefing in London was common practice for Marine observers in the Middle East, one suspects that a "Former Naval Person" or, at the very least, some senior officers of the RAF wanted to talk to Roosevelt about his views on the Takoradi bottleneck. FDR himself had no hand in the itinerary. In any event, the Americans could not leave Cairo until 31 May on the BOAC flight to Lagos, Nigeria, so they had an additional week's opportunity to watch the Middle East war reach another crisis.[22]

For most of the remainder of his stay in Egypt, Thomas followed the battle for Crete. He shared the frustration and eventual sorrow of his new British friends as Freyberg's defenders valiantly, but unsuccessfully, tried to stem the flood of German paratroopers and gliderborne infantry. On 27 May, Wavell saw no alternative but to order Freyberg to save the remnants of his force and leave the island, courtesy of the embattled Royal Navy. During the fight for Crete, the Luftwaffe ravaged the British forces and sank nine warships and several transports during the evacuation. The battle for Crete, which Thomas discussed with Colonel Peake and the commander of a Highland battalion that had fought there, convinced the Marine that air superiority had become the sine qua non for successful battle in World War II. Thomas also broadened his self-education by meeting with British and South African officers who had been fighting in the Western Desert, by attending briefings and reading British message traffic, and by discussing his observations with other American officers (Marines and Army) who gathered at the Shepherd's bar to compare notes among themselves and with the correspondents. Thomas impressed one of the newsmen, who described him as "a hard-bitten veteran who has sharp eyes," with his grasp of the operational realities of the war and the grand design for Germany's defeat. Thomas agreed with the others that American intervention would be critical, and all wondered when it would come.[23]

The highlight of the last week in Cairo came on 28 May when Roosevelt and Thomas had their thrice-delayed meeting with Gen. Sir Archibald Wavell, General Officer Commanding Middle East. Wavell, fifty-eight, was a short officer who had lost an eye but not his intelligence in his long years of superior service. He was given to long silences and sometimes was inarticulate when he did talk, but he had no trouble convincing Roosevelt and Thomas that the true seriousness of his position was not appreciated in either London or Washington. Although he did not press his points over lunch—the party numbered twenty and included Gen. Charles de Gaulle—Wavell talked to the Americans alone the next day. He could not have been more candid: the loss of Crete would make it even more difficult for the Royal Navy to operate in the Mediterranean because of the Luftwaffe's new bases on the island; the campaigns in Syria and Iraq had diverted scarce forces and thrown him into a tiresome dispute with the Free French; Churchill had ordered him to take the offensive in the Western Desert and to relieve Tobruk, but he doubted that his army and the RAF were up to the task. London also did not appreciate how dependent the Allies were on the goodwill and support of the Egyptian government, which was rife with Arab nationalist and pro-German sentiment. Any strikes or slowdowns that affected the Egyptian transportation and communications systems would be the death knell of the British war effort in the Middle East. Thomas found nothing alarmist about Wavell's assessment and sensed that he had heard a briefing meant for FDR that Jimmy would faithfully report.[24]

The trip back to the United States began on 1 June 1941, after another dinner with the Kirks near the Pyramids, and took almost a month. Thomas found the aerial odyssey full of new impressions. A traveling companion, Capt. Lord Louis Mountbatten, RN, a Royal cousin and gallant destroyer squadron commander, enlivened the trip. The handsome, charismatic Mountbatten had orders home for a new command. He had just lost HMS *Kelly*, his own destroyer, in the evacuation of Crete. Besides filling the hours in the air with amusing stories and his struggle with two lizards he was carrying to his wife, Mountbatten served as tour guide and local organizer because his influence had preceded him to the various colonial officials the party found waiting to greet them. The Sunderland pilot gave the party a view of Karnak and the Valley of the Kings before landing on the Nile near Khartoum; Mountbatten then showed the Americans the historic sites and battlefields at Khartoum and Omdurman. Three days of travel above the rain forests of equatorial Africa brought the Americans, now flying a regular transport, to Lagos, Nigeria, where they found Farrell and Parmalee also waiting for connections to London. During the four-day wait for the BOAC seaplane to Lisbon, the local officials briefed Mountbatten, the center of attention, and the Americans. They took them for tours around Lagos to sample African culture, which reminded Thomas of Haiti. On 8 June, the Americans finally continued their flight, this time north along the coast of West Africa.[25]

In the meantime, the Roosevelt-Thomas mission had stirred unanticipated action in London, for Tedder had apparently reported its interest in the aircraft assembly operation at Takoradi. Churchill had become swamped with ideas from Roosevelt siblings. Jimmy's brother Elliott, an Army Air Corps captain, was then in London with similar plans to ferry aircraft from the United States to Great Britain and the Middle East. With FDR's blessing and Churchill's urging, W. Averell Harriman, Lend-Lease administrator in London, investigated the Middle East air system. Harriman planned to see Jimmy in Lisbon, but he learned that Roosevelt and Thomas had not yet left Bathurst, the Gold Coast, where they had been further delayed by a leaking aircraft engine. Meeting Roosevelt and Thomas at Bathurst on 12 June, Harriman heard their report on conditions at Takoradi and then visited the Middle East himself. After his tour, he arranged for Pan American Airways to contract with the British to handle the American part of the aircraft flow into West Africa, which Tedder welcomed. In the meantime, after eight days' delay in Bathurst, Roosevelt and Thomas finally arrived in Lisbon on 17 June and learned that they had passage three days later by Pan American clipper directly to New York. Delayed again by one day, the Americans toured Lisbon and parts of rural Portugal. Neutral Lisbon, they learned, was a hotbed of espionage. Each time they left their rooms at the Avis Hotel, someone rummaged through their meager baggage but stole nothing. Their notes stayed safely in the American embassy.[26]

Even the final leg home had its moments of excitement. Juan Trippe, the president of Pan American and FDR's unofficial agent for aviation Lend-Lease, warned Thomas that the Navy had two spies, one of them Marine Capt. Thomas G. Ennis, investigating the conditions of the airfields and beaches in the Azores. Ennis and his companion, a Navy ensign, were working under cover as Pan American employees. As Trippe had predicted, Thomas found Ennis at the Pan American hotel in São Miguel. The two officers had a short visit, arranged by Trippe, in a private suite. (A few days later, Portuguese police arrested Ennis and the ensign, but they were released in Lisbon.) The trip to New York City ended without further incident on 22 June 1941. Thomas found Lottie waiting for him, and they returned to Washington together that evening. Thomas then reported to Generals Holcomb and Vandegrift about his trip and found them both pleased with his observations, even though little of what Thomas had learned seemed directly applicable to Marine training. He took great satisfaction from the news that Pan American would soon assume management of Lend-Lease air operations at Takoradi, and Thomas subsequently provided Pan American with additional information about the ferry route across Africa.[27]

In retrospect, Jerry Thomas felt satisfied that he and Roosevelt had completed their mission with discretion and had provided the President (briefed by Jimmy) and the Navy Department with sound impressions of Chinese and British morale and military effectiveness. He basked in the compliments he received from the Commandant with whom he had warm, extended conversations about his trip. However, he worried (and shared his concerns with Vandegrift) that his very success as a military diplomat and instant expert on the leading British personalities in the Middle East would doom him to staff duties at Headquarters or Quantico. Later that same day (27 June 1941), Thomas received orders detaching him from temporary duty at Headquarters and assigning him to the headquarters of the 1st

Marine Division. He had never seen a Marine division—indeed, there had been no Marine divisions until 1941—and he had no idea exactly what he would do on the division staff. As he and Lottie headed south, all he knew was that he would find the 1st Marine Division headquarters embarked on a Navy transport in Charleston harbor. Jerry Thomas had his wish. He was returning to duty with Marine troops.[28]

[CHAPTER XIV]

Once More to War
1941–1942

DURING THE PERIOD of Gerald C. Thomas's labors with the officer candidates at Quantico and his odyssey to observe the Chinese and British at war, Headquarters Marine Corps had readied the Fleet Marine Force for active operations. The transition proved far more difficult than executing a contingency plan for a war with Japan. The U.S. Navy in 1941 faced missions in both the Pacific and Atlantic crucial to Britain's attempt to continue the war. By the summer of 1941, the Navy's operating forces had been divided into an Atlantic Fleet and a Pacific Fleet, the former organized to relieve the British of the responsibility of guarding the Western Atlantic. Reflecting Roosevelt and Churchill's shared concern that Germany and Vichy France might establish air and naval bases in the Western Hemisphere, the Navy studied a strategy of preemptive occupation and reinforcement that would put American troops in the Azores, Iceland, and French-held Martinique. Such operations required the creation of an amphibious corps for the Atlantic Fleet, a force built around a Marine division and two Army infantry divisions. The first step in creating such an amphibious corps demanded the expansion of the 1st Marine Brigade into a full division, a step made in February 1941.[1]

Combat divisions take longer to create in reality than typewriters organize them on paper, but Headquarters at least had a plan. Major General Commandant Thomas Holcomb had approved the plan in April 1941. To support two fleets, Holcomb wanted a peacetime Fleet Marine Force of two divisions (each manned at 70 percent of their full wartime strength of 13,000), two Marine aircraft wings, thirteen base defense battalions, two base defense air groups, and assorted other units. Such a force required a Marine Corps of around 75,000 officers and men. Even with the mobilization of the Marine reserves and increased recruiting, the Corps was still well short of these numbers in June 1941 with an active strength of 54,186. The war-strength Corps would include a third division and require a

Marine Corps three times as large. Although it tripled in size after its activation, the 1st Marine Division had only 8,000 officers and men as it prepared for its first joint exercise in the summer of 1941.[2]

The 1st Marine Division faced an amphibious adolescence unreformed from a troubled childhood. Except for the field grade officers and a small cadre of veteran sergeants, its Marines were brand new officers, mobilized commissioned and enlisted Reserves, and wave after wave of recruits fresh from Parris Island, where the ten weeks of training still focused on discipline, drill, fitness, and rifle marksmanship, not field skills and tactics. There had been few opportunities for unit training since February. Moreover, the division depended on the Army for almost all its combat equipment. Army Chief of Staff George C. Marshall reflected his service's reluctant logistical role: "My main battle is supplying the Marines. Whether we will have anything left after the British and Marines get theirs, I do not know."[3] The division had also outgrown its temporary homes at Quantico and Parris Island, and its planned new quarters along the New River, near Jacksonville, North Carolina, offered little more than 112,000 acres of coastal swamps and pine woods, populated largely by fishermen, moonshiners, timbermen, chiggers, alligators, and snakes. The New River base had three advantages: a potential maneuver area and ranges large enough for a division, a nearby deep-water port with unused capacity at Morehead City, and miles of uninhabited Onslow Beach for amphibious landings. The 1st Division would have to build its own temporary quarters, however, while it prepared for war and waited for Marine quartermasters and civilian contractors to construct a permanent base along the north bank of the New River.[4]

The immediate fate of the 1st Marine Division rested in the hands of two demanding naval warriors, Adm. Ernest J. King and Maj. Gen. Holland M. Smith, the division's commanding general until June 1941. With his career in eclipse and nearing retirement age when World War II began, King returned to sea in command of the Atlantic Squadron in 1940 and became commander of the Atlantic Fleet as a full admiral the following year. Notorious in the Navy for his brilliance, drinking, meanness, and womanizing, King had a wide knowledge of carrier operations and surface warfare, but no amphibious experience. Holland Smith had an ego and temperament to match King, along with hard-learned practical experience as commander of the 1st Marine Brigade. Like King, he had just missed a top command when Roosevelt reappointed Holcomb as Commandant. During the landing exercises of 1940–41 (FLEX 7) in the Caribbean, King had ample opportunity to exercise his ignorance in amphibious operations, and he and Smith battled constantly over the landing plans. Smith won most of the arguments but at high cost to his short supply of patience. The battles continued when he became Commander, I Joint Training Force, U.S. Atlantic Fleet, in July 1941, partly because Smith argued correctly that the greatest defects in amphibious operations remained the Navy's inadequate transports and landing craft. Thrown into close contact with the Army, which he disliked more than the Navy, Smith sent for reinforcements—a new corps chief of staff, Col. Graves B. Erskine, who had mellowed not a whit. Smith turned his attack on his interservice peers while Erskine made sure that the 1st Marine Division would not embarrass his boss.[5]

The new commanding general of the 1st Marine Division, Philip H. Torrey, fifty-seven, appeared to be an apt replacement for Smith, but he had defects in character and professional experience that made his tenure short and unhappy. On the surface, Torrey had ample qualifications: intelligence, striking good looks and military presence, charm, education at the Naval War College and Marine Corps Schools, expeditionary duty in the Caribbean as a junior officer, later command of the 6th Marines, and other high-visibility assignments in barracks posts and naval staffs. He had already served as Smith's de facto deputy commander of the division. Commissioned in 1905, Torrey was a member of the Marine Corps' inner circle, the fourteen generals and seventy colonels who ran the Corps. He had not been promoted to major general in 1941, however, when the regular promotion board selected Smith and Charles F. B. Price for advancement.

Command of the 1st Division, which brought a temporary promotion to major general in November 1941, gave Torrey his chance to win a second star, provided that King, Smith, and Holcomb approved his work. He needed a competent staff because the division faced another round of amphibious exercises in the Caribbean and, perhaps, a contingency operation in the Azores or Martinique. Torrey had no assistant division commander yet; this meant that the next senior officer, his chief of staff, Col. LeRoy P. Hunt, faced off against Bobby Erskine. No one challenged Hunt's reputation as a charismatic, valiant troop leader (he had won four medals for bravery and two Purple Hearts in France), but he was no organizer, no planner. The dominant figure on the division staff was Lt. Col. George E. Monson, the D-4, a supply officer of large administrative ability and energy in the model of his superiors, Quartermaster General Seth Williams and Col. William P. T. Hill, the quartermaster responsible for building the New River base. Torrey favored Monson's advice because he prized administrative efficiency and wanted his division well equipped and well housed. His other principal staff officers—Lt. Col. Robert C. Kilmartin, Jr. (D-1), Lt. Col. Frank B. Goettge (D-2), and Lt. Col. David R. Nimmer (D-3)—did not think that Torrey and Monson had sufficient force and operational knowledge to match Smith and Erskine. Nimmer, who had served as the brigade and division operations officer since 1939, knew that he would soon leave the division to become the commanding officer of a defense battalion. He and Kilmartin welcomed the news that Headquarters had assigned an acknowledged expert in ground warfare training and operations to be the next D-3, a brand new lieutenant colonel named Gerald C. Thomas.[6]

The 1st Marine Division, under new and uncertain leadership, faced several challenges, the first of which was a corps-sized landing in Puerto Rico. In the meantime, it had to form new special units—two tank battalions, two parachute battalions, a scout company, an antiaircraft battery, and an engineer battalion, as well as service troops—and task organize these forces with the division's core of combat troops, the infantry of the 5th and 7th Marines and the four-battalion artillery regiment, the 11th Marines. The third infantry regiment, the 1st Marines based at Parris Island, was only just emerging from cadre status. The rest of the division awaited orders to sail back to the Caribbean. On 5 July, Jerry Thomas boarded the transport *Barnett* (AP 10), a twelve-year-old converted merchantman, on which he found one reinforced battalion of the 7th Marines and part of division headquarters. He learned from Dave Nimmer that the Puerto Rican exercise had been canceled because the proposed maneuver area became malarial during the summer. Instead, the division would gather off Onslow Beach, North Carolina, land there, and use the New River reservation for exercises inland. After taking the lead in rewriting the operations order, Thomas took a shorter version of it to the awaiting subordinate commanders aboard ships at Norfolk, Quantico, Charleston, and Miami, Florida. Thomas briefed them on the changes and returned to the *Barnett* for the landing.[7]

The landings and division maneuvers (4–12 August) did not go well. A summer storm complicated the ship-to-shore movement by placing additional stress on the Navy's amateur coxswains. General Smith and his staff raged at the Navy's small-boat handling, which produced a ragged rank of broached boats along Onslow Beach. Committed to a battle with the Bureau of Ships over the design of infantry landing craft and tank lighters, Smith wanted nothing to dim the performance of his chosen test boats designed by Andrew Higgins. In ill humor, Smith aimed his frustration at Torrey. Although Torrey had nothing to do with the landing craft problem, he did show an uncertain grasp of the division's exercise ashore. To be sure, the 1st Marine Division found the North Carolina woods a tactical challenge. There were few landmarks and no high ground; one sandy path looked like another as the Marines wound into the brush-choked pinewood. As Thomas recalled, "The densely wooded, low lying marshy and snake infested terrain proved a test for troop leaders at all levels."[8]

When the corps staff, principally Bobby Erskine, descended upon the collective head of the division staff, Torrey and Hunt squirmed. Nimmer withdrew sick from the fray, which allowed Thomas to function as the D-3 until the maneuver concluded. Smith's staff found no fault with Thomas's work but reported that the 1st Marine Division lacked sufficient ground warfare training, suffered from too few experienced tactical leaders and too few troops, and lacked any real logistical capability for field operations. The division's communications were inadequate, especially for coordination of supporting fire. Smith judged that the division could not make a successful amphibious assault because of Navy problems with the ship-to-shore movement. While he and his staff worked on improving the Navy's performance—no mean task—the division should concentrate on field training ashore and return to New River as soon as the base could provide minimal support for 10,000 Marines.[9]

Although still officially only Nimmer's principal assistant, Thomas found himself the driving force behind the 1st Marine Division's operational planning. For assistance, he relied on Capt. Wallace M. Greene, Jr., a trusted professional also fresh from the Marine Corps Schools. While awaiting orders to return to New River from Quantico, Thomas made a trip to Martha's Vineyard to assess its suitability as a training area. President Roosevelt wanted the Marines to have a cooler training area and, one suspects, did not mind spending Navy money in the New England area. Thomas confirmed the Navy's official judgment that the site was even worse than Culebra and New River, a finding Holcomb and Vandegrift welcomed, and FDR abandoned the idea. In the meantime, Pete Hill reported that his quartermasters could provide sites for tents, electricity, and fresh water, but that road construction on the new base would slow down barracks construction. If the division could live in a tent camp, it could move to New River. Thomas took a 5th Marines battalion (reinforced) from Quantico to the base in September to erect the tent camp amid the humid heat and mosquito attacks. In October, the rest of the division began to arrive—minus the 1st Marines who were still at Parris Island.

More new Marines slowly joined the division, but the Corps still cried for men. FDR had already mobilized all the Reserves and extended regular enlistments to four years, but the draft (due to expire in October and barely extended that month for another year) encouraged fewer than six hundred enlistments a month. The division force structure expanded more rapidly than its numbers, and it was still short of its authorized training strength of nine thousand when it concentrated at New River. Life in the tent camp proved marginally bearable, especially when the weather turned cold in November. Thomas and the D-3 section tried to balance essential weapons training and small unit tactics with the division's many housekeeping and administrative problems, which Torrey and Monson stressed. Infantry battalions followed a month-long training cycle: two weeks of field training away from the tent camp, a week of leave (buses took the troops to distant East Coast cities), and a week of labor in the tent camp. The artillery battalions went to the Army's Fort Bragg to shoot. In addition, the division provided athletics, boxing matches, band concerts, and movies for the tent camp Marines. Morale ranged from good to surly.[10]

Through the autumn of hardship at New River, Jerry Thomas directed division training. As much as possible, he avoided the distracting influence of the poisoned relations among the division's senior officers and between them and Holland Smith's staff. He developed a routine that he followed for the next twenty months. He awakened early every morning and, neatly turned out and alert, ate breakfast in the division headquarters mess. Except for brief leave periods and one weekend a month when he visited his family in Charleston, he worked seven days a week. He visited units in the field or worked in the D-3 section's office tent and ate a sparse lunch at his desk. At the end of normal working hours, he had a drink or two (bourbon) at the officers' club before dinner in the mess. At one time or another, service in the division brought a flow of friends into the mess: Nimmer, Roy Hunt, John McQueen, Ed Snedeker, Wally Greene, Sam Griffith, Dudley Brown, Joe Fegan, Joe Burger, and L. B. Cresswell. After dinner, Thomas usually returned to his desk for some additional work. He then read, preferably military history, and turned in before 2200. He felt that his staff work improved steadily, and he took great pleasure in directing several division command post exercises and one major maneuver. Within the constraints he faced, largely the administrative obsessions of the Torrey-Monson team and the shortages of men and materiel, he saw the division make slow progress.[11]

In November, the 1st Marine Division received welcome reinforcements, a new assistant division commander, Brig. Gen. A. A. Vandegrift, and his handpicked operations officer, Maj. Merrill B. Twining, the brilliant defensive tactician fresh from the Marine Corps Schools. Vandegrift had persuaded Holcomb to let him leave Washington for field service, and he turned his duties as assistant commandant over to Stover Keyser, a proven Washington operator. Aware of

Holland Smith's lack of rapport with Torrey, Holcomb needed little persuasion to reassign Vandegrift, who (with Torrey's blessing) assumed principal responsibility for the division's training. Vandegrift's arrival promised to give the division staff more effectiveness in dealing with Smith and Erskine but did little to improve its functioning. Hunt, whom Vandegrift admired for his elan and battlefield courage, and Nimmer could not curb Monson's autocratic practice of dealing directly with the regimental and battalion commanders, and Vandegrift did nothing to challenge Monson's power over Torrey. Thomas and Twining, however, forged a close and effective team to support Vandegrift's efforts to improve training, even though Vandegrift rated a staff of his own, a practice Thomas and Twining criticized. (Reflecting European practice, the assistant division commander was supposed to be a de facto infantry brigade commander or "chief of infantry" for the division.) A taut, handsome, slight 1923 Naval Academy graduate, Twining had a command of operational concepts few other Marine officers possessed, but he did not rate as high (by his own admission) in tact, patience, and the art of compromise. Moreover, he had a tendency to tell other officers when they were wrong and he was right (as he almost always was) in words that left little doubt about his judgment of their professional abilities. He could not hide his contempt for Hunt and Monson. In short, Bill Twining needed more protection than Vandegrift, who hated personal confrontations, would provide. Jerry Thomas furnished the shield for Twining's sword, and at New River they forged a relationship that benefited both of them, as well as the Marine Corps.[12]

The bombs that landed on Pearl Harbor on 7 December 1941 sent shock waves across the United States, even into the dreary, wet pinewood along the New River. Word of the attack and America's entry into the war set off an orgy of speculation among the Marines, who had anticipated a relaxed holiday season. The 1st Marine Division still thought it faced a war in the Atlantic, especially when Germany declared war on the United States. The division began to shift to a war footing. The first change came in priorities: training increased and the burden of construction fell from the division's shoulders. New Marines—lieutenants from Quantico, privates from Parris Island—flooded into the division. Popular rage over Pearl Harbor and the subsequent heroic and well-publicized, but unsuccessful, defense of Wake Island brought thousands of would-be Marines into recruiting stations all over the country. Nearly three thousand men enlisted during the week after Pearl Harbor, and the weekly totals through February 1942 climbed to six thousand. The spirited volunteers more easily met and exceeded Corps entrance standards in intelligence and education. World War I Marines remembered the thrill of mobilization in 1917 and rushed the new men through only six weeks of recruit training, then shipped them directly to operational units, principally the 1st and 2d Divisions. The pre–Pearl Harbor oldtimers wondered if the new men, so full of vigor and braggadocio and so empty of discipline and military skills, would enrich or imperil the division's chances to join the battle.[13]

Jerry Thomas found little time for anything but his responsibilities as de facto D-3. He did, however, bring Jerry Junior up to New River from Charleston for a week of living in the field with the Marines. Young Jerry accompanied his father to the firing ranges and exercise areas and enjoyed the cocktail hour (he watched and ate snacks) each evening before dinner in General Torrey's mess, a large white farmhouse in a pecan grove off U.S. 17. He and his father returned to Charleston when Jerry took four days of Christmas leave. Since the division's future was so uncertain, Jerry promised Lottie that he would find the family a home in North Carolina, but housing in New Bern and Jacksonville for a family of six was not easy to find. Not until March did Thomas find a home on Fifth Avenue in Greenville, seventy miles from the base, which meant that he might visit his family on weekends. Wally Greene and Ed Snedeker also rented homes nearby for their families. The Thomas family settled into the social life of Greenville "for the duration."[14]

The first three months of 1942 brought a new level of organizational turmoil to the 1st Marine Division that taxed the entire division staff. In January, General Holcomb, succumbing to FDR's enthusiasm for creating American "commandos," ordered the creation of two complete "special" infantry battalions, which became the 1st and 2d Raider Battalions. The 1st Marine Division lost an entire battalion of the 5th Marines, which returned to Quantico for special operations training under two demanding leaders, Lt. Col. Merritt A. Edson and Maj. Samuel B. Griffith II. The issue of elite troops—raiders and paramarines—split the division staff and pitted Twining and Hunt against one another. Twining thought headquarters had collapsed under political pressure, and Hunt countered by charging Twining with disloyalty and a bookish lack of appreciation for the heroism of Marines. In February, the division's third infantry regiment, the 1st Marines, moved into the tent city from Parris Island. Only its field grade officers and about fifty sergeants had real experience in the peacetime Marine Corps; 90 percent of its enlisted men had joined the Marine Corps after Pearl Harbor. The 1st Marines, commanded by World War I hero Col. Clifton B. Cates and blessed with three good battalion commanders, showed more potential than the 5th Marines. It needed much individual and small unit training before it passed the "Boy Scout phase . . . camping out and cooking weenies," as Twining viewed its field work. In March, the division suffered a serious loss, the detachment of the 7th Marines to form the 3d Marine Brigade. The brigade commander, Brig. Gen. Charles D. Barrett, arrived from Washington with Holcomb's permission to take volunteers from the rest of the division to fill the brigade's ranks, and he carried off a disproportionate share of the division's talented junior officers and NCOs. Bound for Samoa to protect the island from a feared Japanese attack, the brigade also took with it a wartime allowance of weapons, equipment, and supplies.[15]

In the middle of the organizational turmoil, Holcomb relieved Torrey as the division commander and replaced him with Archer Vandegrift, who promptly made several critical personnel changes of his own. Already in Holland Smith's bad graces, Torrey allowed himself to be exploited in a raging feud between George Monson and Col. Pedro A. del Valle, the talented, outspoken, and mercurial commander of the 11th Marines. Since the division's arrival at New River, del Valle and Monson had clashed over the D-4's alleged discrimination against the artillery in matters of housing, equipment, messing facilities, and transportation. Then, adding to the bad blood, Torrey and del Valle exchanged heated words about the commanding general's role at a regimental review. Aware that Torrey wanted del Valle replaced, Monson encouraged Torrey to press Headquarters to investigate citizen reports that the indiscreet Puerto Rican aristocrat had made disparaging remarks about FDR and American policy toward Fascist Italy. Holcomb did indeed send an investigator, who cleared del Valle (barely), but he also discovered that Torrey, an ardent Irish-American, had made similar remarks about FDR's pro-British sympathies. Sensing blood, Holland Smith pressed Holcomb to replace Torrey, which the Commandant did. Holcomb countered by giving Vandegrift, also a rival of Smith's, a temporary promotion to major general and command of the 1st Marine Division.[16]

Vandegrift assumed command on 23 March with Smith and Bobby Erskine present at New River. A stubborn political infighter when sufficiently aroused, Vandegrift told Smith that he would straighten out the division's problems and that he would deal candidly and directly with the corps commander but not with Bobby Erskine. Erskine, however, did not believe that Vandegrift fully appreciated the need to rid his staff of Roy Hunt and George Monson. Vandegrift initially refused to bow to the pressure. Instead, he worked around Hunt and leaned on his new D-3, Jerry Thomas, who had become the division's operations officer a week before Torrey's relief. Vandegrift merged his own staff with Torrey's holdovers and negotiated an amicable reorganization of the D-3 staff, with Bill Twining as Thomas's principal assistant. Despite Thomas's warnings that Vandegrift would support Hunt out of loyalty, Twining encouraged the general to find a new chief of staff and D-4. Vandegrift had no love for Monson but would not relieve him until he was sure of an adequate replacement. Twining found one: Lt. Col. Randolph McCall Pate (Virginia Military Institute, 1921), a forty-four-year-old former division supply officer and logistical planner then stationed at Headquarters. The energetic, intelligent Pate welcomed the change, and he came to the division with a reputation for good work and the benefit of Lemuel C. Shepherd's confidence. Vandegrift solved the Hunt problem by arranging the transfer of the 5th Marines commander, Robert Blake. Vandegrift wanted a warrior to inspire the lackluster 5th Marines, so he gave the job to Roy Hunt, who relished the chance to lead his World War I regiment. His executive officer became Lt. Col. Bill Whaling, a Marine of legendary field skills but little administrative ability. Thomas and Twining doubted the wisdom of the Hunt-Whaling marriage, but Vandegrift and Kilmartin thought the 5th Marines would show new enthusiasm.[17]

Following the "unity and harmony" theme they had established for the division's staff, Holcomb, Keyser, and Vandegrift agreed to assign Col. W. Capers James as division chief of staff when Roy Hunt moved to the 5th Marines. Nothing in James's career suggested that he had any special qualifications to direct the staff of a combat division. A courteous, friendly forty-six-year-old South Carolinian, James was most noted for his efficient service as an administrator. Commissioned in February 1917 after graduation from The Citadel, James had served two years in the Dominican Republic (1917–19) and one year in Nicaragua (1927) but had made his name as a barracks commander in China (1937–39). His most recent assignment had been military secretary to General Holcomb, which meant that Vandegrift knew his work. James's and Keyser's wives were cousins and also cousins of Lottie Thomas. James and Thomas enjoyed good personal relations, but Thomas did not respect James's ability as a field Marine. On the other hand, James would not bar his direct access to Vandegrift with whom Thomas, Twining observed, enjoyed a close association bordering on paternal-filial. Twining suspected that Vandegrift wanted Thomas to be de facto chief of staff, as well as D-3.[18]

    The collapse of the fragile Allied defenses in the western Pacific opened a great oceanic salient that began in the east at the India-Burma border and ended thousands of miles away at the atoll of Midway Island. To the south, Japanese forces captured the Dutch East Indies and Malaya and penetrated the Australian-governed islands of New Britain, New Ireland, New Guinea, and the Solomons chain. The Malay Barrier, along which the Allies had hoped to halt the Japanese, had been breached below the Equator as far as the international date line. Responsive to the alarms of the Australian and New Zealand governments, Winston Churchill pushed Roosevelt to send reinforcements to the South Pacific. Forces originally ordered to the Philippines (which finally fell in May) gathered in Australia; other units stopped along the route to Australia to defend the major islands, such as Samoa and New Caledonia, that protected the lines of communication from the United States. Although the Joint Chiefs of Staff (JCS) and the Navy recognized that the immediate challenge was defensive, Chief of Naval Operations Adm. Ernest J. King ordered his planning staff to look for objectives of opportunity in the South Pacific as early as February 1942. King recognized that he could use the defensive deployments, confirmed in JCS memo 23 (14 March 1942), to build up forces for later offensive operations. In late March, General Holcomb felt sure that the 1st Marine Division would deploy and had Stover Keyser call Vandegrift. Keyser, using a nonsecure telephone, told Vandegrift that "something is going to happen to you people" five days after his (Keyser's) birthday, which happened to be 10 May.[19]

    Following Keyser's cryptic instructions to "send Jerry Thomas to Washington next Monday, and we'll give him the dope on what's going to happen," Vandegrift ordered his curious D-3 to catch the train for Washington. Thomas spent 5 and 6 April 1942 in Washington with Navy and Marine planners, principally Rear Adm. Richmond Kelly Turner and Col. DeWitt Peck, and learned that the 1st Marine Division would depart for New Zealand in mid-May. He and Vandegrift returned to Washington about ten days later to confirm their final plans for deployment. The challenge of the mount-out appeared awesome but not insurmountable because everyone assumed that the division would go to New Zealand to train. The 1st Division was not combat ready; in April, no one believed that it would fight in 1942. Therefore, the division could be organized for administrative efficiency, which meant the prompt and full use of the available shipping and port facilities. Supply ships with small detachments of Marines would sail from New Orleans, Gulfport, Mississippi, and Norfolk. Vandegrift would take one major troop element, the 5th Marines (reinforced), by transport from Norfolk, and the new assistant division commander, Brig. Gen. William H. Rupertus (with Kilmartin as his chief of staff), would lead the 1st Marines (reinforced) by train to California where they would board other transports. In the meantime, Vandegrift sent Bill Twining to New Zealand to plan the division's arrival and movement into training camps. Twining saw a new world when Jerry told him that he was authorized to spend as much money as necessary in New Zealand.[20]

From his first Washington conference to the day he walked aboard the U.S.S. *Wakefield* with General Vandegrift on 15 May, Jerry Thomas supervised the organization of the division for its overseas trip. His functions extended well beyond those of the D-3. He worked with Kilmartin and Kilmartin's assistant, twenty-nine-year-old Capt. James C. Murray, a Yale graduate (1936) with a quick mind and closed mouth, to assign a new flood of officers and enlisted men. He conferred with Frank Goettge, the tireless D-2, a former All-America halfback, whose physical energy and enthusiasm for intelligence work sometimes exceeded his judgment. Thomas and Pate supervised the unloading and distribution of the sudden flood of field uniforms, weapons, equipment, and supplies that arrived by rail into the middle of Tent Camp One, and they went together to New Orleans (7 April) to reorganize the loading of two supply ships. Thomas met constantly with Vandegrift to review details of the deployment. He stayed in touch with Bill Twining by radio, and Twining confirmed that the division should bring everything it needed with it, including a whisky ration. (Vandegrift doubted this advice; he told Thomas he had never served anywhere he couldn't buy a drink.) Throughout the preparatory period, Thomas enhanced his position as Vandegrift's principal advisor and judge of staff ideas, good and bad. Bill Twining thought Thomas could say "no" more easily than any other officer he knew, and yet he could move more forcefully (often too stubbornly, Twining also thought) when he was certain he knew what course of action to take. By the time the *Wakefield* hit the first ocean swells off Cape Henry point, Thomas had demonstrated his ascendancy within the 1st Division staff.[21]

[CHAPTER XV]

The Road to CACTUS
June–August 1942

BELOW THE CONGESTED streets around Washington's Farragut Square, a portrait of Gen. Gerald C. Thomas, looking out over the basement corridor of the Army and Navy Club, guards the club's guest book and a gallery of photographs of other American military leaders. Painted in 1975 by Peter Egeli, a Maryland portraitist favored by officers in the Washington area, the picture shows Thomas in retirement, resplendent in dress blues and a career's worth of decorations, domestic and foreign. The portrait is a good likeness. Thomas's iron gray hair is combed to the rear, his bushy eyebrows prominent above his clear hazel eyes. Commissioned by several of his Marine comrades, the Thomas portrait also shows a kidney-shaped, two-toned green island that dominates the background. The brass plate below the painting tells the visitor that General Thomas served twice as the club president (1955 and 1971) and fought in three major wars and "numerous expeditions beyond the seas," but the portrait shows only one of the many places where Thomas heard the sound of the guns. The island is the place where Jerry Thomas's career moved into the nation's history. The island is Guadalcanal, code-named CACTUS.

Although Franklin D. Roosevelt and the Joint Chiefs of Staff in March 1942 approved a Navy plan for an offensive in the South Pacific, Adm. Ernest J. King did not like the pace or organization of the preparations for the offensive. Other priorities intruded: the buildup of American forces in the British Isles; the forlorn reinforcements for Gen. Douglas MacArthur, who was physically in Australia but whose heart was still in the Philippines; the deployment of air and ground forces to protect the line of communications to Australia and New Zealand through New Caledonia, the Tongas, Samoa, the New Hebrides, and the Fijis. In the meantime, the studies flowed from the War Plans Division, headed by the brilliant but irascible Rear Adm. Richmond Kelly Turner. When the JCS finally ordered MacArthur and his fellow theater commander, Adm. Chester W. Nimitz

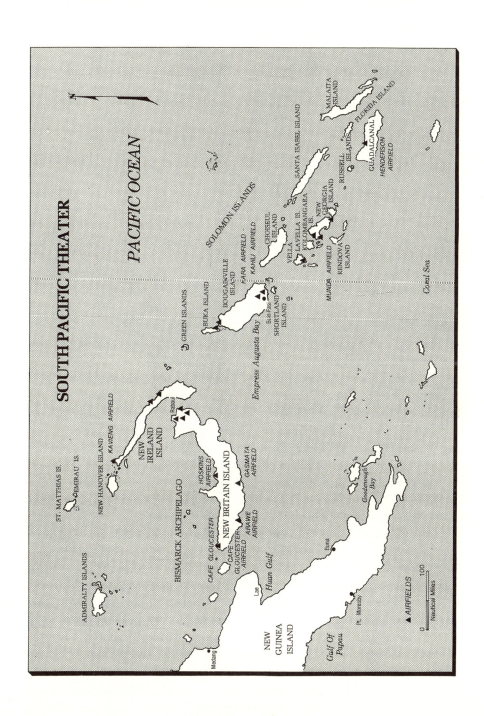

(Commander Pacific Ocean Areas), to begin their own general planning, King already had a fair idea of where he wanted the first counteroffensive and how he wanted it to be conducted. By mid-April, King's gaze fixed on the lower Solomon Islands and the Santa Cruz islands to the east, between 550 and 250 miles to the northwest of the New Hebrides. The Japanese high command in Tokyo read the same maps. Concentrating a part of the Combined Fleet in southern waters, the Japanese attempted a coup de main against the remaining Allied positions on New Guinea, an offensive that produced the battle of the Coral Sea (4–8 May 1942). As part of this operation, Japanese naval forces occupied the small island of Tulagi in the southern Solomons and changed it from a rustic colonial port and British administrative center into a base for seaplanes and reconnaissance vessels.[1]

Despite their setback in the Battle of the Coral Sea, the Japanese did not surrender their plan to eliminate Australia and New Zealand as threats to their new conquests along the Malay Barrier. On 18 May, Imperial General Headquarters (IGHQ) ordered the Japanese Army and Navy commanders in the South Pacific to prepare for a major attack against New Caledonia, Fiji, and Samoa. The primary Japanese effort, however, would come in the central Pacific where Adm. Isoroku Yamamoto sought a decisive engagement with the U.S. Pacific Fleet near Midway Island. The Japanese radio traffic flowed in torrents across the Pacific; Navy radio intelligence listening stations recorded it, and Admiral Nimitz's code breakers and analysts waded through the intercepts in order to determine both enemy capabilities and intentions. Amid the information they gleaned was that the Japanese planned to occupy Guadalcanal, seventeen miles south of Tulagi. When the first Japanese from Tulagi crossed the straits and landed on Guadalcanal on 28 May, they found the handful of white settlers gone and the Melanesian natives in short supply. On 19 June, a Japanese survey party started work on airfield planning. By the end of the month, the engineers and Korean laborers had begun to build a single runway strip and supporting installations. Coastwatchers, British and Australians recruited for stay-behind intelligence operations, reported the activity by radio, and Allied reconnaissance aircraft confirmed the Guadalcanal construction project in the last week of June.[2]

In the meantime, King and Nimitz forced the issue of a Solomons offensive, with the unlikely support of MacArthur, against the predictable reluctance of Army Chief of Staff George C. Marshall. They gained another ally in the British Chiefs of Staff Committee, which did not relish a major offensive against the Germans in 1942 and saw the Navy's ardor for the Pacific war as a useful way to defer Marshall's "Germany First" campaign until the Wehrmacht had bled a little more in Russia. The U.S. Navy's stunning victory in the Battle of Midway (4–5 June 1942) opened the way for a little strategic opportunism, if only to disrupt the Japanese plans to attack the islands east of Australia. MacArthur, as was his wont, proposed a direct strike on the Japanese stronghold of Rabaul on the eastern tip of New Britain, a plan well beyond anyone's capabilities. On June 25, even before he was sure that Marshall and Roosevelt would accept a more conservative plan (Cartwheel) for the capture of Rabaul, King ordered Nimitz to use his own forces to seize and occupy Tulagi and the Santa Cruz islands (specifically Ndeni, a suitable airbase site) as early as 1 August. The first hint that Guadalcanal might also be an objective came on 26 June when the JCS approved a theater boundary change that brought the island into Nimitz's theater or, more precisely, a subsidiary theater, the South Pacific Area (SoPac). The Marshall–King negotiations continued until both were satisfied that they had a workable plan involving both MacArthur and Nimitz and employing Army ground and air forces under Nimitz's command. The JCS issued formal orders on 2 July to commence Task 1 of Cartwheel, which directed MacArthur to clear New Guinea and Nimitz to seize and occupy Tulagi, the Santa Cruz group, and "adjacent areas."[3]

Within Nimitz's headquarters, known as Commander in Chief Pacific Fleet (CinCPac), the task of bringing operational form to Task 1 fell to Kelly Turner, released from his war plans assignment in Washington for sea duty in the Pacific. A tall, beetle-browed, heavy-drinking, intimidating surface line officer, Turner glared from behind his glasses at the outside world and flooded his harried subordinates with operational opinions in which he deeply believed, whether he knew anything about the subject or not. Although most often he did, amphibious operations were not his specialty, a deficiency he shared with almost all of the Navy's 1942 admirals. Campaign planning, however, was his forte, even though he often assumed he knew the enemy's intentions as well as his own. He knew King's plans for a Solomons offensive because he had drafted them. He also knew that he was supposed to be an amphibious force commander, but he did not know his mission and task organization. Coming off a shortened leave en route to Hawaii, he learned on 30 June that the JCS would issue a binding directive for a South Pacific offensive and that he would be responsible for the amphibious portion of Task 1 in the Solomons. He also learned that he would have to brief Nimitz and King at a 3 July conference in San Francisco. With only a skeleton staff, he produced a general concept for Operation Pestilence—the occupation of undefended Ndeni and the seizure of defended Tulagi and Guadalcanal, as well as related operations in the lower Solomons and the Ellice Islands, eight hundred miles east of Ndeni. Although Turner's concept was vague on priorities and timing, he identified Guadalcanal as important as the other islands.[4]

Some uncertainty about the extent and pace of Japanese airfield construction on Guadalcanal may have persisted, but Turner needed little of his vaunted genius to understand that he needed land-based air support to complete his mission. The prevailing wisdom on carrier operations in the Pacific was that carriers could conduct raids on bases and carry the burden in sea battles but that they were too vulnerable to submarines, aircraft, and warships for sustained support of land operations. Some pessimists even thought that carriers could not operate safely beyond the support of land-based aircraft. The reality was that the Navy had already lost two of its six carriers in the Pacific. Although Guadalcanal and Ndeni eventually proved worlds apart in value, they had one thing in common: each could be the site of airfields. Tulagi and Florida Island, which glowered above Tulagi, were either too small or too mountainous for air bases. Whether Turner divined the air imperative on his own—which he might have—is uncertain, but he had the expert counsel of five staff officers, three of whom were Marines well schooled in amphibious operations. Approving Turner's general plan, King and Nimitz ordered him to report to his immediate superior, Vice Adm. Robert L. Ghormley, Commander South Pacific Area (ComSoPac), and further develop the plan. Ghormley had already received a warning order (25 June) that Pestilence would soon arrive to plague the Japanese; Turner headed for a prearranged conference with him in Auckland, New Zealand. Turner also knew that he would find the 1st Marine Division awaiting him "down under."[5]

In blissful ignorance, the advanced echelon of the 1st Marine Division, which included division headquarters, passed through the Panama Canal from 25 to 28 May. The Marines watched the jungle fade behind as the *Wakefield* set course for New Zealand. The major enterprise of the Canal transit was the purchase of four hundred cases of scotch and bourbon for the officers mess. The next excitement occurred ten days out of New Zealand when the transport ran into heavy seas and a large wave flooded the open troop compartments. The war seemed far away, even though the troops held the usual emergency drills, did some minimal physical training, and cared for their equipment and weapons between eating and vomiting. Jerry Thomas shared a stateroom with Frank Goettge, Ran Pate, and Capers James. Thomas had plenty of time to read military history because there was little business. Before dinner he went to General Vandegrift's adjoining stateroom for a drink. He thought about his family and looked forward to the end of the voyage and the inactivity.

On Sunday, 14 June, the *Wakefield* made landfall at North Island. Before she turned into Wellington harbor, the Marines gazed in wonder at a land of sharp hills, fields of sheep and yellow gorse, pastures so green they looked painted, and neat villages. The transport tied up at Aotea Quay and disgorged its excited Marines. Among the first down the gangplank were Vandegrift and Thomas, eager to talk with Bill Twining, who awaited them with information on off-loading and billeting. Twining had good news and bad news, all of it administrative. New Zealand authorities had built and provisioned a cantonment for the 5th Marines (reinforced) and would have quarters ready for the second echelon when it arrived from California. The local longshoremen, however, worked only union hours and at English speed, so off-loading would take days unless the Marines did it themselves. Vandegrift promptly ordered the Marines to stevedore duty, despite civilian protests. His own headquarters, the Hotel Cecil of Victorian decor and aged inhabitants, had not yet been readied. He and his staff stayed aboard the *Wakefield*, the better to see it unloaded and the troops marched off to their camp and some welcome liberty in Wellington. On 19–20 June, the 1st Marine Division advanced echelon had cleared the *Wakefield* and settled in ashore.[6]

As Vandegrift made his courtesy calls on the New Zealand authorities and the American ambassador, Thomas simultaneously managed the tasks of planning division training and drafting contingency plans for the defense of North Island. The first task took priority. Because James had not taken hold as division chief of staff, Jerry found himself also working with Jim Murray and Pate on personnel and logistical matters. Thomas sent Twining on an aerial reconnaissance in Vandegrift's Beechcraft; when Twining reported he could find no good beaches on North Island for amphibious training, Jerry himself reconnoitered another site on South Island and found it suitable. He and Twining were totally absorbed with getting training under way. Even an earthquake that rocked the Hotel Cecil and disconcerted Vandegrift only annoyed them because it interrupted their sleep and forced them to persuade the commanding general not to move his command post

(CP). While Thomas was making his aerial reconnaissance, however, Admiral Ghormley on 25 June radioed Vandegrift that he must see him the next day at ComSoPac headquarters at Auckland. The message did not surprise Vandegrift, although Ghormley had earlier indicated that there was no hurry for them to meet in person. He had been reading ComSoPac's message traffic, decoded and brought to him by Lt. Sanford B. Hunt, his cryptographic officer. Vandegrift took Thomas, Goettge, and Snedeker with him in the Beechcraft to Auckland and the biggest surprise of their lives.[7]

Dropping his staff at a hotel in downtown Auckland, Vandegrift rode the remaining two blocks to Ghormley's headquarters in anxious silence. Ghormley, a fifty-eight-year-old battleship admiral noted for his staff skills and high intelligence, greeted Vandegrift with uncharacteristic directness and told him he had bad news. He then handed the Marine general Admiral King's 24 June (Washington date) message to Nimitz directing him to prepare an offensive in the southern Solomons (Tulagi) and Santa Cruz islands, to commence as early as 1 August. The message also suggested the "information addressees," Ghormley and MacArthur, confer on objectives, forces, command structure, and timing. The message implied that further official guidance would follow, as it did with the 2 July JCS directive on Operation Pestilence. Vandegrift read the message several times, then called Thomas and told him, Goettge, and Snedeker to hurry to ComSoPac headquarters. There Thomas read the King message. "Everyone seemed amazed. . . . COMSOPAC [was] flabbergasted."[8] Vandegrift and Thomas explained to Ghormley, his chief of staff (Rear Adm. Daniel J. Callaghan), and his plans officer (Marine Col. DeWitt Peck) the difficulties the 1st Marine Division would have in concentrating and reorganizing for a landing presumably only five weeks away. The conference quickly agreed that ComSoPac, who was supposed to fly to Australia to see MacArthur, should ask for a temporary delay in the landing. The meeting broke up, and Thomas went off with Peck to discuss planning while Goettge and Snedeker met with their counterparts.[9]

Returning to Wellington the same day, Vandegrift and Thomas made the basic decisions that started their division toward Guadalcanal. They did not know that Kelly Turner would be their commander or what the admiral might have as a campaign plan. They knew virtually nothing about the Japanese order of battle in the southern Solomons or the topography of the islands. Vandegrift sent Goettge to Australia on an intelligence fishing expedition, especially to learn what he could from refugees and the coastwatchers' reports. Maps, coastal charts, aerial photographs, and live guides were the highest priority. Thomas could not do detailed planning without more information, but he thought through the implications of King's warning order while he awaited more guidance. He could, however, get the division moving. At Thomas's recommendation, Vandegrift ordered Roy Hunt's 5th Marines to reembark on three assault transports, much to the troops' dismay. Vandegrift and his staff announced that the 5th Marines (reinforced) would stage an amphibious exercise; in the meantime, working parties labored around the clock on Aotea Quay to unload ten cargo ships arriving with the division's supplies and heavy equipment. Their task was to load twenty-three transports and supply ships. The Marines received some help from skilled New Zealand heavy equipment operators and enjoyed superior cooperation with Capt.

Lawrence F. Reifsnider, USN, commander of the SoPac transport divisions. Even without a firm landing plan, the division could at least reload for combat operations and assess what it could take and what it must leave behind. These concerns were magnified by ten days of cold spring rain and the sloth of the sulking 5th Marines.[10]

Vandegrift and Thomas spent part of each dripping day on the docks. They consulted with Ran Pate, the D-4, and watched the equipment and palletized cargo lift from the quay and swing toward the ships' holds. Neither liked the way the 5th Marines had turned to, and Vandegrift had hard words with Roy Hunt. Thomas and Twining dealt even more abruptly with two of Hunt's battalion commanders, who showed little interest in the reloading or the well-being of their troops. The quay itself was a jumble of equipment and disintegrating cardboard boxes; packing labels from cartons and cans slid into the goo on the docks. The division staff concluded that the division could not sail with all its impedimenta. It would have to go without much of its personal baggage, tentage, and comfort supplies. More critical was the decision to leave behind trucks, smaller vehicles, and engineering equipment and to cut bulk consumables (fuels, lubricants, and food) to sixty days of resupply and to reduce the ammunition allowance to ten days of fire. It also planned to leave a rear echelon composed largely of excess headquarters troops, service details, the MP company, part of the tank battalion, and the 150-mm heavy guns of the 4th Battalion, 11th Marines. The rear echelon in Wellington had 112 officers and 1,617 enlisted men. The division staff shared other planners' estimate that the Solomons operation deserved to be called "Shoestring."[11]

Thomas and Twining spent much of their time in a chill room of the Hotel Cecil working on a draft operations order. They had little assistance. The only other officers in the D-3 section were Capt. Clarence R. Schwenke, one of Vandegrift's aides, and Maj. Henry W. Buse, Jr., whom Thomas had taught at The Basic School. Thomas told Buse that the 1st Tank Battalion (Buse was the executive officer) was not likely to embark and that Buse was now an assistant D-3. The D-3 section worked in splendid isolation, for ComSoPac had little additional guidance for it or Snedeker's communications planners. When Goettge returned to Wellington on 15 July, CinCPac had still not provided more information.

Nevertheless, Thomas decided before he returned to Auckland on 1 July for another meeting with DeWitt Peck that Guadalcanal should be the focus of the campaign. He was not yet aware that Kelly Turner had come to the same conclusion and would put Guadalcanal by name into his 3 July concept paper for King and Nimitz. Conferring with Peck, Thomas proposed that Guadalcanal and Tulagi be seized simultaneously; Guadalcanal would require the major effort to ensure capture and exploitation of the airfield. Ghormley agreed to the concept before Thomas returned to Wellington the next day.

Nimitz and Turner returned to Pearl Harbor on 5 July. The most recent radio intelligence had convinced them that Guadalcanal was indeed the most *pressing* objective for Task 1, now code-named Watchtower. Whether they thought it was the most important objective of the campaign remained to be seen. In any event, CinCPac flooded message centers from California to New Zealand with directives assigning forces to Watchtower before Turner left Pearl Harbor on 8 July. The major reinforcements for the landing force would be the 1st Raider Battalion, the 1st Parachute Battalion, the 3d Defense Battalion, and (most welcome) a third infantry regiment, the 2d Marines. Additional information about the task organization, including the assignment of amphibious shipping, made Thomas's detailed planning less uncertain but no less anxious. Basically, he and Peck had to carry the planning burden because Turner and his staff had left Hawaii by plane without drafting an operation order; harried by poor weather they did not arrive in Auckland until 15 July. ComSoPac had the responsibility of organizing and tasking land-based air support and the complete naval expeditionary force, which would include three carrier task forces and the amphibious forces of cruisers, destroyers, and the amphibious shipping. Thomas attacked the problem of making two landings the same day, seizing the division's initial objectives, and then working backward from the scheme of maneuver ashore to a landing plan and a detailed loading plan. He had to ensure that the ComSoPac operation order reflected the division's views on the campaign. He also probably recognized the benefits of having at least the ComSoPac order ready and approved by Ghormley before Turner arrived. Time could not wait on Kelly Turner.[12]

From the "Black Room" in the Cecil, Thomas's work took shape in the form of a draft operation order, the required annexes and appendices, and the supporting crude maps and overlays. Frank Goettge returned from Australia with eight Guadalcanal "experts," some rough maps and charts, and mounting radio intelligence about the Japanese order of battle. He had arranged for a detailed aerial map of the area around the mouth of the Lunga River and the Japanese airfield, the focus of Japanese activity on Guadalcanal. Other initial objectives, Tulagi and the smaller islands of Gavutu-Tanambogo, received close analysis. The enemy situation on the ground looked strong. There might be as many as 2,500 Japanese combat troops on Guadalcanal. The rest of the garrison was composed of 2,500 engineering troops and Korean laborers. Tulagi and its environs were defended by one of the Japanese Navy's elite special landing forces. As Thomas and Twining deduced—and convinced Vandegrift—the key to the operation was to get ashore as quickly as possible, establish defenses against a counterlanding, get Allied aviation on Guadalcanal as soon as possible, and await the predictable Japanese air, naval, and amphibious onslaught. They remained uncertain just how long it would take the division to get ashore but estimated that it would probably require four or five days. They also quickly saw that they badly needed control of the 2d Marines, assigned to the expeditionary force but not yet attached to the 1st Marine Division.[13]

When Kelly Turner arrived in Auckland on 15 July to meet with Ghormley, he found ComSoPac Op Order 1-42 ready and awaiting only Ghormley's signature and his own hurried blessing. He also learned that Ghormley, having conferred with MacArthur, had serious reservations about Watchtower. Ghormley and MacArthur had urged reconsideration of the operation. The JCS had done this on 10 July and confirmed everything but the landing date, which it allowed to slip to 7 August. Certainly, the 1st Marine Division needed every additional day. Its second echelon did not arrive in New Zealand until 11 July, and other reinforcements still remained at sea. Vandegrift had done all he could to prepare General Rupertus and the 1st Marines (reinforced) for a strange reception; a radio message to Rupertus suggested his force faced a dockside reorganization and instant reembarkation. After welcoming the second echelon amid the soggy rubbish on Aotea Quay, Vandegrift and Thomas returned again to Auckland to meet with Ghormley and Turner on 15 July. The same day, they dispatched Bill

Twining and Maj. William B. McKean of Reifsnider's staff on another aerial reconnaissance of Guadalcanal and Tulagi. The Marines found Ghormley pessimistic and Turner assertive. Vandegrift, under great pressure but always the soul of courtesy, took an immediate disliking to Turner, who held forth at length on all the unsatisfactory aspects of the operation, including Thomas's concept of the landing and operations ashore. Nevertheless, Turner, without a plan of his own, could not stop Ghormley from signing the Watchtower order on 16 July. Turner accepted Thomas's concept of operations, probably because he saw that he could not land on 7 August if he demanded the reloading a change would require.[14]

By the time Thomas and the rest of Vandegrift's staff embarked on Turner's flagship *McCawley* (AP-10) on 19 July, Thomas had a much clearer picture of the problems Vandegrift faced with Kelly Turner. His counterparts on Turner's staff, Capt. James H. Doyle, USN, and Lt. Col. Henry D. Linscott, USMC, proved eager to use the division draft operations order as the basis for their own order, but Thomas postponed delivery three days until he was satisfied that the order was correct and even less likely to be changed. For one thing, Thomas suspected Linscott would encourage Turner to force unwanted revisions. He pressed DeWitt Peck to insist that Ghormley back up Vandegrift if Turner insisted on changes. No sooner had the Marine command group embarked than Turner began to lecture the officers about their exaggerated emphasis on taking and defending the Guadalcanal airstrip; he told Vandegrift that the Marines' concept of the operation was too bookish, which angered even Vandegrift. Turner made his point by refusing to give Vandegrift the 2d Marines and providing only one battalion of the regiment as a temporary reserve during the landing. The first confrontation with Turner drove home to Vandegrift and Thomas their gnawing suspicion that Ghormley had not made clear enough that the land operations should be Vandegrift's province after the landing phase ended. Turner intended to play general as well as admiral. He also insisted that Vandegrift and Thomas eat with him aboard the *McCawley*, which meant that the admiral could ruin every meal with long sermons on the principles of war. Thomas found it difficult not to talk back, his ill temper heightened by his constant concern about the Commander Amphibious Force South Pacific (ComPhibForSoPac) operation order.[15]

Tension and anticipation built around Wellington harbor like thunderheads above the mountains of North Island. By 21 July, most of Turner's Task Force (TF) 62 had made the rendezvous, including five cruisers and seven destroyers, the heart of Rear Adm. (Royal Navy) V. A. C. Crutchley's covering force. The *McCawley* swung at anchor, ready to depart for the rehearsal on 28–30 July at Koro, Fiji Islands. Thomas and Capers James signed the division operation order on 20 July, but it took another week to have it duplicated, assembled, and distributed throughout TF 62. Turner's own operation order did not appear until 30 July. For better or worse, the 1st Marine Division had its plan in final form. The Guadalcanal Group (Vandegrift) would land across Red Beach, six thousand yards east of the mouth of the Lunga and the airfield, with two battalions of the 5th Marines in the lead and the whole 1st Marines to follow, supported by the guns of the 11th Marines and the 1st Special Weapons Battalion. The 5th Marines would pivot west and take the airfield while the 1st Marines would make a deeper pivot inland to take the high ground south of the airfield. Although Roy Hunt's objective was clear enough, Clifton Cates's was not. Guadalcanal residents identified the critical high ground as "the grassy knoll," a ridge about two miles from the airfield, but photo and map analysis pointed to higher ground (Mount Austen) much farther from the field. In careless usage, "the grassy knoll" became Mount Austen and the distant height became the 1st Marines' objective. A Support Group (Pedro del Valle) would provide a quick beach defense and unload the flow of vehicles and supplies. The Northern Group (Rupertus with Robert Kilmartin as chief of staff) would clear two promontories on Florida Island (probably undefended) with a 2d Marines battalion and capture Tulagi with the 1st Raider Battalion and 2d Battalion, 5th Marines. The 1st Parachute Battalion would seize Gavutu-Tanambogo.[16]

Thomas chose the Red Beach landing site, and Bill Twining thought he picked the wrong place to come ashore. If the beaches were defended, the concave Red Beach would provide the Japanese with interlocking fields of fire; a convex point nearer the Lunga had an adequate (if smaller) beach and reduced the fields of fire. If the beaches were undefended, the alternate landing site put the 5th Marines nearer the airfield and shortened the distance that equipment and supplies would have to travel to the proposed logistical sites ashore. Convinced that landing at Red Beach would postpone a serious battle until most of the division was ashore, Thomas told Twining, before Twining left on his Guadalcanal reconnaissance, that the issue was no longer debatable. Thomas also probably believed that the Navy's inexperienced boat crews and poorly maintained boats would need all the beach they could find to land the Marines. Because the division embarked less than half of its vehicles, moving supplies from the beach was a risk taken and known.[17]

The division staff looked in vain for more definitive information on the enemy situation, but a series of events blurred Japanese deployments in the objective area: Radio intelligence information faded when the Japanese finally changed some of their codes; on the run from Japanese patrols, the principal Guadalcanal coastwatcher, Capt. Martin Clemens, shut down his radio; the detailed photo map taken by the U.S. Army Air Forces (USAAF) became lost in transit to the *McCawley*. The Twining reconnaissance over Guadalcanal, flown on 17 July, produced some angry Zeros, but little new information except that the beaches appeared unobstructed and the airfield nearly complete. When Twining joined the *McCawley* in the Fijis on 26 July, he found the enemy situation no clearer. He also learned that Watchtower had developed serious problems beyond those he already knew.[18]

On the afternoon of Sunday, 26 July, Vice Adm. Frank Jack Fletcher, USN, called his principal subordinates of the Solomons expeditionary force to a conference aboard the *Saratoga*, one of three carriers in his TF 61. Fletcher had not had a good war; he had already lost two carriers under his command. The one great victory in which he had participated, Midway, was not his handiwork, and the Japanese had forced him to shift his flag by sinking the *Yorktown*. Marines blamed him for failing to relieve Wake Island. Critics then and now thought that he would rather fuel than fight, a reference to his uncanny ability to avoid contact. In Fletcher's defense, Nimitz had warned him to be cautious with TF 61 with no second Midway in prospect. Fletcher had little taste for putting TF 61 in harm's way in the lower Solomons, where it could be reached by Japan's land-based aircraft, submarines, battleships, and cruisers. When Turner and Vandegrift told him they needed five days for the amphibious assault and off-loading, Fletcher

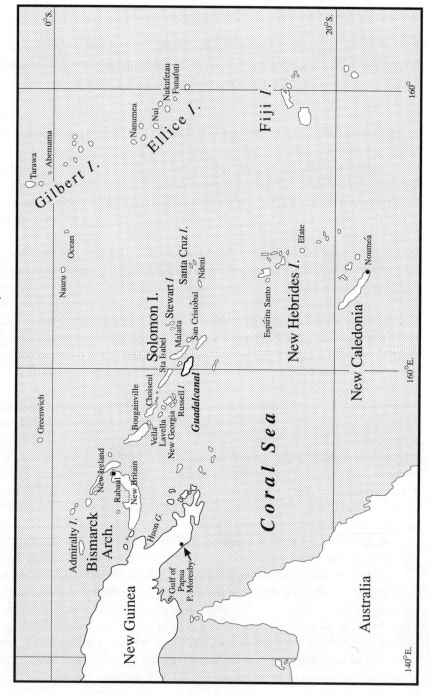

announced that he would provide forty-eight hours of air support. The conferees listened in shock, then argued that this decision endangered Watchtower. Ghormley had vested tactical command afloat in Fletcher the day before; only ComSoPac himself could overrule Fletcher, and he was not present. Indeed, Ghormley had decided to come no closer than his anchored flagship, a destroyer tender, in Nouméa Harbor, New Caledonia, one thousand miles from Guadalcanal. Turner, however, could have appealed the decision to Ghormley by message or through Callaghan, who was present. After he failed to dissuade Fletcher in passionate argument, Turner simply gave up the fight. Not silent himself, Vandegrift listened in dismay to a second admiral say that he had no faith in Watchtower. Vandegrift in turn told Thomas, who was not present at the meeting, of the further decline of air support. The best the Marines could hope for was that Rear Adm. John S. McCain, commander of all South Pacific land-based air, would make good on his promise to send Marine and Army squadrons to Guadalcanal as soon as the Marines could get the strip operational. No one doubted McCain's sincerity, but his promise depended on Ghormley's approval.[19]

Throughout the final preparations off Koro, including an ill-managed rehearsal on 28 and 30 July, Thomas retained his optimism. On 29 July, he briefed the unit commanders of the division on board the *McCawley* with complete composure. He warned the officers on the D-3 section that they should concentrate on events they could influence, not those they could not. He and Vandegrift worked as amicably as possible with Turner, who had taken out his considerable and justified wrath on the transport commanders until they repaired their landing craft and trained their crews to work more quickly. In truth, there was not much that could be done now, 1,100 miles and one week away from Dog-Day. Thomas might have thought about Guadalcanal, 90 miles long and 30 miles wide, divided by a volcanic spine of mountains that radiated rivers and ridges down to the island's northern plain. Where the well-spaced coconut trees of the plantations along the Lunga surrendered to the jungle, the trees and vines of tropical rain forest alternated with coral ridges bristling with sharp kunai grass. Although the temperature seldom reached ninety degrees, the humidity, fed by eighty inches of annual rainfall, did reach that figure. For men unaccustomed to jungle warfare, Guadalcanal would be a test but less so than the strain of combat itself.

Perhaps Thomas thought about the Japanese. He knew them well from his days in Peiping and probably had no illusions about their tenacity. He might also have remembered their arrogance and inflexibility, their incredible conviction in their own spiritual superiority, and their contempt for the white man's softness. Thomas most certainly thought more about the defense of the airfield, for him the central and only *fact* of the campaign. When Twining returned to the *McCawley*, Thomas ordered his assistant to draw up a defense of the airfield. With misgiving, Twining organized a conventional sector defense in depth, according to current doctrine. The forces at hand seemed inadequate to the task, and the terrain and conditions inappropriate. Thomas did not like the plan either and told Twining so, but he did not yet have an alternative—at least not one that he believed Vandegrift and Turner would accept. Perhaps Thomas thought about Belleau Wood and Soissons and the anxiety of young Marines facing first battle as the transports slid through the dark waters of the Coral Sea toward the retreating horizon. As Thomas knew from experience and study, planning remained prologue.[20]

[CHAPTER XVI]

Division Operations Officer on Guadalcanal
7 August–22 September 1942

RUNNING IN RADIO SILENCE and with ships darkened, the seventy-five warships and transports of Admiral Fletcher's Task Force 61, concealed by low clouds, turned north in the Coral Sea and headed for Guadalcanal. To the embarked Marines, the task force looked like an invincible armada, the largest massing of American naval power yet deployed against Japan. Only the senior commanders knew that this fleet represented a cutting edge that had no blade behind it. Adm. John McCain's land-based air force could offer little help beyond an occasional (and probably ineffectual) B-17 bombing raid and long-range reconnaissance until it received further air reinforcements from Admiral Nimitz and, more grudgingly, from the Army Air Forces. The plans for the logistical support of the landing force were, at best, incomplete. For the first weeks ashore, the 1st Marine Division would have to depend on the equipment and supplies in the holds of its transports and cargo ships. Its own depot remained two thousand miles away in New Zealand; the 1,700-man depot force was its only source of replacements. Given the risks Ghormley, Fletcher, Turner, and Vandegrift had assumed, they and their forces had to be both expert and lucky. They were neither.[1]

While the Navy worried about Japanese submarines and reconnaissance aircraft, Jerry Thomas, Frank Goettge, and Bill Twining worked in their cramped office in the bowels of the *McCawley* on several variations of their original operation order. The conditions aboard the hot, packed transport added to the tension. When the executive officer, a zealot, tried to kill the D-3's lighting one night, Thomas and Goettge threw him out of the compartment. Their immediate problem was to anticipate what changes they would have to make in the landing if one or more of the troop transports stopped a torpedo. Given the multiple tasks the Marines faced, such planning only emphasized the thin troop list and the understrength infantry battalions. Any emergency would require another con-

[172]

The Solomon Islands

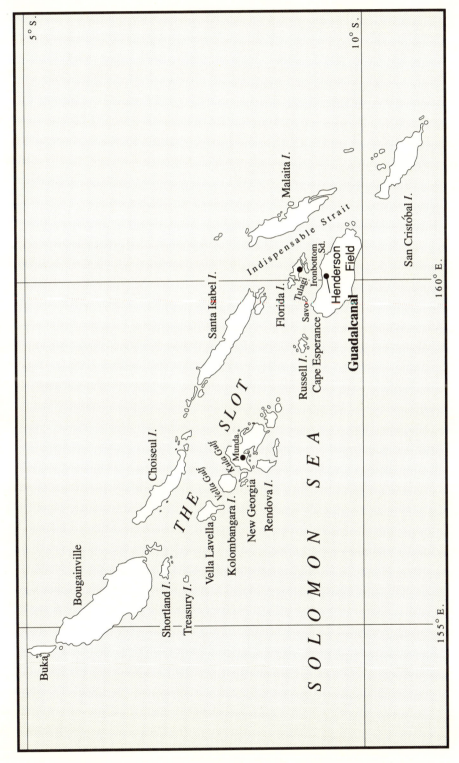

frontation with Kelly Turner over control of the 2d Marines. None of the lieutenant colonels relished the prospect, but they also feared allowing Vandegrift to deal with the admiral alone because they knew he had little taste for personal battles, a trait seen in New Zealand and at the Koro conference. They did not welcome the news, either, that Turner intended to establish his own headquarters ashore. Turner also said that he needed to see the Marines' plan to defend Guadalcanal, but Thomas argued that the plan had not been finished. This raised the admiral's ire. Although Thomas accepted the criticism (the plan was actually complete), he did not show Turner the plan until the day before the landing when, Thomas knew, it would be too late to change it. He wanted to preserve whatever tactical flexibility Vandegrift had left, at whatever risk.[2]

The dawn of 7 August 1942 brought a rain of bombs and shells on the Japanese positions on Guadalcanal, Tulagi, and Gavutu-Tanambogo. To all appearances, Watchtower began with a sound and fury that promised victory. The Japanese base defense and engineering troops surprised at Kukum, the settlement nearest the airfield at Lunga Point, ran for the hills and jungle and left their pigs and cattle to stop the deluge of fragments. After a 0330 breakfast of steak, eggs, and jam sandwiches, the Marines crawled down the nets into the awaiting landing craft, circled until the wave commanders reached their departure times, and then headed for Red Beach, which jumped before their eyes under the pounding of naval gunfire. Across Sealark Channel, Rupertus's Northern Group headed for its objectives and three days of hard fighting, but the 5th Marines hit Red Beach—Thomas thought the landing looked like an exercise—and found it undefended as predicted. Capers James and Bill Twining went ashore to establish a small division command post near the beach in midmorning, but Thomas stayed with Vandegrift and Turner aboard the *McCawley* because it provided the only reliable radio links with all of the landing forces. At midday, the task force endured two Japanese bombing attacks—the first response from the Japanese air bases at Rabaul and on Bougainville—that cost the attackers thirty of their fifty-one aircraft and left the transports undamaged. The Navy, however, lost three hours' unloading time. In the midafternoon, Vandegrift, Thomas, and much of the division staff reached the advanced CP on Red Beach and assessed the ground situation.[3]

After its textbook beginning from the line of departure to the high watermark, the amphibious assault on Guadalcanal had changed from a charge to a stagger. As experienced field Marines, Vandegrift and Thomas anticipated that the real world would not conform to their operation order, but the division's problems did not yet include a fight with the Japanese, an ominous indicator. One battalion of Roy Hunt's 5th Marines had organized a temporary defense inland, but the other battalion's advance westward toward the airfield quickly demonstrated its inexperience and the inept leadership of the battalion commander, William E. Maxwell. Thomas had warned Vandegrift and Hunt that Maxwell would not drive his battalion, and now he saw his prophecy turn to reality. Vandegrift himself ordered Maxwell to get moving. The order sent the handsome Maxwell, whose taste for field work did not match his love for garrison-style soldiering, groping again through the coconut groves. Some of his men amused themselves by shooting coconuts and phantom Japs around the CP.

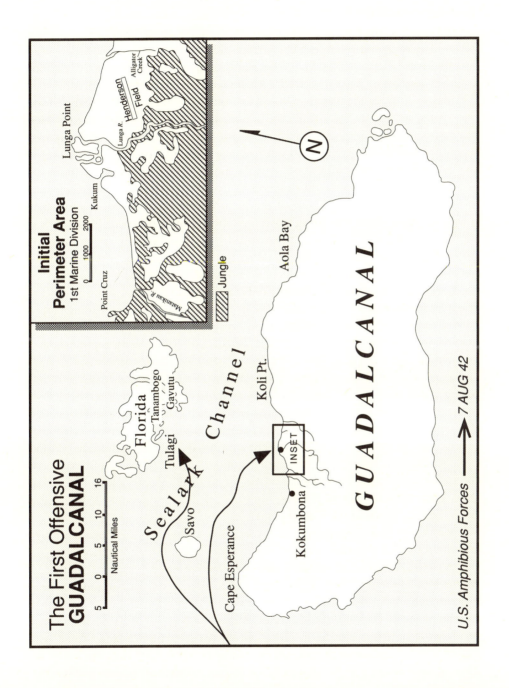

Although far better commanded, the 1st Marines did not make much progress. Too many weeks at sea (there had been nothing but wharf work in New Zealand), poor food on the way from California, heavy loads, and heat had brought Col. Clifton B. Cates's regiment to the brink of physical exhaustion before it fired a shot in anger. The terrain did not cooperate. Cates discovered that the river labeled as "the Ilu" on his sketch map could not be crossed without engineer assistance. According to the Australians, the Ilu River was fordable, not a bayou swamp. In the planning, however, the division staff had mislabeled the two rivers, so "the Ilu" was really the Tenaru and vice versa. The Tenaru, which ran across the left and rear of Red Beach, proved a major obstacle that required a pontoon bridge to cross. The result was that both infantry regiments jammed the beachhead area and moved off into the jungle behind schedule.

The artillery and logistical situation added to the confusion. Although two 75-mm pack howitzer battalions of the 11th Marines managed to wrestle their guns and some shells into firing positions, the 105-mm howitzer battalion had difficulty getting off the beach. The available vehicles could not move the guns through the sand; only amphibian tractors could do that. In the meantime, bulk supplies not preloaded in light vehicles overwhelmed the pioneer battalion of hard-driving Lt. Col. George Rowan and the attached sailors, a condition exacerbated by some of the transport commanders, who began general unloading before Rowan approved it. The beach area soon became a vast, unorganized dump and vehicle park, sealed on one side by the Tenaru and the infantry regiments and blocked at the waterline by a jumble of landing craft, wandering troops, and abandoned mounds of cargo. Vandegrift wisely ordered the Marines ashore to halt and prepare a hasty defense with the advance to continue toward the airfield in the morning. He and Thomas also conferred with Cates and decided to change the 1st Marines' mission. Instead of advancing toward the "grassy knoll" (in reality, Mount Austen), which they knew now lay miles inland, Cates should pivot to the right and head for the high ground (the real "grassy knoll") south of the airfield, thus protecting the 5th Marines' left flank. Vandegrift had begun to think they would find few Japanese, but if they did they would likely emerge from the hills south of the coastal plain.[4]

Vandegrift had ample reason to revise the operation with Thomas's urging, and the second day started with the right mix of optimism and caution. During the evening, Turner had released the two uncommitted battalions of the 2d Marines to clean up the die-hard Japanese resistance on Tulagi and Gavutu-Tanambogo, which had already bloodied the 1st Raider Battalion, 1st Parachute Battalion, and 2d Battalion, 5th Marines. A major action on Guadalcanal appeared unadvisable until the Northern Group completed its action because Vandegrift had only one battalion of the 5th Marines in reserve. Nevertheless, such a battle did not seem likely. The division had now taken a handful of Japanese and Korean prisoners, and they reported through interpreter Captain S. F. "Pappy" Moran that the airfield and Kukum campsite west of the Lunga River had been abandoned. They also verified the growing impression that the defenders numbered far less than five thousand men. Thomas issued a revised order for Maxwell's battalion to hug the coast and go straight for Kukum; the 1st Marines would envelop the airfield and establish a loose area defense along the upper waters of the Lunga.

When the infantry regiments started to move after first light, Vandegrift and Thomas followed the movement by radio. Although they did not then realize it, Cates soon lost contact with his leading battalion, but his reassuring reports masked his own worries. Thomas and Twining suspected Cates did not have the 1st Marines under tight control, but they did not raise the issue with Vandegrift because they had confidence that Cates would correct his problems. They had no such confidence in Roy Hunt. Again, Maxwell dallied, and Thomas and Hunt found his Marines moving with unjustified sloth because the only resistance they met consisted of a few snipers and rampaging pigs, which they riddled with fury. Thomas warned Hunt that he should relieve Maxwell if the battalion did not move more rapidly. Instead Hunt, a true warrior and charismatic leader, gathered his command group and pushed ahead of his lead battalion to the Lunga. At about the same time (late morning), reconnaissance patrols from the 11th Marines and the lead elements of the 1st Battalion, 1st Marines (L. B. Cresswell), reached the airfield. Following its fearless regimental commander, the 1st Battalion, 5th Marines then crossed the Lunga and occupied Kukum. The division's five infantry battalions and three artillery battalions then went into defensive positions while the division staff turned its attention to the logistical mess between the airfield and Red Beach. During the afternoon, Thomas and Bill Buse looked for a permanent division CP and eventually selected a coral ridge with some trees for concealment about a mile northwest of the airfield. Thomas selected the location because the Lunga protected the CP's western edge and the twisting ridge offered tent sites and bunkers that would be safe from direct fire from the sea or across the Lunga.[5]

In the meantime, the Japanese naval aviators struck again at Turner's Task Force 62 in Sealark Channel. Fletcher's fighters rose from the carriers hovering off Guadalcanal to meet the Japanese in an air battle that began at midday and ended in the early evening. The Japanese attack force of forty aircraft flew into the Navy Wildcats and antiaircraft fire with abandon, fatally damaged the transport *Elliott*, and largely perished, but the campaign had now cost Fletcher one-fifth of his fighter strength (twenty-one of ninety-nine planes) and most of his nerve. In the late afternoon, he informed Ghormley by message that he would leave Guadalcanal twelve hours earlier than he had planned, which meant immediately. Ghormley did not object. Furious over Fletcher's departure, Turner called Vandegrift and Admiral Crutchley to the *McCawley* to review the operation. Vandegrift and Thomas left the island just as nightfall plunged the channel into darkness, and their uncertain coxswain took three long hours to find the flagship. In addition to being unhappy about the course of the general unloading, the admiral had more bad news: at least three Japanese cruisers had been sighted in the waters to the north, and Fletcher had departed. Turner expected a sea battle on the morrow, and he wanted a better grasp of the situation. Vandegrift and Thomas found him combative, if anxious, and they encouraged him to continue unloading the next day. They also asked that they visit Rupertus at his headquarters on the *Neville* off Tulagi.

Vandegrift and Thomas, after switching passage to an old destroyer-minesweeper, sought Rupertus. The night, now darkened by rain, erupted in gunflashes, explosions, and searchlights off Savo Island. Not until the next day did they learn that the Japanese force—seven cruisers and one destroyer—had surprised Admiral Crutchley's covering force and sunk four of his six cruisers and a destroyer. The ferocity of the battle, however, dampened Adm. Gunichi Mikawa's enthusiasm for an attack on the transports, and he turned away north, probably to escape the morning's attack by Fletcher's aircraft—an attack, of course, that never came. The Battle of Savo Island, however, forced Kelly Turner to gather his task force and flee south behind Fletcher's carrier groups. After a flurry of last-minute unloading and moving small craft into the scratch bases at Kukum and Tulagi, Turner's surviving ships pulled their anchors and abandoned, at least temporarily, the 1st Marine Division. Sealark Channel had begun its gruesome history as "Ironbottom Sound," and rubbish and corpses from the U.S. Navy bobbed in the oily scum that lapped up on Guadalcanal. Few of the Marines knew exactly what had happened, but Vandegrift, who had badly hurt his leg in a fall that evening, and Thomas knew that Watchtower was in full jeopardy on that bleak morning of 9 August 1942.[6]

Amid the dripping bamboo and vine-laden trees along the coral ridge that protected the CP, Vandegrift and Thomas met their senior commanders even before the last transports had cleared Sealark Channel. The grim commanding general, his eyes gray with fatigue but his jutting chin set with the classic Vandegrift look of determination, briefed his officers on their peril and set their common goals: curtail all offensive operations except patrolling; establish a defense of the airfield oriented to the threat of attack from the sea; complete the airfield for Allied aviation; and move all the supplies inside the perimeter. The confusion of the last forty-eight hours had given the division some advantages, however meager. First, the battles of the Northern Group had put all three 2d Marines battalions ashore, even though Turner still claimed control of them. The 2d Marines (reinforced) could defend Tulagi, which could release the 1st Raiders, the 1st Parachute Battalion, and the 2d Battalion, 5th Marines, for Guadalcanal. The Tulagi transport group, commanded by aggressive Navy officers, had off-loaded all their supplies and equipment before departing; this meant that the first available supply dump was seventeen wet miles away on Tulagi. In addition, the Japanese had left their camps without destroying their own equipment and supplies, including beer, canned fish, and seaweed. Another advantage was that Vandegrift received Turner's hurried permission to land the heavy shore defense and antiaircraft guns of the 3d Defense Battalion on Guadalcanal, not Tulagi, their intended destination. Last, Kelly Turner, tainted by the disasters at Pearl Harbor and Savo Island, left Sealark Channel a driven man, determined to avenge his defeats. Although he remained difficult to deal with, he now saw Guadalcanal (if not the airfield), rather than Tulagi or Ndeni, as the focus of the campaign. He vowed to Vandegrift that he would return.[7]

After Vandegrift finished his briefing, Thomas issued the basic defense order, which he himself had conceived to replace Twining's earlier effort. The 5th Marines would defend the coast and the perimeter west of the Lunga; the 1st Marines would defend the coast and the eastern line along the "Tenaru" River, actually the Ilu or Crocodile Creek, east of the airfield and the Lunga. One 1st Marines battalion remained in division reserve, as did the one tank company; the three artillery battalions would prepare positions along the southern edge of the perimeter at the fringe of the rain forest. The artillerymen would have to share the responsibility for patrolling the open southern edge with the amphibian tractor battalion, some infantry, and the engineer and pioneer battalions. This defense order cemented a similar order Thomas had given the day before to Cates and Hunt: the key mission was to defend the airfield at all costs, for air superiority would eventually decide the campaign. To Vandegrift, the plan made intuitive common sense; to Thomas, it represented two decades of thought about the conduct of war. The challenge would be to see that their vision of the campaign prevailed in the face of all challenges, Japanese and American.[8]

As the 1st Marine Division prepared itself for—who knew?—Vandegrift and Thomas assessed their operational situation. Although they were unable to see all the lessons of the Guadalcanal campaign in perfect post hoc clarity, their long experience and professional expertise gave them a sure feel for their division's capabilities and limitations. Thomas wrote his wife that "we are in the war up to our necks," but he had full confidence the Marines would win. The 1st Marine Division (reinforced) was large, even without its third infantry regiment and two of its five artillery battalions. It began the campaign with about seventeen thousand officers and men, but it could not become larger unless higher commanders made decisions they had not yet made. Admiral Turner controlled the first source of reinforcements: the 2d Marines (reinforced) on Tulagi and the nearly five thousand Marines still aboard his amphibious ships or held in New Zealand. There were no plans to bring individual replacements. Vandegrift badly wanted his own third infantry regiment, the 7th Marines (reinforced), but it still guarded Samoa. Like other Marine formations (principally the 2d Marine Division, less the 2d Marines), the Samoan Marine brigade belonged to either Admiral Ghormley or Admiral Nimitz, as did the Army ground combat units (loosely grouped as the "Americal Division") defending other islands north of New Zealand. In sum, the 1st Marine Division faced an uncertain future in fighting strength, and its leaders had to conserve its manpower by avoiding casualties.[9]

The structure of the 1st Marine Division also made it an apt instrument for defending the broad coastal plain and coconut plantations on either side of the Lunga, but not for extended offensive operations into the jungles and hills to the south. Until the division recovered the 1st Raider Battalion, 1st Parachute Battalion, and 2d Battalion, 5th Marines, from Tulagi and Gavutu-Tanambogo, it still had only five small infantry battalions for jungle attacks. The artillery of the 11th Marines, to be sure, could provide accurate fire support, but the artillery regiment was not large or heavily gunned by later Pacific war standards. By September, the 11th Marines had three full battalions (1st, 2d, and 5th) on the island; in firing guns, however, this force deployed only twenty-four 75-mm M1A1 pack howitzers (range 9,000 yards, shell weight 14 pounds) and twelve 105-mm M2A2 howitzers (range 12,000 yards, shell weight 33 pounds). This force could hardly afford much damage from Japanese bombing and counterbattery fire. In fact, the 11th Marines artillerymen had serious doubts about their ability to support infantry fighting in triple-canopy jungle. The defensive potential of the 11th Marines was important, however, and it had help from the 1st Special Weapons Battalion, with two batteries of 37-mm antitank guns, one battery of half-track–mounted 75-mm guns, and one battery of 40-mm dual-purpose cannon. The direct fire defensive capability of the special weapons battalion was enhanced by other cannons in the hands of each infantry regiment weapons company and the infantry's nearly two hundred mortars, as well as the company of M2A4 light tanks. The last important firepower asset was the allowance of .30-caliber and .50-caliber machine guns in division hands. The division deployed with nearly one thousand machine guns, half of them allotted to the small amphibian tractor battalion. Many of these guns—they could not be manned by their legal owners—went to the infantry regiments for defensive deployment. In sum, if the division fought defensive battles with fields of fire within the relatively clear and flat expanses of the Lunga plain, the Japanese would be in for some very nasty experiences.[10]

The state of morale and training of the division's Marines made the division better suited for defense than attack. The troops had not had meaningful training or physical conditioning for months; the 1st Marines had even lost weight aboard the transport *Ericcson*, whose food would have disgraced a Depression soup kitchen. Except for some field grade officers and a handful of aging sergeants, the division had no proven combat leadership. The Marines had no conception of the terrors of war or the physical and emotional collapse those terrors could inflict on the most hardy souls among them. As one corporal recalled, he and his comrades could not have been more innocent: "War was killing. Seeking out the enemy and killing. Killing without mercy. . . . It was something like being a Boy Scout. You camped out. You killed for God and Country. There was no plan to die."[11]

These Marines had much to learn, but they would know more and live longer if their classroom was a well-dug foxhole protected by mortar and artillery barrages and interlocking machine gun fire. They would learn offensive tactics, even patrolling, slowly and carefully because the division leadership had a healthy regard for Japanese infantry in the jungle. The enlisted men and junior officers did not yet recognize that the Japanese army had its flaws (e.g., an inability to combine arms and coordinate attacks), but they had heard from their intelligence officers that the Japanese fought without fear or pity. The Marines faced the enemy with a mixture of contempt, anxiety, and anticipation. Even if the Marines lacked the skills for the attack, their preference was to close with the Japanese, an ardor (real and imagined) that sometimes flowed upward through their officers in a demand for more aggressive operations. Vandegrift, Cates, and Hunt responded at a visceral level to such pleas for action. Thomas and Twining shared their empathy but tried to prevent the calls to battle in the name of morale from jeopardizing the reasoned plan to defend the airfield.[12]

The defense of Guadalcanal required air support; on 9 August, it had none. Fringed with coconut trees and brushy coral ridges, the unfinished airstrip east of the Lunga could not be used until it was 2,600 feet long, and the entire runway required another two weeks' work to complete it to 3,800 feet. The first 2,600 feet might be finished in a couple of days, which meant that the field could handle at least some fighters, promised by Kelly Turner for 11 August. The naval retreat of 9 August, when the transports took away most of the 1st Engineer Battalion's heavy equipment, rendered the estimate of 8 August so much wishful thinking. (Only one bulldozer, for example, got ashore.) Abandoned Japanese equipment filled some of the needs (especially rollers), but most of the earth moving had to be done by hand, and even handcarts and shovels were in short supply. Revetments for aircraft protection and fortified storage sites for fuel and ordnance would have to wait. On 12 August, the Marine labor force had its work tested by a PBY flown by Admiral McCain's aide, who declared the strip fit for aircraft. During the night of 14–15 August, three destroyer-transports, the first Navy vessels to return to Guadalcanal, arrived off Lunga point with aviation fuel, spare parts, lubricants, and ordnance, as well as a Navy construction unit and a small detachment of Marine aviation support personnel. The Japanese did not allow the airfield construction to proceed unmolested. Flights of bombers appeared daily when the weather allowed. They arrived predictably around noon because they had a five- to six-hour run from their airfields at Rabaul and Bougainville. The three batteries of 90-mm antiaircraft guns of the 3d Defense Battalion (Col. Robert H. Pepper) kept the bombers at around twenty thousand feet, no boon to bombing accuracy, but real air defense required fighters. On 20 August, the very day of the first heavy Japanese ground attack on the perimeter, Marine air charged to the rescue. Carried within range on the light carrier *Long Island*, the nineteen F4F Wildcats of VMF-223 and twelve dive-bombers of VMSB-232 dropped through the clouds and landed on the airfield, soon named Henderson Field. The first echelon of a gallant interservice aviation command, dubbed "CACTUS Air Force," prepared for its own desperate battle to interdict Japanese naval forces and the reinforcements they carried and to protect CACTUS from air attack.[13]

The logistical situation of the 1st Marine Division offered little comfort and few quick fixes. Again, the flight of the transports had frayed Operation "Shoestring" to the breaking point. After assessment of the frantic off-loading of 7–9 August and inventory of the captured Japanese food and supplies, Vandegrift found little comfort in the reports of his D-4, Lt. Col. Ran Pate, and division quartermaster, Lt. Col. Raymond P. Coffman. Coffman's first estimates proved unduly pessimistic, especially on food supplies, but the real condition, known by 11 August, set serious limits on the division's initial operations. The Marines had about half their allotted ammunition, which meant they had enough for five days of intense fighting. With captured Japanese food, they could eat for a month and a bit more, provided they did not gorge. Vandegrift put the division on two meals a day, a rationing that lasted six weeks, in part because he did not want noon chow lines awaiting the midday Japanese bombers. The reduced caloric intake contributed to fatigue and vulnerability to tropical disease, both enemies of fighting ardor. The stock of general supplies and equipment appeared adequate, but such critical items for defensive operations as sandbags, barbed wire, hand shovels, and field telephone wire had almost all disappeared with the transports. Medical supplies, especially Atabrine and quinine, were marginally adequate; the division surgeon, the redoubtable Capt. Warwick T. Brown, MC, USN, entered the campaign as concerned about malarial mosquitoes as he was about the Japanese, a concern justified by time. Only immune Caribbean campaigners like Vandegrift and Thomas could be relatively sure they would not contract malaria, and other perils, including dengue fever and unknown tropical diseases, might spare no one.[14]

If the division's operational and logistical condition brought little comfort, its communication situation was no less troubling. The internal communication system had its own weaknesses (wire and radio battery shortages), but the constricted nature of the perimeter meant that the commanders could meet in person or communicate through message-bearing runners at least during the day when movement proved reasonably safe. There were larger problems. Air-ground communications, for example, depended on one jeep-mounted radio; this jeep had to stay mobile during bombing raids. A repaired Japanese radio station offered the only communication with Turner, Ghormley, and Navy forces at sea because the Navy's planned radio station had not disembarked. Even though the 5th Marines riddled the abandoned Japanese radio complex on 8 August, Marine radiomen repaired the modern Japanese equipment and, by using Morse code, established a dependable station, NGK. The fear that the Japanese might capture American cryptographic materials, however, worried those officers responsible for communications security. The division received "Ultra" radio intelligence information sparingly; most often it came—slowly—by messenger. The limited secure external communications had one unintended advantage: it forced the division to develop its own sources of information about Japanese intentions and activities on Guadalcanal.[15]

With limited resources, all to be husbanded for the battles that really counted, the division had to fight smart, not just hard. Vandegrift and Thomas needed reliable, time-urgent, and relevant intelligence about the Japanese. Early in the campaign, they faced one disaster and received one blessing. The enthusiastic D-2, Frank Goettge, organized the disaster. Prisoner interrogations and a patrol report convinced Goettge that a Japanese unit west of the Matanikau River wanted to surrender. He took a patrol of twenty-five men from his staff section and the 5th Marines intelligence section and led them by small boat on the night of 12–13 August to a landing spot near the Matanikau. The Japanese greeted them with bullets, not white flags, and all but three Marines of the Goettge patrol (including the D-2) perished, thus stripping the division of irreplaceable intelligence experts. Lt. Col. Edmund J. Buckley, a Reserve artilleryman, became the D-2 and did well in the role, although his taste for risky reconnaissance patrols and his professional limitations worried Thomas and Twining, who keenly felt Goettge's death. On 14 August, the division received its intelligence blessing when Capt. Martin Clemens, district officer for Guadalcanal and a Cambridge-educated Aberdeen Scot, and sixty Melanesian native scouts reached the perimeter from their observation post east of the division. Personable, athletic, and clever, Clemens soon functioned as unofficial D-2, as well as Thomas's close friend and collaborator in organizing reconnaissance missions that joined Marines and his scouts. If some Marines did not like or trust the natives, Thomas had no such reservations, for he quickly decided that only Clemens knew Guadalcanal well enough to be a trusted advisor on Japanese movements and the nature of the terrain.[16]

From all outward appearances, Vandegrift dealt with the discouraging news from his division, the growing enemy pressure from the sea and air, and the uncertainty of naval support with characteristic poise and determination. On 11 August, he called in his field grade officers for a confidential talk. He emphasized the advantages of their situation without minimizing the enormity of the challenges they faced. He was satisfied that their first defensive arrangements would prevent another Bataan or Wake Island and assured them that the Navy would return, Marine aircraft would arrive, and the 3d Defense Battalion's 5-inch coastal guns, backed by the 11th Marines and the 1st Special Weapons Battalion, would smash any direct amphibious assault on the Lunga perimeter. Vandegrift then gathered the forty other officers for a group picture against a coral outcropping. None smiled for the camera. Dressed in stained gray-green dungarees and soiled khakis, the senior officers presented a collective portrait of determination that reflected their leader's personality. With few exceptions, they had all served as career officers since World War I or the 1920s; Vandegrift and Pedro del Valle had belonged to the pre–1917 Marine Corps. Only four of them, however, had heavy combat experience in France: Jerry Thomas, Bill Whaling, Clifton Cates, and Roy Hunt. Few of the majors had served even in the Caribbean or Nicaragua. Although they all knew that Vandegrift had little formal education in military operations, they respected his integrity and force. Only a handful, including Thomas, could have guessed that Vandegrift had physical limitations that worried his staff and might influence his judgment. In addition to his sensitive eardrums, which made bombing and shelling an unpleasant experience, the commanding general was growing blind at night. Moreover, Vandegrift wanted to command at the front, not from the CP, and he felt most at home talking to officers and men, inspiring them, and gauging their skills and morale. Thomas and Twining worried about Vandegrift's health and safety. With Bill Rupertus still on Tulagi, the next senior officer was del Valle, whom the D-3 section regarded as excitable and inconsistent. Thomas and Twining trusted Cates but believed that Hunt counted on his friendship with Vandegrift to protect him from criticism.[17]

Thomas himself settled quickly into a routine he followed through most of the campaign. By Guadalcanal standards, he lived well; he had a tent, cot, and mosquito net. He went to bed early and arose early for the first of many cups of coffee and cigarettes, shaved, showered briefly in an extemporized open-air barrel and spigot arrangement built for Vandegrift, and dressed as neatly as possible. After he and Vandegrift breakfasted on biscuits and, perhaps, a piece of meat, they examined the message traffic, discussed operations, and issued any needed orders. Vandegrift then toured the division, sometimes with Thomas in tow, but Thomas and Twining normally manned the operations tent, built against a hillside. They worked closely with their assistants, Bill Buse and Ray Schwenke, and their principal enlisted clerks, Sergeants Robert Brandt and Richard C. Kuhn. The most relaxed time of the day came in the late afternoon after the midday Japanese air raid. Like Thomas, Vandegrift did not care for formal staff conferences, and neither trusted Capers James, the chief of staff, whose only operational opinion was that patrolling was too dangerous. Instead, Vandegrift and Thomas preferred to talk individually with other staff members before dinner, a time sometimes brightened by a short sortie into the headquarters mess liquor supply. Thomas usually washed down his daily quinine dose with a shot of bourbon. He took no Atabrine, which made him ill. Always sociable, Thomas often led the discussions, usually a mix of operational talk and reminiscence. He also listened closely to Vandegrift for clues to the general's judgments of people and situations. Thomas chose his own words carefully, if clearly, and seldom openly criticized any of his fellow officers. He saved his opinions for Vandegrift and Twining.

Convinced that the campaign would end in an American victory—a conviction he never surrendered even on the bleakest of many "purple nights" as Japanese naval shells and infantry attack buffeted the perimeter—Thomas wisely paced himself and his commanding general. A busy man who developed the nervous habits of tugging at his trousers and jerking his head as he talked, he used force and candor in dealing with his fellow officers. He kept his mind on essential business, avoided the distraction of personal feuds, and resisted the temptation to conduct the campaign through the newspaper reporters who had accompanied the division. His concentration had never before been so tested; at the peak of his intellectual power, he fused his own experience, formal training, and force of character into an ability to shape operations that was matched only by Vandegrift's talent. If his sense of urgency became excessive, Vandegrift calmed him. Although Thomas and Twining occasionally disagreed, especially on the importance of the Matanikau flank, they became allied in the battle for the heart and mind of Alexander Archer Vandegrift. They had no challengers in the CP, but they worried that, during Vandegrift's trips to the regiments, del Valle, Hunt, and Cates would wring a decision from the commanding general that would unnecessarily kill Marines and do nothing to strengthen the division's position. By the end of September, Thomas dominated not only the division staff but the entire division. He did not seek power for its own sake, but he rose to this position because he believed the division had come to Guadalcanal to give the United States its first offensive victory over Japan.[18]

Between 18 August and 18 September 1942, the Japanese and the Allies fought a vast, episodic air-land-sea campaign in the lower Solomons for control of Guadalcanal, an engagement won by the U.S. Navy and U.S. Marine Corps. Although the campaign did not end in September, 1st Marine Division headquarters believed (at least, after the fact) that these four weeks of battle proved the division's ability to hold Henderson Field against a ground attack, provided American air and naval forces could keep the Japanese army from bringing overwhelming numbers of soldiers to Guadalcanal. After the battles of the Tenaru (20–21 August) and Raider Ridge (12–14 September), the Marines had no doubts about their competence in smashing the most determined Japanese attacks. Japanese ardor and skill, which had destroyed more numerous Allied forces in Malaya and the Philippines, no longer provided a tactical edge, even in the jungle. As operations officer of the 1st Marine Division, Lt. Col. Gerald C. Thomas was one of the handful of Marine officers who shaped the battle for the island. His sure-handed, clear-headed management of the defense made him second only to General Vandegrift as the architect of victory. To play this role, he not only outthought the Japanese commanders he faced but outmaneuvered some Marines as well, including Vandegrift himself.

Surprised by the initial landings, the Japanese Army and Navy commanders at Rabaul and the IGHQ in Tokyo struck back with air and naval forces, but quickly (10–12 August) determined that they would need a ground campaign to recapture their lost Lunga base with its invaluable airfield. Aware that they had temporary air and naval superiority, the Japanese commanders rushed a force of about 1,400 soldiers and naval infantry south on destroyer-transports. American radio intelligence picked up and analyzed some of the message traffic for this operation, but the Navy's radio security system prevented a rapid transmission of the information to Vandegrift. In any event, he had no way to stop the convoy, which arrived during the night of 18–19 August, and the Navy made no effort to intercept it. The division staff realized that the Japanese had brought in reinforcements only when Marine lookouts reported vessels in Sealark Channel; no one knew exactly where the Japanese had landed or how many had come ashore. The Japanese also worked in the fog of war. Although they had some idea of the dispositions within the Lunga perimeter (an observation team on Mount Austen identified most of the Marine artillery positions), they had little knowledge about the Marines' strength ashore or the position of Vandegrift's five infantry battalions. Patrols from the two forces groped toward each other in their efforts to gain information. The Marines won the intelligence edge before they had to fight the battle itself.[19]

By nightfall on 19 August, Vandegrift and Thomas knew they had Japanese forces in action off both the western and eastern flanks of the perimeter. They had to decide which threat was the most immediate. After the Goettge patrol disaster, the 5th Marines had mounted a series of patrols across the Matanikau toward the coastal village of Kokumbona; they found Japanese naval infantry, but no Marine survivors. In the most ambitious of these operations, a three-company raid on 19 August, the Marines fought a day-long battle with inconclusive results, largely because of the inept management of the battle by Lt. Col. Frederick E. Biebush, commander of the 3d Battalion, 5th Marines. The three infantry companies fought their way back to the perimeter with captured documents and eyewitness reports from missionaries, however, that convinced Vandegrift he faced no immediate threat from the "Matanikau front." The same day, a large 1st Marines patrol marched east along the coastal track toward Koli Point, the estimated landing site of the new Japanese troops, and ambushed an enemy reconnaissance patrol of thirty-five. Killing all but three or four Japanese, the Marines returned with maps and orders that identified the Japanese infantrymen, the first encountered on Guadalcanal, as members of the "Ichiki Detachment," a 900-man reinforced battalion from the 28th Infantry Regiment. Clemens's scouts provided more warning of a likely Japanese attack on the 1st Marines lines along the Tenaru River. Under Thomas's direction, Cates reinforced his positions with the 1st Special Weapons Battalion while the 11th Marines prepared defensive fires in front of his line. Thomas alerted Cresswell's 1st Battalion, 1st Marines (the division reserve), for several counterattack missions and brought the eager, energetic Cresswell (an old friend) back to the CP with him. As darkness dropped, the Marines awaited the certain attack.

In a furious battle that lasted twelve hours, the 2d Battalion, 1st Marines (Lt. Col. Edwin A. Pollock), held the Tenaru River line with withering artillery and machine gun fire (including 37-mm canister rounds that approximated big shotgun blasts), and the infantry battled the small groups of Japanese that actually penetrated the line. Thomas and Cates conferred throughout the action by phone. When not talking to Cates, Thomas paced in front of the D-3 tent as he listened to artillery and watched flares pop above the coconut trees. He joked with Cates that the two of them would have to learn a whole new set of artillery sounds because their World War I senses no longer sufficed. Cates asked for his 1st Battalion, but Thomas told him there could be no help until daylight came and the course of battle cleared. After three banzai charges fell along the mouth of the

Tenaru, Cates and Thomas felt that they had held their lines and that the Ichiki Detachment had dangerously massed at the shoreline. They then decided that Cresswell's battalion should counterattack from the south and pin the surviving Japanese against the coast, which the 1st Battalion did. Thomas furthered the slaughter by requesting air strikes and releasing a tank platoon to Cates, who sent the tanks with 2d Battalion infantry to close the trap. When the battle ended, only about one hundred desperate survivors of the Ichiki Detachment remained. Thomas visited the battlefield and found more than eight hundred mangled corpses, broken trees, and shattered weapons. Few of the weapons belonged to the Marines, and only thirty-four of the dead wore dungarees. The 1st Division had its first big victory.[20]

Although relieved from any immediate threat of ground attack, the 1st Marine Division faced a campaign still in doubt and its prospects remained dubious. The CACTUS Air Force and the U.S. Navy could not stop the Japanese from bringing more troops to Guadalcanal. To be sure, American air and naval forces extracted a price—and paid a price—in the interdiction battle. At first the campaign tilted toward the Americans because the 1st Marine Division received welcome supplies from Turner's amphibious force, protected by a carrier task force that met the Japanese navy in a carrier battle (Eastern Solomons, 23–25 August) and allowed the American transports to escape attack. On the other hand, the Japanese reinforcement transports did not make Guadalcanal during the night and lost the rest of the 28th Infantry Regiment and more Japanese naval infantry to dive bombers from CACTUS. The U.S. Navy, however, temporarily lost the carrier *Enterprise* to bomb damage; fortunately, its SBD squadron diverted to Henderson Field where it was joined by two more Marine fighter squadrons and the headquarters of Marine Aircraft Group (MAG)–23 on 30 August. Another American supply convoy arrived at the end of August, but its protection cost the Navy the carrier *Saratoga*, damaged and out of action from a Japanese torpedo. The threat of air attack forced the Japanese to plan that the last leg of reinforcement trips end at night, for which the Americans did not yet have an answer. In the meantime, air attacks on Henderson Field took their toll of aircraft and logistical support, although Marine fighters, given the required forty-minute warning from the coastwatchers, made the runs a one-way trip for many Japanese bombers. The Marine air effort received a welcome boost when the commander of the 1st Marine Aircraft Wing, Brig. Gen. Roy S. Geiger, arrived with part of his staff (including Jerry Thomas's old friend, Col. Louis E. Woods) to take charge of the CACTUS Air Force. Before Geiger arrived, Thomas pressed Vandegrift to demand more from the aviators, who still held cautious standards about flying weather and pilot fatigue. After Geiger arrived, Thomas never again worried about whether the Marine pilots would press their attacks to the point of mutual annihilation. The Japanese recognized the potency of CACTUS by increasing their efforts against Henderson Field. They sent warships (the Tokyo Express) down "The Slot" to bombard the airstrip at night and destroy the American transports bringing in aviation fuel and ordnance.[21]

The opposing land force commanders used their delicate, temporary advantages in air-sea control to build up their forces for another battle for Henderson Field. The Japanese commander, Maj. Gen. Kiyotaki Kawaguchi, chose to land troops both west and east of the Lunga perimeter and, in early September, had a reinforced brigade of more than six thousand soldiers on Guadalcanal. Vandegrift had more limited options, but he used them quickly. On 21 August, the 2d Battalion, 5th Marines, crossed from Tulagi, followed by the 1st Raider Battalion and the 1st Parachute Battalion on 31 August, which increased the division's strength by two maneuver battalions (the Raiders and Paramarines functioned as one battalion) of about 1,800 crack Marine infantrymen. With more reserves, Thomas used the 5th Marines to probe west again past the Matanikau River to Kokumbona on 27–28 August. The 3d Battalion, 5th Marines, would attack along the Matanikau, while the 1st Battalion, 5th Marines, landed from the sea at Kokumbona, beyond the range of the 11th Marines' guns. Thomas believed that he had made it clear to Roy Hunt that the two battalions should fight through to a linkup, but somehow Hunt and Maxwell believed the 1st Battalion was off on a limited raid and should withdraw at nightfall by landing craft. In any event, Maxwell did not press his attack against organized Japanese resistance. His battalion fought a confused, inept, and uncontrolled battle. Faulty communications made the tactical situation sound even worse than it was, and Vandegrift, truly enraged, sent Hunt to the beachhead to take charge and relieve Maxwell. Vandegrift finally thought he might get rid of Hunt, too, but Thomas suggested he at least postpone the decision until the 1st Battalion could be withdrawn. The "second battle of the Matanikau" ended without serious damage to the battalion, but with hard feelings all around.[22]

Thomas could hardly afford to deal overlong on the Matanikau fiasco because he had decided from patrol reports and other evidence that Kawaguchi's attack would come from the east, not the west. He was beginning to suspect that the Japanese had discovered that the southern (jungle) edge of the perimeter was open and that an attack there would make it difficult for the Marines to break the next banzai charges with artillery and automatic weapons fire. To meet such an attack, Thomas would have to persuade Vandegrift to reorient the whole defense, a prospect he did not relish. He could count on Twining's support in any discussion with Vandegrift, but his assistant still favored a defense weighted more to a threat west of the Lunga. Moreover, Thomas thought that the concept of defense in depth, which might now be fully created with two additional infantry battalions, was fundamentally unsound, given the nature of the terrain and the enemy's penchant for night infiltration attacks. The personal dynamics were as difficult as divining Kawaguchi's intentions. Buoyed by its success in the Battle of the Tenaru, the 1st Marines would resist any fundamental change in its own disposition, a stubbornness reinforced by Cates's and Pollock's antipathy to Twining, who had continued to criticize the 1st Marines' shortcomings. Thomas, however, had a new ally, Col. Merritt A. "Red Mike" Edson, forty-five-year-old commander of the 1st Raider Battalion and conqueror of Tulagi. Thomas knew Edson only by reputation, but he trusted the judgment of Edson's executive officer, Sam Griffith, an old friend from Peiping, and Griffith believed that the Marine Corps had no better tactician than Edson.

In early September 1942, Jerry Thomas and Mike Edson formed a limited partnership that won the Battle of Raider Ridge and continued through other battles until Edson's death in 1955. Edson had joined the Marine Corps in 1917

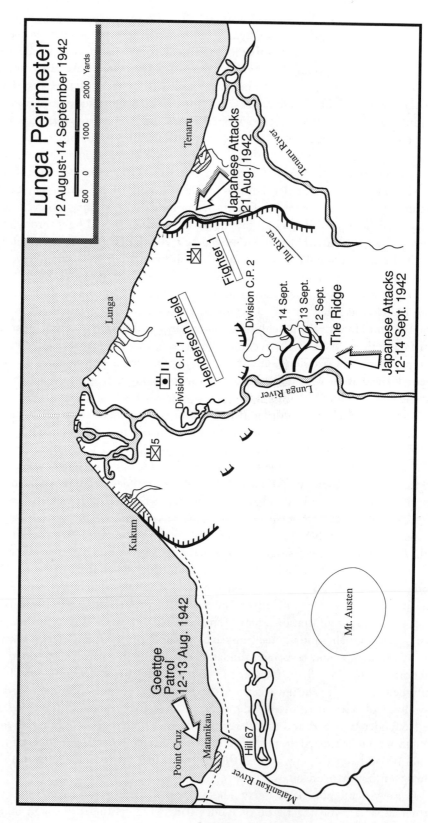

after a brief 1916 tour on the Mexican border with the Vermont National Guard. With one year of college, he had qualified for a commission in the Marine Corps in October 1917 and served in France. Like Thomas, he had survived the machinations of the Russell and Neville boards and remained a regular officer (slightly senior to Thomas) in the 1920s. Edson became a pilot and flew until grounded for physical problems. His career in eclipse, he went from sea duty to service in Nicaragua in 1927 where he won a Navy Cross and Corps-wide fame as the leader of the Coco River patrol that drove the Sandinistas from eastern Nicaragua. He then became captain of the national championship Marine Corps Rifle and Pistol Team, 1936–37, and a Distinguished Marksman. After completing the Senior Course at Quantico, he had served as R-3 of the 4th Marines in Shanghai and commander of the 1st Battalion, 5th Marines, before that battalion became the 1st Raider Battalion. In uniform, Edson always appeared misshapen but neat, and his superficial carriage would have impressed no one except that he routinely transfixed other Marines with his icy gaze, soft voice, and quiet air of menace. Not all Marine officers belonged to the "Red Mike" fan club. Offended by his diffidence, they recoiled from his driving ambition and perfectionism. One of his nonadmirers was Edwin A. Pollock, also a veteran of the Coco River Patrol and now the outstanding battalion commander of the 1st Marines and "the lion of Tenaru." Some of the Raiders called Edson "Mad Merritt the Morguemaster."[23]

After he discussed the tactical situation with Edson, Thomas proposed that the Raiders mount a major combat patrol by amphibious landing at Tasimboko, a small village on the east coast that, to Clemens's scouts, appeared to be a major Japanese staging area. Clemens, Buckley, and Twining thought the operation risky, but Thomas persuaded Vandegrift that a one-day operation (8 September) was feasible if the Navy could sneak the Raiders down the coast at night in two destroyer-transports and two patrol craft. Vandegrift approved the proposal on 6 September, and the next day the Raiders embarked. On 8 September, the Raiders, supported by air strikes, landed without resistance and attacked a Japanese base camp. Although surprised by the landing, the Japanese of the Kawaguchi Detachment rallied and fought the Raiders all day. Apparently convinced by two passing large Navy transports that the landing was a major assault, the Japanese fought only a delaying action, which allowed the Raiders to capture and destroy supplies and grab incriminating maps and documents. The most ominous find, Japanese artillery pieces, consisted of both captured guns and guns that had shelled the Raiders. Although Edson wanted to press the attack, Vandegrift ordered him to withdraw that afternoon. The Raiders returned with vital information at the cost of only six casualties. The information Edson recovered indicated that his battalion had fought only the rear guard of a force that might be as large as four thousand soldiers. Thomas was now certain that the next Japanese effort would come against the southern perimeters east of the Lunga.[24]

Thomas was clear in his own mind that Kawaguchi would strike somewhere between the Tenaru and the Lunga, thus avoiding the thickened positions of the 1st Marines, but he would have to convert Vandegrift to a radical change in the division's defensive posture. Vandegrift played into his hands by deciding on 5 September to move the division command post against the advice of his staff. As Japanese bombing and naval shelling against Henderson Field mounted, Vandegrift became less happy with the location of his headquarters near the airfield. He complained about the location to Cates, who encouraged him to move. While the Raiders visited Tasimboko, Vandegrift directed his engineers to build a division CP well south of the airstrip and to tuck his staff sections among the ravines east of a barren ridge that ran south-north from the jungle to the airfield. Just east of the Lunga, the ridge was the real "grassy knoll" of D-Day fame and an obvious avenue of approach into the heart of the Marine perimeter. (On various occasions before 8 September, del Valle, Edson, Thomas, and Twining had identified the ridge as key terrain.) To Vandegrift, however, the edges of the ridge, well forested and protected by natural cover, appeared a splendid place to escape the shelling and bombing that plagued the old CP. The issue of the CP displacement came up again during the evening of 8 September when Edson debriefed Vandegrift and Thomas about the Tasimboko raid. Tutored by Clemens and Griffith, Edson thought the move ill advised because he believed the Japanese would make the ridge their prime objective in an attack from the southern jungle line. Vandegrift rejected his advice. Thomas suggested, however, that Edson move his composite battalion to the southern nose of the ridge for a well-deserved rest and to provide security for the CP. Vandegrift agreed that Edson's battalion should also leave its airfield bivouac area at the same time the CP moved, but he did not view the change as a basic shift in the division's defensive posture. Thomas, on the other hand, saw the Raider deployment as only the first step in preparing the southern flank for a major Japanese attack.[25]

Although heavy rains made 9 September an uncomfortable moving day, Vandegrift pushed forward with his plan to move the CP to the ridge, despite growing intelligence from Clemens's scouts that the jungle held Japanese. Sam Griffith also reported that the Raiders might have to fight for their "rest area" because Japanese outposts already held part of the position. Bill Twining went to the general and urged him to postpone the move to the "Robber's Roost," as the new CP was dubbed, but Vandegrift cut Twining off with harsh words suggesting that Twining might think about another assignment. Thomas quickly cautioned Twining not to press the issue. The CP move did not develop in an orderly way, however, and not until the early afternoon of 10 September did Vandegrift announce to the rest of the division that he had shifted the CP. In the meantime, the Raiders and paramarines moved to company positions on the ridge and into the jungle on either side of it. Thomas kept his counsel, but he took time to warn division historian and press officer Herb Merillat that he thought the division's history could be even more interesting in a few days.

While division CP personnel settled into their new quarters, Thomas quickened his attack to strengthen the defenses of the southern perimeter as Kawaguchi's troops toiled through the jungle for the attack on Henderson Field. He held a rare conference at the CP on 10 September to discuss defensive doctrine. The discussion flowed back and forth among the division staff and Vandegrift until Edson said that the proper interval for a jungle defense should be about fifteen yards; anything else invited catastrophic infiltration. The Japanese themselves added to the discussion by sending reconnaissance patrols right up to the Raiders' positions and by bombing the ridge for the first time on 11 September. Vandegrift approved Thomas's proposal to move the 3d Battalion, 1st Marines (Lt. Col. William N.

"Spike" McKelvey, Jr.), from the coast to fill the gap between the Raiders and the Tenaru and to reorient the 11th Marines' defensive fires to the south. In the meantime, Edson had his Raiders and paramarines dig in and establish barbed wire and booby traps on either side of the ridge, as well as establish fallback positions along the ridge all the way to the division CP. Marine patrols and Clemens's scouts continued to report a massing of Japanese forces to the south.

Into the gathering storm on the afternoon of 12 September came Rear Adm. Richmond Kelly Turner, who flew in from New Caledonia to confer with Vandegrift on the progress of the campaign. Although he himself still believed the campaign winnable and worth winning, Turner brought with him two alarming messages from Admiral Ghormley for the 1st Division leaders. Ghormley had just reported to Nimitz that he thought that Watchtower might just result in another Philippines and that the Navy could not guarantee reinforcements and supplies for CACTUS at its current level of losses. Ghormley also sent Vandegrift a personal note that described the Guadalcanal situation in dire terms and suggested that Vandegrift might have to surrender. The import of the messages was clear to all the Marines: they should think about either surrender or some sort of guerrilla campaign waged from the mountains of Guadalcanal. Vandegrift and Thomas had a different agenda. They wanted Turner to give them the 7th Marines (reinforced), released by Ghormley from the defense of Samoa. Another source of reinforcements rested in Kelly Turner's hands. He could allow Vandegrift to draw battalions of the 2d Marines from Tulagi, studiously ignored by the Japanese, and cancel not only his Ndeni plans but his subsequent schemes to use one or both regiments to open another enclave along the east coast of Guadalcanal at Aola Bay or to turn the 2d Marines into raider battalions. Having delivered his bad news, Turner wanted to drink with Vandegrift and discuss the situation, which he himself regarded with more optimism. Thomas took an obligatory drink and cornered Bill Twining. He told his assistant to draft a plan for a retreat to the headwaters of the Lunga but not to spread any talk of defeatism. Although he changed the concept to a withdrawal along the east coast, Twining did as he was instructed while Thomas attended to the operations of the moment. More reports suggested that the Japanese would attack that night. Serious shelling of the ridge by a cruiser and four destroyers that pummeled the new CP area through a driving rainstorm reinforced these reports. When a considerably dampened and slightly shell-shocked Kelly Turner departed on 13 September, he told Vandegrift he would do all in his power to get the 7th Marines to Guadalcanal. Vandegrift could also draw on the 2d Marines on Tulagi.[26]

As Turner and Vandegrift conferred, General Kawaguchi launched his first attack on the Raider positions no more than two miles from the CP. Thus began two nights of battle for what the Marines called "Edson's Ridge." The attack of 12–13 September penetrated the positions in the jungle on either side of the ridge, but Edson did not believe his two battalions had seen the worse attack because the Japanese had not driven hard into his position. (In fact, Kawaguchi was supposed to make his maximum effort that night, but his main body was not ready.) While Vandegrift, Turner, and Thomas held their last meeting at the 1st Marines CP on the morning of 13 September, the division made additional preparations for the next attack the staff knew would come that night. Despite an air raid, the 2d Battalion, 5th Marines, moved forward to a blocking position on the north rim of the ridge; when a bomb injured its commander, Vandegrift put the regimental executive officer, that ultimate warrior Bill Whaling, in command of the battalion. In the meantime, 11th Marines artillery fire combed likely assembly areas in the jungle and routes to the ridge. Edson pulled the Raiders back from the jungle and occupied alternate positions 500 yards from the holes they had occupied the night before. After darkness came on 13 September, the Japanese plunged forward against the Marines. Japanese destroyers in Sealark Channel threw shells against the ridge, and some Japanese infiltrators actually reached the division CP area. Throughout the battle, Edson directed his Raiders with sangfroid and skill. Marine artillery fire smashed attack after attack, but some Marines and Japanese reached muzzle-blast distance and killed each other in close combat. Thomas responded to Edson's requests for help by sending forward two companies of the 5th Marines, but Thomas also had to monitor a secondary attack against McKelvey's battalion to the east and a probe against the 5th Marines. Dawn found the Raiders bloodied but unbroken and the 5th Marines ready to take up the fight if the Japanese made one more banzai attack. With daylight, Thomas ordered air attacks, supported by more artillery fire, on the remnants of the Kawaguchi Detachment. Around the ridge and in the jungle were the bodies of 1,200 Japanese soldiers. During the day of 14 September, Vandegrift ordered a return to the old CP. Before the move had been completed, Jerry Thomas, at the division surgeon's urging, had collapsed on a stretcher for some welcome sleep. He had been on his feet and locked in combat with Vandegrift, Turner, and the Japanese for two nights. Even if Thomas had not awakened to face a new set of problems on 15 September 1942, he had earned his place in the history of Marine Corps combat operations.[27]

The battle of Raider Ridge brought another breathing spell for the 1st Marine Division. General Vandegrift seized the opportunity to make some dramatic changes among the senior officers of the division. Until mid-September, he had avoided any decision about how he would respond to a message from Headquarters Marine Corps that directed him to release "excess" colonels for reassignment. Even before the division landed on Guadalcanal, a promotion board at Headquarters had published a list of 61 promotions to temporary colonel. The board had considered 219 ground lieutenant colonels for temporary promotion. It had not included Jerry Thomas, whose date of rank placed him outside the zone of consideration. Among the board's selections for new colonels of officers assigned to the 1st Marine Division (reinforced) were George Rowan, Bill Whaling, Robert Kilmartin, Frank Goettge, Bob Pepper, and Merritt A. Edson. Vandegrift thus could use the Headquarters directive as an opportunity to pick and choose those colonels he wanted to keep and those he wanted reassigned. No one doubts that Vandegrift discussed his options with Thomas; no one is sure that Thomas made the critical recommendations, but many suspect he did. Vandegrift argued that he sent back the most senior officers with longest service in the division, which is not true. He kept Cliff Cates and Pedro del Valle. He released Capers James and Roy Hunt from his colonels and Rowan and Kilmartin from the new temporary colonels. He kept Whaling, Pepper, and Edson of the new colonels. In early

September, Vandegrift had already recommended that Thomas be made a temporary colonel, a rank appropriate to his new position as division chief of staff. General Holcomb approved all the changes; as of 15 September 1942, Thomas received a "spot" promotion to colonel.[28]

With his promotion to colonel coming barely fourteen months after promotion to lieutenant colonel, Jerry Thomas had ample reason to savor his success. He did not bask, however, even though he now had the rank and formal assignment to go with his informal authority. His elevation depended on his personal relationship and the favor of Alexander Archer Vandegrift, whose own star (and stars) depended on the 1st Marine Division's continued success on Guadalcanal. Moreover, Thomas had made enemies on Guadalcanal because of his influence on Vandegrift. Cliff Cates respected his expertise, with qualifications. Roy Hunt and Capers James left Guadalcanal as his bitter enemies; George Rowan and "Killy" Kilmartin were more realistic and resigned. Part of the problem was Vandegrift's generous nature. In the autumn of 1942, he and the other Marine generals answered Commandant Holcomb's request that they examine the sixty-eight most senior ground colonels and recommend fifteen of them for promotion to brigadier general. Vandegrift chose three colonels from the most senior twenty-nine and twelve of the next nineteen. Among his selections were Roy Hunt, who was promoted, and Capers James, who was not. The rate of success was about fifty-fifty among the other colonels Vandegrift recommended. From Thomas's perspective, the other important nominees (all promoted) were Clifton B. Cates, Lemuel C. Shepherd, and Graves B. Erskine. Shepherd and Erskine remained Thomas admirers, but Cates did not view him with equal enthusiasm. Whether Thomas's influence and power ran beyond the 1st Marine Division remained to be seen.[29]

Jerry Thomas gauged the reassignments and certainly knew the *Lineal List* that ranked Marine officers by seniority. Lt. Sanford B. Hunt kept the division's copy of the *Lineal List* and suspected that Thomas had it memorized. Bill Twining knew that Thomas had strong opinions about who should remain with the division on Guadalcanal. Thomas was more interested, however, in the fact that the 3d Battalion, 2d Marines, arrived from Tulagi on 12 September and that, despite the sinking of the carrier *Wasp* in the covering force, a convoy delivered the entire 7th Marines (reinforced) on 18 September. Unless the 1st Marine Division won its part of the battle for Guadalcanal, Jerry Thomas had no future, whatever his rank.

[CHAPTER XVII]

Division Chief of Staff on Guadalcanal

22 September–10 December 1942

AFTER SIX WEEKS OF inconclusive battle, the Japanese and American high commanders in the Pacific, Washington, and Tokyo simultaneously decided that the campaign for Guadalcanal should receive more resources, which produced an escalating stalemate until the Japanese conceded the island in early December. Like most campaigns, Guadalcanal became a test of will and resources; in the end, the Americans had more of both. Two unsuccessful attacks against the Lunga perimeter had not dampened the Japanese commitment to seize Henderson Field. In fact, the buildup in the northern Solomons, Rabaul, and Truk that sent Admiral Ghormley into a defeatist swoon reflected a Japanese decision to emphasize operations in the Solomons rather than New Guinea. Imperial General Headquarters assigned Gen. Haruyoshi Hyakutake and his Seventeenth Army headquarters to Guadalcanal and ordered him to move two divisions, an independent brigade, and support troops to the island. For the first time, this force would bring heavy artillery and tanks into the battle. Japanese warships and army and naval aviation units would increase their efforts to halt American reinforcements and destroy Henderson Field.

In Washington, President Roosevelt's increased concern about Guadalcanal sharpened the attention of the JCS. Weighing the balance between the buildups in the South Pacific and Europe, the JCS sanctioned requests from MacArthur and Nimitz to move forces already assigned to the Pacific war into the theaters of active operations. The JCS had approved a landing in North Africa for November and recognized that it might find some extra planes and logistical shipping, too, because the buildup in Britain had been slowed by changing plans and German submarines. In fact, the shipping proved more important than the tiring and largely irrelevant arguments about USAAF squadrons, for Admirals Nimitz and Ghormley had adequate ground forces and ground-based fighters and dive bombers for the task at hand. By massing their forces, the Japanese made American

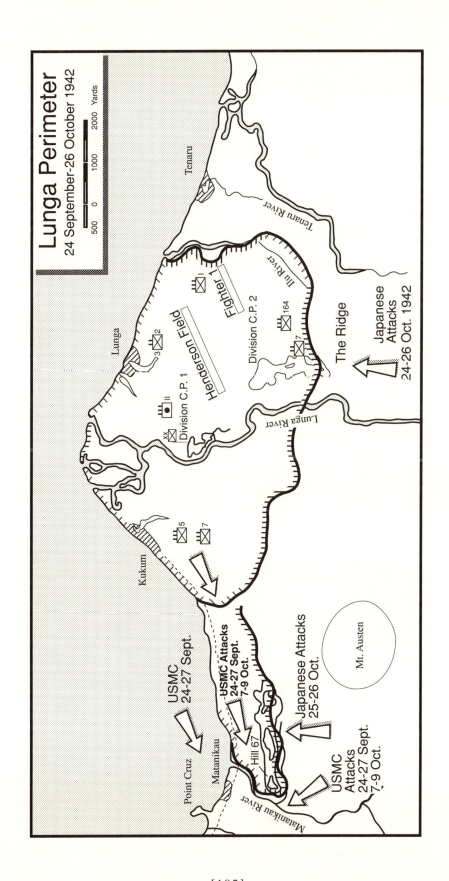

redeployment decisions easier. The islands on the Australia–United States line of communication now looked less vulnerable to attack. The critical question, from the planners' viewpoint, was whether Richmond Kelly Turner could get the reinforcements into Guadalcanal. Turner's problem was also simple to define: could the Navy and CACTUS Air Force cover his convoys? Air superiority really depended on CACTUS Air Force because the Navy had only one operational carrier, the *Hornet,* left in the theater. In mid-September, Roy Geiger had around sixty aircraft in six squadrons (four Marine) and about one thousand aviation personnel. Planes and pilots required constant replacement, for flight operations were costing CACTUS Air Force an average of three aircraft a day. In addition, nighttime shelling by Japanese warships endangered airplanes, air crews, and the field's primitive facilities and scanty supplies.[1]

The security of Henderson Field depended on American successes in three dimensions: defense against air attack, defense against nighttime naval shelling, and defense against ground attack. By mid-September, the CACTUS pilots (assisted by the Marine antiaircraft batteries) had proved that they could keep the damage of bombing attacks acceptable by shooting down bombers and their escorts at loss ratios the Japanese could ill afford. As long as Commander Aircraft South Pacific (ComAirSoPac) could keep replacement F4Fs and pilots coming, the air superiority battle need not be lost. The imponderable was Japanese domination of the night. Their cruisers and destroyers had thus far sailed with slight molestation to shell Henderson Field. These nighttime attacks usually covered the movement of barges and transports bringing Japanese ground forces down "The Slot." The more the Japanese reduced the threat to their reinforcement effort—primarily by American aircraft, secondarily by submarines—the greater their chances of taking Henderson Field by ground attack. The Japanese interdiction attempts, principally by warships and submarines, against American transports required relative freedom from American air attack. Happily, the Japanese Navy had no more taste than the U.S. Navy for carrier operations in the southern Solomons, and the Japanese interdiction effort inflicted only logistical losses. Not one American reinforcing infantry battalion perished in transit; the Japanese probably lost the equivalent of eight or nine. Without some effort to fight the IJN at night, however, the U.S. Navy could not slow the Japanese barges and transports enough to make them vulnerable to daylight air attack from CACTUS—assuming that shelling had not put CACTUS Air Force out of business, even temporarily. The delicate balance of operational factors guaranteed that the local commanders felt that they waged war on a knife-edge of risk in which small opportunities might bring ringing victory or crashing defeat.

No one appreciated the realities of the campaign better than the Marine Corps team of A. A. Vandegrift and Roy Geiger, and they understood that they faced two different sorts of tasks to hold Henderson Field. One set of tasks involved the operational handling of their own forces. They had to use all the skill and endurance of the 1st Marine Division and CACTUS Air Force to prevent the Japanese from capturing the airfield by ground attack, which meant a combination of air and land operations to prevent the Japanese from arriving in the first place or to mount a successful offensive after they landed. Both generals were stubborn optimists and had proved their power of leadership and tactical skill to use their forces with prudence and effect. Their second set of problems involved persuading other American commanders, principally admirals of the U.S. Navy, to wring the same sort of effort from *their* forces so that the Americans, not the Japanese, would win the reinforcement battle. Vandegrift and Geiger received unqualified support from only one colleague, Rear Adm. John S. McCain, the land-based aviation commander, although they also won over the commander of Army forces in the theater, Maj. Gen. Millard F. Harmon. Kelly Turner proved difficult throughout the campaign. No one worked harder to bring supplies to Guadalcanal, but Turner retained his compulsion to divert ground reinforcements to other schemes. The key to the battle to control the waters around Guadalcanal remained the judgment of the theater commander, Admiral Ghormley, and CinCPac himself, Admiral Chester W. Nimitz. Unless they were willing to commit the surviving carrier and surface forces to a battle to the death with the Imperial Japanese Navy, even in night actions in which the Navy hardly excelled, Henderson Field might indeed fall. Vandegrift and Geiger would then be forced to withdraw from the Lunga enclave and wage guerrilla warfare, as they had agreed on 14 September. The Battle of the Ridge had bought them more time, and they used it to take the initiative against the Japanese and the U.S. Navy.[2]

Gerald C. Thomas, colonel and division chief of staff by the grace of Vandegrift and twenty-four years of exemplary professional growth, pulled the reigns of power tautly to headquarters, the better to serve his commanding general and strengthen the division's high command for the ordeals to come. Enjoying his meager rewards for becoming chief of staff, he moved into Vandegrift's more spacious personal tent. Friends sent an occasional bottle of bourbon and notes of well-wishing. Vandegrift recommended him for a Distinguished Service Medal for his performance as D-3. He began to hear talk from other officers that he was sure to become a general, but, as he wrote Lottie, "I do not worry about such things."

The division staff was his to direct, and it was loyal to a man; Capers James's departure made the work less complicated in personal terms. Avoiding grand conferences, Thomas preferred quiet and firm conversations with his section chiefs. Although worn by the campaign and twenty pounds thinner, he had lost none of his intellectual acuity. He talked with a directness and force that impressed his staff. He also listened and pondered the officers' advice as he pulled at his belt and scratched his body. The staff, hard men hardened more by battle, had no weaklings. Jim Murray performed with energy and discretion as the D-1, no "yes" man even to Thomas. Ed Buckley worked as D-2 with competence, ably assisted by "Pappy" Moran, the expert interpreter, and Martin Clemens, who ran both the native scout force and several hundred native bearers with the assistance of the other Australians attached to the division. Bill Twining, back in Vandegrift's good graces after the CP fiasco and the Battle of the Ridge, directed the D-3 section with high skill and outspoken advice. He and Thomas continued their close collaboration, although they disagreed about the control of Clemens's scouts and the importance of the Matanikau front. As D-4, Ran Pate performed yeoman work until broken by illness and evacuated. His replacement, Lt. Col. Raymond P. Coffman, proved ideal as logistics officer; he worked with persistence, care, and quiet skill to ensure that the division husbanded its supplies and knew exactly what it had and what it needed. Coffman's principal assistant, Lt. Col. John D. Macklin, an extrovert with a dramatic flair, provided the fire when any logistical crisis arose and extraordinary measures (such as hoodwinking the Navy and Army) seemed necessary. Warwick T. Brown managed the division's medical effort with consistent competence in the face of a growing sick rate. The division communications system worked as well as the equipment allowed under the tender care of Ed Snedeker, Lt. Robert Hall, and Sandy Hunt, who also functioned as Thomas's assistant and cryptographic officer. Bonded by their service on Guadalcanal, most of the staff remained "Thomas men" for the rest of their careers.[3]

Other reassignments, worked out by Vandegrift and Thomas, strengthened the division's tactical leadership at the regimental level. Merritt Edson took command of the 5th Marines to see if he could give it some cohesion and esprit, but even the formidable "Red Mike" could not bring the regiment up to his exacting standards, as Thomas had hoped. Cliff Cates had the 1st Marines, not seriously engaged as a regiment since the Battle of Tenaru, under firm control. Thomas watched the battalion commanders closely, especially "Spike" McKelvey of the 2d Battalion, whom he liked and understood. Thomas knew that McKelvey had a tendency toward depression, exacerbated by drinking, and he made it a point to see McKelvey often for a pep talk and one carefully rationed drink. In turn, McKelvey would have stormed hell with his battalion if Thomas had ordered the attack. The 1st Marines could spare some talent, so Vandegrift shifted the executive officer, Julian C. Frisbie, a Marine's Marine and World War I veteran, to the same job (then vacant) in the newly arrived 7th Marines, commanded by the dapper and mediocre Amor L. Sims. Sims had his hands full with two independent battalion commanders who had stellar reputations in Caribbean "bush warfare," Herman H. Hanneken and Lewis B. "Chesty" Puller. (Puller further embellished his own legend by marching his battalion from the beach into the jungle with showy disdain for a map orientation. "Hell, let's go get 'em!" In fact, Puller had trouble—as did others—in reading the aerial photograph map.) The 11th Marines remained under Pedro del Valle, a proven quantity even when he was excited, as on his 1 October promotion to brigadier general. The division still had one unassigned colonel, Bill Whaling, whom Thomas moved under his direct orders. At Whaling's suggestion, Thomas had him organize a scout-sniper unit of one hundred volunteers for close patrolling. An aggressive troop leader and woodswise, Whaling became available to take over any task force organized for special missions or any battalion that faltered. His reputation frayed through association with Roy Hunt and the 5th Marines, Whaling owed his professional rebirth to his old friend from World War I, Jerry Thomas.[4]

With his division high command reorganized, Vandegrift, always an aggressive commander in the operational sense, saw an opportunity to shift to the offensive before more Japanese reinforcements arrived. He no longer feared a direct amphibious assault against his enclave. Thomas encouraged the general's instincts because he believed that the Marines—like those he had seen in World War I—might lose their fighting edge sitting in their defensive positions. Always aware of the vulnerability of the southern (jungle) side of the perimeter, Thomas did not share Twining's and Vandegrift's enthusiasm for more serious advances west across the Matanikau, but Vandegrift accepted Twining's recommendation that the perimeter would not be secure from ground attack until the Marines dominated the terrain between the Matanikau and Kokumbona village. The division had the resources for an offensive, at least a limited one. The 7th Marines (reinforced) were fresh and eager for battle, if untested. The 11th Marines now had four full battalions. The 3d Battalion, 2d Marines, did not return to Tulagi but stayed in division reserve. Ammunition supplies appeared adequate, as did air support. The Navy's small craft fleet at Kukum and Tulagi offered the option of attack from the sea. Although short rations, lack of sleep, and heat had begun to take their toll, disease and battle casualties had not yet sapped the division's strength. Fewer than three hundred 1st Division Marines had died in six weeks of battle, and about the same number had been evacuated by air. Disease problems, especially malaria and dengue fever, appeared bothersome (1,800 hospital admissions by 18 September), but Vandegrift judged his men's health as good. Nevertheless, he worried that prolonged exposure to malaria and nighttime bombardment would eventually erode the division's effectiveness. He wanted the division withdrawn from Guadalcanal, but he also wanted to use it to end the defensive phase of the ground operation.[5]

In two separate offensive operations along the Matanikau (23–27 September and 7–9 October 1942), the 1st Marine Division attempted without success to dislodge the Japanese from their major position west of the Lunga perimeter. At a cost of 350 Marine casualties, the division punished the defenders (probably 1,000 casualties) and eliminated a Japanese bridgehead east of the Matanikau, but Vandegrift and Thomas agreed that more ambitious commitments might endanger the defense of Henderson Field by exhausting their infantry. They also learned that, in the tactical sense on Guadalcanal, it was wiser to defend than attack. The scheme of maneuver in both operations, worked out by Twining, looked better on a map than among the broken ridges, thick jungles, and muddy slopes along the Matanikau. Even staunch spirits like Edson, Whaling, Puller, Hanneken, and Sam Griffith could not overcome the intrinsic problems of uprooting a determined enemy from jungle defenses with inexperienced, overburdened Marines who collapsed from heat exhaustion or fell from snipers and hidden machine guns. The basic plan in both operations looked much the same, whether by design or extemporized. One force would cross the Matanikau near its headwaters at the base of Mount Austen, then attack downhill toward the coast and the heart of the Japanese defenses; another would fix the defenders with an attack across the mouth of the river. A third force would envelop the Japanese from the sea with an amphibious assault. The second operation eliminated the amphibious assault and strengthened the envelopment from the southern flank, a change that provided the battle with its greatest success, the artillery slaughter of a Japanese infantry battalion caught in a pincers west of the Matanikau on the coastline. In the first operation, the division almost lost its amphibious assault force, but naval gunfire and the opportune arrival of Chesty Puller and part of his battalion rescued another part of his battalion that appeared ready to repeat the annihilation of the Goettge Patrol. Although the second operation produced better tactical performance by the infantry, aided by crushing artillery fire support from three 11th Marines battalions, Vandegrift decided to reestablish a strong defense east of the river rather than a salient to the west. Thomas encouraged such prudence; he and Vandegrift had read a growing body of intelligence analysis suggesting that the Japanese had at least a reinforced division ready for another attack on Henderson Field.[6]

In the middle of the two Matanikau operations, the 1st Marine Division received a welcome visitor on short notice, CinCPac himself. Nimitz's visit allowed Vandegrift to present his case for reinforcement and relief directly rather than through his superiors, Kelly Turner and Robert H. Ghormley, who still viewed the campaign in very different terms. The 1st Division staff had become adept at impressing visitors, whether civilian reporters or Army and Navy flag officers, largely because Vandegrift and Thomas believed in the division's ultimate victory and because of the resilient spirit of all the Marines, down to the privates in the foxholes. Reports from the "rear," including not only Ghormley's defeatist headquarters but the radio and press in the United States, appalled the division, which did not share the judgment that Guadalcanal might become another Bataan. Nimitz, ever wise if not open, had decided to see the situation for himself. He had already discovered that Ghormley did not have a firm grip on his command and had not fully committed the forces already in his theater. Kelly Turner was aggressive enough, but his experiment in campaign management still had not focused clearly on Henderson Field. (Turner was even then planning another enclave along Guadalcanal's eastern coast at Aola Bay that would use scarce Navy engineers and part of the 2d Marines.) Admiral McCain and General Harmon shared Vandegrift's assessment that Henderson Field was the key position, but without Nimitz's intervention they could not commit more naval aviation or Army ground and air units to the 1st Marine Division sector.

In a conference at Nouméa, Nimitz had listened and pondered. He then flew to Guadalcanal (arriving on 30 September) with his logistical advisor, senior air officer, and two senior Marine colonels, Omar T. Pfeiffer and DeWitt Peck, the Marine planners from his own and Ghormley's staff. Vandegrift and Thomas showed Nimitz their position and guided him through a classic Henry V visit with the troops. They talked at length with the admiral about their problems, not minimizing their difficulties but remaining optimistic. Pfeiffer thought that Vandegrift described Turner's generalship too gently, but Thomas impressed him with his professional grasp and pragmatic determination. Nimitz talked with enthusiasm about the battle and awarded Navy Crosses to representative Marine heroes. When Nimitz departed, Thomas believed the 1st Marine Division would soon receive more support.[7]

Although Nimitz wanted to think more about the Solomons campaign before he made any radical changes, he galvanized Ghormley and Turner to extra efforts to reinforce Vandegrift, and the two admirals quickly organized another major relief expedition. The American naval forces joined a race for Henderson Field; General Hyakutake had ordered a maximum effort by the 2d Division (Lt. Gen. Masao Maruyama) and all other units to capture Henderson Field on 17 October. The Imperial Japanese Navy and all army and navy aviation units in the Solomons would support the ground attack with round-the-clock bombardment of the Marines' enclave. The Japanese revealed a new dimension to their ground attack on 13 October. From positions west of the Matanikau, they opened fire with a battalion of 150-mm guns, which outranged the 11th Marines. Japanese artillery fire posed an additional threat to Henderson Field. The battle opened with another midnight grapple between the American and Japanese warships screening the two converging convoys. The Battle of Cape Esperance (11–12 October) ended with both fleets reeling apart with three ships sunk (two Japanese) and damage to the other engaged cruisers and destroyers. The convoys landed their reinforcements unmolested. The 1st Division welcomed the newcomers, who were well equipped and supplied and numbered more than four thousand. The major unit was the U.S. 164th Infantry Regiment, North Dakota National Guardsmen of sturdy stuff, a heroic tradition, and well commanded by the quiet and professional Col. Bryant Moore (United States Military Academy, 1917). The Army infantrymen brought thousands of M-1 rifles into the battle, bad news for charging Japanese infantry. Thomas and his staff found the 164th Infantry comparable with the 7th Marines and developed an instant liking and respect for Colonel Moore and his staff as they directed the Guardsmen toward positions along the southern perimeter.[8]

While the Americans made a short maximum effort to get more reinforcements and supplies to CACTUS, the Japanese had organized a sustained campaign to destroy Henderson Field and to police up the shattered remnants of the 1st Marine Division (reinforced) with a ground attack. The campaign reached its worst crisis. Even as the 164th Infantry landed, Japanese bombers, after about a week's lull, returned to bomb Henderson Field and Fighter One, an auxiliary strip east of the main airfield. That night (13–14 October), the "Tokyo Express" also arrived, now reinforced with two battleships. It did not retreat, and Jerry Thomas spent the next two days at the CP under a bombardment worse than anything he had experienced in World War I. One 14-inch shell landed near the CP tent but did not explode. During the day, Japanese bombers pounded the two airstrips, abetted by the distant 150-mm guns, dubbed "Pistol Pete." The night naval shelling, however, did the most damage. The first night's bombardment almost put the CACTUS Air Force out of business; by 16 October, Roy Geiger had lost twenty-three of thirty-six dive bombers and all but nine of his fighters. Almost all of his torpedo planes could not fly. With nearly one thousand 14-inch shells and a nice assortment of smaller ordnance, the IJN had provided a grace period for Hyakutake's reinforcements, who streamed ashore in daylight from destroyers and transports. The following night, two IJN cruisers took up the bombardment, followed the next day by another bombing. Although Geiger pieced together enough airplanes and scarce aviation gasoline to continue the air battle and destroy three transports, the Japanese bombardment had returned the initiative to the Japanese.[9]

Between the naval shells and the bombs, Jerry Thomas assessed the ground situation and weighed the gathering information that the Lunga perimeter would soon receive another attack. He strengthened the jungle line with battalions of the 7th Marines and 164th Infantry and called for two batteries of 155-mm guns to deal with "Pistol Pete." He probably had no idea that the Japanese had a full battalion of 150-mm guns ashore (Twining was amazed when he later saw the captured guns and stocks of shells), but he did know that the Japanese had tanks west of the Matanikau. Thomas let small notes of doubt creep into his letters home: "However it may end I am proud to have had such a part in the blows that have been struck here." He worried whether CACTUS Air Force could stem the tide of Japanese ships and planes and believed that the pilots were the greatest heroes of the campaign. He held no illusions that the grinding campaign of attrition would soon end, but he still believed in ultimate victory. He and Vandegrift conferred with Geiger constantly about the air situation and watched with awe as the remnants of CACTUS Air Force tackled the Japanese air attacks until reinforced with a Marine fighter squadron on 16 October. Thomas became concerned about the state of the 11th Marines, who also shared "Impact Central" with the aviators. Although the artillerymen had experienced little physical damage and limited casualties, they had become rattled by the shelling. Jerry's close friend John Bemis, the regimental executive officer, had barely survived a near-miss and had to be evacuated with shell shock; through battle stress and collapse, the 11th Marines also lost three battalion commanders in October. The 3d Defense Battalion and 1st Special Weapons Battalion had fared somewhat better, and even Roy Geiger admitted that Marine antiaircraft artillery had blunted the bombing attacks. Few along the front lines, largely spared the bombardment, doubted that the infantry regiments faced the next test. They only dimly realized that the Japanese infantrymen, pushing through the jungle toward them, had themselves suffered to the extent that the attack had been postponed.[10]

Although not the shell-shocked, sickly, and cowardly remnant the Japanese imagined, the Marines of the 1st Division and the 1st Marine Aircraft Wing needed another lift. They received two bits of good news while they awaited another ground assault. On 18 October, Nimitz relieved Ghormley and replaced him with a thunderstruck Vice Adm. William F. Halsey, recently recovered from illness and awaiting command of another carrier task force. In Washington, Adm. Ernest J. King thought the change overdue and approved the appointment of the pugnacious and personable Bill Halsey, already lionized by the press and admired by officers and men alike for his thirst for victory, if not always for his skill as a commander. The 1st Division, from CP to foxhole, celebrated the change. In the CP, the cautious optimism increased with the visit three days later (21 October) by the Lieutenant General Commandant, the much-beloved and badly aging Thomas Holcomb. The Commandant had his detractors, but they were not on Guadalcanal. Vandegrift felt his own spirits soar with Holcomb's arrival, and Thomas again rose to the challenge of briefing Holcomb and his staff on the division's condition. Malaria had become a major problem, two thousand cases in the past five weeks. The division needed relief, an issue that again raised the question of Kelly Turner's grandiose plans to put ground forces everywhere but into the Lunga enclave. The matter was important, for the 2d Marines and 164th Infantry were but the vanguard now of their parent divisions, the 2d Marine Division and the Americal Division, released for battle in the Solomons. In addition, the Army 25th Infantry Division had left Hawaii, as had smaller Marine units, such as the 2d Raider Battalion, sent south by Nimitz.

Holcomb urged Vandegrift to see Halsey about reinforcements and about curbing Turner's premature plans for dispersed ground and air operations. He also promised Vandegrift that he would get Nimitz and King to review the problem of command relationships in amphibious operations, thus sharpening the guidance of FTP-167 and forcing Turner to surrender his claim to generalship. In truth, the doctrinal guidance did not cover extended campaigns like Guadalcanal, and Ghormley had made the ambiguity worse by failing to provide active operational leadership. Such would not be the case with Halsey, who always sailed to the sound of the guns. The Marine generals also talked about their own futures. Holcomb planned to retire in 1943 (he would be beyond statutory retirement age, but so were George C. Marshall and Ernest J. King), and he wanted FDR to make Vandegrift the next Commandant. Because they had discussed this possibility before, this part of the conversation brought no surprises except to Jerry Thomas, who learned that both Holcomb and Vandegrift expected him to return to Washington, too, as a brigadier general and director of the Plans and Policies Division. Other discussions turned to tactical matters. Thomas ably defended his commitment to the cordon defense concept for jungle operations, seconded by Edson, who added that the new M-1 rifle would be the perfect antidote for the banzai charge. Comforting discussions of tactics, however, invariably gave way to the main issue, reinforcements and relief.[11]

Vandegrift agreed with Holcomb that he should return to Nouméa with the Commandant to see Halsey, who also wanted to talk with Vandegrift. The division commander, however, could sense another battle building. On the day before Holcomb's visit, a Japanese combat patrol with two tanks had probed the positions of the 3d Battalion, 1st Marines, at the mouth of the Matanikau, but McKelvey's outposts easily drove them off. Twining felt confident that the Japanese main effort would be across the bar of the Matanikau, a more professional repeat of the Tenaru attack covered with heavy artillery and supported by tanks. Thomas was not so certain and ensured that the D-3 placed adequate forces facing the jungles along the ridges between the Matanikau and the Lunga. Vandegrift approved the shifts before boarding a plane for Nouméa on 23 October. He left Bill Rupertus, who had come over from Tulagi to see Holcomb, as acting commanding general of the division with Roy Geiger as acting commander of all CACTUS forces. Rupertus collapsed with dengue fever even before Vandegrift took off, and Geiger now had both commands. As Vandegrift's plane lifted off Henderson Field, Geiger turned to Thomas and told him to fight the land battle as it developed. "Jerry, you know what you're supposed to do. You go ahead and do it." Geiger said that Thomas could reach him at CACTUS Air Force headquarters if he needed him. Otherwise, he wanted only a morning brief on the situation. For all intents and purposes, Jerry Thomas had just become the de facto division commander on the eve of the 1st Marine Division's last great defense of Henderson Field.[12]

While Vandegrift won an overdue victory over Kelly Turner, Jerry Thomas won a battle against the enemy. The Japanese commanders simplified his task by attacking without adequate coordination. On the evening of 23 October, a reinforced brigade made its major effort across the Matanikau in best World War I fashion with tanks and an artillery barrage. McKelvey's battalion, heavily supported with antitank weapons and artillery, smashed the attack. The Japanese lost eleven tanks and hundreds of infantrymen. To strengthen the Matanikau front, Thomas and Twining shifted the 2d Battalion, 7th Marines, toward the river's mouth, thus putting three battalions on that line, but changed their minds on 24 October. They then turned the battalion toward the south to face Mount Austen because scouts reported that another Japanese force was moving east of the Matanikau and north toward the shoreline to flank the Marines. The 2d Battalion, 7th Marines, blocked this move. In the meantime, the line east of the Lunga had thinned to only one battalion, Chesty Puller's 1st Battalion, 7th Marines, which covered a 2,500-yard front. Puller's contact with the 164th Infantry to his left along the Tenaru was tenuous at best. The field of battle was just east of Raider Ridge. Late in the afternoon of 24 October, Puller readied his battalion for an attack. He faced two Japanese infantry regiments but no artillery and few mortars, for most of the supporting arms had been abandoned in the jungle. Thomas followed the battle by phone with Puller's headquarters and with the CP of the 7th Marines. Puller, going mad, as usual, with the lust of battle, inspired his men and disconcerted his superiors, who wanted to help him.

As soon as Thomas could be sure that Puller faced the Japanese main effort, he put into play a decision he had reached at the start of the attack. He had Twining order a battalion of the 164th Infantry into the 7th Marine's sector and put under Puller's operational control. Already blessed with more machine guns than his battalion rated, Puller used the GIs and their M-1s to thicken his defense and seal off several slight penetrations. Because the nighttime battle was fought in a rainstorm, Puller's excitement was understandable and the movement of the 3d Battalion, 164th Infantry, predictably slow. Nevertheless, the Japanese infantry could not bear all the artillery and machine gun fire that ravaged its ranks and caused at least 1,500 casualties. Operations orders taken from dead Japanese officers in Puller's position confirmed that only half of the Japanese forces moving against the southern perimeter had made the plunge toward Raider Ridge. When another attack came the next night, Thomas and Twining had two battalions of the 164th Infantry ready to meet it. The attack died with the Japanese, who now had almost 2,000 casualties against a total of 250 Americans east of the Lunga.

In the meantime, other battles raged. Japanese aircraft and destroyers raided Guadalcanal throughout 25 October, but they retreated before the concentrated counterfires of the 3d Defense Battalion and air attack. Although heavy rains slowed the Marine air response until the strip at Fighter One dried, the Wildcats then drove off enemy aircraft while dive bombers attacked the Japanese warships and transports. The ground action continued that night when a Japanese regiment assaulted 2d Battalion, 7th Marines, east of the Matanikau and overran one company. A counterattack led by the battalion executive officer retook the position the next morning. When Vandegrift arrived back at the CP on 26 October, Thomas delivered him another victory.[13]

As the land battle sputtered and died with a hundred firefights along the southern perimeter on 26 October, Admiral Halsey engaged a larger Japanese fleet lurking off the Santa Cruz islands that awaited the signal for a final naval effort against Guadalcanal and the U.S. Navy. Adm. Thomas C. Kinkaid's two carrier groups, bearing the brunt of the fighting, lost seventy-four planes against the Japanese loss of more than one hundred planes. American pilots hit three carriers, but Kinkaid lost the *Hornet* (sunk) and the *Enterprise* (damaged) in a near-run thing. Once again, the Japanese Navy grabbed defeat from the jaws of victory and withdrew to the north, thus sparing Guadalcanal. Halsey withdrew, too, but only to push more reinforcements north while he prepared his remaining surface forces for the one type of battle the Navy had not yet won—a night engagement with big guns.

The defeat of the Japanese in their third attempt to take Henderson Field left Vandegrift and his staff optimistic but still cautious. Even though the Japanese Army had lost another 3,500 men and its tank force, General Hyakutake had most of the 38th Division available for transport down "The Slot." Between 2 and 10 November, the Japanese Navy brought more reinforcements to Guadalcanal without major interruption. In the second week of November, the opposing forces each had 30,000 men facing one another, although the Americans held the advantages of a concentrated position, immediate air support by the CACTUS Air Force, a better logistical situation, and much greater firepower. The IJN still had the advantage at night, which meant that it could shell Henderson Field and protect its own convoys until daybreak. General Hyakutake used this advantage to complicate the 1st Marine Division's tactical situation by reviving the front on the Lunga perimeter's eastern flank. Remnants of earlier attack forces had established a base near Koli Point, fifteen miles from the enclave, and the Japanese brought more troops to this beachhead, as well as to the enclave around Kokumbona. Heartened not only by his own reinforcements (the 7th Marines and 164th Infantry) but by the promised arrival of two additional regiments (8th Marines and 182d Infantry), Vandegrift had no intention of ceding the initiative to the Japanese. Although Thomas remained the most prudent of the three minds directing the division, he worried about his own judgment. He found himself swinging from moods of great weariness to moments of excessive exhilaration when a battle raged. He wrote Lottie that he thought more about retiring after the war and observed that the job of division chief of staff forced him to deal with a host of difficult problems and difficult people.[14]

Vandegrift and Twining had good reason to give the Matanikau front primary emphasis, even though Thomas thought their clarity of tactical vision sometimes bordered on the obsessive. The majority of Japanese troops, including the 150-mm artillery battalion, held the seafront and hills from Point Cruz westward. The Japanese guns could still harass air operations on Henderson Field and a new grass strip west of the Lunga, Fighter Two. Another factor argued for a shift to the attack. Despite the Holcomb-Halsey agreement to curb Kelly Turner's influence on the land campaign, Turner's basic directive for Watchtower would not be changed until Halsey, Nimitz, and King agreed to do so in December 1942, when operations on Guadalcanal shifted to the control of the Army's XXIV Corps. As for a permanent definition of relations between the amphibious force and landing force commanders when Marines waged an extended land battle as part of a naval campaign, that change would have to await consultation in Washington and a formal revision of FTP-167, the operative doctrinal statement. In other words, Kelly Turner could still play general unless Halsey overruled him. And Turner had a project: opening another enclave, complete with an airfield, at Aola Bay on Guadalcanal's eastern coast, a long forty-five miles from Lunga. On 4 November, Turner landed the 2d Raider Battalion (Lt. Col. Evans Carlson), a Marine defense battalion, Army artillery, Navy construction troops, and the first elements of the

U.S. 147th Infantry Regiment at Aola Bay, despite Australian advice that the ground was unsuitable for an airfield. Additional offensive operations, especially against the Koli Point enclave, would thus serve two purposes for the 1st Marine Division: (1) create a potent rationale for curbing the Aola Bay buildup and (2) stake a claim to the forces already landed there. Jerry Thomas saw no point in confronting Kelly Turner, especially because Vandegrift thought he had taken care of the Turner problem, but he could shape operations to the east that would discomfit the Japanese and Commander Amphibious Forces South Pacific.[15]

Reflecting Vandegrift's preference for a drive to the west, however, the 1st Marine Division welcomed November with a four-battalion attack across the Matanikau by the 5th Marines and another Whaling Group of the scout force and a battalion of the 7th Marines. When the 5th Marines pinned a Japanese force at Point Cruz, Vandegrift committed his reserve, two fresh battalions of the 2d Marines brought over from Tulagi and a battalion of the 164th Infantry, to the westward drive while Edson's regiment annihilated the Japanese in the pocket. At the same time, Vandegrift, at Thomas's urging, ordered another 7th Marines battalion to mount a reconnaissance-in-force toward Koli Point. This battalion ran into fresh Japanese troops and watched more come ashore at night (2–3 November); heavily engaged, it fought in a downpour without radio contact with the CP and the 11th Marines. Vandegrift, Thomas, and Twining agreed that two major, simultaneous actions made one action too many, especially because Navy radio intelligence had warned of a potential attack directly on the Lunga perimeter. They called Edson's force back to the Matanikau and pushed reinforcements to the east. The 11th Marines displaced again to shift the weight of its fires from the west to the east. Vandegrift also won Turner's permission to use the 2d Raider Battalion for an epic combat patrol that would march westward from Aola Bay all the way to the Lunga. It was just the sort of operation Turner could not refuse, given his raider-mania; Evans Carlson himself was eager for the assignment because it would prove the validity of his concept of irregular warfare. While the 7th Marines concentrated along a river line near Koli Point, the 2d Raiders entered the jungle to fall on the Japanese rear. To further strengthen the eastern operation, Vandegrift also committed two battalions of the 164th Infantry to a deep envelopment through the jungle against the Japanese coastal position. Because he now had two infantry regiments (four battalions) in the Koli Point offensive, Vandegrift put Brigadier General Rupertus in command. Rupertus again fell ill, however, and turned his assignment over to Brig. Gen. Edmund B. Sebree, USA, assistant division commander of the Americal Division, with Bill Whaling as his chief of staff. Vandegrift also reorganized his reinforced division, now almost a corps, into two basic commands, with Rupertus in command west of the Lunga and Sebree east of the river.[16]

While Sebree Force shifted from the defense to a major attack east past Koli Point, Admiral Halsey made his first visit to Guadalcanal. He met with Vandegrift and Thomas and took the obligatory tours and visits to the troops, at which he excelled. In their private conversations with ComSoPac, Vandegrift and Thomas convinced Halsey that the land campaign required a concentration of forces at the Lunga enclave, not diversions like the Aola Bay project. They bolstered their argument with persuasive reports from the Aola Bay engineers that the site was unsuited for air operations. Pleased that they had wrested the newly arrived 8th Marines and the 2d Raider Battalion from Turner's grasp, they made a successful plea for the 182d U.S. Infantry Regiment (scheduled for Aola Bay) and the eventual transfer of the whole Aola Bay force to the Lunga position. They also discussed whether the Navy could stop the nighttime runs of the "Tokyo Express," even though the Japanese Second and Third Fleets had now closed on the Solomons with large carrier and battleship task forces. Halsey assured them that he would mount another maximum effort to break the IJN's attacks on Guadalcanal. Even though the Koli Point operation had not yet finished, Vandegrift ordered a resumption of the offensive west of the Matanikau for 10 November. He had major actions under way on two fronts that day—a first for the division. Neither action went well enough to satisfy Vandegrift and Thomas. Much of the Japanese force to the east broke through a gap in the encircling Marines and soldiers and disappeared into the jungle, where some five hundred eventually died at the hands of the 2d Raider Battalion. The Point Cruz force recovered some lost ground, but it had not met the main Japanese defense forces when Vandegrift postponed the operation on 11 November. Again, the battle had shifted to the sea.[17]

In two naval engagements interspersed with air attacks, the U.S. Navy and CACTUS Air Force broke the back of the "Tokyo Express" between 12 and 15 November with a sacrificial ferocity that amazed the Japanese admirals and forced the senior commanders at Rabaul toward the conclusion that Guadalcanal was lost. A Navy task force of five cruisers and eight destroyers smashed into a Japanese fleet of two battleships, a cruiser, and fourteen destroyers on the night of 12–13 November. In a melee off Savo Island, the American squadron won no prizes for tactical skill but ravaged a Japanese battleship and sank two destroyers, while losing two cruisers and four destroyers. The other three cruisers suffered substantial damage, as did three of the four remaining destroyers. Two American admirals and more than seven hundred other officers and men died, but Henderson Field had not been shelled. As the remnants of the American squadron withdrew, a Japanese submarine sank one of the damaged cruisers, thus adding another seven hundred American sailors to the list of dead. The next night, the IJN returned and shelled Henderson Field and the fighter strips without opposition. The attack destroyed eighteen aircraft of CACTUS Air Force, but almost one hundred American aircraft survived. In the meantime, a Japanese convoy of eleven transports with a heavy destroyer escort steamed south down "The Slot" for western Guadalcanal. Another crisis had come. Bill Halsey, however, had not conceded defeat. His one carrier, the damaged *Enterprise*, arrived to provide limited air support. His main force, however, consisted of two battleships and four destroyers, the last of his operational combatants. On the night of 14–15 November, the American squadron engaged an IJN force of a battleship, four cruisers, and nine destroyers and defeated it, destroying the battleship and one destroyer. With one battleship and one destroyer still in action, the U.S. Navy held control of the waters off Guadalcanal and opened the way for the final aerial slaughter of the Japanese transports. On 14 November, the American pilots had sunk six transports and damaged a seventh; the next day, they destroyed the remaining four, which the Japanese had run aground in desperation. Only two thousand Japanese reached

Guadalcanal, and they did so without much heavy equipment and food. Halsey produced an operational assessment that said it all: "We've got the bastards licked!"[18]

Thomas watched the climactic naval and air battles from a hillside on Guadalcanal. He had supervised the landing of reinforcements on 12 November and ensured that the ground troops got away from "Impact Central" as quickly as possible. He felt confident that with seven infantry regiments and eleven artillery battalions, plus thousands of combat-capable supporting troops, the perimeter itself was safe from a landing. Thomas and Vandegrift did not know the details of Rear Adm. Norman Scott's plans for a night engagement except that he would seek one; they received this word from scout plane pilots dispatched from their parent cruisers before the battle began. During the night of 12 November, Thomas watched the ceaseless flicker of gunfire and heard the rumble of explosions around Savo Island. The next morning, he and other Marines saw a Japanese battleship dead in the water near Savo Island and two crippled American cruisers just off Lunga Point. Navy small craft from Vandegrift's Kukum naval station plowed about Sealark Channel and rescued hundreds of American sailors. Among them was Comdr. Murray Stokes, an old friend and captain of the destroyer *Laffey*, now at the bottom of "Ironbottom Sound." Stokes told Thomas what he knew of the battle, and his account, along with the other messages, gave Thomas a sense of the magnitude of the engagement and the threat that the Japanese Navy still posed.

There was not much Vandegrift and Thomas could do that was not being done. CACTUS Air Force, along with B-17s from Espíritu Santo, were in the air—dueling with Japanese fighters and bombing Japanese warships and transports. Thomas went down to the 1st Marine Aircraft Wing headquarters, now being run by its new commander and his old friend, Louie Woods. There, Thomas and Woods collected intelligence information from the pilot debriefings and concluded that at least four transports and a covering force would reach Guadalcanal the night of 14–15 November, an assessment they passed on to Halsey. On the evening of 13–14 November, Thomas and the headquarters personnel survived a 1,000-shell bombardment of Henderson Field. Little did they know that it would be their last uplifting experience. The next night, Thomas again watched a great naval battle—or at least heard it. The following morning he and Vandegrift observed the air attacks that blasted the last four transports, given the coup de grace by a surviving American destroyer. Another opportunity beckoned for an offensive west of the Matanikau. Thomas and Twining promptly organized a task force built around the 8th Marines, the 2d Marines, and 182d Infantry and commanded by Maj. Gen. Alexander M. Patch of the Americal Division and Vandegrift's designated successor as commander of all Guadalcanal ground troops.[19]

Even though further reinforced by the 164th Infantry, the offensive did not go well, largely because the green 182d Infantry did not press its attack behind a close artillery barrage. Hearing reports that suggested tactical inertia, Thomas drove out to Patch's CP for a conference and learned that the Japanese were present and fighting, although not yet in force. Vandegrift, furious, wanted the attack pressed, but Thomas persuaded him to grant Patch's request for a postponement until the Army general could deploy his own 132d Infantry in the offensive. One advantage of the postponement was that it allowed Vandegrift to disengage the 8th Marines, who had not fared well between two Army battalions that paid little attention to their flanks. Elsewhere, the tactical situation looked promising. After a series of running battles outside the perimeter, the 2d Raider Battalion entered the enclave, tired but exultant, and Carlson accurately reported that the Japanese had no effective forces anywhere but on the western coastline. CACTUS Air Force made good its losses with more USAAF fighter reinforcements. The only real concern was the 1st Marine Division's health; its hospitals had admitted more than three thousand Marines with malaria during November. On 29 November, the JCS confirmed that the U.S. 25th Infantry Division would come directly to Guadalcanal as a relief for the 1st Marine Division. As soon as the Navy could provide transports, the Marines would head for a rest camp in Australia. Jerry Thomas and his comrades found a future, after all.[20]

With the end of its ordeal in sight, the 1st Marine Division turned surly as well as cynical. Vandegrift and Thomas worked closely to make the turnover as smooth as possible, but even they found it difficult to keep an even temper when dealing with the Army and their own colonels. Vandegrift did not like the vague guidance he received about shipping schedules, equipment transfers, and his destination in Australia. He showed one particularly opaque ComSoPac message to Thomas: "I must rank with an admiral. They won't give me an order."[21] He and Patch decided to make 9 December the official change-of-command day; the arrival of the 132d Infantry meant that Army troops would then outnumber the Marines. In the meantime, Bill Twining and Capt. Donald L. Dickson, adjutant of the 5th Marines and premier artist of the campaign, designed the division's informal campaign decoration, the "George Medal." It featured an admiral, a Marine, a cactus, a hot potato shaped like the island, the stern of a cow, and a whirring fan. The medal, which became a collector's item, bore the motto in Latin, "Let George Do It." "George" was the 1st Marine Division's self-inflicted nickname. Even one last nighttime defeat for the U.S. Navy (the Battle of Tassafaronga, 30 November–1 December) did not quench the urge to move toward the beaches once the division knew that its transports were safe. After their last night at General Rupertus's headquarters near Lunga Point, Vandegrift, Thomas, Twining, and four other key officers of the division headquarters mounted a DC-3 at Henderson Field and flew—in a sky no longer disturbed by Zeros—without incident to Nouméa and a final meeting with Admiral Halsey. For Vandegrift and Thomas, Guadalcanal marked the fulfillment of their professional careers and the deepening of an association that would soon win other battles for the United States Marine Corps.[22]

Although the 1st Marine Division left Guadalcanal before the end of the campaign in February 1943, the men knew they had won their part of a decisive victory. When General Vandegrift issued a clear, heartfelt message of congratulations to his division on 7 December 1942, he could not know how deeply the Marines had wounded the Japanese war effort. Before the end of the month, the high commanders at Imperial Headquarters admitted to themselves that they could not continue to expend their forces for Guadalcanal. The Japanese Army lost 21,000 men on the island (8,500 battle deaths); the Japanese Navy lost around eight hundred aircraft and 2,400 pilots and crewmen in the battle for air superiority, and Army aviation also took serious losses; the Imperial Japanese fleet dropped twenty-four warships and thousands of sailors from its rolls. The campaign ended any concern about Japanese invincibility and inflicted irreplaceable losses on the surface fleet and aviation force of the Imperial Navy. The U.S. Navy paid the highest part of the American butcher's bill: twenty-four warships and the lives of probably 5,000 sailors. For the 1st Marine Division and the 1st Marine Aircraft Wing, the campaign had not been too costly, given the results; about 1,500 Marines died or became missing in action on Guadalcanal, with another 3,000 wounded in battle. More than half of Marine casualties occurred when the division began to mount serious offensive operations after the Battle of the Ridge (12–14 September). Like most great military campaigns of the twentieth century—the age of mass military organizations and lethal technology—individual contributions to victory and defeat are difficult to fix. Yet, among the senior officers of the 1st Marine Division, two giants stand out, then and now, as the architects of victory, Alexander Archer Vandegrift and Gerald C. Thomas.[23]

[CHAPTER XVIII]

Marines in the South Pacific 1943

For almost a year after the 1st Marine Division shook the slime of Guadalcanal from its field shoes, the fate of the Marine Corps in the war with Japan drifted. Although Marine Corps aviation and some specialized ground combat units, such as the raider and defense battalions, participated in the campaign for the central Solomons, the divisions of the Fleet Marine Force did not make an amphibious assault until the landing on Bougainville (1 November 1943) in the northern Solomons and the assault on Tarawa (20 November 1943) in the Gilberts. The 1st Marine Division made its next assault at Cape Gloucester on New Britain Island (26 December 1943). The months between the winter and late autumn of 1943 became a time of uncertainty at the strategic level, a time of transition in the leadership of the Marine Corps at Headquarters, a period of plans made and discarded for organizations and individuals. For Col. Gerald C. Thomas, the year began in Australia and ended in Washington. Like the fortunes of the Marine Corps, Thomas's career took some unexpected turns before it found its place in the drive for final victory over Japan.[1]

For Maj. Gen. Alexander Archer Vandegrift and six of his most trusted staff officers (including Thomas), the road from Guadalcanal led first to Headquarters, South Pacific Theater, at Nouméa, New Caledonia, and a visit with Vice Adm. William F. Halsey, who welcomed the Marines as conquering heroes. Wined, dined, and lionized, Vandegrift and his staff spent three busy but gratifying days in Nouméa before flying on to Brisbane, Australia, and the 1st Division's rest camp. The business conducted by the staff of the 1st Division consisted primarily of conferences with Maj. Gen. Clayton B. Vogel, commanding general of the I Marine Amphibious Corps (I MAC), and his staff, which included several of Jerry's best friends, Archie Howard, Dudley Brown, and John T. Selden. Established in October 1942, Vogel's corps headquarters had the responsibility for the administration, training, and logistical support of the Marine ground forces in the

[211]

South Pacific, but Commandant Thomas Holcomb and Admiral Halsey expected it to also serve as a landing force headquarters for future amphibious operations. One of the senior permanent major generals in the Marine Corps, the bluff, gregarious Vogel had ample recent experience in corps command. He had directed the 2d Joint Training Force, a Marine-Army amphibious corps, for a year before coming to Nouméa. Vogel, however, had more intuition than education in amphibious matters and more energy for liberty than for work. He complicated his problems by avoiding airplane flights whenever possible, which did nothing to enhance his efficiency or his reputation with Halsey.[2]

Amid the compliments and promises of assistance they received from Halsey and Vogel—and the confirmation that both of them would soon receive prestigious decorations for their leadership on Guadalcanal—Vandegrift and Thomas also learned from Vogel's staff that interservice rivalry in the South Pacific had increased with the tempo of operations. During the stop at Nouméa, Bill Twining visited with his older brother, Brig. Gen. Nathan F. Twining, USAAF, and other army officers, including Maj. Gen. J. Lawton Collins, the brilliant and ambitious commanding general of the U.S. 25th Infantry Division. Bill Twining listened in dismay as the Army officers described their plan to limit the role of the Fleet Marine Force (FMF) in the war with Japan and their postwar intent to control all air forces and to reduce the FMF to a small expeditionary force incapable of performing major war missions. Even with his Guadalcanal experience behind him, Vandegrift might have ignored Twining's concerns (he regarded his D-3 as an alarmist), but he received the same news from Holcomb, who feared that neither the Army nor the Navy would allow Vogel or Maj. Gen. Holland M. Smith to command an amphibious corps. (Smith had succeeded Vogel as commander of Amphibious Corps, Pacific Fleet, at San Diego in August 1942.) However worrisome these questions, Vandegrift faced more pressing problems in Australia, where his division, on the verge of collapse, awaited him.[3]

As part of the arrangement that had brought Army divisions to Guadalcanal, the 1st Marine Division changed theaters and sailed for Australia, not back to New Zealand, to recuperate and reorganize. The Southwest Pacific theater commander, Gen. Douglas MacArthur, wanted the Marines to encamp near Brisbane, Queensland, where the division, in theory, could serve as a reserve force should the Japanese try to regain the initiative in the continuing battle for New Guinea. The division's long-range mission was to train for another amphibious assault as part of MacArthur's drive towards Rabaul. When Vandegrift and Thomas arrived in Brisbane, site of MacArthur's major (and massive) administrative headquarters, they found much to dislike about the division's situation, an assessment heartily shared by all their Marines. The division tent city, Camp Cable, rested in a wooded marshland twenty-five miles from the city; the Marines thought their base at New River, North Carolina, had been a better campground. Although the Army supply services tried to make the camp livable, the major objection to Camp Cable became medical. Despite earlier reports that the area was free of malaria-bearing mosquitoes, American and Australian medical authorities concurred that the Marines and the mosquitoes had found one another. The troops raised the incidence of malaria cases by neglecting to stay on their regime of Atabrine and quinine. The division surgeon, Capt. Warwick Brown, USN, soon reported that malaria and related fevers had reached epidemic proportions, far worse than at Guadalcanal. Vandegrift sent two officers to search for another cantonment and visited MacArthur to plead for a movement south to healthier climes. Navy commanders added similar recommendations. MacArthur, however, would not relent in his decision that the Marines must make do at Brisbane.[4]

Exhausted and twenty pounds thinner from his service on Guadalcanal, Jerry Thomas did his best to manage the division's movement and rehabilitation, but he shared the general lethargy that struck the 1st Division. His own morale took several shocks. He had not heard from Lottie for weeks; the division's mail had not yet arrived. He learned that his trunk in New Zealand had been lost and with it most of his service uniforms and, more importantly, his family photographs and personal effects. Although he and the division staff moved into large rooms in a hotel in Brisbane, he took no comfort as long as the men's health and living conditions remained deplorable. He did not relish a Christmas season apart from his family in North Carolina. His sense of duty, however, moved him to tackle his business with a degree of concentration that distinguished him from many of the division's senior officers. He worked closely with MacArthur's G-3 and G-4, the latter a Leavenworth classmate, to improve Camp Cable and to mount a convincing case that the division should move south. From his forward headquarters at Port Moresby, MacArthur finally relented on the division's further redeployment, with Admiral Halsey's promise to provide the shipping for the move from his own transport force. With the enthusiastic endorsement of the Australians, MacArthur's own rear headquarters, the U.S. Navy, and the American ambassador to Australia (Thomas's friend Nelson T. Johnson), the 1st Marine Division arrived in Melbourne in mid-January 1943 for the real beginning of its rebirth as a fighting force.[5]

The anabasis to Melbourne provided just the tonic the chief of staff and the rest of the division required to restore their morale. Vandegrift and his staff took rooms and offices in a downtown hotel and the City Cricket Club, but then moved to the villa of an American businessman. One infantry regiment camped inside the city, a model of cleanliness and "Olde English" floral splendor. Two infantry regiments and the 11th Marines went to camps of considerable comfort just outside the city. The division found special friends in the U.S. Army 4th Base Section, which made up for the division's alarming defects in equipment and uniforms and provided fifty cars. Staffed by doctors and attendants from the prestigious Cleveland [Ohio] Clinic, the 4th Base Hospital occupied one of the most modern, complete hospitals in Australia and provided exceptional care as another wave of recurrent malaria struck the division. Thomas believed that his personal relationship with the colonel who commanded the 4th Base Section, another Leavenworth friend, helped to ensure Army hospitality. Australian graciousness left nothing to be desired, even when the restored Marines began their ambitious assault on the city's bars and lovelorn women. Thomas himself followed a regime suitable for a Marine colonel. He organized the general's small mess, held daily meetings and conferences, met with Australian and American civilian and military officials, attended social gatherings, and amused himself by going to the local theater and movies, musicals preferred. He read some, walked a lot, and reported to Lottie that he was feeling much more energetic. His pilfered trunk arrived without his uniforms, but with his photographs and personal items intact. He also learned that Holcomb wanted Vandegrift and him to return to the United States immediately.[6]

The two Marines left Australia in its summer warmth and, after eighty hours of chilling flight, landed in Washington, D.C., in the middle of a snowstorm. Vandegrift and Thomas received no guidance on the nature of their recall; in Brisbane, Vandegrift asked MacArthur if he had requested his relief because of his strenuous arguments for moving the division to Melbourne. Surprised, MacArthur replied that he had not, that he thought Vandegrift's return was political. MacArthur's instincts were correct. President Roosevelt and General Holcomb wanted to display the hero of Guadalcanal to a government and public thirsty for victorious generals. For almost two months, Vandegrift—under the sure guidance of Undersecretary of the Navy James V. Forrestal and Holcomb—conducted briefings and press conferences, addressed Congress and the JCS, made round after round of public appearances, and spoke to live and radio audiences. On 4 February 1943, Roosevelt decorated Vandegrift with the Medal of Honor at a White House ceremony. For Thomas, the Washington visit (the American equivalent of a Roman triumphal parade) had its own high moments. Working from a room in the Army and Navy Club, Thomas found his operational views in great demand at Headquarters and the Marine schools at Quantico. He enjoyed seeing old friends and spent some time with his father, but he also longed for Lottie and his children. In early February, he took twelve days' leave to see his family in Greenville, North Carolina, which hailed him as a native son. Returning to Headquarters, Jerry received his own speaking assignments, a Veterans of Foreign Wars meeting in Washington and a Red Cross convention in Philadelphia. He believed that he played his public role to Forrestal's satisfaction. Certainly his own morale took a jump when he finally received the Distinguished Service Medal from Holcomb on 20 February.[7]

Always attuned to the demands of duty, Thomas used his Washington interlude to study the people, policies, and procedures at Headquarters. Neither he nor Vandegrift heard anything that modified Holcomb's commitment to retire and turn the Marine Corps over to Vandegrift. The Washington trip, indeed, allowed them to make a reconnaissance and to reinforce Vandegrift's popularity in the capital. Thomas kept his counsel. As he left the city, he thought of the challenges ahead as Director, Plans and Policies Division. He enjoyed one more event on the way west, a sentimental visit to Bloomington and Illinois Wesleyan University and a reunion with his brother Shelton. After Vandegrift gave one last speech in Chicago, the two Marines left for San Francisco by train, arriving on 19 March. Jerry used the trip to begin reading the first volume of Douglas Southall Freeman's *Lee's Lieutenants*, which he enjoyed immensely. The air trip back to Australia went at a leisurely pace and allowed Vandegrift and Thomas to have long talks and visit an exotic island or two. They discussed the organization of the Marine Corps Headquarters staff and personnel matters. Their only uncertainty about Vandegrift's appointment as Commandant related to its timing. Jerry's spirits received another boost when he arrived in Melbourne on 29 March and found his Christmas packages and twenty letters awaiting him.[8]

The staff of the 1st Marine Division welcomed its commanding general and chief of staff back to Australia with warm pleasure and pressing problems. Malaria had revisited the division and forced delays in the training schedule. As the 4th Base Hospital medical staff and Captain Brown's corpsmen put the Marines on a strict malaria-suppression regime, Vandegrift and Thomas accepted the doctor's advice that the troops would recover more rapidly with exercise, specifically long hikes in the crisp Australian autumn. With the predictable grousing of veterans, the Marines took to the roads. Within a month, Thomas observed a definite improvement in the troops' endurance, spirits, and interest in training. In the meantime, he tackled another major difficulty, restoring the division to Marine Corps levels of weapons, equipment, and spare parts. Army quartermasters shrank before the requisitions the Marines submitted. The 1st Marine Division demanded more of everything than an Army infantry division, which could expect logistical services at corps level that a Marine amphibious division could not. Thomas spurred his own logistical staff to imaginative efforts both within and outside normal channels, while he made many trips to Sydney, the location of the Army supply center, and Brisbane, the site of the U.S. Sixth Army headquarters (Lt. Gen. Walter Krueger). As the parent command for the 1st Marine Division, the Sixth Army could, and did, help with the supply problems. Thomas felt that his own personal diplomacy smoothed the way; six of Krueger's principal staff officers were his Army friends from Benning and Leavenworth. By June 1943, Thomas believed that the 1st Marine Division had reached combat readiness as the division started training with the Seventh Fleet's amphibious ships. Few doubted that the division would once again meet the Japanese somewhere in the South Pacific, but no one had a clue about the place and time. Thomas had an additional concern. He and Vandegrift had not yet received orders to return to Washington. In fact, Thomas received another assignment that pushed his return to the United States into the indefinite future.[9]

Between January and April 1943, Roosevelt, Churchill, and their military planners hammered out a set of fluid agreements that shaped operations against Japan for the rest of the year. Although still limited by the "Germany First" strategy, the Allied leaders wanted to keep the initiative in the Pacific, but they had very different ideas about how they might advance against Japan. The British wanted more emphasis on the reconquest of Burma and Malaya; the Americans (principally the U.S. Navy) wanted to open a new theater in the central Pacific where they could bring the Combined Fleet to decisive battle. No one had the resources for all of the operations endorsed in principle at Casablanca in January. More detailed planning continued and culminated with the Pacific Military Conference in March 1943, where the JCS planners examined the options with representatives from South West Pacific (SoWesPac), SoPac, and CinCPac.

The basis for discussion became MacArthur's basic plan, code-named Elkton, for the isolation and possible capture of Rabaul by thirteen operations in eight months. As always, MacArthur's concept accepted major risks, underestimated the Japanese, and placed inordinate faith in land-based air power. Admirals Nimitz and Halsey favored a slower, more calculated advance that avoided a direct assault on the most heavily defended Japanese air bases and with its operations keyed to the forces already available, not those MacArthur hoped to pry from the JCS. The Navy representatives also wanted to husband their forces for the first advances in the central Pacific. By the end of March, the JCS approved a modification of the July 1942 strategic guidance for the Pacific war that confirmed the South Pacific dual advance and promised more forces. MacArthur would continue to provide strategic direction, but Halsey retained considerable latitude in designing the right-hand advance up the Solomons. Unlike MacArthur, Halsey did not fancy a drive directly to heavily defended Bougainville in the northern Solomons. Instead, he preferred a series of more limited attacks in the central Solomons, with the capture of New Georgia as the centerpiece of the concept of operations. Supported by King and Nimitz, Halsey eventually received approval from MacArthur to take New Georgia before the SoPac forces tackled Bougainville.[10]

The renewed offensive in the Solomons put new stress on Halsey's SoPac staff, which had little experience in amphibious operations. Although Halsey had his own Marine planner, DeWitt Peck, he properly turned to General Vogel's I MAC headquarters to do the preliminary studies of the New Georgia operation. The operational discussions did not go well for Vogel and his staff, which turned in pessimistic (though realistic) estimates of the ground forces necessary to isolate, then capture, New Georgia. The landing forces would come primarily from SoPac's Army contingent. Perhaps Vogel did not take the planning seriously because he thought I MAC would not command the landing. In any event, the Army's XIV Corps assumed the planning mission by promising to do more with less. When Vandegrift and Thomas passed through Halsey's headquarters on their way back to Melbourne, the bullish admiral discussed Vandegrift's availability to command I MAC and warned the Marines that he would request that Holcomb change the senior Marine officers assigned to SoPac.[11]

The New Georgia operation brought a summer of discontent to SoPac headquarters as the XIV Corps did less with more and further strengthened Halsey's conviction that he wanted I MAC to organize the forthcoming Bougainville invasion. The two principal commanders, Maj. Gen. Oscar W. Griswold (XIV Corps) and Maj. Gen. John H. Hester (43d Infantry Division), did not perform up to Halsey's aggressive standards. Even Admiral Nimitz, ever alert to Army sensitivities about command, agreed that the XIV Corps showed little expertise in amphibious operations and the management of a jungle campaign. Halsey's impatience forced the issue of General Vogel's fitness to direct the next major operation. As the battle for New Georgia raged, Vogel dramatized his own limitations by touring Marine commands in SoPac by ship. By early July, he had been absent from his headquarters for six weeks, and his chief of staff, Archie Howard, had simply postponed many critical decisions and left key planning documents and directives unsigned until Vogel's return. Halsey asked Holcomb whether Vandegrift could postpone his return to the United States to become the Marine Corps Commandant and replace Vogel at I MAC. Nimitz supported his request. Holcomb decided he could delay his retirement from August until the end of December (others wanted him to remain Commandant until the end of the war), and he feared that only Vandegrift's prestige would save the principle that Marine generals should command amphibious corps. Aware of Halsey's intentions since March, Vandegrift finally received orders on 1 July assigning him as Commanding General, I Marine Amphibious Corps. Vogel returned to the United States to a training command.[12]

Vandegrift kept his Guadalcanal team with him when he left the 1st Marine Division for Nouméa. William Rupertus, promoted to major general, moved up to division commander and deserved to pick his own staff, which included other Guadalcanal veterans: Amor L. Sims (chief of staff), Ed Buckley (D-2), Al Pollock (D-3), and William S. Fellers (D-4). Lem Shepherd, a new brigadier, arrived to become assistant division commander. Cliff Cates, also a new brigadier, departed to command a separate brigade, and "Red Mike" Edson moved to the 2d Marine Division to become its chief of staff. Vandegrift kept his most trusted officers with him: Thomas (chief of staff), Bill Twining (C-3), Jim Murray (staff secretary), Ed Snedeker (communications officer), and Ray Schwenke (aide and assistant operations officer). To the moving music of the 1st Division band, which specialized in "The Marines' Hymn" and "Waltzing Matilda," Vandegrift's group departed by plane for its new headquarters on 7 July. Thomas understood why he would not be returning to Washington and his family, and he warned Lottie that his assignment to Headquarters might be changed permanently. The I MAC chief of staff found his "in" basket filled to overflowing, and he moved with the same urgency as Vandegrift to change the pace of Marine planning in Nouméa. The new I MAC staff pleased them both. One of Thomas's old friends, Lt. Col. Joseph C. Burger, remained from Vogel's staff to serve as C-1. Lt. Col. Frederick L. Wieseman, a Guadalcanal veteran with the 7th Marines and former division assistant D-4 in Australia, arrived to be the C-4. Thomas wanted Dudley Brown to stay in the South Pacific, but Vogel took Brown to be his chief of staff in California. Thomas plunged into his new job with complete confidence that Vandegrift's staff could meet any challenge.[13]

Vandegrift provided the active leadership for I MAC that Halsey sought. He first asked Halsey for his own command plane and received an amphibian PBY-5A, which he and Thomas used to visit every major Marine command in SoPac during July and August. Vandegrift focused especially on the 3d Marine Division (Maj. Gen. Charles D. Barrett) and the newly established Marine Service Command South Pacific, ably commanded by Brig. Gen. Earl C. Long. He also intervened to prevent Vice Adm. Richmond Kelly Turner, still commander of Amphibious Force South Pacific, from using two unsuitable anchorages (both too far from the objective) to load the 2d Marine Division in amphibious craft for the forthcoming assault on Tarawa. Although the I MAC staff already knew the sites were poor, Halsey required an additional reconnaissance that sent Thomas and part of his staff on another long plane ride to the Fijis. A navigational error almost put the aircraft into the ocean, but the trip produced compelling evidence that Halsey could use to stop Turner's plans. Although Thomas judged his own relations with Turner happy, or at least unintimidated, the I MAC staff did not go into mourning when Turner went off to the central Pacific. His replacement was Rear Adm. Theodore S. Wilkinson, Halsey's deputy and a thorough professional of even temperament. For all the administrative energy the I MAC demonstrated, Vandegrift had come to Nouméa to plan another offensive, the assault on Bougainville.[14]

From the I MAC perspective, the Bougainville operation posed special planning problems. MacArthur still believed in a direct attack on Rabaul and wanted Halsey to eliminate the five Japanese air bases on the island (and two others on the neighboring Shortlands and Buka) and to do so in six weeks, prior to the SoWesPac invasion of New Britain Island before the end of 1943. Concerned by the slow pace, casualties, and interservice tension with the Army that characterized the summer campaign in the central Solomons, Halsey tacked away from any decision that committed his SoPac forces to a direct assault on the most significant Japanese bases on Bougainville's southern tip in the Buin area and Faisi on the Shortlands. His planners floated all sorts of other options that focused on landing on the Treasury Islands, Buka, and neighboring Choiseul Island—in effect, proposals to isolate Rabaul by isolating Bougainville. MacArthur could read maps when he chose to, and he found all these indirect approaches unacceptable because they did not neutralize Japanese air or provide adequate Allied fighter coverage for his own anticipated operations against Rabaul. Halsey's staff reluctantly concluded that I MAC would have to assault Bougainville directly, a conclusion Vandegrift and Thomas thought unavoidable. Detailed planning, however, could not progress, despite the press of time, because the planners at all levels wanted more information about possible objective areas. This required a flurry of reconnaissance activity by aircraft, submarines, and patrols that actually landed on Bougainville. Until Halsey made up his mind where I MAC's main effort would be, Vandegrift and Thomas could direct only limited preparations, principally ensuring that their tactical organizations (the 3d Marine Division and corps troops) and service units were ready for a major, complex operation.[15]

Hardly had Vandegrift's Guadalcanal team arrived in Nouméa to take charge of I MAC when Vandegrift learned from Holcomb that he would return soon to Washington, as planned, to be Commandant. On 22 July, Thomas wrote his wife that she should have a birthday cake ready for him, which meant that he expected to be home by the end of October or before the projected date of the Bougainville landing. Holcomb and Vandegrift made the command arrangements for I MAC early in Vandegrift's service as the corps commander, with the assistance of the Commandant's decision on the latest group of new brigadier generals. Vandegrift would turn over I MAC to Major General Barrett, who would bring along his division chief of staff, Alfred H. Noble (a new brigadier), to serve in the same role for I MAC. Barrett would turn over command of his division to his assistant division commander, Allen Hal Turnage, fifty-two, a gracious, widely respected North Carolinian of equal intelligence and energy. Oscar R. Cauldwell, a former Thomas comrade from World War I, moved up to assistant division commander from command of the 3d Marines. Robert Blake replaced Noble as division chief of staff. Bill Twining, Ed Snedeker, and Fred Wieseman would remain on the I MAC staff to provide continuity and combat experience. The leadership of the 3d Division and I MAC had few peers in the Marine Corps for quiet competence, and Vandegrift felt no reluctance to let these officers bear the major role in shaping the Bougainville operation. On 23 July, Vandegrift split I MAC headquarters. He moved the planners to Guadalcanal and left the administrative and logistical staff at Nouméa. The move fused I MAC headquarters with the 3d Marine Division planners, as well as those of the 1st Marine Aircraft Wing

(Maj. Gen. Field Harris), which bore the task of developing an allied airfield on Bougainville.[16]

Thomas relished the triumphal return to Guadalcanal, now a modestly comfortable base area, but he also found plenty of problems for the I MAC chief of staff to tackle. He worked closely with Twining, Barrett, and Noble on the Bougainville planning and played a major role in adding one nuance to the Corps' concept of operation, a diversionary raid on Choiseul island. The Choiseul diversion sprang from the fertile mind of Jim Murray, but Thomas immediately recognized the potential effect of the operation. He probably remembered the considerable benefits of Evans Carlson's 2d Raider Battalion patrol east of the Lunga perimeter. The issue of utilizing I MAC's corps troops also focused Thomas's attention on the whole problem of the FMF's current force structure. When Vandegrift became Commanding General I MAC, he inherited four raider battalions, three parachute battalions, and six defense battalions, most of whom participated in one way or another in the defense of Guadalcanal and the central Solomons campaign. Thomas doubted that I MAC could find enough missions for these special operations battalions, and they contained an inordinate amount of officer and senior enlisted talent. Encouraged by Thomas, Vandegrift came to the same conclusion. By the end of the year, these units had begun their transformation into regular divisional units or, in the case of the defense battalions, antiaircraft or heavy artillery battalions. Thomas made his own position clear by arranging for Headquarters to transfer a select group of majors from the defense battalions to the United States for staff training and subsequent assignment to the two newest Marine divisions.[17]

Convinced that he had done all he could to advance the Bougainville planning and already thinking ahead to his tour as Commandant, Vandegrift saw no reason to stay desk-bound on Guadalcanal when he could be assessing other aspects of amphibious operations. He had no delusions that the Guadalcanal landing could be repeated in terms of surprise. On 7 August 1943, he held a major press conference on Guadalcanal to recognize the first anniversary of Watchtower; he told the assembled reporters that the Fleet Marine Force faced Japanese defenders who would now be better prepared for any landing. A week later, he and Thomas joined Admiral Wilkinson on his flagship *Cony* (DD 508) for the invasion of Vella Lavella by a composite Army-Marine Corps task force. Barrett joined the party at Vandegrift's invitation. Although the Japanese ground defense did not materialize, the amphibious task force endured a heavy air attack, and the *Cony* barely avoided two close bomb hits. Soaked by the near misses, Vandegrift's party came away impressed by the continued ferocity of Japanese resistance—Admiral Halsey's subsequent scolding for taking unnecessary risks reinforced this impression. Japanese air and naval attacks continued for four more days and took some toll of the amphibious shipping, but the landing succeeded. (Japanese propagandists later announced that Vandegrift had been killed on 15 August.) In the meantime, the I MAC staff returned to Guadalcanal by way of Munda as Vandegrift continued his final tour of Marine units in SoPac and SoWesPac. He and Thomas flew on to Australia, New Guinea, and Nouméa, where Vandegrift officially turned over I MAC to Barrett on 15 September, and then went to New Zealand for a last visit with the 2d Marine Division, bound for Tarawa. Afterward,

Vandegrift's party started home with intermediate stops to visit Marine units stationed between New Zealand and Hawaii.[18]

Weeks after Charlie Barrett assumed command of I MAC, Halsey finally decided that the 3d Marine Division (reinforced) would land at Empress Augusta Bay halfway up Bougainville's relatively undefended (and swampy) western coast. The decision reflected Barrett's preference for anything but a Buin-Faisi landing. Halsey's decision set off a tragic chain of events that would delay Thomas's return to the United States well past his birthday. Before he and Vandegrift could take over Headquarters, they had to retrace their steps to the South Pacific to perform a second rescue operation of I Marine Amphibious Corps. Neither of them foresaw the seeds of potential trouble. The first omen might have been Bill Twining's return to the United States for his second treatment for stomach cancer, but Ed Snedeker took his place as corps operations officer. Snedeker, still battling a case of Guadalcanal malaria, found the planning behind schedule. None of the I MAC staff could fault Barrett and Noble for their close examination of the Bougainville operation. Barrett, in fact, had the major influence on choosing Empress Augusta Bay as the amphibious objective area, but he also remained keenly aware that Wilkinson's amphibious task force faced potentially heavy Japanese air and naval attacks. Moreover, he watched ominous signs of stiffening Japanese beach defenses in the area. An amphibious planner of legendary brilliance in the Marine Corps—Barrett, more than any other officer, shaped the *Tentative Manual for Landing Operations*—he took only Noble into his confidence. The rest of the I MAC staff on Guadalcanal often watched these two officers work late into the night on details of the landing plan. Where Barney Vogel had done too little, Charlie Barrett did too much, and it cost him his life.

The more Barrett worked on the Bougainville landing, the more profound became his doubts that it would succeed or that it would succeed only with heavy casualties. His obsession with casualties, which predated his command of the 3d Marine Brigade, mounted in the South Pacific. His depression deepened a level of fatigue difficult for a fifty-eight-year-old general to manage. Holcomb had already cautioned him, while he had commanded the 3d Marine Division, to relax and to pace himself and his troops. Barrett could not take the advice, and the irritable and excitable Noble did nothing to ease his emotional stress. Summoned to Nouméa to discuss the operation again with Halsey—and aware that time would not allow more consideration—Barrett worked late into the preceding night of 7 October, then departed by air for the long trip to Halsey's headquarters. He met with Halsey on the afternoon of 8 October and learned that Halsey intended to sign a final directive for the Empress Augusta Bay assault. Halsey may have suggested that he was considering relieving Barrett with Vandegrift. Uncharacteristically quiet, Barrett returned to the I MAC rear echelon headquarters, a comfortable villa in Nouméa, and discussed the remaining problems with his logistical staff. Excusing himself from the group, he went to the second-floor balcony and, apparently deep in thought, sat on the short restraining wall. None of his staff bothered him. Later in the evening, his officers discovered to their horror that Barrett had fallen from the balcony and died of a broken neck and fractured skull. Some suspected suicide, others that he had suffered a stroke that caused the fall. More likely, he had simply fallen asleep and plunged to his accidental death. Whatever the cause, Barrett's death, a tragic end to a career of immeasurable value to the Corps, threw SoPac headquarters into a panic. The Bougainville landing was less than a month away.[19]

Vandegrift and Thomas learned of Barrett's death on their first day at Nimitz's headquarters at Pearl Harbor. Neither found surprising Halsey's recommendations that Vandegrift return immediately to I MAC for the Bougainville landing and that Roy S. Geiger replace him as soon as possible as the permanent commander of I MAC. Thomas had, in fact, already discussed the question of I MAC command, should something happen to Barrett, with Bill Riley, the Marine colonel serving as the new SoPac plans officer. Both of them thought Geiger the obvious choice and probably available because he could be replaced at Headquarters as the Commandant's director of Marine aviation with another senior air officer. That a pilot should command an amphibious corps might strike some as shocking, but Geiger had proved his competence at Guadalcanal. He had started his career as an infantry officer of great repute and had studied the ground aspects of amphibious operations before the war with an attention unusual among Marine aviators. More importantly, he enjoyed the complete confidence of Halsey and Vandegrift. Riley had reinforced Halsey's inclination to request Vandegrift and Geiger in tandem, and Nimitz, King, and Holcomb approved the arrangement. Vandegrift's entire party returned to its command aircraft and flew back to Nouméa in time for Barrett's funeral on 10 October. Without a rest, Vandegrift and his staff flew on to Guadalcanal and reassumed command of I MAC.[20]

Vandegrift returned to the South Pacific ready to exploit Halsey's relief upon his emergency assignment, and Thomas pushed the future Commandant's advantage to full effect. That the 3d Marine Division would assault Empress Augusta Bay was fixed. Vandegrift had no choice but to accept Barrett's basic concept; on 12 October, Halsey confirmed 1 November as D-Day. That a New Zealand brigade group would invade the Treasury Islands on 27 October was also a given. Vandegrift, at Thomas's urging, could still influence the operation, however, and he did. Barrett had canceled the Choiseul raid, but it reappeared in the corps operations order approved by Vandegrift on 18 October. The mission of raiding Choiseul went (at Jim Murray's urging) to the well-trained but underutilized 2d Parachute Battalion (Lt. Col. Victor H. Krulak), unhappily stationed on Vella Lavella with the New Zealanders. Krulak seized the dangerous operation with characteristic enthusiasm, energy, and intelligence, and his subsequent strong leadership of the Choiseul raid insured "Brute" Krulak a combat reputation and membership on the Vandegrift-Thomas team. More importantly in the short term, Thomas, as the corps chief of staff (Noble had moved to deputy corps commander to make room), took the initiative in pushing the Navy to provide shipping for reinforcements to the 3d Division's Cape Torokina beachhead. From his Guadalcanal experience, Thomas thought that the initial assault would get ashore but that the Japanese would mount a rapid, violent air and sea attack to interdict reinforcements. The concept Vandegrift had inherited, however, provided for a leisurely movement of Hal Turnage's third infantry regiment and the reinforcing U.S. 37th Infantry Division to the beachhead. When Thomas found Wilkinson's staff insensitive to the problem, he urged Vandegrift to take the issue directly to the amphibious task force commander. Vandegrift raised the question at a conference on Guadalcanal; Halsey had joined the advanced command group and immediately endorsed the change of plans. Turnage, therefore, could push the assault, confident that he would get timely reinforcements.[21]

Thomas also forced another issue of more significant consequence to the Marine Corps, the question of command relations in any future amphibious operations. Prewar doctrine, at least as understood in the Marine Corps, implied that Marine organizations would conduct initial amphibious assaults and that Army headquarters would then control the following land campaign, if extended and requiring Army divisions. Although unsettled in doctrine and practice, this relationship had prevailed in Guadalcanal. It had become unraveled, however, in the summer of 1943 when the Army's XIV Corps assumed responsibility for the New Georgia landing and also laid claim to the Bougainville assault. Even as the planning for Bougainville staggered forward, Halsey's staff examined other, subsequent landings that would contribute to the isolation of Rabaul. When Thomas learned of these plans, he encouraged Vandegrift to seize the moment and insist that I MAC control not only the Bougainville landing but any other SoPac amphibious assaults. In another conference on Guadalcanal in late October 1943, Vandegrift raised the issue with Halsey in the presence of senior Army officers. Halsey passed the matter to Wilkinson, who said he preferred that XIV Corps take control of the Bougainville operations after the landing and the arrival of the 37th Division, thus releasing I MAC to plan any further operations. Halsey approved Wilkinson's choice. The precedent stood not only in the denouement of the South Pacific campaign but for central Pacific operations as well. Of course, Holland M. Smith, the senior Marine commander in the central Pacific, needed few precedents to argue the same point, but Thomas had at least made his own contribution to a critical interservice doctrinal issue.[22]

When Vandegrift and part of the I MAC staff embarked with Wilkinson and the 3d Division for the Bougainville landing on 30 October, Thomas remained on Guadalcanal with Roy Geiger, recently arrived from Washington. Thomas did not relax. He saw to it that the reinforcement plan worked as organized, despite Japanese air attacks and a major surface action (won by the U.S. Navy) on 2 November. Although he was uncertain whether he influenced Halsey's decision, Thomas urged ComSoPac to make a second carrier strike on Rabaul on 5 November, a strike far more successful because it involved land-based fighter support that was absent during an earlier attack on 1 November. He followed the progress of Krulak's Choiseul raid that began on 28 October and supported Krulak's request that his battalion be withdrawn by Navy PT boats and landing craft on 3 November after a series of successful battles with the Japanese. Thomas also monitored all Marine air operations in the northern Solomons and demonstrated his continuing conviction in the crucial support that tactical aviation provided Marine operations. In sum, he showed that his performance on Guadalcanal was not a one-time phenomenon but a reflection of professional competence and strength of character, fully justifying his anticipated early promotion to brigadier general and the subsequent award of the Legion of Merit for his service as I MAC chief of staff.[23]

★★★★

With Roy Geiger and Hal Turnage in firm control and the Bougainville beachhead secure, Vandegrift surrendered the command of I Marine Amphibious Corps on 10 November for the second time. He then returned to Guadalcanal for the last time to celebrate the Marine Corps birthday and reassemble his personal staff for the long trip to Washington. On Guadalcanal, Vandegrift and Thomas conferred with Halsey and watched with pleasure as the admiral pinned a Navy Cross on "Brute" Krulak, crippled for the moment with a painful leg injury. The Marine officers (including Krulak, who needed medical leave) flew back to Nouméa with Halsey and then, using the admiral's comfortable PB2Y seaplane, headed north for a conference with Admiral Nimitz and Holland M. Smith before Smith's headquarters departed for Tarawa. If Smith felt any disappointment that the younger Vandegrift would be Commandant, he did not let it color his discussion of building the Fifth Fleet's amphibious corps. Smith and Vandegrift shared a similar determination that Smith control the fate of the Fleet Marine Force ground forces, not Kelly Turner, whose lust for generalship had returned as soon as he left the South Pacific. Opposites in personal style, Smith and Vandegrift knew that their goals coincided, and they used the meeting to demonstrate to one another full trust and confidence in the other's role. Thomas also took comfort from the fact that his old friend, Brig. Gen. Graves B. Erskine, led Smith's able staff.[24]

The Vandegrift party reached San Francisco on 16 November. Thomas accompanied the general on a round of inspections, official calls, conferences, media appearances, and social events in the San Francisco area, Camp Pendleton, and the San Diego–area Marine bases. The trip gave Thomas his first opportunity to see the expanding Marine presence in southern California, and he expressed some doubt that the Marine Corps could hold so much choice real estate after the war ended. He enjoyed visiting the new 4th Marine Division, just completing training before its departure for the central Pacific war zone. After about two weeks on the West Coast, Vandegrift and Thomas took a train for Washington and the host of problems Holcomb had saved for the new Commandant and his staff. Holcomb's retirement and Vandegrift's appointment did not become effective until the end of December, which allowed Thomas time for a welcome leave to visit his family in Greenville, with side trips to Camp Lejeune, the Marine air station at Cherry Point, and Parris Island. He returned to Washington for meetings at Headquarters and some frustrating house hunting in the overcrowded capital, but he returned to his family in time for Christmas. He did not underestimate the challenges ahead and shared with Lottie his irritation over Admiral King's persuading Vandegrift that Thomas could not become a brigadier general until January because of arcane Navy Department policies on seniority and temporary promotions. Still only a permanent lieutenant colonel, Thomas recognized that his rapid advancement was not necessarily cost free. As Vandegrift wrote Holland Smith: "I imagine this [Thomas's promotion] will create quite a bit of talk by officers who believe in seniority promotion, but that leaves me absolutely cold, as I do not believe I could find a better person for that job [Director, Division of Plans and Policies], irrespective of rank than Thomas; and the rank is necessary in order to transact the business."[25]

Although Thomas had no illusion that his approaching tour of duty at Headquarters Marine Corps would be any less difficult than his service in the Solomons, he relished the prospect of again living with Lottie and his children in some semblance of life as it had been in the prewar Marine Corps. Such would not be his future. Gerald C. Thomas might have traded his green field desk for a government-issue oak desk heavy enough to crush a Japanese platoon, but he had only moved from one battlefield to another. In the new jungle of Washington, D.C., the enemies were no less determined, the stakes for the Marine Corps no less high, and the dangers no less real for his own professional survival.

[CHAPTER XIX]

The War at Headquarters Marine Corps 1944–1946

An admiring throng in the offices of the Secretary of the Navy at "Main Navy" on Constitution Avenue witnessed Lt. Gen. Alexander Archer Vandegrift take the oath of office as eighteenth Commandant of the Marine Corps from Frank Knox on 1 January 1944. The Secretary also read Thomas Holcomb's retirement orders and his final promotion to general. Holcomb became the first Marine officer to wear four stars (even if only in retirement), but his successor had an even greater distinction. Vandegrift was the first Commandant to be a national celebrity. The media covered his appointment with unabashed enthusiasm; *Time* magazine had already made him a cover story. National organizations were deluging his office with speaking invitations. Slightly dazzled by the swearing-in ceremony and the public attention that Vandegrift was receiving, Col. Gerald C. Thomas later attended the traditional New Year's reception at Commandant's House, Marine Barracks, and then fled to visit Bill Twining and Sam Griffith at Quantico to relax and talk shop. His mind whirled with putting together his own team in the Division of Plans and Policies. He wanted no officer in his division that had been senior to him in the old Corps. More importantly, he wanted the best talent in the Corps fresh from the battlefields of the Pacific. He already had arranged for Ed Snedeker and Joe Burger to leave I Marine Amphibious Corps, and he had his eye on other officers from the "Guadalcanal gang." He knew that he would need a talented staff in order to win the forthcoming battles at Headquarters.[1]

Vandegrift inherited a Marine Corps near its top wartime strength, materiel richness, and training excellence. In November 1943, the Joint Chiefs of Staff approved a peak 1944 strength of 478,000. The ground and air units of the Fleet Marine Force shared the productivity of American industry as it hit top effectiveness the same year. Holcomb left the new Commandant a sound, if slightly chaotic, training establishment and base structure in the United States, most of it in California. In every impressive statistic and report of organizational activity, however, lay obvious problems. The personnel authorization did not match the Corps' request for 559,000 because Army and civilian personnel planners had convinced the JCS that all of the services had neared the limit of available, qualified recruits. Marine Corps procurement, managed by Brig. Gen. Seth Williams's Quartermaster Department, drew materiel from the Army (65 percent of the total items), from the Navy (5 percent), and directly from civilian contractors or its own production (30 percent). Transporting the equipment and supplies to the field and then managing it still presented substantial, often embarrassing, problems. The training system, especially for technical specialists and aviation personnel, seemed bloated and designed for the convenience of base commanders, not the FMF. Headquarters Marine Corps, the focal point of shaping policies and coping with the policies of others, numbered around 2,400 officers and enlisted personnel, supplemented by 862 civilian employees. Another 350 to 400 Marines served in other billets in the Navy Department and the Joint Chiefs of Staff organization. Sixteen generals (1945) and sixty-some colonels provided the inner core of Headquarters leadership. They bore responsibility for the Corps' problems—some of their own making and others created by circumstance and inattention.[2]

Although Vandegrift had no operational authority over the Fleet Marine Force, consisting of half of his Marine Corps of 32,804 officers and 440,599 enlisted personnel, the Commandant had a deep interest in how the Pacific theater commanders intended to use his four divisions and four aircraft wings. (A fifth division was in the process of forming, and two independent regimental combat teams had also joined the war.) The strategic dilemma of the war against Japan remained the question of how to divide objectives and forces between Admiral Nimitz and General MacArthur. Rabaul no longer interested MacArthur, who cast his eyes to the liberation of the Philippines. The Australian and New Zealand armed forces inherited the dubious mission of squeezing the remaining Japanese on New Guinea, New Britain, and Bougainville. Admirals King and Nimitz favored a central Pacific drive aimed roughly along the Equator through the Gilberts, the Marshalls, and the Palaus to the Philippines. They regarded that former American colony, however, as only a stepping stone to Formosa and mainland China, from which the Navy proposed to isolate Japan from the critical raw resources of Southeast Asia. The Joint Chiefs of Staff had a different vision that did not exclude the Philippines and Formosa but did include a vector to the northwest to the Marianas (Guam, Saipan, and Tinian), an island group that could be used to develop bases for the USAAF long-range bomber, the B-29. The JCS favored a strategic bombing campaign on Japan to supplement the continuing submarine offensive against the Japanese merchant marine. Somebody would have to seize the Marianas, and that somebody would be the V Amphibious Corps (Holland M. Smith) and the III Amphibious Corps (Roy S. Geiger), composed predominately of Marines.[3]

Vandegrift and Thomas received a quick introduction to the interaction of strategy and politics, Washington-style, as soon as they reached home. They had inherited a public relations crisis caused by the successful but costly capture of Betio Island, Tarawa atoll, in November 1943. Informed about the battle by reports from Holland Smith and Julian C. Smith, the 2d Division commander, Vandegrift felt nothing but pride in the sacrificial determination with which the 2d Division had annihilated a die-hard Japanese garrison of 4,600 at the cost of around 1,000 Marine dead. For the first time in World War II, the Marine Corps had fought a battle with the fury of Belleau Wood and Soissons, simply because there was no other way to fight for a small coral island that someone had decided it was necessary to take. Tarawa exposed operational problems that could be fixed: changing naval gunfire to pinpoint destruction fire, providing better land-based control of air strikes, supplying each division with more amphibian tractors, improving tactical communications, providing the infantry with better training for assaulting fortified positions, and prepositioning Marine artillery on neighboring islands for more fire support. All of these lessons became obvious before the Navy, the Army, and the press decided that Tarawa had been a disaster. Vandegrift went to the pro–Marine Corps press in early 1944 to assure the public that Tarawa was a necessary objective and a needed learning experience, which quieted Congressional anxiety. He soothed Chester W. Nimitz, who had been traumatized by a visit to the unpoliced battlefield. He backed Holland M. Smith, who warned the Commandant that part of the problem was the Army's determination to deny Corps command to Marine generals. The crisis provided only the first of three such interservice conflicts during the Pacific war that convinced Jerry Thomas that the Marine Corps faced two enemy armies.[4]

The Tarawa crisis demonstrated a fact of life for senior officers at Headquarters Marine Corps: immediate media and bureaucratic battles stole time and credibility from more important long-term issues. Thanks to Vandegrift's heroic stature and the informed reporting of David Lawrence (*U.S. News*) and Robert Sherrod (*Time-Life*), the Marine Corps weathered the season of discontent, but Thomas faced other problems. One, simply, was finding a home for his family in Washington, a problem that found no resolution until February 1944. The Thomas family left Greenville, North Carolina, for a rented row house in Georgetown where they waited for their permanent home, a five-bedroom brick house at 4412 Volta Place, Foxhall Village, to be vacated and repainted. On a salary of $483 a month (1944 dollars), Thomas found it a challenge to finance a house, buy a car, help support his father, and send his oldest daughter to college. He planned to send his oldest son to prep school. Thomas had no money for frivolity, and the new brigadier general (4 January 1944) did not relax his iron control of his family's fortunes. He still talked about postwar retirement to the Charleston area, but his family did not take such musings seriously because he had never relished long vacations. At forty-nine, Thomas also had intimations of noncombat mortality. His annual physical showed signs of emerging problems: the old hearing loss, eyesight deterioration, tooth decay and gum disease, and, ominously, high blood pressure. He made no concessions to advancing age but, instead, plunged into his new Headquarters role as Vandegrift's alter ego.[5]

As General Thomas viewed his charter in the spring of 1944, he had inherited four substantial policy issues that bore on the war effort. The most important was matching personnel procurement to operational needs, still indistinct. He believed that the Marine Corps had too many men in specialist training (except communicators) and that some of these Marines would have to fill less exotic jobs (e.g., infantry) in the FMF. He also thought that the Division of Plans and Policies should be reorganized and become the cutting edge of formulating Corps policy in training and logistical planning. The expansion of 1941–43 had weakened the Commandant's ability to set policy and oversee its execution. Thomas saw no problem in the decentralized execution of policy, but he believed that Headquarters provided too little guidance or ambiguous orders. He intended to remedy that condition if he could. Weak guidance from Headquarters and the lack of field supervision had become particularly bothersome in training. Lessons learned from the Pacific war abounded; unless Headquarters interpreted those lessons and turned them into authoritative training instructions, the experiences of the battlefield would elude some, if not all, of the FMF divisions and aircraft wings. This problem was especially acute in the use of supporting arms, and Thomas believed that only the careful integration of all weapons produced victory and curbed infantry casualties. His last goal was to convert the remaining special operations organizations into line infantry and artillery units for the FMF. These organizations, created as sops to civilian and Navy "armchair generals," had been overtaken by events. The reorganization, standardization, and streamlining of FMF tactical units would bring greater combat effectiveness for sustained land campaigns and reduce the personnel and logistical confusion that accompanied the creation of specialized organizations.[6]

For Thomas to function with any effectiveness as Director, Division of Plans and Policies, he had to preserve his close relationship with Vandegrift, work amicably, if possible, with the other Headquarters departments and divisions, and reorganize his own division, which had become fragmented during the hectic mobilization of 1941–43. Vandegrift, an experienced Washington operator, proved to be even more adept than Holcomb in working harmoniously with the Navy's senior leadership. Thomas profited from this rapport, but he did not depend solely on Vandegrift in his work with the Navy Department. To Vandegrift fell the unenviable task of working directly with the Chief of Naval Operations (CNO) Adm. Ernest J. King, who (despite law and custom to the contrary) wanted to command the Marine Corps, as well as the Navy. The best way to deal with King was not to deal with him. Instead, Vandegrift and Thomas worked with the three admirals who composed King's intimate circle of advisors: Vice Adm. Frederick J. Horne, Adm. Richard S. Edwards, and Vice Adm. Charles M. "Savvy" Cooke, Jr. Thomas thought that he and Vandegrift worked well with King's troika, but he made sure that the senior Marines who worked closest to the Navy's flagpole provided detailed, continuous reports to Headquarters. In 1944–45, they were Brig. Gen. Omar T. Pfeiffer (late of Nimitz's staff), who represented the Commandant in King's office, and Col. David R. Nimmer, whose acute ulcers had forced him home and into the Pacific war plans section of the Joint Chiefs of Staff. Both Pfeiffer and Nimmer proved dependable collaborators in protecting the Corps' interests.[7]

The best way to remind Admiral King that he did not command the Marine Corps was for Vandegrift to maintain close and friendly relations with his true superior, the secretary of the navy. When Vandegrift returned to Washington, he found Secretary Frank Knox, seventy years old, in failing health. A heart attack followed a severe case of the flu, and Knox then died of a second heart attack on 28 April 1944. His successor, Undersecretary James V. Forrestal, fifty-two, had already become the driving force on the civilian side of the Navy Department and a worthy antidote to King's tyrannical instincts. At Forrestal's initiative, the Commandant became a full general in April 1945. Vandegrift and Thomas worked closely and amicably with Forrestal, and Thomas often dealt directly with new Undersecretary Ralph A. Bard, like Forrestal a success in the world of high finance and politics. Although Forrestal and Bard had no influence on strategy and operations, they proved consistent champions of Marine Corps positions on administrative and logistical issues. Vandegrift did not have Holcomb's personal rapport with President Roosevelt, but no issue required direct action in the White House until after FDR's death in April 1945. President Harry S Truman, an AEF veteran and longtime force in Army reserve organizations and the American Legion, lacked FDR's affinity for the naval services, but his naval aide, Commodore James K. Vardaman, Jr., enjoyed the president's trust because they were political associates. Father of a young Marine officer, Vardaman proved, on at least one occasion, a friend of the Marine Corps. As for Congress, Vandegrift knew where all Marine Corps problems went first: Representative Carl Vinson (Democrat of Georgia), chairman of the House Committee on Naval Affairs, then to Senator Harry Byrd (Democrat of Virginia).[8]

Trusted by Vandegrift and the civilians in the Navy Department, Thomas carried his share of the public relations burden at Headquarters, a task he enjoyed because of the opportunities to travel and to meet people. A confident speaker from his teaching days at Quantico, he also wrote his own speeches, which he delivered with force and clarity, if few theatrics. He spoke to a Navy Day luncheon in Los Angeles, an American Legion meeting in Chicago, various university and military student groups, a war loan drive in Utica, New York, and the annual meeting of the American Ordnance Association in New York City. He especially enjoyed another nostalgic return to Bloomington, Illinois, in June 1945, to speak at an Illinois Wesleyan alumni dinner in his honor. Thomas's trip to Los Angeles with Ralph Bard had an extra dividend, a visit to the Navy's ordnance experimental station at China Lake, where Thomas became fascinated with the research and development process.[9]

Thomas's missionary work for the Marine Corps did not distract him from his most pressing problem, reorganizing the Division of Plans and Policies. His internal reforms led to an analysis of the complete organization of Headquarters Marine Corps and a recommendation to Vandegrift in June 1944 that the Marine Corps create a true general staff system. His interest in staff organization won Thomas few friends at Headquarters. In the Division of Plans and Policies, Thomas found the problems relatively easy to identify and remedy. His M-3 (Operations) and M-4 (Logistics) sections had lost power to many specialized subsections, organized by training requirements and equipment procurement. Thomas found small empires of artillerymen, communicators, motor transport and tracked vehicle experts, engineers, and ordnancemen working in Headquarters and managing procurement and training programs on the Marine bases. Thomas broke up these subsections and revived the moribund M-5 section (war plans) as coordinator of all Marine Corps training. He deftly reduced opposition to reform in his division by arranging orders to the Pacific for all senior officers, who, in fact, wanted overseas assignments for the planned 1944 campaign in the central Pacific. He also streamlined his division's operating style by eliminating the ponderous studies process, a procedure of committee analysis guaranteed to pass the initiative to more aggressive and self-confident departments, such as Personnel and Quartermaster.

Thomas found the Personnel and Quartermaster Departments at the peak of their influence at headquarters; both had enriched their staffs and functional authority in reforms during the Holcomb years. The new Personnel Department (1943) merged the Adjutant & Inspector's Department, the Division of Reserve, the Division of Personnel, and the Public Relations Division. The Quartermaster Department soon absorbed the Paymaster Department. During the same years, the Division of Aviation increased its control over aviation matters. Because of its ties to the Navy's aviation establishment, however, this division enjoyed a special status that even the Commandant challenged at his peril. Thomas did not view Personnel and Quartermaster as sacrosanct and tried to convince Vandegrift that someone other than the Commandant should have clear authority at Headquarters to coordinate Personnel, Quartermaster, Plans and Policies, and, perhaps, Aviation. In accordance with general staff theory, which Thomas understood thoroughly from his Army schooling, Headquarters needed a chief of staff and a strong four- or five-section general staff, with a clear understanding that other staff departments concentrate on the execution of plans and not create their own policies. He challenged his subordinates to deal with policy issues, not routine administration, and to prepare thorough policy analysis memoranda and do it quickly. His guidance was always clear, forceful, and infused with urgency. The Quartermaster General functioned as the Corps' budget and fiscal officer; Thomas concluded that no one else had a firm grasp on what the Corps was spending except, perhaps, the Commandant. In the largesse of wartime, this fiscal inattentiveness might be acceptable but not in peacetime. Thomas thought that reform should not be postponed simply because Headquarters had not yet embarrassed itself by mismanaging its money.[10]

Vandegrift saw no pressing reason to reorganize Headquarters as the Pacific war approached its climax. He felt especially comfortable with the new Quartermaster General, Brig. Gen. William P. T. "Pete" Hill, who took office early in 1944. In addition to being an adept administrator, Pete Hill had a photographic memory for budget figures, boasted of many admirers in Congress, and regarded his considerable bureaucratic turf as unconquerable. Jerry Thomas did not regard Hill's power as healthy. In 1944, he unleashed the M-4, Lt. Col. Victor H. Krulak, on the matter of long-term logistical and fiscal planning. Krulak's study, critical of the Quartermaster Department, irritated Hill, who condemned the recommended reforms as untimely. Thomas then honored Krulak's request to return to the FMF as Lemuel C. Shepherd's D-3 in the 6th Marine Division. Krulak's successor, the steady and experienced Lt. Col. Frederick L. Wieseman, found the battlelines with Hill clearly drawn, but he also discovered the Quartermaster Department more cooperative with Plans and Policies. Focused on postwar logistical planning, Wieseman's section enjoyed some advantages, primarily because of Thomas—his access to the Commandant, his excellent connections throughout the Navy Department procurement system, and his refusal to allow Hill's views to go unchallenged. In 1946, for example, another M-4, Col. David M. Shoup, and Thomas discovered that Hill, through error (which seemed unlikely) or malice, had accused Marine commanders in occupied China of illegal expenditures for housing. Thomas and Shoup, after investigating the charges and even flying to China for an inquiry, found them unsubstantiated. Vandegrift, however, refused to discipline Hill. Thomas continued to press the issue for Headquarters reorganization and used Hill's rogue behavior as proof that the Marine Corps needed a chief of staff. When Shepherd became assistant commandant in November 1946, he found Thomas still advocating reorganization. Within the limits allowed by Vandegrift, Shepherd attempted to coordinate the Headquarters departments and divisions. He soon shared Thomas's view that Headquarters needed a general staff system.[11]

Thomas had no greater patience with the work of the M-3 section (Operations), but at least he had no bureaucratic barriers at Headquarters to battle. In fact, his own sense of urgency may have been his worst enemy. His own point of view was that "best" was the enemy of "good enough" in wartime, and he alone knew what was good enough. This perspective irritated other officers. In one instance, Thomas's activism paid dividends in tactical effectiveness. By the summer of 1943, several Marine units, including the Raiders and paramarines, had experimented with the internal organization of the Marine rifle squad and concluded that squads should be further divided into fire teams. Rich debate ensued about whether the fire team should have three or four men and which weapons it should carry. A three-officer board at Quantico reported its recommendations on 7 January 1944 to Thomas, who convened a board of his own composed of Merritt Edson (on temporary duty in the States), Griffith, Twining, and Krulak. They endorsed the four-man fire team built around the Browning automatic rifle (BAR) but changed the assistant BARman's personal weapon from the M-1 to the carbine. (This decision was later reversed so that all members of the team could use the same ammunition.) Four days after Thomas assembled his own board, he won Vandegrift's approval of a new infantry Table of Organization. This change was implemented in time for the Marianas campaign, where the fire team proved its soundness.[12]

Confident of his grasp of combat operations and tactical organization, Thomas pressed the M-3 section to move quickly in integrating lessons from the Pacific war into Marine Corps training and doctrinal publications. Concerned about the length of field training in the United States, Thomas urged extended predeployment training for lieutenants and enlisted personnel, but casualties in the Marianas forced Headquarters to accept shorter training periods than Thomas thought wise. He also thought that this policy increased casualties among replacements. The major activity of the M-3 division, however, was dealing with issues that crossed service lines. These issues mounted in number and severity as the war reached a crescendo during the summer of 1944. The Army wanted a greater share of amphibian tractor production; the Army wanted the FMF frozen at five divisions; the Army wanted Marine draft allocations reduced because it was running short of combat troops in Europe. The War Department complained about Marine Corps supply management in the Pacific, and Chief of Staff George C. Marshall and the Army generals in the field never surrendered their conviction that Marine Corps commanders should not control Army divisions. Although Admiral King generally supported Marine positions, he expected a high degree of gratitude and cooperation on such stateside issues as base use and transportation priorities. Admiral Nimitz remained inconstant in supporting his principal Marine commander, Maj. Gen. Holland M. Smith.

The life of the M-3 was not a happy one. Thomas brought in Ed Snedeker to replace the incumbent, Col. Charles F. Good, Jr., but Snedeker believed that Thomas did not like his pace in handling issues. Thomas arranged for Snedeker to return to the Pacific as a regimental commander in late 1944. He brought Lt. Col. Wallace M. Greene, Jr., D-3 of the 2d Marine Division in the Marianas, back to Headquarters as his M-3 but, without warning, relieved him in July 1945. The next M-3, Lt. Col. Bill Buse of Thomas's Guadalcanal staff, thought that Greene had questioned Thomas's guidance after Thomas considered a decision final. Buse found his former boss even more demanding than he had been on Guadalcanal. When his turn to leave Headquarters came in 1946, Buse turned over the section again to Ed Snedeker, who thought Thomas even more harried and impatient with the thoroughness and timeliness of the section's staff work. Thomas pressed his division's officers to reach new highs of activity and effectiveness, a pace hard to meet after the war ended. Thomas himself showed signs of war wear and tear. His family worried about his health. He worked long hours at the office and also met his politico-social obligations. No one who worked with him during the period of 1944–47 thought Thomas relaxed, despite any special relationship he enjoyed with the Commandant.[13]

Although his bureaucratic foes and personal critics believed Thomas had Vandegrift under a spell, Headquarters politics from 1944 through 1946 limited Thomas's influence and increased his sense of urgency and anxiety. The focal point of the anti-Thomas clique started with Maj. Gen. DeWitt Peck, Vandegrift's assistant. Peck agreed with Thomas that Headquarters needed reorganization but disagreed that the time was right. Instead, he stressed the need to emphasize interservice relations, especially with the Navy. Reorganizational disruption would limit interservice diplomacy. Quartermaster General Hill agreed with Peck.

The anti-Thomas group received a critical new member in the summer of 1945 when Maj. Gen. Thomas E. "Terrible Tommy" Watson came to Headquarters from command of the 2d Marine Division to become Director of Personnel. A fifty-two-year-old Oklahoman who glared at the world through rimless glasses, the short, active Watson had served four years as an enlisted man before becoming an officer in 1916. Although he had missed service in France, which he resented the rest of his life, Watson had seen extensive field service in the Dominican Republic and China. Before leaving for the Pacific war as 3d Brigade chief of staff, he had served in the Division of Plans and Policies. His command of a joint brigade-sized task force at Eniwetok and his driving, highly competent command of the 2d Marine Division on Saipan confirmed his status as a general officer. Success, however, had not reduced his explosive temper or his ability to nurse grievances. Even mean-spirited Marine officers regarded Watson as the meanest of them all, and Watson came to Headquarters with a grudge against Jerry Thomas. He believed that Thomas had isolated Vandegrift from all his old friends, which included Watson. The principal victim of this "alienation of affection" was none other than Brig. Gen. LeRoy Hunt, Watson's much-loved assistant division commander and successor as division commander. Watson, in fact, had created a "Tarawa-Saipan Gang" that resented the dominance of 1st Marine Division officers at Headquarters, especially in the Division of Plans and Policies and the Commandant's personal office, one managed for Thomas by Jim Murray and the other by Joe Burger. Merritt Edson and Dave Shoup did not shift loyalties to Watson from Thomas, their original patron, largely because they were men who felt no special loyalty to anyone but themselves and the Corps in general. Wallace Greene, on the other hand, respected both Watson and Hunt, as well as Thomas. Greene's dispassionate professionalism did not work to his benefit. Some officers of Plans and Policies thought the Thomas–Greene schism stemmed from a policy issue, specifically the organization of the postwar Marine division, but, in fact, Thomas replaced Greene because he thought Greene had become Watson's spy in his division. Thomas gave Greene no more explanation than that Greene had been "disloyal," an idea planted in Thomas's mind by one of Vandegrift's personal staff. Greene could not get Thomas to elaborate on his charges. This rebuff enraged him and the officers of his section, for none of them had discussed M-3's sensitive business with the Watson clique in Personnel and did not understand that Thomas thought they had.

When Watson became Director of Personnel, he lost little time in opening a guerrilla war against the Director, Division of Plans and Policies. First, he brought Capers James back to Washington as his assistant director and a brigadier general. When Greene lost his job as M-3, Watson immediately assigned him to his own staff. Thomas's only ally in Personnel was Col. William J. Scheyer, chief of officer assignments. A defense battalion commander and Roy Geiger's corps C-1, Scheyer had won Corps-wide fame when his antiaircraft artillerymen shot down thirty-nine Japanese planes over Rendova in one month, with thirteen of these destroyed during a single minute's slaughter. Scheyer could keep Thomas informed (and vice versa), but he could not stop Watson from holding "special staff meetings" at the senior officers mess at Marine Barracks. These conferences, which usually focused on blunting Thomas's influence on Vandegrift, included Watson, Peck, Hill, and Col. Walter W. Wensinger, the barracks commander. The Watson group checked Thomas's power in several ways. Although Thomas served on the colonels and lieutenant colonels promotion board in November 1944, Watson excluded him from subsequent boards. Watson went to Vandegrift with personnel matters without coordinating policy issues with the Division of Plans and Policies. He chaired the board to merge the Quartermaster and Paymaster departments, with Pete Hill's blessing, and he contested any effort that Thomas made to reorganize the Headquarters staff. His alliance with Hill made every battle Thomas undertook on personnel and supply issues contentious. Without a Headquarters chief of staff to manage the bureaucratic conflict, only the Commandant could bring order to his fractious staff, and Vandegrift did not relish personal intervention. This leadership trait, along with Headquarters traditionalism, meant that Thomas lost at least as many fights as he won with the Personnel and Quartermaster departments. The risks to his own career, however, did not dissuade him, and he fought for time and better opportunities to confound his enemies.[14]

Vandegrift's plan to shift generals often from overseas commands to Headquarters duty began to work to Thomas's benefit in late 1945. Hal Turnage, a friend, replaced Peck as assistant to the Commandant, retitled assistant commandant. Thomas also finally persuaded Vandegrift that the Marine Corps needed a separate Inspector General's Office to ensure field compliance with Headquarters directives. Pedro del Valle became the first Inspector General. Tommy Watson left Headquarters in the autumn of 1946 to resume command of the 2d Marine Division at Camp Lejeune, North Carolina. Maj. Gen. Franklin A. Hart, if not a Thomas ally, presented fewer problems as Director of Personnel. These personnel changes, however, did not sweep Thomas's rivals from Headquarters. Pete Hill remained entrenched as Quartermaster General, and the new director of information, Brig. Gen. William E. Riley, harbored no love for the reformist activism of the Division of Plans and Policies. Thomas continued to believe that no Commandant could manage the Marine Corps without a general staff system, but Vandegrift remained adamant that Headquarters Marine Corps suited him and worked well. Ironically, as long as the issues clustered around the war effort and the administration of postwar demobilization and redeployment, Vandegrift may have been correct, largely because the Director, Division of Plans and Policies, attempted to operate as de facto Headquarters chief of staff.[15]

When Thomas became division director in 1944, Headquarters Marine Corps had already focused its efforts on building the Fleet Marine Force for the campaign against Japan. The staff, however, had differing views of the ultimate structure and size of the FMF. When Thomas returned to Washington, he held firm beliefs that the requirements of amphibious operations, rather than special operations, base defense, or air operations not connected with landings, should drive personnel and force organizational policy. He could do little about Marine aviation except push for greater expeditionary capability, but he could and did shape ground force policy. He and Vandegrift quickly learned that the JCS would not increase the Corps' personnel ceiling, and they won only two small victories that allowed the Corps to reach its wartime peak strength of 485,000 officers and enlisted personnel in August 1945. They successfully defended the provision that the Marines could recruit seventeen-year-olds as volunteers outside the Selective Service System, and 59,000 young men enlisted under this dispensation. The second victory, supported by Commodore Vardaman in President Truman's office, was to change the personnel counting rules. Headquarters learned that the Army did not count sick and wounded awaiting discharge against its personnel ceiling and asked for equal treatment. In 1945, the White House ruled that the Marine Corps could increase its authorized strength to 503,000 to compensate for casualties that could not be returned to duty.[16]

With a ceiling on total personnel, Headquarters had little choice but to examine its internal allocation of troops in order to field a Fleet Marine Force of six divisions, four aircraft wings, corps troops, and an adequate service establishment in the Pacific. When Thomas took his new post, a fifth division had been authorized but not completed, and a sixth division, at Army insistence, had not even been approved. With Vandegrift's blessing, Thomas tackled the immediate problem of manning the 5th Marine Division, formed in cadre status in California. Thomas designed the scheme that brought the 5th Division to full strength. Through personal action, including trips to Camp Lejeune, Camp Elliott, and Camp Pendleton, he "found" 10,000 Marines in training that Headquarters could reallocate, which it did. Thomas then won Vandegrift's approval to disband the four parachute battalions and assign its elite Marines to officer and NCO slots in the 5th Division. He did the same to the one raider battalion in training and the raider training cadre. In the case of the parachutists, he won their consent by threatening to send them to Eisenhower's army or to MacArthur's command, both of which required parachute units. Thomas's other major target was the defense battalion program. The Navy Department had authorized the formation of twenty-nine defense battalions, and fifteen had already been formed. At Thomas's urging, Vandegrift won Admiral King's approval to cancel the program. The remaining strength (a projected 20,000 Marines) could be used to build other types of FMF units, such as amphibian tractor battalions, and as infantry replacement drafts for the divisions. This program had hardly begun when the larger and more intense battles in the central Pacific created serious personnel shortages, but Headquarters managed to man the FMF even though it had to shorten training programs to do so.[17]

The issue of forming the 6th Marine Division required more finesse and patience, but Vandegrift and Thomas managed this, too, despite the Army's opposition. In mid-1944 they had two infantry regiments and adequate artillery and other units in the Pacific to form a provisional brigade, which Lemuel C. Shepherd commanded as part of Roy Geiger's III Corps in the invasion of Guam. One regiment, the 4th Marines, was the converted raider regiment; the other, the 22d Marines, had been a garrison force for Samoa that replaced the 3d Brigade. Even before Guam, both regiments had been in combat. Thomas made the formation of the 6th Marine Division a personal cause, one suspects, in part, because he guessed that Shepherd would get a second star and be its commanding general. Admiral King said he would not take the issue to the JCS but would back Vandegrift if Nimitz would request a sixth Marine division. Nimitz, with some prompting from Holland Smith, did so. Thomas again turned to Camp Lejeune and the defunct base defense battalion program for the third infantry regiment, the 29th Marines. When the base commander, Maj. Gen. Henry Larsen, protested this second personnel raid, Vandegrift placated him by allowing him to choose a friend, Col. Victor F. Bleasdale, as the regimental commander. The division command, however, could not have pleased Thomas more because it included Lem Shepherd as commanding general, Johnny Clement as assistant division commander (ADC), John McQueen as chief of staff, and "Brute" Krulak as operations officer. All were Thomas's friends and proven officers. Activated in January 1945 on Guadalcanal, the 6th Marine Division might have been called, with justice, "Jerry Thomas's Own."[18]

With mixed emotions and success, Thomas dealt with other personnel issues. When he learned that Navy planners envisioned an invasion of Formosa, followed by an expedition to the mainland of China in order to interdict Japanese maritime trade with Southeast Asia, he took personal action to establish a special program for Chinese translators through the supervision of a friend, Dr. W. B. Pettus, former president of the College of Chinese Studies in Peiping and a faculty member at the University of California–Berkeley. The program died when the JCS decided that the Formosa operation was too risky and of marginal utility (a decision Thomas greeted with relief), but the episode whetted Thomas's urge to return to China. He accepted two other personnel programs with less enthusiasm. He favored the use of women Marines for administrative duties at Headquarters and other stateside bases but pictured their service as only a wartime expedient. A product of his time, Thomas regarded the organization of African-American Marine units, a mix of white officers and black enlisted men forced upon Holcomb by the White House, as an unwarranted political intervention in the Corps' affairs. He had no objection to all-black defense battalions and depot and ammunition companies serving in the Pacific war, but he resisted the proposal that the Marine Corps commission black officers or accept a long-term policy of enlisting black Marines. His prejudice reflected Marine Corps policy and the position of senior Marine officers throughout the Corps.[19]

Although General Thomas did not have a wide range of experience in logistical matters, his strong administrative bent and his experiences in the South Pacific, as well as a lifelong sense of frugality and efficiency, drew him into basic questions of supply and maintenance through the end of the war and into the postwar demobilization. The Commandant held similar values with equal conviction. Alexander Archer Vandegrift had not become Commandant to preside over the reduction of the Marine Corps' wartime base structure. Thomas learned of Vandegrift's tenacity in such matters early in 1944, when the Commandant defeated a Navy attempt to take control of the Marine Barracks and Recruit Depot at San Diego, choice property the Navy wanted because it abutted existing fleet facilities along San Diego Bay. In a meeting with Secretary Knox, Vandegrift surrendered instead Camp Elliott, a training camp north of San Diego but inconvenient for Navy use. To the astonishment of the attending admirals, Knox accepted the offer and declared the issue closed. Thomas applauded Vandegrift's coup. He himself helped with the next major issue, shifting the Corps' major East Coast shipping site from the overcrowded Norfolk area. His division preferred a new supply facility near Gulfport, Mississippi, that the Marine Corps had developed as an alternate shipping point, but he and Vandegrift settled for the construction of a major new supply and maintenance facility at Albany, Georgia, which just happened to be in Carl Vinson's congressional district. The end of the war prevented the immediate development of the Albany base, but Thomas did not forget the reasoning that made it attractive.[20]

Vandegrift's principal concern, however, was the Fleet Marine Force's logistical system in the Pacific. He knew that the Army would argue, as it did, that the Marine Corps should not direct the amphibious campaign in the central Pacific because it could not support the amphibious forces. In June 1945, Vandegrift established Service Command, Fleet Marine Force Pacific, and assigned Brig. Gen. Merritt A. Edson as its commanding general. Thomas and Edson then collaborated to organize Edson's command and to provide able logistical planners and supply officers, no mean feat in the face of Pete Hill's determination to curb Thomas's influence on logistical issues. Thomas believed that career quartermaster officers showed little flair for combat operations, yet Hill insisted on sending to the Pacific senior colonels who could claim the right to serve as logistics officers in the two amphibious corps. Edson would have to find places for them and then relieve those who did not perform. Despite Edson's efforts, Vandegrift never believed that Service Command FMF Pacific met its responsibilities. Thomas and Edson, however, never stopped their herculean efforts to create the right logistical force structure and assign the right officers to manage it.[21]

Thomas's involvement with FMF logistical problems paid an important dividend when the war ended. Although he had no intimate knowledge of the atomic bomb, he suspected that the war would end before the United States would have to invade Japan and received Vandegrift's approval of a draft order halting Marine Corps procurement before VJ-Day. He also had David Shoup, his late-war M-4, draft a logistical redeployment plan for Fleet Marine Force Pacific and to coordinate the plan with Geiger's planner in Hawaii, Lt. Col. Leonard F. Chapman, Jr. (Geiger replaced Holland M. Smith as Commanding General, FMF Pacific, on 3 July 1945.) The concept of the plan was simple: redeploying FMF organizations would bring everything serviceable home with them or turn it over to Service Command. Only under duress would the Marine Corps declare equipment and supplies surplus and turn over these assets to civilian control for sale or other disposition. Instead, the Marine Corps would create a new stockpile of war reserves from World War II materiel and not depend on new procurement. On the other hand, FMF units should not use scarce shipping space for basic consumables but leave them in the Pacific for later disposition, or none at all. If commanders were in doubt about food and items of health, comfort, and recreational well-being, they should allow their troops to use the consumables before they came home without too much attention to conservation. Although Vandegrift did not say so in writing, he implied that he would not be unhappy if the Marine Corps returned to the United States with "abandoned" Army equipment that might be rehabilitated and stored in the Marine Corps war reserves. Vandegrift and Thomas planned to feed the postwar FMF with high quality leftovers.[22]

Alexander Archer Vandegrift, like all great Marine leaders, regarded the troops in the field, not Headquarters, as the temple of the Marine spirit, and he made two major trips to the Pacific during the war. Thomas accompanied him on both trips and found himself involved in issues that had a great deal to do with how he did business in Washington. The first trip (6–23 August 1944) took the two generals to the battlefields of the central Pacific (Eniwetok, Kwajalein, Saipan, Tinian, and Guam), as well as the Marine bases still functioning in the Solomons. Vandegrift departed on the grand tour convinced that he would soon have the correct organization and the right men guiding the fortunes of Fleet Marine Force Pacific: Lt. Gen. Holland M. Smith as commanding general FMF Pacific (PAC), Maj. Gen. Harry Schmidt as commanding general of V Amphibious Corps, Maj. Gen. Roy S. Geiger as commanding general of III Amphibious Corps, and Maj. Gen. Julian C. Smith as commander of FMF PAC Administrative Command. Vandegrift's goal for the war and afterward, he told General Holcomb, was "to retain what we have."[23]

The trip started well in Hawaii. Admiral Nimitz agreed that he could certainly use the proposed 6th Marine Division and took the Commandant's party on a command tour of the Marianas where three Marine and two Army divisions were completing the mop-up of Saipan, Tinian, and Guam. On all three islands, the Headquarters generals observed combat operations, none of them significant. A trip to the Solomons provided a welcome reunion with the 1st Marine Division, which was ready to leave for Peleliu. Even Bill Rupertus's excessive optimism and broken ankle did not dampen the general satisfaction with the coming operation.[24]

When Vandegrift and Thomas arrived in Hawaii on the way home, they found two serious problems awaiting them—one negotiable, the other intractable. The negotiable problem was the future of Marine aviation in the war with Japan. When the focus of operations had been the large islands of the South Pacific, most within aircraft range of each other, the Marines could plan to move aviation squadrons from one island base to another and still get them into the battle as they had on Guadalcanal and Bougainville. The atoll operations of the central Pacific, however, revealed the limitations of Marine air. The battles ended before Marine air entered the action, and Marine air groups had become too heavy, in the logistical sense, to move into the theater of operations until well after the issue had been decided. Marine squadrons had played no role in the assaults in the Gilberts and Marshalls and had moved to the Marianas only with great difficulty and late in the operations. Meanwhile, the Navy's aviation command in the central Pacific had deployed Marine air in peripheral operations, such as bombing bypassed Japanese bases in the Marshalls. At the same time, Marine ground troops depended on Navy carrier-based aircraft for close air support, but the Navy's squadrons, trained for air superiority and antiship operations, showed little interest and expertise in ground support operations. To assist Maj. Gen. Field Harris, director of Marine aviation, Thomas participated in several meetings with Vice Adm. John H. Towers, the dynamic, skilled Commander Aircraft Pacific (ComAirPac), and hammered out an agreement to consolidate Marine squadrons, cut their logistical overhead, and prepare some of them for deployment on the Navy's growing fleet of escort carriers. Before the end of the war the Marine Corps deployed sixteen squadrons on four escort carriers and five *Essex*-class fast carriers. Again, Marine aviation became relevant to the campaign.[25]

The intractable problem centered on Holland Smith, who, with great cause, had relieved Maj. Gen. Ralph Smith, USA, from command of the U.S. 27th Infantry Division during the Saipan campaign. Angered by the division's sloth and operational carelessness, Holland Smith had warned Ralph Smith that he had better find more aggressive and competent leadership at the regimental and battalion level or surrender his command. Ralph Smith agreed that his division lacked aggressiveness and tactical skill but did nothing to improve them. Holland Smith relieved him, after consulting with Admirals Kelly Turner and Raymond A. Spruance. Even with another commander, the 27th Division continued to perform without distinction, a fact reported in the American press, primarily by Robert Sherrod of *Time-Life* and a Tarawa veteran of great personal courage, professional skill, and sound military judgment.

Angered by Holland Smith's action, which was legal and justified, Lt. Gen. Robert C. Richardson, Jr., USA, the senior Army commander in the central Pacific, started a bureaucratic and media counterattack to discredit Holland Smith and challenge the right of any Marine general to command a joint Marine-Army amphibious corps. George C. Marshall, anti-Marine since his service in World War I, supported Richardson's campaign to discomfit the Navy-Marine Corps team in the Pacific. The Hearst (pro-MacArthur) newspaper chain, in turn, supported Richardson. Under official and media attack for his conduct of the Saipan campaign, Holland Smith turned to Nimitz for support and received only mild approval. Thomas conducted his own investigation of the campaign and consulted Army officer friends as well as Marines. He believed that Holland Smith had no recourse but to replace Ralph Smith. Thomas also observed that Chester Nimitz had no stomach for battles with the Army, a bad sign. Vandegrift's own behavior also caused him some concern. Vandegrift, to be sure, was not in the chain of command, but he had consistently backed Holland Smith in the mercurial Smith's ongoing disputes with Kelly Turner. Now the Commandant had become a more modest champion when the battleground shifted to Army-Navy interservice disputes. Thomas knew Holland Smith's personality as well as anyone, and he knew from firsthand experience that Smith could be his own worst enemy in any situation that required some skill at handling people. Nevertheless, on his return from Hawaii, Thomas was disturbed because neither Nimitz nor Vandegrift had pressed the case against General Richardson's vigilantism, thus suggesting to the Army that the judgment of any Marine general was fair game.[26]

The "Smith versus Smith" controversy, still burning by the time Vandegrift and Thomas returned to Washington, dragged on into the autumn of 1944, largely because of a newspaper war over the conduct of the Pacific operations (the MacArthur press versus the pro-Navy press) and a personal feud between Admiral King and General Marshall. Marshall picked up Richardson's arguments that Marine generals were unfit for corps command and that senior Marine officers held unreasonable biases against the Army, not just the inept 27th Division. The Chief of Staff successfully pressed the Navy to appoint a senior Army officer, Lt. Gen. Simon Bolivar Buckner, Jr., as the commander of the U.S. Tenth Army, assigned to capture Okinawa. Buckner had been a willing party to Richardson's campaign against Holland Smith. He had conducted Richardson's personal investigation of the affair, an investigation that had become an anti-Marine witch hunt. Now Buckner would command a force that included the all-Marine III Amphibious Corps.

When Vandegrift and Thomas returned to the Pacific theater seven months later, the war had reached a new level of violence for the Marine Corps in the battles for Peleliu, Iwo Jima, and Okinawa. Hardly a Marine family, especially those of the career officers, had not experienced death in a personal way. General Vandegrift's own son, a battalion commander in the 4th Marine Division, had been wounded twice (Saipan and Iwo Jima), and General Thomas's young cousin, Capt. Archie Norford, had died on Okinawa while leading a rifle company. Gen. Phil Torrey's son was dead; so was "Chesty" Puller's beloved older brother, Sam. The battle for Peleliu, the most questionable of all Marine landings in World War II, had ruined the 1st Marine Division, and Iwo Jima had cost three Marine divisions twenty-three thousand casualties. Vandegrift held rigorously to his policy that all Marines fight in the Pacific war, and more than 90 percent of them did. Vandegrift wanted to see them again. He, Thomas, and Field Harris flew westward to the battlefields (8–28 April 1945), only a week after the climactic campaign for Okinawa began. To their dismay, they found that Nimitz did not want them at the front for fear that they would criticize the U.S. Tenth Army and its commander, General Buckner. He would allow them to visit the 2d and 3d Divisions on Saipan and Guam; this Vandegrift and Thomas did. Nothing they learned from Tommy Watson and Cliff Cates put them in a better frame of mind because Watson's division had been sent back from Okinawa uncommitted. Vandegrift protested to Nimitz that he would appeal to King if the Marine party could not visit Okinawa. Nimitz temporized and allowed them to visit Iwo Jima. Thomas wrote home: "It is the most gosh awful place I ever saw and I do not see how the boys took it."[27]

A crisis on Okinawa convinced Nimitz that Vandegrift and Thomas should accompany him and his own staff to the island for a conference with Buckner and Roy Geiger, whose III Amphibious Corps was safely ashore but not yet committed to the Tenth Army's advance against the Japanese main positions on the southern third of the island. III Amphibious Corps (1st and 6th Marine Divisions and corps troops) had another contingency mission that would have to be changed if Buckner used them in the extended land campaign. By the time the Nimitz-Vandegrift group arrived on Okinawa (23 April), three of Buckner's four Army divisions had lost their combat effectiveness in fierce frontal assaults on the Naha–Shuri Castle–Yonabaru Line. The situation at sea was no more promising because kamikaze attacks had already taken their toll of the Fifth Fleet.

That afternoon Thomas witnessed a commanders conference characterized by gloom and timidity. "It was a spiritless exhibition—dolorous in the extreme—and left me depressed."[28] Although individual members of the group, which included Nimitz, Spruance, Buckner, Kelly Turner, Vandegrift, Rear Adm. Forrest P. Sherman (Nimitz's deputy chief of staff), and Marine Brig. Gen. O. P. Smith (Buckner's deputy chief of staff), had privately discussed an amphibious landing behind Japanese lines, Buckner refused to address the plan. Thomas, for example, had examined the option with Sherman, and they agreed that the 2d Marine Division, which had not unloaded its transports, could make the assault within a week, followed by the rest of Geiger's corps. But Nimitz did not press the issue with Buckner, and Vandegrift and Geiger said little. Buckner, in fact, impressed the Marines as hostile to them and unimaginative in his operational thinking. He simply repeated his position that III Amphibious Corps would have to assume the western half of his southern line and plunge into the battle in the Army's best World War I tradition. The decision sickened Thomas, a sensation undiminished by two days of visits to the 1st and 6th Marine Divisions. Wherever he went he saw old comrades: Pedro del Valle, Lem Shepherd, Dave Nimmer, John Bemis, Johnny Clement, John McQueen, Bob Bare, Ed Snedeker, Jim Murray (commanding 1st Battalion, 1st Marines, and subsequently wounded), Brute Krulak, Bill Whaling, Bob Ballance, and Bob Luckey. He told Krulak that he and Shepherd could not convince more senior officers to challenge Buckner. When he and the Commandant left Okinawa, Thomas felt as if they had left the "Guadalcanal Gang" and their troops to an unkind fate. He discussed the amphibious option again with Forrest Sherman, who said he had raised the issue with Buckner's staff, which replied that the beaches were unsatisfactory. Thomas knew that the Army planners had again misrepresented the problem because the beaches had been the original alternate landing site.[29]

Even though Vandegrift pledged to Nimitz that he would not mention Buckner's questionable judgment, which eventually killed about three thousand Marines and cost Buckner his own life, the issue would not disappear. After the Marine generals returned to Washington, Homer Bigart, an experienced and blunt war correspondent for the *New York Herald-Tribune*, wrote a story critical of Buckner's command. Admiral King called Vandegrift to his office and repeated a charge from Nimitz that Vandegrift (or Thomas) had leaked the story. Nimitz was outraged—but no more so than Vandegrift, who had already investigated the story. His inquiry showed that Bigart had written the story on Okinawa and that Nimitz's own staff had approved it. He persuaded King to use his favorite editor, David Lawrence, to support Bigart's analysis, which Lawrence did after Thomas briefed him. Nimitz and Sherman, however, pleaded with King not to pursue the issue in the name of interservice harmony. The Okinawa episode proved that the problems of Pacific command and Army-Marine Corps relations were not just problems of personalities and the performance of one lackluster Army infantry division.[30]

The Japanese decision to surrender on 10 August 1945 and the formal ceremony of surrender in Tokyo Bay on 2 September found Brig. Gen. Gerald C. Thomas, weary and thankful that there would be no more amphibious assaults, at his desk at Headquarters Marine Corps. The close of the Pacific war ended some problems, created new ones, and postponed others for the Division of Plans and Policies. Thomas no longer had to think about forthcoming combat operations and the men and materiel they required, but he had to examine the temporary requirements for FMF Marines to secure the Japanese surrender and the conflicting pressure to begin demobilization. His division, in collaboration with the Director of Aviation, had the principal responsibility for coordinating plans for the postwar Marine Corps with the planners of the Chief of Naval Operations. Four of the six divisions of the FMF headed for China (Tsingtao and Tientsin) and Japan (Yokosuka, Sasebo, Nagasaki) to accept the Japanese surrender, demobilize and repatriate the Japanese armed forces, and preserve order. The III and V Amphibious Corps took with them appropriate aviation and service support units. The demobilized 3d and 4th Marine Divisions sent their short-service Marines to the western Pacific, thus creating an internal degree of personnel turnover matched only by desperate battle. Regardless of personal preferences, Marine organizational discipline held fast during the demobilization and occupation of late 1945.[31]

In addition to initiating its logistical Operation "Roll Up" and unleashing its first postwar volunteer recruiting effort, which netted 95,000 new Marines by the end of 1946, Headquarters Marine Corps intensified its planning for a stable postwar Fleet Marine Force to be in place by 1948 or sooner. Thomas bore the principal responsibility for this planning. He attempted to divine the Navy's long-range plans and strategic vision, but he used his own judgment, as well, to envision the role of the two naval services in postwar American security policy. Thomas believed that the simultaneous collapse of European and Japanese control in China and Southeast Asia would bring an unpredictable period of political disorder. He knew the Navy planned to resume its activities in western Pacific waters and use the bases seized in World War II. Thomas thought that Okinawa would be especially useful as an American base. Even with their eyes on Asia, the Navy's planners also thought the Navy should establish a permanent and significant presence in the Mediterranean in order to influence events in the oil-rich Middle East. In terms of force size and structure, the Navy planned for a Pacific Fleet of 176 combatants and an Atlantic Fleet of 143 combatants, supported by almost 2,000 other ships and craft. Personnel plans included 58,000 officers and 500,000 sailors. Where contingency planning failed to provide clear guidance, Vandegrift simply invoked the traditional standard that the Marine Corps be one-fifth the size of the Navy. He, Thomas, and Harris settled on a force of 8,200 officers and 100,000 men as adequate and obtainable in the political sense.[32]

As Director of Plans and Policies, Thomas played an active part in virtually every issue with which Vandegrift wrestled in the immediate postwar period, and some of his subordinates thought he often served as de facto Commandant. His division developed a plan to station one division and one brigade, supported by an aircraft wing and air group, with the Pacific Fleet and to develop a division-wing team at Camp Lejeune and Cherry Point, North Carolina, for service with the Atlantic Fleet, with one battalion landing team deployed (at the Navy's request) in the Mediterranean. Thomas argued that the Marine Corps should abandon the "twenty-percent-of-the-Navy" policy for determining personnel needs that Vandegrift had accepted. He also championed the principle that the Marine Corps should be the nation's "minute men . . . held in readiness to be moved instantly with the Fleet to any part of the world to strike hard and promptly to forestall at its beginning any attempt to disrupt the peace of the world."[33] Although he approved of President Truman's decision to support the Nationalists in the rekindled Chinese civil war, he doubted that the administration would offer more than token aid and military materiel assistance.

In July 1946, Thomas returned to China for the first time since 1937 on a fact-finding and inspection trip with Assistant Commandant Hal Turnage and his M-4, David M. Shoup. He especially enjoyed a visit to Peiping and reunion with some Chinese friends. He also relished discussing Chinese affairs with comrades, including Brig. Gen. Arthur Worton and Col. Julian Frisbie. Worton, a China hand, saw little prospect of a Nationalist victory or a mediated settlement, then being pursued by a mission led by former Army Chief of Staff Marshall. Thomas did not let his love of the Chinese or nostalgia for China cloud his vision. He and Turnage reported that unless the United States adopted a more aggressive policy to counter the Chinese Communists, the Marine Corps should reduce its presence and curb its investment in the North China occupation forces.[34]

Thomas did not allow the strategic uncertainties of the demobilization period to deter him from attacking internal Marine Corps issues bearing on the Corps' future. To ensure forceful and knowledgeable representation in the office of the Chief of Naval Operations (now Chester Nimitz), he persuaded the Commandant to bring home Merritt Edson from his forty-four months in the Pacific and assign him to the CNO. With Thomas's urging, Vandegrift reestablished the Marine Corps Equipment Board under the leadership of Brig. Gen. Louis R. Jones and assigned it the high-priority task of developing better antitank weapons for the infantry. The Marine Corps paid special attention to working with the Army on the 3.5-inch rocket launcher, the T80 antitank rocket for the launcher, and the

75-mm recoilless rifle. Thomas also pushed Vandegrift to conduct a complete investigation of the future of Marine Corps aviation because he believed that Marine aviators had lost sight of their ground-support role. Thomas and Harris agreed to the appointment of a high-level board chaired by Maj. Gen. Graves B. Erskine. The Erskine Board's report did not please Harris, who believed that the board had recommended a force of too few squadrons and too few officers, although the board reflected Thomas's belief that thirty percent of the Marine officer corps could be aviators. The Erskine Board, however, produced a recommendation, accepted by Vandegrift, that aviators be assigned throughout the ground FMF and supporting establishment, which would create a larger pool of pilots and advance better air-ground operational integration. Erskine's reforms dismayed aviators, but they reflected Thomas's own view that Marine aviators should be Marine officers, too. He thought they should share the same course of military education and general staff service that had characterized the prewar Corps and produced such distinguished officers as Harris, Louis Woods, and Roy Geiger.[35]

Thomas paid even greater attention to the question of reconstituting the regular officer corps of the Marine Corps for the postwar period. Although the Corps ended the war with almost 38,000 officers, only around 1,800 held regular commissions. To bring this officer corps near its estimated strength of 8,200, Vandegrift (with Thomas's strong support) appointed a board chaired by Maj. Gen. James L. Underhill to select Reserve officers for integration into the regular establishment. Underhill believed that his board selected at least 3,000 exceptional wartime officers for the postwar Corps, an assessment Thomas shared. The remaining officer positions could be filled at a more leisurely pace from other wartime officers or newly commissioned lieutenants, who would have to serve in the infantry for at least one year before becoming specialists or two years before taking flight training. A complementary and vexing issue was the question of which senior officers would remain to lead the postwar Marine Corps. Thomas had an intense interest and a great deal at stake in this issue. Vandegrift's critical decision was to avoid returning generals to their permanent ranks, if possible, but he did not know how many permanent generals the Corps would have. Certainly, they would be fewer than the Corps had in 1946—twenty-nine major generals and forty-two brigadier generals.[36]

The solution to the "excess" flag officer problem, which confronted the Navy as well, became the Naval Services Retirement Act of 21 February 1946 (P.L. 305, 79th Congress). Crafted by the Division of Personnel and the Commandant's counsel and congressional lobbyist, Col. Joseph W. "Buddy" Knighton, the law allowed the Commandant to retire involuntarily generals and colonels at their highest wartime rank and, in cases of distinguished combat service, to promote colonels to brigadier generals at retirement. (The law also provided voluntary retirement incentives for all officers of twenty years' service, ten of which had to be as an officer.) Colonels could choose to complete thirty years' service, but generals would have to retire if not selected for continuation or, if permanent colonels, revert to their regular rank. On 25 March 1946, Vandegrift appointed a board of Holland M. Smith, Roy S. Geiger, and Harry Schmidt (all permanent major generals) to trim the general officer corps. The board, as Vandegrift directed, favored youthfulness and wartime performance, but its results were predictably controversial. (Thomas, for example, wondered why Roy Hunt survived retirement.) Before the end of 1946, sixteen of twenty-nine major generals retired. Thirteen of forty-two brigadiers left the Corps; none of the survivors held permanent general officer rank. Thomas had no reason to fear for his own position in 1946, and the board did, in fact, continue him as a brigadier general in his permanent rank of lieutenant colonel. Thomas ranked twenty-ninth among brigadier generals, but a wave of voluntary retirements brought him up to twelfth in seniority. What Thomas could not have predicted—he followed the board actions closely—was that his status in the Marine Corps would be so uncertain at the very time he ran the greatest risks of his career.[37]

Bloomington (Illinois) High School Football Team, 1910—Gerald C. "Fats" Thomas, second row, second from left. *(Thomas family photo)*

Company B, 1st Battalion, 6th Marine Regiment, 4th Marine Brigade, in Bad Hönningen, Germany, 1919. First Lieutenant Gerald C. Thomas is fifth from right in the first row. *(Thomas family photo)*

Captain Gerald C. Thomas leads Company B, Marine Detachment, in Peking, China, during a pass-in-review, 1935. *(Thomas family photo)*

Second Lieutenant Gerald C. Thomas at home in Marshall, Missouri, 1920. His mother, Virginia Young Thomas, is on his right, and Mrs. Frank Durrett, his mother-in-law, is on his left. *(Courtesy Mrs. Dorothy Durrett Hughes)*

Second Lieutenant Gerald C. Thomas, December 1921. *(U.S. Marine Corps photo)*

Lottie Capers Johnson, Charleston, South Carolina, at debutante ball, January 1924. *(Thomas family photo)*

The Thomas family visits the Great Wall of China in 1936. From left: Gerald C. Thomas, Jr., Lottie Thomas, Tina Thomas, and Jerry Thomas. *(Thomas family photo)*

The senior officers of the Marine Detachment greet the Italian naval attaché, Commander Spagone, at left. Marine officers, from the left, are Captain Gerald C. Thomas, Colonel A. A. Vandegrift, and Major Graves B. Erskine. (*Thomas family photo*)

Captain James Roosevelt and Major Gerald C. Thomas enjoy the veranda of Shepherd's Hotel in Cairo, Egypt, during their 1941 trip around the world. *(Thomas family photo)*

Above right: A group photo on Guadalcanal.

Of the forty-one officers in the photograph, twenty became general officers in the United States Marine Corps either on active duty or upon retirement; of this group thirteen reached at least the rank of major general and served in key Corps billets after World War II, three (Vandegrift, Cates, and Pate) as Commandant. Two officers (Macklin and Fuller) became general officers in the Marine Corps Reserve, and Captain Brown became a vice admiral. One officer (Goettge) died on Guadalcanal. Missing from the picture are officers of the Tulagi Group, which included Brig. Gen. William H. Rupertus, Col. Robert C. Kilmartin, Jr., Col. Merritt A. Edson, Lt. Col. Harold E. Rosecrans, and Maj. Samuel B. Griffith II. None of the officers of the attached 2d Marines were on Guadalcanal on 11 August, and the officers of the 7th Marines were then serving outside the operational area with the 3rd Marine Brigade. *(U.S. Marine Corps photo)*

Senior officers of the 1st Marine Division on Guadalcanal, 11 August 1942, at the division command post.

Front row *(left to right)*: Col. George R. Rowan, Col. Pedro del Valle, Col. W. Capers James, Maj. Gen. A. A. Vandegrift, Lt. Col. Gerald C. Thomas, Col. Clifton B. Cates, Lt. Col. Randolph McC. Pate, Capt. Warwick T. Brown (MC, USN).

Second row *(left to right)*: Col. William J. Whaling, Col. Frank B. Goettge, Col. LeRoy P. Hunt, Lt. Col. Frederick C. Biebush, Lt. Col. Edwin A. Pollock, Lt. Col. Edmund J. Buckley, Lt. Col. Walter W. Barr, Lt. Col. Raymond P. Coffman.

Third row *(left to right)*: Lt. Col. William E. Maxwell, Lt. Col. Edward G. Hagen, Lt. Col. William N. McKelvey, Jr., Lt. Col. Julian N. Frisbie, Maj. M. V. O'Connell, Maj. William Chalfant III, Maj. Horace W. Fuller, Maj. Forest C. Thompson.

Fourth row *(left to right)*: Lt. Col. Francis R. Geraci, Maj. Robert G. Ballance, Maj. Henry W. Buse, Maj. James G. Fraser, Maj. Henry H. Crockett, Lt. Col. Leonard B. Cresswell and (also seated above Cresswell) Maj. Robert O. Bowen, Lt. Col. John A. Bemis, Lt. Col. Kenneth W. Benner (partially hidden behind Bemis), Maj. Robert B. Luckey, and Maj. Samuel G. Taxis.

Fifth row *(all standing, left to right):* Lt. Col. Merrill B. Twining, Lt. Col. Walker A. Reaves, Lt. Col. John DeW. Macklin, Lt. Col. Hawley C. Waterman, Maj. James C. Murray, Lt. Col. Eugene H. Price.

Above: Colonel Gerald C. Thomas, division chief of staff (center), briefs senior Marine officers on planned operations in the division command post, Guadalcanal, October 1942. *(U.S. Marine Corps photo)*

Top left: The commanding general and staff of the 1st Marine Division discuss the Guadalcanal landing, 5 or 6 August 1942, aboard the transport *Charles G. McCawley*. From the left: Major General A. A. Vandegrift, Lieutenant Colonel Gerald C. Thomas, Lieutenant Colonel Randolph McC. Pate, Lieutenant Colonel Frank B. Goettge, and Colonel W. Capers James. *(U.S. Marine Corps photo)*

Bottom left: The 1st Marine Division commander and his staff in Australia after their return from Guadalcanal, January 1943. Seated, from left: Colonel Gerald C. Thomas, Major General Alexander A. Vandegrift, Captain Warwick T. Brown, MC, USN. Standing, from left: Major Guy M. Tarrant, Jr., Lieutenant Colonel Edward W. Snedeker, Major James C. Murray, Jr., Lieutenant Colonel Edmund J. Buckley, Lieutenant Colonel Merrill B. Twining, and Lieutenant Colonel William S. Fellers. *(Courtesy Sanford Hunt)*

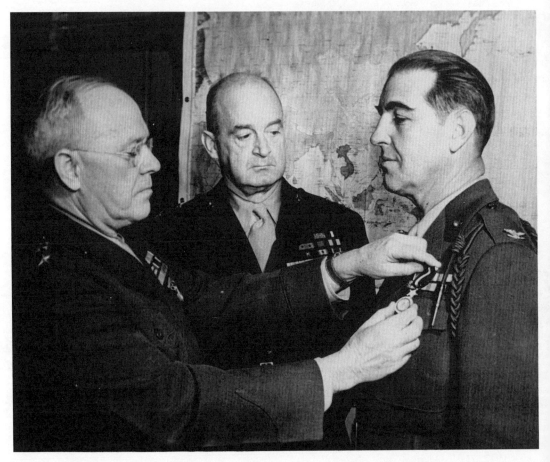

Above: Commandant Thomas Holcomb presents the Distinguished Service Medal to Colonel Gerald C. Thomas as General A. A. Vandegrift looks on. Headquarters Marine Corps, February 1943. *(U.S. Marine Corps photo)*

Top right: Command Post, First Marine Division, north of Inje, Korea, in November 1951. *(Courtesy W. E. Dibble, Jr.)*

Below right: The brain trust of the First Marine Division, August 1951. From left: Brigadier General William J. Whaling, assistant division commander; Major General Gerald C. Thomas, commanding general; Colonel Victor H. Krulak, division chief of staff. *(U.S. Marine Corps photo)*

Above: Home from a third war: Major General and Mrs. Gerald C. Thomas at Washington National Airport in January 1952. *(U.S. Marine Corps photo)*

Top right: A new Commandant, General Lemuel C. Shepherd, Jr. (left), promotes Gerald C. Thomas to lieutenant general and welcomes him to Headquarters Marine Corps and the task of organizational reform, March 1952. *(Department of Defense photo)*

Bottom right: President Dwight D. Eisenhower signs a proclamation establishing an annual Armed Forces Day at the White House, 17 March 1953, as Secretary of Defense Charles E. Wilson looks on. Department of Defense representatives (from left to right in back row) are Under Secretary of the Army Earl D. Johnson; Chief of Naval Operations Admiral William M. Fechteler; Brigadier General Stoyte O. Ross, USAF; Secretary of the Navy Robert B. Anderson; Lieutenant General Gerald C. Thomas; and Vice Admiral Merlin O'Neill, Commandant, U.S. Coast Guard. *(Department of Defense photo)*

Retirement and the last promotion: General Gerald C. Thomas receives his fourth star at his retirement ceremony from Brigadier General Donald McP. Weller (left). Assisting are Mrs. Thomas and Commandant Lemuel C. Shepherd, Jr., at the Marine Corps Schools, Quantico, Virginia, 31 December 1954. *(Thomas family photo)*

Marine Corps elder statesman: General Gerald C. Thomas chats with the Commandant, General Louis H. Wilson, Jr. (left), at the annual reception and serenade, Commandant's House, 1 January 1978. Colonel Joseph A. Bruder, Thomas's son-in-law, is in the background. *(U.S. Marine Corps photo)*

[CHAPTER XX]

The Unification Crisis 1945–1947

RESCUED FROM FAMILY separation and the anxiety of war, the Thomas family of 4412 Volta Place, Foxhall Village, settled into Washington life with no special turmoil, from all outward appearances. Foxhall Village provided genteel comfort and good neighbors. At the Thomas three-story Tudor home, the day began early. In the kitchen at first light, Gerald C. Thomas made a traditional heavy country breakfast of eggs, sausage or bacon, grits, and scrapple for himself and anyone who joined him. Against the first wave of traffic headed into Washington to work, Thomas drove himself across the Potomac to the Navy Annex or shared a car with another officer, often Merritt Edson. Returning home well after regular working hours, he relaxed with a bourbon and water, and ate dinner. In the spring and summer he devoted himself to a new hobby, growing large tomatoes in the family's substantial garden. General and Mrs. Thomas spent many evenings at dinner parties where the general, a conspicuous figure at Headquarters and a hero of Guadalcanal, campaigned with great personal relish. Much of the social whirl involved other Marine officers, and the Thomases enjoyed many parties with the Vandegrifts at Commandant's House, Marine Barracks. They often reciprocated by holding dinners at the Army and Navy Club. The Thomases became especially close to Chauncey G. Parker, Jr., a well-connected Washington lawyer-financier, who also was a former Marine and whose son was then serving in the Corps. Parker admired General Thomas, the handsome, forceful, articulate veteran of the South Pacific, and his attractive, gracious Southern-belle wife. Parker ensured that the Thomases met people important within the inner elite who ran the government and the city.

To his children, Jerry Thomas seemed as autocratic as ever. He was impatient, irritated by the problems of teenagers, and more demanding than Lottie could bear without household help and some respite from the social whirl. A dissatisfied student except in the fine arts, Tina argued that the family finances could not stand the cost of Hollins College (where she had attended for three years) if Jerry Junior, a fine student, was going to attend a first-class university. Leaving Hollins, she took additional courses at George Washington University while she worked as a clerk at Garfinckel's department store and a secretary at Headquarters Marine Corps. She spent much of her emotional energy fending off her parents' efforts to turn her into a Washington debutante. Jerry Junior finished the 1944 school year in Greenville, North Carolina, and then moved smoothly into the academic and social life of Washington's Western High School, which provided a college preparatory curriculum. Perfectly happy with his friends and a summer job as a park maintenance worker, Jerry Junior learned with amazement that his father had arranged for him to attend Philips Exeter Academy for his last year of high school, part of the general's plan to have him enter Yale University. Jerry Junior, however, argued that the family could not afford Yale, and he wanted to attend the Naval Academy instead. The general did not like Jerry's choice, but he bowed to his son's determination and the reality that Annapolis offered his son a free education. The younger children, Ginny and Johnny, on the other hand, enjoyed their neighborhood life with other energetic, bright youngsters like themselves.

When he tired of Washington's politico-military social life and Marine Corps homework in his study, General Thomas loaded the family into the car and drove to Gordonsville, Virginia, to visit his aging father. Vander Thomas lived in a large rooming house famous for its country food, especially what the general called "authentic" Virginia corn bread. Thomas also made the point that he wanted his father, always the handyman, to fix some tool or sharpen some knives. Tina and Jerry Junior did not share their father's enthusiasm for pilgrimages to their grandfather's home, but the Sunday drives at least brought the Thomases together in some semblance of prewar family life. His family may have not ranked first in the general's attention, but he valued their support and affection, even if he did not always show much appreciation for their special problems. His own concerns were awesome enough: the Marine Corps had entered a battle for its survival, and he bore much of the responsibility for winning a secure place for the Corps in the postwar military establishment.[1]

The campaign to control postwar American military policy through the medium of institutional reorganization began in late 1943 when Army Chief of Staff George C. Marshall presented the Joint Chiefs of Staff with a plan to centralize the management of the armed forces. A single executive department would administer the Army, the Navy, the Marine Corps, an independent Air Force, and a joint Service of Supply. A uniformed Chief of Staff to the President and the three service chiefs (the Army never understood that in law the Marine Corps had been a separate service since 1834) would constitute a "United States General Staff" with direct access to the President, although each service would have a civilian secretary. Marshall's proposal did not win official approval in the JCS, largely because of Navy Department opposition, but the JCS conducted the predictable staff studies and authorized a special investigating group, chaired by Adm. J. O. Richardson, to solicit the opinions of senior commanders in the field. The War Department, however, did not wait for the Richardson Committee to complete its report before submitting its plan to Congress, which appointed a

Select Committee on Post-War Military Policy (the Woodrum Committee) to hold hearings on the subject. Although the War Department plan had already gone through some alterations, including the addition of a civilian armed forces secretary, the essence of Marshall's proposal remained intact: the reconstituted Joint Chiefs of Staff would be far more than a committee of equals and would have powers to determine force structure and budgets that would be below only those of the President and Congress. The uniformed chief (not chairman) of the joint staff would be the authoritative voice within the executive branch on matters of military policy, field force organization, strategic planning, budgeting, and service roles and missions. The major lesson of World War II, so the Army argued, was that interservice cooperation had to be imposed from Washington in order to enforce the economic management of the armed forces and eliminate "duplication" of forces and functions.

Commandant Alexander Archer Vandegrift directed that Brig. Gen. Gerald C. Thomas become his personal "action officer" in all matters concerning defense reorganization. Thus, he saddled Thomas with the burden and the glory of three years of crushing responsibility for the future of the Marine Corps. Thomas hoped that defense reorganization would not develop into a major crisis. At first, Navy Department opposition, centered in Under Secretary (later Secretary) James V. Forrestal and Adm. Ernest J. King, seemed to halt the unification movement in its tracks. The Joint Chiefs of Staff committees completed and filed their studies; the Woodrum Committee, whose hearings Thomas attended, ended its investigation without proposing legislation; and the Richardson Committee finished its study in April 1945 and sent its report to the JCS for further consideration. The major barrier to reform, however, was Franklin D. Roosevelt, who sympathized with the Navy Department position on reorganization and who saw no urgent need in disrupting a working system as the war reached its victorious climax. Vandegrift and, especially, Thomas saw alarming signs for the future. Except for FDR and the Navy Department, no one else in the executive branch opposed reform. Even many of the Navy's admirals, often without thorough consideration of the issues involved, had told the Richardson Committee that they favored some change. Moreover, influential members of Congress embraced the War Department's centralization plan on the quaint notion that somehow it would save money and streamline decision making. What most concerned Thomas, however, was the impression that, with the exception of Forrestal, the leadership of the Navy Department did not appreciate the full danger of reform to the Navy and Marine Corps.[2]

Alarmed by the emerging consensus for unification and dissatisfied with the Army's analysis of organizational reform, Secretary Forrestal, in June 1945, asked a trusted friend and Washington bureaucratic veteran, Ferdinand Eberstadt, to prepare a plan the Navy Department could endorse that would preserve most, if not all, of the wartime system, including the Joint Chiefs of Staff and the existing departmental structure. Forrestal acknowledged that an independent Air Force, with its own mission (strategic bombardment) and executive department, could be accepted, if only as a political reality. He wanted to broaden the discussion, however, beyond interservice relations to interdepartmental relations within the executive branch, which he believed needed far more attention than service unification. Eberstadt's plan, submitted to Forrestal in September, recast and complicated debate but did not deflect the Army from its commitment to a powerful single head of the armed forces and a joint staff with far more authority, both legal and practical, than the JCS. Although the Eberstadt Plan had many admirable proposals for improved civilian-military consultation (such as the creation of the National Security Council), it faced a changed political situation that did not bode well for any Navy initiative. Harry S Truman now sat in the Oval Office with his anti-Navy, anti-Marine Corps biases intact; George C. Marshall had retired, but his successor, Gen. Dwight D. Eisenhower, had the same prejudices and great popularity for his role in Germany's defeat; and Adm. Chester W. Nimitz, who had already proved his pliability in interservice matters in the Pacific, had replaced Admiral King. Army champions in Congress also seemed in the ascendancy. Truman himself ended the political speculation in December 1945, when he announced that he favored the Army's plan for defense reorganization.[3]

As Vandegrift and Thomas recognized, the peril to the Navy and the Marine Corps in the Army's proposed plan rested in the power of the proposed joint staff to decide roles and missions, force structure, and program budgeting, or to shape the decisions on these matters by a single civilian secretary or the president himself without Congressional review. The Navy Department feared that no one outside its walls shared its view of the Navy's role in deterring or fighting future wars: a balanced fleet of carrier aviation, surface combatants, and submarines capable of waging a naval campaign, including amphibious operations, with or without the time-consuming and contentious participation of the Army and Air Force. This naval force would include land-based aviation to perform long-range antisubmarine patrols, naval reconnaissance, and administrative and logistical missions. The Marine Corps would have specialized aviation for amphibious assaults, as well as two or more divisions. The Navy recognized that no other world navy menaced the United States in 1945; the Navy created before 1941 to fight Japan would surely have to change because the only potential enemy, the Soviet Union, was not a maritime state like Japan, with all its vulnerabilities. Nevertheless, the Navy wanted no barrier to the full development of aviation forces, including nuclear rockets and missiles, because of the belief that it should continue to be the nation's "first line of defense."[4]

To coordinate the Navy Department's response to the Army's plan and to explain the benefits of the Navy's alternative visions on future defense policy and reorganization, Forrestal established the Secretary's Committee on Research on Reorganization (SCOROR) in early November 1945. He placed it under the leadership of one of the Navy's most able officers, Vice Adm. Arthur W. Radford, Deputy CNO (Air). Brig. Gen. Merritt A. Edson, hurriedly assigned to Nimitz's office (Op-30M), monitored the committee's activities, as well as those of the Navy Department representatives to the JCS planning committees. Thomas trusted Edson, who became the point man on unification politics, but he became concerned that SCOROR had too many senior Navy officers to function well and would not represent Marine Corps interests. He also found that the Marine Corps had virtually no institutional memory or record of its past political and doctrinal problems. Vandegrift had come to the same conclusion in preparing his October 1945 testimony for the Senate. Everyone was calling for position papers from the Marine Corps: the Joint Chiefs of Staff, the Eberstadt Committee, SCOROR, and other parts of the Office of the Chief of Naval Operations. The most pressing problem—from which all issues of roles and missions flowed—was the review and revision of Fleet Training Publication 167, the doctrinal statement on amphibious operations. Following the model of the 1930s, Vandegrift, with Thomas's counsel, established an ad hoc board, designated "Research Section, Marine Corps Schools," and placed it under the leadership of Col. Merrill B. Twining, executive officer of the Marine Corps Schools. To back Twining, still ill and exhausted by his bouts with the Japanese and cancer, Vandegrift and Thomas summoned Brute Krulak from China to join Twining's board. Thomas briefed Krulak at Headquarters on his mission of linking the doctrinal review with the Marine Corps' independent effort to represent its interests in Washington.[5]

Under Thomas's direction, the Marine Corps team on unification policy and postwar roles and missions took form during the winter months of 1945–46. In addition to Twining and Krulak, the Marine Corps board included Lieutenant Colonels Donald McP. Weller, Samuel R. Shaw, James D. Hittle, and E. Colston Dyer, and Maj. Lynford Hutchins. Two officers stationed at the Marine Corps Schools, Colonels Robert E. Hogaboom and James E. Kerr, counseled the Twining-Krulak group, but the schools commandant, Brig. Gen. O. P. Smith, remained aloof and ambivalent about the board's work when it moved into political action. At Headquarters, the focal point was Thomas's personal office in the Division of Plans and Policies. Jim Murray and then Lt. Col. DeWolf Schatzel served as Thomas's special assistants on unification matters. Murray not only wrote papers but maintained liaison with General Edson and Lt. Col. E. Hunter Hurst, Thomas's representative to SCOROR. The intellectual core of the group, however, remained the Quantico group, dubbed the "Little Men's Chowder and Marching Society" by Colonel Kerr, who found the inspiration in a current comic strip and Krulak's height. The label stuck, and the Twining-Krulak group and its studies became "Chowder." Although membership changed during the next two years, Twining and Krulak remained key members and set the pace in zeal and commitment.[6]

With the Marine Corps unification team barely in place, the tempo of the struggle over defense organization and roles and missions increased dramatically during the winter of 1945–46. Thomas found himself in the middle of a growing crisis. In the process of its own consideration of service functions, the Joint Chiefs of Staff accepted Army testimony, forcefully presented by General Eisenhower, that the Marine Corps should be organized for small-scale naval raids, minor landings, and its traditional naval security duties but not for division or corps amphibious operations. The role of the Fleet Marine Force in World War II had been an anomaly. In fact, the Army description of the future Marine Corps drew its inspiration from the functions of the British Royal Marines, which assisted the Royal Navy in amphibious operations and conducted commando operations of battalion scale or smaller. As General Eisenhower was later to state publicly, the Marine Corps should not be "a so-called amphibious army." Since twenty-eight Army divisions had made amphibious assaults in World War II, "I feel that the United States cannot afford to provide and maintain two great forces, both of which have identical missions, conducting great landing operations."[7] Privately, as Eisenhower wrote Army friends, he wanted the Marine Corps abolished, but he feared public reaction to such a proposal. The Army was quite serious because it proposed an ambitious amphibious training program in 1946 for its own forces. Even more alarming, Admiral Nimitz, a naval El Cid who failed to come alive on interservice issues, actually suggested that the Marine Corps consider a Fleet Marine Force designed as the Army proposed.[8]

Counseled by Thomas and Edson, Vandegrift filed strong rejoinders, drafted by "Chowder," to the Army position. He appeared before the JCS to argue the Marine case for an integrated ground-air team especially trained and organized for major amphibious operations, either as part of a naval campaign or for the opening stages of a ground campaign. Any future war was likely to require the seizure of advanced naval and air bases around the Eurasian land mass, and a sea-based amphibious force prepared for such a major war contingency could also perform more limited military missions, including service with the United Nation's peacekeeping forces, because it could be quickly deployed and did not depend on fixed land bases. Vandegrift also presented a detailed critique of the Army position papers (JCS 1478/10 and JCS 1478/11) that satisfied him and Thomas. Any reasonable military planner should find the Corps' argument for the postwar Fleet Marine Force unassailable in terms of strategic logic and doctrinal soundness.[9]

Marine Corps confidence in its amphibious mission received a severe shock from the Navy-sponsored nuclear tests, Operation Crossroads, at Bikini atoll in the summer of 1946. The senior Marine observer, Lt. Gen. Roy S. Geiger, reported to Vandegrift that nuclear weapons had made the World War II–style amphibious assault a bloody anachronism because no amphibious force could mass offshore in the face of nuclear threat. Vandegrift and Thomas received Geiger's report with alarm, and the Commandant immediately created a special board of senior officers (Generals Lemuel C. Shepherd, O. P. Smith, and Field Harris) to reexamine amphibious doctrine. Thomas ensured that the Shepherd Board received the ardent educational attention of the Twining-Krulak group. After weeks of deliberation, the Shepherd Board reported to Vandegrift that a worst case (a nuclear weapons threat) ship-to-shore movement could be salvaged by the adoption of the troop-carrying helicopter, an operational concept eventually labeled vertical envelopment. Although the Army and the Navy had already begun evaluating experimental helicopters, the lift limitations of these aircraft made the vertical envelopment concept truly visionary, but Thomas embraced it immediately and thus became one of a handful of senior officers to champion helicopter development by the Marine Corps.

The future role of the helicopter, however, muddied the roles and missions controversy because it complicated aviation planning and divided Marine officers over the balance between fixed-wing and rotary-wing aircraft in the future Fleet Marine Force. The Navy's aviation community, itself embattled, pondered the costs of helicopters and the availability of carriers to employ them. Marine officers argued over the merit of armed helicopters as tank killers, as well as troop carriers; this alarmed Marine fighter-bomber pilots. Some Marine officers thought Thomas, Twining, and others of their circle placed too great an emphasis on close air support by whatever means, which discomfited both aviators and artillery officers. The vertical envelopment concept, on the one hand, gave the Marine Corps added incentive to champion the cause of naval aviation but, on the other, made naval aviators (Navy and Marine) suspicious that senior Marine ground officers close to the Commandant, such as Erskine, Shepherd, and Thomas, could not be trusted to preserve an all-purpose naval aviation force that included aircraft capable of carrying nuclear weapons from land bases or carriers.[10]

As the Marine Corps entered the critical legislative year of 1946, Jerry Thomas found himself faced with a delicate and complex political situation. He, Edson, and Vandegrift at Headquarters were the only senior officers who grasped the full danger to the Fleet Marine Force. Other generals, such as Tommy Watson and Pete Hill, had personnel and logistical problems of such size that they probably saw the unification issue as an unhappy intrusion on their own legislative program on officer strength and postwar stockpiling. Some officers probably underestimated the threat and viewed the frenetic work of the Twining-Krulak group as the product of a self-important, over-intellectual clique of ambitious colonels whose major mission was to curry favor with the Commandant and his self-appointed alter ego, Jerry Thomas. ("Wheels within wheels," O. P. Smith once muttered darkly to Krulak.) The aviators had three major studies directed by Twining, Erskine, and Shepherd with which to deal; none made the Marine pilots happy. Secretary of the Navy Forrestal had his own agenda that might not include a vigorous defense of the Fleet Marine Force, even though Forrestal's commitment to naval aviation was total. (Might Forrestal accept a deal that protected naval aviation by compromising on the Fleet Marine Force?) Although Admiral Radford proved a constant defender of the Marine Corps, his strong views made Nimitz nervous, and the Chief of Naval Operations turned more often to another deputy CNO (DCNO), Vice Adm. Forrest P. Sherman, for advice on unification matters. Nimitz had an especially able group of DCNOs (three later became CNO and another chairman of the JCS), but they could hardly challenge Forrestal, who discouraged dissent on defense reorganization, and Nimitz on such a major policy issue as unification. Vandegrift and Thomas hoped they could count on the Navy; in 1946 they concluded, however, that the Marine Corps would have to save itself—and that meant winning the support of Congress.[11]

In the spring of 1946, the Senate Military Affairs Committee (the War Department's favorite Congressional committee) planned hearings on the latest version of a defense reorganization bill (S. 2044). The draft bill had all the signs of a White House–Pentagon origin. Secretary of War Robert Patterson assigned an Army Air Forces planner of reputed brilliance, Maj. Gen. Lauris Norstad, to tutor the committee, and Forrestal countered with Admiral Radford. The Navy's position was especially desperate because Truman had ruled that all land-based air should be included in the new, independent Air Force, which in World War II had already shown its lack of interest in maritime missions. Truman had conceded that the Marine Corps could continue, but his language on this point was as vague as it was strident. Although the President had accepted most of the interdepartmental proposals of the Eberstadt Plan and weakened the powers of the single service secretary and chief of staff, he had not answered critical questions about how the services would split the restricted defense budget or how roles and missions would be assigned.

The prospect of another Congressional effort to pass a defense reorganization act set off a flurry of activity within the executive branch that narrowed, but did not eliminate, the differences between the Army and the Navy. Secretaries Patterson and Forrestal conferred (along with Assistant Secretary of War for Air Stuart Symington), and Norstad and Radford negotiated with ardor. Radford's dogged battle for naval aviation and weakened central powers outside the service departments made him unacceptable to the War Department, and Forrestal replaced him with Nimitz's alter ego, Admiral Sherman, the DCNO (Plans). Radford's political eclipse alarmed Vandegrift and Thomas; Radford had been an ardent champion of limiting any executive branch official, including the president, from deciding roles and missions without Congressional approval. Forrestal and Sherman, on the other hand, thought an executive order should establish roles and missions. The Marines found this concept no less dangerous because it still placed the Corps' future in the hands of political appointees, Army and Air Force generals, and Navy admirals. Truman, however, still provided ample stimulus for dissent by holding fast to his stand that land-based air belonged to the Air Force, but he complicated his position by a statement suggesting that the admirals could challenge this decision. He then became outraged when the admirals took him at his ambiguous word and made public statements in opposition to S. 2044. Truman ordered Forrestal and Nimitz to silence their subordinates, which they promised to do in July 1946.[12]

The newest Congressional battle on defense reform ended in the summer of 1946 as a short-term victory for the Navy Department's champions; the Marines contributed heavily to the successful delaying action. Predictably, the Senate Military Affairs Committee reported that S. 2044 met its liking, but Forrestal arranged for the Senate Naval Affairs Committee to hold subsequent hearings, which produced the opposite result. (The White House already knew that the House of Representatives tended to be pro-Navy.) The Senate Naval Affairs Committee hearings resulted in Vandegrift's finest hour, as orchestrated by Jerry Thomas and the Twining-Krulak group, during the unification controversy. Vandegrift, armed with a speech written by Twining and Krulak, appeared before the committee on 6 May 1946. Vandegrift thought the speech too strong, too likely to antagonize Truman and the War Department. Much of it focused on the Army's case against the Corps and required intimate knowledge of the classified JCS 1478 papers, to which Headquarters did not have official access. Even as the Commandant's limousine crawled through traffic toward the Hill, Vandegrift and Thomas discussed the speech. That Vandegrift gave it as written was largely due to Thomas's persuasiveness. A model of rectitude and sincerity, Vandegrift drew the media attention that Thomas and "Chowder" hoped he would. His closing paragraph became a historic statement of the Corps' political position:

> The Marine Corps, then, believes that it has earned this right—to have its future decided by the legislative body which created it—nothing more. Sentiment is not a valid consideration in determining questions of national security. We have pride in ourselves and in our past but we do not rest our case on any presumed gratitude owing us from the nation. The bended knee is not a tradition of our Corps. If the Marine as a fighting man has not made a case for himself after 170 years of service, he must go. But I think you will agree with me that

he has earned the right to depart with dignity and honor, not by subjugation to the status of uselessness and servility planned for him by the War Department.[13]

In the discussion that followed his speech, Vandegrift reluctantly acknowledged (to a planted question) the existence of the JCS 1478 papers, as did Admiral Nimitz under close and insistent grilling. The White House and the War Department were not amused at the revelations, but the press played the story to the hilt. The day after the "bended knee" speech, Truman recognized that S. 2044 in its current form could not become law.[14]

With the progress on S. 2044 delayed, if not yet ended, Truman ordered Patterson, Forrestal, and their senior military advisors to propose revisions to the bill that might improve its chances of passage. The newest round of executive branch negotiations produced substantial revisions that pleased Forrestal and Nimitz by weakening the powers of the proposed "Secretary of Common Defense" and strengthening departmental civilian and military powers in service management, budgeting, and policy formulation. The issues of land-based naval aviation, the amphibious mission, and the structure of the Marine Corps remained unresolved, however, even after Truman issued a public statement and released private correspondence that implied he would accept a naval aviation force and Marine Corps much like those existing at that time. Truman also announced that Forrestal and Nimitz would cooperate in advancing the administration's reform plan. Angered by an apparent sellout by their two senior leaders, a line of admirals (active and retired) expressed their public dismay when the Senate Naval Affairs Committee resumed hearings on 2 July. So obvious was the rebellion in the Navy Department and the opposition in the Senate that, two weeks later, Truman, on the advice of the Democratic Senate leadership, agreed that S. 2044 (revised) should wait until another Congress convened in 1947.[15]

Although the immediate crisis had passed, Thomas saw ominous indications that, although wounded, S. 2044 might not be dead. There were omens that the Marine Corps still faced a desperate struggle to preserve the Fleet Marine Force and its general war amphibious mission. Two powerful Senators, Lister Hill (Democrat of Alabama) and Harry Byrd (Democrat of Virginia), had promised Marines that they would champion legislative protection for the Corps, but neither had done so. In addition, Forrestal appeared ready for a final compromise that would not include legislative protection of service roles and missions but settle instead for an executive order on the subject. Truman's threats against admirals and Marine generals who opposed unification seemed serious when Nimitz transferred Radford from Washington and took punitive action against other admirals.

Thomas, Twining, and Krulak worried most, however, about Vandegrift's political will and endurance. They suspected that Truman had cowed the Commandant with some sort of threat. Truman had several options he could take against Vandegrift: refuse to appoint his recommended successor as Commandant, intervene in the retention and selection of general officers, cut the strength of the Corps in the budget process, and fail to support officer personnel legislation. By the autumn of 1946, Vandegrift appeared exhausted by his service as Commandant. He was becoming progressively blind and deaf (glasses helped his eyesight, but he hated to wear them). The necessity of sending many of his old friends into involuntary retirement had disheartened him. His spirits sank even more with the death of Roy Geiger (23 January 1947), a close friend since they entered the Marine Corps together in 1909. To help with the burdens of his office, he brought Lemuel C. Shepherd, Jr., up from Quantico to become assistant commandant. Shepherd, one of Thomas's closest friends in the Marine Corps, did not displace Thomas as the unofficial leader of "Chowder" and its Headquarters allies. Thomas himself showed signs of nervous exhaustion, with his blood pressure climbing ever higher, but he had plenty of fight left. When he learned that a new agreement between the Navy and the Army provided no protection for the Marine Corps, he arranged for Vandegrift to meet with him, Twining, and Krulak in order to map strategy for the 1947 legislative session. At Thomas's insistence, Vandegrift created a new board, led by Merritt Edson and composed of leading members of "Chowder" and Thomas's personal staff, to represent the Marine Corps. Thomas was to coordinate the Edson Board's activities as the Commandant's personal representative.[16]

When the 80th Congress began hearings on defense organization in March 1947, the Edson Board went to work in its primary mission—developing a group of Marine Corps champions in Congress, feeding information to the friendly media, and arguing (officially and unofficially) to anyone on the Hill who would listen. All members of the Edson Board had been on the unification barricades since early 1946, with the exception of Lt. Col. Robert D. Heinl, Jr., its historian and public affairs expert, and Maj. Jonas M. Platt, its recorder. Coached by Lieutenant Colonel Hittle (a student of general staff organization), the members had concluded that if Congress passed the latest version of S. 2044 (now S. 758), it would surrender much of its constitutional control over military affairs. Some Marine officers, especially Edson, Twining, Hittle, and Heinl, thought that unification under the terms of S. 758 would lead to the end of effective civilian control of the military in America. This belief gave them a sense of mission and zeal beyond the mere survival of the Fleet Marine Force. They faced a daunting task, even though the Republicans had taken control of Congress after the 1946 elections, because Congress had already merged the Military Affairs and Naval Affairs committees into two reorganized Armed Services committees. The Senate committee was under the control of pro-Army members, and the House committee, despite its mild pro-Navy stance, no longer enjoyed the leadership of Carl Vinson. Both the Truman administration and Congress, moreover, wanted a final resolution to the defense reorganization question, for they believed that the growing confrontation with the Soviet Union in early 1947 required prompt military restructuring. As the Edson-Thomas group realized, the risk was growing that the Marine Corps would appear as an obstructionist malcontent, spoiled by its World War II publicity.[17]

As feared, the Edson-Thomas group could not derail Senate passage of S. 758; it bore the approval of the White House, the War Department, and the Navy Department. Despite their best efforts to discredit the legislation and mount a public furor on the issue of civilian control and the future of the Corps, the Marine officers could count only limited victories for their point of view. Largely through the efforts of Senators E. V. Robertson (Republican of Wyoming) and Styles Bridges (Republican of New Hampshire), they did win crucial admissions from Forrestal that the law allowed a future secretary of defense to reassign roles and missions without congressional approval and from General Eisenhower that he still believed in a strong military chief of the armed forces who would have substantial authority to determine service functions. The Edson-Thomas group arranged for General Vandegrift to testify again about the threat of extinction to the Corps, but the Commandant's testimony was a pale imitation of the "bended knee" speech. In fact, he refused to use an aggressive statement prepared by Twining and Krulak. Outside support from the Veterans of Foreign Wars, the National Rifle Association, the National Guard Association, the American Legion, and the Marine Corps Reserve Officers Association did not fundamentally change the direction of the hearings. After Vandegrift's appearance, the Edson-Thomas group, with Thomas's approval, arranged for Senator Robertson to call Edson to testify. On 7 May 1947 Edson presented the testimony (originally prepared for Vandegrift), including a full description of the import of the JCS 1478 papers, and enlarged upon his own conviction that S. 758 would lead to militarism and defense ineffectiveness. Nevertheless, the only change engineered by the Edson-Thomas group was a loosely constructed amendment to S. 758 that "the provisions of this act shall not authorize the alteration or diminution of the existing relative status of the Marine Corps (including the fleet marine forces) or of naval aviation." After more testimony, the committee unanimously reported out S. 758 in substantially unaltered form on 5 June, and the Senate approved the bill four days later by voice vote.[18]

The Edson-Thomas group felt not just defeated but betrayed by the Commandant and the Navy. And it took a casualty, none other than General Edson himself. Weakened by a back operation and a hookworm infection, bored by peacetime assignments, and convinced that he might damage the Marine Corps, Edson had planned to retire before his Senate appearance. His militant attack on S. 758 was true to character, an act of great personal courage. It was a verbal battle of Raider Ridge with the ice-calm Edson, wearing his Medal of Honor, at his best. After this testimony, Secretary Forrestal, through General Vandegrift, suggested that Edson might be subject to some sanction for his testimony and media statements. Edson did not fall silent, but Vandegrift did not accept his retirement request until a month after his Senate testimony. As commissioner of the Vermont highway patrol and, later, executive director of the National Rifle Association, he preached against defense reorganization until his death in 1955. His retirement, however, deprived "Chowder" of an institutional spokesman with public celebrity equal to—if not greater than—Vandegrift.[19]

What the Edson-Thomas group did not win in the Senate, it accomplished in the House of Representatives. Despite the opposition of the Watson-Hill clique of generals at Headquarters that now included Brig. Gen. William E. Riley, the director of information and a Thomas foe, the surviving colonels of "Chowder" coordinated their congressional lobbying with continued media exploitation through such Corps champions as editor David Lawrence. Jerry Thomas, however, did not remain at Headquarters to direct the final political offensive. The Commandant sent him off to command the remaining Marines in China, a truncated brigade in Tsingtao designated Fleet Marine Force Western Pacific (FMFWesPac). On the surface, the assignment appeared routine, and Thomas thought he was China-bound as early as 1947. Thomas had served at Headquarters more than three years and was due for overseas service; the last tactical unit he had commanded had been a company in China before the war. The Commandant would be doing him a favor by giving him a brigade in an area where combat threatened. Thomas himself favored the forward deployment of FMF units in troubled areas, and he thought that some American presence might improve the Nationalist government's will to fight the Chinese Communists. Nevertheless, the timing of Thomas's departure from Washington suggests that he and Vandegrift had reached the point where they could no longer work together, in good conscience, for the benefit of the Corps. Twining and Krulak certainly thought that Vandegrift had decided to curb the colonels of "Chowder" by transferring the one general officer at Headquarters who truly understood that only Congressional protection of the Fleet Marine Force would save the Marine Corps from eventual extinction.[20]

The congressional managers of S. 758 gave the Edson-Thomas group its last opportunity to work a major modification of the defense reorganization legislation, and the Marines and their allies seized it with a vengeance. Instead of asking the House Armed Services Committee to hold hearings on the House version of the law (H.R. 2319), the managers referred the bill to the House Committee on Expenditures in the Executive Department, chaired by Representative Clare E. Hoffman (Republican of Michigan) but dominated in military matters by pro-Army Representative James W. Wadsworth, Jr. (Republican of New York), a former senator. The political envelopment failed, largely because Colonel Hittle's father was a friend of Hoffman and because Representative John W. McCormack (Democrat of Massachusetts), the minority whip and former majority House floor leader, had an equally close relationship with Brig. Gen. Arthur Worton, a Thomas intimate and Edson's successor on the CNO's staff. Hoffman and McCormack organized a bipartisan coalition on the committee to check Wadsworth's influence on the H.R. 2319 hearings. Before the review ended on 1 July 1947, the revised version of the bill contained a statutory definition of service roles and missions drafted by Twining, Krulak, and Hittle.

The entire matter was a near-run thing. The subcommittee approved the administration's bill by a vote of 4–3, but voted 5–1 for legislative protection in the markup. When the bill went before the full House, naval aviators joined the fray in support of legislated roles and missions and the pro-Marine lobbyists supported Hoffman's successful effort to enter on the record, finally, the full set of JSC 1478 papers. In Senate-House conference on the revised bill, Hoffman held fast to the concept of legislated service functions and eventually won his point. Title II, Section 206(c), of the final version of the National Security Act of 1947 read as the Marines had written it:

> The United States Marine Corps, within the Department of the Navy, shall include land combat and service forces and such aviation as may be organic therein. The primary mission of the Marine Corps shall be to provide fleet marine forces of combined arms, together with supporting air components, for service with the fleet in the seizure and defense of advanced naval bases and for the conduct of such land operations as may be essential to the prosecution of a naval campaign.

The Marine Corps also had the responsibilities of developing amphibious warfare doctrine and equipment in cooperation with the other services, providing ships guards and other naval security detachments, and performing additional duties as the President might assign it. These duties should not interfere, however, with its general war missions, which might require the mobilization of reserves and the expansion of the Fleet Marine Force. The surviving members of the Edson-Thomas group assembled at Krulak's quarters for a victory celebration on the evening of 26 July 1947, the date Truman signed the National Security Act. There was no dissent among them about the significance of the accomplishment. They also agreed that Jerry Thomas, then on his way to China, deserved major credit for the Marine Corps' salvation.[21]

The question remains: What had brought about the rift between Vandegrift and Thomas during House hearings on the National Security Act? Neither general then or later discussed the matter for the record. The evidence suggests, however, that Thomas believed Vandegrift had lost his moral courage to see the battle for legislative protection to its conclusion. Edson had been pressured to retire, and Nimitz had made similar threats against Arthur Worton, who eventually retired in 1949 to become police chief of Los Angeles. In the spring of 1947, Vandegrift, believing that S. 758 was minimally acceptable, refused to take counsel from the Edson-Thomas group, and instead turned for political advice to Col. Joseph W. "Buddy" Knighton and Samuel Meek, the former Marine who ran the J. Walter Thompson advertising firm. Knighton, the Commandant's legal advisor and a personnel expert, did not understand the roles and missions crisis and saw it only as a barrier to pending personnel legislation. To be sure, Vandegrift had a discouraging budget situation to handle and wanted some resolution of the defense reorganization issue before the Marine Corps lost even more ground in Congress. Basically, Vandegrift would have accepted an executive order on roles and missions, and Thomas would not.

Faced with a Commandant who would not risk one more effort at legislative protection—a risk the Edson-Thomas group accepted—Thomas "just quit in disgust," as Bill Twining saw the situation. At the time Thomas left Headquarters, he still held no permanent status as a Marine general officer. Not until the passage of the Officer Personnel Act of 7 August 1947 (P.L. 381, 80th Congress)* could Thomas and his peers be appointed, approved by the White House, and confirmed by the Senate as generals. His role in orchestrating the Marine Corps opposition to the National Security Act might have ended Thomas's career. His break with the Commandant, however, did not come until June 1947, when the tide in the House hearings had swung in favor of the Marine Corps. Whether he took another assignment of his own volition or accepted exile to China as an acceptable alternative to retirement, Thomas did not flee the field. He must have left Washington reasonably certain that Vandegrift saw the wisdom of legislated protection, even if the Commandant thought Buddy Knighton had produced the political miracle. The result was the same. At a minimum, the Marine Corps could continue the fight.[22]

---

* The legislation provided the Marine Corps with twelve permanent major generals (including the Commandant as a general and two lieutenant generals for the operating forces in the Atlantic and Pacific) and twenty unrestricted line brigadier generals.

★ ★ ★ ★

As Vandegrift approached the end of four trying years as Commandant, he held no illusions that his successor would have fewer trials. The most recent appropriations had left the Corps short 1,000 officers and 8,000 enlisted. In a three-month period (1 April–30 June 1947), the Corps had lost another 369 officers and 11,000 enlisted Marines as the last of the wartime noncareer veterans left the service. The Marine Corps had met its enlistment quotas in 1947 only because its authorized strength had shrunk. Although Vandegrift believed that he had a sound officer procurement and recruiting system in place, that the training establishment at the recruit depots and Quantico was sound, and that the war stockpiles looked bullish, he reported to the new Secretary of Defense, James V. Forrestal, that the lack of personnel and training funds had brought the units (especially aviation) of the Fleet Marine Force to the brink of ineffectiveness. The next Commandant might move into Commandant's House, but he could not escape four years of misery unless the nation's security policy changed sea-state.[23]

In August 1947, while Forrestal still served as secretary of the navy and Nimitz as chief of naval operations, Vandegrift submitted his analysis of the question of who should be the next Commandant. He complied with Forrestal's request for multiple nominations by sending forward briefs and comments on six generals: Lemuel C. Shepherd, Jr., Clifton B. Cates, Harry Schmidt, Graves B. Erskine, Allen H. Turnage, and Franklin A. Hart. Vandegrift recommended Shepherd, and he reported that Schmidt, who was too old to serve a full term as Commandant, had requested retirement in 1948. The other five generals had records of distinguished service, especially in World War II, in which all but Hart had commanded divisions in combat. Nimitz supported Vandegrift's nomination of Shepherd, but with his usual tepidness. Forrestal made no recommendation at all. Harry Truman made no decision. In November, Vandegrift asked Secretary of the Navy John L. Sullivan to press the White House for a decision. Finally, Truman summoned Generals Shepherd and Cates to his office without prior warning. Shepherd was Assistant Commandant and Cates the commanding general at Quantico, so the interview posed no problems. Truman saw the two generals in the Oval Office and admitted he knew nothing about either of them, but he liked their splendid combat records in World War I. He also mentioned that he had received political pressure to appoint someone else (probably Erskine, who had become a favorite of Congress in his role as administrator of veterans' rehabilitation), but that he would appoint Cates since he was slightly senior and slightly older (three years) than Shepherd. Shepherd would have to wait four years, a prospect that must have alarmed Shepherd because Harry Truman was not exactly a sure bet for reelection in 1948. Cates left the room dazed by his good fortune and no less surprised than Shepherd.[24]

The change of Commandants could not have been worse for Jerry Thomas. Shepherd remained one of his longtime friends and admirers, no less so because Thomas had kept the Assistant Commandant clean of political taint during the unification crisis. Cates, on the other hand, still regarded Thomas with suspicion. The new Commandant moved his best Guadalcanal battalion commander, Edwin A. Pollock, from Quantico to be his military secretary and then (as a new brigadier general) Director of the Division of Plans and Policies. Shepherd and Cates simply switched bases. The problem was Hal Turnage, Commanding General Fleet Marine Force Pacific, who decided to retire as soon as Cates became Commandant. Cates then appointed Thomas E. Watson, one of the senior major generals, to Turnage's billet. This meant that Watson had now become Thomas's reporting senior. The change of general officers also moved LeRoy Hunt closer to a short appointment as lieutenant general before he retired. The ripple effect of Cates's appointment could hardly have worked to more disadvantage than it did for Gerald C. Thomas, a junior brigadier on his way to the field from Headquarters Marine Corps.

[CHAPTER XXI]

Watch on the Yellow Sea
1947–1949

While Brig. Gen. Gerald C. Thomas and all of his family, except Jerry Junior, were driving west toward the Pacific and another voyage to Asia in June 1947, American forces in China had begun their inexorable withdrawal. Thomas arrived at his command in Tsingtao, Shantung Province, just in time to manage the departure from North China, a recognition of the victory of Mao Tse-tung's Communists in the twenty-five-year Chinese civil war. A decade of military and financial support for Chiang Kai-shek's Nationalist government, fueled by the faint hope that China might play a major role in Japan's defeat, could not restore Nationalist control of North China—stronghold of the Communist party and the People's Liberation Army (PLA). After V-J Day, the III Amphibious Corps (the 1st and 6th Marine Divisions, the 1st Marine Aircraft Wing, the 7th Force Service Regiment, and other reinforcing corps troops) deployed to North China to disarm and repatriate the Japanese Army and to provide some security for the cities, railroads, and coal mines of the region. In fact, the Marines covered the redeployment of the elite divisions of the Nationalist Army, committed to a final campaign (so Chiang Kai-shek planned) to crush the Communists.[1]

By August 1947, when the Thomas family arrived in China after ten years' absence, the Truman administration had discovered the limits of its ability to strengthen the Nationalist position. During 1945 and 1946, it had poured more than $1 billion into the Chinese treasury to strengthen the Nationalist Army, stabilize the economy, and fund the government but without much demonstrable improvement. It had established a Joint United States Military Assistance Group (JUSMAG), which advised and trained the Nationalist Army, also with minimal results. General of the Army George C. Marshall, who enjoyed President Truman's unadulterated confidence, had spent a frustrating year in an attempt to negotiate a peace settlement. Although Mao Tse-tung showed no inclination to

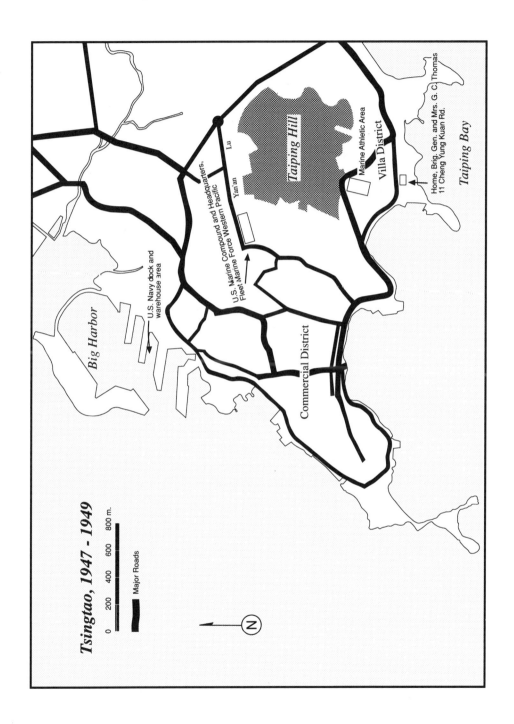

compromise, the Nationalists proved equally obdurate against power-sharing and wealth distribution outside the closed structure of the Kuomintang. The Truman administration, however, faced an awkward domestic political situation. The rival Republican party, although split in its support of containment and collective security in Europe, demanded a strong commitment to Nationalist China. The most partisan Republican leaders in Congress suspected that the "Old China Hands" of the State Department secretly favored a Communist victory and made "losing" China a political issue of dramatic proportions, regardless of the damage such vigilantism would do to the bipartisan coalition that supported the Truman Doctrine, the European Recovery Program of 1948, and, eventually, the creation of the North Atlantic Treaty Organization in 1949. In effect, the Truman administration felt that it had to pursue any hope, however faint, that the Nationalists might at least retain control over central and southern China. The American armed forces remained a major instrument in the government's rearguard action.

Within the military, the China commitment offered few benefits and many risks. Although individual senior officers held varied views about the wisdom and feasibility of supporting Chiang Kai-shek, the Joint Chiefs of Staff had shifted their global vision to Europe and the Mediterranean. They wanted few of their scarce combat units and ships held on mainland China, which the Joint Chiefs did not view as essential to America's long-term security. They doubted that the Communists could be defeated without the direct commitment of American air and ground combat units. A major war in Asia—to use Gen. Omar Bradley's later phrase—was the wrong war at the wrong place at the wrong time against the wrong enemy. The State Department, however, argued against rapid redeployment of the III Amphibious Corps. Instead, the diplomats and the JCS compromised. By the spring of 1947, most of the Marines, after losing ten dead and thirty-three wounded to PLA raiding parties, had left north China with the exception of Tsingtao. The U.S. Navy had several reasons for maintaining at least one strong enclave in Shantung: a defensible safe haven for American and foreign civilians, a site of extensive communications facilities for the fleet and intelligence activities (including monitoring Chinese radio communications), a good location for ship maintenance and logistical support, as well as recreation facilities for its sailors. If for some reason the United States reversed its policy of military intervention, Tsingtao could provide a bridgehead for the return of the Fleet Marine Force Pacific, which maintained skeleton forces on Guam and Hawaii, and in California. Reflecting the reduction of the forward deployed naval forces in China in 1947, the U.S. Seventh Fleet became simply Naval Forces Western Pacific (NavForWesPac) and the garrison of four thousand Marines in Tsingtao took the designation Fleet Marine Force Western Pacific (FMFWesPac). As former director of the Division of Plans and Policies, Thomas had an intimate knowledge of Marine affairs in China and approved the extended deployment of Marine forces at Tsingtao.[2]

When the Thomases had left Washington for San Francisco and passage on a Navy transport to Tsingtao, they had been excited for different reasons by the return to China. As they left their home in Foxhall Village, the general had announced their time of arrival at Marine headquarters in San Francisco as 1000

2 July. This bit of planning did not immediately concern Lottie and the children because the trip began in leisurely enough fashion. After spending the first night in a Wheeling, West Virginia, rooming house of Victorian decor, they drove westward on U.S. 40 into Indiana and turned north for a two-night stay on the Shoup farm north of Lafayette at Battleground, Indiana, the site of the Battle of Tippecanoe. Dave Shoup's parents proved genial hosts, even if Battleground offered little more than cornfields, a railroad crossing, and a cluster of country stores. The trip continued with a stop in Bloomington, Illinois, for a visit with Jerry's brother Shelton and his wife Irene, as well as another reunion with the admiring townspeople of Jerry's hometown and alma mater. Then the rains and the troubles began, abetted by flooded roads and altered routes. Perhaps Jerry responded to deep memories of his truck drive with the Army over the Appalachians in 1928, for he drove on with relentless concentration. The quality of roadside accommodations deteriorated as the Great Plains heat increased. The family got food poisoning; Tina's new hat blew off and disappeared into the brush; Lottie forgot a new nightgown at one motel, but her request to retrieve it fell on the convoy commander's deaf ears. On he drove. The Thomases, exhausted and cross, arrived in San Francisco two minutes early at 0958 on 2 July 1947 to Jerry's satisfaction. As he reported in to Maj. Gen. LeRoy Hunt, Lottie suggested that, since they had arrived early, perhaps they should try the trip again. The general was not amused. The mutiny subsided after four days at the Saint Francis Hotel and three weeks at sea on board the transport U.S.S. *President Jackson*. As the ranking passengers, General and Mrs. Thomas enjoyed the best stateroom, with the three children billeted next to them. The ship made calls to Hawaii and Yokosuka, Japan, before arriving at Tsingtao on 2 August. The Commanding General, Fleet Marine Force Western Pacific, took over from his predecessor, Brig. Gen. Omar T. Pfeiffer, in leisurely fashion and assumed command two weeks after he arrived. The return to China and the Fleet Marine Force brought Thomas a degree of peace he had not found in Washington.[3]

Built in a beautiful natural harbor on the southern coast of the Shantung peninsula near the tip, Tsingtao retained much of its Old World charm in 1947, but that charm was more European than Chinese. The city, particularly the business and governmental districts of the inner city and nearby residential districts, had been built by the Germans after they had obtained a leasehold in 1898. The Japanese had captured the city in 1915 as part of their whirlwind World War I campaign against Germany's Asian colonies, but they had maintained and beautified it until forced to withdraw by the League of Nations in 1922. Under Chinese governance until the Japanese returned in 1938, Tsingtao had continued to thrive as a center of commerce and shipping, run largely by its European inhabitants because it retained its status as a treaty port. Local police and a force of foreign volunteers prevented the Nationalists from destroying the city in 1938 and curbed looting. The Japanese made their own peace with the city's power structure during the war, and they surrendered the city to the 6th Marine Division and the Nationalists much as it had existed in 1938. The Navy and Marine Corps inherited offices and quarters that might have been built in Prussia or Bavaria but landscaped by Japanese gardeners. Most of the Americans settled in the Villa

District between Taiping Hill and Taiping Bay, bordered by pleasant beaches and parks. The major portion of the Marine garrison occupied the former Bismarck Barracks, converted to become the Shantung University, on Yan'an Road about three miles from the Villa District. The quarters of the CG FMFWesPac did not quite match the opulence of the billets of ComNavForWesPac, but the Thomas home at 11 Cheng Yung Kuan Road offered the family rare comfort and ascribed social status. Set in a walled compound of almost a full acre of well-kept lawns, gardens, ornamental woods, and an orchard, the three-story brick and stucco commanding general's quarters had once belonged to a German millionaire, Tsingtao's leading sausage manufacturer. The compound included a badminton court, summer house, servants' quarters, gardener's hut, greenhouse, and outdoor courtyard designed for garden parties. A staff of eight servants provided Lottie and the children with ample freedom to enjoy Tsingtao's lively European society and sights. For about a year, the Thomas family lived the gracious life enjoyed by senior American officers in China prior to 1937 but one that was now disappearing for the second time in the sweep of war.[4]

Jerry Thomas had come to China to command a Marine brigade, not just live well. He quickly assessed his mission and forces; he found the first demanding and the second in sore need of training. He received his operational guidance from Admiral Charles M. Cooke, Jr., ComNavForWesPac. The Marines had the responsibility for providing security detachments (sentries and patrols) for all naval facilities in Tsingtao and the Marine airfield at nearby Tsang Kou. The greatest security problem, however, was guarding the American warehouses and storage areas scattered about the city by the Navy and the 6th Marine Division—tempting targets for Chinese midnight entrepreneurs. Under pressure from anti-American agitators, along with the obvious disparity between American affluence and Chinese poverty, the people of Tsingtao could not be regarded as passive and friendly. As one of Admiral Cooke's staff put it, "Some abatement of the enthusiasm of the general public over the presence of our forces had become apparent."[5] While China's economy deteriorated and the city (normally about 200,000 people) doubled in size from refugees, the Marines found it increasingly difficult to beat back the thieves. Thomas reduced the number of supply depots, but his Marines still found themselves harassed, shot at, and distracted by raiders. The rules of engagement, determined by Admiral Cooke, required sentries to challenge any intruders six times in English and Chinese before they opened fire with their shotguns, loaded with nothing more lethal than bird shot. Internal security proved more difficult than any external threat. The Nationalist Army adequately blocked the limited approaches to the city from the north, aided by a defensible line created by the Bai Sha river and the Lao Shan mountains. Unless they mounted urban riots, which they did not, the Communists were not an immediate threat to the city.[6]

As the civil war turned against the Nationalists in 1948 and the safety of Americans in north China assumed growing importance, FMFWesPac received additional missions. Thomas had to provide an alert platoon available for airlift in an hour, to be followed by a full battalion landing team within six hours. This force would hold an airhead to which American diplomatic personnel and the soldiers of JUSMAG could retreat for evacuation to Tsingtao. In addition, the

Marines should prepare to receive and process American private citizens and foreign nationals who found their way to Tsingtao; these civilians would be sent by ship either to Shanghai to the south or away from China altogether. Should Tsingtao itself require evacuation, the Marines would provide a shield for the Navy's withdrawal and destruction of its communications stations, support facilities, and all administrative service installations.[7]

Thomas's brigade shrank as its missions expanded. When he assumed command, Thomas had inherited a headquarters and service battalion, three reinforced infantry battalions with attached artillery batteries, a service regiment, a service battalion, a three-squadron aircraft group, and assorted headquarters units, in all about 4,000 officers and enlisted personnel. By November 1947, he had lost one of the infantry battalions and the service regiment. For most of 1948, FMFWesPac consisted of two reinforced infantry battalions (1st Marines and 3d Marines); an air group composed of a headquarters and service squadron, a Corsair squadron (VMF-211), and a composite utility squadron of R5C transports and OY light observation planes; the 12th Service Battalion; and the Force headquarters. (In the postwar reorganization of the FMF, individual battalions assumed regimental identities much like the British army system.) The brigade now numbered around 3,500 officers and enlisted personnel. The brigade structure could not conceal organizational problems. The two six-gun artillery batteries of 105-mm howitzers were not manned; the brigade cadre of artillerymen (fewer than 100 officers and enlisted) served in the infantry battalions. The single tank platoon guarded the airfield and seldom trained. More importantly, the two infantry battalions seldom mustered more than 50 Marines for training; the others served either on the guard detail or on working parties.[8]

Before he could do much about his brigade's marginal state of readiness, Thomas had to find some relief from his logistical and administrative burdens. He fumed that the Marine Corps supply system had reverted to peacetime tempo and that competent supply officers were in short supply in China. His plan showed imagination and energy. He rescued Marine Corps funds sequestered in banks all over China to fund barracks improvements and thus lower maintenance needs. Reducing the number of fleet and Marine supply facilities lightened the guard requirements. He pushed his supply officers to cut inventories by transferring their holdings as surplus or aid to the Nationalists. His pragmatic, if risky, approach to logistics problems heartened his supply officers, who had found General Pfeiffer a legalist and stickler for administrative regularity.[9]

Drawing on his experience with the Peiping legation guard, Thomas initiated a demanding training program for his infantry battalions. He rejected the pleas of their commanders that they had too few men to make training meaningful; they always needed physical training, drill, small unit tactics, and weapons training and gun drill. Thomas introduced schools for junior officers and sergeants. He ordered training schedules that did not compromise with the stiff Chinese winter weather, and he challenged the infantry battalions to prepare themselves for their summer training with the amphibious force of NavForWesPac that occurred on schedule in May and June 1948. The lack of suitable training areas and beaches placed substantial limits on the quality and complexity of battalion-sized exercises, but Thomas pushed his subordinates to focus on what they could accomplish and not to worry about the obstacles they could not overcome.[10]

Although he took pride in his ability to bring his brigade to higher readiness, Thomas invested even greater interest and effort in assessing the course of the Chinese civil war. His intelligence section, headed by a trusted subordinate from his Headquarters staff, Lt. Col. William A. Kengla, provided routine reports and briefings. In 1948, both of Kengla's assistant G-2s, Capt. John B. Bristow and 1st Lt. Richard A. Cooley, were Chinese-language specialists. Thomas sent his Chinese-language officers off by air to visit the principal cities of north China and the headquarters of the Nationalist Army in the area to provide direct contact with the Nationalist generals and JUSMAG officers. He himself took to the road to consult with other Nationalist generals and American officials. Thomas reinforced his staff with several additional Chinese-language specialists; these Marine officers had trained under his own 1944 program, among them Nicholas G. W. Thorne, John A. Lindsay, Thomas C. Dutton, Palmer M. Rixey, Jr., and William Capers James, Jr., the son of his alienated cousin by marriage, Brig. Gen. Capers James.

Between October 1947 and December 1948, Thomas visited Peiping four times, Tientsin once, Nanking twice, and Shanghai once. In Peiping, he discussed Chinese politics and American policy with the consul general, O. Edmund Clubb, and the assistant military attaché, Col. David D. Barrett, USA, who had served a total of seventeen years in China since 1921. Thomas had first met Barrett in Peiping in the 1930s and relied on his political judgment, particularly because Barrett knew the Communists as well as the Nationalists. In Nanking, Thomas visited with Ambassador Leighton Stuart, former president of Yenching University, also a friend from Peiping and a Sigma Chi. He renewed his contacts with two Nationalist generals who had been his classmates at Fort Leavenworth, Tu Chih Min and Fisher Ho. Thomas thoroughly enjoyed being his own G-2; he had a lifelong addiction to political gossip and personal contacts. His travels around China also provided him with a sound appreciation of the fragility of the Nationalist position, and he recognized the signs of collapse after the decisive battle of Hsuchow in the summer of 1948 more quickly than his naval superiors. He saw the sure indicators of defeat: the flood of refugees into the port cities, the shipment of gold and valuables by Nationalist generals, and the negotiations between local Kuomintang leaders and the Communists in defiance of Chiang Kai-shek. In December 1948, Thomas planned one last trip to Peiping before the city fell to the encircling People's Liberation Army, but he canceled the trip when he learned that the airport was under fire. He told his staff that he had not survived two world wars to die in a civil war in which the United States would not take a stand.[11]

Thomas knew that part of his mission required amiable relations with the Chinese, if for no other reason than to avoid publicity. His biggest challenge was to handle shooting incidents involving his security details because the local press used such episodes to inflame antiforeign sentiment in Tsingtao. The Chinese police in the city tended to shoot at American drivers when they perceived serious traffic violations. American MPs once arrested a drunken Nationalist general who called out his own troops to defend his honor, but officer negotiators from both sides stopped the incident before the shooting started. Thomas did what he could to help Gen. Ting Chih P'An, the administrator of Tsingtao, and Gen. Li Mei, commander of the Nationalist army in Shantung. The Marines passed on American military surplus to the Chinese (Thomas thought most of it worthless) and supported the government and private agencies in their attempts to house, clothe, and feed the refugees. In March 1948, the Marines assisted Chinese authorities to stop a serious fire and treated more than seven hundred injured after a mysterious explosion of a warehouse on Shan Ho Road; the disaster killed more than one hundred Chinese and destroyed or damaged one hundred homes.[12]

The most serious incidents that taxed FMFWesPac relations with the Chinese occurred in the countryside, dominated by the Communist guerrillas of Li Yu. During a fleet exercise in August 1947, three Marine Corsairs from VMF 211 became lost in bad weather; two of the planes ditched at sea, and Navy warships recovered the pilots without incident. The third Corsair, however, landed on the Shantung peninsula. When a Marine landing party went ashore to find the pilot and destroy the aircraft, they exchanged fire with armed Chinese, presumably Communists. Chinese sources reported that the Marines had wounded three men. No Marines fell, but they did not find the pilot either, who remained in Communist hands until Navy intelligence agents negotiated his release the following month. In late December 1947, a four-man hunting party of Marines, driving a jeep, came under fire from a Communist patrol near Lingshan. The brief battle proved hot and confusing, in part because of the arrival of a fifth Marine, Pfc C. J. Brayton, Jr., who had deserted with his M-1. When the shooting stopped, Brayton and two Communist guerrillas lay dead; the guerrillas took the Marines captive and burned the jeep. As soon as he learned of the incident, Thomas organized a rescue party, but the Nationalist authorities would not allow independent military action. Thomas agreed to negotiations and the use of the Nationalist secret service, but he put John Bristow on the case as well, and the Chinese-linguist captain made several journeys to the Lingshan area. The major effort, however, was to air-drop leaflets in Chinese that offered rewards for Brayton's body and the captive Marines. Three leaflet drops occurred in January 1948 with no results. Admiral Cooke followed the recovery operation in detail and complained to Thomas that he (Thomas) had been too aggressive in forming his own plans, managing the Tsingtao media coverage, and communicating with Headquarters Marine Corps. Thomas agreed to work more closely with the Navy, and Cooke approved his efforts to make direct contact with the Communists through Bristow and Tom Dutton. Contact did not occur until April 1948, when the guerrillas returned Brayton's body to a motorized Marine patrol led by Bristow into Communist territory. They did not release the captive Marines until July. Two other incidents involving temporary detention of downed aircrews ended more rapidly through the collaboration of the Nationalist secret police and the Communists. In all, Thomas handled these crises with intelligence and patience, even though his instincts called for less diplomatic action than paying a ransom of medical supplies.[13]

As Commanding General, Fleet Marine Force Western Pacific, Thomas had his first opportunity to hone his professional personality as a senior Marine commander. For the first time in the seven years since his promotion to lieutenant colonel, he did not have to modulate his opinions and behavior to maintain his relationship with Alexander Archer Vandegrift, the ultimate Virginia gentleman whom Thomas had idealized and served. During his tour in Tsingtao, Thomas proved that he could handle the ambiguities and frustrations that inevitably confront general officers. Although Jerry Thomas showed some of the insecurity and rigidity that can accompany flag rank, he also demonstrated his capacity to grow with the job and his uncanny ability to get talented officers to work with him in a common cause.

Thomas's relations with his nominal Navy and Marine Corps superiors produced mixed results, not all under his control. His first operational commander, Admiral Cooke, was a staff officer of renown in the Navy but not exactly a hardened sea dog—he had spent most of the war in Washington. Thomas had known him well during their service together in the Navy Department. Although he understood that Cooke was not a risk taker, he soon learned that Cooke tended to see Marine carelessness as the cause of any incident with the Chinese. Each incident, even if initiated by a Chinese, required an immediate American public apology. Thomas seldom forced issues to the confrontation stage with Cooke, a sure way to lose the policy argument. Instead, he defended his positions with persistence but not insistence: ". . . we fought all the things out, and I got along with Admiral Cooke in pretty good fashion. I believe I've always been smart enough to keep my seniors from running over me, but have also been smart enough not to fight with them, and that's not always done. Cooke and I got along very well."[14]

In March 1948 Adm. Oscar C. Badger replaced Admiral Cooke as ComNavForWesPac. A battleship admiral and the third generation of his family to fly his flag aboard American warships, Badger took a no-nonsense, uncomplicated approach to the same problems that agitated Cooke, principally the lack of guidance from the theater commander, General of the Army Douglas MacArthur, who preferred reforming Japan to losing China. Thomas and Badger had no serious difficulties during their association. If a problem remained unresolved to his satisfaction, however, Thomas never hesitated to threaten an appeal to the Navy Department for a decision. Admirals Cooke and Badger reported Thomas's performance as superior in every way.[15]

Lt. Gen. Thomas E. Watson, Commanding General, Fleet Marine Force Pacific (FMF Pac), did not share the admirals' enthusiasm for Thomas. Watson became Jerry Thomas's reporting senior for the first time in early 1948. He did not allow this opportunity to pass without exacting revenge for the embarrassment of Roy Hunt on Guadalcanal and his own battles with Thomas at Headquarters. Watson visited Tsingtao once in April 1948. What he saw and heard apparently did not please him. Later the same year, he gave Thomas the worst fitness report of his career. Watson rated him "excellent" in most categories of performance, with a few "outstandings" thrown in for credibility. He gave him only an "above average" in "force," which probably suggested that he did not fight enough with the Navy. Thomas checked with his former assistant in the 1st Division D-3 section, Lt. Col. Henry W. Buse, Jr., now Watson's G-4. Bill Buse reported that alumni of the 2d Marine Division held the key positions at FMF Pac headquarters and that members of the "Guadalcanal gang" found no favor at Headquarters. Watson had made his position very clear by having Col. Bill Twining replaced as chief of staff, FMF Pac, and sent into purgatory as the fleet marine officer, a position of no great moment. Buse sensed that his former bosses would have a tough time in a Marine Corps no longer dominated by Vandegrift.[16]

To his brigade staff, Thomas demonstrated more than enough force, and he pushed his officers as hard as he pushed himself. Thomas demanded speed and intelligence at his headquarters, but he did not use the personal power of a commanding general to make life unpleasant for an able staff that served him loyally. His chief of staff, Col. William J. Scheyer, a colleague from the South Pacific and Headquarters, held the same high standards as Thomas, even though Scheyer took more time to understand complex issues. They expected finished staff work and completed correspondence after they gave broad guidance; if the work did not please them, they sent it back for more study with a few sharp words of criticism but no lasting grudges. Thomas held no mortal fear of paperwork, and he wasted little time copy-editing and revising correspondence if it carried the message he desired. He remained a stickler for military protocol from the prewar Marine Corps. For example, finding his flag flying below that of a visiting admiral, who he learned was a "lower half" rear admiral and his junior, Thomas promptly had the responsible officer reverse the order of the flags.

Even though Thomas had complete confidence in his own judgment, his staff officers could persuade him to change his mind—but only after the most forceful, reasoned, and prolonged arguments they could muster. He accepted a recommendation that headquarters working hours in the summer of 1948 be shortened to 0730–1330, provided the staff completed its routine work, in order for the families and troops to enjoy the weather. During that same summer, Colonel Scheyer and Maj. John R. Chaisson, the force G-1, waged a successful four-week battle to persuade Thomas that his personal evacuation plan for dependents would create dissension in the command because it separated Marine husbands from their dependents. Chaisson learned that Thomas had an explosive temper when challenged and was "profane as hell." The general could quickly calm down, however, usually by talking about football or Guadalcanal, where Chaisson had served as a battery commander in the 11th Marines. Chaisson wrote his wife that Thomas might be worried about his promotion to major general. Thomas had once been "the fair-haired boy" of General Vandegrift, but times had changed. "I think his nerves are slightly raw."[17]

Thomas supported his staff in its relations with the troop commanders, and he would take prompt and decisive action, even outside channels if necessary, on staff recommendations that he approved. Thomas held occasional meetings with his entire staff, but he preferred to deal with his principal staff officers on an individual basis and stopped by their offices each day. He repeatedly pointed out his favorite picture to his staff, a portrait of an ugly turtle. The caption read: "Observe the turtle. He makes no progress unless his neck is extended." He once demonstrated this principle by stripping his command of excess officers without prior approval of Headquarters. Thomas showed the intelligence, force, energy, and presence to draw the best work from his immediate subordinates.[18]

Thomas expected all Marine officers of FMFWesPac to work as hard as his staff. He also pressured senior officers he held in disfavor and asked questions constantly. He especially enjoyed talking with lieutenants, who appreciated his attention. With his G-3, Lt. Col. Thomas J. Colley (another "Old China Hand" from the Peiping legation guard), or another member of his staff, he frequently patrolled the force barracks, working spaces, and training areas. He fretted about adequate officer supervision and insisted that his staff tell him about any officer he did not recognize or know. Few of the two hundred officers and warrant officers in the Thomas command could long remain invisible. The Thomases not only held weekend open houses for officer and family calls but also organized midweek tea parties at their quarters. Thomas showed consistent, sincere interest in his officers and their families. He considered himself the force career counselor for his officers; in this role, he had mixed success. He chided John Chaisson for retaining his primary military occupational specialty (MOS) as an artillery officer and his public affairs secondary MOS, when he could become an infantryman with a general staff subspecialty. Another officer asked for emergency leave to straighten out family business (his father had just died), and Thomas refused the request. The officer—a major—then resigned his commission, to Thomas's surprise. Thomas had also inherited a legal crisis, the court-martial of Col. Leslie F. Narum, who had used his position as 1st Marine Division supply officer in Tientsin to run an elaborate black-market ring. Claiming high influence with Admiral Cooke and Maj. Gen. W. P. T. Hill, the Quartermaster General, Narum tried to bluff his way through the proceedings, but Thomas brought back General Pfeiffer (a lawyer) to run the general court-martial that convicted and cashiered Narum. The Narum court-martial, which brought other senior colonels to Tsingtao to sit on the court and consumed clerical assistance and much time from the officers of FMFWesPac headquarters, concerned Thomas because he wanted a conviction but not a political disaster. The court-martial completed its work without incident.[19]

The enlisted men of FMFWesPac did not escape their commanding general's close attention. Thomas ensured that they stayed busy with training and guard duties. He accepted no excuses for the careless performance of duty, especially for the common problem of sleeping on watch. In his first month of command, Thomas convened twenty-four courts-martial to try derelict Marines. He was not pleased when a court levied a light sentence or dismissed charges for insufficient evidence. From his service in Peiping, he knew that Marines had high skills in finding trouble if not supervised and disciplined. Tsingtao had ninety bars that could legally serve Marines; it also had twice that many "off limits" bars and houses of prostitution. Thomas had inherited a command with 138 cases of venereal disease per thousand troops. In two months, he drove the rate down to 24 cases per thousand, but it climbed back to over 100 per thousand during the raw winter of 1947–48. Thomas encouraged more wholesome activities. The garrison maintained separate clubs for all enlisted ranks, including a privates' club. When the privates' club burned down in November 1947, Thomas made its replacement a command priority. He established an awards program for the enlisted mess halls that created useful competition among mess managers and cooks. He also monitored the quality of goods and services in the post exchange and commissary, the mail delivery, the movie schedule, and the brigade athletic program. Always a firm believer in the benefits of athletics, Thomas insisted on full participation in unit athletics, as well as interunit competition in tackle football, basketball, and baseball. He continued the Marine riding stables, established by General Shepherd (ever the horseman) in 1945. Marines went to the beaches in the summer. They also took liberty trips to Peiping because Thomas thought they should all have an opportunity to see the Imperial City and the Great Wall before the Communists curbed tourism. Thomas wanted the touring Marines to use the old Legation Guard barracks, but Consul General Clubb ordered them to stay in a commercial hotel. With careful policing for prostitution and drugs by older Marines, the liberty parties enjoyed a brief taste of prewar Peiping.[20]

For the Thomas family, the return to China provided a higher standard of living and mixed emotions. The commanding general's villa and domestic staff provided room, comfort, and household assistance far more reminiscent of Peiping than Washington. The physical beauty of the Thomas compound and the skill of the cook made entertaining irresistible. The general and his gracious lady, ever the Southern belle for social occasions, played their social roles to the hilt. The Thomas children, especially Tina, who missed working and more relaxed relations with young adults her own age, liked the formal social occasions less than the opportunity to explore Tsingtao. Ginny and Johnny attended the American dependents school in downtown Tsingtao below Signal Hill but enjoyed plenty of leisure time. The high point of the China tour was the family's sentimental journey in June 1948 to Peiping, where they spent a week at the exclusive Wagon-Lits Hotel. They found three of their 1935–37 household staff, including their "Number One Boy" and personal rickshaw driver. Both of the Chinese devoted themselves to entertaining the Thomases. Ginny's *amah* visited them at the hotel. The family saw familiar tourist sites and patrolled the stores for bargains in artifacts, furniture, and rugs. In a sense, the Peiping trip represented not only the end of an era for Marines in China but for the Thomas family as well. Jerry Junior came to China on leave after his summer cruise but returned immediately to Annapolis to continue his march toward a Marine lieutenant's commission. His sister Tina, tired of her father's lectures about higher education and of her stage-managed social life, departed soon after Jerry Junior's visit for a job in New York City.[21]

As Commanding General Fleet Marine Force Western Pacific, Gerald C. Thomas demonstrated that he deserved his rapid advancement from lieutenant colonel to brigadier general. Placed in command of a Marine force that had real (if ambiguous) missions, Thomas managed to keep his brigade, led by war-weary officers and noncommissioned Marines, in an adequate state of readiness and morale. His effectiveness as a commander, however, received the ultimate test when he learned that he bore the principal responsibility for evacuating Americans, European nationals, and his own force from North China before the Communists completed their conquest of the region and turned the organized withdrawal into a frenzied retreat.

Exploiting their summer victories over the Nationalist Army, the People's Liberation Army and its supporting guerrilla bands tightened their hold in the countryside of North China. By the end of September 1948, the Communists had occupied all of Shantung province, including the capital of Tsinan. Tsingtao alone remained as an enclave of American and Nationalist military control. As the harsh winter approached, the population of Tsingtao doubled again with Chinese fleeing the tender mercies of their Leninist countrymen. Beggars clogged the streets of Tsingtao; street crime increased; and mobs of starving refugees plagued the back doors of all affluent homes, including the quarters of the Commanding General, FMFWesPac. The Chinese banged their tin food cans and cups against the walls and iron fences until they received food, usually some hot tea and millet gruel. Among the peasants, the Thomases saw ragged, but obviously once well-dressed, westernized Chinese families, a sign of true disaster. Some Chinese traded or sold a few precious art treasures in exchange for American money or more food. Johnson Thomas, a schoolboy of eleven, watched in wonder as Tsingtao plunged into poverty:

> Immediately next door to us was a quarter-acre vacant lot grown up in trees and brush. It was usually filled by goat herds. By the autumn it became a small settlement. Shacks of scrap wood or metal were set up and the trees were slowly stripped. It was said that in the spring the Chinese ate all flowers from the trees, in the summer of '48 they stripped and ate the leaves, and by autumn they stripped off the bark to cook for soup. It was not unusual to see bodies on the sidewalk that had died in the night, if you walked a few blocks.[22]

The Nationalist military governor of Tsingtao established an early curfew for the city, and Thomas issued orders that limited the number of Marines who could leave their barracks after working hours. Although neon signs along the streets that catered to Navy liberty parties glowed on, the lights all over Tsingtao began to dim. When the Nationalist currency finally collapsed under the burden of inflation, the banks and stores closed rather than honor Chinese money. American currency could not be officially used for business. Nighttime raids against Marine supply depots increased. It was time for the Marines to leave Tsingtao.[23]

Although the FMFWesPac staff had worked on evacuation contingency plans since April 1948, Thomas and his officers heard little but rumors about their departure until they received a warning order in late October to make arrangements to evacuate willing Europeans and American dependents. In the first week of November, Thomas conferred with both Admiral Badger and CinCPac himself, Adm. DeWitt Ramsey, who had come to Tsingtao to visit the carrier, cruisers, and destroyers of NavForWesPac at anchor in comforting view of the city. Under Admiral Badger's coordination, Thomas would execute a two-phase operation for North China, while Rear Adm. Clyde Crawford, Commander, Amphibious Forces Western Pacific (ComPhibForWesPac), managed all evacuation operations south of the valley of the Yellow River, centered principally on Shanghai. The first task would be to remove eligible civilians (few of whom would be Chinese), then withdraw the American troops and as much of their supplies and equipment as scarce shipping space allowed. Thomas and Crawford received strict instructions to avoid incidents with any Chinese, to prevent the compromise of American communications and intelligence operations, and to mask the withdrawal as best they could from media scrutiny. The senior naval service officers also understood that the Truman administration demanded that the evacuation not reach a level of high drama in the American press until after the presidential election.[24]

Thomas moved rapidly to organize the civilian evacuation. He sent liaison parties, including his Marine Chinese-linguist officers, to join NavForWesPac groups in Peiping and Tientsin that processed evacuees. His headquarters communicated with missionaries, businessmen, and any other Europeans or Chinese who held American passports. On 12 November, he received orders to send home all American military dependents along with the other civilians. This change added another 350 families in Tsingtao alone to the Shantung contingent of evacuees, numbering around 1,500. As additional civilians (including American governmental and military personnel) arrived from Nanking, Peiping, and Tientsin, the flood of anxious Americans and Europeans in Tsingtao swelled. Before the operation ended, FMFWesPac had processed 8,000 American and European refugees, including the numerous (and stateless) White Russian exiles. The plight of the refugees proved heartrending for the Americans. The evacuees left with only what they could carry, and few had any plans or resources to live elsewhere. The Americans, many of them missionaries and missionary families, could go straight to the United States along with the military dependents, but the other evacuees took ships to Shanghai and the control of the International Refugee Organization. In the first phase of the operation, Thomas recognized his biggest problem, an unrealistic schedule for the departure of Navy transports and the limited number of such ships. He and the American consul in Tsingtao conspired to delay the first departure of the Navy's transports by deceiving ComNavForWesPac about their readiness to embark the refugees. The ruse went unchallenged, and Thomas's staff received a welcome few days to make its arrangements.[25]

Concerned about the morale of his command, especially with the departure of Marine families certain, Thomas tightened up his demands for strict discipline and hard work. On 10 November, he staged a parade through Tsingtao by the entire brigade outfitted for combat. Designed to impress the Chinese, the parade also sent a message to the Marines, reinforced that evening at the annual Marine Corps Birthday Ball, held as planned. Speaking with candor and brevity to his officers and their wives—Major John Chaisson noted that Thomas did not indulge in "blarney"—the commanding general reminded them that he and the rest of the Marine Corps and the nation expected them to do their duty without regard for personal preferences in this time of crisis. In an unsettled world, he said, Marines at least had their faith in the standards of the Marine Corps and the knowledge that they shared lasting values of loyalty, devotion, courage, and readiness for war.[26]

Recognizing that few of his officers wanted to put their dependents on the first transport assigned to the United States—scheduled to depart the first week of December, well before the Christmas season—Thomas assigned Lottie, Ginny, and Johnny to passage on the *Henderson*, much to their unhappiness. The *Henderson*, jammed beyond capacity, departed as scheduled on 7 December with the Thomas family, other Marine families, and a large group of missionaries, who made the voyage even more miserable by staging revival meetings for all the passengers. Thomas saw his family off in high choler because his band did not appear on schedule for the sailing. Chaisson also suspected that Thomas did not like the idea of living alone; none of his staff volunteered to live in his quarters and thus work around the clock. Thomas knew his command had a morale problem when the families left because his spirits sank, too. He put his staff on a crisis management schedule with little time for socializing or sulking. Thomas confided to Chaisson "that he had never experienced a more hectic month than this has been even in combat."[27] As Christmas approached and the refugees departed, Thomas faced the second phase of his mission, embarking his own command with as much efficiency and discipline as possible.[28]

Feeling the melancholy of moving the Marines from China and spending another Christmas season apart from his family, Thomas stayed busy with his official duties and personal arrangements. Everything he did gave him a feeling of cloture: packing furniture and precious Chinese art objects; arranging for the last-minute purchase and repair of his uniforms and civilian clothing, canceling one last trip to Peiping, avoiding tiresome social events in the civilian community, and watching the departure of the refugees. Each day, the number of watching Chinese children on the docks dwindled. Thomas opened his Christmas presents alone and found some solace in rereading *Macbeth* and *Hamlet* for leisure, if not joy. As he prepared to move aboard a transport, he learned that Headquarters would give him credit for a full foreign tour and that he would probably be assigned to Washington again after sixty days' leave. This good news helped cushion his sense of defeat and disappointment over the fate of China.[29]

Moving his own command to sea as the last refugees and dependents departed in early January presented Thomas with pyramiding problems, principally logistical. His command had responsibility for its own equipment and supplies, as well as materiel assigned to the Nationalists. His guidance proved either inadequate or unrealistic. How, the commander of the 12th Service Battalion wondered, was he supposed to clean fifty thousand 55-gallon fuel drums for shipment and where were they to go? (They didn't.) Ammunition handling and security, as always, presented special demands. Chinese working parties had few skills and proved more interested in pilferage than labor. Two fires and one explosion slowed the loading. All responsible Marine officers, including the commanding general, fretted about Communist sabotage and a riot in the city, but the Communists did not pressure the withdrawal. The lack of real military threat allowed Thomas to assign a reinforcing battalion landing team (the 9th Marines) to Admiral Crawford's southern evacuation force. The shipping situation improved when the Navy provided fourteen Liberty ships. The G-4, Maj. Edwin B. Wheeler, loaded them with imagination. FMFWesPac eventually took 50,000 tons of materiel with it and left little of value for the Chinese Communists. Thomas had his aircraft group fly away by the end of January 1949. His own shipping arrived at about the same time, so he embarked the 3d Marines as an amphibious ready force, then followed it with Headquarters and Service Battalion and the 1st Marines on 3 February 1949. On 8 February, Thomas and the 1st Marines sailed aboard the transport *Henrico* directly for California and the parent 1st Marine Division. The afloat battalions of the 9th Marines and 3d Marines remained in Asian waters until the Navy declared the withdrawal complete in May.[30]

Jerry Thomas was dismayed by what he regarded as the American betrayal of the Chinese, but he was aware that only an American army of five divisions or more might have stopped the People's Liberation Army in 1948. Even then, he felt there would have been no prospect of victory in the guerrilla war sure to follow. Thomas returned to the United States and his family after accomplishing the last mission of Fleet Marine Force Western Pacific with skill and care and without press criticism of American operations in Tsingtao. More importantly, he had proved that he was not just a general, but a commanding general.

[CHAPTER XXII]

More Wars on the Potomac
1949–1951

ON 26 APRIL 1949, Gerald C. Thomas turned east off U.S. 1 at Triangle, Virginia. When he drove through the modest main gate of Marine Barracks, Quantico, Thomas felt that he was returning to his only true home, the place where he had joined the 6th Marines in 1917 and served with so much satisfaction in the 1930s. The woods bordering both sides of the road into "Mainside" flanked his advance with redbud, dogwood, and budding oaks. Although not exactly a returning hero from China, General Thomas had visited Headquarters and found his stock in good order with the Clifton B. Cates–O. P. Smith group now running the Marine Corps. His new assignment as President, Marine Corps Equipment Board, interested him; he had thought he would receive the same post in Vandegrift's waning tour. For the moment, he had to bear the extemporized title of "chief of staff" of the board until the current president, Brig. Gen. Louis R. Jones, retired in June. Two months would be ample time to catch up on Washington and Quantico politics, observe his new command, and arrange for his family to move from Charleston into quarters at Quantico. His new assignment was not a choice post for an aspiring brigadier, but Thomas liked the location and his administrative commander, who was his old friend, Maj. Gen. Lemuel C. Shepherd, Jr.[1]

It is likely that Shepherd arranged Thomas's assignment to Quantico and that Cates approved his request. When the Commandant made his annual announcement of general officer assignments on 24 March, a matter of great portent because it was Cates's first slate, Thomas's name did not appear on the list. Two East Coast assignments for brigadier generals remained unfilled: President, Marine Corps Equipment Board, and Commanding General, Test and Training Unit, Amphibious Training Command, Atlantic Fleet, Norfolk, Virginia. On 13 April, the Commandant announced that Brig. Gen. Robert H. Pepper, three numbers junior to Thomas but with the same date of rank, would go to Norfolk and

Thomas to Quantico. Serving again with Shepherd, heir-apparent as Commandant since Harry Truman's election in 1948, pleased Thomas, and he believed he would be promoted to major general when the next board met in January 1950. Moreover, the Quantico of 1949 provided a concentration of friends Thomas relished: the Shepherds, the Dudley Browns, the Robert Bares, the William Scheyers, the Edward Snedekers, the Victor Krulaks, the Frederick Wiesemans, the Randolph Pates, the Richard Cooleys, the Lewis Walts, the DeWolf Schatzels, the Merrill Twinings, the Joseph Burgers, and others. At Quantico, Thomas rallied the veterans of "Chowder" and FMFWesPac, along with the survivors of Vandegrift's Guadalcanal staff.[2]

The Marine Corps Equipment Board had drifted outside the mainstream of Marine Corps decision making after World War II, but Thomas recognized its importance. Founded in 1935, the board moved to Quantico in 1937 and contributed to the Corps' readiness for World War II, principally by championing the Higgins landing craft and the Roebling amphibian tractor. Starved for funding, it had not made similar contributions since 1945, but it had pioneered helicopter development, even though helicopter matters still fell under the strong patronage of the Division of Aviation. Although the board's ground warfare interests were eclectic, its principal attention went to antitank weapons for infantrymen, demolitions, and engineering equipment. When Thomas took over the board, its closest collaboration came from its ties to the Army Engineer School just up U.S. 1 at Fort Belvoir, Virginia. The board studied everything that offered some improvement of combat effectiveness; between 1949 and 1951, it completed or initiated 200 different studies. It examined and tested multigraph duplicating machines, electric blankets, roadway matting, vehicle waterproofing kits, the 4.2-inch mortar, shoe dye, ground surveillance radar, field radios, wire-laying devices, water cans, electric typewriters, life jackets, and vise-grip tools. Some of its 1949 projects would bear future dividends for Marines: the 3.5-inch antitank rocket launcher and M20 rocket, body armor, and thermal boots. Thomas had no empire to handle the studies. His staff consisted of twelve officers (colonel to warrant officer), forty enlisted personnel, and fourteen civilians. The board had four functional sections: service and service support, ordnance, electronics, and engineering and general equipment, supplemented by a task-organized experimental group.[3]

Assessing the large menu of projects he inherited, Thomas saw four groups of studies with overriding importance to the Marine Corps: antitank rockets and recoilless rifles; a new family of amphibian-capable motor vehicles, helicopters to carry troops and provide close antitank attack capability, and ground-based radar to guide Marine aircraft to targets regardless of darkness and foul weather. He embraced all four projects with enthusiasm. The motor vehicle and antitank weapons projects required no special action because Headquarters recognized their significance; the new 3.5-inch rocket launcher and rocket were in action against North Korean tanks before the Equipment Board officially reported their usefulness in October 1950.

The aviation projects required Thomas's more personal attention. The politics of research and development and the cost estimates appeared more complex. In the radar-guided bombing project, Thomas backed the principal project officer,

Col. Jack R. Cram (Roy Geiger's personal pilot in the Solomons campaign), who, in turn, backed Maj. Marion C. Dalby, the senior Marine officer assigned to the Navy's Point Mugu, California, missile test center. Thomas visited the Marines working as liaison officers and technicians at Point Mugu, China Lake, McDonnell Aircraft, and Douglas Aircraft, and became an enthusiastic supporter of guided missile and bomb development. Through an epic of improvisation and ingenuity, the Dalby group had the AN/MPQ-14 radar system ready for combat testing in Korea during 1951. Thomas's principal role was to sing the praise of the concept of ground-directed bombing in his visits to Headquarters and his development reports to the Commandant.[4]

Thomas provided the same service for the helicopter pioneers, who already had a toehold in Navy aviation programs. He threw his influence behind raising the tempo of helicopter development, constrained by funding and the technology of helicopter power plants. Thomas embraced the work of Quantico's experimental helicopter squadron (HMX-1) and the visionary experiments with launching helicopters from escort carriers. He supported the aviators' proposal to make helicopters part of the table of equipment for Marine observation squadrons, and he became an ardent convert to the principles of vertical envelopment described in a November 1948 pamphlet written by Colonels Victor H. Krulak and E. Colston Dyer, "Amphibious Operations—Employment of Helicopters (Tentative)" or PHIB 31. Although the concept of bringing troops to battle in helicopters gained good support from ground and air officers alike, Thomas learned that Marine pilots did not like the idea of developing attack helicopters capable of firing machine guns and rockets at ground targets, even after the helicopter developers (Sikorsky and Kaman) replaced flammable wooden rotor blades with aluminum blades. Like most helicopter champions, Thomas preferred to use his influence to advance the cause of a 3,000-pound lift helicopter for troop transportation. Thomas allied himself with the Marine air-ground coalition that successfully won Navy approval of a high-priority helicopter program by the mid-1950s.[5]

Back in the thick of the doctrinal and organizational battles he relished, Jerry Thomas plunged into his role as president of the Marine Corps Equipment Board with his characteristic aggressiveness. He enjoyed the social life at Quantico with equal gusto. In the summer of 1949, he brought Lottie, Ginny, and Johnny north from South Carolina to Quarters 12, a comfortable home along the top of the ridge that dominated "Mainside." He and Lottie organized their first major social event, a cocktail party in their quarters, to honor General Jones on his retirement. As one of Quantico's resident generals, Thomas drew his share of conferences, parades, medal ceremonies, and inspections. His oldest daughter, Tina, still lived and worked in New York City. On a visit, the general took her to Club 21 for dinner and the musical *Kiss Me Kate*. He and she agreed that her plan to save money for art school was not progressing. Jerry persuaded her to visit Quantico more often, a plea advanced in the spring of 1950 by the general's aide. During a weekend visit, Tina watched a debonair Marine major named Joseph A. Bruder sail over a jump that his horse refused. The general conspired to release Tina from her work in New York and found her a secretary's job at the Senior School, where she could pursue her budding romance with Joe Bruder, a well-educated and seasoned officer from New Jersey. Midshipman Second Class Gerald C. Thomas, Jr., visited home to find his father adamant that his oldest son select a Marine commission because the general believed the Navy too anti-intellectual. Thomas thought that naval officers would judge any reading more demanding than *Life* as unwelcome in the wardroom. On another visit, the general took Jerry Junior to the grenade range to show him the latest rifle-grenades, fresh from Belgium and already on their way to the FMF. Thomas impressed his son with his grasp of the destructive properties of antitank weapons and his satisfaction that the Marines would use them with effect on the Communists.[6]

His return to Quantico offered Thomas more challenges than just the work of the Marine Corps Equipment Board. Even before the outbreak of the Korean War in June 1950, Thomas found himself again locked in combat with foes of the Marine Corps, but the enemy—again—was the leadership of the Department of Defense and, in a personal sense, a handful of Marine generals who wanted to see Thomas a professional casualty.

During an orgy of defense budget cutting, the interservice peace promised in the National Security Act of 1947 did not prosper. A series of negotiations took place between the members of the Joint Chiefs of Staff and the civilians of the Office of the Secretary of Defense. Because the Marine Corps did not receive an invitation from the Secretary of the Navy and the Chief of Naval Operations to participate in these negotiations, the Corps steadily lost the battle for service roles and missions. The dominant view in the Department of Defense, formed and expressed by a coalition of civilians and Army and Air Force generals, was that the dual mission of the armed forces was to deter or wage a nuclear air war on the Soviet Union and to stop a non-nuclear invasion of western Europe. The Soviet Union did not possess a blue-water navy and had few important targets within range of an attack from the sea; therefore, the United States did not need a World War II–style fleet for a naval campaign, including amphibious forces. Although the United States might need naval forces—and a Fleet Marine Force—to deal with military contingencies in the Mediterranean, the Middle East, the oceanic rim of Asia, and Latin America, these forces did not need much more relative capability than the Marine landing forces of pre–Fleet Marine Force days. Throughout 1948, the Marine Corps found its role in a future general war diminished in three critical arenas: the joint emergency war plans drafted and approved by the Joint Chiefs of Staff; the roles and missions approved by the secretary of defense and embodied in Executive Order 9877, "Functions of the Armed Forces"; and the authorization and appropriations process. Assuming that President Truman would hold fast to a self-imposed defense budget ceiling of $13 billion in fiscal year 1949, the Army and Air Force thought each of them should have $5 billion, which left $3 billion for the Navy and Marine Corps. The Navy Department quailed at such a prospect, but it had neither the leadership nor the political opportunity to escape the fiscal Pearl Harbor planned for it by the Joint Chiefs of Staff.[7]

The Navy and Marine Corps took no comfort that the budget process and service functions controversy also shaped the question of defense organization. The amendments to the National Security Act strengthened the secretary of defense and the JCS at the expense of the military departments. Even so, the Navy

Department did support a proposal backed by pro–Marine Congressmen that the Commandant of the Marine Corps be made a statutory member of the Joint Chiefs of Staff, which would have provided another maritime perspective in the Pentagon. Instead, the reconstituted JCS of 1949 had three Army–Air Force general war spokesmen with the addition of an Army chairman for the JCS, Gen. Omar N. Bradley. The anti–Navy Department coalition received another important member when Louis A. Johnson, a Truman confidant and former assistant secretary of war, became secretary of defense in March 1949 with presidential instructions to limit defense spending and silence administration critics among the military. Bradley's view of the future Marine Corps was no secret: "I suppose we have to have Marines for sentimental reasons. But I don't know of anything that they can do that the Army can't, and there's certainly no reason for anything bigger than a regiment in the Marine Corps."[8] Bradley doubted that any future major war would require amphibious landings, and, if it did, the Army could perform the operation. Although the Marine Corps retained the primary responsibility for developing doctrine, tactics, techniques, and equipment for amphibious operations, Executive Order 9877 gave it no monopoly on conducting amphibious operations. In fact, the Department of Defense proposed that the Marine Corps maintain only six battalion landing teams and twelve aviation squadrons in the Fleet Marine Force of 1950.[9]

When Jerry Thomas returned from China, he had found Clifton B. Cates emerging from a painful year of learning experience as Commandant and ready to fight more aggressively to preserve a Fleet Marine Force of twice as many battalion landing teams and aviation squadrons as the Department of Defense proposed. Cates also planned to preserve as much non–FMF structure as he could because he knew that in an emergency he could transfer Marines from non–FMF duties into the divisions and wings and mobilize the Marine Corps Reserve. Thomas quickly learned from such confidants as Bill Twining and Brig. Gen. John Taylor Selden, a distant cousin and the combative new director of Marine Corps public relations, that Cates found himself caught between the Marine champions who wanted him on the JCS and a Navy Department that didn't; Cates also preferred more congressional attention to the plight of the Fleet Marine Force. Thomas learned that Cates did not have anything like "Chowder" to provide background position papers or guerrilla political operations. Instead Cates had to depend on Al Pollock and an exhausted, confused Division of Plans and Policies for help, which he was not getting.

In the autumn of 1949, however, Cates grasped his first major opportunity to remind Congress of its 1947 commitment to the Corps. Stripped of money to complete its first postwar supercarrier, the U.S.S. *United States,* the only seagoing platform it would have to carry nuclear-capable bombers, the Navy had challenged the Air Force B-36 bomber program and the strategy of general nuclear war. The Navy lost the budget battle and suffered a leadership decapitation with the resignation of Secretary of the Navy John L. Sullivan and the relief of Chief of Naval Operations Louis E. Denfeld. A 1949 congressional investigation of the Navy's complaints, however, allowed Cates to challenge Congress to exercise its authority in legislating roles and missions, not simply to accept the latest Department of Defense definitions in Executive Order 9877. "In the past, the Marine

Corps has given an exact performance of every obligation assigned it. Its only desire now is to be protected in its right to fight again in the wars of the United States."[10] Cates's October 1949 testimony during "the revolt of the admirals" was the strongest statement from a Commandant since Vandegrift's "bended knee" speech of 1946. In November 1949, Cates told his general officers that he thought Congress would prevent the further emasculation of the Fleet Marine Force and that the administration could not reduce the FMF to a corporal's guard. "Lucky" Cates may have been blessed as a combat commander in two wars, but he won no prizes for prophesy. Two months later, the budget ax fell again. The Commandant, thoroughly aroused, searched for ways to turn the tide of battle.[11]

Early in his tour as president of the Marine Corps Equipment Board, Thomas discussed the fate of the FMF with Cates and accepted the Commandant's request that he assume some of Cates's speaking commitments to public groups, such as the Joint Civilian Orientation Course, as well as to the service war colleges. Thomas took the assignment as routine until he discovered that he was describing World War II landings, rather than future operations, except for vague promises that the helicopters would play a role. "I was talking about large numbers of helicopters while at the same time the helicopter program was lagging with no one really pushing it."[12] He pointed out to Cates that the Commandant would have to throw his personal weight into the fray over helicopters within the naval aviation community—no mean risk—and Cates did so with considerable effect.

Thomas found another problem more worrisome. Although the Marine Corps had the statutory responsibility for developing the operational doctrine for amphibious assaults, Thomas found no authoritative statement of developmental priorities, even for equipment. He conferred with Bill Twining, who had returned from Hawaii to chair the Marine Corps Board. Twining gave Thomas a position paper that he (Twining) had found difficult to sell Headquarters, probably because Cates and Pollock still regarded him with suspicion. Twining advocated the creation of a Marine Corps Development Center at Quantico that would fuse the Marine Corps Equipment Board with a new Tactics and Techniques Board specializing in amphibious operations. Thomas championed the proposal and set out on a missionary effort to convince Headquarters that the reorganization would improve the Corps' political position and show the Department of Defense and Congress that the Marine Corps took its joint functions seriously. Thomas also hoped that a discussion of the organization of a development center might produce more precise guidance for his board's research and development activities. Convinced that the Marine Corps needed to assert its doctrinal and developmental expertise, Thomas pressed Cates to consider the reorganization of the entire Marine Corps Schools system. What made his militancy an act of moral courage was the fact that he had just been passed over for promotion to major general.[13]

Assessing his service reputation and the pattern of general officer promotions since 1947, Jerry Thomas had every reason to expect that he would be selected for promotion when the next major generals board convened in January 1950. Since the general officer ranks had been culled in 1947, the promotions had come almost according to seniority. With the exception of the Quartermaster General, Pete Hill, all the major generals in January 1950 had served in that rank or as brigadier generals senior to Thomas during World War II. The senior brigadier general, Omar T. Pfeiffer, already had been passed over in favor of his own 1942 running mates and two more junior generals, Merwin H. Silverthorn and Ray A. Robinson, so Thomas would not have considered him a likely choice. The second ranking brigadier, William E. Riley, also had been passed over once in favor of Silverthorn and Robinson. Thomas held no special affection for Bill Riley; he and Riley had clashed in the South Pacific in 1943 and at Headquarters in 1946–47. Thomas probably assumed that the two new major generals would come from a group of six brigadier generals with the same date of rank, 7 December 1943. Thomas, third in seniority of all brigadiers, was the senior officer of the group, although one (Henry D. Linscott) was older and one (Edward A. Craig) had entered the Marine Corps (1916) before Thomas had enlisted in 1917. Given what he regarded as his own splendid service reputation and the glowing fitness report that Lem Shepherd had submitted for his work with the Equipment Board, Thomas had reason to be confident.[14]

When the major generals board assembled at Headquarters, however, Thomas knew that his promotion might be in jeopardy. The president of the board was none other than his nemesis, Lt. Gen. Thomas E. Watson, and the next senior Marine was Lt. Gen. LeRoy P. Hunt. The three other Marines on the nine-member board were Major Generals Lemuel C. Shepherd, Field Harris, and William J. Wallace. The four remaining members of the board were Navy admirals; by law, admirals could serve on Marine general officer promotion boards if the Commandant determined that he could not provide enough active-duty Marine generals. The senior officers of the Navy, of course, had reason to influence Marine general officer promotions, at least to limit the advancement of Marines well known for their hostility to the Navy. Jerry Thomas may not have been as unattractive as such Navy-haters as Smedley D. Butler and Lewis B. Puller, but his strong support of Vandegrift in the South Pacific and at Headquarters probably made him suspect. He had no champions among the admirals, certainly no champions courageous enough to offset the biases of Watson and Hunt. One Navy member of the board later told Thomas that the admirals didn't want to promote someone who did not have a college degree. Thomas thought this objection to his fitness irrelevant because he regarded his years at Illinois Wesleyan as a far better education than the marine engineering curriculum at the Naval Academy during the World War I era. Thomas might also have wondered why the Commandant could not find more Marine generals to serve (seven other major generals served on the brigadier generals board) and what role the Assistant Commandant, Maj. Gen. O. P. Smith, might have played in the board's composition.

Whatever the course of its deliberations, which remain confidential (more or less) by law and custom, the major generals board for 1950 selected Bill Riley and Bob Pepper for promotion. The board thus rejected Pfeiffer, Thomas, Linscott, and Dudley S. Brown to reach Pepper, the sixth senior brigadier. Although Pepper enjoyed a fine service reputation, his assignments since Guadalcanal, where he had commanded a defense battalion, had not matched Thomas's in importance. Thomas felt betrayed and rejected. He lost a raise of about $200 a month and some self-confidence. In April 1950, Thomas commented with bitterness to Merritt Edson that "they do not pay off on a scale of values in D.C. today that you or I understand," but four months later he told Edson that he looked forward to fighting for the complete reorganization of the Marine Corps Schools and the creation of a development center. He urged Edson to continue writing and speaking out against the concentration of power in the JCS and Office of the Secretary of Defense and promised to fight on against the Corps' enemies.[15] His fellow veterans of "Chowder" worried about Thomas's morale, but he insisted that he would not let his nonselection blunt his campaign for a better Marine Corps. He intended to press forward with the reforms in which he believed, and he hoped that another board would recognize his fitness to be a major general.[16]

A month after his rejection, Jerry Thomas convinced the Commandant to appoint an Equipment Policy Panel with the mission of providing a comprehensive study of Marine Corps developmental priorities. Convened on 15 February 1950, the panel included the Equipment Board and fifteen specialist officers from Headquarters. To drive the analysis, however, Thomas needed operational guidance from someone who recognized the changes in technology and service roles and missions since World War II. Headquarters had no one to provide it, so he turned to Col. Frederick L. Wieseman, a trusted colleague from the South Pacific and the "Chowder" campaign, for a concept paper. As a former member of the Marine Corps Board, Wieseman knew the advanced concepts argued by Twining and Krulak because he had worked the problem of doing tables of organization. He embodied their ideas in the concept paper that Thomas issued to every member of the Equipment Policy Panel. In essence, the paper argued that strategic and tactical deployment would be characterized by speed and dispersion and that the Marine Corps must be prepared to deploy by amphibious assault shipping, follow-on shipping, and long-range air transports. Equipment must be compatible with such deployment options. Actual operations ashore would require the ability to make an amphibious assault and then sustain operations ashore, characterized by high mobility and heavy firepower, not easily compatible in materiel terms. Mobility, however, should take priority in determining operational requirements. In addition, the Marine Corps should plan to fight the Soviet Union and its proxies, not Third World forces of limited military capability.

Before it finished its work by the end of June 1950, the Equipment Policy Panel had conducted a thorough investigation of the future of amphibious operations. Its members had consulted six Marine generals, all of whom had important operational experience in the Pacific and were Thomas's friends: Franklin A. Hart, Graves B. Erskine, Louis E. Woods, Field Harris, William S. Fellers, and William T. "Johnny" Clement. The collaborative effort produced a clear set of priorities in equipment development. The Marine Corps should stress the following programs: direct firepower for beach assault; helicopters; amphibian vehicles for logistical support; air defense aircraft; amphibious shipping; antitank weapons; ground-based air defense weapons, especially missiles; rapid response communications-electronic systems for command and fire support coordination; and equipment for defense against chemical, biological, and radiological warfare. In addition to the uncounted cost of this developmental effort, the panel recognized that the research and development effort would require continuous interservice collaboration, joint testing, and doctrinal validation. The Marine Corps would require a much more ambitious organization than the Equipment Board to direct such a complex developmental effort. Satisfied with the final draft, Thomas took the report to Headquarters. Before presenting it to Al Pollock, however, he handed Pollock a folder filled with blank paper and told him that it represented prior guidance on equipment policy. Then he gave Pollock the report, *Marine Corps Equipment Policy 1950,* later approved by the Commandant as Headquarters Marine Corps General Order 85 (13 February 1951). Thomas had won another victory to push the Marine Corps into the postwar world of deterrence and enhanced readiness.[17]

While Headquarters reviewed the report of the Equipment Policy Panel, Cates ordered a special board to consider Thomas's recommendation that the Marine Corps Schools be reorganized and that the new organization include a development center. The Thomas-Twining proposal, in fact, would shift developmental responsibilities in doctrine, including manual writing, away from the schools and to the new center. Appointment of the board's president, Lt. Gen. LeRoy Hunt, Commanding General Fleet Marine Force Atlantic, must not have pleased Thomas; however, the other appointees, most of whom had been part of the Equipment Policy Panel investigation, could not have been more sympathetic and knowledgeable about the proposed changes. They were Franklin A. Hart (newly appointed commandant of the Marine Corps Schools), Louis E. Woods, Ray A. Robinson (new commanding general, 2d Marine Division), Edwin A. Pollock, Randolph McC. Pate, and Thomas himself. Col. Samuel R. Shaw, a "Chowder" veteran, served as recorder. The board held its first meeting on 10 July 1950 and completed its final report eight days later, a sure sign that its findings and much of the administrative details were predetermined.

The Hunt Board approved the concept of dividing the Marine Corps Schools into two separate centers, the Education Center and the Landing Force Development Center (LFDC). The Commandant Marine Corps Schools would direct Marine Corps research and development, including the study and promulgation of authoritative doctrine, and serve as the Corps' chief specialist on education and training. Although camouflaging its language, the board reported that the inherent tension between Headquarters Marine Corps and the Office of the Chief of Naval Operations over priorities and resources made it imperative to put research and development outside of Washington and to make the LFDC a truly joint agency with Navy, Army, and Air Force representatives written into its table of organization. It was in the Marine Corps' interest to take the initiative in establishing the LFDC, rather than wait for the JCS to establish a joint center under its direction. On the other hand, the LFDC should focus on "those matters bearing immediately and specifically upon the amphibious subject as opposed to the broad field of general land warfare." The five major developmental sections reflected the amphibious mission: landing force logistics, landing force aviation, ship-to-shore movement, naval gunfire, and landing force assault tactics. Each section would be joint service; the logistics section, for example, would be divided into specialized subsections led by four Army officers, three Marine officers, and one Navy officer. The LFDC would also maintain functional committees to consider close air support, helicopter development, and fire support coordination. The sections and committees would receive their guidance from a new Landing Force Tactics and

Techniques Board and the continued Equipment Board, both operating under the general officer appointed as director of the LFDC, who would continue to maintain active liaison with Headquarters in order to remain current on requirements.[18]

With only two changes, General Cates approved the Hunt Board's report on 16 August and directed the Commandant Marine Corps Schools to establish the Landing Force Development Center and its organic committees, sections, and boards as soon as possible, even though the LFDC might not be fully staffed. The Commandant wanted to think some more about the final structure and function of the Marine Corps Schools and the Education Center, but he wanted the LFDC in business quickly. He promised that Headquarters would arrange the participation of the other services and the assignment of Army, Navy, and Air Force officers to the LFDC. He also directed that the president of the Marine Corps Equipment Board should continue to maintain direct contact with Headquarters because the board still retained developmental responsibilities beyond amphibious operations. Thomas, who remained president of the Equipment Board after he became the first commanding general of the LFDC in September, welcomed the change that gave him an additional measure of independence. In October, the Commandant issued his comprehensive guidance for the functions of the Marine Corps Schools, including mission statements for the Landing Force Development Center, the Landing Force Tactics and Techniques Board, and the Marine Corps Equipment Board. Thomas acknowledged that he read and understood the order, but he did not initial it. He noted on the routing sheet: "I have not initialed the buckship because such might be taken to indicate that we would operate on it." He then had his staff review the guidance for doctrinal matters and rewrite the letters of invitation to the other services to assign personnel to the LFDC. The revisions strengthened Marine Corps domination of the development process.[19]

As he worked to organize the LFDC during the autumn of 1950, Thomas had every reason to feel that he remained a leader of power and repute within the Marine Corps, despite his nonselection to major general. For almost a year he had managed the reorganization of the Corps' research and development effort to a successful conclusion, and he had glowing fitness reports from Lem Shepherd and Franklin Hart in his Officer Qualification Record to verify it. In North China and Quantico, he had proved that he did not depend on Vandegrift's patronage to further his career. He also had survived to serve in a period of Marine Corps history that matched his painstaking, relentless style of command, for the Marine Corps was once more at war.

In the rush to send American air and ground units to the rescue of the Republic of Korea in July and August 1950, the Joint Chiefs of Staff, prodded by Generals Douglas MacArthur, Clifton B. Cates, and Lemuel C. Shepherd, had ordered the 1st Marine Division and 1st Marine Aircraft Wing to the Far East. Both had played a major role in the destruction of the North Korean armed forces by the end of October 1950. The international forces of United Nations Command had poured across the 38th Parallel in euphoric pursuit with the 1st Marine Division (O. P. Smith) and 1st Marine Aircraft Wing (Field Harris) on the cutting edge of X Corps (Maj. Gen. Edward M. Almond) amphibious envelopments along the Korean coast. Thirsty to report victories after the catastrophes of the war's opening months, the American media focused on the Marines, who won battles of high drama and operational significance: the Naktong Bulge, the invasion at Inchon, the liberation of Seoul. Marines of all ages, veterans and new recruits alike, requested orders to Korea. Jerry Thomas felt the pull of the battlefield, too, but he could fill only one billet, commanding general of the 1st Marine Division. In October 1950, Thomas became a major general.[20]

During the stampede of war mobilization in 1950, the Marine Corps received authorization to expand its ranks with recalled reserves, emergency officers, and new recruits. Between 1 July 1950 and 1 July 1951, the Marine Corps grew from 7,284 officers and 67,025 enlisted personnel to 15,150 officers and 177,470 enlisted personnel. Faced with a Congress that could not do enough for the Corps, the Truman administration and the Department of Defense found it unfashionable to continue its guerrilla war to reduce the Corps' political power and military role in the nation's defense. Always a tough-minded gambler and astute leader, Clifton B. Cates seized the moment to request several statutory changes, one enlarging the general officer corps and another changing the composition of general officer promotion boards. In October 1950, the Commandant convened a special promotion board to consider thirteen brigadier generals for four temporary promotions to major general with every expectation that the promotions would be made permanent. Cates also had a new authority to recall retired Marine generals to active duty to serve on the board (rather than Navy admirals) if enough senior active general officers were not available. Thomas believed his case dramatized the need for reform.[21]

Why Headquarters could not find enough active duty generals for the major generals board in January and yet could find an ample number in October remains unclear. Probably Cates had no intention of allowing the Navy Department, even by default, to influence the selection process other than through the statutory review of the nominations by the Secretary of the Navy. In any event, the October board did not include any retirees, although Cates appointed one admiral (Rear Adm. Alfred M. Pride). The board's membership must have pleased Thomas; it included many of his friends and none of his enemies. The president of the board was Lt. Gen. Samuel L. Howard, a Corps legend for his command of the 4th Marines on Corregidor and his heroic behavior as a Japanese prisoner of war. With the possible exception of Houston Noble, the rest of the board were Thomas intimates: Louis Woods, Franklin Hart, William T. Clement, John T. Walker, Merwin H. Silverthorn, and Ray Robinson. Thomas might have wished that more of his admirers were included, but they were busy with the Korean war: Lem Shepherd, Bobby Erskine, and Field Harris. His detractors, LeRoy Hunt, O. P. Smith, Pete Hill, and Bill Riley, were conspicuously absent. The board met and made its recommendations quickly. The four new major generals should be Gerald C. Thomas, Henry D. Linscott, Edward A. Craig, and Christian F. Schilt. The nominations proceeded through the statutory review process, ending with Senate confirmation. During a trip to Camp Lejeune in January 1951, Thomas learned that his promotion had been confirmed, and his friends quickly organized a promotion party in Ray Robinson's quarters. Franklin Hart pinned on the new stars and presented Thomas with his own two-star red flag, much to the pleasure of the assembled onlookers, among them Bill Whaling, L. B. Cresswell, John

Taylor Selden, and many of the officers who had served with Thomas on Guadalcanal, at Headquarters, and in China. Jerry Thomas now held the highest rank his peers could award him, and he must have savored the moment.[22]

Thomas did not let the moment overwhelm his instinct to do a Marine major general's real work, commanding a division in combat. As soon as he returned to Quantico, he requested an interview with the Commandant about his next assignment. Thomas asked Cates to make him the next commanding general of the 1st Marine Division; Cates had already begun to replace the exhausted senior leaders of the division, which had brought added luster to the Corps for its fighting withdrawal from the Chosin Reservoir. Presumably, he pointed out that no other major general had a better claim to command the division than he had because no other major general but Smith and Pepper had served with "The Old Breed" in World War II. He may have pointed out that Bob Pepper was a mere artilleryman and a battalion commander, whereas Jerry Thomas was the former division chief of staff. If Cates made Thomas the division commander, Thomas wanted Bill Whaling, a brigadier and the assistant division commander of the 2d Marine Division, to replace "Chesty" Puller as the 1st Division assistant division commander. The argument for Whaling also rested on sentiment, but only John Taylor Selden of the brigadiers more senior to Whaling could claim comparable service with the 1st Division in World War II. Not given to sentiment, however, Cliff Cates also recognized that a Thomas-Whaling team would give the 1st Marine Division leadership to match its proven valor. He probably saw other advantages in assigning Thomas as the division commander. Thomas was Army trained and had wide contacts with senior Army officers; his operational commanders would be Army corps and Eighth Army generals. Thomas's immediate Marine Corps commander for administrative and logistical matters would be Lemuel C. Shepherd, Jr., the commanding general of Fleet Marine Force Pacific. Thomas had no better friend in the Corps. Whatever the course of Cates's consideration, the Commandant announced on 22 March 1951 that Jerry Thomas would be the next commander of the 1st Marine Division no later than 1 May and that Bill Whaling would be his assistant division commander.[23]

Thomas's assignment sent convulsive ripples through his family. He asked his daughter Tina about the state of her budding romance with Joe Bruder, an instructor at The Basic School. Tina and Joe had made no firm marriage plans, but now they decided to marry before the general left for Korea. Lottie Thomas had to plan a large wedding and then leave her home at Quantico two weeks after the general surrendered command of the Landing Force Development Center. (Fortunately, the Thomas family received a reprieve to stay in quarters until Johnny and Ginny completed the school year in June.) After several weeks of hectic planning and arrangements, Tina Thomas and Joe Bruder wed at the base chapel on 14 April in the full majesty of dress white uniforms, spring flowers, gay dresses, and flashing swords. The guest list gathered the Corps elite: the Vandegrifts, the Cates, the Turnages, the Harts, the Silverthorns, the Julian Smiths, the Pates, the Pollocks, the Kilmartins, the Bares, the McQueens, and the Capers Jameses. After a splendid reception at Harry Lee Hall, the officers club, the newlyweds left "for a short trip." The father of the bride, his bags packed, left the next day for his third war.[24]

[CHAPTER XXIII]

Commanding General, 1st Marine Division 1951–1952

As Maj. Gen. Gerald C. Thomas flew off to his awaiting division, with time allowed for orientation calls to other Marine commanders along his route, he found ample evidence that the Korean War was entering a new phase. From its origin on 25 June 1950, the Korean War had made a habit of entering new phases, usually to the dismay of one or another of the belligerents.* Having blunted the original invasion by the North Korean People's Army (NKPA), General Douglas MacArthur's United Nations Command (UNC), a multinational force built around the remnants of the South Korean army and seven American divisions in the U.S. Eighth Army and the autonomous X Corps, counterattacked in September and drove the NKPA back into North Korea in October. With the sanction of the United Nations, the Truman administration ordered MacArthur to unify Korea, provided neither the People's Republic of China nor the Soviet Union intervened. American euphoria, which spread from MacArthur to the point patrols of the Eighth Army, disappeared in the frozen, snow-choked mountains of North Korea when the Chinese People's Liberation Army (PLA) fell upon the Americans and South Koreans in November 1950, and drove UNC back below the 38th Parallel by the beginning of the new year. Through a series of counteroffensives, the Eighth Army, which had now absorbed the X Corps, ground back toward the prewar boundary. Under its second and most able commanding general, Lt. Gen. Matthew B. Ridgway, the Eighth Army moved north with justified caution. The PLA showed every sign of mounting another major offensive sometime in April 1951.[1]

Jerry Thomas held no illusions that UNC would do anything very dramatic to inflict a defeat on the Chinese of the same magnitude that it had visited on the

---

* Dates and times are hereafter given at the place of origin of messages and correspondence; Korea is one day and thirteen hours ahead of Washington, D.C.

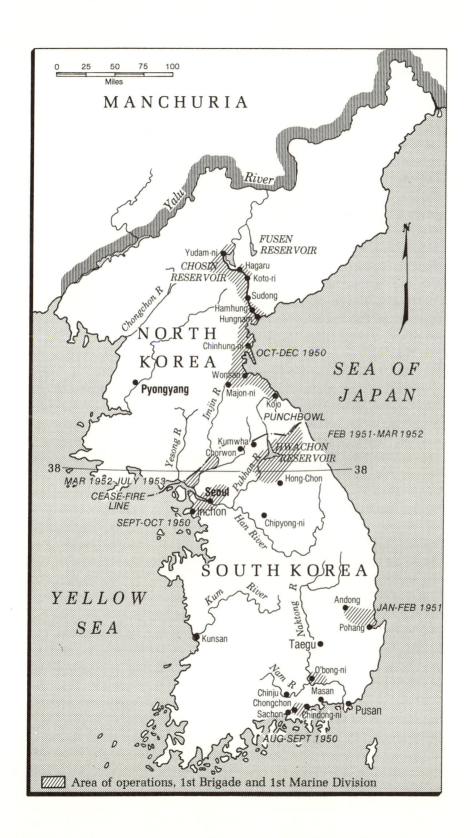

NKPA the previous autumn. By the time Thomas left Quantico to take command of the 1st Marine Division, the Truman administration had reverted to its early war aims to restore the Republic of Korea (ROK) along the political and geographic lines that predated the war. The Joint Chiefs of Staff, deep in a war-justified mobilization to create American forces for the North Atlantic Treaty Organization (NATO) and a global strategic reserve, had adopted a policy that Eighth Army would receive no more American divisions. Air and naval operations would be limited to the Korean peninsula and international waters.

On his arrival in San Francisco on 17 April, Thomas saw living proof of Truman's determination to limit the war. On 10 April, Truman had relieved Douglas MacArthur for waging his own political campaign to change the nation's war aims. Thomas reached San Francisco on the same day as MacArthur, who was bound in the opposite direction for Washington and a date with Congress to protest his relief. The city provided the dethroned general with a boisterous cavalcade and half a million cheering Americans on his route to the Saint Francis Hotel, where Thomas was also staying. More crowds and formal honors sped MacArthur on his way the next day. Thomas found it less dramatic to meet with Maj. Gen. Graves B. Erskine and his staff at Headquarters, Department of the Pacific. Fresh from an extended fact-finding mission in Asia, Bobby Erskine had plenty of information and political advice for his old friend, and Thomas also valued the briefings on the 1st Marine Division's personnel and logistical support system. He enjoyed a similar set of conferences with Lt. Gen. Lemuel C. Shepherd, Jr., at Headquarters, Fleet Marine Force Pacific, outside Honolulu. In a sense, Thomas's trip to Korea was his own triumphal march back to center stage among Marine generals. He wrote Jerry Junior, who had just decided to take a Marine Corps commission after the Naval Academy, that his meetings in San Francisco and Hawaii could not have been warmer. "I believe our standing is such that we will be welcome wherever we go."[2]

Less than a week away from the Saint Francis Hotel, Jerry Thomas sat with Maj. Gen. Field Harris, his old friend, seventh cousin, and commander of the 1st Marine Aircraft Wing, at K-1, a major airbase near Pusan, South Korea. As was their custom, Thomas and Harris talked about all sorts of matters, personal and official. On 23 April 1951, however, the matter that preyed most on their minds was the news of the Chinese launching their vaunted "5th Phase, 1st Impulse Offensive" the night before. That evening Thomas attended the normal debriefing for the Marine pilots, who had flown more than two hundred sorties that day across the most endangered portions of the Eighth Army front. Their excited accounts of the heavy fighting north and east of Seoul convinced Thomas that he might have to abandon his plans to visit the 1st Division's administrative and logistics base at Masan. The next day he started toward the sound of the guns, even though he was not supposed to relieve Maj. Gen. O. P. Smith until 1 May.

The change of command did not proceed smoothly. On 24 April, Thomas made what he thought would be only a courtesy call on Lt. Gen. James A. Van Fleet, the vigorous, muscular, and forceful infantryman who had assumed command of Eighth Army ten days before. The fifty-nine-year-old Floridian, who moved from command of a regiment to a corps in Europe in World War II, shared Thomas's passion for football and combat, which he, too, had first sampled in France in 1918. The two generals appreciated each other's professionalism as Van Fleet briefed Thomas on the situation at the front. The Chinese had made their major effort against the I and IX Corps (Maj. Gen. William M. Hoge, USA), of which the 1st Marine Division was a part. The Communists had destroyed a ROK division, thus driving a wedge that endangered the rear of the U.S. 24th Infantry Division (U.S. I Corps) and the approaches to Seoul. Heavy assaults along the Imjin River threatened the capital, while fixing attacks against the X Corps made it difficult to contain the penetration from the east. On the right flank of the IX Corps, the 1st Marine Division had to prevent any further widening of the gap to the east so that the Eighth Army could focus reinforcements on the western shoulder of the breakthrough. With no mention of his personal concern about O. P. Smith, Van Fleet asked Thomas to change his plans, to go to the 1st Division as soon as possible, and take command. Knowing Smith well, whose style of command was deliberate and whose stature after the Chosin Reservoir campaign was legendary, Thomas must have realized that his early appearance at the division CP near the north bank of the Soyang-gang at Chunchŏn, would not be welcome. Smith had his division well in hand in a hard and unfinished battle. Nevertheless, Thomas honored Van Fleet's request without protest and took a plane back to Masan, where he caught another Marine flight north to Chunchŏn.[3]

Thomas found his reception at the 1st Division CP as cool as a Korean winter wind. Greeted at the division airstrip by Brig. Gen. Lewis B. Puller, whose ungenerous opinions of everyone but Marines like him had not been tempered by his recent promotion, Thomas drove by jeep to meet with Smith and his two principal staff officers, Col. Edward W. Snedeker (chief of staff) and Col. Alpha L. Bowser, Jr. (G-3). When Thomas informed Smith of Van Fleet's preference for an immediate change of command, Smith rejected the proposal. The tactical situation, Smith said, prevented his relief. After two days of hard fighting on its western flank—opened by the evaporation of the 6th ROK Division—the Marines had begun a complex withdrawal to the Soyang-gang and, perhaps, even farther south. The division reserve, the 1st Marines, had moved to the west across the Pukhan-gang, which joined the Soyang-gang just south of Chunchŏn, to refuse the division's left flank and to allow the measured withdrawal of the division's other three infantry regiments (5th Marines, 7th Marines, 1st Korean Marine Corps Regiment), the artillery of the 11th Marines, and all division supporting units. The scheme of maneuver, designed as always by the imaginative Bowser, had its risks because it put major elements of the division in front of two flooded rivers with only one serviceable bridge over each river. The division staff faced a quandary. It regarded both generals with esteem, but viewed Thomas's appearance as premature and unfair to O. P. Smith. Snedeker and Bowser knew Thomas would be a more open, aggressive commander than Smith, but they thought such qualities might not fit the tactical situation.

Thomas admitted to himself that Smith had a point about retaining command, but he held firm in his resolve to take charge. Nevertheless, he left Smith's van without pressing the issue, an act of keen insight into Smith's personality, for Smith responded poorly to direct argument. Thomas went with Snedeker and Bowser to the operations center to examine the maps and go into the situation in detail with the two colonels. He also needed time to think. After several minutes, he decided to renew his conversation with Smith. "O. P.," Thomas said, "The table of organization only calls for one major general in a division. Either you turn over to me, or I'm going to leave." Thomas then left the tent and the silent Smith to continue his talk with Snedeker. Again after some minutes, Smith emerged from his van and told Thomas that he would turn over command the next morning at 0800.[4] Before a handful of witnesses drawn from the division staff, O. P. Smith and Gerald C. Thomas then listened to the orders of relief and assignment and exchanged the division colors in a spartan ceremony later that afternoon. In the chill morning of 25 April 1951, shrouded by the mists of the Soyang-gang, Jerry Thomas assumed command of the 1st Marine Division.

Although the Communist "5th Phase, 1st Impulse Offensive" showed some signs of weakening by the morning of 25 April, James Van Fleet recognized that the Eighth Army faced more challenges before he could honestly report to General Ridgway that United Nations Command had weathered its April storm. To fight his defensive battle and prepare for a following counteroffensive, Van Fleet decided to shift corps boundaries and corps composition because he viewed Korea as a corps commander's war. His most immediate concern was the battle against the four Chinese armies (each equivalent of a UNC corps) pressing against U.S. IX Corps and the embattled U.S. I Corps on the western side of the Communist salient and the approaches to Seoul. Van Fleet passed control of I Corps and Eighth Army reserve forces to General Hoge. These included one brigade of the Commonwealth Division, a regimental combat team from the U.S. 1st Cavalry Division, the 187th Regimental Combat Team (Airborne), the U.S. 24th Infantry Division, and the U.S. 7th Infantry Division, the latter drawn from X Corps reserve. The impatient Ridgway pressed Van Fleet to restore the integrity of the Eighth Army's front across the peninsula. Van Fleet believed he could halt the Communist offensive without again abandoning Seoul, but to do so he needed to strengthen the I and IX Corps. Yet, he could not ignore X Corps (Lt. Gen. Edward M. Almond, USA); the restored NKPA had already pressed hard against the battle-weary U.S. 2d Infantry Division and the 5th and 7th ROK Divisions of X Corps. Van Fleet suspected that the Communists, facing frustration in the drive on Seoul, would commit their reserves (twenty-one of their forty-five divisions) against the Hwachon-Chunchŏn-Hongchon corridor on the east-central front. To stop this anticipated offensive without risking the loss of even a battalion—a requirement levied by Ridgway after the loss of the 1st Battalion, the Gloucestershire Regiment, on the Imjin River—Almond required a division more stalwart than any he then commanded. Ridgway and Van Fleet agreed that once again the 1st Marine Division should come to the rescue.[5]

Van Fleet, however, inherited a problem in reassigning the 1st Marine Division to the X Corps. That problem was Maj. Gen. O. P. Smith himself. While serving together in the X Corps during the Inchŏn-Seoul and the Chosin Reservoir campaigns, Smith and Almond had developed a relationship so poisonous that Ridgway (as Eighth Army commander) had promised Smith that the 1st Marine Division would never again serve under Almond after it returned to the front in early 1951. The Almond-Smith feud stemmed from disagreements over operational matters. Almond, a division commander in Italy during World War II, accepted risks that Smith found imprudent. Part of the difficulty, however, was a matter of personal style as well as operational preference. Holding the dual roles of X Corps commander and MacArthur's Commander in Chief Far East (CinCFE) chief of staff, Almond had a political base that matched his restless, mercurial, aggressive style of command. Not noted for his balance or good humor, he had become even more erratic after the deaths of his only son and son-in-law in World War II. When he felt unfulfilled as a corps commander, Almond liked to command divisions or at least second-guess division commanders. Smith, who had tasted Army paranoia about the Marine Corps in the Pacific war, viewed Ned Almond as an irresponsible meddler. Smith had ample expertise in operations; he had attended the Army Infantry School, as well as the École Supérieure de Guerre, and had participated in three Pacific campaigns. He enjoyed a deserved reputation for personal integrity and moral courage, but he felt no compulsion to exercise personal diplomacy or exhibit any enthusiasm for his corps commander. (In all fairness, some Army generals shared Smith's reservations about Almond's competence.) He believed that Almond was a glory hunter who would fight to the last Marine, provided the press observed the action.[6]

Ridgway and Van Fleet knew that Thomas would take command of the 1st Marine Division and had seen no need to postpone either the change of command or the transfer of the division back to the X Corps just to accommodate O. P. Smith. When Van Fleet had pressed Thomas at their 24 April meeting to take command of his division ahead of schedule, he did not explain the reason for his request. (It was not an order.) Thomas, of course, bore the personal burden of persuading Smith to relinquish command. Shrewd in the matters of high command relations with the U.S. Army, Thomas may have guessed why Van Fleet wanted Smith replaced immediately. In any event, Thomas started his tour as division commander with a reservoir of good will with the Army. He did not, however, become an unquestioning subordinate in matters that affected basic Marine Corps operational principles, as Van Fleet and Ridgway were to learn to their discomfit. In fact, he left his first staff conference with IX Corps appalled at how little discretion a division commander had for the conduct of operations, and he vowed to Al Bowser, his G-3, that he would not accept the Army practice of telling generals not only what to do, but how to do it.[7]

Any Army corps commander in Korea during 1951 would have welcomed the 1st Marine Division in his corps, and Bill Hoge showed genuine regard for Thomas and his Marines. Well he might, for the 1st Marine Division, fighting almost as a corps within a corps, was especially adept at using Marine close air support. At full strength with its own corps reinforcing units, attached Army units, and the 1st KMC Regiment, the 1st Marine Division (reinforced) put nearly 30,000 officers and enlisted personnel in the field. Even when reinforced, a comparable Army division might number 20,000 officers and enlisted personnel. (For some Army divisions, the strength figures went higher when they had operational control of other United Nations contingents that ranged from battalion to brigade strength, but U.S. Army infantry units remained undermanned.) Despite 11,000 casualties during October through December 1950 and subsequent losses in Ridgway's winter counterattacks, the 1st Marine Division started the month of April 1951 with 29,135 effectives. Headquarters scrupulously followed the policy of keeping the division at full strength, something the Army would not do for its divisions. Moreover, the Marines accepted Korean soldiers on far different terms than the Army, which integrated Korean conscripts into American rifle companies where their performance proved uneven at best. The 1st Marine Division, on the other hand, became the patron of the 1st Regiment of the newly founded (1950) Korean Marine Corps (KMC) and furnished skilled advisory teams at the regimental and battalion levels. It assumed responsibility for the Koreans' fire support and logistical needs, even though the Eighth Army and the Korean Army provided some assistance. Because the Korean Marines tried to measure up to the American Marines, the 1st KMC Regiment gave the division a dependable fourth infantry regiment.

The 1st Marine Division had other strengths, some obvious in its structure and others based on experience and Marine Corps tradition. Although its three infantry regiments, artillery regiment (three direct support and one general support battalions), and tank battalion were organized and armed much like their Army counterparts, the division provided much of its own support: amphibian tractor battalion, armored amphibian (artillery) battalion, combat service group, engineer battalion, medical battalion, two motor transport battalions, ordnance battalion, service battalion, shore party battalion, communications battalion, and aviation observation squadron equipped with helicopters and light aircraft. The division headquarters battalion included a military police company and a reconnaissance company. Except for its engineers and medical personnel, an Army infantry division contained service units at company, rather than battalion, strength. This structure and strength gave the 1st Marine Division the advantage of depending on its combat support and combat service support units to provide their own rear-area security or even provide infantry reinforcements, if necessary. The division had proved the soundness of the Corps' adage of "every Marine a rifleman" during the Chosin Reservoir withdrawal, and it retained this principle. In addition, the division enjoyed unparalleled professionalism in its leadership. Its officers in the rank of first lieutenant and above and its senior noncommissioned officers were World War II veterans; its second lieutenants and young enlisted men, who bore the burden of combat and casualties, simply followed the World War II model and their senior leaders. Although Headquarters had begun to rotate the surviving original members of the division back to the United States for reassignment, the quality of the division's Marines at every level left nothing for a commanding general to desire. Jerry Thomas inherited a division from O. P. Smith in "splendid shape," ready to fight successfully in weather and "over some terrain never designed for polite warfare."[8]

In his first week as division commander, and against his better judgment, Thomas executed Eighth Army orders to withdraw the division fifteen miles south of the Soyang-gang to prepared positions in the hills above the river plain, designated No Name Line. With the 1st Marines and an attached battalion of the 7th Marines fighting three Chinese divisions to a bloody standstill west of the Pukhan-gang, the rest of the division moved with discipline and contemptuous ease—with all of its supplies and equipment—to the No Name Line in less than the optimistic forty-eight hours Thomas allowed for the movement. By 29 April, the division had completed its withdrawal across a swollen river in a driving rain and manned the defenses with the 5th Marines, the 1st KMC, and the 7th Marines abreast on the No Name Line. Thomas marveled at the troops' efficiency and morale. Watching the columns of Marine infantrymen pass, conspicuous in their camouflaged helmet covers, he doubted that the withdrawal had been necessary. The ranks were in high spirits and aware that they had again given the Chinese a gory lesson in defensive tactics. Thomas had no doubts that he commanded as good a division as the Marine Corps had ever put into battle and the best division in Korea.[9]

For almost two weeks, the 1st Marine Division awaited the Communist offensive predicted by the Eighth Army. During the period of watchful waiting and defensive organization, Thomas worked out his relationships with his new corps commander, Ned Almond, and his own senior officers. He regarded the first task as his primary concern, and he found ample common ties with Almond, a Virginian and graduate of the Virginia Military Institute. On 1 May 1951, the 1st Marine Division became a part of X Corps as planned; during that day and the next, Thomas and Almond met to establish the ground rules of their collaboration. Thomas had heard all of the Ned Almond horror stories the division staff had to offer, and his first meeting with Almond began on a sour note. One of his assistant G-3s had told an officer on Almond's staff that Thomas did not like some X Corps "guidance" and that Almond "could go to hell." Almond arrived at the 1st Division CP on the day the division joined X Corps and asked Thomas whether he had, in fact, criticized the corps commander. Thomas reinterpreted the question by saying that he would "execute any order proper for a soldier to receive," which meant that he would obey direct orders from the corps commander, not suggestions from staff officers. Almond told Thomas that he was a very active corps commander (no news) and that he planned to visit Marine regimental and battalion CPs on a routine basis (a promise he kept with a vengeance). "Is that all right with you?" Almond asked. Thomas did not respond. Sensing that he was supposed to add something to the conversation, Almond continued: "But I assure you that I will never issue an order affecting one of your units except through you." Thomas replied: "On that basis . . . you are always welcome."[10]

For the next ten weeks, Thomas found Almond omnipresent and "stimulating," but he learned that the corps commander could be converted on operational issues. Thomas did not like two of Van Fleet's existing directives. The first was for the division to establish a battalion patrol base-outpost on a hill mass about halfway between the Soyang-gang and the No Name Line. Even though the site for the base defended a crucial pass through the hills, Thomas regarded the plan as an invitation to wasteful casualties. He chafed at the fact that the outpost would be beyond the range of his 105-mm howitzers, the backbone of his artillery. He could cover the Soyang river plain with aerial reconnaissance and patrols mounted from his principal defensive position. Impressed by the accurate and timely observations of a team from the division reconnaissance company along the Soyang-gang, Thomas asked the veteran team leader, Cpl. Paul G. Martin, what he thought of the battalion outpost concept. Martin thought the plan ill conceived, especially since large numbers of Chinese were already moving south of the river during the night. The accumulated evidence convinced Thomas to challenge the battalion patrol base idea. He won approval of a plan to establish the base with a regiment; he believed a regiment could fight its way clear, if necessary. Although he sent the 7th Marines (Col. Herman Nickerson, Jr.) forward as ordered, he protested that he would have to replace the regiment on the No Name Line with the 1st Marines, which left him no adequate reserve force to backstop twenty-seven miles of front. Almond did approve some shortening of the division's frontage, but he insisted that Thomas maintain the 7th Marines outpost. Thomas did not surrender the argument, especially as his patrols encountered growing numbers of Chinese troops between the outpost and the No Name Line. He ensured that Nickerson received forward support from the 5th Marines and the 1st KMC regiment, so that Nickerson could open the Chunchŏn-Hongchon highway if he had to mount a fighting withdrawal. Thomas made clear to Almond that he had no intention of leaving the 7th Marines isolated if and when the Chinese mounted a major offensive.[11]

Thomas also questioned Eighth Army policy on artillery employment. Van Fleet ordered his artillery battalions to fire a day's allowance of shells every day, whether they had observed targets or not. The headquarters of the 11th Marines (Col. Joseph L. Winecoff) protested the order because the regiment saw no reason to waste scarce ammunition before a likely Chinese attack. Thomas agreed with his gunners, argued with Almond about the policy, and turned a blind eye on shell expenditure reports he knew were inaccurate. During one visit to the division CP, Almond said to Thomas that the 11th Marines didn't shoot enough. Thomas retorted that the real problem was that they didn't hit enough and that the current policy meant that the regiment would have a predictable ammunition shortage when the Chinese attacked. Thomas proved correct on both counts.[12]

Confident that he commanded "the best division that ever wore an American uniform," Thomas waited for the next Communist offensive without special anxiety other than his concern for the 7th Marines. He and his staff expected the blow to fall on the U.S. 2d Infantry Division on their right (the right flank of X Corps). The Chinese attack, mounted by nineteen divisions (each about eight thousand lightly armed and poorly supplied soldiers), actually began on 15–16 May farther to the east against the ROK III Corps. The Chinese offensive scattered two ROK divisions and curled back against the right and rear of the 2d Infantry Division, which once more found itself fighting to avoid disaster. Although X Corps and 2d Division artillery deluged the Chinese with shells, almost fifty thousand on 9 May alone, two more ROK divisions retreated and allowed the Chinese to drive more than thirty miles behind the No Name Line. In the 1st Marine Division sector, two Chinese divisions attempted to slide across the division's front against the left flank of the 2d Infantry Division, but the Chinese ran into a battalion of the 7th Marines. During an all-day battle of 17 May, the Marines prevented any serious penetration of their positions and blunted the movement on the 2d Infantry Division. Ordered by Almond to lengthen his own front so that the 2d Infantry Division could use a fresh regiment to shore up its right flank, now refused back on a sharp north-south axis on the western side of the Communist penetration, Thomas ordered a major redeployment of his division. The 7th Marines returned to the No Name Line to release the 5th Marines for a major movement into the sector assumed from the 2d Infantry Division. As the 5th Marines swung from the division's left flank to its right flank, the 1st Marines withdrew several miles to more favorable terrain in front of the town of Hongchon. Irritated by the movement, the irreverent 1st Marines greeted a new regimental commander, Col. Wilburt S. "Big Foot" Brown, with good-natured catcalls about his timidity. Neither the flamboyant Brown nor his regiment felt like withdrawal. Neither did the division commander.[13]

Although his own frontage allowed his division a reserve of only a battalion or two, Thomas pressed Almond to plan an X Corps counterattack against the base of the Chinese penetration on the Hongchon-Yanggu axis. Almond felt offensive urges, too, but Van Fleet still feared a Chinese major effort against I and IX Corps in front of Seoul. Neither Army general was yet sure that the 2d Infantry Division could prevent the Chinese from widening their penetration. In a series of meetings (17–19 May), Almond, Van Fleet, and Ridgway worked on the broad contours of a counteroffensive along the entire UNC front. Just as Almond pressed Van Fleet and Ridgway to send him reinforcements, Thomas met daily with Almond to urge action, even before the Communist drive had halted. Almond moved cautiously—too cautiously, he later admitted. For one thing, all of his artillery had run short of ammunition; the Eighth Army was supplying only half his estimated needs because of truck shortages and poor road conditions. Even though the Communist advance had slowed from casualties and lack of supplies, Van Fleet released the U.S. 3d Infantry Division to X Corps on the understanding that it would fill the gap in the lines abandoned by the ROK III Corps. The only additional unit sent to Almond—the tank-reinforced 187th Regimental Combat Team (RCT) (Airborne)—was fresh and aggressive but not large enough to bear the offensive burden alone. Unhappy with his division's initial assignment to secure the X Corps left flank and support a IX Corps advance on 20 May, Thomas urged Almond to let the 1st Marine Division lead the attack up the Hongchon-Yanggu corridor and to order it into action before 27 May, the date set for a modest X Corps advance. Thomas saw no purpose in wasting the division on the IX Corps flank when it could add needed muscle in Almond's effort to entrap five Chinese armies and two NKPA corps. Thomas won Almond to his point of view on 20 May and received orders to shift to the offensive three days later, joining the 187th RCT (reinforced) and the bloodied 2d Infantry Division in the X Corps attack to the northeast. Thomas already had the 5th Marines ready to lead the attack, with the three other regiments echeloned behind it. His objective would be Yanggu and the Hwachon Reservoir to the east. Almond gave Thomas authority to deal directly with IX Corps on protecting the corps' left boundary.[14]

With their commanding general watching, the 1st Marines and 5th Marines attacked northward on the morning of 23 May and opened a new chapter in Marine Corps history. This was Jerry Thomas's finest hour as commanding general of the 1st Marine Division. During a week's fighting, the Marines killed about two thousand Chinese soldiers and took the objectives assigned by X Corps. Except for occasional company-scale battles, the division's four infantry regiments, liberally aided by artillery and close air support, as well as tanks, found the terrain more worrisome than the enemy, who fled the battlefield or surrendered (six hundred POWs). In the first four days of the offensive that brought the division back to the banks of the Soyang-gang, the Marines scaled steep mountains, battled rearguard units, overran supply dumps, and, occasionally, pushed along the road in the Hongchon-Yanggu corridor with armed columns of tanks and trucks. Enemy resistance stiffened in front of Yanggu, largely because NKPA units had joined the Communist screening forces, but the Marines pressed forward across the Soyang-gang and dug out the defenders from the commanding heights south of the town and the Hwachon Reservoir. Proud of his Marines' skill and ardor (in all of May, the division had only eighty-three dead from enemy action), Thomas enjoyed showing his units to a flood of visitors, including Generals Ridgway, Van Fleet, and Almond, and Lt. Gen. Lemuel C. Shepherd, Jr., CG FMF Pacific. The 7th Marines mounted the best show by scaling the cliffs near Yanggu to pry out the defenders in close combat. With a tank-infantry assault, the Marines then took the town and left a mess of flame and rubble, in which only the bank safe remained intact. On 31 May, the division held its objectives for the first phase of the X Corps offensive.[15]

Throughout the division's attack, Thomas saw the battle from the front. He proved an active, resolute commander who appeared whenever and wherever firefights flared. He spent little time at his headquarters but preferred to discuss division operations at breakfast and dinner with his new chief of staff, Col. Francis M. McAlister, and his new G-3, Col. Richard G. Weede, who had replaced homeward-bound Snedeker and Bowser. Always on the move by observation helicopter, Thomas divided his time between conferences with Almond and visits to his regimental commanders. Often stopping to confer with battalion commanders, he followed the sound idea that commanders need to watch the action two echelons down the chain of command. He did not allow marginal flying weather, ground fire, or occasional artillery and mortar barrages to deter him from his appointed rounds. Between 26 April and 19 June, he made seventy-three flights over enemy terrain. He set no fashion standards for a modern major general in an army whose generals seemed to vie for the handsomest neck scarves, jump boots, tailored fatigues, and fancy sidearms. Thomas took the field in an old utility cap, a common helmet, an issue field jacket, issue wool sweaters and shirts, a .45 automatic in a black leather shoulder holster (a commonplace rig), baggy utility trousers, World War II canvas leggings, and brown field shoes. The only possible affectation was his Haitian *cocomacaque* walking stick, and even it had a purpose. Thomas amazed younger officers with his vigor. He tackled Korean hillsides with enthusiasm, his muscular legs and flashing walking stick propelling him up slopes that left his juniors gasping. Although the general enjoyed a good meal and one predinner drink (always bourbon), the Thomas mess drew no visitors seeking high cuisine. His division CP of tents and vans was spare, compared with Almond's X Corps headquarters, and he shared the senior officers' shower and head with his staff. Thomas focused on the substance of division command, not its trappings.[16]

Thomas admired the way his Marines fought their way forward to Yanggu and Hwachon Reservoir, but he found much not to like about the employment of the 1st Marine Division and the Eighth Army as a whole. Characteristically, he acted on his ideas. He had his staff conduct a thorough study of the division's

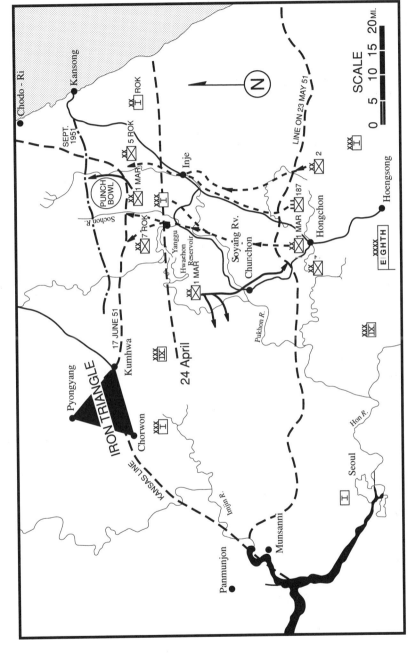

operations that included reports from all regiments and battalions. He reported to General Cates that he lacked MOS-qualified officers and noncommissioned officers in almost every technical specialty. Replacements should be school-trained, not sent directly to Korea. The division also needed more light transport vehicles; even with two thousand Korean bearers attached to the division, resupply in the mountains proved a constant challenge. Thomas wanted more radio jeeps, more detailed topographic maps, and less special equipment. He foresaw problems ahead in fire support, for the Communists showed a growing ability to deliver accurate and heavy artillery and mortar fire for short periods. The new armored vests should be brought to Korea to reduce fragmentation casualties. He saw a growing role for light observation aircraft and transport helicopters in forthcoming mountain operations. Even though the Chinese Communist armies looked beaten, he did not believe his division had seen its last heavy combat.[17]

The most irritating problems Thomas faced, however, stemmed from limitations imposed by American policy, strategy, and his superior commanders. When Almond prepared a plan for another X Corps amphibious envelopment behind Communist lines, Thomas urged the corps commander to press the concept with Van Fleet, who liked the idea, and Ridgway, who didn't. Thomas had full confidence that the 1st Marine Division could make the assault and that such an operation would salvage the stalled effort to ruin the Chinese armies on the east-central front. Ridgway vetoed the idea as inconsistent with his guidance from the JCS to push the enemy back to about the 38th Parallel, even though Shepherd offered to find more Marines (the newly formed 3d Marine Brigade) to make such operations more appealing.[18]

Thomas anticipated heavier combat in mountains that would limit the effectiveness of artillery fire. He reopened the argument, championed by O. P. Smith and Ned Almond earlier in the year, that Ridgway reverse the Air Force policy on close air support (CAS), which worked to the disadvantage of the Eighth Army, in general, and the 1st Marine Division, in particular. Basically, Fifth Air Force commanding generals and their immediate superior, Commanding General Far Eastern Air Forces, regarded close air support as a waste of tactical aviation. Instead, the Air Force generals in 1951 wanted to mount a massive interdiction campaign against Communist troops and supplies on their way to the battlefield. Moreover, Fifth Air Force intended to control all land-based tactical aircraft through its Joint Operations Center—reflecting an Air Force doctrine about centralized employment of aviation that in 1951 had reached the level of service theology. Ground generals might request air missions, but they should not control aircraft or command sorties. (Marine air generals, although sympathizing with the Air Force position, were less doctrinaire on this point. They also eventually had to answer to the Commandant, *always* a ground officer.) Thomas, like Smith, protested that close air support should be an integral, predictable weapon at the ground commander's disposal, that such missions flown for his division should come from the 1st Marine Aircraft Wing, and that the sorties should come rapidly and accurately enough to be worth the risk and effort to infantry and pilots alike. With a time-tested system for directing air strikes from the ground, based on the presence of tactical air control parties (TACPs) at the battalion level, the 1st Marine Division had already proved it could use air strikes with devastating effect, close to the troops locked in combat. The Marine Corps air request and air direction system worked with speed and efficiency because intervening air control agencies seldom interfered with TACP requests. The parallel Army-Air Force system required extensive clearance and approval; by 1951, most Air Force strikes that might qualify as close air support were controlled by airborne controllers, rather than officers working on the ground with infantry commanders. The result was that close air support missions became notorious for being late, inaccurate, and too few in number and were flown by untrained pilots in too few planes with too little appropriate ordnance. From the Fifth Air Force perspective, however, X Corps had become a clique of malcontents who wanted to change the system.[19]

Thoroughly versed in Air Force objections to close air support and briefed on the state of the controversy by Field Harris, Thomas decided in late May 1951 to enter the dispute by expressing his dismay on the inadequate support the division received on its drive toward Yanggu. He discussed the problem with persuasive force with General Shepherd and Adm. Arthur W. Radford, CinCPac, when they visited his headquarters that month. After consulting Almond about Ridgway's reluctance to challenge the Air Force, Thomas wrote an official letter to Almond (intended for Van Fleet and Ridgway) about the poor response time and inadequate number of sorties that the 1st Marine Division received during the late May attack. He made clear that he would not be satisfied until all close air support sorties for the 1st Marine Division came from the 1st Marine Aircraft Wing without clearance by the Joint Operations Center. Thomas did not suggest that the 1st Marine Aircraft Wing fly only for fellow Marines, and he believed that his staff could adequately estimate the number of sorties the division would require, depending on the type of operations it was conducting. He requested only one-third of the Marine daily sorties. He had no strong convictions about various methods of providing quick air support, which centered on the debate over strip alert versus on-call loitering aircraft versus diversion of sorties programmed for interdiction missions. He simply wanted dependable air support, fast. The war, however, would not wait for resolution of the issue.[20]

With the State Department predicting a truce and a negotiated end to the war and Van Fleet reporting that his May counteroffensive had broken Communist military power, the Truman administration called together its principal civilian and political advisors to provide Ridgway clear operational guidance. After a 29 May meeting, the JCS directed Ridgway to continue the offensive but only by advancing to the Wyoming-Kansas Line, a phase line in the mountains north of the 38th Parallel. Although the American divisions in I and IX Corps received the least appetizing assignment, the capture of the Chorwon-Kŭmhwa-Pyonggang area or the "Iron Triangle," X Corps had the task of moving past the Wyoming-Kansas Line through the mountains on either side of an extinct lake, the Punchbowl. The 1st Marine Division, flanked by two doubtful ROK divisions, received the mission of clearing the Punchbowl and the mountains to the west that dominated the Yanggu valley and the Hwachon Reservoir. The configuration of the terrain, however, forced the division's initial advance to clear the mountains between the Soyang-gang valley to the east and the Yanggu valley to the west. These mountains were made for positional defense. Their slopes were sharp, their gullies masked with blue-gray brush and scrub pines, their north-south main spines joined with east-west transverse ridges that allowed a defender to place enfilade fire on any force advancing along the highest ground. The sharp defilades, natural for reverse slope defenses, limited the effectiveness of artillery, which meant that close air support and the direct fire of tank guns would have to play a major role in protecting the advancing infantry from flanking machine gun fire.[21]

On 1 June 1951, the 1st Marine Division began its offensive with the 5th and 7th Marines abreast and no easy way in sight to seize the corps objectives some three miles to the north. The fighting soon took on grim similarities to the Pacific war. Shrinking Marine rifle companies clawed their way through bunker complexes and rifle pits manned by well-armed and stubborn North Koreans. "They fight like Japs," Thomas wrote Merritt Edson. Tank fire helped, but the Koreans had mined the road in the Yanggu valley, so the 1st Tank Battalion paid its own price for the advance. Timely and accurate air attacks often spelled the difference between victory and a halted attack, but close air support errors mounted. On 2 June, the 2d Battalion, 5th Marines, endured four separate attacks on its positions by Air Force F-80 jet fighter-bombers and Marine Corsairs. Fortunately, there were no casualties. The infantry had wisely decided not to trust its own air and took to safety in the hillsides. As Thomas reported, the air strikes were "neither requested nor controlled by this division."[22]

The fighting became so hard that Thomas soon committed the 1st Marines and 1st KMC Regiment and alternated all four infantry regiments in the attack. Hill after bleak and scorched hill, the Marines advanced. When the 1st Marines reached the Wyoming-Kansas Line, Thomas and "Big Foot" Brown could see that the terrain could not be easily defended because of the higher hills dominating it. The advance continued to a new phase line. Thomas spent most of every day forward, conferring with the regimental commanders and gauging his troops' skill, vigor, and morale. He had no complaints about their performance but worried about mounting losses, predominately fragmentation wounds from shells and mortars. The 1st Marines, for example, lost more killed (67) and wounded (1,044) than it suffered in the Chosin Reservoir campaign, although with much less purpose and publicity. Supplying the infantry regiments in the mountains taxed the division. It moved an average of 470 tons (half ammunition) of supplies a day, with the final stage of each resupply mission resting on the sturdy legs of some four thousand Korean bearers, bowed under their A-frames and vulnerable to mortar fire. A Communist division, by contrast, could operate on fifty tons a day. When Thomas left the front, he most often conferred with Almond about the air support problems. He made sure Almond and Van Fleet saw the Marines in action and appreciated the division's ordeal. He did not ask for relief or a change of mission.[23]

In the middle of the battle, Thomas wondered whether the U.S. Army really understood what war was about. Stimulated by a report from the X Corps surgeon, Almond and Van Fleet chided Thomas about taking too many casualties. The Marines were killing Communists at a ratio of more than 10 to 1; Thomas bridled at the suggestion that his men were lazy and careless about taking cover and digging holes, no mean task in the rocky hillsides. He asked Almond and Van Fleet if they wanted the objectives or not. This ended the conversation. Thomas drew no comfort from another event, the visit to the front by Gen. George C. Marshall, the secretary of defense. Thomas thought Marshall appeared tired and dispirited, despite his brave words about keeping the pressure on the Communists even if truce talks began. Almond asked the division commanders to describe their situations; all except Thomas dwelled on casualties and problems. Thomas simply told Marshall, a student of the Civil War, that the three American infantry regiments in the 1st Marine Division fought with the same skill as Stonewall Jackson's brigade. Marshall seemed surprised by his bellicosity, and the meeting dissolved in muted dismay at Thomas's ardor. Returning to his division CP, Thomas was glad to be rid of the defeatism he saw at X Corps headquarters.[24]

On 20 June 1951, the 1st Marine Division held all its objectives and, under new X Corps instructions, turned to the task of creating a solid defensive position along the modified Wyoming-Kansas Line. Thomas again found himself battling the unsound Eighth Army concept of battalion-sized patrol bases. X Corps led the successful effort to persuade Van Fleet to modify his instructions, but not before the 1st KMC Regiment had to fight another hard battle for some dubious terrain forward of the main line of resistance. Finally, after three months of sustained operations, the 1st Marine Division on 17 July surrendered its sector to the U.S. 2d Infantry Division and moved to assembly areas as corps reserve. Thomas left the front a tested, mature division commander. No one was more appreciative of his performance than Ned Almond, who rated him a division commander superior to O. P. Smith and one of the best generals in the Eighth Army. His subordinates also admired his skill and force of character. Upon Almond's recommendation, General Van Fleet awarded Thomas the Army's second highest decoration for gallantry in battle, the Distinguished Service Cross, for his service during the period of 22 May–20 June 1951. Van Fleet pinned the medal on Thomas and eight other Marines at division headquarters on 8 July. The citation applauded Thomas's tactical skill, leadership under fire, and aggressive spirit. Even without the medal, which he appreciated, Thomas felt that no Marine could have a higher honor than command of the 1st Marine Division. Although he enjoyed all the attention he and the division received from visiting generals, admirals, and reporters, he held no illusion that his own war in Korea had ended when the truce talks began in Kaesong on 10 July.[25]

The 1st Marine Division's performance in the Korean War brought major dividends to the whole Marine Corps. In the first year of the war, Congress and the press used the Marines, perceived victims of the Truman administration, to criticize the Department of Defense and the Army for the nation's poor battlefield performance. The political environment in Washington changed in 1951; the size of the armed forces tripled and the defense budget exceeded even this rate of dramatic growth. The Corps grew from less than 100,000 to nearly 200,000 Marines. More importantly, Congress now considered legislation to fix the structure of the Fleet Marine Forces at four divisions and four aircraft wings and to place the Commandant on the Joint Chiefs of Staff. Although Cliff Cates felt obligated to support his Congressional champions, he thought the legislation might be too much, too fast. He wanted to maintain Corps standards during the expansion and transform the new men and weapons into real combat effectiveness, not symbolic victories in Washington. He also needed more exemplary work by the 1st Marine Division.[26]

The division's short respite from combat gave Jerry Thomas a few short weeks to bring it to a higher level of readiness. He liked his command. At the top, he had trusted, experienced leadership. He himself had only two intimates, but they could not have been better men to share Thomas's thoughts and put his thoughts into action. In late May, Bill Whaling replaced Puller as assistant division commander. He renewed a close relationship with Thomas that had begun in Germany in 1919 and had deepened on Guadalcanal. Whaling became a second set of eyes for evaluating tactical situations and training. His easy manner and "good old boy" charm gave him access to troops that Thomas could not and did not have. He conducted "special reconnaissance" missions with his shotgun that kept fresh pheasants and ducks in the generals' mess. Bill Whaling knew how to keep Thomas relaxed and open to others, no mean accomplishment, and he offered complete loyalty to the commanding general and his policies. There was nothing relaxed about the new division chief of staff, "Brute" Krulak, fresh from the wars of Washington and Quantico. With no transition time, Krulak grasped control of the division staff and ran it with his usual relentless search for perfect intellectual performance. He took no time out for contemplating or agonizing. Krulak ensured that Thomas faced no problems in staff functioning. The division's regiments all had strong, proven commanders: Col. Thomas A. Wornham replaced "Big Foot" Brown in the 1st Marines; Col. Richard G. Weede left his post as G-3 to assume command of the 5th Marines; and Herman Nickerson remained in command of the 7th Marines. Col. Custis Burton, Jr., commanded the 11th Marines. Thomas had every reason to feel confident that his division could boast solid professionals in senior staff and command positions.[27]

Thomas developed strong, collaborative relations with the new X Corps commander, Maj. Gen. Clovis E. Byers, a brave, handsome, and charming fifty-one-year-old West Pointer (class of 1920). In addition to his winning personality, Byers appeared to be one of the best Army officers yet appointed to corps command in Korea. During World War II, he had commanded a division, then served as a corps and field army chief of staff. For heroic and distinguished service from 1942 until 1945, the Army had awarded Byers a Distinguished Service Cross, a Distinguished Service Medal, two Silver Stars, two Legions of Merit, three Bronze Stars, and the Purple Heart. Yet, in the faction-ridden general officer ranks of the U.S. Army, Byers had fought the wrong war for the wrong commanding generals. He had served in the southwest Pacific and the Philippines as Gen. Robert L. Eichelberger's trusted subordinate in I Corps and Eighth Army. A fellow Ohioan, Eichelberger felt comfortable with Byers's style and quiet efficiency, but Eichelberger retired in 1948. The Army of 1951 had a new pecking order, arranged by Gen. J. Lawton Collins, the chief of staff, and supported by Gen. Matthew B. Ridgway—American and Allied Supreme Commander in the Far East. Unlike Van Fleet, Byers was not a member of the Collins-Ridgway team; his only senior patron was Gen. Mark W. Clark, commander of Army Field Forces in the United States. One issue drew Byers and Clark together, the question of close air support. As commanding general of the U.S. 82d Division (Airborne),

Byers had criticized the Air Force's pale interest in the mission. Welcoming the opportunity to raise the issue again in Korea, he accepted, without hesitation, Ned Almond's reform mission. Naturally, Thomas and his staff had every reason to cultivate Byers's study of close air support. Thomas, who had met Byers briefly in 1943, had other common interests to exploit. They were fellow Middle Westerners and former football players; they had fought the Japanese; they knew the snakepit of Washington military politics (Byers had been assistant chief of staff, G-1); they had attended the same Army schools. Thomas and Byers developed a strong working relationship that profited the 1st Marine Division.[28]

Thomas tested his rapport with Byers quickly, and the issue was a real one. Under Van Fleet's prodding and concern that the U.S. 2d Infantry Division, locked in another wasting battle for Heartbreak Ridge, might be vulnerable to counterattack, Byers prevented the 1st Marine Division from getting very far from the fighting when it left the front in July. Byers also wondered how he would contain any serious attack on his two committed ROK divisions or against ROK I Corps to the east. He wanted one Marine infantry regiment (5th Marines) to backstop the 2d Division at Inje and another (7th Marines) to work on the defenses behind the ROKs at Yanggu. Because Thomas could still conduct a division training program with these deployments, he did not challenge the orders. He did, however, protest the idea of sending either regiment into battle under Army command, and he also argued against an Eighth Army scheme to send part of the 1st Marine Division (Task Force Able), even if commanded by Bill Whaling, to the ROK I Corps if the Communists attacked it. Byers could make no promises that he could prevent Van Fleet from controlling Task Force Able, but he promised Thomas that no Marine regiment would fight in the X Corps sector under anyone but a Marine general. Thomas liked Byers's sensitivity to such command issues. Byers praised Thomas to an Army friend: "The 1st Marine Division under the command of Major General Gerald C. Thomas, with Brigadier General Whaling as Assistant Division Commander, and Col. Krulak as Chief of Staff, had become a vastly different outfit from that which it was under its former commander. They cooperate with the other divisions in the Corps smoothly and willingly."[29] Thomas and Byers forged a sound, open relationship that gave the 1st Marine Division commander not only greater control over his own division but also allowed him to influence corps operations.[30]

While cultivating X Corps, Thomas put his own division in order. He ordered a crash program of training and logistical rehabilitation that went into effect on 23 July and had to be completed by 20 August. The training focused on small unit tactics and weapons employment with one-third of the exercises at night; Thomas sent twelve special training teams to the 1st KMC Regiment, so that all ROK Marine companies had American advisors. Every division unit received demanding programs to clean and repair its organic weapons and equipment. On 14 August, the division supply officer began distribution of cold-weather clothing and equipment, including the new thermal "Mickey Mouse" boots. (Thomas ensured that Byers received a complete set of new Marine Corps winter clothing.) The Marines participated in an ambitious program of calisthenics and group sports; those with nagging physical and dental problems received priority treatment from the Navy's doctors and dentists. The 1st Marine Division filled with

Table 1. Personnel Comparisons of 1st Marine Division and U.S. 2d Infantry Division—Korean War, 1 June–15 October 1951

	1st Marine Division*	2d Infantry Division**
Authorized strength	25,710	18,313
Average strength (stated as percentage of authorized strength)	96	100+
Battle casualties	4,241	6,247
Nonbattle casualties	5,549	3,264
Casualties returned to duty***	6,706	3,479
Rotation losses	11,637	9,793
Replacements	13,097	14,622

* Does not include 1st Regiment, Korean Marine Corps, with an authorized strength of 3,772.
** Does not include French infantry battalion and Netherlands infantry battalion, authorized strength 1,800 total.
*** 41 percent of U.S. battle casualties returned to duty.
Source: Adapted from G-1, HQ, X Corps, Special Personnel Report, 1 June–15 October 1951, Clovis Byers Papers, Hoover Institution for War Revolution and Peace.

fresh men; between 1 June and 15 October 1951, it rotated almost 12,000 Marines back to the United States and integrated 13,000 replacements. (Table 1 compares personnel statistics between the 1st Marine Division and the U.S. 2d Infantry Division for this period.) A personnel problem was replacement of scarce technicians, and the last veterans of 1950 (some 2,200 officers and men) did not depart until late October and November. Thomas watched morale carefully. He sent a division entertainment troupe to the regimental and battalion camps and checked the food for quality and quantity on his daily inspection trips. He ordered patrols to curb prostitution and illegal liquor sales in the division area. The patrols also burned the abundant local marijuana crop that attracted a handful of avant-garde Marines, but drug use did not become a problem in 1951. In all, Thomas could report with confidence by the end of August that his division could handle any mission that the Eighth Army and X Corps could assign it.[31]

Fully alert to the fact that the North Koreans, the terrain, and the late summer rains would make any operation north of the Wyoming-Kansas Line a tactical misery, Thomas still lobbied for an amphibious operation behind enemy lines. With Byers's blessing, Thomas and his staff flew to Seoul to discuss a landing with Van Fleet's staff, who did not believe the division could mount out in less than four weeks. Assured that the Navy and Marines could mount another amphibious envelopment in ninety-six hours before ice made the operation difficult to support with beaching craft, Van Fleet told Thomas to start detailed planning while he tried to sell the plan to Ridgway. Full of optimism, the division staff completed the operations plan for a corps landing as early as 1 September. (Thomas would command his own division and the 3d ROK Division.) Thomas requested the Eighth Army return the 1st Amphibian Tractor Battalion and 1st Armored Amphibian Battalion to his control from its detached service with the U.S. I Corps, but Van Fleet refused the request. The implication was clear: no landing. Weeks later, Thomas had a chance to ask Ridgway why he had rejected the plan. Ridgway said he had not, that the decision to deny another Inchŏn-like surprise on the North Korean Army had come from Washington where the fear of Russian intervention had mesmerized the JCS, the State Department, and Harry

Truman himself. Once again, Thomas saw a chance to strike the Communists go aglimmering in an atmosphere of strategic timidity.[32]

Instead of an amphibious operation behind the thick North Korean defenses north of the Punchbowl and west of the Soyang-gang, the 1st Marine Division received orders on 21 August 1951 to replace portions of the U.S. 2d Infantry Division and 8th ROK Division on the Wyoming-Kansas Line and to prepare for an attack to seize X Corps Objective Yoke, a steep hill mass north of the Punchbowl. The offensive did not get off to a fast start. Thirty inches of rain during August had turned the roads into slippery quagmires and threatened the Soyang-gang bridges. Conflicting demands to move troops and artillery ammunition plagued division and corps motor transport battalions. No one expected an easy operation. The enemy, two divisions of the NKPA III Corps, had not only fortified the objective and all its abutting ridges but had also organized the battlefield for strong counterattacks. Agents and patrols had penetrated X Corps lines; refugees, deserters, and enemy traffic had disappeared; the North Koreans had imposed radio silence; the enemy had apparently issued new weapons and abundant ammunition and food, as well as stockpiled other supplies in caves and tunnels. Thomas and Krulak looked north from an observation post on the Wyoming-Kansas Line and saw a disheartening maze of 1,100-meter mountains, wrapped in rain and fog, that stretched without interruption (and at higher altitudes) to the north. The 1st Marine Division found little room for tactical imagination and even less for solid accomplishment except duty done in the most difficult missions.[33]

As the initial truce negotiations with the Communists collapsed in late August, the 1st Marine Division returned to the front—the sketchy fortifications of the Wyoming-Kansas Line—prepared for further offensive operations. From 31 August until 20 September, the division fought some of the hardest (and least appreciated) battalion actions of the Korean war. Against the stubborn resistance of the 1st and 2d NKPA Divisions, the Marines captured two hill masses, Yoke Ridge and Kanmubong Ridge, north of the Punchbowl and east of the Soyang-gang, thus establishing the X Corps' portion of a new Eighth Army defensive position, the Hays Line. Against a well-armed and trained enemy fighting from elaborate bunker systems and supported by generous amounts of artillery and mortar fire, the 1st Marine Division again proved that no better division fought in the Eighth Army. Suffering to prove its skill, it became locked into an operational concept from which no commanding general could have provided miraculous relief. On 14 September, at the climax of the attack on Kanmubong Ridge, the Marines lost 39 killed in action (KIA) and 463 wounded, a one-day casualty rate exceeded only by two separate days of battle in the Chosin Reservoir campaign. Veterans of World War II found the battle much like the struggles for Saipan, Iwo Jima, and Okinawa in its ferocity and intensity. The September fighting brought Thomas an immense pride in the fighting heart of his division and a new level of disillusionment in American strategy, the U.S. Air Force, and the operational direction of the Eighth Army.[34]

Struggling against heavy rains and flooded roads, the 7th Marines and 1st KMC Regiment began the offensive on 31 August with assaults on Yoke Ridge.

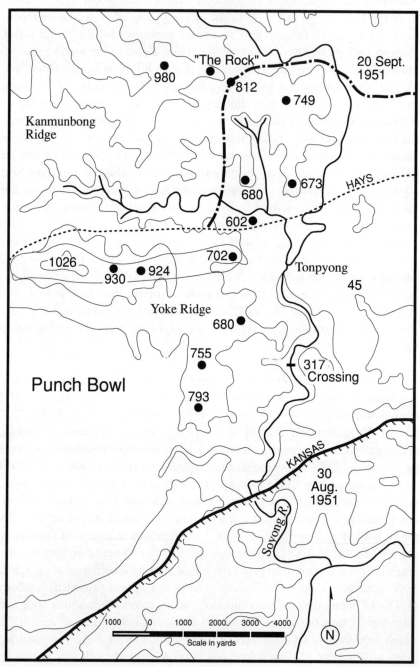# 1st Marine Division
Punch Bowl Operations, 1951

* Contour lines vary by 200 meters

The two regiments attacked with three battalions abreast against the right half of Yoke Ridge. When the KMC Regiment took its first objective, Hill 924, it planned to swing westward along the spine of the ridge and capture, in succession, Hills 1026, 1000, and 930. The 7th Marines would capture Hill 702 above the Soyang-gang valley and hold it against the predicted counterattacks the NKPA might (and did) mount from Hill 602 and the higher positions on Kanmubong Ridge. The Hays Line followed the northern edge of Yoke Ridge, but it was obvious that Yoke could not be easily held unless the Marines captured the NKPA positions on Kanmubong Ridge as well. The battle for Yoke Ridge lasted five days (31 August–4 September) and required the best efforts of 3d Battalion, 7th Marines and all three KMC battalions to capture and hold the objective against a dogged positional defense, continued barrages, and heavy battalion-sized counterattacks. The American Marines did not secure Hill 924 until they had also captured Hill 602 to their front. The battle cost the Marines of both nations over 600 casualties (109 KIA), but the North Koreans lost 656 soldiers dead by actual count and twice as many estimated wounded and missing. Although close air support and saturation artillery fire helped the Marines, they still had to destroy the entrenched North Koreans with infantry weapons in close combat.[35]

Thomas followed the battle but did not intervene in the attack, once joined. He watched the attacks from the division OP and consulted with Herman Nickerson in the 7th Marines CP, but he focused on the operations that would follow the capture of Yoke Ridge. On 1 September, he accompanied Lem Shepherd on a tour of the division and a visit with Byers; two days later he discussed the attack with Byers. The logistical situation had deteriorated with the roads, and the limited amount of transportation meant that fresh troops could not be brought forward until the division and corps artillery had replenished their stockpiles of shells to adequate levels. There had been no lack of artillery fire for the Marines. The 11th Marines and three reinforcing Army artillery battalions fired almost 9,000 shells in a single twenty-four-hour period during the attack; during the month of September, the artillery of X Corps fired 847,000 rounds (24,000 tons). The broken terrain and steep hills, however, limited the number of guns that could be emplaced within effective range and that could deliver devastating fire on fortified positions, especially on reverse slopes. The other major source of fire support, close air support strikes by fighter-bombers, did not arrive with adequate speed and weight to please Thomas and certainly not his embattled infantrymen. Before the 1st Marine Division advanced beyond the Hays Line to Kanmubong Ridge, Thomas wanted some time to reorganize his offensive, and Byers agreed to a pause without complaint. In the meantime, Marines fought off probes on the Hays Line, and the 5th Marines in division reserve along the Wyoming-Kansas Line had to repulse two enemy attacks mounted five miles from the front. The situation was indeed too fluid for comfort.[36]

The concept for the seizure of Kanmubong Ridge assigned the 7th Marines the responsibility for capturing Hills 673 and 948, the commanding heights on the eastern edge of the ridge. The fresh 1st Marines would then pass through the 7th Marines and attack north and west against Hill 1051 and to objectives beyond, which came to include Hills 980 and 812. Thomas did not rush Nickerson; he issued the attack order on 9 September with an execution time of 0300 on 11

September. The battles for Hills 673 and 749 took every bit of fighting heart the 7th Marines could muster. Mines, shells, machine gun fire, and North Korean counterattacks made the battle a two-day slugfest that ended only when Nickerson organized a daring night movement and dawn attack by his reserve battalion and caught the North Koreans between all three of his embattled battalions. Losing almost 300 men in the process, the 7th Marines advanced bunker by bunker. Even so, it dislodged the NKPA from Hill 673 and part of Hill 749 but did not eliminate every position in its zone of action.[37]

On 13 September, the 1st Marines assumed the mission of continuing the attack on Kanmubong Ridge with Hill 749 the first objective. In fighting of mounting intensity, the 1st Marines required three more days to secure Hill 749 and adjoining objectives; in the process, the 2d Battalion, 1st Marines, not only had to fight its way up Hill 749 but then defend it against a regimental-sized counterattack, supported by a NKPA artillery barrage that deluged the hill. When the battle finally ended on 16 September, the division had lost another 800 men, most of them in two battalions of the 1st Marines. The last fresh regiment in the division, the 5th Marines, would have to continue the attack.[38]

The 5th Marines inherited a tactical situation no less dangerous than that faced by the 7th and 1st Marines, an advance of one thousand yards or more through Hills 680 and 673 toward another division objective, Hill 812, almost due west from the positions secured by the 1st Marines. In four more days of attacks and defense against counterattacks (16–20 September), the regiment took its turn in the meat grinder. Although Hill 812 fell on the first day's attack, the 5th Marines ended the day with both its assault battalions out of touch and one of them (2d Battalion, 5th Marines) in tenuous control of Hill 812 and an outlying granite outcropping dubbed the "Rock." The regimental commander, Dick Weede, thought his Marines could advance all the way to Hill 980 on 16 September, but Thomas refused the request since he saw no point in taking a position that would still be subjected to crippling fire from Hill 1052, the highest ground on Kanmubong Ridge. Instead, he ordered the 5th Marines to consolidate its gains, a wise decision since the North Koreans raked the entire front with heavy artillery fire and launched two counterattacks on the 2d Battalion, 5th Marines. The fighting centered around the "Rock," which the Marines captured twice and held against a third counterattack on 20 September. The issue ended at close quarters; grenades and infantry weapons in the hands of Marines decided the fight. The division now held three of its four objectives on the ridge. Suddenly, the battle ended. On 16 September, the Eighth Army had ordered X Corps to suspend all major offensive operations after 20 September. Van Fleet had decided that further attacks along the Hays Line could not be justified. The 1st Marine Division would now have to hold the ground it had seized, however unfinished its work.[39]

Thomas accepted the division's new mission with very mixed emotions. Although he had no desire to see Marines die for one more Korean ridge, he viewed Van Fleet's halt order as tantamount to capitulation to the Communists. He favored a wider war against Communist China that included the employment of the Nationalist army and support for guerrilla warfare against Mao Tse-tung's regime. He wrote his brother Louis that "our guys are off base in D.C. and plenty." The Truman administration might think that the Korean war could be limited to the restoration of South Korea, but "the wounds and worse acquired by Americans here have a real one hundred percent appearance." He found bitter the thought that such sacrifices would not produce an imposed peace but took comfort that the 1st Marine Division had proved as professional and heroic in 1951 as it had been in 1950.[40]

Another great satisfaction to Thomas was the experiment of using transport helicopters in combat. His own experience with the light observation helos of VMO-6 had confirmed his belief that war by vertical envelopment might give the Marine Corps a new dimension of effectiveness, but those helos could perform only reconnaissance, administrative, and casualty evacuation missions. Now, however, he had in hand a new weapon, Marine Transport Helicopter Squadron 161 (HMR-161) equipped with fifteen Sikorsky HRS-1 transport helicopters, each capable of carrying four to six troops or 1,420 pounds of supplies at sea level, but less at Korean altitudes. Arriving in Korea on 31 August, HMR-161 moved onto a rough airstrip, X-83, which it shared with VMO-6 near the division CP along the Soyang-gang. On 11 September, the squadron made its first orientation flights. Thomas and Krulak, ever the helicopter enthusiasts, judged it ready for important missions.[41]

Thomas could hardly wait to find an opportunity to employ HMR-161, for he himself had pressured Cates to send the squadron to Korea as soon as possible. He and Krulak discussed its use long before the squadron arrived at X-83, and Krulak had held planning conferences with the division staff and the 1st Shore Party Battalion that had become tutorials on the principles embodied in PHIB-31, which Krulak had written. On Krulak's recommendation, Thomas decided that the 1st Marines' attack on Hill 749 on 13 September would include the first major helicopter resupply operation in military history. Four hours before the attack, 2d Battalion, 1st Marines, and HMR-161 received their final instructions for Operation Windmill I. While the fight for Hill 749 raged that day, HMR-161 ferried nearly 19,000 pounds of ammunition and supplies to the battalion and evacuated 74 casualties in twenty-eight flights during a period of two and one-half hours. Flying nap of the earth and covered by artillery fire and smoke shells, the squadron completed the operation without a loss. Two days later, HMR-161 flew a similar, if less ambitious, resupply mission for the 5th Marines. On 21 September, as the 1st Marine Division extended its lines to the northeast to replace a ROK regiment, the squadron conducted its first tactical troop lift. In Operation Summit, HMR-161 transported 224 Marines of the division's reconnaissance company (reinforced) and 18,000 pounds of cargo to Hill 884 in four hours. An overland movement to the remote peak would have taken much longer. Shepherd and Byers praised the operation, which also received ample newspaper publicity. Thomas complimented HMR-161 and recognized that the Marines had made history in a war that offered little immediate satisfaction.[42]

General Thomas admired his helicopter squadron, but his dissatisfaction with all other air operations mounted during September. During the last two days of the offensive, he decided to make an official case against the miserable level of close air support his division had received during its trials north of the Hays Line. Since the spring of 1951, he had pursued some change in the Air Force system of centralized control. He had discussed the problem with two commanders of the 1st Marine Aircraft Wing, Field Harris and his successor, Christian F. Schilt, but neither felt powerful enough to fight a guerrilla war against the Fifth Air Force's Joint Operations Center, which had to approve all missions for the Eighth Army. Thomas had gone on record within the Navy and Marine Corps chain of command about the lack of close air support as early as July 1951. In October, however, he embarked on a personal mission to change the system, even if it meant forcing the issue as far away as Washington, D.C., and challenging the Fifth Air Force's massive interdiction campaign, Operation Strangle.[43]

Throughout the battle for Kanmubong Ridge, Thomas's frustration with close air support mounted to an explosive boil. Of 271 separate air requests, only 32 missions had been fulfilled quickly and accurately enough to assist the embattled Marines. In the struggle for Hill 812, one flight of Air Force aircraft had strafed and napalmed a 5th Marines battalion by mistake, but luckily without casualties. Thomas, however, flew into action after more air problems in the waning days of the campaign, 20 and 21 September. With three tired regiments astride the division's objectives, Thomas responded to an X Corps order to expand his frontage to the east by bringing the 1st Marines back to the front and assuming a sector vacated by an ROK division. The movement required delicacy because the ROKs had left behind unmarked minefields (their dismal trademark) and a goodly number of unconquered Communists around Hill 854. On 20 September, the 3d Battalion, 1st Marines, started an attack (air support requested) and met some opposition. The air support arrived in the form of a flight of New Zealand P-51 fighter-bombers that demonstrated an uncertain grasp of the mission by dropping napalm between the advancing lines of Marine infantrymen, again without friendly losses. Watching the incident, the enraged Thomas returned to his headquarters and ordered Krulak to mount a paper offensive against the Eighth Army and Fifth Air Force. His resolution received further ratification the next day when two requested strikes arrived four hours late in one case and not at all in the other.[44]

Thomas began his crusade to improve close air support with the assurance that Shepherd, Radford, and Byers understood and approved of his action. In fact, Shepherd and Radford had already encouraged his protest (he did not need much encouragement), and Thomas reviewed the problem again for Byers on 23 and 28 September. Byers informed him that Eighth Army had just told X Corps that it could expect reduced air support. On 1 October, he raised the issue with General Ridgway at X Corps headquarters during a conference with Gen. Omar N. Bradley, chairman of the JCS. Ridgway suggested that Thomas discuss his complaints with Lt. Gen. Frank E. Everest, USAF, the commander of Fifth Air Force. On 3 October, Thomas reviewed his study with Everest, whom he had met in the South Pacific, and with General Schilt. Thomas thought he had found a sympathetic audience for some change, so he sent a formal message to Everest with the request that only Marines would fly future air strikes for his division. Everest doubted, however, that he could fill another Thomas proposal, that Fifth Air Force assign forty sorties a day to the division whenever the Marines mounted an offensive action. Nevertheless, Thomas decided to press the issue through the chain of command.[45]

His staff completed its air support study; Thomas sent it to Byers on 6 October with a formal request that the 1st Marine Division be assigned forty sorties a day during all offensive actions and that the strikes come only from the 1st Marine Aircraft Wing. He also sent copies of the study to Shepherd and Radford, thus widening the battle at the interservice level in the Pacific command structure. The gist of Thomas's argument was that effective close air support would have sped his advance in September and reduced his casualties, a telling shot at Eighth Army's sensitivity to losses. He also believed every word he said. Byers forwarded Thomas's request and report to Van Fleet and recommended approval. Van Fleet and Everest reacted immediately. They assured Ridgway that they would stand by the existing system.[46]

If he had any illusions that he had pressed a nerve in Eighth Army and CinCFE headquarters, Thomas quickly learned that Van Fleet and Ridgway had no taste for a battle with the Air Force over tactical aviation doctrine, even if a change might save American lives. Byers, on the other hand, firmly stood his ground under pressure from his superiors to abandon his support of Thomas's proposal. Byers also attempted to persuade Van Fleet that Radford and Shepherd were pressuring Thomas to attack Fifth Air Force, which they were not. Thomas doubted that even Schilt, a fellow Marine, would press the 1st Marine Division request. As he wrote his daughter Tina, "One grave weakness is that our fliers frequently do not know which side they are on."[47] He thought Schilt too eager to replace Lt. Col. Edward V. "Mickey" Finn, the division air officer and the principal author of the study. In fact, Schilt thought Thomas exaggerated his problems with the Air Force air support system. Ridgway and Van Fleet quickly informed Thomas and Byers that their criticism of the existing close air support system was not warranted and that the 1st Marine Division request for a dedicated forty sorties, which implied a shift of operational control of aviation to a ground commander, was not acceptable to Gen. O. P. Weyland, the commander of Far East Air Forces and the designer of Operation Strangle. Ridgway's correspondence and personal discussions left Thomas with the impression that Ridgway would have him relieved if the Army general believed he could remove a Marine general from command of a Marine division without controversy, a faint hope. Thomas felt the reflected heat from the Air Force, but it did not come from jet exhausts.[48]

The close air support issue did not fade away. Byers and Thomas would not surrender their position that the Fifth Air Force placed too great an emphasis on interdiction and botched what few close air support missions it flew. Into November, both the division and corps headquarters collected further damning evidence; Byers and Thomas continued to discuss the problem with high-level visitors, including Van Fleet, Admiral Radford, and even the Commandant of the Marine Corps and his aviation directors.[49]

Byers and Thomas may not have known that they had other allies in the U.S. Army. Generals Mark W. Clark and Ned Almond had collaborated on their own studies of close air support that supported the Byers-Thomas position. Clark and Almond used their positions as Commanding General, Army Field Forces, and Commanding General, Army War College, to preach reform throughout the Army, to the discomfiture of J. Lawton Collins and Matthew B. Ridgway. Even Van Fleet and Everest relented and proposed in November that the Marine Corps air request and control system be adopted on an experimental basis in the Eighth Army, with Army ground officers running the tactical air control parties. They even suggested that each American corps receive the operational control of a Marine squadron, a doctrinal heresy. Ridgway was fully aware that a change to accommodate the 1st Marine Division might set off a rebellion among Army corps and division commanders on close air support practices. He would not approve any change because he also knew that Weyland and the Air Force chief of staff, Gen. Hoyt S. Vandenberg, would take the issue to the JCS. The controversy raged on without resolution even after Thomas left Korea. Although the 1st Marine Division saw some small improvements in its own air support, principally because Marine squadrons had moved to a base closer to its position, the existing doctrine for Air Force-Army air-ground operations did not change, and the quality of close air support for the Eighth Army as a whole did not improve. The entire experience further reinforced Thomas's conviction, and the beliefs of other senior Marine officers, that the Air Force would never provide American ground forces the support they required.[50]

Although the possibility of new truce negotiations warmed during the autumn of 1951, the 1st Marine Division felt the first chill winds of the Korean winter from its perch along the sharp ridges of the Taebaek Mountains. Offensive operations also congealed with the Eighth Army's instructions to hold and fortify a Main Line of Resistance (MLR), designated the Minnesota Line, along the X Corps front. Adjusting its dispositions to its defensive mission and the eccentricities of the local terrain and North Korean defenses, the division curled along some thirteen miles of front. Eventually, it placed all four regiments on the MLR with six to eight battalions actually manning the MLR and the combat outposts. The American and Korean Marines dug trenches, fighting holes, and deep bunkers complete with overhead cover; the bunkers received special attention so that they could accommodate rough bunks and small stoves. Barbed wire and mines went into the avenues of approach; direct fire weapons from machine guns to tanks moved into nests of earth and sandbags. The troops began to find many signs of a new, static, and cold war: warm meals on a regular basis, successive waves of cold-weather clothing issues, stockpiles of ammunition, and mounds of engineering equipment and supplies. The fighting did not end but shrank to patrols, from squad to company size. In mid-October, the division ordered a program of aggressive raids by tank-infantry teams against the North Korean forward outpost line; Marine snipers and artillery forward observers searched the hills to the north for targets. In a strange cycle of time and place, Gerald C. Thomas found himself in a war that bore a striking resemblance to his first service in French trenches in early 1918.[51]

As the division commander, Thomas did not live in the trenches, but he saw them often enough on his endless rounds by helicopter to the MLR. He relished the mobility of his command helicopter, which he insisted on using even when foul weather grounded the light planes of his Army counterparts. He did not spend much time around the division command post, a city of tents, huts, and graded streets along a branch of the Soyang-gang behind a ridge east of the Punchbowl and only a half mile from the main supply route (MSR) in the division area. The real appeal of the site was its proximity to the expeditionary airfield,

X-83, home of VMO-6 and HMR-161. Thomas used his transport helicopters at every opportunity. They flew hot meals to isolated Marines along the MLR and provided emergency resupply of ammunition and supplies in externally slung loads. Helicopters from both squadrons evacuated casualties with growing proficiency. Thomas also subdued guerrilla activity within his area—a minor but constant problem—with heliborne patrols from the reserve battalions and noninfantry units. He enjoyed pointing out to visiting VIPs how the Marines had adapted the helicopter to land warfare and ensured that visitors to X Corps had an opportunity to see the battlefield from the noisy, chill interior of an HRS-1. Thomas continued to exchange visits with Byers, his corps commander, by helicopter. When he returned to the CP to sleep and eat and for Krulak's briefings, Thomas enjoyed Bill Whaling's company, especially the bag of game birds the "provider" brought to the general's mess. Thomas loved his surprise fifty-seventh birthday party on 29 October, especially when the division band played "The Sweetheart of Sigma Chi" in Lottie's honor. His only serious regret was that he would miss the 1951 football season in the states.[52]

The commanding general kept his hand on the pulse of the division's personnel administration and logistical operations. Satisfied that he would receive adequate numbers of Marines—Headquarters maintained its policy of keeping the division over strength—he inspected the entire replacement system, from the MLR to Japan, to ensure that the troops and their personal baggage received proper handling and that the last of the 1950 Marines returned to the states before Christmas. He personally bid farewell to the last veterans of the Chosin Reservoir campaign around Thanksgiving. He kept close personal track of his officer corps, especially field grade officers, to ensure equity in line and staff assignments. A bleak moment came at the death of his highly regarded G-1, Col. Wesley M. Platt, on 27 September. A hero of the defense of Wake Island and almost four years of captivity by the Japanese, Platt died in a shell burst while on a jeep trip near the front. (Platt was the most senior Marine officer killed in the Korean War.) Thomas also followed his division's materiel condition closely through Krulak and his able G-4, Lt. Col. Frank P. Hager. With the division in a fixed defensive position, its logistical tail spread into a wide net of vehicle parks, workshops, depots, and supply dumps. Thomas, in fact, thought his division had too few fighters and too many service troops. In a November review of the division's experience, he concluded that the division required some sort of fourth maneuver unit (he favored a fourth battalion in each regiment) and fewer tanks and heavy artillery in the division structure. He did not believe that the growing similarity of his limited operations to those of the artillery-dominated Western Front should set a precedent for future division organization; instead, it should be shaped by the requirement for helicopter mobility. Thomas had a way of working well in the present while preparing for the future.[53]

Thomas also thought about his own next assignment. He knew from his talk with Cates in October that President Truman would make good on his promise to Lem Shepherd and appoint Shepherd the next Commandant on 1 January 1952. Shepherd visited Thomas again on 16 November and said that he wanted Thomas to return to Headquarters to assume the position of Assistant Commandant and chief of staff with the rank of lieutenant general. Shepherd and Cates had not decided who would take Thomas's place, although Shepherd wanted Thomas back in Washington as soon as possible. Shepherd also wanted Krulak to return to Headquarters immediately to begin planning the major reorganization of the Commandant's staff on clean general staff lines, and Krulak left the division on Thanksgiving Day. Thomas relished the opportunity to rejoin the battle for control of Headquarters. He and Krulak worked on a draft statement that Shepherd could use when he assumed office. Thomas urged Shepherd to act quickly before he lost the advantage of surprise, and he himself pondered his own role as chief of staff, especially another round of bureaucratic warfare with Quartermaster General William P. T. Hill.[54]

Before he could leave Korea, however, Thomas found himself commanding X Corps. Ridgway, without warning, had relieved a stunned, shaken Clovis E. Byers. Thomas and his corps commander still enjoyed a warm relationship, fused by their common desire to provide the corps better close air support. On 10 November, Byers had celebrated the Marine Corps Birthday at Thomas's CP, complete with Commandant's message, the traditional Lejeune birthday message, cake cutting, and an 11th Marines one-gun salute that fell on the North Koreans. Thomas visited Byers on 24 November to help host another party of VIPs that included Vice President Alben Barkley and Generals Ridgway and Van Fleet. Van Fleet used the occasion to tell the commanding general of the U.S. 7th Infantry Division and Byers that they would be replaced with two officers in greater favor with Collins and Ridgway, Major Generals Lyman L. Lemnitzer and Williston B. Palmer, both Europeanists. Ridgway told Byers he would come with him to Japan to take command of another corps, but his smooth delivery of the message of professional doom did not soothe Byers. Both Byers and Thomas concluded that the close air support issue had cost Byers dearly, although it is also likely that Collins and Ridgway had decided that Byers was at the limits of his usefulness. Because Palmer had to travel from Germany to join X Corps, Thomas might hold the corps command for three or four weeks. Leaving Bill Whaling as acting commander of the 1st Marine Division, Thomas, accompanied by only one aide, moved to corps headquarters on 28 November. As he assumed his new duties, Thomas was angry at the injustice visited on Byers, an officer whose professional competence Thomas respected.[55]

Although Thomas commanded X Corps only until Palmer's arrival on 5 December, he did not just sit around with Byers's gloomy staff to await the new commanding general. He visited all of the division commanders for operational briefings, and he even modified the corps orders for raids on Korean outposts. He discussed patrolling policies and ammunition expenditure limitations with Van Fleet. Nevertheless, he returned to the 1st Marine Division with pleasure. The rest of the month passed without a major crisis, and Thomas celebrated Christmas with Francis Cardinal Spellman, vicar of the American armed forces. He observed New Year's Day with another division one-shot salute on the NKPA. Thomas could hardly wait to turn over command to his relief and friend, Maj. Gen. John Taylor Selden, who arrived on 8 January. Thomas and Selden held a modest change of command ceremony three days later at the division CP. Departing Korea by plane in the middle of a winter storm, Thomas immediately started his journey back to the United States.

Thomas left Korea with his reputation as a combat field commander refurbished and extended; this would add moral authority to his struggles in Washington. Shepherd thought Thomas had clearly demonstrated his fitness for higher responsibility and promotion to lieutenant general. Despite their differences, Ridgway thanked him "for your conspicuously superior performance of combat command duty." An endorsement from Almond, who called him "the best Marine officer who has ever served under my command," might not win Thomas friends in the Corps, but more respected Army generals appreciated his force and professionalism. Van Fleet applauded his vigorous leadership, tactical skill, resourcefulness, ability to build moral aggressiveness, and administrative competence. Clovis Byers called Thomas a team player highly qualified for unified command but an officer who "carefully safeguarded the best interests of his division insofar as its traditional Marine Corps functions are concerned." Williston Palmer found all these traits and others: "I would be happy to serve under his command." Although he thanked Ridgway by message for his complimentary farewell remarks, Thomas turned his concentration from the Korean war to another campaign along the Potomac.[56]

[CHAPTER XXIV]

Reforming the Marine Corps

1952–1954

GERALD C. THOMAS returned for his third tour at Headquarters eager to assault all the unfinished business he had left behind in 1947 when he departed, exhausted, for his command in Tsingtao. His professional reputation assured by his command of the 1st Marine Division and his power at its peak through his intimate friendship with Commandant Lemuel C. Shepherd, Jr., Thomas arrived in Washington in mid-January 1952. He took a week's leave with his wife and daughters to visit South Carolina and then assumed his new post as Assistant Commandant and Chief of Staff, Headquarters U.S. Marine Corps, by the end of the month. After a routine nomination and review by the secretary of the navy and the president, Thomas became a lieutenant general on 8 March 1952. The promotion made him the fifth ranking general officer in the Marine Corps and second only to the Commandant in responsibility for managing the Corps' business throughout the world. His high office carried with it all the symbols of military authority: a suite of offices along the long north corridor on the second floor of the Navy Annex with direct access to the Commandant's offices in the building's northwest corner, a chauffeured limousine at his beck and call, and a home in spacious Quarters One within the compound of the Marine Barracks at 8th and I Streets.[1]

For the Thomas family, the general's promotion (which brought no increase in his $993 base pay) and comfortable living conditions could not stop the Korean War or halt the maturation of the Thomas children and their own pressing concerns. Virginia returned home from Bryn Mawr for a gala debutante party in December 1953. Tina Bruder waited in Florida for Joe to complete his own Korean tour. Before Joe left, Tina had given birth to the first of eleven Thomas grandchildren, a girl named Anne, on 2 April 1952 at Quantico. Jerry Junior, a second lieutenant serving with the 1st Battalion, 5th Marines, fell with multiple fragmentation wounds and left Korea in June 1952 for a short convalescence at

Bethesda Naval Hospital. The youngest Thomas son, Johnny, also fought his own battle against his father's plans for his education and development of character. Marched off to Mercersburg Academy in Pennsylvania at the age of almost fifteen, the free-spirited Johnny survived two and a half years of an academic regime he found uncongenial, then enlisted in the Marine Corps in April 1954. His father administered the oath. Whatever his dismay at Johnny's revolt, General Thomas himself remained a dutiful son, still sending money to and visiting his father in northwestern Virginia. During his tour as Assistant Commandant, the general also became an Episcopalian, and he and Lottie joined the congregation of St. John's Church at Washington's Lafayette Square.[2]

Although concerned about the happiness of his wife and children, Jerry Thomas embodied thirty-five years of Marine Corps discipline and focused his energy on a Corps again in transition, a process Thomas intended to manage in the name of Commandant Lemuel C. Shepherd. Shepherd and Thomas returned to Washington convinced that the Marine Corps had entered a new era in which it could enjoy relatively stable size, a clarity of mission, and a steady march toward greater combat readiness that would not be held hostage to the confusions of wartime expansion and wild swings of funding. For twelve years, the Marine Corps had gorged, starved, and again gorged in two wars and a five-year period of peacetime malnourishment. Because the Korean War had not yet ended (and would not until July 1953), the Marine Corps neared the zenith of its most recent expansion, which reached the strength of 261,343 active duty Marines in June 1953. The quality of officers and enlisted personnel always concerned Shepherd, but he recognized that this troop base could support the 1st Marine Division and 1st Marine Aircraft Wing in Korea and also provide adequate personnel for two more uncommitted divisions and aircraft wings. No doubt the Marine Corps would shrink when peace came, but he thought a personnel strength of 215,000 was likely for the rest of the decade.

Reflecting public acclaim for the combat record of the Marines in Korea, Congress passed the Douglas-Mansfield Act (introduced and debated throughout 1951) by an easy voice vote on 20 June 1952. Public Law 416 (82d Congress, 2d Session) dictated that the Marine Corps should provide no fewer than three divisions and three aircraft wings in the Fleet Marine Force. The Marine Corps, therefore, became the only service with its force structure written into Title 10, U.S. Code. Congress had debated whether it should also dictate the active-duty size of the Marine Corps with figures ranging from 300,000 to 400,000 personnel, but even Headquarters thought that a force of this size would prove too large for peacetime missions and traditional Marine Corps standards. In addition, Congress wanted the Commandant to participate in the Joint Chiefs of Staff formal decision-making process, with full statutory membership, an idea that distressed the other services. Instead, the Commandant could examine the JCS agenda, declare agenda items of interest to the Marine Corps, and then sit with the other chiefs when these items were reviewed. General Shepherd found this arrangement acceptable. He reported to his general officers that P.L. 416 and the Department of Defense (DOD) "Functions Paper" (Executive Order 9950) gave the Marine Corps as much legal authority as it was likely to receive. Without compromising its special amphibious capabilities, the Fleet Marine Force, along with other operating units, would stress combat readiness without mobilization while the Corps continued to pursue its doctrinal charge of research and development in landing operations. The Corps would especially work on the integration of ground combat and aviation forces, not just in amphibious operations but in land campaigns as well. Shepherd charged his senior leadership to provide the elite Marine Corps they had all promised the nation since World War II.[3]

From his own experience at Headquarters, Shepherd did not think the staff system he inherited in 1952 could provide him with the timely, expert advice the Commandant of the new Marine Corps would require. He had discussed the matter often with Thomas and Victor H. Krulak during their year together in FMF Pacific. When he knew he would be the next Commandant, Shepherd again reviewed the problems of Headquarters with Thomas and Krulak, who agreed completely that the Commandant required a real general staff, not just a fragmented, overworked Division of Plans and Policies. On his first working day as Commandant (2 January 1952), Shepherd, using a speech that Krulak and Thomas had written in Korea, announced that a major goal would be the reorganization of Headquarters Marine Corps. Gerald C. Thomas, whom Shepherd considered "an outstanding staff officer" and "a very close personal friend of mine," would serve as chief of staff in order to implement this plan. As Assistant Commandant, Thomas could also issue binding orders in Shepherd's name, and Shepherd trusted him implicitly. Neither Shepherd nor Thomas, however, believed that their relationship and formal powers would make the task easy.[4]

On his fifth day as Assistant Commandant and chief of staff, Jerry Thomas held the first of three conferences with the fifteen senior officers (eight generals, seven colonels) who bore the responsibility for making the reorganization of Headquarters work. Thomas found them cooperative and largely recovered from the shock of Shepherd's 2 January announcement that reform would be executed, not studied. He emphasized that the traditional "operating divisions" of Headquarters would continue to enjoy direct access to the Commandant and would execute policy free of general staff supervision. These agencies included the Division of Aviation, Supply (Quartermaster General's) Department, Personnel Division, Division of Reserve, Administrative Division, and Division of Information. In addition, Headquarters would create two new divisions; one of these, the Fiscal Division, also would be outside the general staff system. In theory, the only operating divisions left for the general staff to supervise were the Inspection Division, the Director of Women Marines, the Office of the Legislative Assistant, and the newly established Policy Analysis Division. As Assistant Commandant and chief of staff, of course, Thomas himself supervised the operating divisions in the name of the Commandant, but he promised that Shepherd would chair conferences of senior staff generals and deal with them directly as often as he could.

Convinced that Headquarters needed far more expert planning and much less frenetic executing, Thomas and Shepherd stressed that policy planning would henceforth rest in the hands of a reorganized Division of Plans and Policies, which would dissolve and reappear under the chief of staff, a deputy chief of staff (Maj. Gen. Walter W. Wensinger), and a secretary of the general staff (Col. Victor H. Krulak) as four functional divisions: G-1 (personnel), G-2 (intelligence), G-3 (operations and plans), and G-4 (logistics). All of the division heads would be

Headquarters Organization, 1952

- **HEADQUARTERS U.S. MARINE CORPS** / **COMMANDANT OF THE MARINE CORPS**
  - BOARDS
  - AIDES de CAMP
  - ASSISTANT COMMANDANT (AIR) (Concurrently Director, Division of Aviation)
    - OFFICE OF THE DIRECTOR OF WOMEN MARINES — DIRECTOR
    - OFFICE OF THE LEGISLATIVE ASSISTANT — LEGISLATIVE ASSISTANT
  - **CHIEF OF STAFF AND ASSISTANT COMMANDANT**
    - LIAISON FOR MARINE CORPS MATTERS WITH CHIEF OF NAVAL OPERATIONS (OP-09M)
    - OFFICE OF THE DEPUTY CHIEF OF STAFF — DEPUTY CHIEF OF STAFF
    - OFFICE OF THE SECRETARY OF THE GENERAL STAFF — SECRETARY OF THE GENERAL STAFF
    - G-1 DIVISION — ASSISTANT CHIEF OF STAFF G-1
    - G-2 DIVISION — ASSISTANT CHIEF OF STAFF G-2
    - G-3 DIVISION — ASSISTANT CHIEF OF STAFF G-3
    - G-4 DIVISION — ASSISTANT CHIEF OF STAFF G-4
    - ADMINISTRATIVE DIVISION — ADMINISTRATIVE OFFICER
    - FISCAL DIVISION — DIRECTOR
    - POLICY ANALYSIS DIVISION — DIRECTOR
    - DIVISION OF PUBLIC INFORMATION — DIRECTOR
    - DIVISION OF AVIATION — DIRECTOR
    - DIVISION OF RESERVE — DIRECTOR
    - INSPECTION DIVISION — INSPECTOR GENERAL
    - PERSONNEL DEPARTMENT — DIRECTOR
    - SUPPLY DEPARTMENT — QUARTERMASTER GENERAL

*Source: Headquarters Manual 1952

brigadier generals except the G-2, who would remain a colonel. This organizational scheme meant that all the staff sections of technical specialists that had proliferated in World War II would disappear. Supervision of the execution of policies—an issue that had bedeviled all earlier reform plans—would rest with the Commandant, Assistant Commandant, and the officers of the operating divisions, not members of the G divisions. As Thomas had observed in his studies of the War Department General Staff, the besetting sin of the general staff system was the compulsion of general staff officers to become "operators" in their messianic zeal to see their plans come to life. Thomas hoped the Headquarters staff officers could be educated to their "true" function of long-term policy planning and analysis. On the other hand, Thomas also intended to see that the operating divisions executed the approved G division plans and to use his personal office as the place where planning and execution would fuse.[5]

In most respects, the reorganization of Headquarters proceeded smoothly under Thomas's guidance and Krulak's relentless and omnipresent pressure. The changes did not lead to a swollen general staff; the 1,041 military personnel at Headquarters at the end of 1952 represented a decline of 200 Marines since 1950, but the force of 1,785 civilians had more than doubled. The four G division heads proved able and cooperative, in part because several of them were already Thomas protégés. The first G-1, Col. Thomas J. Colley, turned over his office in September to Brig. Gen. Nels H. Nelson, who served until 1955. Colonels F. R. Moore (February 1952–July 1953) and Wilbur J. McNenny (July 1953–1 August 1955), a Thomas friend from Peiping and I MAC, served as G-2s. The first G-3, Col. Eustace R. Smoak (February–March 1952), went off to Korea to command a regiment, and a strong Thomas colleague, Brig. Gen. Thomas A. Wornham, held the G-3 post until June 1955. Brig. Gen. Arthur H. "Tex" Butler became the G-4 on 20 February 1952 and remained in that post until July 1954. As he had in other assignments, Thomas demanded quality staff work, personal probity (especially on official trips), and military decorum. He did not associate long hours at Headquarters with completed staff action. The G divisions worked hard, but the officers believed that Thomas appreciated their efforts and used their plans.[6]

Maj. Gen. William P. T. Hill, Quartermaster General of the Marine Corps, still loomed as a colossus at Headquarters, and he saw no reason why he should surrender his considerable power to any other Marine officer, let alone the chief of staff or his representative. From his service as Director, Division of Plans and Policies, Thomas had felt Hill's bite before, and he did not underestimate Hill's strength, which had grown since their last battle in 1947. In fact, Hill combined three functions. He handled all the Corps' supply functions (less some aviation items, such as aircraft), all its disbursing functions, and all budgeting and accounting functions. His considerable legal powers, collected between 1944 and 1949, gave him the same degree of autonomy as the Navy's Chief of the Bureau of Supplies and Accounts, and he had borne the formal title of Fiscal Director of the Marine Corps since 1944. Blessed with a fabled memory for numbers (mostly attached to dollar signs) and Congressional contacts beyond accounting, Hill could not believe that Shepherd really wanted to divide the fiscal division from the Supply Department, which Shepherd announced in his 2 January speech to his staff. He and Shepherd had always enjoyed close and cordial relations, and indeed Shepherd held Hill's skills and dedication to the Corps in great esteem. He also saw that Hill's efficiency depended on Hill's skill alone, and he would someday have to retire. (Hill was not so sure.) Moreover, Shepherd thought that the Commandant needed an independent fiscal division to make budgeting more structured and accountability much more clear throughout the Marine Corps. Thomas and Krulak agreed, and so did Col. David M. Shoup, a former section head in the Division of Plans and Policies, who now commanded The Basic School.[7]

Thomas put together the plan to separate the Fiscal Division from the Supply Department and, perhaps, remove it from Hill's personal control. He persuaded Shepherd to appoint Shoup to produce a study of the organization of a fiscal division. When Shoup produced his report—predictably recommending a separate budgeting agency—in May 1952, Shepherd directed Hill to produce a plan for a separate fiscal division before 1 November 1952 with an implementation date of 1 January 1953. To see the plans through, Shepherd, to Hill's dismay, appointed Shoup deputy fiscal director in July 1952 and announced that he expected Shoup to become fiscal director a year later. In the meantime, Thomas advised the Commandant that the Quartermaster General should no longer have the power to issue "letters" in his own name but route his policy correspondence through the Commandant's office. Even Tex Butler, the G-4, did not see how Hill could function under these constraints and questioned the legality of curbing Hill's autonomy. Hill himself challenged Thomas's ruling on "letters," and Shepherd relented some on the point. But Hill saw the danger that he might lose more than the fiscal function. In the face of Hill's intransigence, Shoup pressed forward with his planning, which took the form of a special Headquarters manual on budgeting. Thomas had picked the right man for the fray, for he knew that Shoup was "stubborn" and "mean . . . mean as hell."[8] As Hill's hostility deepened, Shoup dealt directly with the Commandant through Thomas's office. In April 1953, Shepherd approved Shoup's budget manual without Hill's prior agreement. The Commandant announced that Shoup, newly selected to the rank of brigadier general, would coordinate the preparation of the fiscal year 1955 budget for Headquarters, even though Hill still held the legal responsibility for this task. Thomas immediately directed all staff departments and divisions to prepare their requests in accordance with the new manual and to submit them to Shoup for analysis and review. By September 1953, the Fiscal Division began its existence independent of the Supply Department.[9]

General Hill may have extracted some small revenge for the Thomas-Shoup victory in the dispute over the Marine Corps budget process. Close friend to Congressmen Carl Vinson and L. Mendel Rivers, Hill may have encouraged speculation in November 1953 that Shepherd might be removed as Commandant at the end of two years. Certainly, the Eisenhower administration, which did not reappoint any of the members of the JCS after it took office, wanted a new set of chiefs. Shepherd was not on the purge list, however; for Secretary of Defense Charles E. Wilson and his civilian deputies thought the Commandant an able and cooperative officer. When Wilson heard the rumor about Shepherd's removal in favor of Lt. Gen. Franklin A. Hart, he alerted the President and proposed that his office mount a campaign to discredit the rumor. Eisenhower found the rumor annoying: "I never heard of it—I'd never consider such a thing except on the recommendation of D.O.D." Wilson assured the press that General Shepherd retained his complete confidence.[10]

One of Thomas's duties was to serve as chief administrator at Headquarters, and he worked closely with the Administrative Division throughout his tour to streamline Marine Corps administration. He and Shepherd agreed that the Marine Corps showed all the signs of peacetime administrative arteriosclerosis, the clogging of its veins of communication with reams of paperwork. Thomas started his campaign for efficiency with a revision of the *Headquarters Manual*. Despite a bureaucratic row over the control of "electric accounting machines," the revised manual reached its users in late June 1952, and Thomas supervised subsequent annual revisions. He also initiated a Corps-wide study of the utility of the reports required by Headquarters after Shepherd's visits to the field commands. The Commandant had concluded that "an excessive portion of commanding officers' time" passed behind a desk doing paperwork. Although Thomas focused his attention on reducing the reporting requirements of Headquarters, he made scant progress. He urged division heads not to waste their clerks' time producing perfectly typed internal correspondence, but the compulsion for aesthetic perfection in naval letters lived on. In one administrative area, Thomas made no concessions and responded to every one of the one thousand congressional inquiries a month, most of which concerned questions about the release dates of Korean War enlisted Marines.[11]

Much of the torrent of reports and correspondence that besieged Headquarters focused on Marine Corps personnel problems. In 1952, the Corps faced a post–Korean War crisis easily identified by the assistant chief of staff (G-1) and the director of the Personnel Department. Coming on the heels of World War II and requiring the mobilization of Reserves and the promotion of sergeants to temporary officer status, the Korean War had re-created a surplus of officers from the ranks of general to lieutenant. The Commandant, however, wanted to make room in the career officer ranks for qualified Reservists and former NCOs, but such a policy required some relief from the provisions of the Officer Personnel Act of 1947. Another complexity was the fact that the Corps had acute shortages of officers with technical skills, who had a tendency not to be selected for promotion to lieutenant colonel because of their lack of formal military and civilian education and their shortage of command time. The problem, then, was to cull out the least fit officers for a peacetime Marine Corps, provide opportunities for others to remain on active duty, and reduce the officer corps from its wartime high of 19,536 (1953) to some lower figure. Although the Eisenhower administration provided legal relief through its powers under the Korean War declaration of national emergency (December 1950), this selective suspension of the Officer Personnel Act allowed officers to be retained, not separated, if they held regular commissions. Brought to Headquarters on temporary duty, Maj. Gen. Merrill B. Twining, still a trusted troubleshooter for Shepherd and Thomas, proposed a major revision of the promotion system so that senior officers of World War II vintage might be separated more rapidly. Bill Twining found that Shepherd and Thomas did not want to add promotion reform to their plate of travails. As a partial result of this decision, the Marine Corps entered the post–Korean War period with a field grade officer "hump" and almost as many officers (18,417 in 1955) as it had during the war.[12]

Another personnel problem for which Thomas had no magic cure involved the catastrophic turnover in the enlisted ranks as the Korean War ended. In 1953, largely through the use of two-year enlistees and draftees, the Marine Corps reached an enlisted strength of 241,343. In fiscal year 1954, however, this force would separate an estimated 116,000 enlisted personnel; this meant that 85 percent of the remaining enlisted Marines (including new recruits) would have less than three years' service. If temporary officers who were not integrated as regular officers chose not to return to NCO rank and wartime NCOs (especially Reservists and draftees) did not stay, the result would be an inexperienced enlisted force with too few leaders and technical specialists. The Fleet Marine Force still would be larger than that of 1946–50 but it would have less real capability in terms of training and morale. The Corps could hardly admit that it was unable to supply personnel for three divisions and aircraft wings after the passage of P.L. 416, and it required a major training effort and redeployment to bases that could support such training.[13]

The general problems of the Marine officer corps especially concerned Thomas when he examined the future of Marine Corps aviation, and he made a special effort to avoid controversy with the senior air officers. Thomas's principal goal was to encourage Marine aviators to accept a future aviation force that would be balanced between fixed-wing aircraft (especially jet fighter-attack planes) and helicopters. He supported with enthusiasm the appointment of Maj. Gen. William O. Brice, his former deputy in the Division of Plans and Policies, as deputy chief of staff for aviation. Thomas then successfully lobbied to have Brice's position formally designated Assistant Commandant (Air) and raised to the rank of lieutenant general. Thomas dealt with Brice as an equal and did not challenge his direct access to the Commandant. Although Thomas and Krulak regarded the aviation officers as oblivious to Marine Corps-wide issues of doctrine and training, they accepted the political reality that naval aviators now ran the Navy and gave Marine aviators important levels of power on aviation issues. On the other hand, Brice also respected Thomas and recognized that "Jerry Thomas was running the Marine Corps more or less."[14] Thomas, Brice, and Krulak attempted to bring Marine aviation planning and planners into the general staff structure and to ensure that Marine aircraft procurement programs that emerged as a component part of the Navy's plans did not distort Marine Corps personnel and logistics planning, a perennial problem for the Corps. Their work, however, brought protests from the aviation community that Headquarters paid no attention to the opinion of senior air officers.[15]

The fate of Col. Frank H. Schwable made it difficult for Thomas to work with complete trust with Marine aviators. Schwable was a Marine Corps "junior," a distinguished World War II pilot who had pioneered in creating the first Marine night fighter squadron and a thorough professional. He became chief of staff of the 1st Marine Aircraft Wing in May 1952 and then fell into Communist hands on 8 July 1952 when he was shot down by flak. Identified by his uniform and personal papers as a Marine colonel (and the senior Marine captured in the Korean war), Schwable found himself in solitary confinement until his release on 6 September 1953. Communist interrogators gave him special attention. Schwable was constantly sick with dysentery, subjected to long hours of interrogation, malnourished, denied medical treatment, and forced to squat in a small unheated cage. He feared that he would have a nervous breakdown and provide important information to the Communists, who knew he was the wing chief of staff (from information published in American newspapers) but did not know that he had been a nuclear war planner in an earlier tour. After five months of depressing confinement, Schwable "confessed" on camera and tape that he had participated in germ warfare, an obsession with Chinese propagandists. Schwable hoped that the patently false admission would be recognized as such in the United States and that the interrogators, presented with such a prize, would reduce their efforts to extract real information from him. (Schwable, in fact, guessed correctly.) On his return to American control, however, Schwable found himself under investigation for criminal collaboration with the enemy, which enraged him. He came to Headquarters to a meaningless job while Shepherd examined his case.[16]

Although the Commandant took great pride in the dogged resistance of Marine prisoners of war (194 of 221 captured Marines survived), Shepherd wanted Schwable prosecuted and turned the case over to Thomas to manage. Shepherd found this decision painful because he knew Schwable and his wife and their families, but he wanted to make a point with Marine aviators that they were part of the Marine Corps in every respect. He also wanted to avoid any suggestion of toleration of POW collaboration, a public issue of much heat during 1953 and 1954. In early 1954, however, a naval court of inquiry reported to the Commandant that prosecuting Schwable for collaboration did not look sound on legal grounds. The Uniform Code of Military Justice (Article 104) did not specifically state that Schwable could be tried for providing *false* information to the enemy, and the judge advocates thought that Schwable's postrelease interrogation by intelligence officers amounted to self-incrimination and thus tainted the evidence. Other than Schwable's own admissions and a Chinese propaganda film and voice recording, there was no other evidence, and the court of inquiry reported that Schwable had been subjected to intense stress before "confessing." It recommended no prosecution. Shepherd, however, wanted Schwable disciplined in some way, and he directed Thomas to arrange for an entry in Schwable's records that his conduct as a POW had compromised his utility to the Corps and that he should receive no important assignments, including command. Schwable blamed Twining and Krulak for his internal exile, not Shepherd or Thomas, but other aviators believed Thomas had arranged Schwable's insignificant assignments until his retirement in 1959. Thomas did nothing to shift responsibility to Shepherd.[17]

Thomas also managed another delicate assignment he received from the Commandant, the completion and placement of the Marine Corps War Memorial in Washington to honor all Marines who had served and died in America's wars. The subject was heroic—a 100-ton bronze statue by Felix de Weldon of Joe Rosenthal's photograph of five Marines and one corpsman raising the American flag on Mount Suribachi, Iwo Jima. The intent could not have been more noble, but the funding proved uncertain. When Thomas and Krulak confirmed that Shepherd had promised Gen. Clifton B. Cates that he would see the project through, they also learned that the Marine Corps had a projected and unpledged debt of at least $500,000 for the monument and that the Department of Interior had not yet granted a site for the memorial. The first challenge was to revive the scandal-plagued committee that was supposed to be mounting the project as a private effort. Thomas enlisted his old comrade, Merritt A. Edson, to chair the group. Edson's organization served as the official voice and banker for the project, but Thomas knew that he would have to solicit money from the only people who could provide money now, active-duty Marines. Aware that asking the troops to donate to a private cause risked unwelcome publicity and potential legal action against the Corps, Thomas quietly used the chain of command to collect a first installment of $250,000 to keep the project alive. He and Edson then negotiated a site on a knoll north of Arlington National Cemetery and conducted a second solicitation for another $250,000 to complete the work, even though all the bills were not paid. Eventually, individual Marines contributed $800,000 to the project. On 10 November 1954, the memorial, popularly known as the Iwo Jima monument, took its place among the most visited of Washington sites.[18]

From his office on the second floor of Headquarters, Jerry Thomas could see the gravestones along the wooded slope of Arlington National Cemetery's southwest corner. His view did not include another more relevant symbol of life, death, and rebirth for the Marine Corps. The Pentagon, erected on a Potomac swamp about a mile from the Navy Annex, was the burial yard of service hopes and fears. During his tenure as Assistant Commandant and Chief of Staff, Headquarters U.S. Marine Corps, Thomas played a major role in preventing a quartet of potential gravediggers—Secretary of Defense, Chairman of the Joint Chiefs of Staff, Secretary of the Navy, and Chief of Naval Operations—from shoveling the dirt of disapproval over the corpse of Marine Corps plans and programs. Thomas proved that he had lost none of the deftness he had shown in service politics from 1944 through 1947. He and the Commandant, no mean operator himself, proved a potent team in ensuring that the Marine Corps would not pass through another ordeal like the one it had barely survived after World War II.

The key to the political challenge that the Corps faced, as Shepherd and Thomas saw it, remained the Commandant's authority to command the Marine Corps as the head of a separate service with a unique mission. When Congress passed the Douglas-Mansfield Act (P.L. 416) in 1952, Shepherd believed that the Corps now had about all the legislative protection it needed. In fact, he and Thomas did not have to intervene in the legislative process upon taking office because the pro-Marine congressional leaders who backed the law had the issue well in hand. They did not restrain some of the officers who remained from "Chowder" from cultivating the media, veterans organizations, and pro-Marine lobbyists, but they did not have to do much more than express their personal satisfaction with the compromise bill. When P.L. 416 became effective in the summer of 1952, Shepherd and Thomas agreed that the time had come to consolidate the political victory with restraint and caution. They wanted to make the Marine Corps capable of performing its functions, rather than gloat over its success or alienate the civilian and military leaders with whom the Corps shared the challenge of preparing the armed forces for a period of extended Cold War.[19]

When Shepherd raised the issue of his right to attend JCS meetings with the chairman, Gen. Omar N. Bradley, he learned that Bradley (an opponent of P.L. 416) would accept the verdict of Congress and do nothing to obstruct Shepherd's participation under the law. As long as Bradley remained JCS chairman (until August 1953), Shepherd or Thomas, serving as the Commandant's deputy, attended few JCS meetings. They did nothing to change the Marine Corps representation on the Joint Staff or the JCS secretariat, 12 of 250 officers. When Adm. Arthur W. Radford replaced Bradley as Eisenhower's chairman, Shepherd continued to proceed with caution in designating agenda items of Marine Corps interest. He also did not join the other chiefs at the huge oblong table in "The Tank" (the JCS conference room in the Pentagon) but sat at a separate table; he left when the chiefs turned to items he had not declared of Marine Corps interest. Thomas followed the same practice when he represented the Commandant as a stand-in or in meetings of the chiefs' operational deputies. Thomas told a Marine captain detailed as Bradley's aide that Shepherd wanted no conflict with the JCS. A close friend of Shepherd's and valued co-manager of the Korean War from their days as CinCPac and Commanding General, Fleet Marine Force Pacific (CG FMF Pac), Admiral Radford insisted that the Commandant remain in the room for all JCS discussions and directed Shepherd to offer his advice when appropriate. The Commandant, however, remained circumspect and seldom offered his opinion on matters of no direct interest to the Corps. Between June 1952 and December 1956, the Commandant identified only 1,306 of 4,369 agenda items as being of Marine Corps interest and actually discussed only 918 items of interest during the course of 516 meetings. Shepherd attended only about one-fourth of Bradley's JCS deliberations; even with Radford's encouragement, he and his successor, Randolph McC. Pate, participated in less than one-half of the agenda items. Whether the other chiefs appreciated such restraint is uncertain, but Shepherd and Thomas believed they avoided another round of interservice acrimony.[20]

Shepherd and Thomas dealt with JCS matters with restraint, in part, because they had a bigger battle to win within the Navy Department, a running conflict with the chief of naval operations regarding his influence over Headquarters Marine Corps. The villain was P.L. 432, 1947 legislation relating to naval administration, that gave the CNO unprecedented authority over the Navy Department bureaus and other support agencies. Adm. Forrest P. Sherman, despite a 1947 agreement to exempt the Marine Corps from the CNO's powers, tried to run the Corps during his 1949–51 tenure as CNO, but his successor, William M. Fechteler, dropped the battle. In August 1953, Adm. Robert B. Carney replaced Fechteler as Eisenhower's CNO and immediately insisted that P.L. 432 gave him administrative authority over the Marine Corps. The entire Department of Defense was in the usual upheaval that follows a presidential inauguration, complemented this time by a major reorganization of the Office of the Secretary of Defense (OSD), and Carney pressed new Secretary of the Navy Robert B. Anderson to apply P.L. 432 to the Marine Corps. A lawyer and businessman from Texas and an experienced public servant, Anderson took no position until he studied the issue, which Shepherd urged him to do. Because the Navy Department had to match its organization with new agencies in OSD, Anderson convened a board headed by Undersecretary of the Navy Thomas S. Gates, Jr., an investment banker and former naval officer of talents comparable to Anderson's. Gates convened his committee of eight in October 1953. The Marine Corps representative was Lt. Gen. Gerald C. Thomas.[21]

Through six months of meetings, the review of management studies, and the testimony of fifty administrators, Thomas pursued a single goal: the revision of Navy Department General Order (GO) No. 5. The version then in effect, published by Anderson in June 1953, still bore the taint of P.L. 432. An aggressive CNO like "Mick" Carney might be able to persuade an inexperienced secretary like Bob Anderson that Congress meant for the CNO to be the single authoritative voice of the naval services on matters of departmental administration, including programming and budgeting. Shepherd and Thomas did not think that the definitions of authority, responsibility, and functions of the Commandant and CNO in GO 5 adequately reflected the intent of P.L. 416 and the National Security Act of 1947. They believed that these laws gave the Commandant of the Marine Corps equal status with the chief of naval operations as chief of service in all matters affecting the management of the Marine Corps within the Department of the Navy. As the Gates Board conducted its investigation, Thomas cultivated his fellow members and won four of them to the Marine Corps position on GO 5. One morning in early 1954, Gates announced that it was now clear that one serious organizational problem had emerged from the hearings: the relationship between the chief of naval operations and the Commandant. No witness had addressed the problem, but it existed. Gates asked Thomas what he thought, and Thomas replied that CNO-CMC relations "were no worse than they had been for some years."[22] Gates wanted to discuss the matter with Anderson before the board continued its work. At Gates's suggestion, Anderson called Carney and Shepherd to his office and instructed them to provide him with their personal positions on their relationship under GO 5. He also asked the Judge Advocate General of the Navy to provide him with copies of all the legislation, executive orders, and court decisions that bore on the issue. He immediately began his own study of the question.[23]

Within a week Anderson wrote a memorandum on his interpretation of GO 5 that followed the Marine Corps position and ordered Gates to publish it as authoritative guidance until a new version of GO 5 could be written. He directed Carney and Shepherd to appoint one officer each to revise GO 5. Carney selected Rear Adm. Ruthven E. Libby, a member of the Gates Board, and the Commandant chose Col. Victor H. Krulak. When Gates published the Anderson memorandum, he himself signed it, but Thomas persuaded Shepherd that Anderson should at least initial the memorandum. The Commandant hand-carried his copy to Secretary Anderson, who did initial it. Libby, who championed the P.L. 432 position, and Krulak labored off and on for more than a year on the revision of GO 5. Thomas and Krulak knew exactly the wording they wanted, but Libby was probably playing for time in the hope that he and Carney would outlast Anderson and Gates. They almost succeeded in blunting the Marine Corps attack. In March 1954, Anderson became deputy secretary of defense. Charles S. Thomas, an assistant secretary of defense and former protégé of James V. Forrestal, succeeded Anderson as secretary of the navy. When both the Navy and Marine Corps pressed the new secretary to take a position on GO 5, he wisely turned to

Congressman Carl Vinson for advice. Vinson told Thomas that GO 5 should draw its inspiration from P.L. 416, not P.L. 432. Congress had intended for the CNO to have greater authority within the Navy, but it wanted the secretary of the navy and the Commandant to run the Marine Corps. On 20 November 1954, the secretary of the navy published the new GO 5:

> The Commandant of the Marine Corps is the senior officer of the Marine Corps. He commands the Marine Corps and is directly responsible to the Secretary of the Navy for its administration, discipline, internal organization, unit training, requirements, efficiency, and readiness, and for the total performance of the Marine Corps.[24]

In the meantime, Thomas completed his work on the Gates Board, which issued its final report in April 1954. The report described the role of the Commandant with the same language later inserted in the new version of GO 5. It also reported that the Anderson memorandum had already clarified the CNO-CMC relationship. In addition to recommending revision of GO 5, the Gates Board thought that GO 19, which determined the relationship of shore-based support activities with each other and the operating forces, also needed clarification. Bill Twining, who had become deputy chief of staff at Headquarters in January 1954, thought that Headquarters should also press for a revision of GO 10, which outlined fiscal relationships within the Navy Department. But Shepherd, Thomas, and Krulak decided to take the victory on GO 5 and let the other issues ride. They thought the time had come to pause in the struggle to enhance the Commandant's power.[25]

The battles at the Pentagon exacted their toll on Thomas. Although his health remained good, he occasionally showed the strain of work. Late one afternoon, he returned from another interminable meeting at the Pentagon, walked past his secretary and staff without a word, and slammed the door of his office behind him. Finally, one of his officers entered Thomas's office with appropriate stealth to recover a memorandum that required a signature that day. As the officer reached for the "Out" basket, Thomas looked up and to no one in particular loudly said: "Damn . . . Damn! There is *nothing* more frightening than a *new* idea!"[26] If he had trouble persuading the Headquarters staff or the Department of Defense bureaucracy to examine change, Jerry Thomas had every intention to force the rest of the Marine Corps to meet the intellectual challenge of a new era in defense policy.

Even though the Korean War dragged on for the first eighteen months of his service at Headquarters, Gerald C. Thomas looked well beyond the conflict and the immediate problems of sustaining the war effort of Fleet Marine Force Pacific. He and the Commandant (and their most trusted associates) tried to reshape the entire Fleet Marine Force for the years of recurring crises they saw ahead for the United States in its relations with the Soviet Union, Communist China, and their Marxist-Leninist surrogates. Although Asia provided two hot wars (Korea and Indochina), the first strategic priority remained Europe and the strength of NATO's military forces. As the amphibious force for the Atlantic Fleet (2d and 6th Fleets), the division and aircraft wing of Fleet Marine Force Atlantic were well established. The major change to support European and Middle Eastern contingencies came in 1952 with the creation of the massive Marine Corps Supply Center in Albany, Georgia. The status of Fleet Marine Force Pacific was more complex because the strategic situation was more complicated. Before the end of the Korean War, General Shepherd moved the new 3d Marine Aircraft Wing from Florida to the base at El Toro, California, and, in August 1953, deployed the new 3d Marine Division from Camp Pendleton to camps near Mount Fuji, Japan. The Navy wanted FMF Pac to remain deployed forward of the United States, but Shepherd insisted that he could not maintain a ready force unless he used California as a major training area. He added a desert warfare training center (Twentynine Palms) and a mountain warfare training center (Bridgeport) to Camp Pendleton as sites for tactical exercises and live firing. After its withdrawal from Korea in 1955, the 1st Division returned to Camp Pendleton. The 3d Division established permanent residences on Okinawa (still under American administration) and Hawaii, with the 1st Marine Aircraft Wing split among bases on mainland Japan, Okinawa, and Hawaii.[27]

With this reorganization of the Fleet Marine Force already under way, the Marine Corps faced the challenge of adjusting to a new administration and a Congress seized by the irresistible urge to cut defense spending even before the Korean War ended. Although the Eisenhower administration had not yet produced its own strategic design, it reduced the military requests for fiscal year 1954 (which assumed no war) from $42 billion to $36 billion. In July 1953, Congress authorized only $34.3 billion for military spending; a little more than $1 billion would go to the Marine Corps. Four months later, the Eisenhower administration attempted to rationalize future budget cutting with a national security policy, labeled the "New Look" and sanctified on 30 October 1953 in National Security Council (NSC) Memorandum 162/2. The essence of NSC 162/2 rested on the assumption that the United States would base its security on strategic nuclear deterrence; forward collective security with allies that girdled the Eurasian land mass; limited deployment of naval, air, and ground forces in support of its alliances; and early use of tactical nuclear weapons anywhere that deterrence failed. The major challenge the Soviet Union now posed was not war but the erosion of American economic strength in a prolonged arms race, complemented by the subversive effect on American political will that distant "foreign wars" like Korea would bring. The Eisenhower Administration wanted to create a defense posture that would provide adequate deterrence "for the long haul."[28]

General Shepherd accepted the vision of the "New Look." He saw a future of nuclear stalemate, for " . . . total war is completely outside the realm of national policy." Instead, the United States faced the challenge of "war by proxy, war by satellite, war by threat and subversion." Only by the exploitation of a maritime strategy could the United States make forward, collective defense work. The "New Look," however, posed serious problems of internal organization for the Fleet Marine Force. First, the Corps had to create a minimal tactical nuclear capability to fulfill its "force-in-readiness" mission, but this requirement, whether the nuclear weapons came from aircraft or ground-based artillery or rockets, limited strategic mobility. Shepherd and Thomas already agreed that the FMF had more weight than fight, and they sought new ways to squeeze more combat capability from the operating forces. A second problem stemmed from the fact that any major reduction in total Corps personnel, another feature of the "New Look," would make it difficult to maintain Headquarters' goal for field personnel. It wanted a minimum of 60 percent of all Marines in the FMF and other field operational units, such as ships guards and security detachments. Last, the functional specialty of the amphibious assault required review. The Commandant recognized that the FMF did not have a nuclear-age amphibious capability requiring helicopter-borne forces and a new generation of fast amphibious shipping and landing craft and amphibian vehicles. The margin for miscalculation in long-range force planning and doctrinal development shrank with the size of the challenges.[29]

Dissatisfied with the existing structure for producing basic conceptual studies, Thomas convinced Shepherd to create a special "think tank" at Quantico. Thomas, in turn, took his cue from his longtime protégé, Lt. Col. James C. Murray, and his own conclusion that the Landing Force Development Center and the Joint Landing Force Board (established in 1951) would not, or could not, escape their bureaucratic inertia. In January 1953, Shepherd announced that he would sponsor a "special" year of "additional" study for ten junior colonels and senior lieutenant colonels, who would assemble at the Marine Corps Schools for the equivalent of a year of senior service school education. Nominally, this Advanced Research Group (ARG) fell under the supervision of the Commandant Marine Corps Schools, but the group would receive its instructions and make its reports directly to the Commandant through the Chief of Staff, Headquarters Marine Corps. The first set of officers assigned to the ARG (dubbed the "Double Dome School" by its detractors) reflected a strong Thomas preference for officers with a bent toward doctrinal risk taking and proven personal loyalty: Thomas J. Colley, John P. Condon, August Larson, Joseph N. Renner, Carson A. Roberts, Samuel R. Shaw, George R. E. Shell, Eustace R. Smoak, William J. Van Ryzin, and Richard G. Weede. The Commandant assigned the ARG three major study areas, but he and Thomas gave primary emphasis to Project I: "Develop a concept of future amphibious operations that will require maximum utilization of the Fleet Marine Force as a mobile force in readiness."[30]

Although the Advanced Research Group studied the structure of the FMF ground forces and the organization of Headquarters Marine Corps and the Navy Department, it put its intellectual energy into Project I and Project IV, an additional study of its own choosing on future helicopter development and utilization. The colonels knew just what results Thomas wanted from their deliberations. In the spring of 1954, the ARG produced its Project I report, complemented by its Project IV report. It concluded that the future of the Fleet Marine Force depended on developing the ability to mount future amphibious operations (at least the initial assault phase) entirely by helicopters. It envisioned a division force beachhead area in such operations that might be as deep as one hundred miles and as wide as fifty miles. The fire support for these operations would have to come from fighter-attack aircraft and helicopter-borne artillery, not naval gunfire. The operations would also require the Marine Corps to give first developmental priority to the Sikorsky HR2S. This new helicopter might carry as much as four times the payload of the currently operational HRS, the same helo that Thomas and Krulak had used with such imagination in Korea in 1951. To Thomas's satisfaction,

General Shepherd endorsed the concept of the all-helicopter amphibious assault in April 1954 and announced that all future FMF planning, force structure changes, and amphibious training would stress helicopter operations. The decision was the most important change in Marine Corps doctrine since Commandant John A. Lejeune endorsed the concept of the waterborne amphibious assault in 1921.[31]

In addition to the lack of Navy approval of the concept (which did not come until December 1955) and the active skepticism of the Army and Air Force, the champions of vertical envelopment—with General Thomas in the first rank—faced considerable resistance within the Marine Corps. The aviation community, lead by General Brice, did not want helicopter development to distort its plans for aircraft modernization, including the adoption of aircraft with nuclear capability. Thomas's critics believed that his position on vertical envelopment reflected his hostility to the growing influence of artillery officers in the inner core of Marine senior leadership. A shift to helicopter-capable ground combat forces only exacerbated the raging debate over the organization of infantry crew-served weapons units and the creation of four-battalion infantry regiments. Thomas, for example, wanted the new infantry tables of organization to reflect a new emphasis on mobility. Lieutenant Generals Clifton B. Cates, Franklin A. Hart, and O. P. Smith, however, did not want to abolish the infantry battalion weapons company, and their support for the four-battalion regiment was lukewarm at best. Thomas reported to Shepherd that these officers represented thoughtless reaction.[32] Thomas knew that the vertical envelopment concept had only worsened a dispute about whether Marine aviators should command integrated air-ground tactical units. He and the Commandant also cautioned other Marine generals that they should not discuss the new concepts of divisional organization by comparing Marine Corps divisions with Army infantry divisions, which had different functions. To push the Marine Corps into an uncertain future required a high order of determination and conviction, characteristics that Jerry Thomas had in abundance and demonstrated almost every day at Headquarters.[33]

In the face of internal opposition, Shepherd and Thomas pressed forward with their plans to adapt the Fleet Marine Force to the "New Look." Through their participation in the Joint Chiefs of Staff planning process, they arranged for Marines to participate in the testing of tactical nuclear weapons in the Desert Rock exercises at Yucca Flats, Nevada. The first Marine troop participation in May 1952 consisted simply of providing two thousand infantrymen to occupy trenches in the blast area; the purpose of these tests was to judge the adequacy of protective measures and radiation monitoring. For Desert Rock IV (July 1954), Headquarters created a special regimental-sized task force, supported by two helicopter squadrons, that could actually conduct tactical exercises on a nuclear battlefield. This force, designated Marine Corps Test Unit No. 1, had the special mission of determining how helicopter-borne forces could operate effectively without succumbing to blast overpressures and residual radiation. Participation in the Desert Rock exercises did not exhaust the interest of Headquarters in a more demanding and centrally controlled exercise schedule. Again at Thomas's urging, Headquarters initiated a series of annual Corps-wide mobilization and deployment tests named Marex. Organized as global command post exercises, Marex began in 1952 and required major Marine commands to test their plans to respond to contingencies in Korea, Iran, Iraq, the Philippines, and Guatemala. The first Marex in 1952 assumed that the 3d Marine Division would deploy to Korea; when the Joint Chiefs of Staff asked the Commandant in 1953 how long it would take to send the division to Japan, he answered with confidence (based on Marex I) that he could assemble the forces—if the Navy could provide shipping—in ten days. Rather than wait for the U.S. Army to provide a division in months, the JCS gave Shepherd an "execute," and the 3d Marine Division headed for the Far East, where it remained into the 1990s. The tests provided critical data on the ability of the FMF to respond to crises.[34]

On 11 January 1954, Commandant Lemuel C. Shepherd, Jr., held his third New Year's review of the state of the Marine Corps for his staff. Although he did not minimize the problems foreseen for the years ahead, he told his staff that he and they could look back with enormous pride on the accomplishments of the past two years. He believed that the Marine Corps had made the transition from the Korean war service to an organization committed to purposeful change appropriate to the assumptions of the "New Look." Nevertheless, the Corps' leaders must press ahead with his plans to reshape the Fleet Marine Force. "There is no doubt that we are in a period of change—of rapid change—and we must not be caught asleep. Too often, in times such as these, the cold hand of reaction is mistaken for sound reasoning or mature conservatism. We cannot afford to run with the pack. If we are to survive, we must be ahead." The words reflected the views of the next ranking officer in the room, Lt. Gen. Gerald C. Thomas.[35]

Commandants of the Marine Corps sow and reap in two cycles. If they want to reshape the Corps, they tend to act quickly. They know that the element of surprise will confound their opponents, who need time to wear down a Commandant with an antireform coalition or to produce an alternative vision (and different leadership) that challenges the Commandant's power. If an incumbent Commandant wants to ensure some continuity in his reforms, he thus faces the task of reassigning his senior general officers to billets that both suit their abilities (and his preferences) and offer some hope that his reforms will prevail during the last two years of his term and, perhaps, beyond. The process is complicated by the fact that he has limited power to choose his major generals, who, by law, are the only pool he can tap for lieutenant generals (and now one general to serve as Assistant Commandant), his principal subordinates at Headquarters and in the field. Major generals are chosen by a promotion board, and even the most powerful Commandant cannot dictate a promotion board's selections. Moreover, senior generals have their own agendas and problems that often include ill health, family considerations, retirement plans, a strong preference not to change station (usually to Washington), and skepticism that they can work effectively with the incumbent Commandant and his staff. The mid-tour reassignments are further complicated by the Commandant's desires to position his favorite or favorites to be the next Commandant and to remove those officers he wants to eliminate from consideration as his successor.

Shepherd faced an additional problem. The Korean war emergency had brought a suspension of voluntary retirements, and this executive order did not expire until early in 1954. Therefore, lieutenant generals and major generals had to serve until they reached the mandatory retirement age of sixty-two, regardless of the Commandant's preferences. Of the five lieutenant generals, Clifton B. Cates had already served four long years as Commandant, and he applied for retirement as soon as he could in 1954. Franklin A. Hart and O. P. Smith, the next senior generals, were both too old to complete a term as Commandant, even if Shepherd supported their candidacies, which he did not. That left Jerry Thomas as next senior general. Shepherd talked about his successor with Thomas. He even said he would like Thomas to be Commandant, but Thomas had the same problem as Hart and Smith. He would turn sixty-two before he could complete a tour of his own in 1960. He also believed that he had outlived his usefulness at Headquarters after two years. He himself had considered retirement in 1954, rather than serve until his sixty-second birthday on 29 October 1956.

The Commandant's immediate problem concerned finding a replacement for Cates as Commandant Marine Corps Schools, and he convinced Thomas that he could help the Shepherd reform program through his command at Quantico. Given Thomas's love of Quantico and his strong attraction to the role of teacher-mentor, one doubts that Thomas required much arm-twisting. He was a natural for the assignment. Moreover, if Thomas held the Quantico post until 1956—and the end of Shepherd's tour—the Commandant did not have to create a Commandant candidate in the lieutenant general's post at Quantico. Instead, he could appoint a new Assistant Commandant and chief of staff from among the senior major generals, and this officer would have valuable Washington exposure before a new Commandant would be chosen in 1955. Shepherd nominated Maj. Gen. Randolph McCall Pate, a fellow VMI graduate and commander of the 1st Marine Division, for Thomas's post. Pleased that he would finish his career as the schoolmaster of the Marine Corps, Jerry Thomas prepared to leave Headquarters—the vale of tears—and move to Quantico and his last assignment in June 1954.[36]

[CHAPTER XXV]

The Last Tour
1954–1955

THE HUMID WIND blowing off the Potomac River whipped the red and gold flags that marked the units drawn up on the runway of the Marine Corps Air Station, Quantico. Five thousand men and women in khaki summer service uniforms faced the stand of spectators and the handful of senior officers gathered to review them. The parade, held on 30 June 1954, honored the retirement of a Marine Corps giant, Gen. Clifton B. Cates, a former Commandant and the current Quantico commander. Standing with Cates to receive the honors of the passing troops, who swept by the reviewing stand in 30-inch strides, Lemuel C. Shepherd, Jr., and Gerald C. Thomas knew that they, too, would leave active service in another eighteen months. As Jerry Thomas heard Cates's retirement and final promotion orders read, he probably thought of how much he wanted to do at Quantico and how little time he had to do it. He had no intention of taking up his last command without moving the Marine Corps Schools into the postwar era of enhanced professionalism and operational readiness.[1]

The base at Quantico to which Jerry Thomas returned—for the fourth and last time—little resembled the camp of raw barracks and muddy streets that he found in 1917. The original 5,300 acres between U.S. 1 and the Potomac River had exploded in World War II with the addition of 51,000 acres (the Guadalcanal Area) west of the highway. Much of the permanent construction of large buildings and warehouses of red brick and officers quarters of white wood was on Mainside, but the enlarged base offered many possibilities for building more ranges and training areas and dispersing the crowded organizations strung out along the river westward to the Guadalcanal Area. Although construction had slowed during the 1950s, the Marine Corps Schools had just added Earl H. Ellis Hall, a special building for amphibious warfare training in miniature scale, to James C. Breckinridge Hall, the home of the library and the Senior School. The Junior School had just moved into new quarters in Roy Geiger Hall located on a hill north of

Mainside between the U.S. Naval Hospital and the post golf course and an enlisted housing area. When Thomas assumed command, another classroom building for the Communications Officers School had entered construction above the riverbank north of Ellis-Breckinridge halls. With all aviation activities now transferred to Turner Field (Marine Corps Air Station, Quantico), the landfill north of Chopawamsic Creek, the old air station at Brown Field had been converted for the use of The Basic School, which not only trained new second lieutenants but also ran the various officer candidate programs that the Marine Corps offered young men and women.[2]

In some ways, life at Quantico still reflected the more stately life of the prewar Marine Corps. The base maintained an active intermural athletic program. It fielded a football team that played other service teams and several universities, a special delight for a football fan like Jerry Thomas, who gloried in his role as de facto "owner" of the Quantico Marines. Marines could fish, hunt, sail, golf, and even ride aboard the base. The Marine Corps preserved a stable at Quantico under the delightful subterfuge that it needed to teach lieutenants the fine art of mule packing, instruction continued as late as 1960. By Marine Corps standards, base housing—apartments, duplexes, and single homes—provided families with living conditions superior to those on boomtown Fleet Marine Force bases like Camp Lejeune and Camp Pendleton. The Marines of the largest permanent organizations at Quantico, including Headquarters Battalion, Service Battalion, the Schools Demonstration Troops, the Air Station, and the school support troops of the Education Center, tended to be older, to hold higher rank, and to have more technical skills than their FMF comrades, and they caused fewer disciplinary problems. As one prewar Marine general once said to Thomas, Quantico would be a perfect post if it were not for all the students.

Unlike his predecessors, Thomas took command with the intention of running the schools, not enjoying the base. He assigned his chief of staff, Col. Donald McP. Weller, all routine housekeeping tasks that came with the assignment. He himself, with General Shepherd's enthusiastic support, served as the mentor and chief instructor for the students who came under his control, for he had strong ideas about what they needed to learn and how they should learn it.[3]

Day in and day out—there were few days when he was on post that he did not rove—Jerry Thomas visited the classrooms and auditoriums of Breckinridge and Geiger halls to sample the instruction of the Senior and Junior schools. In addition to the majesty that accompanies the rank of lieutenant general at Quantico, he enjoyed close personal relations with his major school directors. During most of Thomas's tour, Brig. Gen. Robert O. Bare was director of the Education Center. Col. Herman Nickerson, Jr., his favorite Korean regimental commander, ran the Senior School for colonels and lieutenant colonels, and Col. Max J. Volcansek, an aviator, directed the Junior School, another curriculum in amphibious operations designed for majors and captains. Twice an instructor and five times a student, Jerry Thomas relished his role as leader of the Marine Corps Schools. Although he did not demand a curriculum revision of the two advanced schools, a temptation few senior Marine officers can resist, he insisted that the faculty include more military history in the instruction (Thomas found virtually none) and stress broad operational concepts based on that history rather than technical details and the rote teaching of staff planning methods. Thomas resurrected his old Gallipoli presentation (actually he couldn't find his own notes in the archives, so he relied on a later version prepared by Col. Arthur T. Mason) and presented five hours of lectures over a two-day period on one of his favorite subjects. He marveled at the improvements in audiovisual support for lectures since the 1930s, but his students marveled even more at the fact that a lieutenant general on the eve of retirement would organize and give such a bravura performance on the stage of Little Hall, the jammed base theater.[4]

Thomas also reviewed the instruction, especially the annual command post exercise Packard, to see that the students learned how to integrate air and ground combat capabilities, a point of no compromise. He ensured that the instruction stressed battlefield dispersion and the capabilities of the helicopter-borne force in the vertical envelopment. He used his influence at Headquarters to place his disciples in the Advanced Research Group in positions where they could carry the message of the all-helicopter assault concept. John A. Saxten went to Headquarters G-3; Bill Van Ryzin took command of the Advanced Base Problem team, which made presentations not only at Quantico but to other service schools and joint and combined headquarters all over the world. John P. Condon became the Education Center chief of staff. Although the Advanced Research Group did not have the same prestige at Headquarters as when Thomas was Assistant Commandant, its officers clearly enjoyed the favor of the Commandant Marine Corps Schools and found that Thomas used their skills to educate Marine officers about the new operational concepts they championed.[5]

General Thomas did not ignore the selection of the Marine Corps' newest officers, who flooded into Quantico for precommissioning screening (the officers' equivalent of boot camp) and postcommissioning training at The Basic School. During the 1954–55 term, 7,800 student Marines matriculated at Quantico; 3,130 lieutenants attended The Basic School, while 3,164 officer candidates persevered and survived (or did not survive) the trials of the various officer candidate courses for college students (Platoon Leaders Course), college graduates and meritorious NCOs (Officers Candidate Course), midshipmen from university-based NROTC programs, and a warrant officers screening course. The Basic School, commanded by Col. Lewis W. Walt, had the responsibility for training the lieutenants and officer candidates. Thomas found that Walt and his hard-pressed staff had both too much and too little to do. First, Thomas agreed that The Basic School had a training load that exceeded its time, staff, and resources. He inherited a plan to move Basic School lieutenants from their barracks at old Brown Field south of Mainside and send them into semiexile in the wilds of the Guadalcanal Area where they would live close to their training areas—and isolated from just about everything and everyone else. The lieutenants found their quonset hut quarters and Butler building classrooms set in a muddy pinewoods; their cars sank to their hubcaps in the swamp labeled a parking lot. Life at Camp Upshur held few attractions, but, in the meantime, the Marine Corps began construction on Camp Barrett, a permanent home for The Basic School in the Guadalcanal Area. With the move also came an extension of the training syllabus from twenty-two to thirty-two weeks. Executing a policy he had shaped at Headquarters, Thomas divided The Basic School's training mission when Walt and his staff moved to Camp Upshur. To manage all of the officer candidate programs, concentrated at the Brown Field site, Thomas supervised the creation of the Training and Test Regiment, which later became the Officer Candidate School.[6]

In his investigations of The Basic School, Thomas learned that Walt did not control his own mess halls or train his lieutenants in rifle marksmanship. Observing that the lieutenants did not eat or shoot to Marine standards, Thomas reorganized both functions. The rifle range situation begged for change because the regular coaches lacked the marksmanship qualifications of The Basic School instructors and NCOs. Thomas told Walt to teach his own lieutenants, a decision that sent the rifle range commander into early retirement. The qualification rates, however, improved under the new arrangement. So did satisfaction with the food.[7]

In addition to his duties as educational manager, Thomas followed the work of the Landing Force Development Center. Since the Joint Landing Force Board had moved to Camp Lejeune in 1952, the center had had fewer administrative headaches, but its work load remained high because Headquarters continued to give it responsibility for an ascending number of technical evaluations. Thomas's principal interest in the Development Center's work stemmed from his concern that current instruction should incorporate an awareness of potential technological advancements in the amphibious art. As always, he kept thinking about the future. If he remained a traditionalist on many issues related to the Corps' military standards, his operational preferences focused on the years ahead, not those behind.[8]

Throughout his tour as Commandant Marine Corps Schools (CMCS), Thomas showed interest in the improvement of the schools system. The changes that he originated or managed proved both beneficial and lasting. If he did not set off a frenzy of reform at Quantico, he also did not function simply as a caretaker for the Marine Corps Schools. As the commanding general of the Corps' major Washington-area base, he also assumed a wide range of assignments that advanced the Corps' interests beyond officer education.

From its earliest days as a major Marine Corps installation, Quantico had received visitors from Washington. Coming by boat, train, and automobile, the visitors sought the promise of Marine hospitality and time to hide in the Virginia woods from their real and imagined burdens in the nation's capital. After he took office in early 1953, Secretary of Defense Charles E. Wilson chose Quantico as an admirable site for a "retreat" (the word itself was *not* used) for the senior civilian and military leadership of his department. Thomas assumed the role of host for Wilson's third conference in July 1955. Although Wilson's office organized the three days of formal and informal discussion attended by 167 VIPs, Thomas directed all the local arrangements, including meals, accommodations, recreational events, and cocktail parties. Pleased that his staff ran a smooth meeting, Thomas basked in the reflected power of President Eisenhower; Vice President Richard M. Nixon; Secretary of the Treasury George M. Humphrey; Allen Dulles, director of the Central Intelligence Agency (CIA); and Adm. Arthur W. Radford, chairman of the Joint Chiefs of Staff. Generals Shepherd and Pate led the Marine delegation, but Thomas probably most enjoyed seeing Bobby Erskine, now serving as Secretary Wilson's personal assistant for special operations and counter-guerrilla warfare.

Thomas also served as host for another Department of Defense program, the Joint Civilian Orientation Conference (JCOC), an annual pilgrimage by civic and business leaders to military bases. He had watched this program develop as a wartime initiative by James V. Forrestal within the Navy Department. Thomas had presented a briefing in New York City as part of the first JCOC in 1943. At Quantico, he welcomed two JCOC tours in October 1954 and in May 1955. He made certain that the VIPs all received helicopter rides and watched carefully orchestrated demonstrations of firepower by the Marine air-ground team. He and Lottie held receptions in their quarters for the guests and fed them at Harry Lee Hall, a BOQ providing a spectacular view of the Potomac. Thomas believed that he and Lottie more than met "Old Corps" standards for hospitality and graciousness, an opinion shared by his staff.[9]

Quantico made all sorts of demands on the CMCS, but Thomas played his social and ceremonial roles with his usual verve. He welcomed senior foreign military officers who wanted to observe Marine Corps officer education and training. On one occasion, Thomas did not even let a hurricane ruin an evening with a British delegation because he timed the gala reception with the eye of the storm. Thomas used his position to entertain old friends—in the line of duty. He provided a base tour and tactical demonstration for 450 members of the National Rifle Association, whose executive director was Merritt A. Edson. Thomas enjoyed football weekends, especially Quantico's games with other Marine teams from Camp Lejeune and Parris Island. After the 1955 Parris Island game, the Thomases entertained the Erskines, the Hal Turnages, the Bares, the David Shoups, the David Nimmers, the Robert Kilmartins, the L. B. Cresswells, and the Chester Allens. In June of the same year, Thomas welcomed Secretary of the Navy Charles S. Thomas to Quantico to dedicate the new golf clubhouse. He paired his best senior officer-golfer, John Condon, with the secretary, and Condon ably matched the secretary's 84 in a masterpiece of sport and diplomacy. The Thomases also held at least three receptions a year for the Quantico student officers and two receptions for senior active and retired officers from the Washington and Quantico area. Thomas also performed his almost daily tasks of appearing at promotion, retirement, and graduation ceremonies, awarding decorations to Marines and citations to civil servants, and receiving visitors at his headquarters office, a converted brick barracks on Barnett Avenue. Mrs. Thomas also had a demanding schedule of talks and appearances before base women's groups.[10]

The Thomas children responded in different ways to all the "pomp and circumstance" that came with their father's social position in the Washington-area military community. Capt. Gerald C. Thomas, Jr., stationed at Quantico, married the attractive and vivacious Lydia ("Deanie") Dubbelde, the daughter of an Army colonel, at the base chapel at Fort Myer in August 1954 with all the customs dictated by service etiquette. His sister Virginia, a student at Bryn Mawr, dismayed her parents by eloping to Baltimore in January 1955, to marry 2d Lt. John Richards Andrews, U.S. Marine Corps Reserve, a native Minnesotan who had graduated from the University of Virginia with a degree in architecture. The strain of her sister Tina's wedding in 1951 may have influenced Ginny's decision to elope, but the anticipated paternal dismay that she would leave college without graduating probably contributed to her secretiveness.[11]

For all the trappings of office that came to the CMCS, General Thomas did not turn regal in his last assignment. He used his power to help others; for example, he ordered the base housing officer to provide his G-3, Col. William K. Jones, with quarters adequate for his four young children, quarters that should have gone to a more senior colonel. Thomas also enjoyed walking to work from Quarters One rather than taking the car that was always at his beck and call. Thomas used his walks not just for exercise but to talk with Marines and their dependents along his route to the office. One day, he stopped to talk with a young girl, who asked him who he was. He replied that he was General Thomas, the base commander. The girl responded sharply: "No, you're not! You have to walk to work, and General Thomas has a nice, big official car!" Thomas told the story to his staff with great humor.[12]

As Commandant Marine Corps Schools, Thomas traveled as a representative of the Marine Corps, a task to which he had become accustomed during his tour as Assistant Commandant. General Shepherd, also a frequent traveler, often asked him to pinch-hit. While Assistant Commandant, Thomas had developed a reputation as a menace to Marine officers who found curious ways to spend en route time in European and Asian cities that had little military merit. In his last tour, he relaxed a bit. Within the United States, he simply took leave to attend meetings of the 1st Marine Division Association, in which he became a dominant force. In the line of duty, Thomas made speeches in 1955 at the Naval War College and Army War College, respectively, as well as attending the Global Strategy Conference in Newport, Rhode Island, and the National Strategy Seminar in Carlisle, Pennsylvania. That same year, Thomas visited Europe twice. His first visit in August became a reprise of a 1953 visit he had made to the NATO Defense College, colocated with the École de Guerre in Paris. The August 1955 trip started with an appearance of the U.S. Amphibious Warfare Presentation Team at the Royal Marines' amphibious training base at Fremington, England. This first stop gave the general and Lottie an opportunity to visit their son, Johnny, a member of the Marine guard for the U.S. Navy Europe Headquarters in London. (Mrs. Thomas flew to England on commercial air.) The Thomases and the Quantico team then went to Paris and Naples for additional performances. The Paris visit allowed General and Mrs. Thomas to visit Joe and Tina Bruder and their children. Joe was then serving as a planner at Supreme Headquarters Allied Powers Europe. The Bruders planned a gala reception, but Paris in August is a ghost town for the political, military, and economic elite of every nationality. One of the guests who attended, however, had the dubious taste of bringing a friend, a former German army doctor who had served in Belleau Wood. Tina Bruder thought her father knew immediately that "the enemy" had infiltrated the party, for he did not show his normal courtly party manners when he met the German.[13]

The second trip to France in 1955 brought Thomas again to his memories of Belleau Wood. He had previously revisited the site of his first great battle in 1953 and, characteristically, had presented an analysis of the battle for his Marine escorts. His November 1955 pilgrimage, however, was full of special meaning. Standing at the edge of retirement, he made the visit as a representative of the Corps, along with other Marine veterans of the battle. The occasion was the dedication of a special monument to the 4th Marine Brigade, a bas-relief of a 1918 Marine cast by the Marines' sculptor of choice, Felix de Weldon. General Shepherd led the delegation, which included Thomas, retired Generals Houston Noble and Arthur Worton, de Weldon, and Col. Rathvon M. Tompkins, a World War II hero and former colonel of the 5th Marines. Members of the Thomas family, Lt. Col. and Mrs. Joseph A. Bruder and Pfc William H. J. Thomas, assigned as his father's personal orderly, contributed to the party. The mission was to recapture the historic identity of the Bois de la Brigade de Marine. The German occupation during World War II and some egregious monument planting by the U.S. Army after the war had eliminated any formal recognition that *this* woodlot belonged to the Marine Corps. Informed that Belleau Wood cried for recapture, Shepherd had raised the money for a de Weldon monument and invited veterans of the battle to join him for its dedication.[14]

After a ceremonial appearance with the Royal Marines in London for the gala opening of the movie *Cockleshell Heroes,* the Marines flew to Paris as guests of the French government. General Thomas, his son Johnny, and Arthur Worton rode together in the same car to Belleau Wood, and the two veterans of the 6th Marines regaled the young Marine with their memories of the campaign. General Worton, always a bon vivant of the first order, set the tone of the day by demanding that their Parisian *hotelier* open his bar before 0700 to accommodate two old veterans of the Great War. All three Marines started the day with a "whiskey neat," but the Thomases declined Worton's invitation to a second drink. In a cold morning full of nostalgia, the dedication ceremony proceeded with proper reverence and military precision. Later, the party repaired to the *mairie* of Château-Thierry for wine toasts and hors d'oeuvres. The day ended with another party at the American embassy in Paris. In a sense, Jerry Thomas ended his Marine Corps career that day in France—shrouded in the memories of the battle that made him a Marine.

Thomas might have wished that the Marine Corps would be unable to function without his services, but he concluded in the summer of 1955 that his decision to retire could not be recalled. He did not relish the inevitable, but the inevitable pressed down upon him. In June 1955, he completed an annual physical examination. Although he learned that he was holding his own against high blood pressure and related cardiovascular problems, he remained a potential casualty to circulatory complications, some of which had appeared as nagging skin problems. Mortality pressed in upon him. Long ill with heart disease, Stover Keyser had died at seventy-one in April. In the summer of 1955 "Chesty" Puller, a major general, retired for disability. Johnny Clement, already retired, died of a heart attack at sixty-one. The sharpest blow came with the suicide of Merritt Edson on 14 August. At age fifty-eight, with no apparent illness or psychological problem that predicted suicide, Edson had gone to his garage in the early morning hours, turned on his car's ignition, and died of carbon monoxide poisoning. One of his two sons (both Marine officers) found him. The car engine remained warm, but the fuel tank still held half its capacity. Probably in his last moment of consciousness, Edson had turned off the ignition. In December 1955, Thomas dedicated the new Communications Officer School building as Edson Hall with the Edson family present.[15]

Thomas looked for post-retirement employment in July 1955, as the end of his Quantico tour approached. He had already begun negotiations with a college in Georgia to be its president, but the negotiations produced nothing, probably because Thomas did not have a baccalaureate degree. Thomas wrote General A. A. Vandegrift, in genteel retirement in Charlottesville, Virginia, that he would need "a connection" in January and that he had written twenty-five friends of his availability. Although Thomas preferred to remain on the East Coast, he was willing to move anywhere if a job interested him. Thomas knew that he had no technical expertise, but he felt confident that he had proved his ability to direct large, complex enterprises. "It is my hope that I can find something in which the pressure under which I have worked for nearly fifteen years will be relaxed a bit. In addition, a life of service prepares one only for the doing of a job which needs doing. . . . I believe that the enclosed summary of my service will indicate to a man experienced in business what I am probably qualified to do."[16]

The autumn of 1955 passed quickly for the Commandant Marine Corps Schools. The Quantico Marines football team looked invincible but ended the season 8-3. In October, the Commandant announced that he would be succeeded by Randolph McC. Pate, the Assistant Commandant and chief of staff. The next month, Shepherd followed with the news that General Thomas would retire as planned on 31 December. Thomas had returned from France to preside over the Quantico Marine Corps Birthday Ball at Larson Gym, preceded by cake-cuttings, parades, and receptions around the base. On 31 December 1955, a Saturday marred by snow and harsh winds, General Shepherd came to Quantico to bid Jerry Thomas good-by in his last official act as Commandant. Shepherd filed Thomas's final fitness report, which made the same observations that earlier fitness reports had contained: ". . . a brilliant officer—highly qualified in both staff and command duties, who by his devotion to duty and professional attainments has contributed materially toward the efficiency and high standards of the Marine Corps. His retirement from active duty will be a distinct loss to the Marine Corps."[17]

Before a large audience in front of post headquarters, Shepherd eulogized Thomas. He told the spectators that the "scholarly" Thomas, "revered" in the Marine Corps, had proved himself in nine battles in three wars. Shepherd and Thomas stood together to hear the adjutant read Thomas's retirement orders. Shepherd and Thomas bid the Marine Corps good-bye with their usual poise. They left a Marine Corps they had pushed into the postwar era, a Corps that could have stagnated in the afterglow of World War II and Korea.[18]

[CHAPTER XXVI]

Sunset Parade
1956–1984

Even for general officers not wedded to the regal trappings of their rank, the march into retirement can be a night patrol without a compass. For men who have spent their adult lives within the United States Marine Corps, the transition to a new routine not dictated by duty can be as disconcerting as boot camp. The dramatic change of pace is a welcome novelty, but the freedom from responsibility often pales quickly and changes into a sense of uselessness that no hobby or postponed personal agenda can replace. The first key as to what a retired general intends to do is where he chooses to live. Although recreational facilities, climate, home ownership, and medical care may influence the decision, the location offers strong clues about how much real work a retired general wants to do. "Working generals" stay in Washingtion unless they have cultivated business arrangements elsewhere in the country. Early in 1956, General and Mrs. Gerald C. Thomas rented a house on Quebec Place in northwest Washington and began an active retired life.

The first concern for a retired lieutenant general, in addition to finding work, would be his retired rank, not just a matter of prestige in 1956. For the first time since 1908, the law governing military pay provided lieutenant generals and generals, active and retired, with pay higher than that of a major general. (General Pershing and the five-star generals and admirals of World War II, as well as General Vandegrift, already enjoyed special pay provisions by acts of Congress.) A pay bill, passed in April 1955, provided a lieutenant general with $100 more a month ($1,076) than a major general, and a general received an additional $100 a month above a lieutenant general's pay. As a percentage of base pay, the increases were not trivial, but a general needed a presidential nomination and Senate confirmation before the retired rank became the same as the retiree's highest active rank. By virtue of "commended service" in combat in World War II, Thomas qualified for promotion to general, but the second promotion brought no added retirement pay. In February 1956, the Navy Department recommended Thomas for promotion on the retired list as a lieutenant general by virtue of his service as Assistant Commandant, U.S. Marine Corps, and Commandant Marine Corps Schools, followed by promotion to the rank of general in recognition of his service in World War II. The request received routine sponsorship from the secretary of defense and White House and subsequent Senate confirmation.[1]

Thomas may not have been well known in the Eisenhower White House, but he did have modest access to the President. That access led to his first postretirement employment and, in fact, brought him out of retirement for active service as a general. Eventually, this duty meant an additional increment of retirement pay, which Thomas relished as a bureaucratic victory.

On his first trip to the White House in March 1953, Thomas (the only Marine general present) attended a luncheon that President Eisenhower held for his West Point classmate, Gen. James Van Fleet. Eisenhower used the occasion to discuss the Korean War with the Secretary of Defense and his assistants, the members of the Joint Chiefs of Staff, and seven of the most influential members of Congress.[2] Thomas's prominence as a senior Korean War commander then brought him several speaking engagements to veterans' groups in Illinois that included Republicans who corresponded with Eisenhower's political operatives. One of these groups, the Illinois Republican Veterans League, lauded Thomas and recommended his consideration for an administration appointment. An Eisenhower political organizer then asked the President's naval aide: "Can you tell me who Lt. Gen. Gerald C. Thomas is?" As Commandant Marine Corps Schools, Thomas invited White House notables, including Sherman Adams, to give graduation speeches at Quantico.[3]

As smooth a politician as ever wore a Navy uniform, Adm. Arthur W. Radford, chairman of the Joint Chiefs of Staff, probably knew that Thomas found the Republicans congenial, even though Thomas had crossed swords with Eisenhower during the unification crisis of 1946–47. Radford had a job for Thomas, one that required White House approval. During a meeting with Eisenhower in March 1956, Radford suggested that the president meet Thomas and approve Radford's recommendation that he be recalled to active duty as the staff director of the Net Evaluation Subcommittee of the National Security Council. Eisenhower agreed to the meeting, which must have gone well. On 1 April 1956, Jerry Thomas returned to active duty as a general and staff member of the National Security Council. Although he intended to serve only through 1957, Thomas remained on active duty until 1 January 1959.[4]

For all his commitment to the "New Look," Arthur Radford retained considerable doubt about the planning assumptions and bureaucratic politics that characterized the administration's military planning. Radford recognized a growing demand for civil defense and for active air defense by the Army and Air Force. He supported the concept that some agency provide an annual assessment of the damage the Soviet bomber force (and, later, intercontinental ballistic missiles) might do to American targets against varying levels of air defenses and civil preparations, such as shelters and evacuation plans, but did not like the idea of the assessment being done outside of military control, in part for security reasons.

The JCS accepted the idea of the assessment as long as Radford directed the process, rather than the director of the CIA. At Radford's initiative, the National Security Council approved planning for a "net capabilities evaluation subcommittee" that would estimate the results of a nuclear war between the United States and the Soviet Union, should such a war be fought three years hence (i.e., 1957). Although the NSC asked that the first report be prepared by November 1954, President Eisenhower did not approve the subcommittee's organization until February 1955. The president charged the Net Evaluation Subcommittee with preparing an annual report for the NSC on "the net capabilities of the USSR, in the event of general war, to inflict direct injury upon the continental U.S. and key U.S. installations overseas . . ." and to report any significant changes in these capabilities. Although the initial guidance included the mission of considering "all types of attack, overt or clandestine," the subcommittee guidance actually applied only to nuclear war, initiated under varying degrees of strategic warning, directed at the United States. Under the direction of the subcommittee, chaired by the Chairman, Joint Chiefs of Staff, and including the Director of Central Intelligence, Director of the Office of Defense Mobilization, Federal Civil Defense Administrator, chairman of the NSC's interdepartmental intelligence conference, and chairman of the interdepartmental committee on internal security, the real work would be conducted by a staff drawn from the armed forces and CIA. Although Radford would supervise the staff, the choice of a staff director remained in the President's hands.[5]

Shortly after reporting to his office on the Pentagon's second floor, E Ring, Jerry Thomas learned that his staff (seven military officers, one CIA representative) faced a daunting task, for the process of net assessment remained in its infancy. Admiral Radford and Allen Dulles argued about the significance of different intelligence estimates (varying by a factor of three) of the projected Soviet nuclear warhead stockpile, but they agreed that operational analysis and damage assessment needed much refinement. The key uncertainty remained the pace and scope of Soviet missile development—opinions were varied and hard intelligence highly ambiguous. To reduce interdepartmental meddling with the staff, Radford and Thomas won NSC approval of their proposal that only Radford would decide whether the annual report went directly to the President. Unresolved differences, therefore, could not stop the annual report short of the White House.[6]

Under Thomas's direction, the staff of the Net Evaluation Subcommittee produced three annual reports, each more pessimistic about the growing ability of the Soviet Union to ruin the United States by a preemptive nuclear strike with intercontinental ballistic missiles. In his first appearance on 20 December 1956 before the National Security Council (five statutory members) and an invited audience that included virtually every important national security official in the administration, Thomas described how the report had been drafted and explained the significant military variables in the Soviet offensive forces and the American defensive forces. He also described the problems of the estimating process and the sensitivity of the study results to changes in assumptions. He reviewed the war games and statistical analysis his staff used to test hypothetical Soviet attacks against existing American contingency plans. Thomas's staff gave a detailed analysis of the damage that the United States would suffer under differing conditions of alert. Admiral Radford then praised Thomas and his staff for a much improved analysis and stressed the obvious: American air defenses and civil defenses could not protect the nation from "terrific destruction." Eisenhower concluded the briefing with the observation that he wondered "why we should put a single nickel into anything but developing our capacity to diminish the enemy's capacity for nuclear attack."[7]

The 1957 and 1958 briefings of the Net Evaluation Subcommittee reflected the growing complexity of assessing the possible courses of a nuclear war between the United States and the Soviet Union and the political sensitivity of such calculations. Eisenhower found the analysis useful, however, and provided personal guidance on the types of assumptions that the staff should make about Soviet capabilities and American defense programs. He further widened the staff's access to information throughout the executive branch and the staff director's powers to recruit military officers for his office. He approved the staff's increased size; by 1958, Thomas had an Air Force brigadier general as deputy director, eight military members, a civilian, and an administrative officer. In substantive terms, the President directed that Thomas's staff produce a more sophisticated analysis of what mix of urban-industrial targets and Soviet strategic military targets would offer the United States the greatest deterrent advantages and limit damage to the United States in case of war. Thomas and his staff devoted much of their time to educational travel, with visits to civil defense officials, the officers of the Army's air defense missile programs, and the Air Force nuclear planners of Strategic Air Command. In other words, Thomas's staff grappled with the strategic nuclear perplexities of the late 1950s that dogged the planners of the Strategic Air Command, the analysts of the RAND Corporation, and members of the Security Resources Panel (Gaither Committee) of the Science Advisory Committee, but it did its work in greater obscurity.[8]

The three annual strategic nuclear war net assessments that Thomas's staff produced for the Net Evaluation Subcommittee proved the value of the net assessment process. Even though Admiral Radford retired in 1957 (replaced by Air Force Gen. Nathan F. Twining), the Net Evaluation Subcommittee survived the change. The basic fact was that Eisenhower appreciated the analytic effort and found it useful. As Thomas neared his second retirement, the president wrote him that he and other members of the NSC and the White House staff valued Thomas's "outstanding performance" in preparing complex, but comprehensive, studies. To General Twining, Eisenhower praised Thomas's staff's work on the 1958 briefing: "It was, I believe, the best of the reports and was clear and easily understandable." The next director of the Net Evaluation Subcommittee staff, Lt. Gen. Thomas F. Hickey, USA (Retired), recognized that the 1956–58 reports had set a high standard for future reports. In appreciation of Thomas's work, Eisenhower ruled that Thomas, having served on active duty as a general, was eligible for retirement pay as a general, an honor thus far accorded only to former Commandants. With some risk to his health, for he still suffered from skin problems related to nerves and circulatory problems, Jerry Thomas had made one last—and lasting—contribution to the nation's security planning before he left government at the end of 1958. He believed his service with the NSC had been a perfect transition to real retirement.[9]

★ ★ ★ ★

Although he found his work on the Net Evaluation Subcommittee fascinating and a wonderful way to stay informed on military gossip and defense intrigue, Thomas wanted to try his hand at making some money in business. Early in his retirement, he joined two investment enterprises. One failed, but the other prospered and added substantial income to his retirement pension. Even while he worked for the Eisenhower administration, the general agreed to participate in the formation of an investment company that would sell variable annuities. His sponsor for his appointment as chairman of the board of the company, a job in which he intended to work hard, was an Army officer on his staff, a relative of the Kentucky insurance man who planned the venture. The company depended on an anticipated change in the federal income tax law that did not eventually occur, however, and it went out of business in 1961. In the meantime, another group of business and professional men from the Washington area asked Thomas to serve on the board of advisors to their new company, the Washington Real Estate Investment Trust (WRIT), which began operations in November 1960. The group of initial investors valued Thomas's counsel and his local reputation for shrewd judgment and high personal probity. He also gave the company an elder statesman image that the group badly needed, given the investors' relative youthfulness. Thomas's sponsor in this case was Benjamin Dorsey, an attorney and the older brother of Thomas's Quantico aide, Captain Joshua Dorsey, III. WRIT prospered, and Thomas, compensated in part with company stock, prospered as well.[10]

However active his business career—at times Thomas thought it too demanding—the general preserved his intense interest in Marine Corps affairs through the traumatic 1960s and the postwar renaissance of the 1970s. As long as his son, his son-in-law, and his protégés remained on active duty well into the 1970s, he remained in touch with Marine Corps policy issues and offered his counsel when sought. Thomas stayed in contact with Headquarters and Quantico through Bobby Hogaboom, Bill Twining, Bill Buse, Bill Jones, Joe Platt, John Condon, Brute Krulak, and Don Weller, all active-duty generals. When David M. Shoup became Commandant on 1 January 1960 with a mandate to restore the Corps' fighting trim, which had been shaken by the manpower reductions of the "Second New Look" and Randolph McC. Pate's weak leadership, Thomas took great pride in seeing a protégé become Commandant (although Shoup did so at Bill Twining's expense) and in dining at the Commandant's House. Relations between Thomas and the next Commandant, Wallace M. Greene, Jr., were properly cordial, but the two were not close, probably because of their tiff at Headquarters. As a dedicated Marine and convinced Cold Warrior, Thomas supported the American intervention in Vietnam. He did not rupture his personal relationship with Dave Shoup, as did other Marines, when the former Commandant became an outspoken critic of the Vietnam war and the Johnson administration.[11]

By the mid-1960s, Thomas had become the central figure in a close circle of friends, all retired or senior active-duty officers, who gathered for lunch at least once a week at the Army and Navy Club to discuss Corps affairs, politics, international relations, and Washington gossip. While he had a business office downtown, Thomas simply made the short walk to the club. Later, he hiked downtown to Farragut Square from his last home on 44th Street N.W. in Foxhall Village, northwest of Georgetown and across Rock Creek. His routine seldom varied. He had one or two drinks (normally one and always a martini or old-fashioned) and a chef salad, participated with verve in the talk, and took a cab home before rush hour. The luncheon group might vary, but it had common bonds: service in the Solomons, membership in "Chowder," and association with Thomas during the reform days at Headquarters and Quantico. Members of the luncheon group depended on who was in town, but among the "regulars" were Jones, Weller, Condon, Platt, Hunter Hurst, DeWolf Schatzel, and Bob Heinl. When they attended, Warren Baker and Don Hittle, both of whom had active post-retirement careers in Washington, brought news from Congress and the Department of Defense. Thomas so enjoyed the fellowship that he also formed a regular retired officers lunch group at the club that heard invited speakers and discussed national issues of interest. In later years, the informal "Tuesday group" often shifted the luncheon site to a favored Chinese restaurant in Alexandria, but the change of location altered only the menu, not the vigorous discussions.[12]

One of the most faithful members of the "Tuesday group" became an officer Thomas did not know well until late in his career and early in his retirement, Col. Angus M. "Tiny" Fraser. Commissioned a Reserve lieutenant in 1939, the massive Fraser had served in the 8th Marines on Samoa early in World War II and returned to the Pacific as a regimental operations officer on Okinawa and in the occupation of China. The Thomas-Fraser relationship probably began during Fraser's extended service at Headquarters (1954–58) as general staff secretary, policy analyst in the G-3 division, and special projects officer for General Pate. Thomas and Fraser shared a love of China, and Fraser had developed a knowledge of the Chinese language and politics that allowed him in retirement (1964) to work for the Institute for Defense Analysis as an Asian defense expert and to become the author of a respected book on the People's Liberation Army. An urbane intellectual with many interests and wide expertise, Fraser, along with Bob Heinl, became one of the general's greatest admirers and closest friends.[13]

Prolific authors themselves, Heinl and Fraser encouraged General Thomas to try his own hand at writing—a lure to learning and teaching reinforced by Sam Griffith, who returned from England with a doctorate in history and a contract to write a history of the Guadalcanal campaign. Thomas needed little urging to write history, still his great love, as well as read it. Writing in longhand on yellow legal pads, he began his own autobiography after his retirement, and this project stretched into the 1960s. He also discussed writing a book on important Marine leaders for Harper & Row, but the project never materialized. (Thomas's choices were Archibald N. Henderson, L. W. T. Waller, Charles Heywood, John A. Lejeune, Smedley D. Butler, Roy S. Geiger, and Merritt A. Edson.) Another publishing arrangement, made by Bob Heinl, produced the first edition of *The Marine Officer's Guide* (1956). Heinl did the writing, but used Thomas (most willingly) to offset the influence of Rear Adm. Arthur A. Ageton, USN (Retired), assigned to the project by the publisher, the U.S. Naval Institute. Thomas preferred to read others' work than to write himself, and he had not written for publication while a serving officer. He did, however, review the manuscripts for the Marine Corps' official histories of the Solomons campaign and the Korean War, 1951, and provided terse, candid judgments to the authors of three volumes published by the Historical Branch, G-3 Division, Headquarters Marine Corps. In 1966 he dictated his memoirs to Benis M. Frank for inclusion in the Marine Corps oral history project, sponsored by the Historical Branch. He also showed keen interest in the establishment of the Marine Corps Historical Foundation (1979) and the teaching of military history in the Marine Corps Schools.[14]

Thomas preserved his close relationship with Generals Vandegrift, Erskine, and Shepherd as all four of them battled the ravages of aging. In his published memoirs, *Once a Marine* (1964), Vandegrift acknowledged Thomas's contributions to his own career without mentioning the tension between them in 1947. The Erskines and Shepherds remained fast friends of the Thomas family, but the Shepherds moved to California for business and health reasons. The Vandegrifts remained in nearby Virginia. The former Commandant lapsed into an isolation imposed by blindness and deafness, abetted by his second wife, who brought some strain to Vandegrift's contacts with his service friends. Whatever his personal opinions of his contemporaries—and theirs of him—Thomas did his best to be friendly with other retirees. The only officers he regarded as devoted enemies were LeRoy P. Hunt and Thomas E. Watson, and he relished the fact that he outlived both of them. He especially enjoyed traveling to reunions of the 1st Marine Division Association, the 2d Infantry Division Association (where he could reminisce about World War I and Korea), and his Sigma Chi fraternity brothers from Illinois Wesleyan University. Thomas also maintained ties with military and civilian veterans of China service (including the missionaries) in the Washington area, nurtured by the Republic of China, which welcomed the Thomases to social events at its Washington embassy.

General and Mrs. Thomas remained concerned parents and grandparents, although Thomas showed little inclination to tell war stories to his grandchildren or to dote on them. Ginny and Rick Andrews, who established himself as a Washington architect, were the most accessible of the family, although Tina and Joe Bruder also settled in the Washington area when Joe retired as a colonel. Jerry Junior's career in the Marine Corps took him (and his family) to Taiwan for language training in Chinese and work as an aide-interpreter for Commander, Taiwan Defense Command. He immediately started plans to bring his parents to Taipei for a visit in 1961. The plans collapsed, to Jerry Junior's disappointment, when his grandfather, Vander Thomas, collapsed in August, and Jerry Thomas refused to leave the United States until he found a suitable and affordable nursing home for his father in Fredericksburg, Virginia. (Vander Thomas died in 1964 at the age of ninety-two.) When Jerry Junior returned from Taiwan, he learned that his orders for further schooling had been changed by General Shoup himself, who dictated that Jerry Thomas's son belonged in the Fleet Marine Force. Jerry Junior then served as the operations officer of the 1st Reconnaissance Battalion and executive officer of a 7th Marines battalion bound by the transplacement schedule for thirteen months on Okinawa or afloat in the western Pacific. Thomas agreed with Shoup that his son (whatever his own disposition for educational assignments) should be a field Marine.[15]

★★★★

Having escaped the bullets of three wars, Jerry Thomas could no longer avoid the perils of advanced age, but he did reach his fiftieth wedding anniversary in 1974 without incapacity. He and Lottie, surrounded by family and friends on the roof of the Army and Navy Club, celebrated the occasion with gusto. In May of the same year, both Vandegrift and Erskine died at the U.S. Naval Hospital, Bethesda, Maryland. In June 1974, Thomas suffered a slight stroke but recovered, although not completely. In December 1975, the general's son Johnny, then living in Charleston, South Carolina, and working as a free-lance writer, found his parents having difficulty maintaining their home. Neither had any desire to move to an apartment or face the demoralization and expense of a nursing home. Johnny decided to move in with his parents in order to spare them the ordeal of moving and to ease the physical demands of housekeeping. With Johnny's aid, General and Mrs. Thomas remained as active as the general's health and energy permitted.[16]

Thomas retained as much of his routine schedule as possible. In 1977, he attended the opening of the new Marine Corps Historical Center in the Washington Navy Yard as the oldest living Marine general (83) in attendance. The occasion took a strange turn when a reporter from *The Washington Star* described him as a doddering old man "shuffling in baby steps" toward the drinks and "soggy . . . sandwiches," his cane over his arm. The rest of the story was no more complimentary and showed no understanding of the importance of Marine Corps history to Marines. Angered by the article, Tiny Fraser wrote to the *Star* (as did others) and protested the reporter's lack of respect for Thomas and all of the Marines honored by the center and its first-floor museum. Fraser's outrage did not end with the publication of his letter in the *Star* on 23 May 1977. He planned to write a biography of Thomas. By 1979, he was interviewing Thomas to supplement the general's unpublished autobiography. Fraser produced an article, "Conversations with the General," for the *Marine Corps Gazette* in November 1979 and received a grant from the Marine Corps Historical Foundation to write a book. Working with Johnny and the general, Fraser collected documents on some of the general's more dramatic adventures, especially those during World War I and Thomas's trip around the world with Jimmy Roosevelt. Other admirers continued to call at the Thomas home, 1606 44th Street N.W., among them Bill Jones, Hunter Hurst, Don Weller, and Bob Heinl, until Heinl died of a heart attack in 1979. His death saddened Thomas, who always overlooked Heinl's eccentricities and appreciated his caustic wit and worldly opinions.[17]

The biographical project seemed to give Thomas new strength, but in May 1983, either because of an accidental fall or another stroke, he became a semi-invalid from back trouble. His illness took him to and from Bethesda Naval Hospital and Georgetown University Hospital for the rest of the year. Several more strokes made it difficult for Thomas to leave his bed at home, but he remained lucid. Colonel Sanford B. Hunt, his personal communications assistant on Guadalcanal, visited him in December 1983 and found him "physically shot but still brilliant in his thinking" and ever interested in the Marine Corps. The two 1st Division veterans shared some laughs about Hunt's antics as a young officer on Guadalcanal while the colonel sat by Thomas's bed and held his hand. Early in the morning of 7 April 1984, Gerald C. Thomas died in his sleep at home from another stroke. Four days later, the Marine Corps buried one of its finest officers with appropriate honors in Arlington National Cemetery after a memorial service in the base chapel at Fort Myer, a short walk from Headquarters Marine Corps. Mourners packed the chapel, and sixteen Marine officers served as pallbearers: Wallace M. Greene, Jr., Robert E. Hogaboom, William K. Jones, Frederick L. Wieseman, William J. Van Ryzin, Lewis J. Fields, Henry W. Buse, Robert C. Kilmartin, Charles L. Cogswell, Jonas M. Platt, Samuel R. Shaw, John P. Condon, E. Hunter Hurst, Angus M. Fraser, Custis Burton, Jr., and Warren P. Baker. The ceremony, perfected by generations of Marines serving at Headquarters and the Marine Barracks, proceeded with grief, appreciation, communal ritual, patriotism, and reverence for Corps and country. On the kind of balmy spring day that makes Washington memorable—with the cherry blossoms in full bloom—Gerald C. Thomas came to rest in his last foxhole at the intersection of Grant Drive and Roosevelt Drive, near the graves of three of his Guadalcanal comrades, Alexander Archer Vandegrift, Roy S. Geiger, and Merritt A. Edson.[18]

At 090701Z April 1984, Commandant of the Marine Corps General P. X. Kelley had issued ALMAR 77/84, which announced General Gerald C. Thomas's death. In accordance with Marine Corps Order P10520.3A (*Flag Manual*) and the standing instructions for the burial of general officers of the Marine Corps (CMC MHP-10), the Commandant directed that every Marine installation throughout the world drop its national colors to half-staff from 1000 Washington time until sunset of the same day in honor of General Thomas.[19] Just how many Marines, lowering the colors throughout the world that day, knew who Jerry Thomas was or had the slightest inkling of what he had done for their Marine Corps is beyond knowing. The answer is probably that few of them did. Marine generals come, serve, and retire—and eventually die—with a rapidity the public can hardly appreciate. One can ask whether they really make a difference to the Marine Corps, let alone the military history of the United States. If they had not performed their duties with special distinction sometime in their careers, they would not have become generals. That is not the same as saying that as generals, they then left the Marine Corps a better service than they found it. For Jerry Thomas, however, there should be no doubt. He made a difference and left a heritage that should inspire all Marines—and all Americans—as long as there is a United States Marine Corps. Semper Fidelis!

Bibliographical Essay

A bibliography is found in the chapter notes of the book. This essay reviews primary archival and documentary sources that provided the greatest contributions to a biography of General Thomas and the Marine Corps of his era. It also lists the most significant printed primary sources and secondary works used in the book.

Gerald C. Thomas

General Thomas wrote an extensive autobiography after his retirement in 1955; copies may be found in the Personal Papers Collection, Marine Corps Historical Center, Washington Navy Yard, Washington, D.C. The internal evidence in the manuscript and the general's son, William H. Johnson Thomas (who typed the autobiography in the 1970s), suggest that Thomas began the autobiography in 1956 or 1957 and completed it about ten years later. Thomas wrote the entire manuscript (over 400 typed pages) in longhand on legal pads. Some of these notes survive. In 1966, Benis M. Frank, former director of the Marine Corps oral history program, conducted an interview with the general over several days, and the transcript, numbering 989 pages, constitutes a second autobiography. Multiple copies of the oral memoir and the original tapes are maintained in the Marine Corps Oral History Collection, Marine Corps Historical Center. In 1981, Thomas provided a much shorter interview (transcript of 41 pages) on the organization of Headquarters Marine Corps and his views of the Commandants he knew. In 1983, he discussed operations in the South Pacific with Gibson Smith, who was conducting research on Col. Evans Carlson; although not transcribed, the tape is in the Oral History Collection. When Col. Angus M. Fraser, USMC (Ret.), began research for a biography of Thomas in 1979, he conducted additional interviews with the general. He carried on some correspondence with the general's associates and collected a few relevant documents. Both Thomas and Fraser died before this collaboration produced much information beyond that found in the original autobiography and oral memoir. Colonel Fraser's letters, clippings, interview notes, and fragments of two draft chapters are filed with the Thomas autobiography. With the permission of the Thomas family, I had full use of the Officer Qualification Record (OQR) of Thomas, Gerald Carthrae (0984), at the National Personnel Records Center, St. Louis, Missouri. The OQR provides rich documentation: a detailed chronology of assignments, official correspondence, fitness reports, citations, and medical records. It provides little evidence of Thomas's personal thoughts about his service.

Fortunately, the general's wife, Lottie Capers Johnson Thomas of Washington, D.C., preserved and retains possession of a collection of private letters the general wrote to family members during his wartime service abroad. His letters to his mother, Virginia Young Thomas of Bloomington, Illinois, and Marshall, Missouri, from 1917–19 offer a contemporaneous account and assessment of his service with the 4th Marine Brigade in France and Germany. Letters to his wife, two brothers, and children provide essential information on his service in the South Pacific (1942–43) and Korea (1951–52). Mrs. Thomas also preserved correspondence from shorter periods of family separation, including the general's sea duty on the gunboat USS *Tulsa* (1923–25), attendance at the Army Motor Transport and Infantry Schools (1927–28, 1931–32), service with the 1st Marine Division (1941–42), and the last days of his command of Fleet Marine Force Western Pacific (December 1948–January 1949).

My description of the Thomas family comes from several sources. General Thomas himself wrote about his ancestry and life before the Marine Corps in "Family Notes," probably written in the 1960s, supplemented by "A Partial Genealogy" of the Johnson and Capers families written by his father-in-law, William H. Johnson, M.D., of Charleston, South Carolina, and his brother, Rev. Louis O'Vander Thomas. The general's son William inherited the mantle of family genealogist, and he and I corresponded extensively about family matters from 1986 to 1990. Mrs. Thomas and her other children, Lottie Capers (Tina) Thomas Bruder; Gerald C. Thomas, Jr.; and Virginia Thomas Andrews, provided critical perspectives on Thomas's career and family life in letters and memoranda that remain in the author's possession. The archives of Illinois Wesleyan University, especially the files of the registrar and the alumni association, furnished additional personal data.

To see Thomas through the eyes of his Marine Corps contemporaries, I sent an extensive questionnaire (in 1986 and later) to officers whom the Thomas family and I identified as his closest associates. In several cases, the questionnaire opened an extensive correspondence about the general's personality, habits, attitudes and values, and military performance. Not all of the respondents were unabashed admirers, but even those who disagreed with the general, whether on a personal issue or matter of policy, did agree that his dedication to the Marine Corps and his duty (whatever it happened to be) was total. I received responses from the following Marine officers: Gen. Wallace M. Greene, Jr., a former Commandant; Gen. Merrill B. Twining, whose knowledge of the Guadalcanal campaign and the unification struggle is unparalleled and whose candor is unmatched; Gen. Robert E. Hogaboom; Lt. Gen. Alpha L. Bowser, G-3, 1st Marine Division,

1950–53; Lt. Gen. Victor H. Krulak, whose close association with Thomas began at The Basic School in 1934 and continued through their creation of a Headquarters Marine Corps general staff in 1952–54; the late Lt. Gen. Henry W. Buse, Jr.; Lt. Gen. Edward W. Snedeker; Lt. Gen. William K. Jones; Maj. Gen. John P. Condon; Maj. Gen. Jonas M. Platt; Brig. Gen. Frederick P. Henderson; Col. Drew J. Barrett, Jr.; Col. Warren P. Baker, who first met Thomas on Guadalcanal and whose career contacts with the general continued through 1954; Col. Sanford B. Hunt, a communications officer for Thomas on Guadalcanal and at Headquarters Marine Corps; the late Col. DeWolf Schatzel, a veteran of the unification wars; Col. Clarence R. Schwenke, a veteran of staff service with the 1st Marine Division and I Marine Amphibious Corps; Col. Jeremiah A. O'Leary, veteran Washington newspaperman and public information officer for the 1st Marine Division in Korea; and Lt. Col. Sherman W. Parry, 1st Marine Division artillery officer in the division fire support coordination center in Korea during 1951. I am especially in debt to W. F. Martin Clemens, CBE, MC, former Australian army major and de facto chief of scouts for the 1st Marine Division on Guadalcanal, for his views of the campaign and the Marine officers with whom he served, including General Thomas.

The private papers of Marine general officers held by the Personal Papers Collection, Marine Corps Historical Center, provided references to Thomas and his performance of duty, as well as essential contextual information explaining the issues with which he dealt. The most important collections in this regard are the papers of the two Commandants he served so well, Gen. Alexander Archer Vandegrift (1944–47) and Gen. Lemuel C. Shepherd, Jr. (1952–55). I also found significant materials in the following collections: Gen. Clifton B. Cates, Gen. Thomas Holcomb, Lt. Gen. Edward W. Snedeker, Gen. Oliver Prince Smith, and Maj. Gen. William P. T. Hill.

Other personal papers contributed to a rounded view of Thomas at various stages of his career. They are the collections of Adm. Charles M. Cooke, Gen. David M. Shoup, Lt. Gen. John R. Chaisson, and Lt. Gen. Clovis E. Byers, USA, at the Hoover Institution for War, Peace and Revolution, Stanford, California; Gen. Matthew B. Ridgway, USA, and Lt. Gen. Edward M. Almond, USA, U.S. Army Military History Institute, Carlisle Barracks, Pennsylvania.

Personal papers, however, did not exhaust the range of individual opinion on General Thomas's career and his eventual contributions to Marine Corps history. The following oral history memoirs of Marine officers, held in the Marine Corps Oral History Collection, provided essential information: Maj. Gen. Chester R. Allen (1969); Brig. Gen. Charles L. Banks (1969); Lt. Gen. Robert O. Bare (1968); Maj. Gen. Robert Blake (1968); Lt. Gen. Alpha L. Bowser (1970); Gen. William O. Brice (1971); Maj. Gen. Wilburt S. Brown (1967); Lt. Gen. Joseph C. Burger (1969); Lt. Gen. Henry W. Buse, Jr. (1971); Gen. Clifton B. Cates (1967); Maj. Gen. John P. Condon (1970); Lt. Gen. Pedro del Valle (1966); Brig. Gen. E. Colston Dyer (1968); Gen. Graves B. Erskine (1970); Lt. Gen. Lewis J. Fields (1971); Brig. Gen. Samuel B. Griffith II (1970); Col. Robert D. Heinl, Jr. (1972–78); Brig. Gen. Frederick P. Henderson (1974–76); Lt. Gen. Leo D. Hermle (1968); Maj. Gen. Louis R. Jones (1970); Brig. Gen. Robert C. Kilmartin, Jr. (1979); Lt. Gen. Victor H. Krulak (1970); Lt. Gen. Robert B. Luckey (1969); Maj.

Gen. John H. Masters (1971); Lt. Gen. John C. McQueen (1969); Lt. Gen. Herman Nickerson, Jr. (1973 and 1978); Maj. Gen. David R. Nimmer (1970); Gen. Alfred H. Noble (1968); Maj. Gen. DeWitt Peck (1967); Maj. Gen. Omar T. Pfeiffer (1968); Gen. Edwin A. Pollock (1971 and 1973); Lt. Gen. Carson A. Roberts (1971); Gen. Ray A. Robinson (1968); Gen. Christian F. Schilt, Jr. (1969); Brig. Gen. Samuel R. Shaw (1970); Gen. Lemuel C. Shepherd (1967); Lt. Gen. Merwin H. Silverthorn (1969); Lt. Gen. Julian C. Smith (1968); Gen. Oliver P. Smith (1969); Gen. Merrill B. Twining (1967); Gen. A. A. Vandegrift (1962); Maj. Gen. William J. Van Ryzin (1975); Maj. Gen. Donald McP. Weller (1971); Lt. Gen. Frederick L. Wieseman (1971); Lt. Gen. Thomas A. Wornham (1968); and Maj. Gen. William A. Worton (1967).

Documents relating to Thomas were found in three Presidential libraries. The Personal Papers Collection, Franklin D. Roosevelt Library, Hyde Park, New York, contains correspondence about the James Roosevelt-Thomas observation mission of 1941. File 18-E (Marine Corps), Roosevelt Presidential Papers, contain general policy documents on policy and personnel matters that affected Thomas. The office correspondence files of the Truman White House contain scattered Thomas letters and references to his appointment as Commanding General, 1st Marine Division, and Assistant Commandant and Chief of Staff, as well as a few clippings about his service in Korea. These papers are held in the Harry S Truman Library, Independence, Missouri. The Dwight D. Eisenhower Library in Abilene, Kansas, has Thomas-related correspondence in the White House Office Files and Central Files, the Personal Papers Files, the Sherman Adams Papers, and the Records of the Special Assistant for National Security Affairs. The Ann Whitman Files (National Security Series), the Staff Secretary Records, and the National Security Staff Papers contain material on the Net Evaluation Subcommittee.

Organizational and Agency Records

The organizational records of the U.S. Marine Corps are either held by the user offices of the Corps or transferred to the Military Records Division, National Archives and Records Administration, for inclusion in Record Group 127, portions of which are stored in the National Archives building in Washington, D.C., and in the Washington National Records Center, Suitland, Maryland. These records are divided into three general groups: Headquarters Marine Corps; Marine Corps installations, bases, posts, and stations; and operational commands. For this book, I used the following records from Headquarters Marine Corps: correspondence of the Office of the Commandant, 1919–54; correspondence of the Office of the Adjutant and Inspector, 1917–41; records of the Division of Operations and Training and its successor agency, the Division of Plans and Policies, 1940–49, and the correspondence and office files of the Office of the Assistant Commandant and Chief of Staff, 1952–54. I consulted subject files, compiled by Headquarters Marine Corps according to function and place of origin ("Ells-Dran" filing system), that included officer recruitment, promotions, officer education, schools assignments, training exercises and maneuvers, wars plans, personnel recruitment policy, and joint operations. Also, I researched the files of the Marine Corps Schools in Philadelphia and Quantico for the periods that Thomas was a student or faculty member and for the period during which he was Commandant Marine Corps Schools.

Among the records of operational units that normally include files of reports and documents considered of historical importance, I used the following command records: 1st Marine Brigade, Haiti; Marine Detachment, Peiping, China; Marine detachment, USS *Tulsa*; 1st Marine Division for the Solomons campaign, especially the important five-part summary of operations submitted by the commanding general; 1st Marine Division for Korean operations, April 1951–January 1952, which includes monthly historical reports, war diaries, and special studies; I Marine Amphibious Corps for operations in the Solomon Islands, especially Bougainville historical file and after-action report; and Fleet Marine Force Western Pacific, Tsingtao, China, 1947–49.

Official documents of historical importance, many of them drawn from Record Group 127 or suitable for inclusion therein, may be found outside the National Archives and Records Administration. The History and Museums Division, Headquarters Marine Corps, maintains three offices at its Washington Navy Yard center that assist documentary research: archives section (unit historical reports), reference section (subject and biographical files), and library (bound reports, manuals, general orders, and other issuances). Another important archive is located in the James C. Breckinridge Library, Marine Corps Training and Education Center, Marine Corps Combat Development Command, Quantico, Virginia. Part of the Breckinridge archive is organized and indexed as the "Historical Amphibious File," which contains subject matter files related to the development of amphibious warfare and the specialization in that function by the Marine Corps. The library also has extensive collections of operational reports from the Fleet Marine Force that date from World War II and many materials related to the history of the Marine Corps Schools and education within the Marine Corps.

The official records of the Army and Navy also provided essential documents for this book. Army documents in the National Archives include Records of the American Expeditionary Forces (RG 120) to supplement the printed documents for the 4th Marine Brigade and 2d Division, AEF; Records of the War Department General Staff (RG 165) for the interwar period; Records of The Adjutant General's Office (RG 94), especially the central correspondence files for the interwar period for Army schools; and U.S. Army Command Reports, 1949–54 (RG 407) for X Corps operations in Korea, 1951–52. Records of the Joint Chiefs of Staff (RG 218) contain significant materials on post-World War II contingency planning and defense organization. Navy documents include Records of the Bureau of Navigation (RG 24) for the operations of the Special Service Squadron in the Caribbean and Central America; General Records of the Navy Department (RG 80) and U.S. Navy Flag Files (RG 313) for the records of Commander Naval Forces Western Pacific (China), 1947–49. The Command Files, Operational Archives, Naval Historical Center, also contain collections of documents on the Fleet Marine Force and Navy operational commands for World War II and the Korean War.

I found relevant material on Thomas's service in Haiti and China, as well as his 1941 trip with James Roosevelt, in the Decimal File, General Records of the

Department of State (RG 59) and Records of Posts and State Stations, Department of State (RG 84).

SERVICE IN THREE WARS

Most of the information about the wartime experiences of General Thomas comes from the personal and official primary sources already cited, but I consulted other sources to put Thomas's service in the proper tactical and operational context.

For World War I, Thomas himself provided critical data in 2d Lt. G. C. Thomas, "Data Regarding My Service with the American Expeditionary Forces," 24 June 1919, prepared for his application for a regular commission (Thomas OQR). Other important primary sources are "A Brief History of the Sixth Regiment, United States Marine Corps" (1918–19), by the regimental adjutant, Capt. David Bellamy, who also preserved his own "World War I Diary of David Bellamy," both in the Marine Corps Historical Center; Historical Section, Army War College, *Records of the Second Division (Regular)*, nine volumes, Fort Sam Houston and Washington, D.C. (1924–28), and the accompanying *Translations of War Diaries of German Units Opposed to the Second Division (Regular)* (1930–32); and Historical Division, Department of the Army, *United States Army in World War I,* seventeen volumes (Washington, D.C.: Government Printing Office, 1948).

Two secondary sources are especially important: Maj. Edward N. McClellan, *The United States Marine Corps in the World War* (1920, and reissued 1968, History and Museums Division, Headquarters Marine Corps); and Col. Oliver L. Spaulding, USA, and Col. John W. Wright, USA, *The Second Division, American Expeditionary Force in France, 1917–1919* (New York: Hillman Press, 1937). Robert B. Asprey, *At Belleau Wood* (New York: Putnam, 1965), remains the best available account of the battle for Belleau Wood. With the aid of maps available in the Historical Section, War Department, *2d Division Summary of Operations in the World War* (Washington, D.C.: Government Printing Office, 1944), the author walked the battlefields of Belleau Wood and Soissons in August 1987.

Among the 1st Marine Division records that survived the Guadalcanal campaign, the division staff logs and diaries should be matched against Commanding General, 1st Marine Division, to Commandant of the Marine Corps, "Final Report of the Guadalcanal Campaign," in five parts, April 1947, in the 1st Marine Division organizational records (RG 127). Valuable secondary accounts are numerous. Two were written by participants: Brig. Gen. Samuel B. Griffith II, *The Battle for Guadalcanal* (Philadelphia: Lippincott, 1963), which is notable for its use of Japanese sources; and Herbert C. Merillat, *Guadalcanal Remembered* (New York: Dodd, Mead, 1982), which includes the author's 1942 diary notes, as well as his personal observations that were not in an earlier work, *The Island* (Boston: Houghton Mifflin, 1944).

Official Marine Corps histories are: Maj. John Zimmerman, *The Guadalcanal Operation* (Washington, D.C.: G-3, Headquarters Marine Corps, 1949), a monograph completed too quickly after the war to avoid errors; and Lt. Col. Frank O. Hough, Maj. Verle E. Ludwig, and Henry I. Shaw, Jr., *Pearl Harbor to Guadalcanal*, Volume I in the five-volume *History of U.S. Marine Corps Operations in World War II* (Washington, D.C.: Historical Division, G-3, Headquarters Marine Corps,

1958–71). Other useful official histories are Samuel Eliot Morison, *The Struggle for Guadalcanal*, Volume V in the fifteen-volume *History of United States Naval Operations in World War II* (Boston: Little, Brown, 1947–62); and John Miller, Jr., *Guadalcanal: The First Offensive* (Washington, D.C.: Historical Division, Department of the Army, 1949), the first book of the Pacific war volumes of the *United States Army in World War II*, a projected eighty-volume collection. The semiofficial history of Marine aviation during the war is Robert Sherrod, *History of Marine Corps Aviation in World War II*, available in two editions (Washington, D.C.: Combat Forces Press, 1952; Baltimore, Md.: Nautical and Aviation Publishing Co., 1987). Jeter A. Isley and Philip A. Crowl, *The U.S. Marines and Amphibious War* (Princeton, N.J.: Princeton University Press, 1951) remains essential.

The official after-action report for Bougainville is Commanding General, I Marine Amphibious Corps, to Commandant of the Marine Corps, "Bougainville Operation," March 1944, in the I MAC organizational records (RG 127). The official histories, parts of the service series already cited, are: Henry I. Shaw, Jr., and Maj. Douglas T. Kane, *Isolation of Rabaul* (Washington, D. C.: Historical Branch, G-3, Headquarters Marine Corps, 1963); John Miller, Jr., *CARTWHEEL: The Isolation of Rabaul* (Washington, D.C.: Department of the Army, 1959); and Samuel Eliot Morison, *Breaking the Bismarcks Barrier* (Boston: Atlantic, Little, Brown, 1950).

The official history of Marine Corps participation in the Korean War is Lynn Montross, et al., *U.S. Marine Operations in Korea, 1950–1953* (Washington, D.C.: Historical Branch, G-3, Headquarters Marine Corps, 1954–72), a five-volume series. For the period during which General Thomas served as Commanding General, 1st Marine Division, the fourth volume in this series is the appropriate volume: Lynn Montross, Maj. Hubbard O. Kuokka, and Maj. Norman H. Hicks, *The East-Central Front* (1962). The role of the air war is told in Robert F. Futrell, *The United States Air Force in Korea, 1950–1953*, revised edition (Washington, D.C.: Office of Air Force History, 1983). The strategic and organizational context of the American war effort is covered thoroughly in James F. Schnabel and Robert J. Watson, *The Korean War*, Volume III of *The History of the Joint Chiefs of Staff* (Wilmington, Del.: Michael Glazier, 1979); and Doris M. Condit, *The Test of War, 1950–1953*, Volume II of *History of the Office of the Secretary of Defense* (Washington, D.C.: Office of the Secretary of Defense, 1988).

THE MARINE CORPS IN THE TWENTIETH CENTURY

Since the end of World War II, the Marine Corps has been the subject of four comprehensive histories. Three were written by Marine Corps officers, and all of them are characterized by unique strengths and weaknesses. The first, Col. Robert D. Heinl, Jr., *Soldiers of the Seas: The United States Marine Corps, 1775–1962* (Annapolis, Md.: U.S. Naval Institute, 1962), reflects the author's interest in the use of history to support organizational morale and policy preferences, his dogged defensiveness about the Corps, and his distrust of all the other services. Colonel Heinl, who died in 1979, also liked any good story that related to origins of Corps customs and tradition, but original documentary research was not his strong suit. As an officer and Corps historian, however, he knew much of the "inside story" of Marine Corps affairs from the 1930s to the 1960s. Brig. Gen. Edwin H.

Simmons, who retired in 1971 to become the director of the History and Museums Division, wrote the second book, *The United States Marine Corps, 1775–1975* (New York: Viking Press, 1975), with a verve comparable to Heinl's, but he incorporated more comprehensive research and more cautious judgments of Marine personalities and policies. The book is especially notable for its operational assessments; the author, a three-war veteran, had more field experience than Heinl but knew the Corps' senior leaders just as well. In the third work, J. Robert Moskin, *The U.S. Marine Corps Story* (New York: McGraw-Hill, 1977; revised 1987), focuses on Marine battlefield heroics. It provides no special advance in the research done by Heinl and Simmons but profits from the author's ability as a prose stylist and his experience as a correspondent and writer of popular history. Although the fourth book suffers from stylistic density and some academic pretentiousness, Allan R. Millett, *Semper Fidelis: The History of the Marine Corps* (New York: Macmillan, 1980 and 1991), sets a new standard for original research, especially in the checkered history of the Corps before World War II, and deals with Marine Corps history with less awe than its predecessors. This history places less emphasis on operations and focuses instead on the development of the Corps as an institution driven to find a useful place in national defense policy and dedicated to its own preservation.

Although it does not pretend to be a full history of the Marine Corps, Lt. Gen. Victor H. Krulak, *First to Fight: An Inside View of the U.S. Marine Corps* (Annapolis, Md.: Naval Institute Press, 1984), is an exceptional effort to catch the uniqueness of the Marine Corps and to draw examples of that special character from the author's own distinguished career.

For their contributions as views of Marine Corps history through the experiences of individual officers, noteworthy memoirs and biographies are:

Lt. Col. Merrill L. Bartlett, *Lejeune: A Marine's Life* (Columbia: University of South Carolina Press, 1991).

Norman V. Cooper, *A Fighting General: The Biography of Gen. Holland M. "Howlin' Mad" Smith* (Quantico, Va.: Marine Corps Association, 1987).

Hans Schmidt, *Maverick Marine: General Smedley D. Butler and the Contradictions of American Military History* (Lexington: University Press of Kentucky, 1987).

Gen. A. A. Vandegrift with Robert Asprey, *Once a Marine* (New York: W. W. Norton, 1964).

Brig. Gen. Robert H. Williams, *The Old Corps: A Portrait of the U.S. Marine Corps between the Wars* (Annapolis, Md.: Naval Institute Press, 1982).

Of the many monographs published by the History and Museums Division, Headquarters Marine Corps (HQMC), and its predecessors, the most important works that bear on General Thomas's career are:

Lt. Col. Kenneth J. Clifford, *Progress and Purpose: A Developmental History of the U.S. Marine Corps, 1900–1970* (Washington, D.C.: History and Museums Division, HQMC, 1973).

Kenneth W. Condit, Maj. John H. Johnstone, and Ella W. Nargele, *A Brief History of the Headquarters Marine Corps Staff Organization*, revised edition (Washington, D.C.: Historical Division, HQMC, 1971).

Lt. Col. Edward C. Johnson and Graham A. Cosmas, *Marine Corps Aviation: The Early Years, 1912–1940* (Washington, D.C.: History and Museums Divison, HQMC, 1977).

Lt. Col. Eugene W. Rawlins and Maj. William J. Sambito, *Marines and Helicopters, 1946–1962* (Washington, D.C.: History and Museums Division, HQMC, 1976).

Lt. Col. Charles A. Fleming, Capt. Robin L. Austin, and Capt. Charles A. Braley, III, *Quantico: Crossroads of the Marine Corps* (Washington, D.C.: History and Museums Division, HQMC, 1978).

Periodicals that cover Marine Corps affairs are *Marine Corps Gazette* (the journal of the Marine Corps Association), U.S. Naval Institute *Proceedings*, *Army and Navy Journal* and its successor magazines, and *Fortitudine*, the newsletter and journal of the History and Museums Division. A bibliography of Marine Corps history can be found in several subject bibliographies published by the History and Museums Division since the 1950s, as well as in the expert assessments in Graham Cosmas's two essays: "The United States Marine Corps" in Robin Higham and Donald J. Mrozek, compilers, *A Guide to the Sources of U.S. Military History: Supplement I* 199–233 (Hamden, Conn.: Archon Books, 1981); and *Guide to the Sources in U.S. Military History: Supplement II* 230–240 (Hamden, Conn.: Archon Books, 1986).

Notes

Abbreviations

AAF	Army Air Forces
AC/S	Assistant Chief of Staff
AEF	American Expeditionary Forces
AFB	Air Force Base
AFF	Army Field Forces
AG	Adjutant General
A&I	Adjutant & Inspector, U.S. Marine Corps.
ALNAV	All Naval Addressees
ARG	Advanced Research Group
ARND	Annual Reports of the Navy Department
ARWD	Annual Reports of the War Department
BAR	Browning automatic rifle
CAS	Close Air Support
CCS	Combined Chiefs of Staff (World War II)
C&GSS	Command and General Staff School, U.S. Army
CG	Commanding General
CinC	Commander in Chief
CinCFE	Commander in Chief Far East
CinCPac	Commander in Chief Pacific
CinCPAO	Commander in Chief Pacific Ocean Areas
CMC or Cmdt.	Commandant of the Marine Corps
CMCS	Commandant, Marine Corps Schools
CNO	Chief of Naval Operations
CO	Commanding Officer
COMINCH/CNO	Commander in Chief U.S. Fleet/Chief of Naval Operations
ComNavForWesPac or ComNavWesPac	Commander Naval Forces Western Pacific

CP	Command Post
ComPhibForPacFlt	Commander Amphibious Forces Pacific Fleet
ComSoPac	Commander South Pacific
C/S	Chief of Staff
DP&P	Director, Division of Plans and Policies, HQMC
EXO	Executive Officer
FEAF	Far East Air Forces
FMF	Fleet Marine Forces
FMF LANT	Fleet Marine Forces Atlantic
FMF PAC	Fleet Marine Forces Pacific
FMFWesPac	Fleet Marine Forces Western Pacific
FO	Forward Observer
FY	Fiscal Year
GHQ	General Headquarters
GPF	Grand Puissance Filloux [French-manufactured 155-mm. artillery piece]
HAF	Historical Amphibious File
HDR	Historical Division (Reference) [now RS MCHC]
H&MD	History and Museums Division, HQMC
HMSO	Her Majesty's Stationery Office
HQ	Headquarters
HQMC	Headquarters Marine Corps
I MAC	I Marine Amphibious Corps
JAG	Judge Advocate General
JCS	Joint Chiefs of Staff
JPC	Joint Planning Committee
LANTFLT	Atlantic Fleet
LC	Library of Congress
LFDC	Landing Force Development Center
MarDiv	Marine Division
MCG	*Marine Corps Gazette*
MCHC	Marine Corps Historical Center
MCOHC	Marine Corps Oral History Collection
MCPPC	Marine Corps Personal Papers Collection
MCSC	Marine Corps Systems Command
MCTEC	Marine Corps Training and Education Command, Quantico, Va.
MD/LC	Manuscript Division, Library of Congress
MG	machine gun
MG Bn	Machine Gun Battalion
MHI	Military History Institute (U.S. Army)
NA	National Archives of the United States
NavForWesPac	Naval Forces Western Pacific
NHC	Naval Historical Center
NHD	Naval Historical Division

OA or OA NHC	Operational Archives, Naval Historical Center, Washington, D.C.
OHC	Oral History Collection
OpO	Operations Order
OQR	Officer Qualification Record
P.L.	Public Law
PPC	Personal Papers Collection
QM	Quartermaster
RAF	Royal Air Force
RAN	Royal Australian Navy
RG	Record Group
RS or RS MCHC	Reference Section, Marine Corps Historical Center
SecNav	Secretary of the Navy
SecState	Secretary of State
SecWar	Secretary of War
SHRC	Simpson Historical Research Center
TAGO	The Adjutant General's Office, U.S. Army
TFP	Thomas Family Papers
USAC&GSC	U.S. Army Command and General Staff College, Fort Leavenworth
USAF	U.S. Air Force
USNIP	U.S. Naval Institute *Proceedings*
WPA	Works Progress Administration

Preface

1. Allan R. Millett, Williamson Murray, and Kenneth H. Watman, "The Effectiveness of Military Organizations," in Allan R. Millett and Williamson Murray, eds., *Military Effectiveness,* 3 vols. (Boston: Allen & Unwin, 1988), 1:1–30.
2. Allan R. Millett, *The General: Robert L. Bullard and Officership in the United States Army, 1881–1925* (Westport, Conn.: Greenwood Press, 1975).
3. Forrest C. Pogue, *George C. Marshall,* 4 vols. (New York: Viking Press, 1963–87); D. Clayton James, *The Years of MacArthur,* 3 vols. (Boston: Houghton Mifflin, 1970–85).
4. Stephen E. Ambrose, *Eisenhower: Soldier, General of the Army, President-Elect, 1890–1952* (New York: Simon & Schuster, 1983); E. B. Potter, *Nimitz* (Annapolis, Md.: Naval Institute Press, 1976); Thomas B. Buell, *Master of Sea Power: A Biography of Fleet Admiral Ernest J. King* (Boston: Little, Brown, 1980); Barbara Tuchman, *Stilwell and the American Experience in China, 1911–1945* (New York: Macmillan, 1970); Martin Blumenson, *Patton* (New York: William Morrow, 1985); Donald Smythe, *Guerrilla Warrior: The Early Life of John J. Pershing* (New York: Charles Scribner's Sons, 1973); *Pershing: General of the Armies* (Bloomington: Indiana University Press, 1986).
5. Lloyd Lewis, *Captain Sam Grant* (Boston: Little, Brown, 1950); Bruce Catton, *Grant Moves South* (Boston: Little, Brown, 1960); Bruce Catton, *Grant Takes Command* (Boston: Little, Brown, 1968).

6. Anton Myrer, *Once an Eagle* (New York: Holt, Rinehart, & Winston, 1968).
7. Hans Schmidt, *Maverick Marine: General Smedley D. Butler and the Contradictions of American Military History* (Lexington: University Press of Kentucky, 1987); Norman V. Cooper, *A Fighting General: The Biography of Gen. Holland M. "Howlin' Mad" Smith* (Quantico, Va.: Marine Corps Association, 1987); Lt. Col. Merrill L. Bartlett, USMC (Ret.), *Lejeune: A Marine's Life* (Columbia: University of South Carolina Press, 1991); George Barnett, "Soldier and Sailor, Too," unpublished autobiography, George Barnett Papers, Personal Papers Collection, Marine Corps Historical Center (MCHC); John A. Lejeune, *The Reminiscences of a Marine* (Philadelphia: Dorrance, 1930); A. A. Vandegrift, with Robert Aspry, *Once a Marine: The Memoirs of General A. A. Vandegrift* (New York: Norton, 1966); Burke Davis, *Marine: The Life of Lt. Gen. Lewis B. (Chesty) Puller, USMC (Ret.)* (Boston: Little, Brown, 1962); Roger Willock, *Unaccustomed to Fear: A Biography of the Late General Roy S. Geiger, USMC* (Princeton, N.J.: Roger Willock, 1968). Shepherd's biographer is Lt. Gen. Victor H. Krulak, USMC (Ret.), who contributed a shorter version of his work for Allan R. Millett, ed., *Commandants of the Marine Corps* (Annapolis, Md.: Naval Institute Press, forthcoming).
8. Gen. Gerald C. Thomas, oral memoir (1966), Marine Corps Oral History Collection, Marine Corps Historical Center; Allan R. Millett, *Semper Fidelis; The History of the United States Marine Corps* (New York: Macmillan, 1980, 1991).
9. Col. DeWolf Schatzel, response to General Thomas questionnaire, 17 March 1986, in author's possession.

Chapter I. Molding the Man

1. E. E. Pierson and J. L. Hasbrouck, eds., *McLean County, Illinois in the World War, 1917–1918* (Bloomington, Ill.: McLean County Publishing Co., 1921), 6–8; *Illinois Wesleyan Argus* (Bloomington, Ill.), 3 May 1917; *Daily Pantagraph* (Bloomington, Ill.), 1 March–17 April 1917.
2. *Illinois Wesleyan Argus*, 3 May 1917.
3. Ibid.; *Daily Pantagraph*, 19 April 1917.
4. Ibid.
5. Missouri Writers Project (WPA), Missouri State Highway Department, *Missouri* (New York: Duell, Sloan, & Pierce, 1941), 480–1.
6. Gen. G. C. Thomas, "Family Notes," 7–10, manuscript written by General Thomas, 1973, with supporting "Notes on Thomas Family" by Dr. W. H. Johnson and "Chart on Thomas and Young Lines" by the Rev. Louis O'Vander Thomas, Thomas Family Papers (TFP), held by Mrs. G. C. Thomas, Washington, D.C., and Col. G. C. Thomas, Jr., USMC (Ret.), The Plains, Virginia. General Thomas's "Family Notes" and unpublished memoir are more accurate than his oral memoir (1966), Marine Corps Oral History Collection (OHC), Marine Corps Historical Center, Washington Navy Yard.
7. Thomas, "Family Notes," 1–4, 6–7.
8. Ibid., 10–11.
9. Ibid., 11–13.

10. "Bloomington and Normal," Federal Writers' Project, *Illinois: A Descriptive and Historical Guide* (Chicago: A. C. McClurg, 1947), 161–68; Donals F. Tingley, *The Structuring of a State: The History of Illinois* (Urbana and Chicago: University of Illinois Press, 1980), 31, 143–44; J. H. Burnham, comp., *History of Bloomington and Normal, in McLean County, Illinois* (Bloomington, Ill.: J. J. Burnham, 1879); Bloomington Association of Commerce, *Illustrated Bloomington* (Bloomington, Ill.: The Illustrated Publishing Co., 1916).
11. Thomas, "Family Notes," 13–16, and oral memoir, 6–8; *Bloomington and Normal City Directory, 1907* and *1909* (Bloomington, Ill.: Pantagraph Printing Co., 1907, 1909).
12. *Normal City Directory, 1909*, 16–17, 17a.
13. Ibid., 17–18; Gerald C. Thomas, official transcript, Illinois Wesleyan University, furnished by university registrar, 24 July 1986; Elmo Scott Watson, *The Illinois Wesleyan Story, 1850–1950* (Bloomington: Illinois Wesleyan University Press, 1950), 139–54, for the World War I era; Illinois Wesleyan University, *The Wesleyan, 1916–1918* (Indianapolis: Stafford Printing, 1915–1917). Virginia Young Thomas's favorable view of her son and her frustration with her family's life are expressed in V. Y. Thomas to Lt. and Mrs. G. C. Thomas, 13 January 1926, TFP.
14. Thomas, "Family Notes," 18; "Illinois' Quota in First Call under Federal Conscription Act, 1917," *Blue Book of the State of Illinois 1917–1918* (Danville: Illinois Printing Co., 1919), 98–102; *Illinois Wesleyan Argus*, 3 May 1917; Lt. Col. Marvin A. Kreidberg and 1st Lt. Merton G. Henry, USA, *History of Military Mobilization in the United States Army, 1775–1945* (Washington, D.C.: Department of the Army, 1955), 281–83; "Report of the Secretary of War," *Annual Reports of the War Department, 1917*, 3 vols. (Washington, D.C.: Government Printing Office, 1918), I:21–3; "Report of the Chief of Staff," ARWD, *1917*, I:140.
15. Thomas, oral memoir, 9, and "Family Notes," 18. The letters of recommendation are in the Thomas Family Papers. For Marine Corps recruiting policy and advertising in World War I, see Lt. Col. Gary L. Rutledge, USMC, "The Rhetoric of United States Marine Corps Enlisted Recruitment," master's thesis, University of Kansas, 1974, 67–105; "Annual Report of the Secretary of the Navy," *Annual Reports of the Navy Department 1917* (Washington, D.C.: Government Printing Office, 1918), 1, 11–12, 25–7; and "Report of the Major General Commandant of the United States Marine Corps," ARND, *1917*, 835–48.
16. Jack Shulimson, "The First to Fight: Marine Corps Expansion," *Prologue* 8 (Spring 1976), 5–16; Bernard C. Nalty and Lt. Col. Ralph F. Moody, *A Brief History of U.S. Marine Corps Officer Procurement, 1775–1969*, rev. ed. (Washington, D.C.: Historical Division, HQMC, 1970), 4–6; HDR memorandum, "Strength of the Marine Corps," 11 December 1969, Reference Branch, H&MD; U.S. Marine Corps Recruiting Publicity Bureau, *The Recruiters' Bulletin*, April-June, 1917, H&MD Library; Millett, *Semper Fidelis*, 287–90; *New York Times* (using press releases from the Recruiting Publicity Bureau), 4–18 April and 13–21 May 1917. On Marine Corps publicity and World War I, see Robert Lindsay, *This High Name: Public Relations and*

the U.S. Marine Corps (Madison: University of Wisconsin Press, 1956), 23–35.

17. Thomas, "Family Notes," 19, and oral memoir, 9; *Daily Pantagraph*, 16 May 1917; Pierson and Hasbrouck, *McLean County*, 6–8, 196–97.
18. Thomas, oral memoir, 9–10; Gen. Gerald C. Thomas, draft autobiography, "1917–1919," unpublished manuscript, MCHC; *Recruiters' Bulletin* 12 (May 1917).

Chapter II. Becoming a Marine

1. Maj. Gen. Cmdt. G. Barnett to Secretary of the Navy, 21 October 1915, File 2515-10, General Correspondence, 1913–32, Records of Headquarters Marine Corps, Record Group (RG) 127, NA; Barnett, "Soldier and Sailor, Too," Chap. 25; Lt. Col. M. L. Bartlett, "George Barnett," manuscript essay, 1986, in author's possession. The definitive published account of the Marine Corps' participation in World War I remains Maj. E. N. McClellan, *The United States Marine Corps in the World War*, originally printed in 1920, rev. ed. (Washington, D.C.: Historical Branch, G-3 Division, HQMC, 1968). See also Millett, *Semper Fidelis*, 287–318.
2. W. R. Coyle, "Parris Island in the War," *Marine Corps Gazette (MCG)* 10 (December 1925), 187–91; William M. Darden, "Parris Island, S. C.," in Paolo Coletta, ed., and K. Jack Bauer, assoc. ed., *United States Navy and Marine Corps Bases, Domestic* (Westport, Conn.: Greenwood Press, 1985), 415–23; Elmore A. Champie, *A Brief History of the Marine Corps Recruit Depot, Parris Island, South Carolina, 1891–1962*, rev. ed. (Washington, D.C.: Historical Division, HQMC, 1962), 2–6.
3. Kemper F. Cowing, *Dear Folks at Home* (Boston: Houghton Mifflin, 1919), 3.

    For the memories of other recruits who went through Parris Island and joined the 6th Marines with Jerry Thomas in 1917, see Levi E. Hemrick, *Once a Marine* (New York: Carlton Press, 1968); J. E. Rendinell and G. Pattulo, *One Man's War* (New York, 1928); Martin G. Gulberg, *A War Diary* (Chicago: Drake Press, 1927); Maj. Gen. Melvin L. Krulewitch, USMC, memoir (1970), 10–53, Marine Corps Oral History Collection (OHC), MCHC; Gy. Sgt. Don V. Paradis, memoir (1973), OHC.
4. G. C. Thomas to Mrs. V. Y. Thomas, 17 and 19 May and 6 June 1917, TFP; G. C. Thomas, autobiography, "1917–1919," 1, Thomas Family Papers; Thomas, oral memoir, 10; medical record of Gen. G. C. Thomas, USMC, National Personnel Records Center, St. Louis.
5. G. C. Thomas to Mrs. V. Y. Thomas, 6–25 June 1917, TFP.
6. G. C. Thomas to Mrs. V. Y. Thomas, 29 June and 15 July 1917, TFP.
7. Ordnance Department, U.S. Army, *Description and Rules for the Management of the U. S. Magazine Rifle Model of 1903, Caliber 30* (reprint, Union City, Tenn.: Pioneer Printing, 1979); Robert E. Barde, *The History of Marine Corps Competitive Marksmanship Training* (Washington, D.C.: Marksmanship Branch, HQMC, 1961), 57–80; *New York Times*, 4 November 1917; D. Michael O'Quinlivan and Benis M. Frank, *The Lauchheimer Trophy* (Washington, D.C.: Historical Branch, G-3, HQMC, 1962); Pvt. Raymond Howard

Stenback, diary, entry of 22 December 1917, with appendices on marksmanship training, 1917–1919, in 6th Marine Regiment file, 2d Division Collection, World War I Survey Collection, U.S. Army Military History Institute, Carlisle Barracks, Penn. Private Stenback, who eventually served in the 6th Marines' regimental machine gun company in France, constructed a journal from his diary and his detailed letters home. His memoir is one of the best sources for the experience of a Marine enlisted man during World War I.

8. G. C. Thomas to Mrs. V. Y. Thomas, 19 July and 10 August 1917, TFP. Cpl. Leonard O. Prather reached France as a member of the 13th Marines on 25 September 1918 but did not see combat.

9. Secretary of War N. D. Baker to Secretary of the Navy J. Daniels, 16 May 1917, and Headquarters AEF General Orders 31 (3 September 1917) and 38 (17 September 1917), in File 16.7, G-3, GHQ, AEF, Correspondence File, Records of the American Expeditionary Forces, RG 120; Brig. Gen. C. L. McCawley, QM USMC, to Col. D. E. McCarthy, USA, 23 May 1917, File 29, AG AEF, Correspondence File, RG 120; "Excerpts from the Statement of the Major General Commandant, U.S. Marine Corps, before the Committee on Naval Affairs of the House of Representatives on the Estimates of the Marine Corps," 23 January 1918, *MCG* 3 (March, 1918), 67–85; Barnett, "Soldier and Sailor, Too"; Col. Oliver L. Spaulding, USA, and Col. John W. Wright, USA, *The Second Division, American Expeditionary Force, 1917–1919* (New York: Hillman Press, 1937), 6–28.

Technically, the regiments of the 4th Brigade (Marine Corps) were the 5th Regiment of Marines and 6th Regiment of Marines, but I have adopted the usage official since 1930, the 5th Marines and 6th Marines, in referring to these Marine regiments, which was also the popular usage in 1917–18.

10. Lt. Col. Charles A. Fleming, Capt. Robin L. Austin, and Capt. Charles A. Bradley III, *Quantico: Crossroads of the Marine Corps* (Washington, D.C.: History and Museums Division, HQMC, 1978), 8–37.

11. "History of the 6th Regiment (Marines)," 1919, probably written by Capt. David Bellamy, first 3d Battalion adjutant, then regimental adjutant, 6th Marines Historical File 10.2–32.16, Organizational Records, AEF, RG 120; Brig. Gen. Albertus W. Catlin, *With the Help of God and a Few Marines* (Garden City, N.Y.: Doubleday, Page, 1919), 18–20; G. C. Thomas to Mrs. V. Y. Thomas, 14 August 1917, TFP.

12. Three letters, G. C. Thomas to Mrs. V. Y. Thomas, 4–14 September 1917, TFP; Thomas, oral memoir, 11–12, and "1917–1919," 2–3.

13. "History of the 6th Regiment (Marines)" (RG 120); Gulberg, *War Diary*, 5.

14. Thomas, "1917–1919," 3–5; G. C. Thomas to Mrs. V. Y. Thomas, 5 October 1917, TFP; Thomas, oral memoir, 13–14.

15. Maj. Robert L. Denig, "Diary of a Marine Officer during the World War," 112, Brig. Gen. Robert L. Denig Papers, MCPPC.

16. CG AEF to Maj. Gen. Cmdt., 10 November 1917, File 5414, AG AEF, General Correspondence, 1917–1920, RG 120; AG AEF, memorandum, 10 January 1918, Ibid.; Maj. Gen. J. F. Morrison, memorandum for the C/S USA, December 1917, Correspondence of the Chief of Staff, 1918–1921, Records of the War Department General Staff, RG 165; Adm. W. S. Benson,

USN, to Maj. Gen. J. Biddle, USA, 12 January 1918, Correspondence of the Chief of Staff, RG 165; Frederick Palmer, *America in France* (New York: Dodd, Mead, 1918), 97–9.

17. Five letters, G. C. Thomas to Mrs. V. Y. Thomas, 10 October 1917–3 January 1918, TFP; Thomas, "1917–1919," 5–6, and oral memoir, 14–16.

Chapter III. Marine Sergeant at War

1. For the background for the 1918 campaign on the Western Front, see especially Office of the Chief of Staff, GHQ AEF, "A Strategical Study on the Employment of the A.E.F. against the Imperial German Government," 25 September 1917, GHQ AEF Secret General Correspondence, File 681, RG 120; Gen. John J. Pershing, *My Experiences in the World War*, 2 vols. (New York: Frederick J. Stokes, 1931), I:38–272; B. H. Liddell Hart, *The Real War, 1914–1918* (Boston: Little, Brown, 1931), 364–469; Allan R. Millett, "Over Where? The AEF and the American Strategy for Victory, 1917–1918," in Kenneth J. Hagan and William R. Roberts, eds., *Against All Enemies: Interpretations of American Military History from Colonial Times to the Present* (Westport, Conn.: Greenwood Press, 1986), 235–56; Edward M. Coffman, *The War to End All Wars: The American Military Experience in World War I* (New York: Oxford University Press, 1968); Robert H. Ferrell, *Woodrow Wilson and World War I, 1917–1921* (New York: Harper & Row, 1985); Historical Section, U.S. Army War College, *The Genesis of the American First Army* (Washington, D.C.: Government Printing Office, 1938); Barrie Pitt, *1918: The Last Act* (New York: Norton, 1962); John Toland, *No Man's Land* (Garden City, N.Y.: Doubleday, 1981); Donald Smythe, *John J. Pershing: General of the Armies* (Bloomington: Indiana University Press, 1986).
2. Harvey A. DeWeerd, *President Wilson Fights His War: World War I and the American Intervention* (New York: Macmillan, 1968), 257–87.
3. Smythe, *Pershing*, 60–95.
4. Thomas, "1917–1919," 6–8, and oral memoir, 15–19; G. C. Thomas to Mrs. V. Y. Thomas, 20 January 1918, TFP; Gulberg, *A War Diary*, 10–12.
5. Thomas, "1917–1919," 7–8, and oral memoir, 19–24; Carlton Burr, Summary of Qualifications, 25 February 1918, Burr File, MCHC. See also 2d Lt. Gerald C. Thomas, "Data Regarding My Services with the American Expeditionary Forces," 24 June 1919, Thomas OQR. For detail on the 6th Marines' service, see especially Capt. David Bellamy, "World War I Diary of David Bellamy, 1888–1960," PPC, MCHC.
6. "History of the 6th Regiment (Marines)," 1919, 6th Marines Historical File, RG 120; Spaulding and Wright, *Second Division*, 13–28.
7. Catlin, *With the Help of God*, 33.
8. G. C. Thomas to Mrs. V. Y. Thomas, 19 April 1918, TFP; Thomas, "1917–1919," 10–12; "History of the 6th Regiment (Marines)," RG 120; Battalion Intelligence Officer to CO, 6th Marines, 11 April 1918, 6th Marines Historical File, RG 120.

   For a detailed account of trench warfare operations, see Maj. E. N. McClellan, "The Fourth Brigade of Marines in the Training Areas and the Operations in the Verdun Sector," *MCG* 5 (March, 1920), 81–110. The

battlefield is described in American Battle Monuments Commission, *American Armies and Battlefields in Europe* (Washington, D.C.: Government Printing Office, 1938), 105–66.
9. Smythe, *Pershing,* 96–104.
10. Thomas, "1917–1919," 12–13, and oral memoir, 24; "Brig. Gen. Maurice E. Shearer," 1954, Shearer File, MCHC. On the gas attack, see Capt. B. C. Goss, Chief Gas Officer, to C/S, 2d Div. 14 April 1918, and 6th Marines, "Report on Gas Attack," 21 April 1918, 6th Marines Historical File, RG 120.
11. Charles R. Shrader, "Harbord, James Guthrie," in Roger J. Spiller, ed., *Dictionary of American Military Biography,* 3 vols. (Westport, Conn.: Greenwood Press, 1984), II:437–41; Brig. Gen. J. G. Harbord to Maj. Gen. C. R. Edwards, 11 May 1918, General Clarence R. Edwards Papers, Massachusetts Historical Society; James G. Harbord, *Leaves from a War Diary* (New York: Dodd, Mead, 1925), 280–1; Catlin, *With the Help of God,* 56–9. For favorable evaluations of the 4th Brigade, see Fifth Section, HQ AEF, memorandum, "Training Marines," 1 May 1918, G-3 Reports, General Correspondence, AEF, RG 120, and "Report of the Sub-Committee for Investigation of Conduct and Administration of Naval Affairs," *MCG* 3 (March, 1918), 76–8.
12. Thomas, "1917–1919," 13–15; Spaulding and Wright, *Second Division,* 33–4; "World War I Diary of David Bellamy," entry, 30 May 1918; Gulberg, *A War Diary,* 21.
13. Quoted in Smythe, *Pershing,* 131.
14. Spaulding and Wright, *Second Division,* 35–7; Smythe, *Pershing,* 131–2; DeWeerd, *President Wilson Fights His War,* 288–95.
15. Spaulding and Wright, *Second Division,* 38–41; Robert B. Asprey, *At Belleau Wood* (New York: G. P. Putnam's, 1965), 81–93.
16. Ibid.; Thomas, "1917–1919," 15–16.
17. Thomas, "1917–1919," 17; Catlin, *With the Help of God,* 83–90; Gulberg, *War Diary,* 22–4; Spaulding and Wright, *Second Division,* 42–3.
18. Thomas, "1917–1919," 18. The physical description of the battlefield is from American Battlefield Monuments Commission, *American Armies and Battlefields in Europe,* 43–8, and *2d Division Summary of Operations in the World War* (Washington, D.C.: Government Printing Office, 1944) with operations maps. The author explored the Belleau Wood battlefield in September 1987 and again in 1991.

Chapter IV. Belleau Wood
1. This account of the Battle of Belleau Wood, officially part of the Aisne Defensive campaign and the Aisne-Marne Counteroffensive campaign, is based principally on these sources: "Aisne Defensive" and "Chateau-Thierry/Belleau Wood" sections of documents in Historical Division, Department of the Army, *United States Army in the World War, 1917–1919,* 17 vols. (Washington, D.C.: Government Printing Office, 1948) IV (hereafter cited as *USA/WW*), IV; HQ 4th Brigade, "Diary of the Fourth Brigade, Marine Corps, A.E.F. . . . May 30, 1918 to June 30, 1918," 4th Brigade File, Reference Section, Marine Corps Historical Center; "History of the 6th Regiment (Marines)," RG 120; Operations summaries, Second Division, 21

May–7 October 1918, General John A. Lejeune Papers, MDLC; Spaulding and Wright, *Second Division; At Belleau Wood*.

    General Thomas wrote two long accounts of the battle from which I have reconstructed his participation: G. C. Thomas to Mrs. V. Y. Thomas, 1 June 1919, TFP, and Thomas, "1917–1919." For other personally observed details about the 6th Marines' experience at Belleau Wood, I have relied especially on Catlin (CO 6th Marines), *With the Help of God;* Maj. Frank E. Evans (Adjutant 6th Marines) to Maj. Gen. Cmdt. George Barnett, 29 June 1918, World War I Subject File, RS MCHC; Gulberg (75th Company), *A War Diary;* and William T. Scanlon (97th Company), *God Have Mercy on Us* (Boston: Houghton Mifflin, 1929). The battle is described in fictionalized form in two classic novels by a member of the 6th Marines, Thomas Boyd, *Through the Wheat* (New York: Charles Scribner's Sons, 1923) and *Points of Honor* (New York: Charles Scribner's Sons, 1925).

2. Thomas, "1917–1919," 17–19; Gulberg, *War Diary,* 24–7. See also Maj. Edwin N. McClellan, "Operations of the Fourth Brigade of Marines in the Aisne Defensive," *MCG* 5 (June 1920), 182–214.
3. Catlin, *With the Help of God,* 101–2; HQ 2nd Div to HQ AEF, 4 June 1918, Report 200-33.1, *USA/WW,* IV:132–3; Spaulding and Wright, *Second Division,* 46–7.
4. Thomas, "1917–1919," 19–21.
5. XXI Army Corps Order 81, 5 June 1918, and HQ 4th Brigade Field Order 1, 5 June 1918, and Field Order 2, 6th Jäger Battalion, in *USA/WW,* IV:143–5, 150, 364–5; Thomas, "1917–1919," 20–1.
6. Maj. Edwin N. McClellan, "Capture of Hill 142, Battle of Belleau Wood, and Capture of Bouresches," *MCG* 5 (September 1920), 277–313; Spaulding and Wright, *Second Division,* 52–5; Asprey, *At Belleau Wood,* 142–89.
7. CG 4th Brigade to C/S AEF, 6 June 1918; 4th Brigade to C/S 2d Division, 6 June 1918; CG 4th Brigade to CO, 6th Marines, 6 June 1918; AC/S III Corps to CG, 2d Division, 6 June 1918; CO 6th MG Bn to CG 4th Brigade, 6 June 1918, all of the above in *USA/WW,* IV:371–6. See also Asprey, *At Belleau Wood,* 190–211.
8. Thomas, "1917–1919," 21–2, and oral memoir, 33–5; two messages, CG 4th Brigade to CO 1st Battalion, 6th Marines, 8 June 1918, *USA/WW,* IV:414–17; CG 4th Brigade to CO 6th Marines and to CO 1st Battalion, 6th Marines, 9 June 1918, *USA/WW,* IV:419; HQ 4th Brigade, FO 3, 9 June 1918, *USA/WW,* IV:422–3; George A. Stowell file, RS MCHC.
9. Maj. E. N. McClellan, "Battle of Belleau Wood," *MCG* 5 (December 1920), 370–404; Spaulding and Wright, *Second Division,* 57–8.
10. CO 6th Marines to CG 4th Brigade, 10 June 1918, and CG 4th Brigade to CO 1st Battalion, 6th Marines, 10 June 1918, *USA/WW,* IV:426–7; Thomas, "1917–1919," 22–3; Asprey, *At Belleau Wood,* 229–42.
11. Thomas, "1917–1919," 23–4.
12. HQ 4th Brigade FO 4, 10 June 1918, *USA/WW,* IV:432; Thomas, "1917–1919," 24–5; Spaulding and Wright, *Second Division,* 58–9.
13. Thomas, "1917–1919," 25–7, and oral memoir, 39–40.

14. Thomas, "1917–1919," 27–8; G. C. Thomas to Mrs. V. Y. Thomas, 1 June 1919, TFP.
15. CO 1st Battalion, 6th Marines to CO 5th Marines and CO 6th Marines, 13 June 1918, *USA/WW*, IV:457; Thomas, "1917–1919," 28–9.
16. Thomas, "1917–1919," 28–9; Franklin B. Garrett File, RS MCHC; Spaulding and Wright, *Second Division*, 60–1; Intelligence report, 2d Division, 12–13 June 1918, *USA/WW*, IV:461–2; Col. W. S. Grant to G-3, AEF, 13 June 1918, *USA/WW*, IV:466–7.
17. Asprey, *At Belleau Wood*, 257–89; Thomas, "1917–1919," 28–9.
18. Spaulding and Wright, *Second Division*, 57–64.

    Although casualty statistics are difficult to assess then and now, the 1st Battalion, 6th Marines, appears to have suffered between 50 and 60 men a day on 10, 11, and 12 June 1918. On the night of 12 June, Hughes reported that he had around 700 effectives. The shelling of 13 June, however, cost the battalion over 200 casualties, many of them from gas. Casualties from 13 through 15 June numbered less than 50. By comparison, the 2d Battalion, 5th Marines, reported that it had only 350 effectives by the night of 12 June after two days of fighting. Total losses for the two Marine infantry regiments (31 May–9 July 1918) were 99 officers and 4,407 men. Brigade losses were 112 officers and 4,598 men, more than half the brigade's original strength.
19. Asprey, *At Belleau Wood*, 243–56, 321–32; Smythe, *Pershing*, 133–41; Spaulding and Wright, *Second Division*, 84–95; report, Intelligence section, *IV Reserve Corps*, 17 June 1918, *USA/WW*, IV:605–8; Millett, *Semper Fidelis*, 306–7, 317–18; Maj. Edwin N. McClellan, *The United States Marine Corps in the World War*, 1920 (Washington, D.C.: G-3, HQMC, 1968), 40–4; "You Wouldn't Dare to Tell It to the Marines Now," *Literary Digest* 57 (June 29 1918), 41–4.
20. Thomas, "1917–1919," 29; Gulberg, *War Diary*, 31; G. C. Thomas to Mrs. V. Y. Thomas, 1 June 1919, TFP.
21. Thomas, "1917–1919," 29–31.

    The conclusions about the influence of Belleau Wood on General Thomas's career are mine, of course.

Chapter V. Soissons
1. This account of the 6th Marines in the Aisne-Marne counteroffensive is based on "History of the 6th Regiment (Marines)," RG 120, NA, and the authoritative Maj. Edward N. McClellan, "The Aisne-Marne Offensive," *MCG* 6 (March 1921), 66–84, and (June 1921), 188–227. The personal narratives of greatest detail and perception are Sgt. A. R. M. Ganoe to A. W. Brown, July 1918, reprinted in Catlin, *With the Help of God*, 196–211; Maj. Robert L. Denig, "Diary of a Marine Officer during the World War," manuscript memoir, PPC, MCHC, 200–14; and Gulberg, *War Diary*, 32–8. General Thomas gave three accounts of the Soissons experience, all in essential agreement: G. C. Thomas to Mrs. V. Y. Thomas, 26 July 1918, TFP; Thomas, "1917–1919," 32–44, and oral memoir, 42–53.
2. The French planning documents from General Foch's headquarters, General Pétain's headquarters, French Group of Armies of the Reserve, French Tenth

Army, and French XX Corps, 14 June–16 July 1918, are reprinted in Historical Division, *USA/WW,* V:223–96. The planning is described and analyzed in Spaulding and Wright, *Second Division,* 96–104.
3. HQ, French Armies of the North and Northeast, 12 July 1919, Instructions No. 14546, 12 July 1918, *USA/WW,* V:235–6; Harbord, *Leaves from a War Diary,* 315–30; Smythe, *Pershing,* 153–60.
4. Spaulding and Wright, *Second Division,* 105–14; "History of the 6th Regiment (Marines)," RG 120.
5. Thomas, "1917–1919," 32–3.
6. Ganoe to Brown in Catlin, *With the Help of God,* 196–211; Gulberg, *War Diary;* Thomas, "1917–1919," 33–5.
7. Thomas, "1917–1919," 35–6, and oral memoir, 45–6.
8. G. C. Thomas to Mrs. V. Y. Thomas, 26 July 1918, TFP; Thomas, "1917–1919," 36–8; Gulberg, *War Diary,* 32–8.
9. Thomas, "1917–1919," 37–8, and oral memoir, 46–7; Spaulding and Wright, *Second Division,* 116–26; 2d Division, operations journal, 18 July 1918, *USA/WW,* V:334–5; Denig, "Diary of a Marine Officer," 200–6.
10. G. C. Thomas to Mrs. V. Y. Thomas, 26 July 1918, TFP; Thomas, "1917–1919," 39–41; Denig, "Diary of a Marine Officer," 206–14. The battlefield and German dispositions are from map, "2nd Division Aisne-Marne Offensive, July 18–20, 1918," in American Battle Monuments Commission, *2nd Division: Summary of Operations in the World War* (Washington, D.C., 1944), and Group of Armies Crown Prince, extracts, war diary 18 July 1918, *USA/WW,* V:678–80.
11. G. C. Thomas to Mrs. V. Y. Thomas, 26 July 1918, TFP; Thomas, oral memoir, 49–51.
12. Thomas, "1917–1919," 41–3. An analysis of the attack is in memorandum, CG, 2nd Division, to CG, XX Corps, July 19, 1918, *USA/WW,* V:336–8, and Spaulding and Wright, *Second Division,* 126–32. One lieutenant of the 75th Company was actually at the front but was separated from most of the company. The author walked the Soissons battlefield in September 1987.
13. Thomas, "1917–1919," 43–4, and oral memoir, 50–2; G. C. Thomas to Mrs. V. Y. Thomas, 26 July 1918, TFP; "Strength Report of Sixth Marines," 21 July 1918, 6th Marines Historical File, RG 120; 2d Division, "Casualties of the Second Division," 1 June 1919, John A. Lejeune Papers, MDLC.

Chapter VI. Surviving
1. The movements of the 6th Marines come from "History of the 6th Regiment (Marines)," RG 120, and Spaulding and Wright, *Second Division,* 133–40. See also Maj. E. N. McClellan, "In the Marbache Sector," *MCG* 6 (September 1921), 253–68. The information on Frederick A. Barker is taken from "Military History of Frederick A. Barker," RS MCHC. Thomas's accounts of the reorganization period appear in his memoir, "1917–1919," 44–5, and supplemental oral memoir (1973), 53.
2. Thomas, "1917–1919," 44–5; Maj. Gen. Cmdt. G. Barnett to Maj. Gen. J. A. Lejeune, 14 August 1918, 4th Brigade Subject File, RS MCHC; *New York Times,* 19 and 23 September 1918; Barnett, "Soldier and Sailor, Too,"

chapt. 25; 6th Marines, 25 August 1918, 6th Marines General Orders, Vol. IX, *2nd Division World War Records,* MCHC.
3. G. C. Thomas to Mrs. V. Y. Thomas, 26 August and 1 September 1918, TFP; Thomas, "1917–1919," 45.
4. Thomas, "1917–1919," 45–6, and oral memoir, 53–4; "History of the 6th Regiment (Marines)," RG 120; Maj. E. N. McClellan, "The St. Mihiel Offensive," *MCG* 6 (December 1921), 375–97; CO 1st Battalion to CO 6th Marines, "Report on Operations between Sept. 12 and 15 inclusive," 17 September 1918, Organizational Records, 6th Marines, RG 120.
5. Thomas, "1917–1919," 46; G. C. Thomas to Mrs. V. Y. Thomas, 21 September 1918, TFP; Gen. G. C. Thomas, entry, medical record, 20 September 1918, Thomas OQR; 2d Lt. G. C. Thomas, commission, 26 September 1918, Thomas OQR; "History of the 6th Regiment (Marines)," RG 120.
6. Spaulding and Wright, *Second Division,* 161–9; John Terraine, *To Win A War, 1918, The Year of Victory* (Garden City, N.Y.: Doubleday, 1981), 119–53; Lejeune, *Reminiscences,* 336–52.
7. Thomas, "1917–1919," 47–8; Lejeune, *Reminiscences,* 346–7.
8. G. C. Thomas to Mrs. V. Y. Thomas, 14 October 1918, TFP, Thomas, "1917–1919," 48–50.
9. G. C. Thomas to Mrs. V. Y. Thomas, 14 October 1918, TFP; "History of the 6th Regiment (Marines)," RG 120; telephone conversation and messages, CO 2d Battalion and CO 1st Battalion with CO 6th Marines, 4–8 October 1918, and report CO 6th Marines to CG 4th Brigade, 8 October 1918, 6th Marines, Organization Records, File 10.2-32.16, RG 120; Maj. E. N. McClellan, "The Battle of Mont Blanc Ridge," *MCG* 7 (March 1922), 1–21, (June 1922), 206–11, and (September 1922), 287–8. Dalton died of pneumonia on 22 October.
10. Smythe, *Pershing,* 212–22; Robert L. Bullard, *Personalities and Reminiscences of the War* (Garden City, N.Y.: Doubleday, 1925), 110–14; Brig. Gen. C. King to Maj. Gen. C. P. Summerall, 22 June 1921, and Maj. Gen. R. L. Bullard to Maj. Gen. C. P. Summerall, 25 June 1921, Charles P. Summerall Papers, MDLC; entry, 11 October 1918, John J. Pershing diaries, John J. Pershing Papers, MDLC; cables, CG AEF to Adjutant General, War Department, 11 and 13 October 1918, "AEF Confidential Cables Sent," Pershing Papers; Brig. Gen. J. McAndrew to Maj. Gen. J. G. Harbord, 21 October 1918, James G. Harbord Papers, MDLC.
11. G. C. Thomas to Mrs. V. Y. Thomas, 14 October 1918, TFP; Thomas, "1917–1919," 50–2; "History of the 6th Regiment (Marines)," RG 120.
12. Lejeune, *Reminiscences,* 367–79; "History of the 6th Regiment (Marines)," RG 120; G. C. Thomas to Mrs. V. Y. Thomas, 20 October 1918, TFP; Thomas, "1917–1919," 51–2; William T. Scanlon, *God Have Mercy on Us* (Boston: Houghton Mifflin, 1929), 304.
13. "History of the 6th Regiment (Marines)," RG 120; Thomas, "1917–1919," 53; entry, 1 November 1918, medical record, Gen. G. C. Thomas, Thomas OQR. Thomas's gassing, which qualified him for an immediate wound stripe, was not officially reported to his family until May 1919. Office of the A&I, HQMC, to Mrs. V. Y. Thomas, 20 May 1919, TFP.

On the AEF combat units and gas warfare, see Charles E. Heller, *Chemical Warfare in World War I: The American Experience, 1917–1918,* Leavenworth Papers No. 10 (Fort Leavenworth, Kan.: Combat Studies Institute, September 1984), 61–90.
14. G. C. Thomas to Mrs. V. Y. Thomas, 15 November 1918, TFP; Thomas, "1917–1919," 54; Gulberg, *War Diary,* 46–7; "History of the 6th Regiment (Marines)," RG 120.
15. Thomas, "1917–1919," 54–5; G. C. Thomas to Mrs. V. Y. Thomas, 15 November 1918, TFP.
16. Thomas, "1917–1919," 55–6; G. C. Thomas to Mrs. V. Y. Thomas, 15 November 1918, TFP; "History of the 6th Regiment (Marines)," RG 120.

The 75th Company seems to have been especially hard hit. The 80th Company had forty-four "originals" present on 11 November, thirty-two of whom had been wounded at least once. The 96th Company had twenty-one "originals" present.

Chapter VII. The Long March and an Occupation

1. Spaulding and Wright, *Second Division,* 223–38, covers the march and occupation duties as does "History of the 6th Regiment (Marines)," RG 120.
2. Thomas, "1917–1919," 56–7.
3. Lejeune, *Reminiscences,* 417–18. See also Second Division, "Operations Report: March to the Rhine," 5 January 1919, John A. Lejeune Papers, MDLC.
4. "History of the 6th Regiment (Marines)," RG 120; G. C. Thomas to Mrs. V. Y. Thomas, 22 November 1918, TFP.
5. G. C. Thomas to Mrs. V. Y. Thomas, 25 November 1918, TFP; Thomas, "1917–1919," 57.

For other details on the "long march," I have used Cpl. Raymond H. Stenback, "The Making of a Marine," manuscript autobiography (1971) with letters and diary entries, 1917–1919, 6th Marine Regiment File, World War I Survey Collection, U.S. Army Military History Institute, Carlisle Barracks, Pa.

6. Lejeune, *Reminiscences,* 426.
7. G. C. Thomas to L. O'V. Thomas, 12 December 1918, TFP; Gen. C. B. Cates, oral memoir (1967), 52, MCOH, MCHC.
8. "History of the 6th Regiment (Marines)," RG 120; Thomas, oral memoir, 56–7.
9. G. C. Thomas to Mrs. V. Y. Thomas, 20 October 1918 and 2 January 1919, TFP.
10. 2d Lt. G. C. Thomas to Maj. Gen. Cmdt. USMC, 23 February 1919, with supporting endorsements, Gen. G. C. Thomas, OQR.
11. G. C. Thomas to Mrs. V. Y. Thomas, 13 March, 3 April, and 4 June 1919, TFP; G. C. Thomas, "1919–1941," 1, manuscript autobiography, TFP.
12. Quote from entry of 29 March 1919, Stenback, "Making of a Marine." Stenback, a member of the 6th Marines machine gun company, was also stationed in Bad Hönningen, and his letters and diary entries give a detailed

picture of the occupation in the Koblenz enclave. See also Spaulding and Wright, *Second Division,* 230–8, and Lejeune, *Reminiscences,* 427–47.
13. Thomas, oral memoir, 57–64; entries of 25 January–24 May 1919, Stenback, "Making of a Marine."
14. G. C. Thomas to R. S. Thomas, 4 and 5 May and 28 June 1919, TFP; G. C. Thomas to Mrs. V. Y. Thomas, 6 April 1919, TFP; "Officer's Rating Card," 13 March 1919, Thomas OQR.
15. G. C. Thomas to Mrs. V. Y. Thomas, 28 June 1919, TFP; Thomas, "1917–1919," 59–60.
16. Lejeune, *Reminiscences,* 458–9.
17. Spaulding and Wright, *Second Division,* 237–8, 293–376; Col. Leonard P. Ayres, comp., *The War with Germany: A Statistical Summary* (Washington, D.C.: Government Printing Office, 1919), 113–18; Second Division Association, *Commendations of the Second Division, American Expeditionary Forces, 1917–1919* (Köln, Germany, May 1919).
18. Brig. Gen. P. B. Malone, USA, to Maj. Gen. J. G. Harbord, USA, 13 June 1919, File 21676-A592, General Correspondence, AEF Adjutant General, 1917–20, RG 120; "Château-Thierry Controversy," File 11112-1327, and SecWar N. D. Baker to SecNav J. Daniels, 6 June 1919, File 11112-1457, General Correspondence, Secretary of the Navy, 1916–26, RG 80, which included General Barnett's letters to various publishers and newspapers; *New York Times,* 13 and 23 April 1919 and 14–16 August 1919; memorandum, Office of the A&I to Maj. Gen. Cmdt., 2 July 1919, File 1740-55, General Correspondence, A&I HQMC, 1913–32, RG 127; J. A. Lejeune to Maj. Gen. Cmdt., (?) 1930, Lejeune Papers; Robert Lindsay, *This High Name: Public Relations and the U.S. Marine Corps* (Madison: University of Wisconsin Press, 1956), 23–35.
19. Thomas, "1917–1919," 60; *New York Times,* 13 August 1919; Lt. Col. Frank E. Evans, "Demobilizing the Brigades," *MCG* 4 (December 1919), 303–14; *Washington Post,* 14 August 1919.

Chapter VIII. Haiti
1. Thomas, oral memoir, 60–2, and "1919–1941," 1; *New York Times,* 31 July 1919.
2. Brig. Gen. R. H. Williams, "Those Controversial Boards," *MCG* 66 (October 1982), 91–6; Maj. Gen. Cmdt. to SecNav, 9 Jan 1920, File 1965, Adjutant & Inspector General Correspondence, 1913–32, RG 127; *New York Times,* 30 August 1919.

In addition to General Williams's article on the Russell and Neville boards, the politics of officer retention and promotion played a major part in Secretary of the Navy Daniels's plan to replace Barnett as Commandant. See especially Benis M. Frank, "The Relief of General Barnett," *Records of the Columbia Historical Society* (Washington, D.C., 1971–72), 679–93; Lt. Col. Merrill L. Bartlett, "Ouster of a Commandant," USNIP, 106 (November 1980), 60–5, and "Old Gimlet Eye," USNIP, 112 (November 1986), 65–72; and Hans Schmidt, *Maverick Marine: General Smedley D. Butler* (Lexington: University Press of Kentucky, 1987), 110–28.

3. Thomas, "1919–1941," 1; Thomas OQR; Maj. Gen. Cmdt. to Rep. R. S. Maloney, with attachments, 5 July 1921, Memo A&I, "Officers to Be Discharged as of Sept 30, 1921 . . . ," and Maj. Gen. W. C. Neville to Rep. R. S. Maloney, 21 June 1921, all in File 1965, A&I General Correspondence, RG 127. The definitive internal document on officer retention is Maj. Gen. Cmdt. memorandum, "Appointment to Commissioned Grades of the Marine Corps," 7 June 1921, File 1965, A&I General Correspondence, RG 127. Barnett's retreat from the findings of the Russell Board may be found in two letters, Maj. Gen. Cmdt. to Judge Advocate General USN, 9 September 1919, and to Secretary of the Navy, 9 January 1920, both also in File 1965.
4. Thomas, oral memoir, 62; Thomas OQR; Brig. Gen. G. Barnett to the Secretary of the Navy, "Report on Affairs in the Republic of Haiti," 11 October 1920, copy in Maj. Gen. George Barnett Papers, MCPPC.
5. "Thomas-Durrett Married at Independence," *Weekly Democrat News* (Marshall, Mo.), 2 October 1919; Thomas-Durrett marriage license, 27 September 1919, Office of Recorder of Deeds, Director of Records, Jackson County, Independence, Mo.; "William S. Durrett" and "John R. Durrett" *History of Saline County, Missouri* (St. Louis, Mo.: Missouri Historical Company, 1881), 749–50, 645–6; Missouri Valley College, *Sabidura 1918* and *1919,* copies in Marshall Public Library; "Mary Ruth Durrett, born Saline County, Missouri, November 17, 1901, died Port-au-Prince, Haiti, December 15, 1920," records of Ridge Park cemetery, Marshall, Mo.; interview with Mrs. John J. Hughes, Marshall, Mo., March 1988; Mrs. Frances D. Tisch, South Bend, Ind., to the author 28 March and 28 April 1988. (Both are nieces of Mary Ruth Durrett.)

   The author thanks Mrs. Marilyn Hazzard Gross of Sweet Springs, Mo., for her thorough search on Mary Ruth Durrett and her family.
6. Mrs. G. C. Thomas to the author, 28 August 1986.
7. Thomas, "1919–1941," 2.
8. Frederick A. Ober, *A Guide to the West Indies, Bermuda, and Panama* (New York: Dodd, Mead, 1920), 265–8; Edna Taft, *A Puritan in Voodoo-Land* (Philadelphia: Penn Publishing, 1938), 47–92; J. Dryden Kuser, *Haiti* (Boston: Gorham Press, 1921).
9. The activities of the 1st Marine Brigade in Haiti, 1919–21, are based on the following primary sources: Headquarters, 1st Brigade, "General Outline of the Work of the Military Occupation of Haiti," 1920, General Correspondence Expedition Commander and 1st Brigade, 1915–20, RG 127; Maj. Gen. Cmdt. John A. Lejeune and Brig. Gen. Smedley D. Butler to Secretary of the Navy Josephus Daniels, report, "Investigation of Alleged Gendarmerie d'Haiti Offenses in Hinche and Massade, 1918–1919," 12 October 1920, Josephus Daniels Papers, MD/LC; Maj. Gen. Cmdt. J. H. Russell, "A Marine Looks Back on Haiti," 1934–35, manuscript history, MCPPC; U.S. Congress, Senate, Select Committee on Haiti and Santo Domingo, "Inquiry into Occupation and Administration of Haiti and Santo Domingo," 2 vols., 67th Congress, 1st and 2d Sessions, 1921–22, which also contains the Barnett Report, Mayo Board Report, and the Lejeune-Butler Report.

   For detailed accounts of the *caco* wars, see John C. Chapin, "The Marines'

Role in the U.S. Occupation of Haiti: 1915–1922," master's thesis, George Washington University, 1967, and Hans Schmidt, *The United States Occupation of Haiti, 1915–1934* (New Brunswick, N.J.: Rutgers University Press, 1971). See also James H. McCrocklin, comp., *Garde d'Haiti* (Annapolis, Md.: U.S. Naval Institute, 1956), which reprints annual reports of the Garde d'Haiti and a manuscript history of the Garde by Gen. Franklin A. Hart, USMC (Ret.).

10. Lt. Col. D. F. Bittner, "John H. Russell," 1991, manuscript in author's possession; Martin K. Gordon, "Louis McCarty Little, 1878–1960," manuscript register, 1971, and "Une Grande Figure Americaine in Haiti: Lt. Colonel Louis McCarty Little," Little File, RS H&MD.

11. Thomas, "1919–1941," 2–3, and oral memoir, 68–70, as verified in the "Chronological Record of Service" section of the Thomas OQR.

Of the 89 enlisted men on the rolls of the 63d Company, Marine Barracks, only 62 were present for duty in January 1920. Muster Roll, 63d Company, January 1920, H&MD.

12. Thomas, oral memoir, 72–4; Thomas OQR, "Chronological Record of Service;" Muster Roll, 63d Company; Barnett, "Report on Affairs in Haiti."

13. Thomas, oral memoir, 75–6. For this and subsequent descriptions of Gen. Alexander Archer Vandegrift (1887–1973), see Gen. A. A. Vandegrift, oral memoir (1962), MCOHC; Gen. M. B. Twining, "Vandegrift," June 1987, manuscript in the possession of B. M. Frank, MCOHC; Thomas interview with B. M. Frank, 4 December 1981, MCOHC; and Vandegrift, *Once a Marine*.

14. Thomas, "1919–1941," 5, and oral memoir, 77–8. Lt. Col. Clyde H. Metcalf, *A History of the United States Marine Corps* (New York: G. P. Putnam's, 1939), 393–401; Brig. Cmdr. to Commanding Officers, 2d Regiment and 8th Regiment, "Provost Courts," 15 September 1920, General Correspondence, Expedition Commander and 1st Brigade, RG 127; Mayo Board, "Record of Court of Inquiry Convened at the Navy Department, Washington, October 19, 1920, by the Order of the Secretary of the Navy, to Inquire into the Conduct of Personnel of the Naval Service That Has Served in Haiti since July 28, 1915," appendix to Senate Select Committee, *Report*, Vol. II, 1585–1842.

The Mayo Board identified forty-two cases of misconduct brought to court-martial, which resulted in twenty-seven convictions. Accused only of hut burning, Cukela, defended by another Medal of Honor winner, Maj. E. A. Ostermann, escaped formal charges.

15. Maj. Gen. Cmdt. to JAG USN, 13 December 1920, File 1965, A&I General Correspondence, RG 127; Maj. Gen. Cmdt., memorandum, "Appointments to Commissioned Grades of the Marine Corps," 7 June 1921, File 1965; Williams, "Those Controversial Boards."

16. Thomas, "1919–1941," 5–6, and oral memoir, 78; Rep. S. C. Major to Maj. Gen. Cmdt., 14 December 1920; Maj. Gen. Cmdt. to Rep. Major and Mrs. V. Y. Thomas, 15 and 16 December 1920, with supporting information, all in Thomas OQR. Thomas's official medical record carries no entry for Haiti, 1920, but later refers to recurrent malaria. The records of the U.S. Naval

Hospital show him as a patient. The incidence of malaria is cited in "Report of the Surgeon General," *Annual Reports Navy Department 1920* (Washington, D.C.: Government Printing Office, 1921), 128. Medical conditions in Haiti in the autumn of 1920 were complicated by a smallpox epidemic. Although American personnel escaped infection, they had to submit to five or six vaccinations.

17. "Death of Mrs. Jerald Thomas," *Weekly Democrat News* (Marshall, Mo.), 16 December 1920; A&I to 2d Lt. G. C. Thomas, 29 November 1920, Thomas OQR.
18. "Funeral of Mrs. Thomas," *Weekly Democrat News* (Marshall, Mo.), 30 December 1920; "Chronological Record of Service," Thomas OQR.
19. Thomas, "1919–1941," 6; Mayo Board, report, "Record of Court of Inquiry," 1921.

    Thomas himself said nothing then or later about the disadvantages of being a married lieutenant, but senior officers discouraged junior officers from marrying for both professional and financial reasons.
20. Maj. Gen. Cmdt. memorandum, "Appointment to Commissioned Grades of the Marine Corps"; "Extracts from the Testimony of the Major General Commandant before the Subcommittee of House Committee on Appropriations on the Naval Appropriations Bill, 1922," 21 January 1921, *MCG* 6 (March 1921), 85–111; Williams, "Those Controversial Boards."

    The information on awards is taken from Maj. Gen. Cmdt. to Board of Awards, Navy Department, memorandum with enclosures, "Officers of the U.S. Marine Corps Who May be Entitled to Advancement on Retirement," 13 May 1936, File 1965, Office of the Commandant, General Correspondence, 1913–38, RG 127. The enclosures list the names and World War I decorations (as of 1936) of all regular officers then in service or who had received disability retirements after the war. The only decorations authorized by the U.S. government at the time of the Neville Board were the Medal of Honor, Distinguished Service Medal, Distinguished Service Cross, and Navy Cross.
21. Thomas, oral memoir, 79–80. My analysis of the impact of the Neville Board on Thomas's career is based on the sources in Note 20 and an examination of the official *Register of Officers of the Navy and Marine Corps* for 1919, 1921, and 1922.
22. Maj. Gen. Cmdt. to 2d Lt. G. C. Thomas, 23 March 1921; 2d Lt. G. C. Thomas to Maj. Gen. Cmdt., 6 April 1921, with endorsements from CO 8th Marines (8 April) and CG 1st Brigade (9 April); telegrams 1st Brigade to HQMC in re: Thomas, 10 April and 8 and 9 May 1921; "Chronological Record of Service," all of the above in Thomas OQR.
23. Thomas, oral memoir, 80–1; Maj. Gen. Cmdt. to 2d Lt. G. C. Thomas, 22 May 1921, with attached appointment; two letters, 2d Lt. G. C. Thomas to Maj. Gen. Cmdt., 4 June 1921, Thomas OQR.

Chapter IX. Renaissance of a Career

1. For naval policy and international diplomacy in the immediate postwar period, see Harold and Margaret Sprout, *Toward a New Order of Sea Power:*

American Naval Policy and the World Scene, 1918–1922 (Princeton, N.J.: Princeton University Press, 1943); William R. Braisted, *The United States Navy in the Pacific, 1909–1922* (Austin: University of Texas Press, 1971); Fred Greene, "The Military View of American National Policy, 1904–1940," *American Historical Review* 66 (January 1961), 354–77; Philip T. Rosen, "The Treaty Navy, 1919–1937," in Kenneth J. Hagan, ed., *In Peace and War: Interpretations of American Naval History, 1775–1978* (Westport, Conn.: Greenwood Press, 1978), 221–36; Thaddeus V. Tuleja, *Statesmen and Admirals: Quest for a Far Eastern Policy* (New York: Norton, 1963); Stephen Roskill, *Naval Policy Between the Wars: The Period of Anglo-American Antagonism, 1919–1929* (London: Collins, 1968); and Gerald E. Wheeler, *Prelude to Pearl Harbor: The United States Navy and the Far East, 1921–1931* (Columbia: University of Missouri Press, 1963).

2. Adm. R. E. Coontz to Maj. Gen. Cmdt. G. Barnett, 28 January 1920, File 432, Records of the General Board of the Navy, Naval Historical Center. See also Louis Morton, "War Plan 'Orange': The Evolution of a Strategy," *World Politics* 11 (January 1959), 221–50, and Frank J. Infusino, Jr., "The United States Marine Corps and War Planning, 1900–1941," master's thesis, California State University San Diego, 1973, 55–93.

3. Maj. Earl H. Ellis, "Advanced Base Force Operations in Micronesia," Operations Plan 712, 1921, endorsed by the Major General Commandant, copy in Historical Amphibious File (HAF) 165, Breckinridge Library, Marine Corps Education Center, Quantico, Va. See also Col. A. T. Mason, "Special Monograph on Amphibious Warfare," 1949–50, manuscript history, Command File, World War II, Naval Historical Center.

4. Maj. Gen. Cmdt. to CNO, quarterly readiness report, 30 June 1921, File 221 (1921), SecNav/CNO Confidential Correspondence, 1919–26, RG 80.

5. Thomas, "1919–1941," 6–7, and oral memoir, 81–2; Lt. Col. Charles A. Fleming, Capt. Robin L. Austin, and Capt. Charles A. Braley III, *Quantico: Crossroads of the Corps* (Washington, D.C.: History and Museums Division, HQMC, 1978), 38–46; Schmidt, *Maverick Marine*, 128–43. As with other chapters, I have verified General Thomas's experiences with "Record of Assignments," Thomas OQR.

6. Thomas, "1919–1941," 17.

7. On the Washington Conference, see Sprout and Sprout, *Toward a New Order of Sea Power*, 149–296; Thomas H. Buckley, *The United States and the Washington Conference, 1921–1922* (Knoxville: University of Tennessee Press, 1970); and Ernest Andrade, Jr., "The United States Navy and the Washington Conference," *Historian* 31 (May 1969), 345–63.

8. Thomas, "1919–1941," 1–8, and oral memoir, 82–4; G. C. Thomas to V. Y. Thomas, 5 December 1921, TFP. The Marine Corps—at least General Lejeune—was skeptical of the treaties' value. See Maj. Gen. Cmdt. memorandum for the General Board, "Future Policy of the Marine Corps as Influenced by the Conference on Limitation of Armament," 11 February 1922, File 432, General Board Records.

9. G. C. Thomas to R. S. Thomas, 2 January 1922, TFP.

10. Lt. Gen. V. H. Krulak, "Lemuel Cornick Shepherd, Jr.," 1988, manuscript

in author's possession; "Record of Lemuel C. Shepherd, Jr.," Shepherd OQR, provided by General Krulak.
11. Thomas, "1919–1941," 8, and oral memoir, 84–7; Thomas OQR; *Washington Post,* 29 and 30 January, 1922.
12. Thomas, "1919–1941," 8–10, and oral memoir, 87–9, 104–5, 966–7; Thomas OQR; Fleming et al., *Quantico,* 41, 47; Maj. Gen. Cmdt., memorandum, "Changes in Marine Corps Manual: Examination of Officers for Promotion," 21 November 1924, File 1520-10, General Correspondence, 1913–32, RG 127.
13. Quoted in Chairman, General Board, to SecNav, memorandum, "Examination of the Organization and Establishment of the U.S. Marine Corps," 10 August 1932, File 1850-40, Office of the Adjutant and Inspector, General Correspondence, 1913–32, RG 127.
14. Maj. Gen. Cmdt., memorandum, "Policy in Regard to Sea Duty of Officers," 14 March 1925; Chief of Personnel to Assistant to the Commandant, 29 October 1924; Capt. L. E. Fagan, CO Sea School Detachment, to Maj. Gen. Cmdt., 20 October 1924, all of the above in File 1515-90, A&I General Correspondence, RG 127. For recollections of sea duty in the era, see Maj. Gen. C. R. Allen, oral memoir (1969), 34; Lt. Gen. A. L. Bowser, oral memoir (1970), 14–21; Lt. Gen. J. P. Berkeley, oral memoir (1969), 55–6, all in MCOHC. For landing operations, see Department of the Navy, *Landing Force Manual 1920* (Washington: Government Printing Office, 1920).
15. *Tulsa*'s characteristics may be found in James C. Fahey, comp., *The Ships and Aircraft of the United States Fleet 1939* (reprint, Annapolis, Md.: U.S. Naval Institute Press, 1976), 22, and entries, logbook, in U.S.S. *Tulsa* (PG 22), 3–31 December 1923, Records of the Bureau of Navigation, RG 24, NA (hereafter cited as *Tulsa* logbook). For *Tulsa*'s mission, see Richard L. Millett, "The State Department's Navy: A History of the Special Service Squadron, 1920–1940," *American Neptune* 35 (April 1975), 118–38.
16. Mrs. G. C. Thomas to the author, 28 August 1986, and Thomas, "1919–1941," 11. For background on the Johnson and Capers families, I have relied on my interviews with Mrs. Thomas and W. H. J. Thomas (her son) to the author, 31 March 1986; W. H. J. Thomas, "Two Families Held House for 166 Years," *The News and Courier* (Charleston, S.C.) June (?), 1910; and W. H. J. Thomas, "Mother and Her Family" and "Charleston: The Area," manuscript notes, February 1988, in the author's possession.
17. Thomas, "1919–1941," 10–11; *Tulsa* logbook, January–May 1924.
18. Mrs. G. C. Thomas to the author, 28 August 1986; Cmdr. Sherwood B. Smith, USN (Ret.), to the author, 6 October 1986.
19. Thomas, "1919–1941," 11; Smith to the author, 6 October 1986; *Tulsa* logbook, June–July 1924.
20. Thomas, "1919–1941," 12, and oral memoir, 92; *Tulsa* logbook, July 1924.
21. Mrs. G. C. Thomas to the author, 28 August 1986; Thomas, "1919–1941," 12.
22. Thomas, "1919–1941," 12–13; Smith to the author, 6 October 1986.
23. Thomas, "1919–1941," 13; *Tulsa* logbook, September 1924.
24. G. C. Thomas to Mrs. G. C. Thomas, 28 October 1924, TFP; Smith to

author, 6 October 1986; Thomas, "1919–1941," 14; *Tulsa* logbook, October 1924.
25. *Tulsa* logbook, November 1924–March 1925; G. C. Thomas to Mrs. G. C. Thomas, 1 February 1925, TFP; Thomas, "1919–1941," 14–15.
26. *Tulsa* logbook, May–June 1925; G. C. Thomas to Mrs. G. C. Thomas, six letters, 23 May–28 June 1925; 1st Lt. G. C. Thomas to Maj. Gen. Cmdt., 5 December 1924, Thomas OQR.
27. Thomas, "1919–1941," 15–16; *Tulsa* logbook, August–September 1925.
28. Thomas, "1919–1941," 16–17; G. C. Thomas to Mrs. G. C. Thomas, three letters, 3–18 October 1925; *Tulsa* logbook, 20 October 1925.

Chapter X. The Long Watch
1. Joint Board, *Joint Action of the Army and the Navy, 1927* (Washington, D.C.: Government Printing Office, 1927), 3. The Joint Board had six members: the Army Chief of Staff, the Chief of Naval Operations, their two deputies, and the two chiefs of each service's war plans division. The Joint Board also had a joint supporting staff, the Joint Planning Committee (JPC), of three members each of the war plans divisions. One of the three naval service officers on the JPC was always a Marine officer. The Joint Board was eventually replaced in 1941 by the Joint Chiefs of Staff and its supporting committees.
2. For the Marine Corps experience with amphibious warfare and service in China and Nicaragua, see Millett, *Semper Fidelis,* 212–63, 319–43. See also Lt. Col. Kenneth J. Clifford, *Progress and Purpose: A Developmental History of the U.S. Marine Corps, 1900–1970* (Washington, D.C.: History and Museums Division, HQMC, 1973), 25–39.
3. Report, Marine Personnel Board (Fuller Board), with memorandum, Maj. Gen. Cmdt. to All Commissioned Officers, "General Discussion of the Commissioned Personnel Situation in the Marine Corps," 10 March 1927, File 1965-75, Adjutant & Inspector's Office, General Correspondence, 1913–32, RG 27.

    The Corps' 1,051 authorized officer strength (it actually had about 1,200 active duty officers) was divided as follows: 6 major generals, 8 brigadier generals, 42 colonels, 84 lieutenant colonels, 158 majors, 315 captains, and 438 lieutenants.
4. Fuller Board, Second Report, 4 November 1927, File 1965-75; "Status of Personnel Legislation," *MCG* 13 (June 1928), 137–42.
5. Maj. Gen. Cmdt., memorandum, "Proposed Marine Corps Personnel Bill," 23 November 1928, with attached summary of the issues and course of proposed legislation, 1928–30, File 1965-75, RG 127.
6. Correspondence, 1913–32, File 1520-10 ("Army Schools"), Adjutant & Inspector's Office, General Correspondence, 1913–32, RG 127.
7. Reports of physical examinations, 1925 and 1926, Lt. Gerald C. Thomas, Thomas medical records, Thomas OQR.
8. Thomas, "1919–1941," 17–18; record of assignments, Thomas OQR; interviews with Mrs. G. C. Thomas and Mrs. Joseph A. Bruder (Lottie Capers Thomas), 1986; Lyon G. Tyler, "Charleston, S.C. Navy Base," in Paolo E.

Coletta, ed., *United States Navy and Marine Bases, Domestic* (Westport, Conn.: Greenwood Press, 1985), 78–102.

9. Thomas, "1919–1941," 18; QMG USMC to Maj. Gen. Cmdt., 15 July 1927, File 1520-10.

10. Thomas, "1919–1941," 18–19, and oral memoir, 95–7; Lt. G. C. Thomas to Mrs. G. C. Thomas, 15 June 1928, TFP; QMG USMC to Maj. Gen. Cmdt., 27 September 1923, Cmdt. QMC MTS to Maj. Gen. Cmdt., 27 September 1923, and Cmdt. QMC MTS to Maj. Gen. Cmdt., 19 June 1928, all in File 1520-10; Daniel R. Beaver, "Politics and Policy: The War Department Motorization and Standardization Program for Wheeled Transport Vehicles, 1920–1940," *Military Affairs* 47 (October 1983), 101–8; Colonel Edgar S. Shayer, QMC, "The Quartermaster Corps Motor Transport School, Camp Holabird, Md.," *Quartermaster Review* 8 (July–August 1928), 35–36.

11. QMG USMC to Maj. Gen. Cmdt., 14 April 1928, File 1520-10; Lt. G. C. Thomas to Mrs. G. C. Thomas, 28 April 1928, TFP.

12. Lt. G. C. Thomas to Mrs. G. C. Thomas, 9 May–1 June 1928, TFP (five letters describe the trip).

13. Lt. G. C. Thomas to Mrs. G. C. Thomas, 1 July 1928, TFP; Thomas, "1919–1941," 19.

14. Thomas, "1919–1941," 19–20; record of assignments, Thomas OQR; "Living Conditions in the Marine Corps," *MCG* 11 (September 1926), 203–9; Lt. G. C. Thomas to QMG USMC, May 1929, Thomas OQR.

15. Thomas, "1919–1941," 20–1, and oral memoir, 99–100; Mrs. Joseph A. Bruder to the author, February 1988; Lt. G. C. Thomas to Maj. Gen. Cmdt., 13 April 1929, and CO Constabulary Detachment USMC Port-au-Prince to American High Commissioner, 14 April 1929, Thomas OQR; "Colonel Richard M. Cutts, USMC," 1955, RS H&MD; "Colonel Richard Malcolm Cutts Passes Away," *MCG* 19 (November 1934), 22, 79.

16. Thomas, oral memoir, 101–2, and "1919–1941," 20–1. The Shepherd, Jackson, and Smith assignments were verified in "Record of Assignments: Lemuel C. Shepherd, Jr.," in the possession of Lt. Gen. Victor H. Krulak, USMC (Ret.), and General Krulak's manuscript biography of General Shepherd, as well as the biographical files for Jackson and Smith, RS MCHC. Command problems may be examined in File 12 ("Misconduct"), 1st Marine Brigade, General Correspondence, 1930–34, RG 127.

17. Schmidt, *United States Occupation of Haiti*, 189–206; Thomas, "1919–1941," 21–2. Thomas's recollections of the 1929 crisis, however, are disappointingly vague on his own role and his observations of the unrest.

18. Thomas, "1919–1941," 22–3. The politics of Trujillo's rise to power, including the Cutts mission, are described in Dana G. Munro, *The United States and the Caribbean Republics, 1921–1933* (Princeton, N.J.: Princeton University Press, 1974), 294–308. At the time of the Cutts mission, Munro was serving as ambassador to Haiti, but his account is also based on the State Department's documents.

19. Thomas, oral memoir, 101–3.

20. My account of Thomas's year at the Infantry School is based on Headquarters, Infantry School, "Annual Report of the Infantry School, 30 June 1932, File

220.63, Central Files 1926–39, The Adjutant General's Office Records, RG 94. The mystique of the Infantry School can best be sampled in the individual experiences of its "giants": see Pogue, *George C. Marshall,* 1:247–69; Gen. Omar N. Bradley and Clay Blair, *A General's Life* (New York: Simon and Schuster, 1983), 63–73; Tuchman, *Stilwell and the American Experience in China,* 123–42; Leslie Anders, *Gentle Knight: The Life and Times of Major General Edwin Forrest Harding* (Kent, Ohio: Kent State University Press, 1985), 109–39; and Gen. J. Lawton Collins, *Lightning Joe* (Baton Rouge: Louisiana University Press, 1979), 47–55. I also consulted the following materials from the archives of the Infantry School library: Col. W. S. Browning to CG IV Army Corps, "Annual Inspection, Ft. Benning," 16 December 1931; Infantry School, "Closing Exercises," 1 June 1932.

21. Thomas, "1919–1941," 24–5.
22. Four letters, Lt. G. C. Thomas to Mrs. G. C. Thomas, 20–28 May 1932, TFP. Lottie had returned to Charleston for the summer and to await another move. Puller's experience is more favorably described in Burke Davis, *Marine: The Life of Chesty Puller* (Boston: Little, Brown, 1962), 67–75. Thomas's letters provide his own evaluation of Puller. See also Gen. O. P. Smith, oral memoir (1969), 44–46, MCOHC.
23. The quote is from "Report of the Major General Commandant of the United States Marine Corps," *Annual Reports of the Navy Department 1932* (Washington, D.C.: Government Printing Office, 1932), 1163. The Corps' own self-assessment is Director, Division of Plans and Training, to Maj. Gen. Cmdt., "Operating Plan, Marine Corps, Fiscal 1933," 16 June 1932, File 432, General Board Records, OA, NHC. The Navy Department's key reports are Chairman, General Board, to SecNav, memorandum, "Examination of the Organization and Establishment of the U.S. Marine Corps," 10 August 1932, File 432; and CNO to SecNav, 2 March 1933, File 1850-40, HQMC, General Correspondence, 1913–38, RG 127. Portions of the Marine Corps Operating Plan and ALNAV 32 (14 July 1932) that describe the personnel reductions are printed in *MCG* 17 (August 1932). For administration policy, see John R. M. Wilson, "The Quaker and the Sword: Herbert Hoover's Relations with the Military," *Military Affairs* 38 (April 1974), 41–7.
24. Lt. G. C. Thomas to TAGO, USA, 13 October 1932; Maj. Gen. Cmdt. to TAGO, 26 August 1932; "Record of Service," all Thomas OQR. See also Philip K. Robles, *United States Military Medals & Ribbons* (Rutland, Vt.: Charles E. Tuttle, 1971), 26–7, 57–8. The data on Marine officers and decorations is from Maj. Gen. Cmdt. to Board of Awards, Navy Department, 13 May 1936, File 1965-85, Office of the Commandant, General Correspondence, 1913–38, RG 127.

The highest number of Silver Stars went to Capt. Gilder D. Jackson (five), one less than the six awarded to Gen. Douglas MacArthur, the Army Chief of Staff who approved the medal.

25. Maj. Gen. Cmdt. to Lt. G. C. Thomas, 6 May 1932, Thomas OQR; Lt. G. C. Thomas to Mrs. G. C. Thomas, 22 May 1932, TFP; Thomas, "Record of Service," Thomas OQR; Thomas, oral memoir, 109; record of medical examination, G. C. Thomas, 5 July 1932, and Chief Bureau of Surgery and

Medicine to JAG USMC, 21 July 1932, both Thomas medical records, Thomas OQR.
26. Cmdt. MCS to Maj. Gen. Cmdt., 20 April 1932, File 1515-95, Adjutant & Inspector's Office, General Correspondence, 1913-32, RG 127; Cmdt. Army Infantry School to Maj. Gen. Cmdt., 6 June 1932, File 1520-10; Thomas, oral memoir, 106; 1st Lt. Anthony A. Frances, "History of Marine Corps Schools," manuscript, 1945, Breckinridge Library, 26-8.
27. Three letters, Lt. G. C. Thomas to Mrs. G. C. Thomas, 15-20 June 1932, TFP; "Living Conditions in the Marine Corps," *MCG* 11 (March 1926), 52-6.
28. Five letters, Capt. G. C. Thomas to Mrs. G. C. Thomas, 12 May-23 July 1934, TFP; Thomas, "1919-1941," 26-7; Bowser, oral memoir (1970), 24-5. Also, responses to author's Thomas questionnaire: Lt. Gen. Victor H. Krulak, USMC (Ret.), 5 March 1986; Maj. Gen. John P. Condon, USMC (Ret.), 19 October 1986; Lt. Gen. Henry W. Buse, Jr., USMC (Ret.), 16 March 1986.
29. Thomas, "1919-1941," 26-7; Clifford, *Progress and Purpose,* 43-8; Millett, *Semper Fidelis,* 329-35.
30. Thomas, oral memoir, 111-13; "Maj. Gen. Ralph S. Keyser," biographical file, RS H&MD.
31. Capt. G. C. Thomas to Mrs. G. C. Thomas, 28 May and 23 July 1934, TFP; Thomas, "1919-1941," 27-8; Marine Corps Personnel Act (P.L. 263), 29 May 1934, and supporting documents, File 1965-75-73; "Legislation: Personnel Situation," *MCG* 18 (February 1934), 16-27. Thomas stood 207 in seniority among 311 captains: Navy Department, *A List of the Commissioned and Warrant Officers of the Marine Corps 1935* (Washington, D.C.: Government Printing Office, 1935), 4-8.
32. Thomas, oral memoir, 108-15.

Chapter XI. Preparing for a War
1. Maj. Gen. John H. Russell, "The Birth of the Fleet Marine Force," USNIP 72 (January 1946), 49-51; Clifford, *Progress and Purpose,* 43-8, 141-3.
2. *Tentative Manual Landing Operations* (1934 and 1935), Historical Amphibious File (HAF) 39, Breckinridge Library, Marine Corps Education Center, Quantico; "Proceedings for Conference . . . January 1934, for the Purpose of Discussing, Approving, or Commenting on the Tentative Landing Operations Manual . . . ," HAF 41; Lt. Col. Benjamin W. Gally, "A History of U.S. Fleet Landing Exercises," 3 July 1939, manuscript history, HAF 73; Gen. Alfred H. Noble, oral memoir (1968), 49-53, MCOHC.
3. Frank J. Infusino, Jr., "The United States Marine Corps and War Planning, 1900-1941," master's thesis, California State University-San Diego, 1973, 55-93; Calvin W. Enders, "The Vinson Navy," Ph.D. diss., Michigan State University, 1970, 25-98; Joint Board, *Joint Action of Army and Navy,* 12-13, 73-4; Maj. Gen. J. H. Russell to Brig. Gen. L. McC. Little, 7 August 1935, and Little to Russell, 9 August 1935, Louis McCarty Little Papers, MCPPC, MCHC; Maj. Gen. Cmdt. to CNO, "Recommended Revision of Joint Action

of Army and Navy, 1935," 11 May 1936, HAF 38; "Marine Corps War Planning Course," *MCG* 14 (March 1929), 57–60.
4. Greene, "Military View," 368–77; Dorothy Borg and S. Okamoto, eds., *Pearl Harbor as History: Japanese-American Relations, 1931–1941* (New York: Columbia University Press, 1973).
5. Fleming et al., *Quantico,* 56–73; Frances, "History of Marine Corps Schools"; Research Section, MCS, "A Brief Historical Sketch of the Development of Amphibious Instruction and Doctrine at the Marine Corps Schools during the Years before World War II," 1949, "Schools" File, RS H&MD; "Field and Company Officers Schools, 1934–1935," MCS report, 1935, "Schools" File, RS H&MD.
6. Thomas, "1919–1941," 28–9; Maj. Gen. DeWitt Peck, oral memoir (1967), 91, MCOHC; Naval War College Advanced Base Problem 1, Dumanquillas Bay, Mindanao, Breckinridge Library archives, MCTEC.
7. Thomas, "1919–1941," 28–9; Cates, oral memoir, 91–7; Naval War College Advanced Base Problem 2, Truk Atoll, Carolines, Breckinridge Library archives, MCTEC.
8. Thomas, "1919–1941," 29; Lt. Gen. Louis E. Woods, oral memoir (1968), 25-65, 74-104, MCOHC; Gen. Vernon E. Megee, oral memoir (1967), 70–121, MCOHC; *A Text on the Employment of Marine Corps Aviation* (Quantico, Va.: Marine Corps Schools, 1935), copy in Breckinridge Library; Lt. Col. Edward C. Johnson and Graham A. Cosmas, *Marine Corps Aviation: the Early Years, 1912–1940* (Washington, D.C.: History and Museums Division, HQMC, 1977), 61–82.
9. Gen. A. A. Vandegrift, oral memoir (1962), 394–8, MCOHC; Thomas, oral memoir, 115; Gen. M. B. Twining, "Vandegrift," manuscript essay, June 1987, property of B. M. Frank.
10. Col. John W. Thomason, Jr., "The Collector," in Thomason, *And A Few Marines,* 2d ed. (New York: Charles Scribner's Sons, 1958), 157–8. Thomason's short stories give a vivid picture of Peiping, China, and the "China Marines" and are collected in two other books: *Marines and Others* (New York: Charles Scribner's Sons, 1929) and *Salt Winds and Gobi Dust* (New York: Charles Scribner's Sons, 1934).
11. The description of life for the Marine Detachment is based on Marine Corps Schools, *Monograph of Peking* (Quantico, Va.: Marine Barracks, 1937), actually completed by the headquarters of the Marine Detachment in March 1937, which meant that Thomas, as the detachment adjutant, probably wrote and edited much of it himself. See also the Detachment newspaper (edited by Thomas), *American Embassy Guard News,* Vols. 3–5, 1935–1937, library, H&MD, and The Peiping Chronicle, *Guide to "Peking"* (rev. ed., Peiping, 1935), property of Col. G. C. Thomas, Jr.
12. Russell D. Buhite, *Nelson T. Johnson and American Policy toward China, 1925–1941* (East Lansing: Michigan State University Press, 1968); Tuchman, *Stilwell and the American Experience in China,* 143–63. See also "A Brief History of the Radio Security Station, Marine Detachment, Peiping, China," 1981, Naval Security Group Study SRH-178, OA, NHD. I also benefited from the advice of Mrs. Kathleen T. Perkins, Washington,

D.C., whose husband served in China with the State Department during the 1930s.
13. Gen. Graves B. Erskine, oral memoir (1970), 128–68, MCOHC, covers his China service. See also "General Graves B. Erskine," biographical file, RS H&MD.
14. Thomas, record of duty assignments, Thomas OQR; Thomas, "1919–1941," 29–30.
15. Thomas, "1919–1941," 30–1. For the life of the Marine Detachment, Peiping, see *American Legation Guard Annual 1935* (Peking, China: n.p., 1935), especially "Reminiscing with Company B," 101–7. I also reviewed the correspondence, 1935–37, in the "Legation Guard" File, American Embassy, Peiping, File 124.9318, State Department Decimal File, 1930–39, General Records of the Department of State, RG 59, NA.
16. For guard policies and operations, see especially Erskine, oral memoir, and Vandegrift, oral memoir, 373–98. See also Vandegrift, *Once a Marine*, 79–86. Thomas's illness is recorded in his medical records, appended to Thomas OQR.
17. Thomas, oral memoir, 117–9; Mrs. J. A. Bruder to the author, February, 1988. The athletic program is outlined in File 400 ("Athletics"), General Correspondence, 1934, Marine Detachment, Peiping, RG 127.
18. Thomas, "1919–1941," 32–6; Thomas, record of duty assignments, Thomas OQR; Gerald C. Thomas, Jr., "Notes on My Father," February 1988; W. H. J. Thomas to the author, April 1988.
19. Ibid.; Lt. Gen. W. J. Van Ryzin, USMC (Ret.), to author, Thomas questionnaire, 1 March 1986.
20. Thomas, oral memoir, 121, verified in oral memoirs of Vandegrift and Erskine; *American Embassy Guard News*, 15 May 1937.
21. Col. J. C. Fegan to Maj. Gen. L. McC. Little, 6 August 1936, Louis McCarty Little Papers, MCPPC; Maj. Gen. Cmdt. J. H. Russell to M. H. Macintyre, 5 November 1936, File OF 18-E, Franklin D. Roosevelt Papers, Roosevelt Library, Hyde Park, N.Y.; Maj. Gen. Cmdt. T. Holcomb to Maj. Gen. L. McC. Little, 18 June 1937, Little Papers; "General Statement of Thomas Holcomb, Major General Commandant of the Marine Corps, at the Budget Hearings on the Marine Corps Personnel Plan," with appendices, 27 May 1937, File 1975-10, Office of the Commandant, General Correspondence, 1933–38, RG 127; John W. Gordon, "Thomas Holcomb," manuscript, 1988, in the author's possession.
22. Maj. Gen. Cmdt. Circular No. 149 to all officers, 14 June 1934, and Adjutant & Inspector to Maj. Gen. Cmdt., 19 July 1937, File 1965-75, A&I, General Correspondence, 1933–38, RG 127, and supporting material on promotions and promotion examinations in the same file, 1937.
23. Thomas, "1919–1941," 37–8; Maj. G. C. Thomas to Mrs. G. C. Thomas, 23 June 1937, TFP.
24. C/S USA to CNO, 19 January 1934, and Maj. Gen. Cmdt. correspondence, 1936–37, File 1520-60-20 ("Fort Leavenworth"), Office of the Commandant, General Correspondence, 1933–38, RG 127; Circular No. 149, 14 June 1934. For the history of Ft. Leavenworth and the Command and General Staff

College, see Boyd L. Dastrup, *The US Army Command and General Staff College: A Centennial History* (Fort Leavenworth, Kan.: USA C&GSC, 1981); Col. Orville Z. Taylor, *The History of Ft. Leavenworth, 1937–1951* (Fort Leavenworth, Kan.: USA C&GSC, 1951); and Timothy K. Nenninger, *The Leavenworth Schools and the Old Army: Education, Professionalism and the Officer Corps of the U.S. Army, 1881–1918* (Westport, Conn.: Greenwood Press, 1978).

I also reviewed the correspondence in Files 210.63 and 352.07, both of which deal with the Command and Staff School, in Office of the Adjutant General, U.S. Army, Central Files, 1926–39, RG 94.

25. Thomas, "1919–1941," 38. See especially Command and General Staff School, *Schedule for 1937–1938 Regular Class* (Fort Leavenworth, 1937); Command and General Staff School, *Instruction Circular No. 1, 1937–1938* (Fort Leavenworth, 1937); and Office of the Commandant, Command and General Staff School, "Annual Report . . . 1937–1938," all in File 352.07, TAGO, cited above, and also in the archives, U.S. Army Combined Arms Center, Fort Leavenworth.
26. Thomas, oral memoir, 122–4.
27. *Democrat News* (Marshall, Mo.), 20 and 27 January 1938. I visited Park Ridge Cemetery on 10 March 1988.
28. Thomas, oral memoir, 122. The evaluation system and class rankings are found in memorandum, Cmdt. C&GSS, "Reports Rendered upon Student Officers at the Command and General Staff School," 23 April 1937; memorandum for C/S USA, "Report on Students, Regular Class, 1937–1938 Command and General Staff School," 15 July 1938; and "Special Report and Recommendations on Members of the Command Staff Schoool, Regular Class, 1937–1938," 19 June 1938, all in File 352.07.

Chapter XII. Inside the Marine Corps Elite
1. Thomas, "Family Notes," 12–14; Col. Gerald C. Thomas, Jr., "Notes on My Father"; Mrs. Joseph A. Bruder to the author, February 1988; Thomas medical examination, 1938, Thomas medical record, Thomas OQR.
2. The faculty and student body of the Senior and Junior Courses for 1938 and 1939 are listed in the *Quantico Sentry* (Marine Corps Base, Quantico) in the issues of 10 June 1938 and 23 June 1939.
3. Thomas, oral memoir, 127–30, and "1919–1941," 39–40; Frances, "History of Marine Corps Schools"; Research Section, "A Brief Historical Sketch of the Development of Amphibious Instruction and Doctrine at the Marine Corps Schools during the Years prior to World War II," 1949, "Schools" File, RS M&HD; Erskine, oral memoir, 168–9; Lt. Gen. R. O. Bare, oral memoir (1968), 40–4, MCOHC, H&MD; Brig. Gen. H. O. Deakin, oral memoir (1968), 15–19, MCOHC, H&MD; Lt. Gen. V. H. Krulak to the author, 3 April 1986; Gen. M. B. Twining to the author, 5 December 1986; Gen. R. E. Hogaboom to the author, 22 April 1986.
4. Thomas, "1919–1941," 40–1; Marine Corps Contributory Plan, C-2, ORANGE, MCWP-2, October 1932, and "Monograph on Guam," 4 vols.,

1937, MCS 13 (2), both in the Marine Corps Schools archives, Records of Headquarters Marine Corps, RG 127, Federal Records Center, Suitland, Md.
5. Thomas, oral memoir, 132–33. For background on the Hepburn Board report, see John Major, "The Navy Plans for War, 1937–1941," in Kenneth J. Hagan, *In Peace and War: Interpretations of American Naval History, 1775–1978* (Westport, Conn.: Greenwood Press, 1978), 237–62; and John Major, "William Daniel Leahy," in Robert W. Love, Jr., *The Chiefs of Naval Operations* (Annapolis, Md.: Naval Institute Press, 1980), 100–17. The report itself is printed: "Report on Need of Additional Naval Bases to Defend the Coasts of the United States, Its Territories, and Possessions," U.S. House of Representatives Document 65, 76th Congress, 1st Session (3 January 1939). The Guam analysis is on pages 27–8. For the LVT story, see Maj. Alfred Dunlop Bailey, *Alligators, Buffaloes, and Bushmasters: The History of the Development of the LVT Through World War II* (Washington, D.C.: History and Museums Division, HQMC, 1986), 25–61.
6. Office of Naval Operations, *Landing Operations Doctrine United States Navy 1938* (Washington, D.C.: Government Printing Office, 1938); Marine Corps Schools, *Tentative Manual for Defense of Advanced Bases,* MCS-3, June 1936, MCS archives, RG 127. The quote is from MCS-3, 15–16.
7. This analysis is based on "Status of Various Grades in Marine Corps," *MCG* 22 (March 1938), 28–9, and my review of the senior officer sections of the Navy Department's *Naval Register* for 1938 and 1940.
8. Headquarters, 1st Marine Brigade, "Notes on the Organization and Activities of the Fleet Marine Force in Connection with Landing Operations," 1938, File 1975-10, Office of the Commandant, General Correspondence, 1933–38, RG 127; Mason, *Amphibious Warfare;* Commander-in-Chief, Atlantic Fleet, "Report on Fleet Landing Exercise No. 6 Conducted at Culebra and Vieques, Puerto Rico," 13 June 1940, LANTFLT Serial C-334, Operational Archives, Naval Historical Center; *Quantico Sentry,* 12 January 1940; Thomas, "1919–1941," 41; Maj. Gen. L. McC. Little to Maj. Gen. Cmdt. T. Holcomb, 7 April 1938, Gen. L. McC. Little Papers, MCPPC; umpires' reports of Fleet Landing Exercise 6, 14–15 February 1940 and 20–23 February 1940, Correspondence of the Division of Plans and Policies, 1940, HQMC, RG 127.
9. "Report on Fleet Landing Exercise No. 6"; Maj. G. C. Thomas to Mrs. G. C. Thomas, 14 January 1940, TFP.
10. Maj. G. C. Thomas to Mrs. G. C. Thomas, five letters, 18 January–11 February 1940, TFP; "Report on Fleet Landing Exercise No. 6."
11. Maj. G. C. Thomas to Mrs. G. C. Thomas, three letters, 25 February–3 March 1940, TFP; "Report on Fleet Landing Exercise No. 6"; Norman V. Cooper, *A Fighting General: The Biography of Gen. Holland M. "Howlin' Mad" Smith* (Quantico, Va.: Marine Corps Association, 1987), 62–6.
12. Thomas, "1919–1941," 42; Mrs. J. R. Andrews to the author, February 1988.
13. "Report of the Board to Study Matters Concerning Regular and Reserve Personnel of the Navy and Marine Corps" (Horne Board), November 1940, Command File, World War II, Operational Archives, NHC; CNO to President F. D. Roosevelt, 19 September 1940, and President F. D. Roosevelt to

Director, Bureau of the Budget, 4 October 1940, File 18-E (Marine Corps) Franklin D. Roosevelt Presidential Papers, Roosevelt Library, Hyde Park, N.Y. The timing and extent of the Marine Corps mobilization for 1941 is confirmed in Maj. Gen. Cmdt. T. Holcomb to CNO, "Strength of the Marine Corps," 27 March 1941, also in File 18-E.

As an interim measure, Congress approved an increase of the Corps to 34,000 officers and men on 11 June 1940, which allowed the mobilization of the Marine Corps Reserve.

14. Bernard C. Nalty and Lt. Col. Ralph F. Moody, *A Brief History of U.S. Marine Corps Officer Procurement, 1775–1969* (Washington, D.C.: Historical Division, HQMC, 1958), 9–10; Public Affairs Unit 4-1, *The Marine Corps Reserve: A History* (Washington, D.C.: Division of Reserve, 1966), 45–7; *Quantico Sentry*, 23 June and 28 July 1939.

15. Thomas, "1919–1941," 42–3; Bare, oral memoir, 45–9; Frances, "History of Marine Corps Schools," 46–55; *Quantico Sentry*, 5 July 1940; Thomas "Record of Assignments" and Shepherd "Record of Assignments," from Thomas and Shepherd OQRs.

16. Thomas, oral memoir, 135–7, and "1919–1941," 43.

17. Thomas, "1919–1941," 43, and oral memoir, 137; Marine Corps Contributory Plan, C-2, Rainbow 1, WPMC-11, 12 November 1940, and Marine Corps Plan C-2, Rainbow 5, WPMC-46, 5 June 1941, MCS archives, RG 127; Kenneth W. Condit, Maj. John H. Johnstone, and Ella W. Nargele, *A Brief History of Headquarters Marine Corps Staff Organization*, rev. ed. (Washington, D.C.: Historical Division, HQMC, 1970), 17; Stetson Conn and Byron Fairchild, *The United States Army in World War II: The Framework of Hemispheric Defense* (Washington, D.C.: Government Printing Office, 1960), 3–155.

Chapter XIII. Observing World War II

1. James MacGregor Burns, *Roosevelt: The Soldier of Freedom, 1940–1945* (New York: Harcourt Brace Jovanovich, 1970), 43–56, 64–78, 84–92; W. Churchill to F. Roosevelt, 7 December 1940; Roosevelt radio address, 29 December 1940; Lend-Lease Act (P.L. 11), 11 March 1941; Excerpts ABC-1 Staff Conversations, 27 March 1941; Roosevelt address, White House Correspondents Association, 15 March 1941; all reprinted in Hans-Adolf Jacobsen and Arthur L. Smith, Jr., *World War II: Policy and Strategy: Selected Documents* (Santa Barbara, Calif.: ABC-Clio, 1979), 127–49.

2. Taped interview, Brig. Gen. J. F. Roosevelt, USMCR (Ret.), with G. Smith, History and Museums Division, 25 October 1979; Spyros P. Skouras to FDR, 10 April 1941; FDR memorandum to E. M. Watson, 16 April 1941; J. F. Roosevelt to FDR, 19 April 1941, and Personal Papers File 3 (PPF 3), Franklin D. Roosevelt Papers, Roosevelt Library, Hyde Park, N.Y.; Department of State to U.S. Embassy, London, 15 April 1941, File 121.5541/163, General Records, Department of State, RG 59. For the diplomatic and strategic background of the Roosevelt-Thomas Mission, see Roosevelt-Churchill letters, 10 March–11 April 1941, in Francis L. Loewenheim, Harold D. Langley, and Manfred Jonas, eds., *Roosevelt and Churchill: Their Secret Wartime Correspon-*

dence (London: Barrie & Jenkins, 1975), 132–8; and Maj. Gen. I. S. O. Playfair et al., *History of the Second World War: The Mediterranean and Middle East*, Vol. II (1941) (London: HMSO, 1956).

3. The quote is from Thomas, oral memoir, 139. Thomas left three separate accounts of the round-the-world trip: letters to his wife 18 April–1 May 1941, TFP; Thomas, oral memoir, 137–217; and an autobiographical chapter, "The Magic Carpet," written probably in 1976. In addition to his own contemporary correspondence and the Smith interview, James Roosevelt wrote a brief account of the trip in James Roosevelt and Sidney Shalett, *Affectionately, F. D. R.* (New York: Harcourt, Brace, 1959), 330–2.
4. Message 209 (21 April 1941) and Message 210 (27 April 1941), Department of Defense, *The "Magic" Background of Pearl Harbor,* 5 vols. (Washington, D.C.: Government Printing Office, 1977), I:A-114.
5. Thomas, "The Magic Carpet," 2.
6. F. B. Sayre via State Department to FDR, telegram, 26 April 1941, and FDR to Mrs. E. Roosevelt, 26 April 1941, PPF 3; Roosevelt-Smith interview, 1979; Thomas, "The Magic Carpet," 3–4; G. C. Thomas to Mrs. Thomas, 26 and 28 April 1941, TFP; Maj. J. M. McHugh, USMC, to L. Currie, 27 April 1941, James Marshall McHugh Papers, Cornell University Library. For American aid to China, see Michael Schaller, *The U.S. Crusade in China, 1938–1945* (New York: Columbia University Press, 1979), 39–85.
7. G. C. Thomas to Mrs. Thomas, 28 April 1941, TFP; Thomas, oral memoir, 147–50.
8. G. C. Thomas to Mrs. Thomas, 1 May 1941, TFP.
9. Thomas, "The Magic Carpet," 9–10, and oral memoir, 153–5.
10. Thomas, oral memoir, 155–8; Thomas, "The Magic Carpet," 10–13.
11. Thomas, "The Magic Carpet," 14–16.
12. Ibid., 16–18.
13. Ibid., 13–14.
14. Secretary of State to FDR, 8 May 1941, PPF 3, Roosevelt Papers; Maj. B. Fellers, USA, to Capt. J. F. Roosevelt, 8 May 1941, PPF 3; Thomas, "The Magic Carpet," 20–1.
15. Thomas, "The Magic Carpet," 20–5, and oral memoir, 164–8. RAF Middle East had almost 1,000 aircraft on its books, but it seldom had more than 400 operational, and even fewer were first-line combat aircraft. Churchill could not understand why the RAF got so little fight from a force of 50,000 officers and other ranks. See John Terraine, *The Right of the Line: The Royal Air Force in the European War, 1939–1945* (London: Hodden and Stoughton, 1985), 301–9, 337–47. Tedder describes his problems in May 1941 in Marshal of the Royal Air Force Lord Tedder, *With Prejudice* (Boston: Little, Brown, 1966), 83–111.
16. Thomas, "The Magic Carpet," 26–9; A. Kirk to SecState, 13 May 1941, File 740.0011, General Records, Department of State, RG 59.
17. Thomas, "The Magic Carpet," 30–1, and oral memoir, 175–6; Playfair et al., *The Mediterranean and the Middle East*, II:117–19.
18. Thomas, "The Magic Carpet," 31–3; Maj. B. Fellers to Roosevelt and Thomas, 15 May 1941, PPF 3, Roosevelt Papers.

19. Thomas, "The Magic Carpet," 33–6.
20. Thomas, oral memoir, 184–8, and "The Magic Carpet," 37–40.
21. Thomas, "The Magic Carpet," 41–2.
22. Capt. J. Roosevelt to Mr. and Mrs. F. D. Roosevelt, 14 May 1941, via U.S. minister, Cairo, and State Department, PPF 3; FDR memorandum for Capt. J. R. Beardall, 20 May 1941, PPF 3; Capt. J. R. Beardall, memorandum for the President, 22 May 1941, PPF 3; Capt. J. F. Roosevelt and Mrs. F. D. Roosevelt, 30 May 1941, and Capt. J. F. Roosevelt to Mrs. J. F. Roosevelt, 3 June 1941, PPF 3; Thomas, "The Magic Carpet," 42.
23. Thomas, "The Magic Carpet," 44–5; diary entries, 24 and 29 May 1941; Cecil Browne, *Suez to Singapore* (New York: Random House, 1942), 36. For the battle for Crete see Playfair et al., *The Mediterranean and the Middle East*, II:121–51.
24. Thomas, oral memoir, 196–9, and "The Magic Carpet," 45–7. The characterization of the principal British officers Thomas met in the Middle East (Wavell, Freyberg, Tedder, Cunningham, and Mountbatten) are drawn from the biographical essays on these officers in Field Marshal Sir Michael Carver, ed., *The War Lords: Military Commanders of the Twentieth Century* (Boston: Little, Brown, 1976).
25. Thomas, "The Magic Carpet," 48–50, and oral memoir, 199–203.
26. Warren F. Kimball, ed., *Churchill & Roosevelt: The Complete Correspondence*, 3 vols. (Princeton, N.J.: Princeton University Press, 1984), I:202–3; Churchill to Roosevelt, 31 May and 3 June 1941, in W. Averell Harriman and Elie Abel, *Special Envoy to Churchill and Stalin, 1941–1946* (New York: Norton, 1976), 308–19; Thomas, "The Magic Carpet," 52–3, and oral memoir, 208–9; J. Roosevelt to Secretary of State C. Hull, 10 June 1941, and Navy communications memorandum for the President, 17 June 1941, PPF 3. See Deborah Wing Ray, "The Takoradi Route: Roosevelt's Prewar Venture Beyond the Western Hemisphere," *Journal of American History* 62 (September 1975), 340–58.
27. Thomas, "The Magic Carpet," 53–4, and oral memoir, 211–13; memorandum for the President, 20 June 1941, PPF 3; Roosevelt-Smith interview, 1979.
28. Thomas, oral memoir, 214a–18.

Chapter XIV. Once More to War
1. Stetson Conn and Byron Fairchild, *United States Army in World War II, The Framework of Hemispheric Defense* (Washington, D.C.: Government Printing Office, 1960), 3–155; Samuel Eliot Morison, *History of United States Naval Operations in World War II*, 15 vols., vol. I: *The Battle of the Atlantic* (Boston: Little, Brown, 1947–1961), 27–67; B. Mitchell Simpson, "Harold Raynsford Stark," in Robert W. Love, Jr., ed., *The Chiefs of Naval Operations* (Annapolis, Md.: Naval Institute Press, 1980), 119–35; Tracy B. Kitteridge, "United States Defense Policy and Strategy; 1941," *U.S. News and World Report* (3 December 1954), 53–139.
2. HQMC, memorandum, "Proposed Peace and War Strength of the Marine Corps to Support a Two Ocean Navy," 18 April 1941, File 432, records of the General Board, U.S. Navy, NHC; Joel D. Thacker, "Outline History of

the First Marine Division," 1945, manuscript history, 1st Division File, RS H&MD.
3. Quoted in Richard M. Leighton and Robert W. Coakley, *United States Army in World War II: Global Logistics and Strategy, 1940–1943* (Washington, D.C.: Government Printing Office, 1955), 65. For the history of Marine Corps mobilization, see especially Historical Section, HQMC, "Marine Corps Administrative History," October, 1946, H&MD, and Kenneth W. Condit, Gerald Diamond, and Edwin T. Turnbladh, "Marine Corps Ground Training in World War II," 1956, H&MD.
4. Thacker, "Outline History of First Marine Division," 1–4; George McMillan, *The Old Breed: A History of the First Marine Division in World War II* (Washington, D.C.: Infantry Journal Press, 1949), 1–8. See also Lt. Col. Frank O. Hough, Maj. Verle E. Ludwig, and Henry I. Shaw, Jr., *History of U.S. Marine Corps Operations in World War II*, 5 vols., vol. I: *Pearl Harbor to Guadalcanal* (Washington, D.C.: G-3 Division, HQMC, 1958–1968), 47–56.
5. Buell, *Master of Sea Power*, 125–41; Cooper, *Gen. Holland M. "Howlin' Mad" Smith*, 57–86. For prewar amphibious developments, see Jeter A. Isely and Philip A. Crowl, *The U.S. Marines and Amphibious War* (Princeton, N.J.: Princeton University Press, 1951), 45–71.
6. "Transcript of Record, Maj. Gen. Philip H. Torrey," (1884–1968), RS H&MD; Maj. Gen. David R. Nimmer, oral memoir (1970), 108–30, MCOHC; Brig. Gen. Robert C. Kilmartin, Jr., oral memoir (1979), 230–41, 251–2, MCOHC. For the relative rank and seniority of Marine officers in 1941, see Department of the Navy, *Navy Register 1941* (Washington, D.C.: Government Printing Office, 1941), 601–12. Thomas joined the 1st Division as the 137th senior of 144 lieutenant colonels, but he was the only officer of that rank to attend five resident military schools. He was junior to Monson, Kilmartin, and Goettge. Bobby Erskine was a junior colonel and the youngest officer of his rank (age forty-four).
7. Thomas, oral memoir, 220–1; Thomas, "Of Coconuts and Their Prelude," manuscript autobiography (1976), 1–2; Thacker, "Outline History of the First Marine Division," 28 May 1941, Historical Amphibious Files (HAF) 146, Breckinridge Library, 1–4. The "growth" of the Navy's amphibious force in 1940 is illustrative of the lack of preparation. The Navy commissioned twelve "new" transports that year, but all of them were converted merchantmen built between 1918 and 1931. The average age of these vessels was nineteen years.
8. Thomas, oral memoir, 221–4, and "Of Coconuts," 2.
9. Thomas, oral memoir, 221–4; Kilmartin, oral memoir, 240–1, 304–5; Cmdt. MCS to Maj. Gen. Cmdt., observations on maneuvers at New River, 25 August 1941, HAF 131; CG Atlantic Amphibious Force to CinC Atlantic Fleet, 27 August and 9 September 1941, HAF 142 and 136; Joint Landing Force Board, "Study of the Conduct of Training Landing Forces for Joint Amphibious Operations during World War II," May 1953, Command File World War II, NHC.
10. Thomas, oral memoir, 224–30; "Marine Corps Administrative History,"

5–105; McMillan, *The Old Breed*, 8–11; *Washington Post*, 28 September 1941; *New York Times*, 20 August 1941; Thacker, "Outline History of First Marine Division," 1–4.
11. G. C. Thomas to Mrs. G. C. Thomas, August–December 1941, TFP.
12. Interview, Gen. G. C. Thomas, with G. Smith, 19 November and 3 December 1978, MCOHC; Gen. M. B. Twining, oral memoir (1967), 85–6, 120–36, 134–6, MCOHC; Gen. M. B. Twining to Col. A. Fraser, April 1983, Thomas Papers, MCHC; Gen. M. B. Twining, Thomas questionnaire in the author's possession, 5 December 1986; Kilmartin, oral memoir, 230–45.
13. McMillan, *The Old Breed*, 11–13; Thomas, "Of Coconuts," 3; "Marine Corps Administrative History," 1–18; Condit et al., "Marine Corps Ground Training," 155–75; *New York Times*, 24 February 1941.
14. Col. G. C. Thomas, Jr., "Notes on My Father in the 1930s," February 1988, TFP; G. C. Thomas to Mrs. G. C. Thomas, 21 March 1942, TFP; W. H. J. Thomas, "Family Notes" (1988), 1–2.
15. Thomas, oral memoir, 238; Twining, oral memoir, 133; Thacker, "Outline History of First Marine Division," 1–4; Cates, oral memoir, 116–28.
16. Kilmartin, oral memoir, 234–41; Erskine, oral memoir, 290–1; Gen. P. A. del Valle, oral memoir (1966), 128–31, MCOHC; Cooper, *Gen. Holland M. "Howlin' Mad" Smith*, 90. The best "inside" account, however, comes from Gen. Merrill B. Twining in various forms: his 1983 memorandum for Col. A. M. Fraser; his oral memoir, 118–42; his memorandum for B. M. Frank, "Vandegrift," June 1987; and his Thomas questionnaire for the author, 5 December 1986. Thomas's only recorded comments on Torrey's relief and the subsequent changes are in his 1978 interview with Gibson B. Smith. Vandegrift wrote nothing of the affair; he was characteristically silent on disagreeable personal problems.
17. In addition to the sources cited above, in 1987 General Twining provided me with his written evaluation of all the principal officers of the 1st Marine Division in 1942. For this paragraph, I used his sketches of Vandegrift, Whaling, Hunt, del Valle, and Pate. See also Maj. Gen. Robert Blake, oral memoir (1968), 85–8, MCOHC.
18. "James, William Capers," biographical file, RS MCHC; Thomas-Smith interview, 1978; Twining memorandum for Fraser, 1983; Twining memorandum, "Vandegrift," June 1987; Kilmartin, oral memoir, 251–2; Twining, "Capers James," 1987 (see Note 17).
19. Thomas, oral memoir, 239; Grace Person Hayes, *The History of the Joint Chiefs of Staff in World War II: The War Against Japan* (Annapolis: Naval Institute Press, 1982), 104–35.
20. Thomas, "Record of Assignments," Thomas, OQR; Thomas, oral memoir, 239–40; Twining, oral memoir, 142–4; Thacker, "Outline History of First Marine Division," 3–4.
21. Thomas, oral memoir, 241–5; Twining, Thomas questionnaire (1986); Twining, "Frank B. Goettge" and "Jim Murray," biographical sketches provided the author; "Record of Assignments," Thomas OQR; Vandegrift fitness report on Thomas, 1942, Thomas OQR.

Chapter XV. The Road to CACTUS

1. For the strategic context of the Solomons offensive, see especially Hayes, *History of Joint Chiefs,* 104–53, supplemented by Buell, *Master of Sea Power,* 194–225. The best single study of the campaign, especially for its use of Japanese materials, is Brig. Gen. Samuel B. Griffith, II, USMC (Ret.), *The Battle for Guadalcanal* (Philadelphia: Lippincott, 1963). An Asian linguist and infantry officer, General Griffith participated in the campaign as executive officer and commanding officer of the 1st Raider Battalion until wounded in action. Comparable, however, is Richard B. Frank, *Guadalcanal* (New York: Random House, 1990). The official history of the campaign is Hough et al., *Pearl Harbor to Guadalcanal.* This volume adds more information and corrects the errors of the earlier monograph of Maj. John L. Zimmerman, *The Guadalcanal Campaign* (Washington, D.C.: G-3, HQMC, 1949). Zimmerman's study is still useful for personal details and its photographs. Also essential for understanding the Pacific War is Ronald H. Spector, *Eagle Against the Sun* (New York: Macmillan, 1985).
2. The rapid and widespread deployment of Japanese forces in May and June of 1942 forced them to use a code (JN-25b) that had been compromised and required a torrent of radio messages, decrypted and analyzed by Fleet Radio Unit Pacific ("Hypo") in Hawaii. On Allied intelligence in the spring of 1942, see Office of Naval Intelligence, *The Role of Communication Intelligence in the American-Japanese Naval War,* vol. III: *The Solomon Islands Campaign,* Part 1 (1 July–9 August 1942), 21 June 1943, NSA/CSS Cryptologic Documents, World War II, RG 457, NA; Rear Adm. Edwin T. Layton, "*And I Was There . . .*" (New York: Morrow, 1985), 457–63; Ronald Lewin, *The American MAGIC: Codes, Ciphers and the Defeat of Japan* (New York: Farrar, Straus Giroux, 1982), 81–111; George C. Dyer, *The Amphibians Came to Conquer: The Story of Admiral Richmond Kelly Turner,* 2 vols. (Washington, D.C.: Naval Historical Division, 1971), I:274–6; W. J. Holmes, *Double-Edged Secrets: U.S. Naval Intelligence Operations in the Pacific during World War II* (Annapolis, Md.: Naval Institute Press, 1979), 67–76; H. P. Willmott, *The Barrier and the Javelin: Japanese and Allied Pacific Strategies, February to June 1942* (Annapolis, Md.: Naval Institute Press, 1983), 291–343; Walter Lord, *Lonely Vigil: Coastwatchers of the Solomons* (New York: Viking, 1977); and Cmdr. Erick A. Feldt, RAN, *The Coastwatchers* (New York: Oxford University Press, 1946).
3. Hayes, *History of Joint Chiefs,* 140–9.
4. Dyer, *Amphibians Came to Conquer,* I:269–76.
5. Ibid., 277–80.
6. For descriptions of the *Wakefield*'s trip to New Zealand and arrival, see Thomas, oral memoir, 245–6, and "Of Coconuts," 5–6; Lt. Col. G. C. Thomas to L. J. Thomas, 2, 9, 13, and 16 June 1942, TFP; Vandegrift, *Once A Marine,* 100–2; McMillan, *The Old Breed,* 15–17; and Herbert Christian Merillat, *Guadalcanal Remembered* (New York: Dodd, Mead, 1982). Merillat served as division press officer and historian and wrote *The Island* (Boston: Houghton Mifflin, 1944), the first "insider's account" of the campaign. His 1982 reprise, however, includes diary entries from 1942 as well as shrewd assessments of the senior Navy and Marine Corps officers he observed.

7. Lt. Col. G. C. Thomas to L. J. Thomas, 22 and 25 June 1942, TFP; Thomas, "Of Coconuts," 6–7; Twining, oral memoir, 144–9; Twining, "Vandegrift"; Vandegrift, *Once a Marine,* 103; Col. S. B. Hunt to author, 22 June 1989. For the most detailed reconstruction and analysis of the division's experience, see CG 1st MarDiv to CMC. "Final Report on the Guadalcanal Campaign," in five parts, July 1943, File A7, war diaries and reports of the 1st Marine Division, FMF, Marine Corps organizational records, RG 127, NA. "Phase I" of "Final Report" covers the period up to 7 August 1942. File A7 also includes the surviving D-2 and D-3 journals, and a headquarters command chronology, all of which were used in the official history, Hough et al., *Pearl Harbor to Guadalcanal;* and in Griffith, *Battle for Guadalcanal.*
8. Thomas, "Of Coconuts," 7.
9. Thomas, oral memoir, 248–50; Vandegrift, *Once a Marine,* 103–4, 109–12; Griffith, *Battle for Guadalcanal,* 26–7.
10. Thomas, "Of Coconuts," 8–10; Vandegrift, *Once a Marine,* 112–13; M. B. Twining, Guadalcanal memorandum for Col. A. M. Fraser, April 1983, 18–22; Griffith, *Battle for Guadalcanal,* 31–2.
11. "Logistics," "Final Report Guadalcanal: Phase I: Preparation," 5–7, and Annexes C and D, File A7-1, 1st Marine Division Organizational Records, RG 127. Marines of the 4th Battalion, 11th Marines, went to fill the understrength 5th Battalion, which had sailed before it had been fully organized as the division 105-mm howitzer general support battalion. The weight of the 155-mm guns and their prime movers drove Vandegrift's decision to leave them in New Zealand. On the employment of the 11th Marines on Guadalcanal, I have relied on Brig. Gen. Pedro A. del Valle, "Marine Field Artillery on Guadalcanal," *Field Artillery Journal* 33 (October 1943), 722–33; and "Marine Corps Artillery on Guadalcanal," *MCG* 27 and 28 (November 1943), 9–13 (January 1944), and 27–30 (February 1944).
12. Thomas, oral memoir, 254–5; Thomas, "Of Coconuts," 10–12; Lt. Col. G. C. Thomas to L. J. Thomas, July 1 and 7, 1942, TFP; Gen. M. B. Twining, "Critical Decisions," January 1987, manuscript in the author's possession; Gen. H. W. Buse, Jr., oral memoir (1970), 39–40, MCOHC. On this point, as others, I have also relied on "Final Report Guadalcanal: Phase I: Preparation."
13. Intelligence Annex, 1st MarDiv OpO 7-42, 27 July 1942, Combat Operations, Documents Collection, Breckinridge Library, Marine Corps Schools; Thomas, "Of Coconuts," 10–12; Twining, oral memoir, 150–2; Zimmerman, *Guadalcanal Campaign,* 14–16.
14. Dyer, *Amphibians Came to Conquer,* I:277–89; Vandegrift, memoir (1962), 543–4, Vandegrift Papers, MCHC; Thomas, oral memoir, 257–9; Griffith, *Battle for Guadalcanal,* 28–32; Twining, oral memoir, 171, 181. For a sketch of Ghormley, see Clark G. Reynolds, *Famous American Admirals* (New York: Van Nostrand Reinhold, 1978), 135–6.
15. Twining, oral memoir, 159–60; Vandegrift, memoir, 543–4, 554; Twining, "Vandegrift," n.p.; Thomas, oral memoir, 261; Col. S. B. Hunt to author, 22 June 1989.
16. 1st MarDiv Op Order 7-42, reprinted in part in Hough et al., *Pearl Harbor to Guadalcanal,* 396–8. The complete order is an annex to "Final Report

Guadalcanal: Phase I: Preparation." The same source reviews the planning, 242–50, and includes the famous sketch map, which actually shows "the grassy knoll" and Mount Austen as two different locations. See also George MacGillivray, "Historical Guadalcanal Maps in Collection, " *Fortitudine* 11–12 (Spring-Summer 1982), 12–13.

17. Twining, "Critical Decisions," and 1983 memorandum on Thomas and Guadalcanal for Fraser discuss the "Beach Red" issue in detail.
18. Twining, oral memoir, 152–7, 165; "Final Report Guadalcanal: Phase I Preparation"; Herbert C. Merillat, "The 'ULTRA' Weapon on Guadalcanal," MCG 66 (September 1982), 44–9.
19. Thomas, oral memoir, 262–3, and "Of Coconuts," 14–15; Vandegrift, *Once a Marine*, 118–21; Dyer, *Amphibians Came to Conquer*, I:299–305; Griffith, *Battle for Guadalcanal*, 34–6.
20. Thomas, "Of Coconuts," 15–18, and oral memoir, 263–5; Twining, "Critical Decisions" and 1983 Guadalcanal memorandum.

Chapter XVI. Division Operations Officer on Guadalcanal

1. In addition to Guadalcanal sources cited in Chapter 15, I have relied on Morison, *History of Naval Operations*, vol. V: *The Struggle for Guadalcanal, August 1942–February 1943* (1948), for the naval context, although Morison worked too quickly and too soon to be always analytical. Especially helpful for the naval campaign are Thomas C. Hone, "The Similarity of Past and Present Standoff Threats," USNIP 107 (September 1981), 113–16, and Michael Vlahos and Dale K. Pace, "War Experiences and Force Requirements," NWCR 41 (Autumn 1988), 26–46. The logistical picture is described in W. R. Carter, *Beans, Bullets, and Black Oil: The Story of Fleet Logistics Afloat in the Pacific during World War II* (Washington, D.C.: Naval Historical Division, 1952), 23–61. Conduct of the Guadalcanal campaign from the Japanese perspective may be found in Paul S. Dull, *A Battle History of the Imperial Japanese Navy (1941–1945)* (Annapolis, Md.: Naval Institute Press, 1978), 175–249, and John Toland, *The Rising Sun: The Decline and Fall of the Japanese Empire, 1936–1945* (New York: Random House, 1970), 345–431, both of which use Japanese interviews and documents.
2. Thomas, "Of Coconuts," 15–16, and oral memoir, 268–71; Twining, "Critical Decisions"; Gen. M. B. Twining, memorandum for Col. A. M. Fraser, April 1983, TFP; Twining, oral memoir, 185–8.
3. CG 1st MarDiv to CMC, "Final Report Guadalcanal, Phase II: 7–9 August 1942: 1942," File A7-2, 1st Marine Division Organizational Records, RG 127; D-2, "Division Intelligence Report on the Guadalcanal Campaign, 7–9 Aug 1942," December 1942, File A8-1, RG 127; Thomas, oral memoir, 266, and "Of Coconuts," 18; Vandegrift, *Once a Marine*, 122–24; Twining, oral memoir, 190–1; Hough et al., *Pearl Harbor to Guadalcanal*, 254–62.
4. Vandegrift, *Once a Marine*, 123–5; Thomas, "Of Coconuts," 18–21, and oral memoir, 282–7; Twining, oral memoir, 191–202; Merillat, *Guadalcanal Remembered*, 52–5. The sketches of Rowan, Cates, and Maxwell come from General Twining, who wrote character appraisals of all the officers in the

famous 11 August 1942 picture for the author in 1988. Whenever possible, I have checked General Twining's evaluation with other participants.

The best source for the operations of 1st Marines is a detailed memoir by its commander, then Col. Clifton B. Cates, "My First at Guadalcanal 7 Aug–22 Dec 1942," n.d., Gen. Clifton B. Cates Papers, MCHC, which is based on his contemporary diary and letters, excerpted in the memoir. Cates's account of 7–9 August is consistent with his oral memoir, 129–33.

5. Thomas, "Of Coconuts," 21–2, and oral memoir, 293–7; Twining, oral memoir, 198–202, and "LeRoy P. Hunt," memorandum for the author, 1988; Vandegrift, *Once a Marine*, 126–8. I have verified the sequence of events in "Final Report Guadalcanal, Phase II," and the D-3 Journal, August 1942, File A7-14, 1st Marine Division Organizational Records, RG 127.
6. The most vivid accounts of the Vandegrift-Thomas odyssey are Vandegrift, memoir (1962), 578–93, Gen. A. A. Vandegrift Papers, MCHC, and Thomas, "Of Coconuts," 21–4. For the naval battles of 8–9 August and Fletcher's withdrawal, see Griffith, *Battle for Guadalcanal*, 56–7; and Dyer, *Amphibians Came to Conquer*, I:319–402.
7. Vandegrift, *Once a Marine*, 130; Dyer, *Amphibians Came to Conquer*, I:382–90; "Final Report Guadalcanal, Phase II."
8. Thomas, "Of Coconuts," 24–6, and oral memoir, 309–11; Gen. M. B. Twining, memorandum on Guadalcanal operations, for Col. A. M. Fraser, 19 April 1983, in author's possession.
9. Lt. Col. G. C. Thomas to L. J. Thomas, 12 August 1942, TFP; Vandegrift, *Once a Marine*, 131–8; Vandegrift, "Memorandum for Colonel Riley," 5 February 1943, a personal campaign assessment, Vandegrift Papers; Col. R. C. Kilmartin to Lt. Col. G. C. Thomas, 31 August 1942, Vandegrift Papers; Thomas, oral memoir, 311–26. The principal source for this section, however, is CG 1st MarDiv to CMC, "Final Report Guadalcanal, Phase III: 10–21 August 1942," RG 127.
10. The organizational strength and equipment of a 1942–43 Marine division may be found in Appendix F of Henry I. Shaw, Jr., and Maj. Douglas T. Kane, *History of U.S. Marine Corps Operations in World War II*, vol. II: *Isolation of Rabaul* (Washington, D.C.: G-3 Division, HQMC, 1963), 571–3.

The 1st Battalion, 11th Marines, remained attached to the 7th Marines in Samoa, and the cannibalized 4th Battalion, 11th Marines (a 155-mm GPF gun battalion), had remained in New Zealand. The pack howitzer shell was not much heavier than that of the 81-mm mortar (ten pounds), the infantry battalion indirect fire weapon. Useful sources for weapons and equipment characteristics are George Forty, *U.S. Army Handbook, 1939–1945* (New York: Charles Scribner's Sons, 1979), and Jack Coggins, *The Campaign for Guadalcanal* (Garden City, N.Y.: Doubleday, 1972).
11. T. Grady Gallant, *On Valor's Side* (Garden City, N.Y.: Doubleday, 1963), 207. See also Robert Leckie, *Helmet for My Pillow* (New York: Random House, 1957), for another classic enlisted man's account of the campaign.
12. McMillan, *The Old Breed*, 45–57, and Robert Leckie, *Strong Men Armed, the U.S. Marines Against Japan* (New York: Random House, 1962), 3–48, catch the troops' attitudes in August 1942. See also U.S. War Department, *Fighting*

on Guadalcanal (Washington, D.C.: War Department, 1943), a compilation of field interviews. Another source for troop psychology is Richard W. Tregaskis, *Guadalcanal Diary* (New York: Random House, 1943), the work of a civilian correspondent who spent most of his time with the 5th Marines. Personal relationships are discussed in detail in General Twining's memorandum on Guadalcanal operations for Colonel Fraser, as well as Twining's 1988 description for me of all the officers in the photograph taken at the division CP. In addition, Robert Asprey, who helped Vandegrift write *Once a Marine* and who was a diligent student of the campaign, discusses personal relationships in a memorandum for K. Hellmer, "Vandegrift," 9 April 1962, Vandegrift Papers. Although Thomas remained guarded in both his autobiography and oral memoir, he discussed personalities with candor in his November 1978 interview with Gibson Smith. For an authoritative view of relationships from outside the CP, see Cates, "My First at Guadalcanal," and Cates, oral memoir.

13. In addition to the aviation portions of Hough et al., *Pearl Harbor to Guadalcanal*, see especially Robert Sherrod, *History of Marine Corps Aviation in World War II*, rev. ed. (Baltimore, Md.: Nautical and Aviation Publishing, 1987), 65–128, and Thomas G. Miller, Jr., *The CACTUS Air Force* (New York: Harper & Row, 1969).

14. The logistical picture is recorded in detail in "Final Report Guadalcanal, Phase III," and in Hough et al., *Pearl Harbor to Guadalcanal*, 274–80.

15. The communications picture is described in Lt. Gen. Edward W. Snedeker, oral memoir (1968), 45–58, MCOHC, and Col. Sanford D. Hunt's letters to H. C. Merillat (8 August 1981) and to the author (8 August 1988), both in the author's possession. General Snedeker and Colonel Hunt were the division communications and assistant communications officers.

16. Lt. Col. G. C. Thomas to L. J. Thomas, 15 August 1942; Thomas, "Of Coconuts," 28–9; Vandegrift, *Once A Marine*, 135–6; Twining, Goettge, and Buckley personal sketches provided the author by General Twining, 1988; Merillat, *Guadalcanal Remembered*, 86–90. I am especially indebted to Maj. W. F. M. Clemens, CBE, MC, Legion of Merit, for his personal letters of 14 and 20 September 1988 on the campaign and for the use of excerpts from his unpublished 1942 diary. Major Clemens also gave me his appraisal of the senior division officers in his letters of 20 and 21 May 1989.

17. Benis M. Frank, "Vandegrift's Guadalcanal Command," *MCG* 71 (August 1987), 56–9; Gen. M. B. Twining to B. M. Frank, 19 February 1987, in Frank's possession; Twining, "Vandegrift" and personal sketches provided the author in 1987; Thomas, oral memoir, and Smith interview; Vandegrift, memoir (1962); Col. C. R. Schwenke (Vandegrift's aide) to the author, 22 March 1989, and his response to Thomas questionnaire. Colonel Schwenke confirms Vandegrift's eyesight problems but not a serious hearing loss.

18. Lt. Col. G. C. Thomas to L. J. Thomas, 15 and 26 August 1942, TFP; Vandegrift, memoir (1962), 691–716; Twining, "Vandegrift"; Twining memorandum on Thomas for Fraser, 1983; Cates, "My First on Guadalcanal," 32–6; Vandegrift, fitness reports on Thomas, September 1942, Thomas OQR; Buse, oral memoir, 40–4; Col. S. B. Hunt, questionnaire for author

on Thomas, 17 July 1988; Maj. W. F. M. Clemens, questionnaire on Thomas, 22 August 1988; Col. C. R. Schwenke, questionnaire on Thomas, 22 March 1989.

19. Griffith, *Battle for Guadalcanal,* 78–88; Hough et al., *Pearl Harbor to Guadalcanal,* 280–6; CG 1st MarDiv to CMC, "Final Report Guadalcanal, Phase IV, 20 August–18 September 1942," RG 127. I have also consulted D-2 and D-3 journals in the 1st Marine Division organizational records as well as the "Enemy Operations Guadalcanal" File, in the Combat Operations Documents Collection, Breckinridge Library, Marine Corps Schools, Quantico. An additional source of analysis from the Japanese perspective is Saburo Hayashi with Alvin D. Coox, *Kogun: The Japanese Army in the Pacific War* (Quantico, Va.: Marine Corps Association, 1959), 58–67. For Japanese order-of-battle data, see A. J. Barker, *Japanese Army Handbook, 1939–1945* (New York: Hippocrane Books, 1979).

20. Lt. Col. G. C. Thomas to L. J. Thomas, 22 August 1942, TFP; Thomas, "Of Coconuts," 31–4, and oral memoir, 332–7; Cates, "My First on Guadalcanal," 20–36; Zimmerman, *Guadalcanal Campaign,* 60–72; Tregaskis, *Guadalcanal Diary,* 132.

21. Hough et al., *Pearl Harbor to Guadalcanal,* 291–8; Thomas, "Of Coconuts," 35–41, and oral memoir, 347a–50; Willock, *Unaccustomed to Fear,* 207–30.

22. Thomas, "Of Coconuts," 39–40; Zimmerman, *Guadalcanal Campaign,* 77–9; Twining, oral memoir, 210–12.

23. Twining, "Critical Decisions" and "Vandegrift"; Thomas, "Of Coconuts," 43; Gen. M. A. Edson biographical file, RS MCHC; Brig. Gen. S. B. Griffith, II, oral memoir (1970), 86–7, 106–7, MCOHC; Cates, "My First at Guadalcanal," 146–7; Twining to author, 16 June 1989; and Maj. Jon T. Hoffman, "The Coco River Patrol and the *Small Wars Manual,*" master's thesis, The Ohio State University, 1989.

24. Thomas, "Of Coconuts," 42; Zimmerman, *Guadalcanal Campaign,* 79–82; Griffith, *Battle for Guadalcanal,* 107–10.

25. Thomas, "Of Coconuts," 43, and oral memoir, 135; Vandegrift, *Once a Marine,* 151–2; Twining, memorandum for Fraser and oral memoir, 248–9; Cates, "My First on Guadalcanal," 145; Twining to author, 2 June 1989; Merillat, *Guadalcanal Remembered,* 129–36. General Twining wrote his only public account of the events of 9–14 September 1942 in "Head for the Hills," *MCG* 71 (August 1987), 46–55. For the sequence of events, I have also used the D-3 Journal, 8–14 September 1942, File A7-15, 1st Marine Division Organizational Records, RG 127, as well as the "Guadalcanal Final Report, Phase IV."

26. Thomas, "Of Coconuts," 44–5, and oral memoir, 356–8; Vandegrift, memoir (1962), 659–64, and *Once a Marine,* 152–4; Twining, "Vandegrift," "Critical Decisions" and oral memoir, 245–8; Dyer, *Amphibians Came to Conquer,* I:440–2, 427–8. The official histories are vague on this meeting, and even General Griffith is unclear on the existence of two messages. General Twining is certain, however, that Ghormley sent Vandegrift a personal letter, which Thomas showed him on 13 or 14 September, that was even more bleak than the ComSoPac-CinCPac message that Turner showed Vandegrift on

the evening of 12 September in the division CP. Vandegrift mentions the Ghormley surrender note in his private memoir but excluded it from his published memoir. The division copies of the ComSoPac-CinCPac message and the Ghormley note do not survive.

27. Lt. Col. G. C. Thomas to L. J. Thomas, 15 September 1942, TFP; Thomas, "Of Coconuts," 45–8, and oral memoir, 359–65; Vandegrift, *Once a Marine,* 152–8; Zimmerman, *Guadalcanal Campaign,* 84–91; Griffith, *Battle for Guadalcanal,* 115–22. Japanese losses were most accurately assessed from Japanese records after the war by General Griffith. Total Marine casualties of 150 reflect not only tenacious ground defense, but more than 3,000 rounds of artillery fired in support.

28. Lt. Col. G. C. Thomas to L. J. Thomas, 22 and 25 September 1942, TFP; Headquarters Marine Corps, *Combined Lineal List,* July 1942; Vandegrift, memoir (1962), 691–3; Maj. Gen. A. A. Vandegrift to Rear Adm. R. K. Turner, 24 September 1942, and Lt. Gen. T. Holcomb to Vandegrift, 29 September 1942, both in Vandegrift Papers; Thomas, "Of Coconuts," 48–9; Buse, oral memoir, 45–6; Twining, memorandum for Fraser and Thomas questionnaire, 1988. All of the new colonels came from the group of lieutenant colonels with dates of rank no later than 1 March 1941; Thomas's date of rank as a lieutenant colonel was 1 July 1941. The new colonels' dates of rank were 21 May 1942. When Thomas received news of his promotion, he learned that his new date of rank was 7 September 1942 (later adjusted to 15 September when the promotion became permanent in 1943) "for present assignment." Therefore, of the colonels who remained in the division after September 1942, del Valle, Cates, Pepper, Edson, Whaling, and A. L. Sims (commander of the 7th Marines) were senior to Thomas.

The truth is that Vandegrift wanted to clean out the 5th Marines and reorganize his staff. Hunt and all three of his original battalion commanders left Guadalcanal, although one, Harold E. Rosecrans, had been badly shaken by a bomb near-miss; in fact, Vandegrift replaced a total of five battalion commanders. To make the Hunt and James relief appear less punitive, he tied it to the release of Rowan and Kilmartin. In Kilmartin's case, Vandegrift (and certainly Thomas) preferred to work with Jim Murray, already the acting D-1 while Kilmartin served on Tulagi.

29. Lt. Gen. T. Holcomb to Maj. Gen. A. A. Vandegrift, 5 October 1942, and Vandegrift to Holcomb, 24 October 1942, Vandegrift Papers.

The selection process for temporary brigadier generals then in effect allowed the Commandant to make nominations without formal board review; he polled all the other Marine generals and then drew up the list.

Chapter XVII. Division Chief of Staff on Guadalcanal

1. Hayes, *History of Joint Chiefs,* 171–97; Griffith, *Battle for Guadalcanal,* 130–9; Hough et al., *Pearl Harbor to Guadalcanal,* 322–30.
2. CG 1st MarDiv to CMC, "Final Report Guadalcanal, Phase V, 18 September–5 December 1942," 1 July 1943, File A7-5, 1st Marine Division Organizational Records, RG 127; Maj. Gen. A. A. Vandegrift to Rear Adm. R. K.

Turner, 24 September 1942, Vandegrift Papers; Dyer, *Amphibians Came to Conquer,* I:403–34; Vandegrift, *Once a Marine,* 149–67.

3. G. C. Thomas to L. J. Thomas, 25 and 28 September and 2 October 1942, TFP; Thomas, "Of Coconuts," 50, and oral memoir, 373–7; Gen. M. B. Twining, biographical sketches of Coffman, Maklin, and Brown for the author, 1988; Gen. M. B. Twining, memorandum on Guadalcanal campaign, for Col. A. Fraser, April, 1983, TFP; Col. S. B. Hunt, Thomas questionnaire for the author, July 1988; W. F. M. Clemens to the author, 22 August and 14 September 1988, with excerpts from Clemens's Guadalcanal diary; Merillat, *Guadalcanal Remembered,* 150–7.

4. Twining, oral memoir, 204–9, 248–9; Twining, biographical sketches of Cates, Whaling, Frisbie, and McKelvey for the author; Thomas, "Of Coconuts," 50, and oral memoir, 378–80; Davis, *Marine: Life of Puller,* 121–2.

5. Maj. Gen. A. A. Vandegrift to Rear Adm. R. K. Turner, 24 September 1942, Vandegrift Papers; Vandegrift, manuscript autobiography (1962), 700–16, Vandegrift Papers; Twining, "Critical Decisions," memorandum on the Guadalcanal campaign for the author, January 1987; Appendix D, "Medical Experience," in Zimmerman, *Guadalcanal Campaign,* 176–80; CG 1st MarDiv to CMC, "Final Report Guadalcanal, Phase V."

6. Thomas, "Of Coconuts," 50–9; Vandegrift, *Once a Marine,* 164–73; Griffith, *Battle for Guadalcanal,* 132–7, 145–8; Hough et al., *Pearl Harbor to Guadalcanal,* 310–21.

7. Potter, *Nimitz,* 190–5; Vandegrift, *Once a Marine,* 170–2; Thomas, "Of Coconuts," 51–54, and oral memoir, 393–9; Pfeiffer, oral memoir, 199–204.

8. Griffith, *Battle for Guadalcanal,* 139–52; Thomas, oral memoir, 414–17; Jerry Cooper, *Citizens As Soldiers: A History of the North Dakota National Guard* (Fargo: North Dakota Institute for Regional Studies, 1986), 278–93.

9. Thomas, "Of Coconuts," 58–61, and oral memoir, 414–20; Vandegrift, *Once a Marine,* 173–8; Sherrod, *History of Marine Corps Aviation,* 98–105; Griffith, *Battle for Guadalcanal,* 152–7.

10. Col. G. C. Thomas, 19 and 27 October 1942, TFP; Thomas, "Of Coconuts," 59–62; del Valle, oral memoir, 132–43; Gen. P. A. del Valle, *Semper Fidelis* (Hawthorne, Calif.: Christian Book Club, 1976), 124–8.

11. Thomas, "Of Coconuts," 62–3, and oral memoir, 428–30; Vandegrift, *Once a Marine,* 181–4; Thomas interview with G. B. Smith, 3 December 1978, TFP; Merillat, *Guadalcanal Remembered,* 186–93.

12. Thomas, oral memoir, 430–2; Twining, Guadalcanal memorandum for Fraser.

13. Thomas, "Of Coconuts," 62–6; Hough et al., *Pearl Harbor to Guadalcanal,* 330–7; Zimmerman, *Guadalcanal Campaign,* 114–23. On Halsey's role as ComSoPac, see E. B. Potter, *Bull Halsey* (Annapolis, Md.: Naval Institute Press, 1985), 148–92.

14. Col. G. C. Thomas to L. J. Thomas, 30 October and 4 and 12 November 1942, TFP; "Final Report Guadalcanal, Phase V"; Vandegrift, *Once a Marine,* 192–5; Thomas, "Of Coconuts," 67–9, and oral memoir, 444–6; Twining, Guadalcanal memorandum for Fraser; Merillat, *Guadalcanal Remembered,* 214–17; Hough et al., *Pearl Harbor to Guadalcanal,* 343–5.

15. Col. G. C. Thomas to L. J. Thomas, 30 October and 4 and 12 November 1942, TFP; Thomas, "Of Coconuts," 70–1, and oral memoir, 449–50; Twining, Guadalcanal memorandum for Fraser; Dyer, *Amphibians Came to Conquer*, I:435–56.
16. "Final Report Guadalcanal, Phase V"; Thomas, "Of Coconuts," 69–71; Charles L. Updegraph, Jr., *U.S. Marine Corps Special Units of World War II* (Washington, D.C.: Historical Division, HQMC, 1972), 19–21.
17. Thomas, "Of Coconuts," 71; Vandegrift, *Once a Marine*, 195–7; Merillat, *Guadalcanal Remembered*, 22–3; Zimmerman, *Guadalcanal Campaign*, 133–41.
18. Griffith, *Battle for Guadalcanal*, 190–206.
19. Thomas, "Of Coconuts," 72–6, and oral memoir, 454–60.
20. Thomas, "Of Coconuts," 77–8, and oral memoir, 460–1; Vandegrift, *Once a Marine*, 198–202; Hough et al., *Pearl Harbor to Guadalcanal*, 357–63.
21. Thomas, oral memoir, 463.
22. Thomas, oral memoir, 463–4, and "Of Coconuts," 78–80; Twining, Guadalcanal memorandum for Fraser, and "Critical Decisions"; letters to the author from Martin Clemens, 22 August and 14 September 1988, and Col. Sanford Hunt, 22 June 1989; Merillat, *Guadalcanal Remembered*, passim.; Col. F. B. Nihart, "The 'George' Medal," *Fortitudine* 3 (Summer 1973), 8–9.
23. Griffith, *Battle for Guadalcanal*, 219–23, 242–5; Hough et al., *Pearl Harbor to Guadalcanal*, 395.

Chapter XVIII. Marines in the South Pacific
1. For a general account of the Bougainville campaign, see Shaw and Kane, *Isolation of Rabaul*. I have reconstructed Thomas's travels and assignments from "Chronological Record of Assignments, Gerald C. Thomas," Thomas OQR. The official Army history of the campaign for the Central and Northern Solomons is John Miller, Jr., *The War in the Pacific: CARTWHEEL: The Isolation of Rabaul* in the series *United States Army in World War II* (Washington, D.C.: Department of the Army, 1959), which is discreetly silent on interservice tensions.
2. Gen. G. C. Thomas, "Post Guadalcanal," chapter in manuscript autobiography (1967), 1–2, TFP; Thomas, oral memoir, 464–7; Col. G. C. Thomas to L. J. Thomas, 11 December 1942, TFP; Vandegrift, *Once a Marine*, 205–6; "Major General Clayton B. Vogel, USMC," biographical file, RS MCHC.
3. Twining, "Vandegrift"; Twining, oral memoir, 221–2; Lt. Gen. Cmdt. T. Holcomb to Maj. Gen. A. A. Vandegrift, 13 and 15 December 1942, Vandegrift Papers.
4. Thomas, oral memoir, 467–70, and "Post Guadalcanal," 2–3; Vandegrift, *Once a Marine*, 205–8; McMillan, *The Old Breed*, 145–8.
5. Col. G. C. Thomas to L. J. Thomas, 21 and 30 December 1942, TFP; Thomas, "Post Guadalcanal," 2–3.
6. Col. G. C. Thomas to L. J. Thomas, 8, 17, and 18 January 1943, TFP; Thomas, "Post Guadalcanal," 3–4, and oral memoir, 472–3; "Claim for Reimbursement for Personal Property Lost in a Marine or Aircraft Disaster," 22 February 1943, Thomas OQR; Col. G. C. Thomas to Rev. L. O'V.

Thomas, 17 January 1943, TFP; McMillan, *The Old Breed,* 148–52; Col. C. R. Schwenke to author, 22 May 1989.
7. Thomas, "Post Guadalcanal," 4–5, and oral memoir, 474–7; Col. G. C. Thomas to L. J. Thomas, 22 and 24 February 1943, TFP; Vandegrift, *Once a Marine,* 209–14; Lt. Gen. Cmdt. T. Holcomb to Maj. Gen. A. A. Vandegrift, Vandegrift Papers; Lt. Gen. Cmdt. T. Holcomb to Adm. C. A. Nimitz, 26 April 1943, Holcomb Papers. Vandegrift's public appearances are described in the newspaper clippings in his personal file, RS MCHC.
8. Col. G. C. Thomas to L. J. Thomas, 26 February and 3, 19, and 30 March 1943, TFP; *The Argus* (Illinois Wesleyan University), 17 March 1943.
9. Col. G. C. Thomas to L. J. Thomas, 25 April and 6, 13, 22, and 28 May 1943, TFP; Thomas, "Post Guadalcanal," 5–7; Vandegrift, *Once a Marine,* 214–18.
10. Hayes, *History of Joint Chiefs,* 278–334; James, *Years of MacArthur,* II:289–321; Potter, *Halsey,* 201–16.
11. Thomas, "Post Guadalcanal," 7, and oral memoir, 480–1; Maj. Gen. O. T. Pfeiffer, oral memoir (1968), 213–19, MCOHC; Lt. Gen. Cmdt. T. Holcomb to Vice Adm. W. F. Halsey, 26 April 1943, Holcomb Papers; Gen. M. B. Twining, "SOPAC," June 1989, memorandum to the author.
12. Thomas, oral memoir, 480–1; Vandegrift, *Once a Marine,* 218; Potter, *Halsey,* 217–31; Potter, *Nimitz,* 245–9; Lt. Gen. Cmdt. T. Holcomb to Maj. Gen. A. A. Vandegrift, 15 July 1943, Holcomb Papers; Brig. Gen. Frederick P. Henderson, oral memoir (1975), 336–7, MCOHC; Lt. Gen. Frederick L. Wieseman, oral memoir (1975), 312–15, MCOHC. Henderson and Wieseman served on the I MAC staff under Vogel, Vandegrift, and Barrett in 1943.
13. Col. G. C. Thomas to L. J. Thomas, 3, 11, 17, and 22 July 1943, TFP; Thomas, "Post Guadalcanal," 7–9; I MAC, "Command List," August–September 1943, Vandegrift Papers.
14. Thomas, "Post Guadalcanal," 7–9; Vandegrift, *Once a Marine,* 219–23. Logistical conditions in the South Pacific are described in Duncan S. Ballantine, *U.S. Naval Logistics in the Second World War* (Princeton, N.J.: Princeton University Press, 1947), 76–93, 99–100, 117–23.
15. Shaw and Kane, *Isolation of Rabaul,* 167–76; Potter, *Halsey,* 248–52; Samuel Eliot Morison, *History of United States Naval Operations in World War II,* vol. VI: *Breaking the Bismarcks Barrier, 22 July 1942–1 May 1944* (Boston: Atlantic Little, Brown, 1950), 279–88.
16. Thomas, oral memoir, 496–9; Col. G. C. Thomas to L. J. Thomas, 17 and 22 July 1943, TFP; Vandegrift, *Once a Marine,* 219–22; Twining, "Vandegrift"; "Major General Allen Hal Turnage," 1944, Turnage File, RS MCHC.
17. Thomas, oral memoir, 493–6; and "Post Guadalcanal," 8–9; Col. G. C. Thomas to L. J. Thomas, 22 August 1943, TFP; Lt. Gen. Joseph C. Burger, oral memoir (1969), 178–82, MCOHC; Lt. Gen. V. H. Krulak, Thomas questionnaire, 3 May 1986, and interview with the author, 16 January 1987.

The operations of specialized units are addressed in Charles L. Updegraph, Jr., *Special Marine Corps Units in World War II* (Washington, D.C.: Historical Division, HQMC, 1972).

18. Thomas, oral memoir, 500–6, and "Post Guadalcanal," 9–10; Vandegrift, *Once a Marine,* 224–7; "Record of Assignments," Thomas OQR; *New York Times,* 8 August 1943.
19. My assessment of the I MAC staff functioning and the Barrett affair is based on the following sources: "Major General Charles D. Barrett, Deceased," biographical file, including casualty report, and newspaper obituaries, RS MCHC; Snedeker, oral memoir, 336–40; Noble, oral memoir, 85–6; Burger, oral memoir, 167–76; Wieseman, oral memoir, 323–6; Henderson, oral memoir, 338–41; Lt. Gen. Cmdt. T. Holcomb to Maj. Gen. C. D. Barrett, 28 June 1943, and Holcomb to H. R. Luce, 6 November 1943, Holcomb Papers; Twining, "SOPAC" memorandum, 1989; Col. C. R. Schwenke to the author, 30 August 1989; Gen. M. B. Twining to the author, 3 July 1989.
20. Potter, *Halsey,* 252–4; Thomas, "Post Guadalcanal," 11–12, and oral memoir, 510–12; Col. G. C. Thomas to L. J. Thomas, 11 October 1943, TFP.
21. Thomas, oral memoir, 512–13, and "Post Guadalcanal," 12; Shaw and Kane, *Isolation of Rabaul,* 176–85.

    It still required seven days to get the first elements of the 37th Division and the 21st Marines to Bougainville.
22. Thomas, "Post Guadalcanal," 12–13, and oral memoir, 517–20.
23. Thomas, "Post Guadalcanal," 13–15; citation, Legion of Merit, Thomas OQR; CG I MAC to CMC, "Bougainville Operation," 21 March 1944, I MAC, Organizational Records, RG 127; Col. G. C. Thomas to L. J. Thomas, 16 November 1943, TFP.
24. Thomas, oral memoir, 521–31, and "Post Guadalcanal," 15; Vandegrift, *Once a Marine,* 230–1; Cooper, *Gen. Holland M. "Howling Mad" Smith,* 98–115; Dyer, *Amphibians Came to Conquer,* II:597–611.
25. The quote is from Lt. Gen. Cmdt. A. A. Vandegrift to Lt. Gen. H. M. Smith, Vandegrift papers. Thomas's travels and views in December are drawn from "Record of Assignments," Thomas OQR; Col. G. C. Thomas to L. J. Thomas, 13, 15, and 17 December 1943, TFP; Thomas, oral memoir, 524–5, and "Post Guadalcanal," 15. Some of the problems at Headquarters are described at length in Lt. Gen. Cmdt. Holcomb to Lt. Gen. A. A. Vandegrift, 19 and 23 November 1943, Holcomb Papers.

Chapter XIX. The War at Headquarters Marine Corps
1. Col. G. C. Thomas to L. J. Thomas, 31 December 1943 and 1 and 3 January 1944, TFP. Vandegrift's press clippings are in the Vandegrift biographical file, RS MCHC.
2. Historical Section, G-3, HQMC, "Marine Corps Administrative History," October 1946, manuscript for the Office of Naval History, MCHC; Kenneth W. Condit, Gerald Diamond, and Edwin T. Turnbladh, "Marine Corps Ground Training in World War II," 1956, manuscript history, MCHC; Thomas, oral memoir, 533–40, and "Post Guadalcanal," 15–23; Rear Adm. Julius A. Furer, USN (Ret.), *Administration of the Navy Department in World War II* (Washington, D.C.: Naval History Division, 1959), 547–95; muster rolls of Headquarters Battalion, Headquarters Marine Corps, January 1944–August 1947, RB MCHC.

3. Hayes, *History of Joint Chiefs*, 543–68.
4. Maj. Gen. J. C. Smith to Lt. Gen. A. A. Vandegrift, 13 December 1943; Lt. Gen. A. A. Vandegrift to Maj. Gen. H. M. Smith, 3 December 1943; Maj. Gen. H. M. Smith to Lt. Gen. Cmdt. A. A. Vandegrift, 6 January 1944; Lt. Gen. Cmdt. A. A. Vandegrift to Maj. Gen. H. M. Smith, 15 January 1944; Lt. Gen. Cmdt. A. A. Vandegrift to Maj. Gen. J. C. Smith, 15 March 1944; all of the above are in the Vandegrift Papers, PPC, MCHC; Lt. Gen. J. C. Smith, oral memoir (1968), 295–301, MCOHC; interview transcripts and articles in Vandegrift biographical file, MCHC, and in the Vandegrift Papers; Vandegrift, *Once a Marine*, 232–7; Cooper, *Gen. Holland M. "Howlin' Mad" Smith*, 116–31; Potter, *Nimitz*, 257–64; Dyer, *Amphibians Came to Conquer*, II:683–731.
5. W. H. J. Thomas to the author, 18 May 1988 and 23 May 1989; Thomas medical record, Thomas OQR; Thomas, "Post Guadalcanal," 15–27; Mrs. J. A. (Tina Thomas) Bruder to the author, 21 August 1989.
6. Brig. Gen. G. C. Thomas to Brig. Gen. M. A. Edson, 14 October 1944, and Brig. Gen. M. H. Silverthorn (C/S, III AC), 7 March 1945, Thomas-Edson Correspondence, Edson Papers, MD/LC.
7. Thomas, oral memoir, 547–55; Pfciffer, oral memoir, 218–20, 233–78; Nimmer, oral memoir, 141–8. For the definitive analysis of King and the Office of COMINCH/CNO, see Buell, *Master of Sea Power*.
8. Thomas, "Post Guadalcanal," 20–1, and oral memoir, 573–5, 603–5, 632, 638; Lt. Gen. Cmdt. A. A. Vandegrift to Lt. Gen. H. M. Smith, Vandegrift Papers. On Knox and Forrestal, see George H. Lobdell, "Frank Knox," and Joseph Zikmund, "James V. Forrestal," in Paolo E. Coletta, ed., *American Secretaries of the Navy*, 2 vols. (Annapolis, Md.: Naval Institute Press, 1980), II: 677–727, 729–44. See also Furer, *Administration of Navy Department*, 36–101.
9. Thomas, "Post Guadalcanal," 29–30; clippings of Thomas speeches, Thomas biographical file, RS MCHC; "Chronological Record of Assignments," Thomas, OQR.
10. Thomas, "Post Guadalcanal," 16–17, and oral memoir, 527–8, 532–3, 607–08; Furer, *Administration of Navy Department*, 551–9; Condit et al., *History of Headquarters Staff Organization*, 17–24; Gen. R. A. Robinson (DP&P, 1941–44), oral memoir (1968), 73–117, MCOHC.
11. Thomas, oral memoir, 527, 587–9, 658–62; Lt. Gen. V. H. Krulak, oral memoir (1970), 86–87, MCOHC, and interview with the author, 16 January 1987; Wieseman, oral memoir, 333–9; Gen. L. C. Shepherd, oral memoir (1967), 427–9, MCOHC.

    On General Thomas's leadership of the Division of Plans and Policies, I used with great profit information on Thomas questionnaires from Col. DeWolf Schatzel (17 March 1986), Maj. Gen. Jonas M. Platt (10 April 1986), Col. Warren P. Baker (6 June 1986), and Lt. Gen. V. H. Krulak (3 May 1986).
12. Thomas, oral memoir, 533–6; Historical Division, HQMC, memorandum AO3E-sd, "Brief History of the Development of the Fire Team in the Marine Corps," 31 August 1955, MCHC.

    Thomas's memory failed him on his retrospective account of this episode. The Quantico Board (headed by Griffith) had already decided that a four-man team had more staying power than a three-man team, so Thomas's group only endorsed this recommendation. The decision to arm the assistant BARman with the carbine rather than the M-1 was a Headquarters initiative, but Thomas, in his oral memoir, says his group ordered the assistant BARman armed with the M-1, which it did not. Its rationale for the carbine was that its light weight would allow the assistant BARman to carry more loaded BAR magazines, as well as his own carbine ammunition.

13. Thomas, "Post Guadalcanal," 18–42, and oral memoir, 547–665; Historical Section, HQMC, "Marine Corps Administrative History," 126–54; Condit et al., "Marine Corps Ground Training"; Snedeker, oral memoir, 69–70, 86–8; Gen. W. M. Greene, Jr., to the author, 11 June 1989; Buse, oral memoir, 63–8; Capt. John E. Simpson, USMCR (Ret.), to the author, 22 May 1990. In addition, I examined the surviving records of the Division of Plans and Policies, 1944–46, Records of Headquarters U.S. Marine Corps, RG 127, NA, but these records contain only a fragment of the division's correspondence. File 1965, however, contains important correspondence on promotion boards and officer assignment, retention, and promotion policies.

14. My assessment of Headquarters politics, 1944–46, is based less on Thomas's own recollections than the following sources: Peck, oral memoir, 131–7; Twining, "Vandegrift"; Wieseman, oral memoir, 293–308; Buse, oral memoir, 63–5; Burger, oral memoir, 187–94; Gen. W. M. Greene, Jr., to the author, 11 June 1989, and interview with the author, 22 February 1982; Gen. W. M. Greene, Jr., memorandum on Thomas-Watson relations, 24 July 1989, Greene Papers, MCHC; Allan R. Millett, "Wallace M. Greene, Jr." (1982), and Howard Jablon, "David M. Shoup" (1988), draft biographical essays for Millett, ed., *Commandants of the Marine Corps* (Annapolis, Md.: Naval Institute Press, forthcoming); "Lieutenant General Thomas E. Watson, USMC (Ret.)," and related biographical information, Watson biographical file, MCHC; "Major General William J. Scheyer, USMC," Scheyer biographical file, MCHC. Watson's influence on personnel matters may be traced in File 1965, general correspondence, Division of Plans and Policies, 1945 and 1946, RG 127.

15. Lt. Gen. Cmdt. to Gen. T. H. Holcomb, 20 June 1945, and to Lt. Gen. R. S. Geiger, 6 July 1945, Vandegrift Papers; Col. R. D. Heinl, oral memoir (1972), 942–76, MCOHC, MCHC.

16. Thomas, oral memoir, 591–3, and "Post Guadalcanal," 19–20; Historical Section, HQMC, "Marine Corps Administrative History," 17–28, 374–90; Furer, *Administration of Navy Department*, 559–75; Condit et al., "Marine Corps Ground Training."

17. Thomas, oral memoir, 537–43, 556–7, and "Post Guadalcanal," 18–19; Historical Section, HQMC, "Marine Corps Administrative History," 425–39; Vandegrift, *Once a Marine*, 232–58.

18. Thomas, oral memoir, 557–60, and "Post Guadalcanal," 23.

19. Thomas, oral memoir, 576–9, 583–7, and "Post Guadalcanal," 27–9. Thomas makes no mention of his position on racial integration of the Corps in his oral memoir or autobiography, but his position is clear enough in File 1965, correspondence of Division of Plans and Policies, HQMC, 1944–45, RG 127,

especially his memorandum to the Commandant, "Colored Officers," 14 April 1944. For studies of the roles of women and blacks in the Marine Corps, see Lt. Col. Pat Meid, *Marine Corps Women's Reserve in World War II* (Washington, D.C.: G-3, HQMC, 1964); Col. Mary V. Stremlow, *A History of the Women Marines, 1946–1977* (Washington, D.C.: History and Museums Division, HQMC, 1986), 1–2; Henry I. Shaw, Jr., and Ralph W. Donnelly, *Blacks in the Marine Corps* (Washington, D.C.: History and Museums Division, HQMC, 1975), 1–46; and Furer, *Administration of Navy Department*, 571–3.

20. Thomas, oral memoir, 543–7, 590–1; Furer, *Administration of Navy Department*, 586–94.
21. Lt. Gen. Cmdt. A. A. Vandegrift to Brig. Gen. E. C. Long, 21 January 1944, Vandegrift Papers; Lt. Gen. Cmdt. A. A. Vandegrift to Lt. Gen. R. S. Geiger, 11 June 1945, General Roy S. Geiger Papers, PPC, MCHC; Brig. Gen. G. C. Thomas to Brig. Gen. M. A. Edson, four letters, 19 March–18 September 1945, Maj. Gen. Merritt A. Edson Papers, MD/LC; Brig. Gen. M. A. Edson to Lt. Gen. Cmdt. A. A. Vandegrift, 27 February 1945, Vandegrift Papers; Historical Section, HQMC, "Marine Corps Administrative History," 440–9.
22. Lt. Gen. Cmdt. A. A. Vandegrift to Lt. Gen. R. S. Geiger, 15 August 1945, Edson Papers; memorandum, Col. D. M. Shoup to Brig. Gen. G. C. Thomas, "Excess and Surplus Materiel in the Hands of the Commanding General, Fleet Marine Force, Pacific," 1 September 1945, Edson Papers; Lt. Gen. M. H. Silverthorn (C/S FMF PAC, 1945), oral memoir (1969), 404–6, MCOHC; Lt. Gen. Cmdt. to Director, Bureau of the Budget, "War Reserves," 24 January 1946, Maj. Gen. W. P. T. Hill Papers, PPC, MCHC.

    The Marine Corps declared about $400 million disposable surplus, a fraction of the value of the materiel under its control at the end of the war.
23. Lt. Gen. Cmdt. A. A. Vandegrift to Gen. T. H. Holcomb, 6 June 1944, Vandegrift Papers.
24. Thomas, "Post Guadalcanal," 23–5; Vandegrift, *Once a Marine*, 267–73.
25. Thomas, oral memoir, 566–8; Lt. Gen. Cmdt. A. A. Vandegrift to Lt. Gen. H. M. Smith, 26 April 1944, Vandegrift papers.

    For studies of Marine Corps aviation in World War II, see especially Sherrod, *History of Marine Corps Aviation;* Gen. Vernon E. Megee, "The Evolution of Marine Air," *MCG* 49 (September 1965), 55–60; and report, Board to Re-examine Marine Aviation [Twining Board], "An Evaluation of Air Operations Affecting the U.S. Marine Corps in World War II," 1945, RS MCHC.
26. Thomas, oral memoir, 568–70; Adm. C. W. Nimitz to Lt. Gen. Cmdt. A. A. Vandegrift, 31 October 1944; Maj. Gen. J. C. Smith to Brig. Gen. G. C. Thomas, 8 July 1944, Gen. Julian C. Smith Papers, PPC, MCHC.

    Thomas followed the Saipan campaign not only from official reports but through long letters written him by Brig. Gen. M. A. Edson (ADC, 2d Marine Division) and Lt. Col. William A. Kengla, an observer from his division. The "Smith versus Smith" controversy is best understood from the perspective of the principals: Vandegrift, *Once a Marine*, 260–5; Cooper, *Gen.*

Holland M. *"Howlin' Mad" Smith,* 156–91, 202–19; Potter, *Nimitz,* 305–9; Pogue, *George C. Marshall,* 447–54. The official reports and correspondence are gathered in Department of the Navy, "Saipan Controversy," a study compiled in 1948, Gen. Holland M. Smith File, RS MCHC. For a sympathetic but telling description of Holland Smith's personality, see Erskine, oral memoir, 183–93, 203–4, 335, 375.

27. Brig. Gen. G. C. Thomas to L. J. Thomas, 20 April 1945, TFP; Thomas, oral memoir, 615–19.

    By the end of the war, 98 percent of Marine officers and 90 percent of Marine enlisted men had served overseas.

    The press controversy over Iwo Jima is preserved in the clippings in the "Iwo Jima" file, RS MCHC.

28. Thomas, "Post Guadalcanal," 35.

29. Ibid., 35–6; Thomas, oral memoir, 620–30; Vandegrift, *Once a Marine,* 288–91; Potter, *Nimitz,* 373–5; Gen. O. P. Smith, "Personal Narrative—Tenth Army and Okinawa, November 8, 1944 to June 23, 1945," 34–46, 88–99, 123, manuscript autobiography and diary, General O. P. Smith Papers, PPC, MCHC. The issue is discussed with restraint in Benis M. Frank and Henry I. Shaw, Jr., *Victory and Occupation,* vol. V, in *History of U.S. Marine Corps Operations in World War II* (Washington, D.C.: Historical Branch, G-3, HQMC, 1968), 195–7.

30. Thomas, "Post Guadalcanal," 38; Vandegrift, *Once a Marine,* 291–2; Potter, *Nimitz,* 375–6.

31. Thomas, oral memoir, 638–45. On the immediate postwar missions and deployments, see Frank and Shaw, *Victory and Occupation,* 441–518. Another essential source for this period is Headquarters Marine Corps, "Administrative History Supplement: History of Various Activities of the U.S. Marine Corps . . . 1 September 1945 . . . 1 October 1946," 2 vols., Command Files, OA NHC.

32. Gen. Cmdt. A. A. Vandegrift to Lt. Gen. R. S. Geiger, 10 August 1946; Gen. Cmdt. A. A. Vandegrift to Fleet Adm. C. W. Nimitz, 28 January 1946; Gen. Cmdt. A. A. Vandegrift to Gen. T. Holcomb, 22 April 1946, all of the above in Vandegrift Papers. I have also consulted the following planning documents: CNO to Distribution List, "Basic Post-War Plan No. 1A," 14 December 1945, Hill Papers; Headquarters Marine Corps, "Navy Subsidiary Postwar Plan—Marine Corps, No. 1," 1 November 1945, and "Navy Subsidiary Postwar Plan—Marine Corps, No. 2," 1 August 1946, both HAF, Breckinridge Library; Division of Plans and Policies, HQMC, "Operating Force Plan—Fiscal—Fiscal Year 1948," File 1965, correspondence of the Division of Plans and Policies, 1946, RG 127; Joint Planning Staff, JCS, "Strategic Estimate and Deployment in the Pacific," 30 August 1946, JPS 757/9, File CCS 323.361, Records of the Joint Chiefs of Staff, RG 218, NA. See also David A. Rosenberg, "The U.S. Navy and the Problem of Oil in a Future War: The Outline of a Dilemma, 1945–1950," *Naval War College Review* 39 (Summer 1976), 53–64, and Vincent Davis, *Postwar Defense Policy and the U.S. Navy, 1943–1946* (Chapel Hill: University of North Carolina Press, 1962).

33. "Navy Subsidiary Postwar Plan—Marine Corps No. l," 12.
34. Cmdt. A. A. Vandegrift to Adm. J. H. Towers, 9 August 1944, Vandegrift Papers; Thomas, "Post Guadalcanal," 42–4. For Marine activities, including limited combat against the Chinese Communists in North China, see Frank and Shaw, *Victory and Occupation,* 521–634.
35. Thomas, oral memoir, 649–50, 806–8. The relationship between Plans and Policies and the Equipment Board is clear from File 2300, correspondence of the Division of Plans and Policies with the head, Marine Corps Equipment Board, 1946, RG 127, which includes "Report, Equipment Board, July–September 1946." For Thomas and Marine aviation, the appropriate source is File 1240 in the same correspondence file; it includes such critical documents as Director, Division of Aviation, to CMC, "Erskine Board," 3 June 1947, and Senior Member to CMC, "Report of Board to Consider Size and Organization of Marine Corps Aviation," 30 April 1947. See also Erskine, oral memoir, 435–9, and Lt. Gen. William J. Van Ryzin (G-1 Section, DP&P 1946–49), oral memoir (1975), 106–16, MCOHC. Thomas's testimony to the Erskine Board is summarized in its final report. Edson's role in the Office of the Chief of Naval Operations is also described in the *New York Times,* 15 and 23 February 1946, as well as material in the Edson biographical file, RS MCHC.
36. Thomas, oral memoir, 648–50; Lt. Gen. James L. Underhill, oral memoir (1968), 194–8, MCOHC.
37. Thomas, oral memoir, 665–8; Burger, oral memoir, 194–200. The description of changes in the general officer corps is based on the *Lineal List* of 1944, 1946, and 1947. The basic correspondence on the question and the text of the law is in File 1965, correspondence of the Division of Plans and Policies, 1945–47, especially Commandant of the Marine Corps to All Commanding Officers, "Retirement of Certain Officers of the Navy, Marine Corps, and Coast Guard," 4 March 1946. Another source of relevant documents is File 52, Maj. Gen. W. P. T. Hill Papers.

Chapter XX. The Unification Crisis
1. Mrs. J. A. (Tina Thomas) Bruder, memoranda on Thomas family for the author, February 1988 and 21 August 1989; W. H. J. Thomas to the author, 14 July 1989; Mrs. G. C. Thomas to the author, "1944–1947—Washington," July 1989, TFP; Col. G. C. Thomas, Jr. to the author, 16 August 1989; Mrs. Sherry Parker Geyelin to Col. G. C. Thomas, Jr., 31 August 1989, TFP.
2. General Thomas left two extended accounts of the unification crisis, a section ("Unification") of his manuscript autobiography chapter, "Post Guadalcanal," 46–54, and his oral memoir, 764–828. The most important personal account by a Marine insider is the diary 1 January–4 June 1947 of Merritt A. Edson, Edson Papers, which forms the basis of two chapters on Edson and unification in Major Jon T. Hoffman's forthcoming biography of Edson, which I read with great profit. Four other accounts (two published), however, provide a detailed picture of the crisis from the Marine perspective and acknowledge Thomas's crucial role in managing the Corps' political campaign

to save the Fleet Marine Force: Lt. Gen. Victor H. Krulak, *First to Fight: An Inside View of the U.S. Marine Corps* (Annapolis, Md.: Naval Institute Press, 1984), 15–51; Col. Gordon W. Keiser, *The U.S. Marine Corps and Defense Unification, 1944–47: The Politics of Survival* (Washington, D.C.: National Defense University Press, 1982); Lt. Col. James D. Hittle, "The Marine Corps and Its Struggle for Survival, 1946–1947," May 1948, manuscript in the "Unification" File, RS MCHC; and 1st Lt. Arthur Ochs Sulzberger, "Unification and the Marine Corps," manuscript history, 1953, RS MCHC.

Of the many general accounts of the genesis of the National Security Act of 1947, the most useful are Demetrius Caraley, *The Politics of Military Unification* (New York: Columbia University Press, 1966); Edgar F. Raines, Jr., and Maj. David R. Campbell, USA, *The Army and the Joint Chiefs of Staff: Evolution of Army Ideas on the Command, Control, and Coordination of the U.S. Armed Forces, 1942–1985* (Washington, D.C.: U.S. Army Center of Military History, 1986); Herman S. Wolk, *Planning and Organizing the Postwar Air Force, 1943–1947* (Washington, D.C.: Office of Air Force History, 1984); Robert G. Albion and Robert H. Connery, *Forrestal and the Navy* (New York: Columbia University Press, 1962); Paul R. Schratz, ed., *Evolution of the American Military Establishment Since World War II* (Lexington, Va.: George C. Marshall Foundation, 1978), the proceedings of a special conference on the thirtieth anniversary of the Act, attended by the author; and James F. Schnabel, *The History of the Joint Chiefs of Staff: The Joint Chiefs of Staff and National Policy,* vol. I, *1945–1947* (Wilmington, Del.: Michael Glazier, 1979).

3. Caraley, *Politics of Military Unification,* 55–6, 86–122. For Truman's role, see Richard F. Haynes, *The Awesome Power: Harry S. Truman as Commander in Chief* (Baton Rouge: Louisiana State University Press, 1973), and Harry S Truman, *Memoirs: Years of Trial and Hope, 1946–1952* (New York: Time, Inc., 1956).

4. CNO to JCS, "Missions of the Land, Sea, and Air Forces," 6 March 1946, JCS 1478/9, 1478 Files, CCS 370, Records of the Joint Chiefs of Staff, RG 218, NA. See also Stephen Jurika, Jr., ed., *From Pearl Harbor to Vietnam: The Memoirs of Admiral Arthur W. Radford* (Stanford, Calif.: Hoover Institution Press, 1980), 73–86, and Michael Palmer, *Origins of the Maritime Strategy: American Naval Strategy in the First Postwar Decade* (Washington, D.C.: Naval Historical Center, 1988), 1–32.

5. Thomas, oral memoir, 781–5; Krulak, *First to Fight,* 28. Edson's billet became Op-09M in 1947.

6. Thomas, oral memoir, 781–5; Twining, oral memoir, 255–84; Krulak, oral memoir, 103–12; Brig. Gen. James D. Hittle, oral memoir (1972), 942–88, MCOHC; Wieseman, oral memoir, 353–5. See also Frank Martullo, "A Good Bowl of 'Chowder' Saved the Marine Corps Following World War II," *MCG* 62 (December 1978), 22–33.

7. Memorandum, C/S USA, "Missions of the Land, Sea and Air Forces," 16 March 1946, JCS 1478/11, File 1478, CCS 370, RG 218; "Statement of General Eisenhower Concerning Mission of Marine Corps, extracted from JCS Pa-

pers," appended to 3 December 1946 entry, Forrestal Diaries, Naval Historical Center; Statement of Gen. D. D. Eisenhower, 11 May 1946, Unification File, RS MCHC.

8. Ambrose, *Eisenhower,* I:443; Cmdt. A. A. Vandegrift to Flt. Adm. C. W. Nimitz, 28 August 1946, CMC-CNO Correspondence File, Vandegrift Papers; CNO to CMC, "Future Amphibious Operations," 23 September 1946, Vandegrift Papers. On Nimitz's service as CNO—a post Forrestal did not want him to hold—see Potter, *Nimitz,* 412–30; and Steven T. Ross, "Chester William Nimitz," in Robert W. Love, Jr., *The Chiefs of Naval Operations* (Annapolis, Md.: Naval Institute Press, 1980), 181–91.

9. MC to CNO, "Comments on JCS 1478/10 and JCS 1478/11," March 1946, JCS 1478/12, File 1478, CCS 370, RG 218; CMC to CNO, "Mission of the Land, Naval and Air Forces," 19 April 1946, JCS 1748/16, File 1478, CCS 370, RG 218; CNO to Secretary of State, "Future Employment of Fleet Marine Force Units," April 1946, File 49, Edson Papers; Thomas, "Unification," 48, and oral memoir, 788–90; Vandegrift, *Once a Marine,* 313–15; Krulak, *First to Fight,* 33–6. On the issues of bases and military planning, see Lester J. Foltos, "The New Pacific Barrier: America's Search for Security in the Pacific, 1945–1947," *Diplomatic History* 13 (Summer 1989), 317–42.

10. Thomas, "Post Guadalcanal," 53, and oral memoir, 677–82; Brig. Gen. Edward C. Dyer, oral memoir (1968), 195–200, 202–9, MCOHC; Krulak, oral memoir, 114–18; Gen. Robert E. Hogaboom, oral memoir (1970), 268–77, MCOHC; Maj. Gen. Louis R. Jones, oral memoir (1970), 152–6, MCOHC; Henderson, oral memoir, 157–9. The official correspondence is CMC to CNO, "Future Amphibious Operations," 19 December 1946, with Special Board, MCS, "Summary of Findings and Recommendations Respecting Future Amphibious Operations," 16 December 1946, enclosed; Op-05 to Op-03, "Future Amphibious Operations," 21 March 1947; DCNO (Air) to DCNO (Operations), 15 April 1947, all of the above in CMC-CNO Correspondence, Vandegrift Papers. See also Clifford, *Progress and Purpose,* 71–7, and Lt. Col. Eugene W. Rawlins and Maj. William J. Sambito, *Marines and Helicopters, 1946–1962* (Washington, D.C.: History and Museums Division, HQMC, 1976), 11–18.

11. Lt. Gen. V. H. Krulak, interview with the author, San Diego, Calif., 23 January 1989; O. P. Smith, oral memoir, 181–6; Krulak, *First to Fight,* 29; Heinl, oral memoir, 987–97.

12. Thomas, "Unification," 48–50, entries, 2 January–16 June, 1946; Jurika, *From Pearl Harbor to Vietnam,* 87–100; Walter Millis, ed., *The Forrestal Diaries* (New York: Viking, 1951), 126–70; Caraley, *Politics of Military Unification,* 125–52. On the Sherman-Nimitz relationship, see Clark G. Reynolds, "Forrest Percival Sherman," in Robert W. Love, Jr. ed., *The Chiefs of Naval Operations* (Annapolis, Md.: Naval Institute Press, 1980), 209–32.

13. "Statement of General Alexander A. Vandegrift, U.S.M.C., before the Senate Naval Affairs Committee at Hearings on S. 2044," memorandum, CMC to All General and Field Officers, 10 May 1946, Vandegrift Papers.

14. Vandegrift, *Once a Marine,* 313–18; Thomas, oral memoir, 795–6; Wieseman, oral memoir, 353–5; Krulak, *First to Fight,* 36–8; Keiser, *Marine Corps and*

Defense Unification, 51–62; Caraley, *Politics of Military Unification,* 131–40; *New York Times,* 7 May 1946.
15. Caraley, *Politics of Military Unification,* 137–43; *New York Times,* 16 June 1946; entries, 4 June and 19 June 1946, in Millis, *Forrestal Diaries,* 168–70; Jurika, *From Pearl Harbor to Vietnam,* 89–94.
16. Thomas, oral memoir, 802–8, and "Unification," 50; Krulak, *First to Fight,* 41–2, and interview with the author, 23 January 1989; Twining, oral memoir, 279–92, and "Vandegrift"; Col. DeWolf Shatzel, Thomas questionnaire for the author, 17 March 1986; Maj. Gen. Jonas M. Platt (Edson Board recorder), Thomas questionnaire for the author, 10 April 1986, and letter, 7 August 1989; Lt. Gen. Lewis J. Fields (Vandegrift's senior aide, 1945–47), oral memoir (1971), 133–48, MCOHC; Shepherd, oral memoir, 431–5; Heinl, oral memoir, 1010–12. The Edson Board's life was 14 March–6 May 1947.
17. In addition to the sources cited in Notes 2 and 3, the most detailed account of the 1947 legislative campaign is Hittle, "Marine Corps and Its Struggle for Survival." See also Heinl, oral memoir, 1027–58.
18. Thomas, oral memoir, 815–19; Hittle, "Marine Corps and Its Struggle for Survival," 1–11; Krulak, *First to Fight,* 40–5; Caraley, *Politics of Military Unification,* 156–70; Keiser, *Marine Corps and Defense Unification,* 81–95; statement of Gen. Cmdt. A. A. Vandegrift to Senate Armed Services Committee, 22 April 1947, Unification File.
19. Diary entries, 30 April–9 May 1947, Edson diaries, Edson Papers; Krulak, *First to Fight,* 43–4; Transcript, telephone conversation, Maj. Gen. M. A. Edson, USMC (Ret.), with Brig. Gen. R. A. Robinson, 17 November 1948, File 106, Edson Papers; Richard Tregaskis, "The Marine Corps Fights for Its Life," *Saturday Evening Post* 22 (5 February 1949): 20–1, 104–5. For an example of Edson's views, see Merritt A. Edson, "Power-Hungry Men in Uniform," *Collier's* 124 (27 August 1949): 16–17, 65; Wieseman, oral memoir, 355.
20. Thomas, "Unification," 50–2; Krulak, oral memoir, 109–12, 119–20, and interview with author, 23 January 1989; Twining, "Vandegrift," and oral memoir, 270–91; Record of Assignments, Thomas OQR; diary entry, 29 January 1947, Edson diaries, Edson Papers.
21. Hittle, "Marine Corps and Its Struggle for Survival," 8–25; Krulak, *First to Fight,* 45–51; Maj. Gen. W. A. Worton, oral memoir (1967), 292–8, MCOHC; Caraley, *Politics of Military Unification,* 170–82; Keiser, *Marine Corps and Defense Unification,* 97–113; U.S. Congress. House (Committee on Armed Forces), National Security Act of 1947 (P.L. 253, 80th Cong., 1st sess., 1947).
22. Vandegrift, *Once a Marine,* 324–32, gives the Commandant's vague retrospective account. Vandegrift refused to explain Thomas's reassignment as other than routine in an interview with Robert Asprey, who assisted Vandegrift in writing the book, before the publication of Vandegrift's memoirs in 1964 (Asprey-Vandegrift interview, MCOHC): "General Thomas wanted to go out, naturally, and have command duty. And I could think of no one who would be more efficient or able to command, nor who knew more about the country to which he would be assigned than Gen. Thomas. It was with deep regret that I saw him leave Headquarters because we had been together for

quite a few years, and a very close and loyal friendship had sprung up between us. His advice, based on clear thinking and able judgement, was beyond compare with any officer I've had serve under me." Vandegrift's general satisfaction with S. 758 and his views on the subsequent travail before the passage of the National Security Act of 1947 are explicit in J. V. Forrestal to R. Dilworth, 17 January 1947; Gen. A. A. Vandegrift to Lt. Gen. H. Schmidt, 22 May 1947; and Gen. A. A. Vandegrift to Adm. L. E. Denfeld, 7 July 1947, all in Vandegrift Papers. On Thomas's reassignment and Vandegrift's role, the most candid interpretations are Twining, oral memoir, 290–9; Krulak, interview with author, 23 January 1989; and Wieseman, oral memoir, 355.

23. HQMC, "Administrative History of the United States Marine Corps for the Period from 1 October 1946 to 1 April 1947," 19 August 1947, Command Files, 1947, OA/NHC; "Annual Report of the Commandant of the Marine Corps," 20 September 1947, File 2295-15, Records of the Director, Division of Plans and Policies, 1947, RG 127.

24. CMC to SecNav, 15 August 1947, with service records appended, and SecNav to the President, "Nomination for Relief of General Alexander A. Vandegrift as Commandant of the Marine Corps," August (?) 1947, both in CMC-SecNav Correspondence Files, Vandegrift Papers; Cates, oral memoir, 206–10; Shepherd, oral memoir, 437–77.

Chapter XXI. Watch on the Yellow Sea

1. For the political and diplomatic context of American military activities in China, 1947–49, see Suzanne Pepper, *Civil War in China: The Political Struggle: 1945–1946* (Berkeley: University of California Press, 1978); Tang Tsou, *America's Failure in China, 1941–1950,* 2 vols. (Chicago: University of Chicago Press, 1963); Warren I. Cohen, *America's Response to China* (New York: John Wiley & Sons, 1971); E. J. Kahn, Jr., *The China Hands* (New York: Viking, 1975); Pogue, *George C. Marshall: Statesman, 1945–1959* (New York: Viking, 1987); and John Melby, *The Mandate of Heaven: China 1945–1949* (Toronto: University of Toronto Press, 1968).

2. Schnabel, *History of Joint Chiefs,* I:393–455; Frank and Shaw, *Victory and Occupation,* V:521–650; Henry I. Shaw, Jr., *The United States Marines in North China, 1945–1949,* rev. ed. (Washington, D.C.: Historical Branch, G-3, HQMC, 1962); ComNavForWesPac, U.S. Pacific Fleet, "Narrative History of Seventh Fleet and Naval Forces Western Pacific, 8 January 1946–24 February 1948," February 1948, Naval Career Office File, 1920–50, Admiral Charles M. Cooke, Jr., Collection, Hoover Institution on War, Revolution and Peace, Stanford, California. General Thomas's own accounts of his service as CG FMFWesPac are his manuscript autobiography, "Post Guadalcanal" chapter, 53–61, and oral memoir, 682–709.

3. Mrs. J. Richards Andrews (Virginia Thomas) to the author, 26 February 1988; William H. Johnson Thomas to the author, "Family Notes," April–May 1988, with appended passenger list, U.S.S. *President Jackson* (APA-18), 10 July 1947; "Record of Assignments," Thomas OQR.

4. I am indebted to William H. Johnson Thomas for his painstaking description of Tsingtao, complete with annotated maps of the city and family home,

written in "Family Notes," 1988, and for contemporary photographs of the city. See also John E. Schrecker, *Imperialism and Chinese Nationalism: Germany in Shantung* (Cambridge, Mass.: Harvard University Press, 1971). Life in Tsingtao from the Marine perspective is also captured in the *North China Marine,* the garrison's weekly newspaper published in Tsingtao in 1947–49 after its redeployment from Tientsin, copies in library, MCHC.

5. ComNavForWesPac, "Narrative History of Seventh Fleet," 17.
6. Thomas, oral memoir, 690–2; HQ FMFWesPac, "Briefing for Major General Shepherd's Party," 28 October 1947, File 1060-10, Correspondence Files, Headquarters Marine Corps, 1939–50, RG 127; CG FMFWesPac to CMC, 15 August 1947, appended to FMFWesPac War Diary, Unit Historical Report File, FMF, RG 127.
7. ComNavForWesPac Op Plan 1-48, 5 April 1948, File Serial 01-5, Flag Files, 1948–Confidential, ComNavWesPac, RG 313, Washington National Records Center, Suitland, Md.
8. FMFWesPac, "Briefing for Major General Shepherd's Party," and CG FMFWesPac to CMC, 15 August 1947 (see Note 6); CG FMFWesPac to CMC, 29 November 1947; War Diary, October 1947, all Unit Historical Report Files, RG 127.
9. Allen, oral memoir, 194–6; Wieseman, oral memoir, 345–51; Blake, oral memoir, 108.
10. Thomas, oral memoir, 692–4; ComPhibForWesPac to ComPhibForPacFlt, 4 July 1948, "Amphibious Training of Battalion Landing Teams, FMF WesPac," File 4-3, Flag Files, 1948–Confidential, RG 313; FMFWesPac, "Briefing for Major General Shepherd's Party" (see Note 6); G-3 Periodic Operations Reports, 1947–48, HQ FMFWesPac, Unit Historical Files, RG 127. I have profited from the evaluation of General Thomas's performance as CG FMFWesPac by the three officers who served as his G-1: Col. Drew J. Barrett, Jr., USMC (Ret.), response to Thomas questionnaire, 22 April 1986; Col. Warren P. Baker, USMC (Ret.), response to Thomas questionnaire, 5 June 1986; and the letters of the late Lt. Gen. John R. Chaisson (1916–72) to his wife Margaret, 23 June 1948 through 30 January 1949, Chaisson Family Papers, John R. Chaisson Collection, Hoover Institution for War, Peace and Revolution. I also found valuable information in letters from other members of FMFWesPac: Lt. Col. Nicholas G. W. Thorne, USMC (Ret.), to the author, 2 May 1990, and Charles Perrault (G-2 clerk) to the author, 9 July 1990.
11. Brig. Gen. G. C. Thomas to L. J. Thomas, 14 December 1948, TFP; Thomas, oral memoir, 688–91, 696–7, and "Post Guadalcanal," 54–6; "Record of Assignments," Thomas OQR; Gen. G. C. Thomas to Col. G. C. Thomas, Jr., 29 May 1971, inscription in Col. David D. Barrett, *Dixie Mission: The United States Army Observer Group in Yenan, 1944* (Berkeley: Center for Chinese Studies, University of California, 1970); Kahn, *China Hands,* 140, 148, 309; Maj. J. R. Chaisson to Mrs. Chaisson, 13 December 1948, Chaisson Papers.
12. Thomas, oral memoir, 686–7, 690–1, 697; entries, 26 December 1947–20 January 1948, Adjutant's logs, HQ FMFWesPac, two volumes, China File (1947–49), RS MCHC; *North China Marine,* 13 March 1948.
13. ComNavForWesPac, "Narrative History of Seventh Fleet," 38–9; Thomas,

oral memoir, 706–7; entries, 26 December 1947–20 January 1948 and 7 April 1948, Adjutant's logs, two volumes, December 1947–July 1948, HQ FMFWesPac, China File (1947–49), RS MCHC; *North China Marine,* 1 May 1948; Maj. J. R. Chaisson to Mrs. Chaisson, 3 July 1948, Chaisson Papers; Charles Perrault (Pfc, G-2 Section) to author, 9 July 1990.

14. Thomas, oral memoir, 694.
15. Fitness reports on Brig. Gen. G. C. Thomas by Admirals Cooke and Badger, 1948 and 1949, Thomas OQR.
16. Thomas fitness report by Lt. Gen. T. E. Watson, 1948, Thomas OQR; Buse, oral memoir, 77.
17. The Chaisson quotes are from his letters to his wife, 26 August and 1 September 1948, Chaisson Papers.
18. Col. Drew J. Barrett, response to Thomas questionnaire, 22 April 1986; Col. Warren P. Baker, response to Thomas questionnaire, 5 June 1986; Maj. John R. Chaisson, letters to Mrs. Chaisson, 12 August–30 October 1948, Chaisson Papers; Capt. C. W. Hollingsworth, USMC (Ret.) (Thomas's aide), "G. C. Thomas, Brigadier General, United States Marine Corps, Tsingtao, China, 1947–1948," August 1983, TFP; Col. T. R. Hill, USMC (Ret.) (Thomas's aide) to Col. A. M. Fraser, 4 October 1983, TFP.
19. Thomas, oral memoir, 698–9, and "Post Guadalcanal," 57; Drew J. Barrett, response to Thomas questionnaire, 22 April 1986; Warren P. Baker, response to Thomas questionnaire, 5 June 1986; Maj. J. R. Chaisson to Mrs. Chaisson, 26 August and 1 September 1948 and 3 January 1949, Chaisson Papers; Col. W. P. Baker to author, 11 January 1990.
20. This section is based on G-1 and G-3 periodic (monthly) operations reports, 1948, File A9, ComNavForWesPac Flag Files, Confidential–1948, RG 313, and the weekly *North China Marine,* 1948, as well as the Barrett, Baker, and Chaisson sources, (see Note 10); Col. W. P. Baker to author, 11 January 1990. I also consulted the correspondence in Files P-7 (Dependents), P-10 (Amusement and Recreation), and P-13 (Misconduct and Discipline) in the NavForWesPac Flag Files for 1948, RG 313.
21. W. H. J. Thomas, "Family Notes," April–May 1988, TFP; Mrs. J. A. Bruder to the author, 21 August 1989; *North China Marine,* 11 September 1948.
22. W. H. J. Thomas, "Family Notes," April–May 1988, TFP.
23. Thomas, oral memoir, 699–702; Major J. R. Chaisson to Mrs. Chaisson, 2 October–12 November 1948, Chaisson Papers. An excellent study of the FMFWesPac evacuation was written by Col. F. C. Thompson, "The Evacuation of Tsingtao, China by FMFWESPAC Jan and Feb 1949," Armed Forces Staff College thesis, 1950, China File (1948–49), RS MCHC. Colonel Thompson commanded the 12th Service Battalion (June 1948–March 1949) and thus bore the major logistical burden for the withdrawal.
24. Thomas, oral memoir, 704–6, and "Post Guadalcanal," 60–1; Maj. J. R. Chaisson to Mrs. Chaisson, 1 and 7 November 1948, Chaisson papers; ComNavForWesPac OpOrder 103, 29 November 1948, File A1, Flag Files Confidential–1948, RG 313.
25. Maj. John R. Chaisson to Mrs. Chaisson, 16 and 19 November 1948, Chaisson Papers; Thompson, "Evacuation of Tsingtao."

26. Brig. Gen. G. C. Thomas, speech, 10 November 1948, appended to Maj. J. R. Chaisson to Mrs. Chaisson, 11 November 1948, which includes a description of the parade, Chaisson Papers.
27. Maj. J. R. Chaisson to Mrs. Chaisson, 4 December 1948, Chaisson Papers.
28. Maj. J. R. Chaisson to Mrs. Chaisson, 6, 8, and 10 December 1948, Chaisson Papers; W. H. J. Thomas, "Family Notes," April–May 1988, TFP, 6; Thomas, oral memoir, 706; Brig. Gen. G. C. Thomas to L. J. Thomas, 9 and 14 December 1948, TFP.
29. Brig. Gen. G. C. Thomas to L. J. Thomas, 14, 22, and 26 December 1948 and 3, 11, 18, 23, and 26 January 1949, TFP.
30. Thompson, "Evacuation of Tsingtao"; Thomas, oral memoir, 707–9, and "Post Guadalcanal," 61; Maj. J. R. Chaisson to Mrs. Chaisson, January 1–30, 1949, Chaisson Papers; Shaw, *Marines in North China*, 24–5; HQ FMFWesPac OpOrder 4-49, January 1949, War Diary File (August 1947–February 1949), RS MCHC.

Chapter XXII. More Wars on the Potomac

1. Thomas's own account of his service at Quantico, 1949–51, may be found in Thomas, oral memoir, 709–30, and "Post Guadalcanal," 62–70.
2. *Quantico Sentry*, 24 March, 14 April, and 23 June 1949; Lt. Gen. V. H. Krulak, "Lemuel C. Shepherd, Jr." (1989), draft essay for Allan R. Millett, ed., *Commandants of the Marine Corps* (Annapolis, Md.: Naval Institute Press, forthcoming); *MCG*, April–December, 1949.
3. Reports of Marine Corps Equipment Board, January–June 1950, File 2300, CMC Central Files, RG 127; L. R. Jones, oral memoir, 152–6; Marine Corps Equipment Board Order 5210.1, 12 March 1962, Breckinridge Library, with appendix listing all projects initiated and completed, 1942–62; *Quantico Sentry*, 10 August 1962.
4. Thomas, "Post Guadalcanal," 62–3, and oral memoir, 711–12; Krulak, *First to Fight*, 113–19.
5. Thomas, "Post Guadalcanal," 62–3, and oral memoir, 711–12; Krulak, *First to Fight*, 113–19.
6. Mrs. J. A. Bruder (Tina Thomas) to the author, 21 August 1989; W. H. J. Thomas to the author, "Family Notes," May 1988; G. C. Thomas, Jr., to the author, 14 May 1989, all TFP.
7. Joint Emergency War Plan, "Halfmoon/Fleetwood/Doublestar," May 1948, and "Off Tackle," May 1949, CCS 381, JCS Series 1844, Records of the Joint Chiefs of Staff, RG 128, NA; CNO to JCS, "Use of Fleet Marine Force Units for Occupation Duty," 28 January 1948, JCS 1829/1, RG 218; the various versions of Executive Order 9877, "Functions of the Armed Forces," published on 26 July 1947, 20 January 1948, 26 March 1948 (the "Key West Agreement"), 21 April 1948, and 21 August 1948 (the "Newport Agreement"), CCS 370, JCS 1478 Files, RG 218; JCS, minutes of meetings on 2–5 October 1948, CCS 370 (1948), RG 218; Secretary of the Navy to Distribution List, "Review of Developments under the National Security Act of 1947," 28 October 1948, Merritt A. Edson Papers; General Board Study 425 (Serial 315), "National Security and the Navy Contributions Thereto for

the Next Ten Years," 25 June 1948, Records of the General Board, NHC; Silverthorn (CNO strategic planning staff, 1947–49), oral memoir, 432–40.

See also Palmer, *Origins of Maritime Strategy;* Paolo E. Coletta, *The United States Navy and Defense Unification, 1947–1953* (Newark: University of Delaware Press, 1981); and David Alan Roseberg, "The Origins of Overkill: Nuclear Weapons and American Strategy, 1945–1960," *International Security* 7 (Spring 1983), 3–71.

8. Quoted in Robert H. Sherrod, "Get the Marines," 13 January 1950, unpublished manuscript, "Unification" file, RS MCHC. Sherrod repeated Bradley's testimony before a Congressional investigation of strategy in October 1949.

9. Office of the Chief of Army Field Forces, "Report of the Army Advisory Panel on Joint Amphibious Operations," 18 January 1949, "Attacks on Marine Corps" File, OP-23, Records of the CNO, NHC; Chairman, General Board, to acting Secretary of the Navy Daniel Kimball, "Unification; Navy's Future Course," 27 July 1949. Records of the General Board, NHC; Statements of General Omar N. Bradley and Secretary of the Navy Francis P. Matthews to the House Armed Services Committee, 19–20 October and 6 October 1949, Francis P. Matthews Papers, Harry S Truman Library; *New York Times,* 18 and 30 October and 5 November 1949, and 10 and 16 January 1950.

See also Steven L. Reardon, *History of the Office of the Secretary of Defense: The Formative Years, 1947–1950* (Washington, D.C.: Office of the Secretary of Defense, 1984), 117–46, 309–422.

10. "Statement of General Clifton B. Cates, Commandant of the Marine Corps, Before the Armed Services Committee of the House of Representatives Investigating the B-36 and Related Matters" and "Testimony Given by General Clifton B. Cates, Commandant of the Marine Corps, Before the House Armed Services Committee Following His Formal Statement Concerning Matters under Investigation by the Committee," 17 October 1949, Clifton B. Cates Papers, PPC MCHC.

11. Thomas, oral memoir, 713–22; Clifton B. Cates, "The Marine Corps and Its Functions," 14 June 1949, speech to 3d Joint Civilian Orientation Conference, and "Opening Remarks, CMC's Conference for Commanding Generals," 29 November 1949, Cates Papers; CMC to SecNav, memorandum, "Annual Report FY 1949," 1 September 1949, Command File 1949, NHC; Paolo Coletta, "Clifton B. Cates" (1988), in Allan R. Millett, ed., *Commandants of the Marine Corps* (Annapolis, Md.: Naval Institute Press, forthcoming).

12. Thomas, "Post Guadalcanal," 63.

13. Ibid., 68–9; Thomas, oral memoir, 719–23; Col. M. B. Twining to Executive Director, Marine Corps Board, memorandum, "Study on Coordination and Integration of Marine Corps Developmental Activities," 1 February 1950, Breckinridge Library.

14. Thomas, oral memoir, 723–4; NAVPERS 15018, *Register of Commissioned and Warrant Officers of the United States Navy and Marine Corps* (Washington, D.C.: Department of the Navy, January 1950), 504; Thomas fitness reports, 1949, Thomas OQR; *Army and Navy Journal,* 3 December 1949.

15. Brig. Gen. G. C. Thomas to Maj. Gen. (Ret.) M. A. Edson, 11 April and 2 September 1950, File 67, Edson Papers.

16. Thomas, "Post Guadalcanal," 69, and oral memoir, 723–4; Heinl, oral memoir, 1131–4; *Quantico Sentry,* 19 January 1950.
17. Thomas, oral memoir, 710–11; Wieseman, oral memoir, 202–4; Marine Corps General Order 85, *Marine Corps Equipment Policy 1950,* 13 February 1951, the final report with appendices of the Marine Corps Equipment Policy Panel as approved by Gen. C. B. Cates, copy in Breckinridge Library. The new emphasis on the development of the amphibious warfare specialty may be found in CMC to SecNav, Annual Report FY 1950, 1 September 1950, Post–1946 Command File, NHC.
18. Report, Board of General Officers to Recommend a Program for Coordination and Integration of Marine Corps Developmental Activities, to the Commandant of the Marine Corps, 18 July 1950, archives, Marine Corps Systems Command (MCSC), Quantico, Va.
19. Commandant of the Marine Corps to Commandant Marine Corps Schools, memorandum, "Reorganization of the Marine Corps Schools . . . ," 16 August 1950; Commandant of the Marine Corps to Commandant Marine Corps Schools, memorandum, "Mission of the Marine Corps Schools," 16 October 1950, with Thomas note, 18 October 1950; Commanding General, LFDC, to Commandant Marine Corps Schools, 28 December 1950, with redrafted letters to the Chief of Staff, U.S. Air Force; Chief of Staff, U.S. Army; and Chief of Naval Operations, all in the MCSC archives.
20. For the mobilization and expansion of the Marine Corps, see Millett, *Semper Fidelis,* 475–500; Thomas, oral memoir, 725–9. Thomas's fitness reports are in his OQR.
21. Thomas, "Post Guadalcanal," 69.
22. My analysis of the *Register of Commissioned and Warrant Officers of the United States Navy and Marine Corps* (the "Lineal List") for 1950 and 1951; *Quantico Sentry,* 12 October and 26 October 1950 and 25 January and 8 February 1951.
23. Thomas, oral memoir, 725; *Quantico Sentry,* 8 February and 22 March 1951.
24. Mrs. J. A. Bruder to the author, 29 August 1989; W. H. J. Thomas to the author, "Family Notes and Fragments," 1988; *Quantico Sentry,* 15 April 1951.

Chapter XXIII. Commanding General, 1st Marine Division

1. For the political and strategic context of the war, see James F. Schnabel and Robert J. Watson, *The History of the Joint Chiefs of Staff,* vol. III, *The Korean War,* in two parts (Wilmington, Del.: Michael Glazier, 1979); Doris M. Condit, *History of the Office of the Secretary of Defense: The Test of War, 1950–1953* (Washington, D.C.: Office of the Secretary of Defense, 1988); James F. Schnabel, *Policy and Direction: The First Year,* in "The U.S. Army in the Korean War" series (Washington, D.C.: Office of the Chief of Military History, 1972). Still useful for their mix of memoir and general history are Gen. Matthew B. Ridgway, *The Korean War* (Garden City, N.Y.: Doubleday, 1967), and Gen. J. Lawton Collins, *War in Peacetime* (Boston: Houghton Mifflin, 1969). Of recent Korean War books, see especially Clay Blair, *The Forgotten War: American in Korea, 1950–1953* (New York: *Times* Books, 1987), which is strong on Eighth Army operations and the personalities and relationships of senior Army commanders. For the 1951 campaign, see Roy E.

Appleman, *Ridgway Duels for Korea* (College Station: Texas A&M University Press, 1990), and Billy C. Mossman, *U.S. Army in the Korean War: Ebb and Flow, November 1950–July 1951* (Washington, D.C.: U.S. Army Center for Military History, 1990). The official history of Marine Corps participation in the war is Lynn Montross, Capt. Nicholas A. Canzona et al., *U.S. Marine Operations in Korea, 1950–1953,* 5 vols. (Washington, D.C.: Historical Branch, G-3, HQMC, 1954–1972). For this chapter, see Montross, Maj. Hubbard D. Kuokka, and Maj. Norman W. Hicks, *The East-Central Front,* vol. IV in the series, published in 1962.

2. Maj. Gen. G. C. Thomas to Midshipman G. C. Thomas, Jr., 6 May 1951, TFP; Thomas, oral memoir, 882; James, *Years of MacArthur,* vol. III: *Triumph & Disaster, 1945–1964,* 560–621.
3. Thomas, "Post Guadalcanal," 70–1, and oral memoir, 732–3; Blair, *Forgotten War,* 804–7, 817–55.
4. Thomas, "Post Guadalcanal," 71, and oral memoir, 733–44; O. P. Smith, oral memoir, 297–8; Bowser, oral memoir (1970), 265–70; Lt. Gen. E. W. Snedeker to the author, 7 July 1990; Lt. Gen. A. L. Bowser, Jr., to the author, 27 July 1990.
5. Memorandum, meeting of CG Eighth Army with U.S. corps commanders, 30 April 1951, CinCFE Correspondence File, Gen. Matthew B. Ridgway Papers, U.S. Army Military History Institute (MHI), Carlisle Barracks, Pa.; April entries, "Personal Notes of Lt. Gen. E. M. Almond Covering Military Operations in Korea, Sept. 1950–July 1951" (hereafter cited as Almond Personal Notes), Lt. Gen. Edward M. Almond Papers, MHI.
6. My analysis of the Smith-Almond tension is based on my own reading of Gen. O. P. Smith, "Aide Memoir . . . Korea," Smith Papers, MCHC, and Almond Personal Notes, but it is corroborated in O. P. Smith, oral memoir, 199–200, 230–4; Gen. Frank T. Mildren, USA (G-3, X Corps), oral memoir (1980), 123–4, Senior Officer Oral History Program, MHI; Thomas, oral memoir, 744; Blair, *Forgotten War,* 32–3, 288, 291–2, 534–6, 579, 611; Bowser oral memoir, 254–8; Shelby Stanton, *America's Tenth Legion: X Corps in Korea 1950* (Novato, Calif.: Presidio, 1989), 1–18.
7. Lt. Gen. A. L. Bowser, Jr., to the author, 27 July 1990.
8. G. C. Thomas to G. C. Thomas, Jr., 6 May 1951, TFP; Thomas, oral memoir, 737, and "Post Guadalcanal," 71–2. The comparison of Marine and Army divisions is based on Montross et al., *East-Central Front,* 267–314, and Department of the Army, Table of Organization and Equipment 7N, "Infantry Division," 7 July 1948, U.S. Army Center of Military History.

   For its performance during three separate operations in 1951, the First Marine Division earned its second Presidential Unit Citation of the war.

   The author visited the Marines' battlefields in Korea during 1991.
9. G. C. Thomas to G. C. Thomas, Jr., 6 May 1951, TFP; Thomas, oral memoir, 736–41, and "Post Guadalcanal," 72–3; memorandum, interview with Gen. G. C. Thomas, USMC (Ret.), 6 February 1958, chapter 6, vol. IV, Comments File, G-3 records, HQMC, RG 127; Montross et al., *East-Central Front,* 108–20; Gen. William M. Hoge, USA, oral memoir (1974), 50–52, MHI; CG 1st MarDiv to CMC, historical diary for April 1951, 1st Marine Division

Command Records, U.S. Marine Corps Records, RG 127, Federal Records Center, Suitland, Md.

10. Thomas, "Post Guadalcanal," 74, and transcript, 6 February 1958 interview. Almond's own notes at the time confirm the substance of the visits and the conversation, Almond Personal Notes, entries, April 1951.

11. Thomas, "Post Guadalcanal," 74–5, and oral memoir, 742–3, 745–9; entries, 1–16 May 1951, Almond Personal Notes; Paul G. Martin, Brooklyn, N.Y., to the author, 2 May 1990.

12. Montross et al., *East-Central Front,* 122; CG 8th Army to CinCFE, 11 May 1951, CinCFE Correspondence 1951, Ridgway Papers; HQ X Corps, "Command Report, May, 1951," Almond Papers; entries, 14–16 May 1951, Almond Personal Notes; Lt. Col. Sherman W. Parry, USMC (Ret.) (1st Marine Division Fire Support Coordination Officer), Thomas questionnaire, 18 July 1989.

13. The quote is in Maj. Gen. G. C. Thomas to Maj. Gen. M. A. Edson, 30 June 1951, Merritt A. Edson Papers, MD/LC. Thomas, oral memoir, 750–3; Maj. Gen. Wilburt S. Brown, oral memoir (1967), 277–90, MCOHC; Brig. Gen. E. H. Simmons, "Big-Foot Brown," *MCG* 57 (September 1973), 19–27; CG 1st MarDiv to CMC, division historical diary for May 1951, 1st Marine Division records, RG 127; HQ X Corps, "Battle of the Soyang River," special report, June 1951, Almond Papers; HQ X Corps, "Command Report: May 1951," Eighth Army Command Reports, 1951, U.S. Army Command Reports, 1949–54, RG 407, Federal Records Center, Suitland, Md.

14. Thomas, "Post Guadalcanal," 76–7; entries, 17–20 May 1951, Almond Personal Notes; Mildren, oral memoir, 141–3; Blair, *Forgotten War,* 878–93.

15. Thomas, oral memoir, 756–61; CG 1st MarDiv to CMC, division historical diary, 1st Marine Division Records, RG 127; entries, 25–31 May 1951, Almond Personal Papers; HQ X Corps, "Battle of the Soyang River," Almond Papers; Montross et al., *East-Central Front,* 127–35.

16. This portrait of Thomas in the field in 1951 is based on photographs attached to the division's monthly historical reports and in the Thomas file, MCHC, as well as Col. Jeremiah A. O'Leary, USMCR (Ret.) and 1st Marine Division public affairs officer in 1951, Thomas questionnaire, 23 December 1988, and my correspondence with Wallace E. Dibble, Jr., Wethersfield, Conn., 1986–89, former lieutenant, USMCR, and division awards officer, 1951.

17. CG 1st MarDiv to CMC, "Special Report on Operations . . . 1 March to 31 May 1951," 1st Marine Division Records, RG 127.

18. Entries, 28 May–7 June 1951, Almond Personal Notes; "Operation Plan Overwhelming—June 1951," UNC Operations File, Ridgway Papers; memorandum for record, conference, Lt. Gen. M. B. Ridgway and Lt. Gen. L. C. Shepherd, 24 May 1951, Korean War Special File, Ridgway Papers; Blair, *Forgotten War,* 897–900.

19. The basic positions on CAS may be found in contemporary private correspondence and studies: United Nations Command, entry, 6 March 1951, Ridgway Diary, Ridgway Papers; Maj. Gen. E. M. Almond to Lt. Gen. M. B. Ridgway, 21 January 1951, and Lt. Gen. M. B. Ridgway to Maj. Gen. E. M. Almond, 6 March, 1951, Ridgway Papers; Maj. Gen. E. M. Almond

to Vice Adm. John L. Hull, Jr., USN, 26 January 1951, CAS File, Almond Papers; entries, 15, 16, and 18 April, 24, 26, and 27 May 1951, Partridge Diaries, vol. IV, Gen. E. E. Partridge Papers, Simpson Historical Research Center (SHRC), Air University, Maxwell Air Force Base, Ala.; Gen. E. E. Partridge, USAF, oral memoir (1974), 601–4, SHRC; O. P. Smith, oral memoir, 284–6; Shepherd, oral memoir, 449–54; HQ X Corps, Report: "Tactical Air Support, X Corps, 10 May–5 June 1951," July 1951, File K239-04291-1, SHRC; HQ X Corps, "Tactical Air Support Studies," 2 vols., October 1950–June 1951, Almond Papers; CG FEAF to C/S, USAF, "Requirements for Increased Combat Effectiveness," 10 June 1951, File K720.161-5, SHRC; Pacific Fleet Evaluation Group Research Memorandum, "An Analysis of the Close Air Support Supplied the U.S. 1st Marine Division in Korea during U.S. Pacific Fleet Operations"; Korean War, 3d Evaluation Report, 1 May–31 December 1951, OA NHC; memorandum, Division of Aviation, HQMC AAT-1737, "Close Air Support, 13 April 1951," CAS File, RS MCHC; Report of the USAF Evaluation Group, "An Evaluation of the Effectiveness of the United States Air Force in Korea," March 1951, File K168.041-1, SHRC; Maj. Gen. Field Harris to CMC, "Report of Board to Study and Make Recommendations on Air-Ground and Aviation Matters," 27 August 1951, HAF B1. See also Allan R. Millett, "Close Air Support in the Korean War, 1950–1953," in Benjamin Franklin Cooling, ed., *Case Studies in the Development of Close Air Support* (Washington, D.C.: Office of Air Force History, 1990), 345–410.

20. Entries, 28 and 29 May 1951, Almond Personal Notes; CG 1st MarDiv to CG X Corps, "Close Air Support," 30 May 1951, Close Air Support File, Almond Papers; Thomas, "Post Guadalcanal," 79; Montross et al., *East-Central Front*, 135–8; Jurika, *From Pearl Harbor to Vietnam*, 256–7.

21. Schnabel and Watson, *History of Joint Chiefs: Korean War*, III(pt. 2):576–89. The battlefield is amply described in CG to CMC, 1st MarDiv historical report for June 1951, 1st Marine Division Records, RG 127.

22. Quotes from Maj. Gen. G. C. Thomas to Maj. Gen. M. A. Edson, 30 June 1951, Edson Papers, and CG 1st MarDiv to CG X Corps, message 021204Z June 51, Miscellaneous Radio Message File, Almond Papers.

23. Entries, 1–18 June 1951, Almond Personal Notes; Thomas, oral memoir, 853–8; CG 1st MarDiv to CMC, 1st Marine Division historical report for June 1951; HQ X Corps, "Distribution of Tonnage Expended during the Battle of the Soyang River," 24 June 1951, Almond Papers; HQ X Corps, "Command Report: June 1951," Army Command Reports, RG 407. I also profited from reading Brig. Gen. E. H. Simmons, "Fight for the Punchbowl, Korea 1951," draft book chapter, 1985.

24. Thomas, "Post Guadalcanal," 80–2, and oral memoir, 862–4. The meeting is verified in entry, 8 June 1951, Almond Papers.

25. Maj. Gen. G. C. Thomas to Mrs. J. A. Bruder, 27 June 1951, TFP; Almond fitness report on Thomas, April–July 1951, Thomas OQR; citation, Distinguished Services Cross HQ FECOM GO 207, 13 August 1951, Thomas OQR; citation, Air Medal (3), Thomas OQR; Lt. Gen. Edward M. Almond, oral memoir, 58, MHI, Carlisle Barracks; entry, 8 July 1951, Almond Personal

Notes; CG 1st MarDiv to CMC, historical report for July 1951, 1st Marine Division Records, RG 127; Lt. Gen. Herman Nickerson, Jr., oral memoir (1980), 186–92, MCOHC; ADC 1st MarDiv to SecNav, 20 August 1951, Thomas OQR; Col. Walter F. Murphy, USMCR (Ret.), to author, 10 March 1990.

26. CMC to SecNav, annual report, 1951, 1 September 1951, Command Files, OA NHC; Policy Analysis Division, HQMC, memorandum, "S. 677—Douglas Bill," 7 April 1951, "Douglas Bill" Subject File, RS MCHC.

27. Thomas, oral memoir, 860–2; interview with Lt. Gen. V. H. Krulak, 23 January 1989, San Diego, Calif.; Col. Jeremiah A. O'Leary, Thomas questionnaire, 23 December 1988.

28. The Thomas-Byers relationship is reconstructed from many sources; Thomas, oral memoir, 873–4, and "Post Guadalcanal," 83–4; Krulak interview, 23 January 1989; "Clovis E. Byers (1899–1973)," *Assembly* (September 1974) 120–1; Lt. Gen. Robert L. Eichelberger, *Our Jungle Road to Tokyo* (New York: Viking, 1950), xxii, 147–9, 250; Ralph D. Bald, Jr., *Air Force Participation in Joint Army-Air Force Training Exercises, 1947–1950*, USAF Historical Studies No. 80, Air University, 1955, 6–31. For relations in the Army, see especially Blair, *Forgotten War*. My portrait of Byers, however, is also based on his diaries and correspondence for 1951 in the Lt. Gen. Clovis E. Byers, USA, Collection (hereafter cited as Byers Papers), Hoover Institution on War, Revolution and Peace, Stanford, Calif. Byers's predisposition to like Marines is expressed in Gen. C. B. Cates to Maj. Gen. C. E. Byers, 23 July 1951, and Maj. Gen. C. E. Byers to Gen. C. B. Cates ("Dear Cliff"), 1 August 1951, Byers Papers. Byers reported his high regard for Thomas and Whaling in Maj. Gen. C. E. Byers to Adm. (CNO) William M. Fechteler ("Dear Bill"), 7 August 1951, Byers Papers. His position on close air support is explicit in Maj. Gen. C. E. Byers to Gen. M. W. Clark, 4 September 1951, Byers Papers.

29. Maj. Gen. C. E. Byers to Lt. Gen. E. H. Brooks, August 1951, Byers Papers.

30. Thomas, "Post Guadalcanal," 83–4; entries, Byers, personal diary, 31 August and 1 September 1951, Byers Papers, and entries, Commanding General, X Corps, diary, 26 and 27 July 1951, Byers Papers. The latter source is a record of events kept by an aide and appended to the HQ X Corps, Command Report for each month, U.S. Army Command Reports, 1949–54, RG 407. Both diaries confirm Thomas's active participation in operational discussions and the substance of those discussions.

31. Thomas, "Post Guadalcanal," 84–5; G-1 HQ X Corps, Special Personnel Report, 1 June–15 October 1951 for the Assistant Secretary of Defense, X Corps Command Report, October 1951, RG 407; CG 1st MarDiv to CMC, Historical Diary for August 1951, 1st Marine Division Command Records, RG 127; Allen (division supply officer), oral memoir, 241–52; Div Supply Officer to CG 1st MarDiv, "Special Historical Report," 16 June 1951, 1st Marine Division Command Records, RG 127; HQ X Corps, Command Reports, July and August 1951, RG 407; Montross et al., *East-Central Front*, 161–72.

32. Thomas, oral memoir, 877–9; CG 1st MarDiv to CMC, "August Historical Diary for August 1951," 1st Marine Division Command Records, RG 127; HQ X Corps, entries 6 and 7 August 1951, "Commanding General's Diary," Army Command Records, RG 1 407; Krulak interview, 23 January 1989; Krulak, oral memoir, 159–63; Operation Plan Wrangler, September 1951, Ridgway Papers; Schnabel and Watson, *History of Joint Chiefs: Korean War*, III(pt. 2):606–12. Actually, the JCS did not disapprove the landing *if* it could be done without publicity.
33. Thomas, "Post Guadalcanal," 86–7; Krulak interview, 23 January 1989; HQ X Corps, entries, 29–31 August 1951, "Commanding General's Diary," RG 407; HQ X Corps, Operations Report, August 1951, RG 407; HQ X Corps, Command Report, 1–31 August 1951, RG 407; G-4 HQ X Corps, Special Report, August 1951, RG 1 407; G-2 HQ 1st Marine Division, "Tactical Study of Weather and Terrain Yanggu-Inje Area," 7 August 1951, 1st Marine Division Command Records, RG 127.
34. The operational narrative is based on CG 1st MarDiv to CMC, historical diary for September 1951, 1st Marine Division Records, RG 127; HQ X Corps, Command Report, September 1951, Army Command Records, RG 407; and Montross et al., *East-Central Front*, 173–98. Thomas provided his own analysis of the offensive in Maj. Gen. G. C. Thomas to the Rev. L. O'V. Thomas, 23 September 1951, TFP; Thomas, "Post Guadalcanal," 87–9, and oral memoir, 879–86.
35. Montross et al., *East-Central Front*, 178–86.
36. Ibid.; Thomas, oral memoir, 883–5; HQ X Corps, entries, 1–4 September 1951, "Commanding General's Diary," RG 407; entries, 4 and 5 September 1951, Byers, personal diaries, Byers Papers; CG 1st MarDiv to CMC, historical diary for September 1951, RG 127.
37. For a participant's account of the fighting, see Jack L. Cannon, "Attack on Hills 673 and 749," *Leatherneck* 72 (March 1989), 22–5.
38. Montross et al., *East-Central Front*, 182–94.
39. Ibid., 194–201; HQ X Corps, entries, 23 and 28 September 1951, "Commanding General's Diary," RG 407; CG 1st MarDiv to CMC, historical diary for September 1951, RG 127; Thomas, "Post Guadalcanal," 88; Maj. G. P. Averill, "Final Objective," *MCG* 40 (August 1956), 10–16; Gerald P. Averill, *Mustang: A Combat Marine* (San Rafael, Calif.: Presidio, 1987), 221–54.
40. Maj. Gen. G. C. Thomas to Rev. L. O'V. Thomas, 23 September 1951, TFP.
41. Ibid.; Krulak interview, 23 January 1989; Thomas, oral memoir, 894–5; CG 1st MarDiv to CG FMFPac, "Special Report: Employment of Assault Helicopters," 4 October 1951, 1st Marine Division Records, RG 127. See also Lynn Montross, *Cavalry of the Sky: The Story of U.S. Marine Combat Helicopters* (New York: Harper & Brothers, 1954), 133–79, and Rawlins and Sambito, *Marines and Helicopters*, 40–58.
42. Thomas, "Post Guadalcanal," 91; Montross et al., *East-Central Front*, 186–90, 206–8; HQ X Corps, entries 19–21 September 1951 "Commanding General's Diary," RG 407.
43. Thomas's own accounts of his crusade for close air support reform are recorded in his oral memoir, 886–92, and "Post Guadalcanal," 89–90; both

accounts are consistent with his 1951 correspondence. For his early analysis, see CG 1st MarDiv to CG FMFPac, 21 July and 25 August 1951, Close Air Support (CAS) File, RS MCHC. In the reconstruction of this controversy, I have relied on two basic collections of documents: Close Air Support File, 1st Marine Division War Diaries and Reports, RG 127, and "Close Air Support," File K239-04291-1, Air Force Simpson Historical Research Center archives, Air University, Maxwell Air Force Base, Ala. In addition to sources already cited, see Alfred Goldberg and Lt. Col. Donald Smith, "Army-Air Force Relations: the Close Air Support Issue," R-906-PR, October 1971, RAND Corporation, HRC library, and Charles W. Dickens, *A Survey of Air-Ground Doctrine*, Historical Study 34, HQ TAC, 1958, HRC. The Air Force perspective may be found throughout Robert F. Futrell, *The United States Air Force in Korea, 1950–1953*, rev. ed. (Washington, D.C.: Office of Air Force History, 1983).

44. Thomas, oral memoir, 886–7; Krulak interview, 23 January 1989; CG 1st MarDiv to CG X Corps, "Close Air Support," 6 October 1951, 1st Marine Division CAS File.
45. HQ X Corps, entries, 23 and 28 September 1951 and 1 October 1951, "Commanding General's Diary, September 1951 and October 1951," X Corps Command Report, October 1951, RG 407; CG 1st MarDiv to CG X Corps, "Close Air Support" (see Note 44); CG 1st MarDiv to CinCPac, 4 October 1951, 1st Marine Division CAS File; Maj. Gen. G. C. Thomas to Lt. Gen. L. C. Shepherd, 4 October 1951, 1st Marine Division CAS File.
46. CG 5th AF to CG FEAF, 6 October 1951; CG 8th Army to CinCFE, 6 October 1951; CG 5th AF to CinCFE, 5 October 1951, all in File K239-04291-1, SHRC. See also Maj. Gen. G. C. Thomas to Lt. Gen. L. C. Shepherd, 4 and (?) October 1951, 1st Marine Division CAS File.
47. Maj. Gen. G. C. Thomas to Mrs. J. A. Bruder, 7 October 1951, TFP.
48. Thomas, oral memoir, 888–92; entry, 18 October 1951, Byers, personal diary, Byers Papers; Maj. Gen. C. E. Byers to Maj. Gen. G. C. Thomas, 10 October 1951, 1st Marine Division CAS File; CG 8th Army to CG X Corps, 7 October 1951, 1st Marine Division CAS File; Gen. C. F. Schilt, Jr., oral memoir (1969), 123–6, MCOHC. Schilt's opinion may have been influenced by his admiration for LeRoy Hunt.
49. HQ X Corps, entries for 11, 16, 18, and 26 October 1951, "Commanding General's Diary," October 1951; HQ X Corps, entries for 7, 14, and 24 November 1951, "Commanding General's Diary," November 1951; HQ X Corps, memorandum, "Close Air Support Analysis," 26 November 1951, in Byers Papers.
50. CG AFF to Lt. Gen. E. M. Almond, 24 October 1951, Almond Papers; memorandum, Van Fleet-Everest conference on close air support, 17 November 1951, File K239-04291-1, HRC; CG 8th Army to CinCFE, 19, 20, and 21 December 1951, Ridgway Papers; memorandum, Weyland-Ridgway conference on close air support, 13 January 1952, Ridgway Papers; Maj. Gen. E. K. Wright (CinCFE G-3) to CinCFE, 15 January 1952, Ridgway Papers; Lt. Gen. J. Van Fleet to Lt. Gen. E. M. Almond, 22 January 1952, Almond Papers; Thomas, "Post Guadalcanal," 89–90.

51. Thomas, oral memoir, 91–2; CG 1st MarDiv to CMC, historical diary for October 1951, 1st Marine Division Records, RG 127; 1st Marine Division Operations Order 45-51 ("Reefer") and Administrative Order 13-51, 31 October 1951, 1st Marine Division Records, RG 127; HQ X Corps, Command Report, October 1951, RG 407.
52. Maj. Gen. G. C. Thomas to Mrs. J. A. Bruder, 7 October and 10 November 1951, TFP; Thomas, "Post Guadalcanal," 92–3; HQ X Corps, entries, 7–24 November 1951, "Commanding General's Diary," November 1951, RG 407; Wallace E. Dibble to the author, 30 August 1989; Davis U. Merwin (former first lieutenant, USMCR), Bloomington, Ill., to Col. A. M. Fraser, 26 August 1983, TFP. The division's experience in October–December 1951 is summarized in Montross et al., *East-Central Front,* 212–25.
53. Thomas, oral memoir, 902–4; Brig. Gen. Gordon Gayle, oral memoir (1988), 385–6, MCOHC; Brig. Gen. Charles L. Banks, oral memoir (1969), 36–40, MCOHC; Krulak interview, 23 January 1989; CG 1st MarDiv to CMC, historical diary for November 1951, 1st Marine Division Records, RG 127; report, General Organization Board, 1st Marine Division, November 1951, HAF 287, Breckinridge Library; CG X Corps to Commanding Generals, LOI, "Operations during Armstice Conference," 14 November 1951, HQ X Corps Command Reports, November 1951, RG 407.
54. Thomas, oral memoir, 910–12; Krulak interview, 23 January 1989; Gen. L. C. Shepherd to Col. A. M. Fraser, 11 May 1983, TFP; Maj. Gen. G. C. Thomas to Mrs. J. A. Bruder, 10 November 1951, TFP; memorandum, "9th Far Eastern Trip, 12–20 November 1951," CG FMFPac Inspection Trips, 1950–51, File A23-9, FMFPac Historical Records, RG 127.
55. Thomas, oral memoir, 905–7; entries, 10 and 24–28 November 1951, Byers, personal diary, Byers Papers; HQ X Corps, entries, 24–28 November 1951, "Commanding General's Diary," RG 407.
56. Thomas, "Post Guadalcanal," 93–5; HQ X Corps, entries, 1–5 December 1951, "Commanding General's Diary," RG 407; HQ X Corps, Command Report, December 1951, RG 407; CG 1st MarDiv to CMC, historical diary for January 1952, RG 127; Maj. Gen. G. C. Thomas to Maj. Gen. M. A. Edson, 26 December 1951, Edson Papers, LC; CinCFE to CMC (Pass to General Thomas) 26 January 1952, and Maj. Gen. G. C. Thomas to CinCFE, 29 January 1952, Ridgway Papers; Gen. M. B. Ridgway to CMC, 25 January 1952; Lt. Gen. J. Van Fleet to CMC, 13 January 1952; Lt. Gen. E. N. Almond to CMC, fitness report on Thomas, 1 May–15 July 1951; Maj. Gen. C. E. Byers, USA, to CMC, 28 November 1951; Gen. L. C. Shepherd, Jr., fitness report on Thomas, 31 December 1951; Maj. Gen. W. B. Palmer to CMC, 11 January 1952, all in Thomas OQR.

Chapter XXIV. Reforming the Marine Corps
1. Gen. G. C. Thomas OQR and "Post Guadalcanal," 95–6; Secretary of the Navy, memorandum, "General Thomas," 16 January 1952, and Robert L. Dennison to the President, 21 January 1952, with subsequent letter of appointment to the rank of lieutenant general, 8 March 1952, File 1285, White

House Office Files, Papers of Harry S Truman, Truman Presidential Library, Independence, Mo.
2. Mrs. J. Richard S. Andrews (Virginia Thomas) to the author, 26 February 1988; Mrs. Joseph A. Bruder (Tina Thomas) to the author, 21 August 1989; W. H. J. Thomas, "Family Notes," 1988, memorandum on the Thomas family for the author; Col. G. C. Thomas, Jr., to the author, 13 July 1990.
3. Conference Report, "Fixing the Personnel Strength of the United States Marine Corps and Establishing the Relationship of the Commandant of the Marine Corps to the Joint Chiefs of Staff," 19 June 1952 (H.R. 2199, 82d Congress, 2d Session); Commandant of the Marine Corps to All General Officers, "A Summary of Problems Confronting the Marine Corps," 1 November 1952, CMC Files, 1947–67, RG 127.
4. Commandant of the Marine Corps to All Marine Corps General Officers, "Remarks by the Commandant of the Marine Corps to Staff," 3 January 1952, Shepherd File, RS MCHC; Shepherd, oral memoir, 477–9; Gen. L. C. Shepherd, Jr. to Col. A. M. Fraser, 11 May 1983, TFP; Thomas, oral memoir, 916–18.
5. Records of proceedings, conferences on Headquarters Marine Corps Reorganization, 5 and 13 February and 1 April 1952, HQMC File, RS MCHC; Thomas, "Post Guadalcanal," 95–6, and oral memoir, 931–3, 957; Condit et al., *History of Headquarters Staff Organization,* 26–30, and Headquarters Marine Corps, *Headquarters Manual 1952.*
6. Lt. Gen. Thomas A. Wornham, oral memoir (1968), 116–20, MCOHC; Lt. Gen. William K. Jones to the author with enclosed memorandum, "General Thomas," 7 March 1986; Krulak, oral memoir, 164–6.
7. My account of the creation of an independent Fiscal Division at Headquarters is based on the following sources: Shepherd, oral memoir, 480–2; Thomas, oral memoir, 918–21, and "Post Guadalcanal," 96–8; interview with Lt. Gen. V. H. Krulak, San Diego, Calif., 23 January 1989; Allen (Assistant QMG and QMG of the Marine Corps, 1954–63), oral memoir, 303–15, 324–5, 350–4; Commandant to Fiscal Director, "Fiscal Director, U.S. Marine Corps," 17 July 1952, Maj. Gen. William P. T. Hill Papers, PPC, MCHC.
8. Thomas, oral memoir, 920.
9. Commandant to Fiscal Director, "Fiscal Director, U.S. Marine Corps," 17 July 1952, Hill Papers, PPC, MCHC; Krulak interview, 23 January 1989; AC/S G-4 to C/S HQMC, memorandum, "Correspondence to the Quartermaster General of the Marine Corps," 28 February 1952, File A6-5, HQMC Central Files, 1950–58, RG 127; Quartermaster General of the Marine Corps to the Commandant of the Marine Corps, "Official Correspondence," 15 September 1953, File A6-5, HQMC Central Files, 1950–58, RG 127; extract, "Notes on Commandant's Weekly Conference," 21 April 1953, and Col. D. M. Shoup to Commandant, "Fiscal Division, U.S. Marine Corps," 16 March 1953, General David M. Shoup Papers, Hoover Institution on War, Peace and Revolution, Stanford, Calif.; Chief of Staff to Staff Division Directors, "Review of Marine Corps Budget Estimates for Fiscal Year 1955," September 1953, C/S Correspondence File, 1953, RG 127.
10. Memorandum for the President with attachments and endorsements, "Gen-

eral Shepherd," 23 November 1953, File 3-B-17, Central File, Official Files of the Office of the President, Dwight D. Eisenhower Library, Abilene, Kan.; Allen, oral memoir, 303–15, 324–5.

Whatever his role in the "dump Shepherd" campaign, General Hill received an extension of his appointment as Quartermaster General of the Marine Corps until February 1955, which meant that he served in that billet for eleven years. The position of Quartermaster General and the office of Supply Department survived until 1973 when the G-4 Division and the Supply Department merged to become the Division of Installations and Logistics.

11. The documents and correspondence on internal administration may be found in File A2-2/2 for 1952 and 1953, HQMC Central Files, 1950–58, RG 127; Commandant of the Marine Corps to Distribution List, "Improvement and Reduction of Administrative Procedures," 23 December 1953, and "Program on Improvement and Reduction of Administrative Procedures," 17 June 1954, File A6-5, HQMC Central Files, 1950–58, RG 127; AC/S G-3 to C/S, "Reduction in Typewriters throughout the Marine Corps," 29 December 1953, with endorsements, C/S Correspondence File, 1953, RG 127; CMC to CG FMF LANT, memorandum, "Congressional Correspondence," File A6-5, HQMC Central Files, 1950–58, RG 127.

12. The focus on personnel issues is reflected in Director, Administrative Division, to Distribution List, "Control of CMC Letters," 16 December 1954 File A6-5, HQMC Central Files, 1950–58, RG 127, which lists and summarizes the 218 CMC letters from March 1952 until December 1954. The personnel problems of the Corps are analyzed in detail in G-1 Report, briefing book and agenda items, CMC Far East Trip (11 September–4 October 1952), CMC Correspondence Files, 1952, RG 127, and Office of the Assistant Secretary of Defense (Legislative and Public Affairs) to Director, Bureau of Budget, memorandum, "U.S. Marine Corps Personnel Matters, 26 May 1955," File 3-B-17, White House Central Files, 1955, and General Counsel, Department of Defense, to Director, Bureau of the Budget, 12 June 1953, along with copies of Executive Orders 10465 (30 June 1953) and 10616 (21 June 1955), in File 3-B-17, White House Central Files, Eisenhower Library. General Twining provides his analysis in his oral memoir, 336–43.

13. G-1 and G-3 briefing papers for the Commandant, September 1952 and February 1954, CMC Correspondence Files, RG 127.

14. Gen. W. O. Brice, oral memoir (1971), 88, MCOHC.

15. Thomas, "Post Guadalcanal," 104–5; Brice, oral memoir, 66–9, 86–90; Secretary G/S to C/S, "Marine Corps Problems," 20 November 1953 and 25 January 1954, C/S Correspondence Files, 1954, RG 127; Brig. Gen. Samuel R. Shaw, oral memoir (1970), 265–73, MCOHC; Dyer, oral memoir, 287; Maj. Gen. V. J. McCaul to Gen. R. McC. Pate, 9 January 1956, CMC Historical Papers, 1948–56, RG 127.

16. Brig. Gen. Frank H. Schwable, oral memoir (1980), 168–89, MCOHC. For comprehensive accounts of Marine Corps POW experiences, see James A. MacDonald, *The Problems of U.S. Marine Corps Prisoners of War in Korea* (Washington, D.C.: History and Museums Division, HQMC, 1988); and Lt. Col. Pat Meid and Maj. James M. Yingling, *Operations in West Korea,* vol. V

of *U.S. Marine Operations in Korea, 1950–1953* (Washington, D.C.: HQMC, 1972), 399–443.
17. Shepherd, oral memoir, 490–4; Schwable, oral memoir, 189–94. For a detailed discussion of the legal problems in prosecuting Korean War POWs, see George S. Prugh, Jr., "The Code of Conduct for the Armed Forces," *Columbia Law Review* 56 (April 1956), 678–707, and "Misconduct in the Prison Camp: A Survey of the Law and an Analysis of the Korean Cases," *Columbia Law Review* 56 (May 1956), 711–94.
18. Thomas, "Post Guadalcanal," 103–4; Brig. Gen. E. H. Simmons, "Dr. De Weldon's Iwo Jima Statue," *Fortitudine* 11 (Fall 1981–Winter 1982), 3–6; National Park Service pamphlet, "The United States Marine Corps War Memorial," 1973; Marine Corps War Memorial Foundation, *A Report of Progress and Accomplishment* (Headquarters Marine Corps, 1954).
19. Thomas, oral memoir, 921–4; Shepherd, oral memoir, 480–3; Commandant of the Marine Corps to All General Officers, "Public Law 416 (S. 677)," 5 July 1952, Hill Papers; AC/S G-3 to C/S with C/S endorsements, "Emphasis of the Marine Corps Position as a Force in Readiness," 28 June 1953, C/S Correspondence File, 1953, RG 127.
20. Thomas, oral memoir, 923–6; Lt. Gen. Robert B. Luckey, oral memoir (1969), 210–14, MCOHC; HQMC, "Marine Corps Representation on JCS," 20 June 1952, CMC Central Files, 1947–67, RG 127; Maj. Gen. Robert H. Bohn, oral memoir (1989), 128, MCOHC; HQMC, *Annual Report of the Commandant of the Marine Corps to the Secretary of the Navy for FY 1954* (Washington, D.C.: HQMC, 1954); C/S (Acting) to CMC, "Data Regarding Marine Corps Participation in JCS/OpDeps Matters . . . ," 4 January 1957, CMC Historical Files, 1947–56, RG 127.
21. Thomas, "Post Guadalcanal," 100–2. The Navy Department principals are described in the following essays: K. Jack Bauer, "Robert Bernerd Anderson," and John R. Wadleigh, "Thomas Sovereign Gates, Jr.," in Coletta, *American Secretaries of the Navy* II:843–55, 877–93; Paul R. Schratz, "Robert Bostwick Carney," in Robert W. Love, Jr., *The Chiefs of Naval Operations* (Annapolis, Md.: Naval Institute Press, 1980), 243–61.
22. Thomas, "Post Guadalcanal," 101.
23. For personal accounts of the revision of GO 5, see Thomas, oral memoir, 934–41; Krulak, oral memoir, 163–5; and Krulak, *First to Fight*, 59–61.
24. Quoted in Krulak, *First to Fight*, 61. Vinson's position is expressed in Carl Vinson to SecNav, 6 May 1954, C/S Correspondence File, 1954, RG 127.

On 10 February 1954, Illinois Wesleyan University awarded General Thomas a Doctor of Laws degree, an honor he shared that day with Secretary of the Navy Robert B. Anderson, who had no prior connection with the university.
25. Twining, oral memoir, 345–7; U.S. Navy Department, *Report of the Committee on Organization of the Department of Navy,* 16 April 1954, copy in the library, Naval Historical Center, Washington Navy Yard.
26. Col. David Randall, USMC (Ret.), to Col. and Mrs. J. A. Bruder, 1989, copy in author's possession, TFP.
27. Annual Reports of the Commandant of the Marine Corps to the Secretary of

the Navy for FY 1954 and FY 1955, copies in library, MCHC; *Army and Navy Journal,* 19 December 1953; G-3 Briefing Book for CMC, Far East trip, September–October 1952, CMC Central Field, RG 127.

28. On the "New Look," see Douglas Kinnard, *President Eisenhower and Strategy Management* (Lexington: University Press of Kentucky, 1977), 1–36; Glenn H. Snyder, "The 'New Look' of 1953," in Warner R. Schilling, Paul Y. Hammond, and Glenn H. Snyder, eds., *Strategy, Politics, and Defense Budgets* (New York: Columbia University Press, 1962), 379–524.

29. Annual Reports of the Commandant of the Marine Corps to the Secretary of the Navy for FY 1954 and 1955, copies in library, MCHC; interviews with Gen. L. C. Shepherd, 12 September and 19 December 1953, *Army and Navy Journal*; Sec G/S to C/S, "Marine Corps Problems," 20 November 1953 and 25 January 1954, with Thomas endorsements and comments, C/S Correspondence File, 1953, RG 127; CMC to CNO, "Concept of Amphibious Assault," May 1954, C/S Correspondence File, 1954, RG 127.

30. Quoted in the report of the Advanced Research Group, summary of the proceedings of the General Officers Conference, Headquarters Marine Corps, 14–16 July 1954, RS MCHC; CMC to CMCS, memorandum, "Marine Corps Advanced Group," 19 January 1953, ARG File, RS MCHC; AC/S G-1 to CMCS, memorandum, "Advanced Research Group," 7 December 1961, ARG File; G-3 Study 5-53, "Policy for Dissemination of Joint Landing Force Board Projects," 29 April 1953, C/S Correspondence, 1953, RG 127.

For summaries of the history of the ARG, see Rawlins and Sambito, *Marines and Helicopters,* 61–5, and Clifford, *Progress and Purpose,* 91–3.

The history of the ARG, however, comes from the oral memoirs of three participants and one critic: Shaw, oral memoir, 262–70; Van Ryzin, oral memoir, 152–9; Lt. Gen. Carson A. Roberts, oral memoir (1971), 90–2, MCOHC; and Buse, oral memoir, 110–11.

31. Commandant's remarks and summary report of the proceedings of the General Officers Conference, 1954 (see Note 30); Landing Force Bulletin 17, "Concept of Future Amphibious Operations," 13 December 1955, HAF 453, James C. Breckinridge Library, MCCDC; CMC to CMCS, memorandum, "1954–55 Marine Corps Advanced Research Group," 30 July 1954, C/S Correspondence, 1953, RG 127.

32. C/S to CMC, memorandum, "Organic Supporting Weapons Structure; Infantry Battalion," 15 December 1953, C/S Correspondence, 1953, RG 127.

33. Shaw, oral memoir, 227–30; Henderson, oral memoir, 382–6; Wornham, oral memoir, 116–20; AC/S G-3 to C/S, memorandum, "Air-Ground Command Relationships," with Thomas endorsements, 16 June 1953, C/S Correspondence, 1953, RG 127; CMC to All General Officers, "Comparison of a Marine Division with an Army Infantry Division," 24 February 1953, C/S Correspondence, 1953, RG 127; *Army and Navy Journal,* 21 March 1953.

34. Rawlins and Sambito, *Marines and Helicopters,* 6–63; AC/S to C/S, memorandum, "Helicopter Participation in Exercise Desert Rock V," 5 November 1953, C/S Correspondence, 1953, RG 127; AC/S G-3 to C/S, memorandum, "Marex II," 23 December 1953, C/S Correspondence, 1953, RG 127; AC/S G-3 to C/S, memorandum, "Marex III; report of," 18 October 1954, C/S

Correspondence, 1954, RG 127; Lt. Gen. William K. Jones, oral memoir (1976), 71–3, MCOHC; Lt. Gen. W. K. Jones to the author, 7 March 1986.
35. CMC to All General Officers, "Remarks by the Commandant of the Marine Corps to Staff on 11 January 1954," 13 January 1954, Hill Papers.
36. Thomas, "Post Guadalcanal," 106; Office of the Secretary of the Navy, Memorandum for the President, 27 April 1954, File OF-3B, White House Central Files, 1954, Eisenhower Library.

Chapter XXV. The Last Tour
1. Thomas, oral memoir, 960–1; *Quantico Sentry,* 24 June and 8 July 1954.
2. The description of the Quantico base and base life in this chapter is drawn from the weekly base newspaper, the *Quantico Sentry,* Breckinridge Library, and Fleming et al., *Quantico,* 74–113. See also File P16 (Quantico), HQMC Central Files, 1950–58, RG 127.
3. Thomas, "Post Guadalcanal," 106–11.
4. Thomas, oral memoir, 961–7; Col. Warren P. Baker, USMC (Ret.), to the author, 16 May 1990. For curriculum matters, see Lt. Col. Donald F. Bittner, *Curriculum Evolution Marine Corps Command and Staff College, 1920–1988* (Washington, D.C.: History and Museums Division, HQMC, 1988). See also Col. Bernard E. Trainor, "A History of Marine Corps Schools," unpublished manuscript, 1967, Breckinridge Library.
5. Van Ryzin, oral memoir, 152–9; Maj. Gen. John P. Condon, Thomas questionnaire for the author, 10 October 1986.
6. Thomas, oral memoir, 967–9; Staff of The Basic School, "The Basic School," manuscript history, rev. ed., 1971, Breckinridge Library; Fleming et al., *Quantico,* 89–90; *Quantico Sentry,* 3 February 1955; *New York Times,* 19 October 1954.
7. Thomas, "Post Guadalcanal," 108–10.
8. Bare, oral memoir, 120–35; *Quantico Sentry,* 20 January 1955; Clifford, *Progress and Purpose,* 84–8.
9. Thomas, oral memoir, 972–4; *Quantico Sentry,* 4 October 1954, 5 May 1955, and 14 July 1955; Lt. Gen. W. K. Jones to the author, 7 March 1986; Burger, oral memoir, 283–4.
10. Thomas, oral memoir, 974–5; Lt. Gen. W. K. Jones to the author, 7 March 1986; *Quantico Sentry,* 17 February 1955, 31 March 1955, 2 June 1955, and 29 September 1955.
11. *Quantico Sentry,* 19 August 1954 and 26 May 1955; Mrs. J. R. Andrews to the author, 26 February 1988.
12. Lt. Gen. W. K. Jones to the author, 7 March 1986.
13. Thomas, oral memoir, 975–7; Mrs. J. A. Bruder to the author, 21 August 1989.
14. Thomas, oral memoir, 977–9; Mrs. J. A. Bruder to the author, 21 August 1989; W. H. J. Thomas to the author, "Family Notes," April–May 1988.
15. Thomas physical, 2 June 1955, Thomas medical record, Thomas OQR; Maj. Gen. Merritt A. Edson, obituaries, Edson File, RS MCHC; *Quantico Sentry,* 15 December 1955.
16. Lt. Gen. G. C. Thomas to Gen. A. A. Vandegrift, 14 July 1955, Vandegrift Papers.

17. Quoted from Thomas fitness report, 1 September–31 December 1955, Thomas OQR; *Quantico Sentry,* 30 October 1956.
18. Thomas, oral memoir, 981–2; *Quantico Sentry,* 17 November 1955; Thomas fitness reports, 1954 and 1955, Thomas OQR.

Chapter XXVI. Sunset Parade
1. Office of the Secretary of the Navy, memorandum for the President, "Gerald C. Thomas," 18 February 1956, and endorsement by the naval aide to the President, 24 February 1956, with notes of subsequent action, File 3–K, White House Office Files, 1956, Dwight D. Eisenhower Papers, Dwight D. Eisenhower Presidential Library, Abilene, Kan.
2. *Washington Post,* 1 March 1953.
3. D. D. Eisenhower to Arthur P. Kane, Bloomington, Ill., 25 March 1953; T. Stephens to Cmdr. E. L. Beach, USN, 24 March 1953; Lt. Gen. G. C. Thomas to H. H. Gruenther, 29 September 1954; H. Pyle to J. M. Taussig, Chicago, Ill., 8 December 1955; J. M. Taussig to S. Adams, 21 November 1955; Lt. Gen. G. C. Thomas to S. Adams, 14 August 1954; S. Adams to Lt. Gen. G. C. Thomas, 17 August 1954, all in White House Central Files, Eisenhower Papers.
4. Brig. Gen. A. J. Goodpaster, memorandum for Mr. Shanley, 13 March 1956, File 1362, Personal Papers Files, 1956, Eisenhower Papers; President of the United States to Gen. G. C. Thomas, March 1956, Thomas OQR; Gen. G. C. Thomas to Capt. G. C. Thomas, Jr., 5 December 1956, TFP.
5. NSC 5423, "Directive for a Net Capabilities Evaluation Subcommittee," 23 June 1954, and NSC 5511, "A Net Evaluation Subcommittee," 14 February 1955, both in Net Capabilities Evaluation Subcommittee File (1954–55), National Security Council Staff Papers, 1948–61, White House Office, Eisenhower Library; Office of the Special Assistant for National Security Affairs, "The Structure and Functions of the National Security Council," 1 July 1957, Records of the Office of the Special Assistant for National Security Affairs, 1952–61, White House Office, Eisenhower Library; Robert J. Watson, *The Joint Chiefs of Staff and National Policy, 1953–1954,* vol. V, in *History of the Joint Chiefs of Staff* (Washington, D.C.: Historical Division, Joint Chiefs of Staff, 1986), 139–41, furnished by Willard J. Webb, chief, JCS Historical Division.
6. NSC Actions 1532–1536, "Record of Actions of the National Security Council at Its Two Hundred and Eighty-First Meeting . . . ," 6 April 1956, File: NSC Record of Actions, 1956, Office of Staff Secretary Records, 1952–61, White House Office, Eisenhower Library; A. W. Dulles to Special Assistant to the President, National Security Affairs, 8 June 1956; Adm. A. W. Radford to Special Assistant to the President, National Security Affairs, 31 May 1956; NSC 5605, "A Net Evaluation Subcommittee," 24 May 1956, National Security Council Staff Papers.

    For the final disposition of the Net Evaluation Subcommittee report and the intelligence estimates, see NSC 5602/1 "Basic National Security Policy," 15 March 1956, in Marc Trachtenberg, ed., *The Development of American Strategic Thought 1945–1969,* 4 vols. (New York: Garland, 1988) I:119–55. For intelligence concerns, see John Prados, *The Soviet Estimate: U.S. Intelligence*

Analysis and Soviet Strategic Forces, rev. ed. (Princeton, N.J.: Princeton University Press, 1986), 51–66.

7. Memorandum, discussion of the 306th Meeting of the National Security Council, Thursday, 20 December 1956, national security series, Ann Whitman File, White House Office, Eisenhower Library; NSC Action 1641, "Records of Actions of the National Security Council at Its Three Hundred and Sixth Meeting . . . December 20, 1956," NSC Record of Actions, 1956, Staff Secretary Records, Eisenhower Library.

  The total number of officials who attended the briefing was forty-three, excluding Thomas and his staff.

8. Memorandum, discussion of the 344th Meeting of the National Security Council, Tuesday, 12 November 1957, Ann Whitman File, White House Office, Eisenhower Library; NSC Action 1815, "Record of Actions by the National Security Council at Its Three Hundred and Forty-fourth Meeting . . . November 12, 1957," File: NSC Actions, 1957, and NSC Action 2009, "Record of Action by the National Security Council at Its Three Hundred and Eighty-seventh Meeting . . . November 20, 1958," NSC Actions, 1958, both in Staff Secretary Records, Eisenhower Library; NSC 5816, "A Net Evaluation Subcommittee," 1 July 1958, National Security Council Staff Papers, Eisenhower Library; Gen. G. C. Thomas to Capt. G. C. Thomas, Jr., 12 February and 20 May 1957, TFP; interview, Gen. A. J. Goodpaster, USA (Ret.), 7 August 1990.

9. D. D. Eisenhower to Gen. G. C. Thomas, 27 November 1958; D. D. Eisenhower to Gen. N. F. Twining, USAF, 8 December 1958; and Lt. Gen. T. F. Hickey, USA (Ret.), to D. D. Eisenhower, 3 December 1958, all in White House Central Files, 1958, Eisenhower Papers; Gen. G. C. Thomas to D. D. Eisenhower, 8 December 1958, Records of the Special Assistant for National Security Affairs, Eisenhower Papers; annual and retirement physical, reports, 10 December 1958, Thomas medical records, Thomas OQR.

  Although the Johnson administration abolished the Net Evaluation Subcommittee and its staff in 1965, the functions of the staff reappeared in 1971 with the establishment of the Office of the Director of Net Assessment, Office of the Secretary of Defense.

10. W. H. J. Thomas to the author, 6 July 1990; Col. G. C. Thomas, Jr., to the author, 13 July 1990.

  Thomas, however, did not become a wealthy man. In 1977, the Illinois Wesleyan University alumni association development office estimated his worth at $150,000.

11. Gen. G. C. Thomas to Capt. G. C. Thomas, Jr., 5 December 1956, 12 February 1957, 14 June 1960, and 31 December 1962, TFP; Lt. Gen. William K. Jones to the author, 22 February 1986; General W. M. Greene, Jr., to the author, 24 July 1990, and personal conversations with General Greene; Col. G. C. Thomas, Jr., to the author, 13 July 1990.

12. Col. G. C. Thomas, Jr., to the author, 13 July 1990; Lt. Gen. W. K. Jones to the author, 22 February 1986; Maj. Gen. J. P. Condon, Thomas questionnaire, 10 October 1986; Col. DeWolf Schatzel, Thomas questionnaire, 17 March 1986; Maj. Gen. J. M. Platt, Thomas questionnaire, 10 April 1986.

13. Col. G. C. Thomas, Jr., to the author, 13 July 1990; W. H. J. Thomas, "Family Notes," April–May 1988, TFP; D. J. Crawford, "In Memoriam: Colonel Angus Malcolm 'Tiny' Fraser," *Fortitudine* 15 (Summer, 1985), 15.
14. Gen. G. C. Thomas to Capt. G. C. Thomas, Jr., 12 February 1957 and 27 February 1961, TFP; G. C. Thomas, Jr., to the author, 13 July 1990; Thomas, "Family Notes," (see Note 13); Gen. Gerald C. Thomas, USMC (Ret.), Col. Robert D. Heinl, Jr., USMC (Ret.), and Rear Adm. Arthur A. Ageton, USN (Ret.), *The Marine Officer's Guide* (Annapolis, Md.: U.S. Naval Institute, 1956).

    I also found General Thomas's comments on the official histories in the History and Museums Division historical files, RG 127.
15. Gen. G. C. Thomas to Maj. G. C. Thomas, Jr., 19 August 1961 and 4 July and 31 December 1962, as annotated by Col. G. C. Thomas, Jr., TFP; Virginia Thomas Andrews to the author, 26 February 1988.
16. Thomas, "Family Notes," 9.
17. Ibid.; John Sherwood, "Our Marines [sic] Big Night: Guests, Ghost Trails and Brand New Library," *The Washington Star,* 13 May 1977; "A Story Rubs Old Wounds," letters to the editor, *The Washington Star,* 23 May 1977; Gen. Gerald C. Thomas with Col. Angus Fraser, "Conversations with the General," *MCG* 63 (November 1979), 82–7.
18. Mrs. G. C. Thomas to the author, 4 February 1986; Col. Sanford B. Hunt to the author, 17 July 1988; Col. G. C. Thomas, Jr., to the author, 25 August 1990; *Washington Post,* 10 April 1984. The definitive obituary is Col. Angus M. Fraser, "Gerald Carthrae Thomas," *MCG* 86 (June 1984), 11–14, reprinted in *The Old Breed News,* Newsletter of the 1st Marine Division Association (June 1984).
19. ALMAR 77/84, Thomas File, RS MCHC.

Index

Adams, Capt. Robert Emmet, 25
Advanced Base Force, advanced bases, 11, 82, 86, 108, 110, 113
Advanced Base Force Operations in Micronesia, 87. *See also* Ellis, Lt. Col. Earl H.
Advanced Base Problem, 114, 338
Advanced Research Group (ARG), 332, 338. *See also* "Double Dome School"
Ahr Valley, 68
Air Force units and commands, 194, 247, 251
   Far East Air Forces, 300, 313
   Fifth Air Force, 300–301, 312; Joint Operations Center, 300–301, 312
   Strategic Air Command, 347
Air-ground operations, 116
Aisne-Marne counteroffensive, 47
Albany, Georgia, 236, 331
Albemarle County, Virginia, 3
Aleutian Islands, 89
Allen, Maj. Gen. Chester, 340
Almond, Maj. Gen. Edward M. "Ned," USA, 285; Lt. Gen., 292–93, 295–98, 300–303, 305, 314, 317
American Expeditionary Forces (AEF), 16–18, 20, 22, 29, 31, 37, 44, 57, 66, 70, 73, 81, 106, 124, 229
   III Corps, 47, 66, 71

XX Corps, 48, 51
XXI Corps, 36–37, 43
1st Division, 15, 20, 22–23, 28–29, 44, 46–47, 62, 66, 72, 106
2d Division, 20, 22–23, 28–29, 31, 34, 36, 38, 46–47, 50, 56–57, 59–60, 62, 64, 66–68, 70–72
   3d Brigade, 44, 48, 51; 7th Infantry, 43, 45; 9th Infantry, 31, 51
   4th Marine Brigade, 22, 28–29, 31, 34, 36–37, 43–44, 46, 48, 54, 56–58, 61, 70–75, 77–78, 81, 87, 108, 111, 119, 131; 5th Marines, 17–20, 35–37, 40, 45, 51, 68, 72; 1st Battalion, 36–37, 43–44; 2d Battalion, 38–42, 44; 3d Battalion, 36–38
   6th Marines, 18, 20, 23, 26–27, 29, 31, 33, 35–39, 48, 50–52, 54–58, 60, 62–69, 71–72
      1st Battalion, 18, 26–31, 33–34, 37, 38–45, 48, 51–55, 57–61, 63–64, 67–69, 71; 74th Company, 19, 28, 43, 59, 61, 68; 75th Company, 22, 25, 29, 33, 35–36, 52–54, 58–59, 61, 64–65, 68, 70–71, 74; 3d Platoon, 39, 50, 63; 76th Company, 19, 39, 40, 42, 53–54, 61, 63; 95th Company, 19, 25, 61, 63
      2d Battalion, 38, 43

[437]

American Expeditionary Forces (AEF) (*continued*)
   3d Battalion, 33, 36–38
   26th Division, 22, 26; 104th Infantry, 45
   27th Division, 39
   28th Division, 39
   32d Division, 66
   33d Division, 62
   36th (Texas National Guard) Division, 59
   42d Division, 22, 25, 62–63
   77th Division, 72
   2d Engineers, 52
   12th Artillery, 33, 35
   23d Infantry, 29, 51, 53, 56
   24th Infantry, 107
   29th Infantry, 107
   461st Infantry, 35
   Services of Supply, 56
American Legion, 255
American School, Peiping, 118
Amiens, France, 28–29
Anderson, Secretary of the Navy Robert B., 328–30
Andrews, 2d Lt. John Richards "Rick," 340, 350
Andrews, Virginia Thomas "Ginny," 350
Aola Bay, 191, 200, 205–7
Aotea Quay, New Zealand, 164–65, 167
Argonne Forest, 59, 63
Arkansas, 132
Arlington National Cemetery, 327, 352
Armed Services committees, 254
Armistice, 66
Army and Navy Club, 160, 214, 245, 348, 351
Army-Navy Joint Board, 98
Army schools
   Command and General Staff School, 100, 122–24, 129
   Engineer School, 277
   Field Artillery School, 100
   Infantry School, 100, 109, 104–10, 121, 126, 129, 293
   Motor Transport School, 100–101
   Signal School, 100
   Subsistence School, 100
Army units and commands
   Commander in Chief, Far East (CinCFe), 293, 313. *See also* MacArthur, Gen. Douglas
   Sixth Army, 215
   Eighth Army, 287–88, 290–92, 294–97, 300, 303–7, 309–10, 312–14

   Tenth Army, 239–40
   I Corps, 291–92, 297, 301, 304, 306
   IX Corps, 291–93, 297, 301
   X Corps, 285, 288, 291–93, 295–98, 300–303, 305–9, 312, 314–16
   XIV Corps, 216, 222
   XXIV Corps, 205
   America Division, 179, 202, 206, 208
   1st Cavalry Division, 292
   2d Infantry Division, 292, 296–97, 303, 305–7
   3d Infantry Division, 297
   7th Infantry Division, 292, 316
   24th Infantry Division, 291–92
   27th Infantry Division, 238–39
   37th Infantry Division, 221
   43d Infantry Division, 216
   82d Division (Airborne), 304
   15th Infantry, 121
   132d Infantry, 209
   147th Infantry, 206
   164th Infantry, 201–2, 204–6, 208
   182d Infantry, 205, 208
   187th Regimental Combat Team (Airborne), 292, 297
   4th Base Hospital, 213
Army War College, 100, 341
Assistant Commandant of the Marine Corps (Air), 325
Auckland, New Zealand, 164–65, 166–67
Australia, 160, 162, 165, 212, 214–15, 219
Australian-New Zealand Army Corps (ANZAC), 129

Bad Hönningen, 68, 71
Badger, Adm. Oscar C., 268, 272
Baker, Secretary of War Newton D., 17, 28, 72
Baker, Col. Warren P., 349, 352
Balboa, Canal Zone, 92, 94, 96
Bar-le-Duc, France, 31
Bard, Undersecretary of the Navy Ralph A., 229
Bare, Col. Robert O., 128, 132, 135; Brig. Gen., 229, 240, 277, 287, 337, 340
Barker, Maj. Frederick A., 56–57, 61, 81, 63, 69, 71
Barkley, Vice President Alben, 316
Barnett, 152–53
Barnett, Maj. Gen. Commandant George, 7, 11, 13–14, 17, 57, 72, 75, 78, 80–81, 86–87
Barnett, Mrs. George, 19
Barrett, Maj. Charles D., 113; Brig. Gen., 136, 138, 156; Maj. Gen., 217–21

Barrett, Col. David D., USA, 266
Barricourt Heights, France, 62
Basra, Iraq, 142–43
Bataan, 200
Bathurst, Gambia, 148
Batraville, Benoit, 77, 79–80
Battle of Belleau Wood, 34–47, 56, 61, 64, 68, 71, 88, 171. *See also* Belleau Wood
Battle of Blanc Mont, 59–61
Battle of Cape Esperance, 201
Battle of Gettysburg, 90
Battle of Midway, 162
Battle of Raider Ridge, 184, 187, 192
Battle of Savo Island, 178
Battle of Soissons, 46–55
Battle of Tassafaronga, 209
Battle of the Coral Sea, 162
Battle of the Eastern Solomons, 186
Battle of the Ridge, 197, 210
Battle of the Tenaru, 184, 187, 198
Battle of the Wilderness, 88
Beaumont, France, 64
Beaurepaire Farm, 50–52
Beauvais, France, 29
Beforterheider, Germany, 67
Belleau, France, 34
Belleau Wood, 227, 341. *See also* Battle of Belleau Wood
Bellegrade, Cadeus, 79
Bemis, Capt. John A., 122, 128, 202; Brig. Gen., 240
"Bended Knee" speech, 252–53, 255, 281. *See also* Vandegrift, Maj. Alexander Archer
Benson, Adm. William S., 13
Berdoulat, Gen. Pierre E., 47, 52
Berkeley, Brig. Gen. Randolph C., 110
Berry, Maj. Benjamin S., 36–37, 40, 63
Bethesda Naval Hospital, 135, 319
Betio Island, Tarawa Atoll, 226
Betts, James E., 128
Biebush, Lt. Col. Frederick E., 185
Bigart, Homer, 241
Bikini Atoll, 250
Bismarck Barracks, 264
Blake, Col. Robert, 131, 157, 218
Blanc Mont, France, 59–61
Blanquillia Reef, 93
Bleasdale, Col. Victor F., 235
Bloomington, Illinois, 1, 5–7, 127, 214, 229
Bluefields, Nicaragua, 97
Bois de la Brigade de Marine, 44, 342. *See also* Battle of Belleau Wood
Bois de la Montagne, 58
Bois du Fond de Limon, 64
Bonchamp, France, 28
Borden, Gy. Sgt. James, 15
Borno, Louis, 104
Boston Navy Yard, 96
Bougainville, 174, 181, 211, 216–23, 226, 238
Bouresches, France, 33–34, 38–39, 44
Bourmont, France, 23
Bowser, Col. Alpha L., Jr., 291, 293, 298
Boxer Rebellion, Boxers, 78, 105
Bradley, Maj. Omar N., 106; Gen., 262, 280, 312, 328
Brandt, Sgt. Robert, 183
Brayton, Pfc. C. J., Jr., 267
Breckinridge, Brig. Gen. James C., 110
Breckinridge Hall, 338
Brest, France, 71
Brice, Maj. Gen. William O., 325, 333
Bridges, Senator Styles, 254
Brisbane, Australia, 211–14
Bristow, Capt. John B., 266–67
British Chiefs of Staff, 162
British Expeditionary Force (BEF), 23, 28, 59
   Third Army, 29
   Fifth Army, 28
British units
   Commonwealth Division, 292
   1st Battalion, the Gloucestershire Regiment, 292
Brown, Alfred, 11
Brown, Capt. Dudley S., 107, 128, 154, 211, 217, 277
Brown, Col. Preston, 31, 36
Brown, Col. Thompson, CSA, 88
Brown, Capt. Warwick T., MC, USN, 181, 198, 212, 215
Brown, Col. Wilbur S. "Big Foot," 99, 297, 302, 304
Brown Field, Quantico, 337–39
Bruder, Anne, 318
Bruder, Maj. Joseph A., 278; Col., 287, 318, 341–42, 350
Bruder, Tina Thomas, 318, 341, 350. *See also* Thomas, Lottie Capers
Buckley, Lt. Col. Edmund J., 182, 189, 197, 217
Buckner, Lt. Gen. Simon Bolivar, Jr., 239–40
Bugge, Maj. Jens, 107
Buin-Faisi, 220
Buka, 218
Bull, Maj. Harold R., 106
Bundy, Maj. Gen. Omar, 31, 43

Bureau of the Budget, 100
Burger, Capt. Joseph C., 122, 128, 154;
    Lt. Col., 217; Col., 225, 233, 277
Burma, Burma Road, 141–42
Burns, Capt. John Francis, 42
Burr, 2d Lt. Carlton, 25–27, 29, 36, 39;
    1st Lt., 51–53
Busby, Sgt. William H., 59
Buse, Maj. Henry W. "Bill," Jr., 166, 177,
    182; Lt. Col., 232, 268–69, 348,
    352
Butler, Brig. Gen. Arthur H. "Tex," 322,
    349
Butler, Brig. Gen. Smedley D., 75, 80–81,
    88, 90, 99, 282
Butler, Congressman Thomas, 75, 81
Button, William R., 77
Buttrick, Brig. Gen. James T., 128
Byers, Maj. Gen. Clovis E., 304–6, 308,
    310, 312–13, 315–17
Byrd, Senator Harry, 229, 253

Cacos, 75, 77, 79–80
CACTUS, 160–210. *See also* Guadalcanal
CACTUS Air Force, 181, 186, 196, 202,
    207–9. *See also* Marine Corps
    units and commands,
    Department of the Pacific *and* 1st
    Marine Aircraft Wing
Cairo, Egypt, 142–43, 145, 147
Calhoun, Mrs. Lucy, 121
Callaghan, Rear Adm. Daniel J., 165, 171
Camp Barrett, Quantico, 338
Camp Cable, Australia, 212–13
Camp Elliott, California, 137, 235–36
Camp Holabird, Maryland, 101–2, 124
Camp Lejeune, North Carolina, 223,
    234–35, 242, 286, 337, 339–40
Camp Merritt, Long Island, 71
Camp Mills, Long Island, 71
Camp Pendleton, California, 223, 235,
    331, 337
Camp Pontanzen, France, 71
Camp Upshur, Quantico, 338–39
Canal Zone, 96–97
Cantigny, France, 29, 44, 47
Cap-Haïtien, Haiti, 104
Cape Gloucester, New Britain, 211
Cape Torokina, Bougainville, 221
Capella, 132
Capers, Rev. Ellison, 92
Capers, Lottie Palmer, 92
Carlson, Lt. Col. Evans F., 205–6, 209,
    219. *See also* Marine Corps units
    and commands, 2d Raider
    Battalion

Carney, Adm. Robert B. "Mick," 328–29
Carthrae, Adeline Addie Sidna, 3
Carthrae, Sidna Brown, 3
Casablanca Conference, 215
Caserne Dartiguenave, Haiti, 104
Casualties, 28, 35, 220, 231, 293, 302
Cates, Capt. Clifton B., 83, 112; Maj.,
    115–16, Col., 131, 156, 169,
    176–77, 179–80, 183, 184–87,
    190, 192–93, 198, 217; Gen., 45,
    240, 258, 276, 280–81, 284–87,
    300, 303, 310, 315, 326, 333,
    335–36
Catlin, Col. Albertus W., 18, 26, 33,
    35–38
Cauldwell, Col. Oscar R., 218
Cayes, Haiti, 104–5
Chaisson, Maj. John R., 269–70, 273–74
Chalons-sur-Marne, France, 60, 62
Champigneulles, France, 23, 25
Chandler, Capt. Henry E., 61
Chapel Saint-Martin, France, 80
Chapman, Lt. Col. Leonard F., Jr., 237
Charleston Navy Yard, 91–93, 101,
    153–54, 156
Château-Thierry, France, 30–31, 46, 72,
    342
Che-Yuan, Gen. Sung, 119
Chemin des Dames, France, 30
Chennault, Col. Claire, 139, 141
Cherry Point, North Carolina, 242
Chiang, Kai-shek, 119, 139, 141, 260, 262,
    266
Chiang, Kai-shek, Madame, 139–41
Chicago and Alton Railroad, 4–7
China, 98, 101, 103–4, 108, 110, 157, 226,
    236, 241, 249, 256, 257, 260, 280,
    287
Chinese People's Liberation Army, 260,
    266, 271, 275, 288, 349
Chinese translators, 235
Chinwangtao, China, 120
Choiseul, 218–19, 221–22
Chorwon, Korea, 301
Chosin Reservoir, 287, 291–92, 294, 302,
    307, 315
"Chowder," 249–50, 252, 255–56, 277,
    280, 283–84, 327, 349. *See also*
    "Little Man's Chowder and
    Marching Society"; Unification
    crisis
Christy, Howard Chandler, 12
Chunchon, Korea, 291–92, 296
Chungking, China, 139–41
Churchill, Prime Minister Winston S.,
    137, 143, 147–48, 150, 158, 215

City Cricket Club, Melbourne, 213
Clark, Gen. Mark W., 304, 313
Clemens, Capt. Martin Clemens, 169, 182, 185, 189–91, 197. *See also* Coastwatchers
Clement, Brig. Gen. William T. "Johnny," 235, 240, 283, 286, 342
Close air support (CAS), 116, 250, 297, 300–302, 304, 308, 310, 312, 314, 316
Clubb, O. Edmund, 122, 266, 271
Coastwatchers, 162, 169, 186
Cochrane, Sir Archibald, 142
Coco River Patrol, 189
Coffman, Lt. Col. Raymond P., 180, 197–98
Cogswell, Brig. Gen. Charles L., 352
Cole, Capt. Glen C., 69–71
College of Chinese Studies, 235
Colley, Lt. Col. Thomas J., 270; Col., 322, 332
Collins, Capt. J. Lawton, USA, 106; Maj. Gen., 212; Gen., 304, 313, 316
Combs, Pvt. Lencil, 79
Command relations, 202, 222
Commandant Marine Corps Schools, 332, 335, 338–39, 343–44
Commandant's House, 225, 258
Condon, Col. John P., 332, 338, 352, 340, 348–49
Conference on the Limitation of Armament, 88. *See also* Washington Conference
Connett, Charles, 90
Conta, General de Infanterie Richard von, 34, 35
Cony, 219
Cooke, Adm. Charles M. "Savvy," Jr., 228, 264, 267–68, 270
Cooley, 1st Lt. Richard A., 266, 277
Coontz, Adm. Robert E., 86
Coral Sea, 172. *See also* Battle of the Coral Sea
Corbett, Murl, 83
Costa Rica, 96
Côtes des Heures, France, 26
Craig, Brig. Gen. Edward A., 282, 286
Cram, Col. Jack R., 278
Crawford, Rear Adm. Clyde, 272, 274
Cresswell, Lt. Col. Lenard B., 154, 177, 185–86, 286, 340
Crete, 143–44, 146–47
Crocodile Creek, 177. *See also* Ilu River; Tenaru River
Crutchley, Rear Adm. V. A. C., RN, 168, 177–78

Cuba, 77
Cukela, Lt. Louis, 80, 82–83
Culebra, Puerto Rico, 132–33
Cunningham, Adm. Sir Andrew B., RN, 144
Currie, Lauchlin, 139
Cutts, Col. Richard M., 103–6, 113

Daily Pantagraph, Bloomington, Illinois, 1, 7
D'Albiac, Air Vice Marshal John J., 145–46
Dalby, Maj. Marion C., 278
Dalton, Gy. Sgt. Jeremiah, 18, 20–21, 59, 61
Daly, 1st Sgt. Dan, 18
Damblain, France, 23
Daniels, Secretary of the Navy Josephus, 11, 13, 17, 73–75, 79–81
Dardanelles, 113
Davies, John Paton, 122
Defense battalion program, 235
Defense reorganization, 251–52. *See also* Unification crisis
Degoutte, Gen. Jean, 31, 36–37
del Valle, Col. Pedro A., 132, 156–57, 169, 183, 184, 190, 192; Brig. Gen., 198, 234, 240
Delaware, 90
Denfeld, Adm. Louis E., 280
Department of Defense, 279–80, 286, 303
Department of the Interior, 327
Desert Rock IV, 333
Dessez, Col. Lester A., 128
Dickson, Capt. Donald L., 209
Director of Central Intelligence, 346
Dominican Republic, 11, 69, 87, 105, 157
Dorman-Smith, Sir Reginald, 142
Dorsey, Benjamin, 348
Dorsey, Capt. Joshua, III, 348
"Double Dome School," 332. *See also* Advanced Research Group
Douglas-Mansfield Act, 319, 327. *See also* Public Law 416
Doyen, Brig. Gen. Charles, 29
Doyle, Capt. James H., USN, 168
Dubbelde, Lydia "Deanie," 340
Dulles, Allen, 339, 346
Dumanquillas Bay, 115
Dunbeck, Charley, 83
Durrett, Frank, 76
Dutton, Thomas C., 266–67
Dyer, Lt. Col. E. Colston, 249; Col., 278

Eastern Platoon Leaders Class, 135
Eberstadt, Ferdinand, 247
Eberstadt Plan, 248–49, 251
École Supérieure de Guerre, 293, 341
Eddy, 1st Lt. William A., 40
Edison, Secretary of the Navy Charles, 130
Edson, Lt. Col. Merritt A. "Red Mike," 99, 156; Col., 187, 189, 191–92, 198–99, 203, 206, 217, 231, 233; Brig. Gen., 236–37, 242, 245, 248–51, 254–55; Maj. Gen., 257, 282–83, 302, 327, 340, 342, 349, 352
Edson Board, 254
Edson Hall, 343
Edson's Ridge, 191
Edwards, Adm. Richard S., 228
Egeli, Peter, 160
Eichelberger, Gen. Robert L., 304
Eisenhower, Gen. Dwight D., 235, 248–50, 255, 323–24, 331, 339, 344, 346–48
Ellice Island, 163
Elliott, 176
Elliott, Rev. J. N., 1
Elliott, James T., 12, 14, 20, 58–59, 62, 64–65, 69
Ellis, Lt. Col. Earl H., 56, 87
Empress Augusta Bay, Bougainville, 220–21
Eniwetok, 232, 237
Ennis, Capt. Thomas G., 148
Enterprise, 186, 204, 207
Ericcson, 180
Erskine, 2d Lt. Graves B. "Bobby," 83; Maj., 119–21; Lt. Col., 122, 125, 128–31; Col., 151–53, 155, 157, 193; Brig. Gen., 223; Maj. Gen., 243, 251, 258, 283, 286, 290, 340, 350–51
Erskine Board, 243
Espiritu Santo, 208
Etheridge, 1st Lt. Charles A., 39, 41–43
European Recovery Program, 262
Evanston Academy, 8, 10
Everest, Lt. Gen. Frank E., USAF, 312–13
Executive Order 9877, 279–80
Exermont, France, 63

Farrell, Lt. Col. Walter G., 143, 145, 147
Fayolle, Gen. Marie Emile, 46
Fechteler, Adm. William M., 328
Fellers, Maj. Bonner, USA, 143
Fellers, Col. William S., 217, 283

Field Service Regulations, 125
Fields, Col. Lewis J., 352
Fighter One (airstrip), 201, 204
Fighter Two (airstrip), 205
Fiji Islands, 160, 162, 217
Finn, Lt. Col. Edward V. "Mickey," 313
First Battle of the Marne, 30
1st Marine Division Association, 341, 350
Fiscal Director of the Marine Corps, 322. *See also* Hill, William P. T.; Shoup, David M.
Five-Power Treaty, 89
Flagg, James Montgomery, 12
Fleet Landing Exercise, 6, 132
Fleet Training Publication 167 (FTP-167), 203, 249
Fletcher, Vice Adm. Frank Jack, 169, 171–72, 177–78
Florida Island, 163, 169
Foch, Gen. Ferdinand, 28, 30, 46–47
Fontaine Saint-Robert, France, 28
Forbes, W. Cameron, 105
Forbidden City, Peiping, 117, 121
Forêt de Retz, France, 47–48, 50, 55
Formosa, 226, 236
Forrestal, Undersecretary of the Navy James V., 214, 226–48, 251–55; Secretary of Defense, 258, 329, 340
Fort Belvoir, Virginia, 277
Fort Benning, Georgia, 106–7, 109, 130, 215
Fort Bragg, North Carolina, 154
Fort de Plenois, France, 58–59
Fort Leavenworth, Kansas, 106, 124, 215, 266
Fort Philip H. Sheridan, Illinois, 10, 12
Frank, Benis M., 350
Fraser, Col. Angus M. "Tiny," 349, 351–52
Fredericksburg, Virginia, 115
Fremington, England, 341
French units
  First Army, 26, 28, 59, 61–62, 106
  Third Army, 66–68, 70
  Fourth Army, 30, 59–62
  Sixth Army, 30–31, 47–48
  Tenth Army, 54
  II Cavalry Corps, 47, 51
  X Corps, 26
  XX Corps, 47
  XXI Corps, 31
  1st Moroccan Division, 47
  33d Division, 26
  167th Division, 37

Freyberg, Maj. Gen. Bernard C., 144, 146
Frisbie, Lt. Col. Julian C., 198; Col., 242
Fuller, Brig. Gen. Ben H., 99; Maj. Gen. Commandant, 108, 110
Fuller, Capt. Edward C., 25, 42
Fuller Board, 99. *See also* Neville Board
"Functions Paper," 319

Gaither Committee, 347
Galliford, Walter, 83
Gallipoli, 87, 114, 128, 338
Galveston, 91, 92
Galveston, Texas, 93, 95
Garde d'Haiti, 104. *See also* Gendarmerie d'Haiti
Garrett, Maj. Franklin B., 43, 45, 64
Gates, Undersecretary of the Navy Thomas S., Jr., 328–29
Gates Board, 329–30
Gavutu, 167, 169, 174, 176, 178
Geiger, Col. Roy S., 116, 144–45, Brig. Gen., 186, 196–97, 201–3, 221–23; Maj. Gen., 226, 233, 237, 240, 243, 250, 254, 278, 349, 352
Gendarmerie d'Haiti, 75, 77, 79–80, 87–88. *See also* Garde d'Haiti
General Board, 86, 108
George II, King of the Hellenes, 143–44
George Medal, 209
German General Staff, 23
German units
 First Army, 30
 Fifth Army, 59, 63
 Seventh Army, 30, 36
  IV Reserve Corps, 30, 34, 44, 66
 Ninth Army, 47
 5th Guards Division, 42, 44
 28th Division, 34, 51; 40th Infantry Regiment, 244
 237th Division, 34
 461st Infantry Regiment, 44
Germanvilliers, France, 23
"Germany First" policy, 215
Germany, occupation of, 66–71
Ghormley, Vice Adm. Robert L., 163–65, 167–68, 171–72, 177, 179, 182, 191, 194, 197, 200, 202–3.
Gilbert Islands, 226, 238
Global Strategy Conference, 341
Gobert Creek, 39
Goettge, Lt. Col. Frank B., 152, 159, 164–67, 172, 182, 185, 192
Goettge Patrol, 199
Gondrecourt, France, 25, 59

Good, Col. Charles F., Jr., 232
Gourard, Gen. Henri, 60, 62
Grand Army of the Republic, 2
Greene, Capt. Wallace M., Jr., 128, 153–54, 156; Lt. Col., 231–33, 348, 352
Griffith, Capt. Samuel Blair, II, 122, 128; Maj., 154, 156, 187, 199, 225, 231, 349
Griswold, Maj. Gen. Oscar W., 216
Guadalcanal, 160–210, 212–13, 218–23, 232, 238, 245, 268, 277, 287, 304, 349. *See also* CACTUS
Guadalcanal Area, Quantico, 336, 338
"Guadalcanal Gang," 240, 269
Guam, 86, 89, 114, 129–30, 138–39, 226, 235, 237, 238, 240, 262
Guantanamo Bay, Cuba, 76, 94, 96
Guardia Nacional de Nicaragua, 99, 109
Gulf of Gonave, 77
Gulick, Col. Mason, 103

Habbaniya, Iraq, 143, 145
Hager, Lt. Col. Frank P., 315
Haig, Field Marshal Sir Douglas, 28, 59
Haiti, 11, 56, 69, 74–85, 87, 98, 106–8, 113–14, 116
Haitian-American Sugar Company, 79
Hall, Lt. Robert, 198
Halsey, Vice Adm. William F., 202–9, 211–13, 215–16, 218–23
Hanneken, Lt. Col. Herman H., 77, 198–99
Harbord, Brig. Gen. James G., 29, 33, 36–41, 43–45; Maj. Gen., 47–48, 51–52, 56
Harding, Maj. Forrest, 89, 106
Harding, President Warren G., 88
Harmon, Maj. Gen. Millard F., 197, 200
Harriman, W. Averell, 148
Harris, Maj. Gen. Field, 219, 238–39, 242–43, 250, 282–83, 285–86, 290, 301, 312
Hart, Col. Franklin A., 112; Lt. Gen., 234, 258, 283–86, 287, 323, 333, 335
Hawaiian Islands, 89, 202, 220, 237–38, 262
Hays Line, 307, 310
Headquarters Manual, 324
Headquarters, U.S. Marine Corps, 11, 13, 29, 57–58, 69, 72, 74–75, 84–85, 87, 105–6, 110–11, 113–14, 122–23, 131–32, 135–36, 138, 148, 150, 152, 156–57, 192, 211, 214, 217, 219–21, 223–46, 249,

Headquarters, U.S. Marine Corps (*continued*)
   251, 255, 259, 267, 269, 276–78, 281–87, 293–94, 315–16, 318–20, 322, 324, 326–28, 330, 332–34, 338–39, 344, 348–49, 352
  Adjutant & Inspector's Department, 82, 84, 230
  Administrative Division, 320, 324
  Director of Women Marines, 320
  Division of Aviation, 116, 230, 277, 320
  Division of Information, 320
  Division of Personnel, Personnel Department, 230, 243, 320, 324
  Division of Plans and Policies ("Pots and Pans"), 225, 228–29, 232–34, 241–42, 249, 258, 262, 280, 320, 323, 325
  Division of Reserve, 230, 320
  Fiscal Division, 320, 323
  Inspection Division, 320
  Inspector General's Office, 234
  Paymaster Department, 230
  Policy Analysis Division, 320
  Public Relations Division, 230
  Quartermaster Department, 230
  Supply Department, 320, 322–23
Heinl, Lt. Col. Robert D., Jr., 254, 349, 351
Helicopter development, 250, 277, 333
Henderson, 19, 273
Henderson Field, 181, 184, 186, 189–90, 194, 196–97, 199–201, 203, 205, 207–9
Henrico, 274
Hepburn, Rear Adm. Arthur J., 130
Hepburn Board, 130
Hester, Maj. Gen. John H., 216
Hickey, Lt. Gen. Thomas F., USA, 347
Higgins, Andrew J., 153
Hill, Senator Lister, 253
Hill, Maj. William P. T., 128–30; Col., 152–53; Maj. Gen., 230–34, 236, 251, 270, 281, 286, 316, 322
Hindenburg, Field Marshal Paul von, 22
Hittle, Lt. Col. James D., 249, 254, 256, 349
Ho, Fisher, 266
Hodes, Capt. Henry, 107
Hoffman, Congressman Clare E., 256
Hogaboom, Col. Robert E., 128, 249, 348, 352
Hoge, Maj. Gen. William M., USA, 291–93

Holcomb, Maj. Thomas, 38; Lt. Col., 43, 45, 48, 69; Maj. Gen. Commandant, 123, 134–35, 138, 148, 150, 152–53, 155–58, 193, 202–3, 205, 212, 214, 218, 220–21, 223, 225, 228, 236–37
Homberger, Dr. Alfred W., 9
Honduras, 94, 96
Hongchon, China, 292, 296–98
Hoover, President Herbert, 105, 108
Hopkins, Harry, 141
Horne, Vice Adm. Frederick J., 228
Hornet, 196, 204
Hotel Cecil, Melbourne, 164, 166
House Armed Services Committee, 256
House Committee on Expenditures in the Executive Department, 256
House Committee on Naval Affairs, 229
House Naval Affairs Committee, 74–75, 81, 110, 130
Howard, Col. Archie F., 128, 135–36, 211, 216
Howard, Lt. Gen. Samuel L., 286
Hsuchow, 266
Huang, Maj. Gen. J. L., 140
Hughes, Maj. John Arthur "Johnny the Hard," 18, 25, 36, 39–44, 48, 50, 52, 54, 56, 78, 80
Humphrey, Secretary of the Treasury George M., 339
Hunt, Col. LeRoy P., 83, 131, 152–57, 165–66, 168, 174, 177, 178–79, 182, 184, 187, 192–93, 198; Brig. Gen., 233, 259; Maj. Gen., 263, 268; Lt. Gen., 282, 286, 350
Hunt, Lt. Sanford B., 165, 193, 198; Col., 351
Hunt Board, 284–85
Hurst, Lt. Col. E. Hunter, 249; Col., 349, 351–52
Hutchins, Maj. Lyford, 249
Hwachon, Hwachon Reservoir, 292, 297–98, 301
Hyakutake, Gen. Haruyoshi, 194, 200–201, 205

Iceland, 150
Illah, Regent Amir Abdul, 14
Illinois Anti-Saloon League, 9
Illinois State Normal University, 7
Illinois Wesleyan University, 1–2, 7–8, 10–11, 214, 229, 282, 350
Ilu River, 176, 178. *See also* Crocodile Creek; Tenaru River
Imjin River, 291–92

Imperial General Headquarters, 162, 184, 194, 209
Industrial War College, 100
Inje, Korea, 305
Institute for Defense Analysis, 349
International Refugee Organization, 273
Interservice conflicts, 227
Iraq, 142, 145
Ironbottom Sound, 178, 208. *See also* Sealark Channel
"Iron Triangle," Korea, 301
Ismailia, Egypt, 143
Iwo Jima, 239, 307, 326

Jackson, Capt. Gilder D., 104, 107; Col., 138
Jacksonville, North Carolina, 156
Jacmel, Haiti, 104
James, 1st Lt. William Capers, 93; Col., 157, 164, 168, 174, 183, 192–93, 197; Brig Gen., 233, 266, 287
James C. Breckinridge Hall, 336
Japan, 86, 98, 114, 241
Japanese Army, 209
 Kwantung Army, 122
 North China Garrison Army, 119
 Seventeenth Army, 194
 38th Division, 205
 Ichiki Detachment, 185–86
 Kawaguchi Detachment, 189, 192
Japanese Navy, 197, 200–201, 204–5, 207, 210
 Combined Fleet, 215
 Second Fleet, 207
 Third Fleet, 207
Japanese Protocol, 119
Johnson, Ens. J. Reid, 92
Johnson, Lottie Capers, 76, 92–93. *See also* Thomas, Lottie
Johnson, Louis A., 280
Johnson, Ambassador Nelson T., 122, 139–41, 213
Johnson, Dr. and Mrs. William H., 92–93
Joint Action of the Army and Navy 1927, 98, 114
Joint Chiefs of Staff (JCS), 158, 160, 162–63, 165, 167, 194, 209, 214–16, 225–26, 228, 234–36, 246–50, 262, 279–80, 283, 285, 290, 300, 303, 312, 314, 319, 323, 328, 333–34, 339, 344, 346
 1478 papers, 250, 252–53, 255
Joint Civilian Orientation Conference, 281, 340
Joint Landing Force Board, 332, 339

Joint Operations Center, 300–301, 310
Joint Pay Act of 1922, 99
Joint United States Military Assistance Group (China), 260, 264, 266
Jones, Lt. Col. Louis R., 128; Brig. Gen., 242, 276
Jones, Lt. Gen. William K., 278, 341, 348–52
Judge Advocate General of the Navy, 81, 329

Kanmubong Ridge, Korea, 307–12
Kawaguchi, Maj. Gen. Kiyotaki, 186–92
Kelley, Gen. Paul X., 352
Kengla, Lt. Col. William A., 266
Kenji, Col. Doihara, 122
Kerr, Col. James E., 249
Keyser, Col. Ralph Stover, 111–12, 154, 157–58, 342
Kilmartin, Lt. Col. Robert C., Jr., 128; Col., 287, 340, 352
King, Adm. Ernest J., 151–52, 157–63, 169, 203, 205, 216, 222–23, 226, 228, 232, 235, 239, 241, 247–48
Kinkaid, Adm. Thomas C., 204
Kirk, Minister Alexander, 143, 145
Kirkpatrick, Edgar, 90
Kittery, 76, 84, 103
Knickerbocker Theater disaster, 90
Knighton, Col. Joseph W. "Buddy," 243, 257
Knox, Secretary of the Navy Frank, 228–29, 236
Koblenz, Germany, 66, 68, 70–71
Kokumbona, 185, 187, 199, 205
Koli Point, 185, 205, 207
Korea, 107, 285–86, 303–5, 314, 316–17, 319, 322, 333–34
Korean War, 279, 288–319, 324–25, 330–31, 344, 350
 5th Phase, 1st Impulse Offensive, 292
Koro, Fiji Islands, 168, 171, 174
Kriegsakademie, 124
Kriemhilde Stellung, 62
Krueger, Lt. Gen. Walter, USA, 215
Krulak, Lt. Col. Victor H., 128, 221–23, 230–31, 235, 240, 249, 251–57; Col., 277–78, 283, 304–5, 307, 310, 315–16, 320, 322–23, 325–26, 329, 332, 348
Kuhn, Sgt. Richard C., 183
Kukum, 174, 176–78, 199, 208
Kumhwa, Korea, 301
Kung, Dr. H. H., 140–41
Kunming, 141

Kuomintang, 266
Kwajalein, 237

La Coupe, France, 77
Laffey, 208
Lake Habbaniya, Iraq, 142
Landing Force Manual, 109
Landing Operations Doctrine United States Navy 1938 (FTP 167), 130
Landing Party Manual, 15
Landres-et-Saint-Georges, France, 64
Larsen, Col. Henry L., 83; Maj. Gen., 235
Larson, Col. August, 332
La Verte Feuille Farm, France, 50
Lawrence, David, 227, 241, 255
Laws, Sgt. Douglas, 42
League of Nations, 115, 263
Leahy, Adm. William D., 130
Lee, Lt. Col. Harry, 38, 52; Col., 38, 41, 43, 56, 59, 69
Le Ferme Paris, 38
Legge, Maj. Barnwell R., 107
Lejeune, Brig. Gen. John A., 13, 56; Maj. Gen., 60, 62, 67, 68, 70, 72; Maj. Gen. Commandant, 80–81, 84, 87–88, 90, 98–100, 109, 111, 333, 349
Lemnitzer, Maj. Gen. Lyman L., 316
Lend-Lease Act, 137, 139, 143, 148
Les Islettes, France, 63
Leyendecker, J. C., 12
Libby, Rear Adm. Ruthven E., 329
Lindsay, John A., 266
Linscott, Lt. Col. Henry D., 168; Brig. Gen., 282, 286
Lisbon, Portugal, 148
Little, Lt. Col. Louis McCarty, 77–78, 80, 83, 105
"Little Man's Chowder and Marching Society," 249. *See also* "Chowder"; Unification crisis
Litzenberg, Capt. Homer L., 124
Long, Brig. Gen. Earl C., 217
Long Island, 180
Longmore, Air Chief Marshal Sir Arthur, 143
Lorraine, France, 28
Louisiana State University, 119
Luckey, Capt. Robert B., 122; Col., 240
Lucy-le-Bocage, France, 31, 33–36, 38–39, 45
Ludendorff, Gen. Erich, 22
Lunga Point, 174, 208–9

Lunga River, 167–68, 176–78, 183, 184–85, 187, 189–91, 194, 197, 199, 201, 204–7, 219
Lyle, Lt. L. Q. C. L., 42

Maas, Representative Melvin, 111
McAlister, Col. Francis M., 298
MacArthur, Gen. Douglas, 139, 160, 162–63, 165, 194, 212–16, 218, 226, 235, 268, 285, 288, 290, 293
McCain, Adm. John, 171–72, 181, 197, 200
McCawley, 168–69, 171–72, 174, 177
McCormack, Representative John W., 256
McDonnell Aircraft, 278
McHugh, Maj. James J., 140
McKean, Maj. William B., 168
McKelvey, Lt. Col. William N. "Spike," Jr., 128, 191, 192, 198, 203
Macklin, Lt. Col. John D., 198
McLean County, Illinois, 2
McNenny, Col. Wilbur J., 322
McQueen, Col. John C., 128, 154; Brig. Gen., 235, 240, 287
Mail guard duty, 90
Main Navy Building, 89
Maine, 18
Maison Blanche, France, 42
Major, Congressman Samuel C., 81
Malaria, 202, 209, 212–13, 215, 220
Malay Barrier, 162
Malta, 143
Manchuria, 114–15
Mangin, Gen. Charles, 46–47
Manila, 138–39
Manley, 132–33
Mare Island, California, 13
Mariana Islands, 86, 226, 231–32, 238
Marine Barracks
  Charleston Navy Yard, 97, 100, 106
  8th & I, Washington, D.C., 318
  Norfolk, 84, 88
  Philadelphia Navy Yard, 109
  Port Royal, South Carolina, 12
  Quantico, 17, 88, 113, 276
  San Diego, 236
Marine Corps Air Stations
  Cherry Point, 242
  Quantico, 336–37
Marine Corps Board, 281
Marine Corps Contributory Plan C-2, ORANGE, MCWP-2, October 1932, 129
Marine Corps doctrine, 333
Marine Corps Equipment Board, 281–82, 284–85

Index

Marine Corps Equipment Policy 1950, 284, 305
Marine Corps Equipment Policy Panel, 283–84
Marine Corps Gazette, 128
Marine Corps Historical Center, 351
Marine Corps Historical Foundation, 350–51
Marine Corps Manual, 109
Marine Corps Personnel Act of 1934 (P.L. 253), 111
Marine Corps, postwar, 241
Marine Corps Recruit Depots
　Parris Island, 13–14, 102, 151–52, 154–56, 223
　San Diego, 236
Marine Corps Reserve, 123, 134, 154, 280; mobilization of, 134
Marine Corps Reserve Officers Association, 111
Marine Corps roles and missions, 86–87, 108, 114, 249–53, 255–57, 279–80
Marine Corps Schools, Quantico, 85, 100, 109–10, 113, 115, 123–24, 127–36, 152–54, 249, 281, 283–85, 332–36, 341, 350
　Amphibious Warfare Presentation Team, 341
　Communications Officer School, 337, 343
　Company Officers Course, 99
　Development Center, 281
　Education Center, 242, 276–79, 284–85, 337–38
　Field Officers Course, 111–12, 115–16, 125
　First Officer Candidates Course, 135
　Junior Course, 128
　Junior School, 336
　Landing Force Development Center, 284–85, 287, 332, 339
　Landing Force Tactics and Techniques Board, 284–85
　Landing Operations Text Board, 110
　Officers Candidate Course, 338–39
　Platoon Leaders Class (PLC), 134–35
　Platoon Leaders Course, 338
　Research Section, 249
　Reserve Officers Course, 135
　Schools Demonstration Troops, 337
　Senior Course, 128, 189
　Senior School, 336
　Tactics and Techniques Board, 281
　The Basic School, 109, 112, 135, 166, 287, 323, 337–39
　Training and Test Regiment, 339
Marine Corps strength, 11, 134, 150, 225, 234, 258, 286, 319
Marine Corps Supply Center, Albany, Georgia, 331
Marine Corps Test Unit No. 1, 333
Marine Corps units and commands
　Department of the Pacific, 290
　Fleet Marine Force, 110, 112–14, 123, 131–32, 134, 136, 150, 211–12, 219, 223, 225–26, 234, 241, 250–51, 253–54, 256–57, 259, 279–81, 303, 319, 331, 333–34, 337, 350
　Fleet Marine Force Atlantic, 284, 330–31
　Fleet Marine Force Pacific, 237, 262, 268–69, 287, 290, 298, 320, 328, 330–32; Service Command, 236–37
　Fleet Marine Force Western Pacific, 257, 264–65, 267, 269, 272–75, 277
　I Marine Amphibious Corps, 223, 225, 322
　III Amphibious Corps, 226, 235, 237, 240–41, 260, 262, 307
　V Amphibious Corps, 226, 237, 241
　1st Marine Aircraft Wing, 186, 202, 208, 210, 218, 260, 285, 290, 300–301, 312–13, 319, 325, 331
　3d Marine Aircraft Wing, 331; Aircraft One, 115
　Marine Aircraft Group (MAG) 23, 186
　Marine Observation Squadron 9 (VO-9M), 104
　Marine Transport Helicopter Squadron 161 (HMR-161), 104, 310
　1st Marine Division, 149, 151–58, 164, 165, 167–68, 172, 178–79, 181, 184, 186, 192–93, 196, 199–203, 205–6, 209–11, 213–15, 217, 233, 238–40, 260, 270, 274, 285–329, 331, 335
　2d Marine Division, 155, 179, 202, 217, 219, 227, 232, 234, 240, 268, 284, 287
　3d Marine Division, 217–18, 220–21, 240–41, 331, 334
　4th Marine Division, 223, 239, 241
　5th Marine Division, 234–35
　6th Marine Division, 230, 235, 237, 240, 260, 263–64
　1st Brigade, 77–80, 82, 103–4, 113–16, 131–33, 150–51

Marine Corps units and commands
(*continued*)
  1st Provisional Brigade, 75
  2d Marine Brigade, 98, 101
  3d Marine Brigade, 98, 104, 156, 232, 235, 300
  4th Brigade, 22, 28–29, 31, 34, 36–37, 43–44, 46, 48, 54, 56–58, 61, 70–75, 77–78, 81, 87, 108, 111, 119, 131, 342
  1st Marines, 152, 154, 156, 158, 167–69, 176–78, 180, 185, 187, 189, 198, 265, 274, 291, 294, 296–97, 302, 304, 309–10, 312
    1st Battalion, 177, 185–86, 240
    2d Battalion, 185, 187, 198, 309–10
    3d Battalion, 190, 203, 312
  2d Marines, 78, 167–69, 174, 176, 178–79, 191, 200, 202, 206, 208
    3d Battalion, 193, 199
  3d Marines, 218, 265, 274
  4th Marines, 99, 189, 235, 286
  5th Marines, 17–20, 35–37, 40, 45, 51, 68, 72, 81, 88, 115, 132, 136, 152, 154–58, 165–66, 168, 174–76, 178, 182, 185, 187, 192, 198, 206–9, 291, 295–97, 302, 304–5, 308–10, 312, 342
    1st Battalion, 36–37, 43–44, 177, 187, 189, 318
    2d Battalion, 38–42, 44, 169, 176, 178–79, 186, 192, 302, 309
    3d Battalion, 36–38, 185, 187
  6th Marines, 18, 20, 23, 26–27, 29, 31, 33, 35–39, 48, 50–52, 54–58, 60, 62–69, 71–72, 90, 101, 108, 115, 119, 136, 152, 276, 342
    1st Battalion, 18, 26–31, 33–34, 37, 38–45, 48, 51–55, 57–61, 63–64, 67–69, 71
      74th Company, 19, 28, 43, 59, 61, 68
      75th Company, 22, 25, 29, 33, 35–36, 52–54, 58–59, 61, 64–65, 68, 70–71, 74; 3d Platoon, 39, 50, 63
      76th Company, 19, 39, 40, 42, 53–54, 61, 63
      95th Company, 19, 25, 61, 63
    2d Battalion, 38, 43
    3d Battalion, 33, 36–38
  7th Marines, 152–53, 156, 179, 191, 193, 198–99, 201, 204–6, 217, 291, 294–96, 302, 304–5, 307, 309–10, 350
    1st Battalion, 204
    2d Battalion, 203–4
    3d Battalion, 308
  7th Force Service Regiment, 260
  8th Marines, 77–78, 80, 104, 205, 207–9, 349
  9th Marines, 274
  10th Marines, 115, 132
  11th Marines, 152, 156, 168, 176–77, 179, 182, 185, 187, 191–92, 198–99, 201–2, 206, 213, 269, 291, 296, 304, 308, 316
    4th Battalion, 166
  22d Marines, 235
  29th Marines, 235
  1st Amphibian Tractor Battalion, 306
  1st Armored Amphibian Battalion, 306
  1st Engineer Battalion, 180
  1st Parachute Battalion, 166, 169, 176, 178–79, 187
  1st Raider Battalion, 156, 166, 169, 176, 178–79, 187, 189–91
  1st Reconnaissance Battalion, 350
  1st Shore Party Battalion, 310
  1st Special Weapons Battalion, 168, 179, 182, 185, 202
  1st Tank Battalion, 166, 302
  2d Parachute Battalion, 221
  2d Raider Battalion, 156, 202, 205, 206–7, 209, 219
  3d Defense Battalion, 166, 178, 181–82, 202, 204
  6th Machine Gun Battalion, 28
  12th Service Battalion, 265, 274
  Marine Detachment, American Embassy, Peiping, China, 116–17
    Company A, 120
    Company B, 120, 121
    Company C, 120
    Horse Marines, 122
Marine Corps War Memorial, 326
Marne River, 30–31, 37, 44, 46, 48
Marshall, Lt. Col. George C., 106–7, 110; Gen., 151, 162, 203, 231, 239, 242, 246, 248; General of the Army, 260, 303
Marshall, James Robert, 4
Marshall, Margaret Young Dawes, 4, 76
Marshall Islands, 86, 226, 238
Marshall-King negotiations, 163
Marshall, Missouri, 2, 127
Marston, Col. John, 123
Martha's Vineyard, Massachusetts, 153
Martin, Cpl. Paul G., 295

Martinique, 150
Maruyama, Lt. Gen. Masao, 200
Masan, South Korea, 290
Mason, Capt. Arthur T., 128; Col., 338
Matanikau River, 182, 184–85, 187, 197, 199–200, 203–4, 206–8
Maund, Air Vice Marshal A. C., 145
Maxwell, Brig. R. H., 145
Maxwell, Lt. Col. William E., 128, 174, 176–77, 187
Mayo, Adm. Henry T., 62, 80
Mayo Board, 82
Meaux, France, 30–31
Megee, 1st Lt. Vernon E., 116, 128
Mei, Gen. Li, 267
Melbourne, Australia, 213–14
Mellon Institute, 9
Mercersburg Academy, 319
Merillat, Capt. Herbert C., 190
Metz-Paris highway, 38
Meuse-Argonne campaign, 61, 66–67
Meuse River, 23, 59, 64, 66
Mexico, 78, 80, 96
Midway Island, 130, 138, 158, 162, 169
Mikawa, Adm. Gunichi, 178
Military Affairs Committee, 254
Miller, Lt. Col. Ellis B., 110, 111, 113
Milne, Cdr. MacGillivary, 93; Capt., 93, 96
Min, Tu Chih, 266
Mindanao, 115
Minnesota Line, 314
Mirebalais, France, 77–78, 81
Mon Plaisir Ferme, France, 58
Monson, Lt. Col. George E., 152, 154–57
Montdidier, France, 29
Montreuil-aux-Lions, France, 31–32, 46
Moore, Col. Bryant, USA, 201
Moore, Col. F. R., 322
Moran, Capt. Sherwood F. "Pappy," 176, 197
Mosel, France, 66
Mount Austen, Guadalcanal, 169, 176, 185, 199, 204
Mountbatten, Capt. Lord Louis, RN, 147
Mount Fuji, Japan, 331
Mount Gretna, Pennsylvania, 110
Mount Suribachi, 326
Muhl, Frederick L., 1
Munda, New Georgia, 219
Murray, Capt. James C., 159, 164, 197, 217, 219, 221; Lt. Col., 233, 240, 249, 332
Myers, Brig. Gen. John Twiggs "Handsome Jack," 105–6

Nagasaki, Japan, 241
Naha, Okinawa, 240
Naktong Bulge, 286
Nancy, France, 57
Nanking, China, 266, 273
Nanteuil, France, 37
Nanteuil-le-Haudouin, France, 56
Nanteuil-sur-Marne, France, 44
Narum, Col. Leslie, 270
National Defense Act of 1916, 10
National Guard Association, 255
National Rifle Association, 255, 340
National Security Act of 1947, 256–57, 279, 329
National Security Council, 248, 344, 346
  Memorandum 162/2, 331
National Strategy Seminar, 341
Nationalist China, 262
  Nationalist Army, 260, 264, 266–67, 271
Naval Act of 1916, 11
Naval Affairs Committee, 254
Naval Appropriations Act
  for 1920, 74
  for 1921, 81
Naval Courts and Boards, 109
Naval Disciplinary Barracks, 103
Naval Examining Board, 123
Naval Expansion Act of 1938, 130
Naval Mission, United States Embassy, London, 138
Naval Services Retirement Act of 21 February 1946, 243
Naval War College, 78, 86, 114–16, 124, 128, 152, 341
Navy Annex, 245, 327. *See also* Headquarters, U.S. Marine Corps
Navy Department, 14, 100, 139, 286, 328
  Bureau of Ships, 153
  Bureau of Supplies and Accounts, 322
  General Order No. 5, 329–30
  General Order No. 10, 330
  General Order No. 19, 330
  General Order No. 241, 113
  War Plans Division, 160
Navy units and commands
  Commander in Chief, Pacific Fleet (CinCPac)/Commander in Chief, Pacific Ocean Areas (CinCPOA), 162, 197, 200, 272, 328. *See also* Nimitz, Adm. Chester W.
  Amphibious Corps, Pacific Fleet, 212
  Commander, Aircraft Pacific, 238

Navy units and commands (*continued*)
  Commander, South Pacific Area (ComSoPac), 158, 160, 162–67, 169, 171–72, 179, 191, 194, 197, 200, 202, 205–6, 209, 212, 215–16, 221, 223, 226–28, 231–32, 237, 239–42, 248, 250–53, 257–58. *See also* Ghormley, Vice Adm. Robert L.; Halsey, Vice Adm. William F.
  Amphibious Forces South Pacific, 217
  Commander, Aircraft South Pacific (ComAirSoPac), 196
  Atlantic Fleet, 136, 150–51, 242, 330
    Amphibious Corps Atlantic Fleet I Joint Training Force, 151
  Pacific Fleet, 162
  Second Fleet, 330
  Fifth Fleet, 240
  Sixth Fleet, 331
  Seventh Fleet, 215, 262
  Task Force 61, 169, 172
  Task Force 62, 168, 177
  Special Service Squadron, 86, 92–94, 96, 97
  Naval Forces Western Pacific, 262, 265, 272–73
  Amphibious Forces Western Pacific, 272
Ndeni, 162–63, 191
Neidle, Barnett, 12
Nelson, Brig. Gen. Nels H., 322
Net Evaluation Subcommittee, 344–48
Neufchateau, France, 23
Neville, Col. Wendell C. "Buck," 45, 48; Brig. Gen., 56, 73, 81, 111
Neville, 177
Neville Board, 81, 83, 90, 100, 131, 188. *See also* Russell Board
New Bern, North Carolina, 156
New Britain Island, 158, 162, 211
New Caledonia, 158, 160, 162, 191
New Georgia, 216, 222
New Guinea, 162–63, 194, 212, 219
New Hebrides, 160–62
New Orleans, 158–59
New River, North Carolina, 151, 153–55. *See also* Camp Lejeune
New York, 132
New Zealand, 158, 160, 162, 164, 172, 174–76, 179, 212, 219–21
Newport, Rhode Island, 78
Nicaragua, 80, 96–99, 101–4, 108, 110, 113, 157, 182, 189

Nickerie, 106
Nickerson, Col. Herman, Jr., 296, 304, 308, 337
Nimitz, Adm. Chester W., 160, 162–63, 166, 169, 172, 179, 191, 194, 197, 200, 202, 205, 215–16, 221, 223, 226–28, 232, 237, 239–42, 248, 250–53, 257–58. *See also* Navy units and commands, Commander in Chief, Pacific Fleet (CinCPac)/Commander in Chief, Pacific Ocean Areas (CinCPOA)
Nimmer, Maj. David, 128; Lt. Col., 152–55; Col., 228, 240, 340
Nixon, Vice President Richard M., 339
No Name Line, 294–96
Noble, Lt. Alfred Houston, 83; Maj., 131–32; Lt. Col., 128, 131–32; Brig. Gen., 218–21; Gen., 286, 342
Norfolk, Virginia, 84, 88, 153, 158
Norford, Capt. Archie, 239
Norford, Madeline Thomas, 3
Normal State University, 11–12
Norstad, Maj. Gen. Lauris, 251–52
North Africa, 194
North Atlantic Treaty Organization (NATO), 262, 290
  NATO Defense College, 341
North China, 99, 260, 285
North Island, New Zealand, 164, 168
North Korean People's Army, 288, 290, 292, 298
Noumea, New Caledonia, 171, 200, 203, 209, 211–12, 217–20
Nuber, Lt. H. D., 94
Nuevitas, 76

O'Brien, 1st Sgt. Daniel, 18
Office of the Chief of Naval Operations, 284
Office of Defense Mobilization, 346
  revision of, 205
  role of, 249
Officer Personnel Act of 1947 (P.L. 381, 80th Congress), 257, 324
Okinawa, 239–41, 307, 331, 349–50
Onslow Beach, North Carolina, 151, 153
Operations
  Cartwheel, 162–63
  Crossroads, 250
  Elkton, 215
  Pestilence, 163, 165
  "Roll Up," 241

Operations (*continued*)
　Shoestring, 166, 181
　Strangle, 312–13
　Summit, 310
　Watchtower, 166, 168–69, 171, 178, 191, 205, 219. *See also* CACTUS; Guadalcanal
　Windmill I, 310
Operations Plan 712, 87
Our River, Germany, 67–68
Ourcq River, France, 30, 47
Overton, 1st Lt. Macon C., 39–42, 53–54, 61; Capt., 63

P'An, Gen. Ting Chih, 267
Pacific Military Conference, 215
Palmer, Maj. Gen. Williston B., 316–17
Pan American Airways, 148
Pan American Union, 96
Panama, Panama Canal, 80, 94, 164
Parcy-Tigny, France, 52–53
Paris-Metz highway, 30, 34, 36
Parker, Chauncey G., Jr., 245
Parmalee, Capt. Perry O., 143, 145, 147
Parris Island, South Carolina, 13, 340. *See also* Marine Corps Recruit Depots, Parris Island
Patch, Maj. Gen. Alexander M., USA, 208–9
Pate, Lt. Col. Randolph McCall, 157, 159, 164–66, 181, 197; Col., 277, 284, 287, 328; Commandant, 335, 339, 343
Patterson, Secretary of War Robert, 251–53
Peake, Col. Roger, 143, 146
Pearl Harbor, Hawaii, 138, 155, 166, 221
Peck, Col. DeWitt, 158, 165–67, 168, 200, 216; Maj. Gen., 232–34
Peiping, China, 78, 99, 117, 119–22, 171, 235, 242, 266
Peleliu, 238–39
Pepper, Lt. Col. Robert H., 180, 192; Brig. Gen., 276, 282, 287
Peralte, Charlemagne, 77
Pershing, Gen. John J., 16, 20, 22–23, 28–29, 43, 47, 56–57, 59–62, 66, 344
Pétain, Gen. Henri Philippe, 46–47, 59
Peter II, King of Yugoslavia, 145
Petit-Goave, Haiti, 104
Pettus, Dr. W. B., 235
Pfeiffer, Col. Omar T., 200; Brig. Gen., 228, 263, 265, 282
Philippine Islands, 89, 114, 158, 160

Platt, Maj. Jonas M., 254, 348–49, 352
Platt, Col. Wesley M., 315
Plattsburg Movement, 10
Point Cruz, 205–7
Policia Nacional Dominicana, 87, 104–5
Pollock, Lt. Col. Edwin A., 185, 187, 189, 217; Col., 258, 280–81, 284, 287
Port-au-Prince, Haiti, 77–76, 79–82, 103–4, 116
Port Moresby, 213
Prather, Leonard O., 12, 14, 16
Pratt, Adm. William V., 108
President Jackson, 263
President Polk, 119
Price, Col. Charles F. B., 152
Pride, Rear Adm. Alfred M., 286
Protocol of 1904, 118
Psi, Gen. Pai Chung, 141
Public Law 416, 325, 328–30. *See also* Douglas-Mansfield Act
Public Law 432, 328–30
Puerto Cabezas, 97
Puerto Cortez, 94
Puerto Mexico, 97
Puerto Rico, 152–53
Pukhan-gang (river), 291, 294
Puller, 1st Lt. Lewis B. "Chesty," 99; Lt. Col., 107, 198–99, 204; Brig. Gen., 239, 282, 287, 291, 304, 342
Puller, Lt. Col. Samuel D., 239
Punchbowl, 301, 307
Pusan, South Korea, 290
Pyonggang, Korea, 301

Quantico, Virginia, 17, 72–73, 75, 82, 85, 87, 90, 100, 109–10, 112, 114–16, 126–27, 129, 133–35, 148, 150–51, 153–56, 189, 214, 225, 229, 231, 242, 254, 258, 277–79, 281, 285, 287, 290, 304, 332, 335–43, 338–40, 348–49. *See also* Marine Barracks
Quartermaster General of the Marine Corps, 101. *See also* Hill, Maj. William P. T.; Williams, Quartermaster General Seth
Quick, Sgt. Maj. John, 18
Quinan, Lt. Gen. E. P., 142

Rabaul, 162, 174, 181, 184, 194, 207, 212, 215, 218, 222, 226
Radford, Vice Adm. Arthur W., 248; Adm. 251–53, 301, 312–13, 328, 339, 344, 346–47

Raider Ridge, 192, 204
Ramsey, Adm. DeWitt, 272
RAND Corporation, 347
Red Beach, Guadalcanal, 168, 174, 176–77
Redford, 2d Lt. David A., 18, 21, 26, 30, 36, 53–54
Reifsnider, Capt. Lawrence, USN, 166, 168
Renner, Col. Joseph N., 332
Renya, Col. Mataguchi, 119
Republic of Korea, 290
  Armed Forces
    I Corps, 305
    III Corps, 296–97
    1st Korean Marine Corps Regiment, 291, 293–96, 302–3, 305, 307
    3d Republic of Korea (ROK) Division, 306
    5th ROK Division, 292
    6th ROK Division, 291
    7th ROK Division, 292
    8th ROK Division, 306, 270–71, 273–74, 322
Revolt of the Admirals, 281
Rheims, 46
Rhine River, 66, 68
Richardson, Adm. J. O., 246
Richardson, Lt. Gen. Robert C., Jr., USA, 238–39
Richardson Committee, 246–47
Ridgway, Lt. Gen. Matthew B., 288, 292–93, 297–98, 300–301, 304, 312–13, 316–17
Riley, Brig. Gen. William E. "Bill," 221, 234, 255, 282, 286
Rivers, Congressman L. Mendel, 323
Rixey, Col. Palmer M., Jr., 266
Rixey, Col. Presley M., 116–17, 119–21
Robber's Roost, 190
Roberts, Lt. Gen. Carson A., 332
Robertson, Senator E. V., 254–55
Robinson, Lt. Col. Ray A. "Torchy," 128; Lt. Gen., 282, 284, 286
Rockey, Capt. Keller E., 83
Roebling, Donald, 130
Roebling amphibian, 277
Rogers, Lt. Col. William Walter, 136
Romagne Heights, France, 62
Roosevelt, Elliott, 148
Roosevelt, Assistant Secretary of the Navy Franklin D., 71, 78; President, 123, 134, 136–37, 144–45, 147–48, 153–54, 156–57, 160, 162, 194, 203, 214–15, 229, 247
Roosevelt, Capt. James, 123, 137–46, 351
Rosecrans, Lt. Col. Harold E., 128

Rosenthal, Joe, 326
Rota, 138–39
Rowan, Lt. Col. George, 176, 192–93
Rowe, Dr. Leo S., 96
Rowell, Maj. Ross, 116
Roy Geiger Hall, 336
Rupertus, Col. William H., 132; Maj. Gen., 238
Russell, Col. John H., 74, 77–78, 80, 83; Brig. Gen., 104, 158, 167, 169, 174, 177, 182, 203, 206, 209, 217; Commandant, 110–11, 113, 123
Russell Board, 74–75, 81, 188. *See also* Neville Board

Saar River, 67–68
Saesebo, Japan, 241
Saint-Étienne-à-Arnes, France, 61
Saint Mihiel salient, 23, 26, 28, 57–59, 62
Saint Nazaire, France, 19, 21, 66
Saipan, 129, 226, 232, 237–40, 307
Saline County, Missouri, 3–4
Samoa, 156, 158, 160, 162, 179, 191, 235, 349
San Diego, California, 87, 134
Sandinistas, 99, 189
Sandino, Augusto Cesar, 98
Santa Cruz, 162–63, 165, 204
Santo Domingo, 56, 78
Saratoga, 169, 186
Savo Island, 177, 207–8
Saxten, Col. John A., 338
Sayre, Francis B., 139
Schatzel, Lt. Col. DeWolf, 249, 277, 349
Scheyer, Col. William J., 233, 269, 277
Schilt, Maj. Gen. Christian F., 286, 312, 313
Schmidt, Maj. Gen. Harry, 237, 243, 258
Schwable, Col. Frank H., 325–26
Schwenke, Capt. Clarence R. "Ray," 166, 183, 217
Science Advisory Committee, 347
SCOROR, 248. *See also* Secretary's Committee on Research and Reorganization
Scott, Rear Adm. Norman, 208
Sealark Channel, 174, 177–78, 185, 192, 208. *See also* Ironbottom Sound
Sebree, Brig. Gen. Edmund B., USA, 206
Sebree Force, 206
Second Battle of the Marne, 46
Second Caco War, 77, 80, 82. *See also* Cacos
Secretary's Committee on Research and Reorganization, 248. *See also* SCOROR

Security Resources Panel, 347
Sedan, France, 59, 64
Selden, Col. John T., 211; Brig. Gen., 280, 287; Maj. Gen., 316
Select Committee on Post-War Military Policy, 247. *See also* Woodrum Committee
Selective Service Act, 10
Selective Service system, 234
Senate Military Affairs Committee, 251–52
Senate Naval Affairs Committee, 100, 252–53
Seoul, South Korea, 286, 290–92, 297
Service, John Stewart, 122
Shanghai, 99, 117, 189, 266, 272–73
Shantung, Shantung Peninsula, 86, 115, 267, 271
Shantung University, 264
Shaw, Lt. Col. Samuel R., 249; Col., 128, 284, 332, 352
Shearer, Maj. Maurice E., 28–29, 31, 36
Shell, Col. George R. E., 332
Shepherd, Capt. Lemuel C., Jr., 45, 83, 90; Maj., 104; Col., 128, 131, 135, 157, 193, 217; Maj. Gen., 230–31, 235, 240, 250–51, 254, 258, 271, 276–77, 282, 285–87, 290, 298, 300–301, 308, 310, 312–13, 315–17; Commandant, 318–20, 322–24, 326, 328, 331, 333–34, 336–37, 339, 341–43, 350
Shepherd Board, 250
Sherman, Rear Adm. Forrest P., 240–41; Vice Adm., 251; Adm., 252, 328
Sherrod, Robert, 227, 238
Ship-to-shore movement, 114
Shortland Islands, 218
Shoup, 1st Lt. David M., 121, 128–29; Col., 231, 233, 237, 242, 263, 323, 340; Commandant, 348, 350
Shozo, Lt. Gen. Kawabe, 119
Shuri Castle, 240
Sibley, Maj. Burton, 37–39
Sigma Chi, 8
Silverthorn, Col. Merwin H., 83; Maj. Gen., 282, 286–87
Sims, Col. Amor L., 198, 217
Sims, Adm. William S., 78
Slade, Maj. Lawrence, 124
Slater, Missouri, 2
Slim, Brig. William, 142

Smith, Maj. Holland M., 19; Brig. Gen., 133; Maj. Gen., 151–53, 155–57, 212, 222–23, 226–27, 232, 235, 238–39, 243
Smith, Maj. Gen. Julian C., 227, 237, 287
Smith, Capt. Oliver P., 104, 107, 128; Brig. Gen., 240; Maj. Gen., 249–51, 276, 282, 285–86, 290–94, 300, 303; Lt. Gen., 333, 335
Smith, Maj. Gen. Ralph, USA, 238
Smith, Ens. Sherwood, 93–95
Smoak, Col. Eustace R., 322, 332
Snedeker, Col. Edward W., 154, 156, 165–66, 198, 217–18, 220, 232, 240, 277, 291–92, 298
Soissons, 31, 50, 52, 54, 57, 60–62, 68, 76, 107, 227. *See also* Battle of Soissons
Solomon Islands, 128, 158, 162–63, 165, 200, 216, 238
Sommedieue, France, 26
Somme-Py, France, 60
Sommerance, France, 63, 66–67
Somme River, 28
Soong, Ambassador T. V., 139–40
Souilly, France, 26
South Island, New Zealand, 164
South Pacific, 282–83
Soyang-gang (river), 291, 294–95, 298, 301, 307–8, 310
Spellman, Francis Cardinal, 316
Spruance, Adm. Raymond A., 238, 240
Steele, Capt. Franklin, 84
Steele, Col. Matthew F., USA, 91
Stilwell, Lt. Col. Joseph W. "Vinegar Joe," USA, 106–7, 110; Col., 122
Stokes, Cdr. Murray, 208
Stone, Hal M., 1
Stowell, Capt. George A., 38–39, 61, 63; Maj., 66
Stuart, Ambassador Leighton, 266
Suez Canal, 137
Suippes, France, 60
Sullivan, Secretary of the Navy John L., 258, 280
Summerall, Maj. Gen. Charles P., 62–63
Swanson, Secretary of the Navy Claude A., 113
Symington, Assistant Secretary of War for Air Stuart, 252
Syria, 145

Taboga Island, 94
Tacoma, 93

Taebaek Mountains, 314
Taiwan Defense Command, 350
Takoradi, Gold Coast, 143–44, 146, 148
Tampico, Mexico, 96–97
Tanambogo, 167, 174–75, 178
Tang-ku, China, 120
Tarawa, 211, 217, 219, 223, 226–27, 238
Tartar Wall, Peiping, 117
Tasimboko, 189–90
Tedder, Air Marshal Arthur W., 143, 148
Tela, Honduras, 95
Tenaru River, 175, 177, 185–86, 189–90, 203–4. *See also* Ilu River; Crocodile Creek
Tent Camp One, New River, 159
Tentative Manual for Defense of Advanced Bases, MCS-3, 130–31
Tentative Manual for Landing Operations 111, 113–16, 128, 130, 220
Texas, 132
The Citadel, 157
The Slot, 186, 196, 205, 207
Thiacourt, France, 58
Thomas, Secretary of the Navy Charles S., 329, 340
Thomas, David Wyatt, 3
Thomas, Frances Ellen Wood, 3
Thomas, Gerald C., Jr., 155, 246, 260, 271, 279, 290, 318, 340, 350
Thomas, Ginny, 246, 271, 273, 278, 287, 318, 340. *See also* Thomas, Virginia
Thomas, Inez, 5
Thomas, Johnny, 246, 271–73, 278, 287, 319, 341–42, 351. *See also* Thomas, William H. Johnson
Thomas, Joseph, 3
Thomas, Lemuel, 3
Thomas, Lottie, 94, 124, 128, 132, 148, 156–57, 197, 205, 213, 217, 223–24, 245, 263–64, 273, 278, 287, 315, 319, 340–41, 351. *See also* Thomas, Lottie Capers
Thomas, Lottie Capers, 101, 103. *See also* Thomas, Tina
Thomas, Louis, 309
Thomas, Louis O'Vander, 5, 7, 69, 125, 127
Thomas, Mary Frances, 5, 7, 125, 127
Thomas, Mary Ruth Durrett, 76, 78, 81–82
Thomas, Robert Shelton, 4, 7–8, 69, 81–82, 90, 124–25, 214, 263
Thomas, Tina, 245, 263, 271, 278, 287, 313. *See also* Thomas, Lottie Capers

Thomas, Vander Wyatt, 3–7, 69, 82, 246, 350
Thomas, Virginia, 7, 124–25, 134
Thomas, William H. Johnson, 121
Thompson, J. Walter, 257
Thorne, Nicholas G. W., 266
Tientsin, China, 99, 120, 241, 266, 270, 273
Tigny, France, 52
Tinian, 129, 143, 147, 226, 237–38
Tokyo, 162, 184, 241
Tompkins, Col. Rathvon M., 342
Tonga, 160
Torcy, France, 31, 33–35, 36–38
Torrey, Maj. Gen. Philip H., 128, 151–56, 239
Toul, France, 59
Toulon, 26, 28–29, 34
Towers, Vice Adm. John H., 238
Treasury Islands, 221
Tresavaux, France, 26, 28
Trinidad, 129
Trippe, Juan, 148
Trujillo, Honduras, 96
Trujillo Molina, Rafael, 105
Truk, 115–16, 194
Truman, President Harry S., 229, 234, 242, 248, 251–53, 258, 260, 262, 277, 279–80, 286, 288, 290, 301, 309, 315
Truman Doctrine, 262
Tsang Kou, 264
Tse-tung, Mao, 260
Tsinan, 271
Tsingtao, 241, 255, 260, 266, 262–73, 318
Tulagi, 162–63, 165, 168, 169, 174, 176–79, 183, 187, 191, 193, 199, 203, 206
Tulsa, 91–97, 109, 120
Turnage, Brig. Gen. Allen Hal, 218, 221–23; Lt. Gen., 234, 242, 258–59, 287, 340
Turner, Capt. Arthur H., 28, 57
Turner, Rear Adm. Richmond Kelly "Terrible," 158, 160–68, 172, 174, 177–80, 182, 191–92, 196–97, 200, 202, 205–7, 217, 223, 238–40
Turner, Col. Thomas C., 116
Turner Field, 337
Twentynine Palms, California, 331
Twining, Maj. Merrill B., 128, 154–56; Lt. Col., 158–210, 212, 217–20; Col., 225, 231, 249–57, 269, 277, 280–81, 283–84; Maj. Gen., 324, 326, 330, 348

Twining, Brig. Gen. Nathan F., USAAF, 212; Gen., 347
Two-Ocean Navy Act, 134

Underhill, Maj. Gen. James L., 243
Unification crisis, 245–59. *See also* "Chowder"
Union Medical College Hospital, 118
United Fruit Company, 94
United Nations Command, 250, 285, 288, 292. *See also* Army units and commands, Commander in Chief, Far East (CinCFe) *and* Eighth Army
United States, 280
United States Naval Academy, 11, 77, 155, 246, 282, 290
University of California, 236

Vandegrift, Maj. Alexander Archer, 79–80, 90; Lt. Col., 116–17, 119–23, 138, 148; Brig. Gen., 153–54; Maj. Gen., 155–223; Commandant, 225–30, 232–37, 240–43, 245, 247–48, 250–53, 255–58, 268–69, 276, 281–82, 285, 287, 343–44, 350, 351–52
Vandenberg, Gen. Hoyt S., USAF, 314
Van Fleet, Gen. James, 290–93, 295–98, 300–302, 305–6, 313, 316–17, 344
Van Ryzin, Col. William J., 332, 338, 352
Vardaman, Commo. James K., Jr., 229, 234
Vaux, France, 44, 47
Vella Lavella, 219, 221
Veracruz, Mexico, 18, 96–97
Verdun, 22–23, 26, 28
Vermont National Guard, 188
Vertical envelopment, 250–51, 278, 310, 333, 338
Veterans of Foreign Wars, 255
Vieques, Puerto Rico, 133
Vierzy, France, 51
Vietnam, 348
Vinson, Congressman Carl, 13, 110, 229, 236, 254, 323, 330
Virginia Military Institute, 11, 90, 157, 295, 336
V-J Day, 237
Vogel, Maj. Gen. Clayton B., 211–12, 216–17
Volcansek, Col. Max J., 337

Wadsworth, Congressman James W., Jr., 256

Wagon-Lits Hotel, 271
Wakefield, 159, 164
Wake Island, 130, 138, 155, 169, 182, 315
Walker, Maj. Gen. John T., 286
Wallace, Maj. Gen. William J., 282
Waller, L. W. T., 349
Walt, Col. Lewis W., 277, 338–39
Wang, Dr. C. T., 140
War Department, 114, 130, 139, 231, 246–47, 252
   General Staff, 16, 124, 130
War Plan ORANGE, 86, 89, 114–15, 129
Ward, Sir John and Lady, 142
Washington Conference, 89, 98, 114. *See also* Conference on the Limitation of Armament
Washington Real Estate Investment Trust, 348
Washington Treaty, 111
Wasp, 193
Watson, Maj. Gen. Thomas E. "Terrible Tommy," 232–40, 251, 259; Lt. Gen., 268–69, 282, 350
Wavell, Gen. Sir Archibald, 143, 146–47
Weede, Col. Richard G., 298, 304, 309, 332
Wei, Dr. Yu Ta, 141
Weldon, Felix de, 326, 342
Weller, Lt. Col. Donald M., 249; Col., 337, 348–49, 351
Wellington, New Zealand, 164–65, 168
Wensinger, Col. Walter W., 233; Maj. Gen., 320
Western Desert (World War II), 143
Western Front (World War I), 23, 28–29, 44
Western Hills, China, 121
Weyland, Gen. O. P., USAF, 313–14
Whaling, Lt. Col. William J., 128, 157, 183, 192, 198–99, 240; Brig. Gen., 286–87, 304, 305, 315–16
   Whaling Group, 206
Wheeler, Maj. Edwin B., 274
Wheeler, 1st Lt. Frederick C., 53
White, J. P., 53–54
Wieseman, Lt. Col. Frederick L., 128, 217–18, 230; Col., 277, 283; Lt. Gen., 352
Wilkinson, Rear Adm. Theodore S., 217, 219–22
Williams, Lt. Col. Robert H., 128
Williams, Quartermaster General Seth, 152, 226
Wilson, Secretary of Defense Charles E., 323–24, 339

Wilson, Lt. Gen. H. M. "Jumbo," 145
Wilson, President Woodrow, 1, 73
Winecoff, Col. Joseph L., 296
Wise, Maj. Frederic M., 39–44; Col., 88
Women Marines, 236
Woodrum Committee, 247. *See also* Select Committee on Post-War Military Policy
Woods, Capt. Louis E., 115–16; Col., 186; Brig. Gen., 208, 243, 283–84, 286
World War I, 10–73, 86, 155, 218
Wornham, Col. Thomas A., 128, 304; Brig. Gen., 322
Worton, Col. William Arthur, 128; Brig. Gen., 256–57, 342
Wyoming, 132

Wyoming-Kansas Line, 301–3, 306–8

Yamamoto, Adm. Isoroku, 162
Yanggu, 297–98, 301–2, 305
Yenching University, 266
Yoke Ridge, Korea, 307, 309
Yokosuka, Japan, 241
Yonabaru, 240
Yorktown, 169
Young, Fred, 8
Young, Jacob Harrison, 4
Young, Virginia Harrell, 3–4
Yowell, Laura Thomas, 3
Yu, Li, 267
Yui, O. K., 13

Zimmerman Brothers, 5

About the Author

Allan R. Millett, Raymond E. Mason, Jr., Professor of Military History and associate director, the Mershon Center, at The Ohio State University, specializes in the history of American military policy and institutions. He is the author or coauthor of numerous books, studies, essays, and articles, and has edited or co-edited several others. His previous publications include the books *Semper Fidelis: The History of the United States Marine Corps* (1980, revised edition 1991) and *For the Common Defense: The Military History of the United States of America* (1984), and articles in *Military Affairs, International Security,* and the *Marine Corps Gazette*.

A colonel in the U.S. Marine Corps Reserve, Dr. Millett retired from the Ready Reserve in 1990 with twenty-nine years of service, eleven in infantry battalions.

Dr. Millett holds a Ph.D. from The Ohio State University. He is the former president of the Society for Military History and former national president of the Marine Corps Reserve Officers Association.

The **Naval Institute Press** is the book-publishing arm of the U.S. Naval Institute, a private, nonprofit society for sea service professionals and others who share an interest in naval and maritime affairs. Established in 1873 at the U.S. Naval Academy in Annapolis, Maryland, where its offices remain, today the Naval Institute has more than 100,000 members worldwide.

Members of the Naval Institute receive the influential monthly magazine *Proceedings* and discounts on fine nautical prints and on ship and aircraft photos. They also have access to the transcripts of the Institute's Oral History Program and get discounted admission to any of the Institute-sponsored seminars offered around the country.

The Naval Institute also publishes *Naval History* magazine. This colorful quarterly is filled with entertaining and thought-provoking articles, first-person reminiscences, and dramatic art and photography. Members receive a discount on *Naval History* subscriptions.

The Naval Institute's book-publishing program, begun in 1898 with basic guides to naval practices, has broadened its scope in recent years to include books of more general interest. Now the Naval Institute Press publishes more than sixty titles each year, ranging from how-to books on boating and navigation to battle histories, biographies, ship and aircraft guides, and novels. Institute members receive discounts on the Press's nearly 400 books in print.

For a free catalog describing Naval Institute Press books currently available, and for further information about subscribing to *Naval History* magazine or about joining the U.S. Naval Institute, please write to:

Membership & Communications Department
U.S. Naval Institute
118 Maryland Avenue
Annapolis, Maryland 21402-5035

Or call, toll-free, (800) 233-USNI.

THE NAVAL INSTITUTE PRESS
IN MANY A STRIFE
General Gerald C. Thomas and the U.S. Marine Corps, 1917–1956
Designed by Karen L. White

Set in Bembo and Cochin
by TCSystems, Inc.
Shippensburg, Pennsylvania

Printed on 50-lb. Glatfelter eggshell cream
and bound in Holliston Roxite B
by The Maple-Vail Book Manufacturing Group
York, Pennsylvania